REVOLUTIONS OF THE
LATE TWENTIETH CENTURY

REVOLUTIONS OF THE
LATE TWENTIETH CENTURY

EDITED BY

Jack A. Goldstone
Ted Robert Gurr
Farrokh Moshiri

Westview Press

BOULDER • SAN FRANCISCO • OXFORD

Copyright © 1991 by Westview Press, Inc.

Published in 1991 in the United States of America by Westview Press, Inc., 5500 Central Avenue, Boulder, Colorado 80301, and in the United Kingdom by Westview Press, 36 Lonsdale Road, Summertown, Oxford OX2 7EW

Library of Congress Cataloging-in-Publication Data
Revolutions of the late twentieth century / edited by Jack A.
  Goldstone, Ted Robert Gurr, Farrokh Moshiri.
    p. cm.
  Includes bibliographical references and index.
  ISBN 0-8133-7597-5 — ISBN 0-8133-1299-X (pbk.)
  1. History, Modern—1945–   . 2. Revolutions. I. Goldstone, Jack A.
II. Gurr, Ted Robert, 1936–   . III. Moshiri, Farrokh, 1961–   .
D848.R48   1991
909.82—dc20   91-17945
                                                                            CIP

Printed and bound in the United States of America

 The paper used in this publication meets the requirements
of the American National Standard for Permanence of Paper
for Printed Library Materials Z39.48-1984.

10   9   8   7   6   5   4   3   2   1

To Hamid Moshiri
(1928–1987)

CONTENTS

TABLES AND ILLUSTRATIONS

PREFACE

This book, like most revolutions, was many years in the making. While at Northwestern University in 1984, two of the volume's editors—Ted Robert Gurr and Farrokh Moshiri—conceived the idea for a comparative study of recent revolutions. The plan was to design a common framework, based on extant academic theories of revolution, and to invite political scientists to apply it to cases with which they were closely familiar. Events of the 1980s amply confirmed our initial idea, derived from what we knew then of revolutions in Iran and Nicaragua, that both the theory and the practice of revolution had changed dramatically since the 1960s. We put the project aside until 1987, when Jack A. Goldstone, also at Northwestern University, became intrigued by the project and took the lead in implementing it.

We have avoided the temptation to let our pet theoretical assumptions or the specifics of the cases we knew best dictate the shape of this project. Instead, the theoretical and concluding chapters present and use a general framework that identifies key variables and combinations that appear significant in all contemporary revolutions. The framework, developed by Goldstone, evolved through a series of confrontations with the facts of particular cases and the interpretations of our contributors. It has proved flexible enough to guide the analysis of ten very diverse revolutions and rigorous enough that it can be used to make systematic comparisons across them.

One distinctive feature of the project, which we had in mind from the outset, is that we relied as much as possible on contributors who are native to the countries and regions in which the revolutions occurred, as we believed that nationals of revolutionary countries who are trained in Western social sciences are especially well suited for analysis that informs theory with cultural and political understanding. Eight of the ten case studies are by nationals, and in a number of instances, their contributions provide distinctive insights that reflect their firsthand knowledge.

The original plan also called for inclusion of several revolutions in progress, that is, ones in which a transfer of power to new leaders had not yet occurred. In our working outlines, Poland was included as an "aborted revolution," South Africa as potentially revolutionary. Events have dramatically changed the character of these revolutionary situations and amply justified our decision to include them.

According to the same logic, this volume also includes a case study of the Palestinian *intifada*. We also note that the revolutions in Afghanistan, Cambodia, and Nicaragua have taken sharp and unexpected turns from the courses they were on in the mid-1980s. Observing our cases over the decade of this volume's preparation has brought home forcefully to us that "revolution" is not a neat analytic category of events with a finite beginning and end. At most, revolutions are climacterics in long, irregular processes of political conflict over who will hold power and for what purposes. Only in distant retrospect can one say that a particular revolution was decisive for a country's future.

The preparation of this volume was funded by a generous grant from the United States Institute of Peace. Most important, this grant provided the contributors an opportunity to present and discuss their interpretations of particular cases at a conference in September 1988, and we are grateful to the Overseas Development Council, and particularly to the council's vice president, Richard Feinberg, for hosting that conference. Of course, the opinions, findings, and conclusions or recommendations expressed in this volume are those of the authors and do not necessarily reflect the views of the United States Institute of Peace or the Overseas Development Council.

The administration of this project was handled by the expert staff of Northwestern University's Center for Urban Affairs and Policy Research, to whom we are grateful. We also owe thanks to Kelli Jensen—the executive officer of the Center for Comparative Research in History, Society, and Culture at the University of California, Davis—who coordinated the authors' chapters, converted various texts and tables into a single uniform format, and assembled the final manuscript, and to Wava Haggard—of the Sociology Department at the University of California, Davis—who assisted in the manuscript's preparation.

Far more than most edited volumes, this book was indeed a team effort. The authors of the various chapters had a chance to review each others' efforts at the 1988 conference, and they also critiqued the editors' introduction and conclusion. They were also extraordinarily gracious in responding to heavy editorial demands to maintain a tight focus on common issues and problems. The editors therefore thank these contributors, not only for their specific chapter contributions, but also for their less obvious, but no less important, contributions to the coherence and quality of this volume as a whole.

Jack A. Goldstone
Ted Robert Gurr
Farrokh Moshiri

INTRODUCTION

JACK A. GOLDSTONE

Revolutions startle us with their unexpectedness and their impact. The sudden falls of the shah in Iran and Somoza in Nicaragua, the persistence of the Afghan resistance movement, and the bravery of the participants in the Polish Solidarity movement inspire wonder. The mass starvation in Cambodia, the brutal conflicts in South Africa, and violence in the Middle East inspire alarm. How capable are we of understanding, or of influencing, the causes and outcomes of these events?

This volume brings together a variety of scholars in search of answers. Two of the editors—Ted Robert Gurr and Jack A. Goldstone—are theorists of revolution. Studying many revolutions, they have sought recurring patterns to provide answers to the general questions of why revolutions take place and what results are likely to follow. The third editor—Farrokh Moshiri—and the authors of Chapters 4 through 13 are area specialists who have studied particular countries and their revolutions in depth. These two approaches are both necessary and complementary. Area specialists rarely encounter more than one revolution in the history of each country they study. Hence, they may not recognize, among the many factors that accompany revolutionary turmoil, which factors are unique to their nation and which are more general. On the other hand, theorists are dependent on the expertise of area specialists to avoid false generalizations. The contributors to this volume collectively bring both kinds of skills to bear on unraveling the complexities of modern revolutions.

We have focused on revolutions—and potentially revolutionary situations—that have occurred since 1970. There have been many studies of the "great" revolutions in England, France, Russia, and China,[1] and there are several surveys of the postcolonial revolutions that followed World War II, and of the twentieth-century revolutions in Latin America.[2] The more recent events in Poland, Afghanistan, Iran, Nicaragua, Zimbabwe, the Philippines, Cambodia, and Palestine and the ongoing struggle in South Africa have not been the object of the same kind of comparative study. Yet more than mere novelty recommends such a focus.

The revolutions in the years since 1970 have taken place in very different circumstances than the great upheavals in France, Russia, and China, which usually form the basis for the study of revolutions. Whereas the latter marked the end of ancient, traditional royal or imperial regimes, the cases discussed in this volume are revolutionary movements that arose in various kinds of nontraditional, semi-modern states.[3] In Nicaragua and the Philippines, state leaders ruled through a combination of electoral, bureaucratic, and military methods. In 1979 and 1986, respectively, these methods failed to ensure either the continuity of rule or peaceful transitions of power. In Iran, a modernizing, industrializing government was overthrown by an avowedly traditional, antiliberal, Islamic movement. In Afghanistan and Poland, broad-based antigovernment movements arose in states governed by Communist parties closely allied with the Soviet Union. In Zimbabwe and South Africa, revolutionary struggles arose out of majority opposition to racial-minority rule. These events are unlike any of the great revolutions that have been the grist for many political scientists' model building. They therefore pose a challenge to current theories of revolution. More than that, they sharply raise the question of whether our existing theories have any value as a guide to contemporary revolutionary crises. Our goal in this volume is to develop concepts and theories that illuminate the distinctive kinds of revolutionary situations that have developed, and are likely to further develop, in our day.

The cases covered in this book also suggest a further historical divide. Not only are most contemporary revolutions internally different from the classic revolutions, but their international context is different as well. From the French Revolution of 1789 to the 1960s, revolutions in smaller states were largely guided by the great powers. France fostered revolutionary regimes in Belgium and Germany under Napoleon; the USSR fostered revolutionary regimes in Mongolia and Eastern Europe and suppressed attempted regime changes in Czechoslovakia and Hungary; China fostered a revolutionary regime in North Korea; the United States fostered a revolutionary regime in Bolivia after 1952 and suppressed attempted regime changes in Nicaragua in the 1920s, Iran in 1953, and the Dominican Republic in 1965. Yet it is possible that the revolutionary crises of the two decades since 1970 mark a shift in the ability of superpowers to impose their international policies by manipulating or suppressing revolutionary movements. The loss of important regional allies by the United States in Vietnam, Iran, and Nicaragua has raised critical questions about the ability of U.S. foreign policy to foresee, comprehend, and react constructively to domestic struggles overseas. For the Soviet Union, the breadth and persistence of the Solidarity movement in Poland and the effective resistance of the Afghans to the Soviet-sponsored regime raised the first doubts about the Soviet Union's ability to maintain its informal "empire" in Eastern Europe and central Asia. Is the era of superpower dominance of smaller nations' politics coming to an end? What will be the implications for strategic policy? Will revolutions become more likely, and more dangerous, as the superpowers' ability to extend their authority around the world weakens? Are the tragedies of Cambodia and Ethiopia the likely outcome of revolutions in isolated states? What implications do these trends hold for the future of South Africa and for future U.S. policy toward shaky regimes in Africa, Latin America, and the Middle East? These are some of the issues the following chapters address.

Much of the confusion and dismay that the revolutions since 1970 have engendered among scholars derives from the long-cherished belief that revolutions are inherently progressive, often necessary steps on the path to economic and political modernization. The contributors to this volume, by and large, do not share this notion. They approach the issues of how a particular conflict situation occurs, how it gives rise to revolution, and whether the outcome is likely to be greater democracy and economic progress or not as empirical problems with a variety of answers. Indeed, one main theme of this volume is that *revolutions are highly varied phenomena*, whose results—some happy, some sad—reflect particular constellations of causal factors and background conditions.

This volume begins by examining theories of revolution, shifts to particular cases, and then returns to theory. Chapter 2 presents a survey of theories of revolution from Marx to the present, demonstrating how changes in the nature of revolutions have often shaped contemporary theorizing. Chapter 3 then distills a framework for the comparative study of contemporary revolutions. The goal of that chapter is to suggest the key elements that lead to revolutions and govern their outcomes. In it, I argue that one needs to be aware of a variety of factors and of their ability to combine in different ways to produce a revolutionary crisis. Not all revolutions stem from the same causes. Thus, to foresee the coming of a revolution, it is necessary to be able to perceive critical *combinations* of elements that may, in isolation or in different combinations, otherwise be innocuous. Similarly, forecasting the outcome of revolutions depends on recognizing how a variety of distinct factors—the power of contending groups, ideology, and international conditions—act together to produce a particular result.

Chapters 4 through 13 examine particular cases of revolution and potentially revolutionary situations, evaluating the framework and drawing attention to the unique factors in each case. The variety of cases covered—ranging from revolution against a neocolonial regime in Vietnam, to revolutions against modernizing neopatrimonial regimes in Iran, Nicaragua, and the Philippines, to rebellions against Communist regimes in Afghanistan and Poland, plus examination of the struggles against racial domination in Zimbabwe and South Africa, the limited revolt against Israeli occupation in Palestine, and the genocidal outcome of the revolution in Cambodia—provides a severe test for any general framework.

The final chapter offers an evaluation of what we know, and can hope to know, about the factors that govern contemporary revolutions. Despite the variety of cases and outcomes, common patterns do emerge. Certain motivations, certain actions, and certain errors are often repeated, and suggestions are offered regarding the leading causal factors, indicators for forecasting, and actions that may influence the outcomes of modern revolutions.

NOTES

1. See Brinton (1965); Eisenstadt (1978); Goldstone (1986b); Skocpol (1979).
2. See Chaliand (1977); Dunn (1972); Eckstein (1982); Miller and Aya (1971); Paige (1975); Walton (1984); Wolf (1969).
3. See Dix (1983); Farhi (1990); Goodwin and Skocpol (1989); Gugler (1982); Liu (1988); Shugart (1989).

2

REVOLUTIONARY CONFLICT THEORY IN AN EVOLUTIONARY PERSPECTIVE

FARROKH MOSHIRI

Ted Robert Gurr's 1980 *Handbook of Political Conflict* highlights the "veritable explosion of conflict research" that began in the early 1960s. The *Handbook's* survey of books about conflict reveals that the number of published works increased from 128 prior to 1964 to 692 works in the 1964–1975 period (Gurr, ed. 1980: 16). This massive literature inspired the publication of a number of critical review articles,[1] but these articles provide too little analysis of the evolution of conflict theory as a specific field. In examining the development of conflict theory we need to ask; How did key works contribute to succeeding theoretical models of conflict? How was each of these works influenced by both the world historical and the intellectual environments within which the author lived?

This chapter is not intended to be a typical critical review. Nor is it primarily an intellectual history or a traditional historiography. Rather, it has elements of all three. My main concern is to lay out the essentials of each theoretical model and to interpret them in their historical and intellectual contexts. To achieve my purpose, I have relied extensively on paraphrasing and quotation from the works reviewed. I attempt to show how each theoretical model was affected by the world historical and intellectual environments of the author and, more important, to indicate how each theoretical model relates to successor models.

By "revolutionary conflict theory" I mean that part of the conflict theory literature that either deals exclusively with revolutions or has an important bearing on the subject. I have chosen to focus on a few works by major conflict theorists: Marx/Engels, Crane Brinton, Chalmers Johnson, Ted Robert Gurr, Charles Tilly, Theda Skocpol, and Jack Goldstone. In discussing Marx and Engels, I have relied on a number of works;[2] for each of the other theoreticians, I relied primarily on one influential work that contains the essentials of his or her theory. In addition, I have relied on a number of historical works to assess the contexts in which these theories were formed.[3]

If one views the literature of conflict theory in an evolutionary perspective, it is evident that some important variables reoccur in the major works. Thus, the development of conflict theory has depended less on discovering previously neglected variables than on assessing different *combinations* of variables that are known to be important and further specifying their operationalization.

KARL MARX AND FREDERICK ENGELS: NO ANTAGONISM, NO PROGRESS

A. S. Cohen has written with truth that the "Marxian revolutionary tradition is perhaps the most significant of any of the schools of revolutionary thought" (Cohen 1975: 54), but why is this so? At least in four overlapping yet important ways Marx contributed to the evolution of conflict theory. The first is his own theory of social revolutions as being parsimonious and "uni-causal" yet powerful and appealing. The second consists of "Marxian" approaches to revolutions by social scientists ranging from Tilly (1978), Skocpol (1979), Barrington Moore, Jr. (1966), and Eric Wolf (1969), with their all-encompassing interest in collective action, social revolutions, determinants of political systems, and peasant rebellions to historians of the great French Revolution of 1789 such as Georges Lefebvre (1962–1963) and Albert Soboul (1975). The third is Marx's influence on professional revolutionaries ranging from Lenin, Mao, and Castro to Frantz Fanon. Finally, and this might be considered Marx's greatest contribution to social sciences in general, there is his emphasis on empiricism.

Through these four concrete contributions Marx and Engels made yet another contribution, the value of which no one will ever be able to determine. For much of this century, approximately one-third of the world's population has lived under the domination of governments influenced by the ideas of Marx and Engels, and most other governments have been engaged in recurring struggles to prevent the creation of a world outlined in the *Manifesto of the Communist Party* (1848). This world order would be based on:

- abolition of property in land and application of rents of land to public purposes
- a heavy progressive or graduated income tax
- abolition of all rights of inheritance
- confiscation of property of all emigrants and rebels
- centralization of credit in the hands of the state
- extension of factories and instruments of production owned by the state, the bringing into cultivation of wasteland, and the improvement of the soil generally in accordance with a common plan
- equal liability of all to labor; establishment of industrial armies, especially for agriculture
- combination of agriculture with manufacturing industries; gradual abolition of the distinction between town and country by a more equitable distribution of the population over the country
- free education for all children in public schools; abolition of children's factory labor in its present form; combination of education with industrial production (Tucker 1978: 490)

Ironically, the governments opposed to Marx's ideals have perhaps prevented the creation of a Marxian world partly by implementing some of Marx's goals, particularly in the areas of public education and welfare. But to understand Marx, as one critic of Marx has suggested, it is necessary to understand the origins of Marx's ideas. To do so we must go back to Marx's world: a world, as Ferdinand Tonnies pointed out, that could be encapsulated in the famous phrase, no antagonism, no progress (Tonnies 1974: x).

Marx's World

Early and mid-nineteenth-century Europe was an age of contradictions. It was an age of internationalism, and the expansion of Europe's culture, political hegemony, and market system was so important an influence that one historian suggests that "the internationalism of political philosophy of Karl Marx and Frederick Engels was a true child of this age of international political and ideological fronts" (Holborn 1951: 36). Yet the nineteenth century was also an age of nationalism. The German and Italian unifications, the Polish revolution of 1830, the struggle of the Balkans to break the ever-weakening yoke of the Ottoman Empire, and the Hungarian effort to achieve equality in the Austro-Hungarian Empire were all largely owing to powerful nationalist movements. Nineteenth-century Europe was also the age of revolutions. The French revolutions of 1830 and 1848, the Polish revolt of 1830, the German revolution of 1848, and the Paris Commune of 1871, to name the more important ones, all occurred as aftershocks of the great French Revolution of 1789. Yet nineteenth-century Europe was also the age of reaction. In 1815, the Congress of Vienna not only created a model balance-of-power system but also represented a deliberate attempt by the European governments to restore the social status quo that had existed before the French Revolution.

Mid-nineteenth-century Europe witnessed an unparalleled rate of capital accumulation, yet the conditions of the working men and women of Europe worsened. In his "Inaugural Address of the Working Men's International Association," Marx used statistics provided by the British government to prove precisely this point. He quoted William Gladstone, the chancellor of the exchequer: "From 1842 to 1852 the taxable income of the country increased by six percent; in the eight years from 1853 to 1861, it has increased from the basis taken in 1853 20 per cent. . . . This intoxicating augmentation of wealth and power . . . is entirely confined to classes of property" (Tucker 1978: 514).

The British child labor situation was especially damning. Moreover, Marx believed that the British "head . . . the Europe of commerce and industry" (Tucker 1978: 515). The working people of the rest of Europe had benefited even less from the "augmentation" of wealth, but as Marx put it, "if however, the German reader shrugs his shoulders at the condition of the English industrial and agricultural laborers . . . I must plainly tell him 'de te fabula narratum' [the story is about you]" (Tucker 1978: 295–296).

Nineteenth-century Europe was also the age of science, which seemed to be triumphant everywhere. Engels, in his essay "Socialism: Utopian and Scientific," wrote of Darwin's impact on the world around him: "Nature . . . does not move in eternal oneness of a perpetually recurring circle, but goes through a real historical evolution. In this connection Darwin must be named before all others. He dealt the metaphysical conception of nature the heaviest blow by his proof that all organic beings, plants, animals, and man himself are the products of a process of evolution going through millions of years" (Tucker 1978: 697).

Marx, however, believed in practical science and practical philosophy. His eleventh thesis on Feuerbach makes this point explicitly: "Philosophers have only interpreted the world; the point however is to change it" (Tucker 1978: 145). This point is further elaborated upon in "Contributions to the Critique of Hegel's Philosophy of Right: Introduction" (1844):

> Just as philosophy finds its material weapon in the proletariat so the proletariat finds its intellectual weapon in philosophy. And once the lightning of thought has penetrated deeply into this virgin soil of the people, the Germans will emancipate themselves and become men. . . . Philosophy is the head of this emancipation and the proletariat is its heart. Philosophy can only be realized by the abolition of the proletariat, and the proletariat can only be abolished by realization of philosophy. (Tucker 1978: 65).

This belief represents a sharp contrast with the view of those scholars who believe in theory for the sake of theory, science for the sake of science, and art for the sake of art.

Yet nineteenth-century Europe was frightened by what the progress of science could do to humankind, and the utopian movements, socialist or otherwise, were influenced by the negative impact of an increasingly scientific world. Nineteenth-century Europe was the age of hope and despair of science. The hope was that science might some day enable people to overcome nature and improve their lot; the despair was over what industrial society was doing to humankind itself. Nineteenth-century Europe was thus an age of contradictions, and it was from such an epoch that a theory of society based on the contradictions of society was born. Marxist theory claimed to be scientific, international, progressive, optimistic, and confrontationalist—and so was one side of the coin of the world. It wanted to combat ignorance, parochialism, exploitation, and despair—the other side of the coin.

Marxian Conception of Society

Essential to our understanding of the Marxian notion of society are Marx's conceptualizations of historical materialism, the capitalist mode of production, and classes and their objective interest. Simply put, historical materialism means that all social, political, and cultural aspects of society are really based on the particular economic structure of that society: its mode of production. The mode of production that most concerned Marx was industrial capitalism, and in 1887, Ferdinand Tonnies referred to Karl Marx as "the discoverer of the capitalist mode of production" (Tonnies 1974: xv). Although ideas such as Hegelian dialectics and Ricardo's notion of surplus value were in existence before Marx "discovered" the capitalist mode of production, it was Marx's understanding of the nature of capitalist production and its impact on nineteenth-century Europe that lay at the heart of much of Marx's writing.

In essence, the capitalist mode of production is an exploitation of labor that earlier propertied classes would have found inconceivable. By reducing the laborer to a commodity and cutting all bonds between the laborer and master except for the "cash nexus," capitalism makes the laborer into part of a machine, a machine that has as its sole purpose the accumulation of capital. The worker is separated from any meaningful connection with his or her product, thus increasing the alienation of labor (discussed in the next section). The capitalist mode of production inexorably results in the polarization of society into two warring camps, workers and capitalists, which are distinguished by their differing relationships to the production process.

Marx was also the first social theoretician to explicitly define classes on the basis of their relations to the mode of production and exchange, and ever since, Marxian analysis has used classes as its most powerful analytical tool. By isolating groups within society that have their role in production as their most important common feature, Marxian analysis has provided an appealing explanation of conflict that is dogmatically opposed to structural-functionalist and aggregate-psychological interpretations. Socialist revolution will come when the masses recognize this objective class structure and act to end its injustices; in other words, when they become a class in and for themselves.

The Marxian Theory of Revolution

In its essence, the Marxist theory of revolution is parsimonious. Consider the following summary of the Marxist theory of revolution by Theda Skocpol: "Marx understood revolution not as an isolated episode of violence or conflict but as a class-based movement growing out of objective structural contradictions within historically developing and inherently conflict-ridden society" (Skocpol 1979: 7). Every element of Marx's definition of a social revolution is present in that summary. There is, however, one qualifying note. Marx in his later years did foresee the possibility of a social revolution that does not necessarily involve violence. On September 8, 1872, Marx delivered a speech in which he specifically pointed out the possibility of nonviolent revolution. "You know that institutions, mores, and traditions of various countries must be taken into consideration and we do not deny that there are countries—such as America, England, and if I were more familiar with your institutions, I would perhaps also add Holland—where the workers can attain their goal by peaceful means" (Tucker 1978: 522). However, this potentially nonviolent type of a Marxist revolution is rarely mentioned.

For the proletariat to unite and bring about a social revolution, its members must first become aware of their structural position—they must develop class consciousness—and the attainment of class consciousness is facilitated by a mode of production that "alienates" the worker. By alienation Marx meant three at least complementary concepts. First, the capitalist mode of production "transforms" the worker into a commodity (Cohen 1975: 63). As Marx wrote, "The bourgeoisie has resolved personal worth into exchange value" (Tucker 1978: 475). Second, it has separated the worker from his or her own product through an extensive use of machines, the "loss" of the product by labor once the product is complete, and the fact that private property is the bourgeoisie's property. Third, even the worker has become like a machine in an ever-increasing division of labor. It is when the workers realize that this "inhuman existence" is caused by the capitalist mode of production that they have gained class consciousness.

The capitalist mode of production, as well as the alienation produced by it, was, however, more entrenched in the cities of nineteenth-century Europe. Marxist theory generally overlooked the countryside. In the *German Ideology*, Marx wrote, "The greatest division of material and mental labour is the separation of town and country" (Tucker 1978: 176). In thus emphasizing the poverty, backwardness, and desperation of the country, one would think that the peasants would play an important role in Marxian revolutionary theory. However, the reality of nineteenth-century Europe was that peasants were as much an obstacle to social revolution as they were essential to its success. What most peasants wanted was to have precisely what a Marxist revolution is supposed to destroy: private property. They would go along with revolution only so long as it helped them get rid of the landlord and take over property. Classical Marxist theory was very much affected by this perception of the peasantry as essentially conservative, indeed as a drag on the forces of change. Subsequently, the revolutionary role was reserved for the urban proletariat, the working class of the cities, and peasants—along with other lower classes—were considered nonrevolutionary. The *Manifesto of the Communist Party* states:

> Today, the proletariat alone is a really revolutionary class. The other classes decay and finally disappear in the face of modern industry. The proletariat is its special and essential product. The lower middle class, the small manufacturer, the shopkeeper, the artisan, the peasant, all these fight against the bourgeoisie to save from extinction their existence as fractions of the middle class—they are therefore not revolutionary, but conservative. Nay more, they are reactionary, for they try to roll back the wheel of history. (Tucker 1978: 482)

The Marxist distinction between town and country contributed to somewhat of a neglect of peasant revolts until the recent works by Moore, Wolf, and Skocpol. Furthermore, it affected revolutionary strategy by Marxists. For agrarian societies, such as in China, it actually retarded revolutionary strategy until the pressures of the revolutionary struggle led Mao to revise the doctrine.

The target of revolution remains somewhat ambiguous in Marx—should revolutionaries attack the dominant class or must they first attack the state? Who is in control of the social order? In Marx's and Engels' own writings, both views exist. The view that the state is simply a tool of the dominant class is explicitly expressed in the *Manifesto*: "The bourgeoisie has at last, since the establishment of modern industry and of the world market, conquered for itself, in the modern representative state, exclusive political sway. The executive of the modern state is but a committee for managing the common affairs of the whole bourgeoisie" (Tucker 1978: 475).

Yet, Engels also wrote about the state as an autonomous structure, such as in the United States of America. In the *Civil War in France*, the introduction by Engels explicitly points out that "it is precisely in America that we see best how there takes place this process of state power making itself independent in relation to society, whose mere instrument it was originally intended to be . . . this transformation of the state and the organs of the state from servants of society into masters of society" (Marx 1972: 16). But in the very same introduction Engels goes back to the other notion of the state, not as an independent organ but an instrument of class oppression. "In reality, however, the state is nothing but a machine for the oppression of one class by another, and indeed in the democratic republic no less than in monarchy" (Marx 1972: 17).

Hence, classical Marxist writing, as that of Marx and Engels, seems to provide for both an autonomous state structure and a state structure that is essentially an instrument of class oppression. These two views of the state are not only un-contradictory, they are complementary. The state is an instrument of class oppression, but it suppresses classes for its own purposes and those purposes are more often than not also in line with the interests of the bourgeoisie.

Contributions to Revolutionary Strategy: Emphasis on Organization and Identification of Revolutionary Classes and the Notion of the Vanguard

With regard to revolutionary strategy, Marxist contributions were of critical importance in how socialist revolutions, especially in Russia, occurred. There are several key concepts involved, one being the focus on organization. Time after time Marx declared that the workers must "unite to achieve victory." In the "Address to the Central Committee of the Communist League" in 1850, Marx said, "The worker's party . . . must act in the most organized, most unanimous and most independent fashion possible if it is not to be exploited and taken in tow again by bourgeoisie as in 1848" (Tucker 1978: 502). In the *Manifesto* he had written: "Now and then the workers are victorious, but only for a time. The real fruit of their battles lies not in the immediate result, but in the ever-expanding union of the workers. . . . This organization of the proletarians into a class, and consequently into a political party, is continually being upset. . . . But it ever rises up again, stronger, firmer, and mightier" (Tucker 1978: 481). If Marxian conflict theorists have picked up on organization as a key variable in successful revolutions, so did Marxist revolutionaries such as Lenin and Mao (Cohen 1975: 80). Even today Communist parties are among the best organized parties of the world.

Marx also identified revolutionary versus nonrevolutionary classes, which also affected revolutionary strategy. As stated before, in China the lack of a significant proletariat actually retarded revolutionary progress until Mao argued that when the proletariat is insignificant, "other classes which may be in a similar relationship with the dominant class . . . may have revolutionary potential" (Cohen 1975: 95). Finally, Marxist theory contributed the notion of the vanguard party. That idea is not a purely Leninist addition as some would argue, as the Communists' role in leading the proletariat is specifically pointed out by Marx in the *Manifesto*: "The communists, therefore, are on the one hand, practically, the most advanced and resolute section of the working class parties of every country, that section which pushes forward all others; on the other hand, theoretically, they have over the great mass of the proletariat the advantage of clearly understanding the line of march, the conditions, and the ultimate general results of the proletarian movement" (Tucker 1978: 484).

Internationalism of Marxist Theory

The Marxist theory of revolution does not deal with one particular country or only a few, as the conditions that lead to a socialist revolution are supposed to develop everywhere. More important, Marxist theory is international in the sense that—for the first time—social, political, and economic conditions everywhere in the world are connected to the developments everywhere else. In "On Imperialism in India" (1853), Marx pointed out that this interrelationship is owing to the specific mode of production of the capitalist system.

> The destructive influence of that centralization upon the markets of the world does but reveal, in most gigantic dimensions, the inherent organic laws of political economy now at work in every civilized town. The bourgeois period of history has to create the material basis of the new world—on the one hand the universal intercourse founded upon the mutual dependency of mankind, and the means of that intercourse; on the other hand the development of the productive powers of man and the transformation of material production into a scientific domination of natural agencies. Bourgeois industry and commerce create these material conditions of a new world. (Tucker 1978: 663–664)

One can no longer ignore the international system when analyzing revolution. Not surprisingly, Marxian approaches to revolution, such as Skocpol's, place a significant emphasis on the world market and the international system. This emphasis also serves as the starting point for dependency theory, which is essentially Marxist in its analytical approach. Lastly, radical political economy as we know it today explains the poverty in Third World nations as the result of "structural violence" created by the capitalist mode of production.

Summary of Marx/Engels

It was the inhumane nature of nineteenth-century capitalist production that made Marx devote his entire life to struggling to overthrow the very existence of capitalism. *Das Kapital* could not possibly have been written in another era. Similarly, every contribution of Marx to conflict theory derived from the fact that Marx was a child of nineteenth-century Europe. Even his very focus on revolutions was largely shaped by the fact that early and mid-nineteenth-century Europe was constantly fought over by revolutionaries and reactionaries. Marx wrote about the objective world as he saw it.

CRANE BRINTON: THE THERMIDOR

Crane Brinton's last edition of *The Anatomy of Revolution* (1965), Ted Robert Gurr's Ph.D. dissertation, which was the foundation of *Why Men Rebel* (1970), and Chalmers Johnson's first edition of *Revolutionary Change* (1966) all appeared during 1965 and 1966. Also in 1965, David Truman delivered a presidential address to the American Political Science Association (APSA) entitled, "Disillusion and Regeneration: The Quest for a Discipline," in which he raised the issue of an emerging paradigm in political science. The relationship between the three influential works on revolutionary conflict theory and Truman's presidential address is related to a revolution within political science itself. The behavioral revolution was at its peak and already under attack by forces that four years later David Easton was to label the post behavioral movement in his 1969 APSA presidential address, "The New Revolution in Political Science." What was at stake, and why was this debate important for the evolution of revolutionary conflict theory?

The Behavioral Impact on Conflict Theory

What do we mean by the behavioral revolution? Some critics charged that behavioralism meant "dealing in trivialities," lack of "concern with values," "ignoring institutions," and mere counting. A few of the behavioralists might have been guilty of such offenses, but most, especially the distinguished behavioralists such as Howard Lasswell, David Truman, and David Easton, simply wanted to shift the focus of political science from "prescription, ethical inquiry, and action to description, explanation, and verification" (Easton 1969: 1053). Their argument was that reliable knowledge must be accumulated before action can be prescribed, and the only way such knowledge can be obtained is through rigorous, empirical research "modeled" after the physical sciences. Hence, the first implication for conflict theory research was that the methodology of conducting research received more attention. Second, objectivity—in the sense that the social scientist must try to remain as unattached from the subject of his or her research as possible— became a guiding light. It is in these respects that Brinton, Gurr, and Johnson can be argued to have been influenced by the behavioral movement.

The behavioral era included a third component, the growth of interdisciplinary exchange, especially in the cases of Chalmers Johnson and Gurr. Gurr postulated a sequence—relative deprivation, discontent, politicized discontent, political violence—which is a more detailed and "controlled" version of the psychological frustration–aggression hypothesis of John Dollard and others (Dollard et al. 1939). Similarly, Johnson's systems theory approach has its origins in neurology, where systems theory was developed to explore the functioning of the human brain. B. F. Skinner's stimuli, organism, response sequence is an analog of the input, system, output structure of systems analysts. Finally, Brinton's conceptualization of revolutions as "fevers" had its roots in pathology (Brinton 1965: 5).

Crane Brinton's last edition of *The Anatomy of Revolution*, Johnson's first edition of *Revolutionary Change*, and Gurr's *Why Men Rebel* also have a common world-historical context.[4] All were written in a period when civil strife and international instability were endemic. To this end Brinton wrote, "We live in the midst of the alarums of war and revolution, of what can be not unfairly called world-wide revolution" (Brinton 1965: 5). Civil strife was the rule, especially in the United States where "antiwar violence, campus turmoil, ghetto riots, and a contagion of political assassinations generated a kind of apocalyptic perception that the seams of American society were coming apart" (Graham and Gurr 1979: 13).

All of these authors believed that understanding such violence required analyzing more and better data. They were aided by the fact that the 1960s witnessed the computer revolution, as this technology enabled the social scientist to process massive amounts of data on numerous cases or countries. That might have been critical for the empirical testing of Gurr's *Why Men Rebel*, but how would it have helped Brinton? *The Anatomy of Revolution* does not rely on computer analysis of quantitative data; rather, it is a comparative historical treatment. Nonetheless, the 1965 edition came out at a time when much more historical data was available and access to historical data was much easier. "Even in the field of history," Brinton wrote, "our existing supply of facts is surprisingly good" (Brinton 1965: 13).

Scientific History and Comparative Research

Brinton's greatest contribution to conflict theory is his demonstration that comparative historical analysis could be conducted on a scientific basis, and he devotes three sections of his introductory chapter to the discussion of scientific method. To him "the bare elements of scientific thinking" are "conceptual scheme, facts, especially 'case histories,' logical operations [and] uniformities" (Brinton 1965: 13). Particularly interesting is his defense of historical facts. He points out that "you cannot draw Cromwell back to life, but neither can you call the dinosaurs back to life. What we know about Cromwell from the written record is in many ways as reliable as what we know about dinosaurs from the fossil record" (Brinton 1965: 13). He then argues that the social sciences have a good supply of facts. But since these facts must be put in a "conceptual scheme," he identifies the concept of "equilibrium." In effect, he seems to view revolution as synonymous with disequilibrium. "As new desires arise, or as old desires grow strong in various groups, or as environmental conditions change, and as institutions fail to change, a relative disequilibrium may arise, and what we call a revolution breakout" (Brinton 1965: 16). Later, though, he dismisses the concept of equilibrium, preferring to use a conceptual scheme borrowed from pathology and view revolutions as a "fever." Signs of the coming disease (revolution) appear, then the symptoms, and finally the crisis accompanied by a reign of terror and eventually recovery (the thermidor).

Brintonian Theory of Revolution: The Uniformities

Brinton sought to develop a theory of revolution by seeking uniformities in the pattern of events in four cases: The English (1640), American (1776), French (1789), and Russian (1917) revolutions. According to Brinton's theory, structural weaknesses are a critical uniformity, an idea later theoreticians (Skocpol in particular) built upon. All four prerevolutionary societies had governments that faced financial difficulties (Brinton 1965: 24). As a further point, a symptom of revolution in such societies is a group feeling of frustration with existing structures: "Certain economic grievances—usually not in the form of economic distress, but rather a feeling on the part of some of the chief enterprising groups that their opportunities for getting on in this world are unduly limited by political arrangements—would seem to be one of the symptoms of revolution" (Brinton 1965: 34). There are two important notions in that passage: Collectively or group-based perceptions are what really matter, and the barriers to a group's expectations are viewed as illegitimate. This conception is similar to Gurr's notion of just expectations.

Next, Brinton talks about the importance of mobilization (critical to Tilly 1978) and the politicization of discontent (critical to Gurr 1970). Collective discontent "must, of course, be raised to an effective social pitch by propaganda, pressure-group action, public meetings, and preferably a few good dramatic riots, like the Boston Tea Party" (Brinton 1965: 34). How does the structural part of a government's bankruptcy relate to group-based discontent? Brinton says that financial difficulties make governments inefficient and subsequently unable to address this discontent. Governments do realize the problem; hence, they try to reform, one uniformity that Brinton mentions in passing and Skocpol develops fully (Brinton 1965: 39). Finally, a good part of the intellectual community in a prerevolutionary society turns against the government and subsequently expresses "ideas" that shape and formulate the group-based discontent. This "transfer of allegiance of the intellectuals" is a critical uniformity and a symptom that Brinton stresses.

Although Brinton takes exception to a narrow economic conception of the term "class," he nonetheless proposes that intensified class antagonism is another important uniformity. Marx before Brinton, as well as Skocpol and Tilly after him, also emphasize class struggle, but "class" enters Brintonian theory in another way. The ruling class lacks solidarity and is divided, and some among the ruling class feel that they are unjustly in power (Brinton 1965: 55). Essentially, the Brintonian uniformities can be summarized as follows.

- fiscal crisis makes government inefficient
- the inefficiency frustrates an important group's aspiration for advancement
- the group becomes discontented
- the discontent is politicized by "desertion of intellectuals" and mobilization
- government initiates reforms to improve its efficiency, but reforms fail; perhaps they only increase group frustration
- class conflicts become more intensified
- the ruling class becomes divided over how to cope with the crisis
- the government is consequently inconsistent in its behavior, which only makes the situation worse
- what happens at this point, according to Brinton, is that revolution is "in the air." People actually "talk about" it, and then the revolution occurs (Brinton 1965: 66)

Brintonian Theory of Revolution:
The Stages of the Revolutionary Process

After describing the source of revolution, Brinton talks about how the revolution actually progresses. There are four stages: the actual overthrow of the government, the rule of the moderates, the accession of the extremists and an accompanying reign of terror, and finally, the thermidor.

The first stage is preceded by an increase in antigovernment protests and ends with the victory of the revolutionary party. It contains the following set of uniformities:

- government failure to raise revenue through taxation (Brinton 1965: 78)
- polarization of society into revolutionary and status quo parties
- government reliance on force and the failure of force to curb discontent (Brinton 1965: 86)

The last generality is quite an important one in revolutionary conflict theory. Brinton added that "no government has ever fallen before attackers until it has lost control over its armed forces or lost the ability to use them effectively" (Brinton 1965: 89). Chalmers Johnson refers to this condition as an "accelerator." Somehow government control over coercive means, Johnson argues, must break down before the revolution succeeds (see later discussion of Johnson). An empirical study by Russell (1974) supports the hypothesis proposed by Brinton and Johnson.

The second stage begins with the revolutionary party in power. The uniformity that Brinton proposes here is that a centrist, moderate reform party takes power but as soon as the "moderates" are in control, they are attacked by extremists from both sides of the political spectrum. An important concept Brinton introduces here is the notion of "dual sovereignty," defined as "[two] conflicting chains of institutions providing two conflicting sets of decisions" (Brinton 1965: 133). The one set of institutions is the legal government headed by the moderates; the other is the extremist organization, which while illegal, usually commands more support and is better staffed. The English revolution had the Long Parliament and the New Model Army, the French had the Feuillants (constitutional monarchists) and the Jacobin societies, and in Russia there was a struggle between the provisional government and the workers' councils (soviets) controlled by the Bolsheviks and their allies. At this point, the legal government becomes a liability for the moderates, since, as the people responsible for maintaining law and order, they often have to oppose the aspirations of the masses.

The concept of dual sovereignty is an important uniformity—which also holds true in the case of the recent Iranian revolution (Moshiri 1985: chap. 7)—and Tilly develops the concept more fully and introduces his own notion of multiple sovereignty (Tilly 1978). It is in the fact of dual (or multiple) sovereignty where the logic of the demise of the moderates lies. Dual or multiple sovereignty paralyzes a moderate government's effectiveness as there can be counter orders issued by the competing sovereign body. Unable to effectively command, and therefore unable to solve the problems that spurred the revolution, the moderates grow unpopular, weak, and vulnerable to a radical coup.

In the crisis stage of the revolution, dual sovereignty is ended by an extremist coup d'etat. Extremists replace the moderates, Brinton argues, because of their effective organization (disciplined, few in number, and solidly behind their leader) and their fitness (adaptability to a crisis situation, some degree of experience in government, and endurance under oppression). The extremists then impose their own dictatorship through a "centralized executive commission" (e.g., committee of public safety). Finally, they institutionalize terror. The reign of terror, besides ruthless persecution of all opposition parties, includes a social revolution. The extremists try to destroy "everything of the contaminated past" (Brinton 1965: 174) and to institute a new social order internally, and they devote some of their resources to spreading their "gospel" abroad (p. 192). Brinton suggests, that "perhaps the most important uniformity" is the fact that all revolutions are "universalist in aspiration and nationalist, exclusive in ultimate goal" (p. 196). The extremist reign is also marked by an acute economic crisis (p. 200), heightened class struggle, an uncompromising stand on the part of the leadership (p. 202), and finally an "extraordinary mixture of spiritual fury, of exaltation, of devotion and self-sacrifice"—the reign of virtue (pp. 202–203).

"A convalescence from the fever of revolution," is the final stage of the Brintonian process model. Brinton calls this stage "the thermidor," after the month in the French Revolutionary calendar in which the radicals lost power. Its beginning is marked by the fall of the extremists, who are eventually replaced by a "tyrant." Terror continues, but it is relaxed. Amnesty is granted to formerly persecuted "pure radicals, then the moderates, then the moderate conservatives, until the final restoration brings back remnants of the old gang" (Brinton 1965: 209). The terror is now aimed at only "the convinced and persistent extremists." (p. 211). The thermidor is also marked by the return of the church and a certain degree of toleration for the recognized religion of the old order. At the same time, there is a relaxation of social controls, and a "search for pleasure" begins as the reign of virtue has ended.

Brinton on the Outcome of Revolution: Strengthened States and Varying Types of Revolutions

A social revolution, Brinton argues, creates more powerful institutions than existed before. This achievement of government efficiency is really the most striking uniformity we can note in estimating the political changes effected by a revolution (Brinton 1965: 239). Socially, revolutions do result in some changes in distribution (p. 241), but these really amount to a transfer of economic power from one group to another and not a total change in the class structure of the society. Intellectually, the revolution establishes "a tradition of successful revolt" and a number of ideas that "weigh heavily" on the new ruling class (pp. 248–249).

Brinton differentiates between popular revolutions (England, America, France, Russia, and China), rightist or fascist revolutions (Italian and German), territorial-nationalist revolutions (Algeria), and abortive revolutions (American Civil War). What is important in Brinton's typology is that the outcome of a revolution does not serve to classify it; rather, it is the ideology of the group involved in the revolutionary struggle that is crucial. This is a critical point for it stands in sharp contrast to conceptualizations of revolution, such as Skocpol's, in which it is explicitly denied that the ideology of the revolutionary group plays any part in determining the outcome (Taylor 1984: 43). The latter view is problematic for it takes away a certain degree of predictive power. The former is useful for it allows us to speculate on the kind of order that a successful revolution might bring about. If we want to know the outcome of a major social conflict, Brinton seems to be telling us, all we have to do is to consider the ideology of the revolutionary group and the possibility of their success. The French, Russian, and English revolutions are classified as social revolutions, not so much because of their outcomes, but because of their class-based ideology (Brinton 1965: 26).

Summary of Brinton

Brinton revised *The Anatomy of Revolution* for the 1965 edition in a world that was more unstable than ever before, in an intellectual environment sharply divided over the role and functions of the intellectual, and in a social science context influenced by behavioralism. His most important methodological contribution was to show that scientific historical research on revolution can be done using qualitative comparisons. To revolutionary conflict theory he made the following specific contributions: (a) an elaboration of the transfer of allegiance by intellectuals, (b) a process theory of revolutionary stages, and (c) a discussion of outcomes.

CHALMERS JOHNSON:
SYSTEMS THEORY AND REVOLUTION

One year after Brinton's 1965 edition of *The Anatomy of Revolution*, Chalmers Johnson's influential work, *Revolutionary Change*, was published, and the points made earlier about the world historical and intellectual context surrounding Brinton, Johnson, and Gurr find explicit support in the foreword and preface of this work. The foreword, written by Sheldon S. Wolin, discusses behavioralism. Wolin writes:

> A quarter-century ago only a few voices challenged the prevailing consensus regarding the methods of political science, the choice of problems, and the relative weight [of] factors shaping political events, custom, and behavior. Since then a revolution of uncertain proportion has occurred, one that has been variously described as "the behavioral movement" or "social science." . . . It has visibly altered the climate of political science . . . today's political scientist is receptive to quantitative classification of empirical data. . . . No longer does [the political scientist] believe that political science is a self-contained field. It has become second nature for him to utilize methods, concepts, and data drawn from a wide range of academic disciplines. (Johnson 1966: v, vi)

The interdisciplinary context in which Johnson wrote becomes evident in his preface when he writes, "Because I have borrowed extensively from the theoretical literature of scholarly fields other than my own, I hope that my interpretations do not pain greatly the sociologists, anthropologists, philosophers, and social psychologists to whom I am indebted" (Johnson 1966: xii).

The fact that Brinton, Johnson, and Gurr all wrote in a world historical context of widespread conflict is also explicit in Johnson's preface. The concluding pages of the preface deal with the student rebellion at Berkeley in autumn of 1964: "In the autumn of 1964, the university was racked by a student rebellion that it was my good fortune to observe and to learn from . . . more important than being a locale of revolution, Berkeley has influenced me and this book, through my education there" (Johnson 1966: xiv).

Johnson's Contributions to Conflict Theory

Johnson contributed to the evolution of conflict theory in the following respects: first, his synthesis of coercion and value theories of society; second, his application of systems theory to the analysis of conflict, including his model of revolution; and third, his development of the important concept of accelerators. According to Johnson, his theory of revolutionary change combines the Weberian and value theories of society (Johnson 1966: 17). Revolutions are viewed as "antisocial" events, occurring in a society in which the harmony of values is no longer in existence. The system has become disequilibrated. However, coercion can still maintain the system, provided that the elite undertakes a set of policies to redress the causes of value disharmony in the society and direct the social system toward homeostatic equilibrium. The contrast to theories of society that rely exclusively either on the value theory approach or the coercion theory approach is indeed dramatic. Social systems are not purely "moral communities" that will maintain themselves at all times. Authorities must use coercion at certain points to ensure the continued existence of the social system, but coercion alone can not indefinitely maintain the system. The system must rely on the shared values of its members, which legitimize its injustices. A critical implication of Johnson's synthesis of coercion theory and value theory concerns the outcomes of revolution. Revolutions occur and succeed eventually because the political leadership of the polity has failed to perform its tasks. Revolutions do not need to occur and, more important, do not need to succeed.

Johnson's complex model of the causes of revolution (Figure 5-1 in the 1966 edition) is essentially an elaborated version of systems theorists' approaches to the political system. What Johnson does is to use the concept of a system as a theoretical framework to present his ideas about the causes of revolution. Systems theory was best represented in the work of David Easton, who presented a simplified graphic version of his arguments (see Figure 2.1). This is essentially the model that Johnson uses. The environment, according to Johnson, contributes to social change by affecting either the values or the pattern of division of labor. "Rise of external reference groups" and "foreign conquest" are two examples of environmental contributions to social change (Johnson 1966: 106). Within the system itself, values and division of labor can also be altered (religious innovation or technological innovation are examples). These changes enter the social system as inputs. Normally the social system, like a biological unit, possesses mechanisms to adapt to these inputs. However, if these mechanisms fail, the system becomes disequilibrated. Disequilibrium can occur if one, socialization is incoherent; two, roles have been inappropriately assembled; three, the society no longer agrees on goals; or four, resulting conflicts are not solved peacefully (Johnson 1966: 106). Elite reaction to this disequilibrium will then have a feedback effect to the very source of disequilibration. For instance, if the elite decides to use coercion without regard to the lack of value agreements, the result is a further disintegration of consensus among the society's members, which in turn moves the system further from equilibrium. The best summary of Johnson's theory is provided by Johnson himself.

Figure 2.1   A Simple Model of a Political System

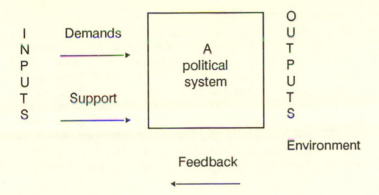

Environment

	Demands		O
I		A	U
N	——→	political	T
P		system	P
U			U
T	Support		T
S	——→		S

Environment

Feedback

←———

Source: David Easton, "An Approach to the Analysis of Political Systems," *World Politics* 9 (April 1957). Used by permission of The Johns Hopkins University Press.

There are two clusters of mutually-influencing necessary . . . causes of any revolution. First there are the pressures created by a disequilibrated social system—a society which is changing and which is in need of further change if it is to continue to exist. . . . The second cluster of necessary causes revolves around the quality of the purposeful change being undertaken while a system is disequilibrated . . . the final, or sufficient, cause of a revolution is some ingredient, usually contributed by fortune, which deprives the elite of its chief weapon for enforcing social behavior (accelerator). (Johnson 1966: 91)

The first situation, a disequilibrated social system, results in what Johnson calls "power deflation," excessive use of force. The second situation results in "loss of authority"—which occurs if the elite is intransigent and continues to rely on force. What is interesting about the last factor, accelerators, is its probabilistic connotation within a specified framework of time yet the certainty of its occurrence somewhere along the line. In a formula, "power deflation + loss of authority + an accelerator = revolution" (Johnson 1966: 119).

An accelerator is a factor that destroys the deterrent effect of governmental force, which can happen in a number of ways. "Defeat in war" or "a belief that the army can be crippled" are two examples of accelerators (Johnson 1966: 104). What is important about this concept is that it focuses attention on the armed forces. No modern revolution will ever succeed if the armed forces of the government have remained intact (have not suffered from some serious loss) or if the revolutionaries do not believe that they could somehow reduce the coercive power of the armed forces. The focus on the role of armed forces is a critical variable in Brinton, Ted Robert Gurr (his notion of coercive balance), and Skocpol (her reliance on the impact of foreign wars on the state). What all these theories emphasize, in varying degree, is that analysis of revolution must focus on who has the guns, how many guns, and under what circumstances the guns will be used.

Johnson in Evolutionary Perspective

Brinton, Johnson, and Gurr wrote in the same world historical and intellectual contexts. They also all believe that revolutions occur "contingently" upon certain factors; they are not inevitable. Despite the fact that Johnson's theory is characterized as structural-functionalist,[5] he is nevertheless far from the deterministic approach of Marx. In Johnson's world, it matters what kind of people occupy these structures, especially the institutions of the state. Even if a disequilibrated social system is in existence, the elite can still prevent a revolution from occurring. The elite has choices open to it. Gurr moves even further from the deterministic view of social action; in Gurr's world, revolutions occur because people purposely decide to make revolutions. In Gurr's vision of society, the mind of the individual is a critical factor.

TED ROBERT GURR: *WHY MEN REBEL*

The Theory of Relative Deprivation

The core of Gurr's theory is quite parsimonious. The widespread perception of relative deprivation leads to discontent, which tends to lead to politicization of discontent, which tends to lead to political violence (Gurr, 1970: 12–13). Nowhere in Gurr's writings, contrary to many common interpretations, is relative deprivation presented as both a necessary and a sufficient cause of civil strife. Relative deprivation itself is defined as "a perceived discrepancy between [people's] value expectations and their value capabilities. Value expectations are the goods and conditions of life to which people believe they are rightfully entitled. Value capabilities are goods and conditions they think they are capable of attaining or maintaining, given the social means available to them" (Gurr 1970: 13).

There are two important points in that quotation. First, expectations must be just expectations; that is, people must not only want something but really think they are "entitled" to it. Second, the whole concept is based on peoples' "perceptions" and not on how things actually might be. The latter is where the strengths and weaknesses of the concept lie and is one of Gurr's major contributions to conflict theory: focusing on the dynamics of human behavior as dictated by people's perceptions of the world. Gurr argues that when people define situations as real, they are real in their consequences. If we accept that argument, then the advantages of bringing in focus the dynamics of human behavior far outweigh the possible error associated with our measurement techniques.[6]

The theory itself elaborates on the discrepancy between expectations and capabilities. First, there are three forms of the gap: decremental deprivation, in which the group's value expectations remain relatively constant but value capabilities are perceived to decline; aspirational deprivation, in which capabilities remain relatively static while expectations increase or intensify; and progressive deprivation, in which there is substantial and simultaneous increase in expectations and decrease in capabilities (Gurr 1970: 46). The critical point here is that the resulting discrepancy from all three forms of relative deprivation is temporary: "over the long run [people's] value expectations tend to adapt to their value capabilities" (p. 58). The intensity and persistence of the short-term feeling of frustration that results from any of the three forms of relative deprivation depends upon (a) the "average degree" of the gap, (b) the "average importance" of the set of values affected by the gap, (c) the number or proportion of "value classes" affected by the gap, and (d) time.

With regard to the hierarchy of values, Gurr proposes that in any heterogeneous population, the intensity of relative deprivation is greatest with respect to discrepancies affecting economic values, less with respect to security and communality values, and least with respect to participation, self-realization, status, or ideational coherence values (Gurr 1970: 71). A number of other qualifications are also introduced. As time passes, the intensity of relative deprivation (hereafter RD) first increases and then declines. The importance of a value position varies positively and directly with "the effort invested in attaining or maintaining the desired position" (p. 73). Finally, and with regard to the particular form of aspirational RD, "the closeness of the desired value position at the time discrepancy is first experienced" intensifies the resulting frustration (p. 73).

The intensity of RD for a collectivity is said to be the average amount of anger felt by all members of that collectivity. This is the psychological component. How many members of a collectivity are affected by the anger resulting from RD is a question of scope and thus a sociological variable (Gurr 1970: 83). In any society some people will feel deprived about something. The first step in analyzing their potential for collective action is to determine what proportion of the population shares the same feelings of intense deprivation, and about what (pp. 86–91).

Operationally, one should begin by identifying the relevant classes, economic strata, and demographic and communal groups in each society. The groupings that are relevant will vary among societies. The proportional size of each group is determined (from census-type data, if available). Then the pattern of political and economic deprivation affecting the group is judged based on information about conditions such as economic adversity, deprivational government policies (for example, confiscatory fiscal policies or restrictions on political activities), and degrees of inequality across ethnic or religious barriers. The proportion of each group affected by one or more such conditions is the indicator of the scope of RD; intensity is a function of the severity of the policies or conditions. The product of the scope and intensity measures for each group is an index of their magnitude of discontent—and of their potential for collective action.

As Gurr put it, "The potential for collective violence would be greatest in a nation most of whose citizens felt sharply deprived with respect to their most deeply valued goals, had individually and collectively exhausted the constructive means open to them to attain those goals, and lacked any non-violent opportunity to act on their anger" (Gurr 1970: 92). Some degree of RD is present in any population at all times. What is crucial to the onset of conflict is the intensification of RD owing to conditions that either raise expectations or cause declining capabilities in key population groups.

Gurr identifies four sources of rising expectations. One is the demonstration effect of exposure to the material culture of Western societies through the media or through literacy and Western education. Gurr, however, modifies the demonstration effect by proposing that one must consider "the intensity and scope of pre-existing Relative Deprivation in the group" when examining the demonstration effect (Gurr 1970: 101). Even when preexisting RD is intense in a given group, the demonstration effect is likely to be a powerful source of rising expectations only when people believe there is some chance of obtaining these new value goals (p. 102). Second, similar effects can occur as the result of the introduction of a new ideological belief, such as the appeal of communism to peasants who are made subjectively aware of their own privation (p. 104).[7] A third kind of demonstration effect occurs when the position of a group's reference group is improved (p. 105). Finally, rising expectations can occur if a group has different value positions on different axes of values; say, a high economic value position and low political and status positions (p. 109).

A critical point is that revolution becomes most likely when expectations have risen, owing to some limited reform process, after a prolonged period of intense deprivation but then expectations are crushed (Gurr 1970: 117). "Only a great genius can save a prince who undertakes to relieve his subjects after a long oppression" (de Tocqueville quoted in Gurr 1970: 117). Gurr suggests that to avoid a revolutionary outcome in such instances, "value outputs and opportunities" must be continually expanded while institutional loyalties are strengthened and authority is maintained (Gurr 1970: 121). The occurrence of RD, however, is not only dependent upon rising expectations. A decrease in the capabilities and opportunities available to a group can also contribute to the creation of discontent. An example of the former is the sudden imposition of austerity measures, which has the effect, for example, of reducing the capability of the poorest Latin Americans to realize their welfare values.

Once discontent has been created, whether or not it becomes politicized depends on a variety of intervening factors. Loss of government legitimacy, which was critical for Brinton and Johnson, is regarded by Gurr as an important factor in explaining civil strife events. Whether or not a discontented group resorts to violent action depends in part on the availability of normative (cultural or value-based) justifications for undertaking violent action. The legitimacy of the political regime is one of the most important of these normative factors. Furthermore, Gurr incorporates rational choice arguments, proposing that the cost-benefit calculations of discontented groups, especially of their leaders, shape the likelihood of political action. Finally, the balance of coercive forces, that is, the relative military power of government versus opposition parties and the presence or absence of organized structures for the support of the opposition party as compared to support mechanisms for the government, interacts with politicized discontent to determine the extent, magnitude, and general forms of political violence.

Gurr in Evolutionary Perspective

Why Men Rebel is an exemplar of the contributions of the behavioral revolution, not only in its reliance on empirical quantitative analysis, but in the sense of the deliberate attempt by Gurr to distance himself emotionally from the subject of his analysis. Brinton's words echo in Gurr's writing when the latter writes that his work could be used by both governments and rebels. Epistemologically, Gurr sharply differs with scholars such as Alasdair MacIntyre and Sheldon S. Wolin in the sense that unlike the latter, he does believe that revolution is subject to objective and systematic analysis. He also differs from Marx in the sense that he does not explicitly argue for a practical philosophy that would change the world as well as interpret it.

Substantively, Gurr's work is much closer to Brinton and Johnson, especially the latter. In fact, Gurr later wrote that "social structural theories [e.g., Johnson, Smelser, etc.] differ in emphasis rather than kind from the social-psychological theories," for example those of Gurr and Ivo and Rosalind Feierbend (Gurr 1973: 359–392). Both schools of thought agree on the critical role of social change in the creation of "strain" or dislocation; both emphasize the importance of norms, beliefs, and values in society; both focus on the balance of institutional support (structural conduciveness); both argue that elite intransigence is likely to worsen the prospects for a nonviolent outcome; and both pay critical attention to the armed forces. Gurr and Johnson would disagree only over whether and how the psychological level of analysis should be considered.

In later works Gurr moves away somewhat from his initial emphasis on psychological variables. In his model for forecasting domestic political conflict, he argues that the extent of political conflict depends upon (a) discontent, which is inferred from structural inequalities in societies, (b) dispositions toward conflict, and (c) organizational strength. The revised theoretical model stipulates an interactive relationship among the three characteristics of conflict groups. Disposition toward conflict in turn depends on rational calculations regarding such factors as the history of successful challenges, the balance of strength of forces, and the availability of normative justifications for attacking the regime (i.e., illegitimacy of the regime). Organizational strength, on the other hand, depends upon the size, cohesiveness and coercive capability of the particular group. However, discontent remains at the core of the theoretical model: Groups will not rebel unless their members share intense discontents. This psychological underpinning of the theory has been intensely criticized by a number of conflict theoreticians, among whom Charles Tilly and Theda Skocpol are most prominent.

CHARLES TILLY AND THEDA SKOCPOL

Charles Tilly and Theda Skocpol share more than a strong opposition to the social-psychological school of thought as both claim to be working in what is generally referred to as the Marxian tradition. In particular, they pay explicit attention to concepts such as class interest and focus on structures rather than individuals. Both share the views of the postbehavioralists. They question, as did

Wolin and MacIntyre, the feasibility of a unified analysis of different categories of conflict (this is especially true in the case of Skocpol). In addition, they are both sociologists with a thorough knowledge of the history of particular cases and a strong belief that such knowledge is crucial for theory building.

Each has made very important specific contributions to conflict theory. Tilly focuses our attention on group mobilization; Skocpol reminds us of the importance of the world historical context and of the need to look at the international and domestic scenes simultaneously. In a larger perspective, Tilly provides a synthesis between structural and individual orientations; Skocpol provides the connection between international and domestic arenas.

Tilly—Resource Mobilization

Tilly's 1978 *From Mobilization to Revolution* is based on two important models: the polity model and the mobilization model. The polity model defines politics as interaction among groups and it consists of the following parts: government, contenders (challengers and members of polity), the polity, and coalitions (Tilly 1978: 52). Government is defined as the organization that has the greatest coercive capacity in the polity. Challengers and members are organized groups; they are members of the polity if they have routine access to resources controlled by the government and challengers if they lack access. When any number of these groups decide to act together they have formed a coalition. What is important about the polity model is that it is the conflict between and among groups that is the key to understanding revolutions. As early as 1973 Tilly had laid out this central point (Tilly 1973: 436). The specific claims and counterclaims being made on an existing government by various mobilized groups are more important than the general satisfaction or discontent of these groups, and such claims for established places within the structure of power are crucial.

The polity model describes the behavior of all the polity's contenders. A single contender's behavior is explained by the mobilization model, which has the following parts:

- interests: shared costs or benefits of a particular course of action
- organization: shared values, identities, unifying structure
- mobilization: "the extent of resources" under group "control" (normative, coercive, and utilitarian)
- power: gaining relative to other groups as a consequence of interaction with them
- repression: the cost of interaction with other groups
- opportunity/threat: likelihood of interaction with other groups (Tilly 1978: 54–56, 66, 69)

In the mobilization model, the extent of a group's collective action is based on its degree of mobilization, opportunity, and power (as defined above), whereas the degree of mobilization is determined by organization, interest, repression, and opportunity (Tilly 1978: 57). In essence, a highly mobilized group is able to demand vast resources from its members and have them delivered. The most important independent variable in the entire model is interest. Tilly argues that in the long run, individuals' interest is determined by their "real" interest, which is their social position in connection to the "relations of production," whereas in the short run, their interest is what they say it is. He then addresses the conflict between individual interest and group interest by proposing that such a conflict will affect the cost of collective action for the group (pp. 61–62).

The models nicely lead us to what Tilly calls a revolutionary situation—or a situation of "multiple sovereignty," defined as a situation in which the existing government of a polity "becomes the object of effective, competing, mutually exclusive claims on the part of two or more distinct polities" (Tilly 1978: 191). The causes of the existence of a revolutionary situation are:

1. the appearance of contenders, or coalitions of contenders, advancing exclusive alternative claims to control over the government, which is currently exerted by members of the polity
2. commitment to these claims by a significant segment of the population
3. incapacity or unwillingness of the agents of the government to suppress the alternative coalition and/or commitment to its claims (Tilly 1978: 200)

Tilly then distinguishes between a revolutionary situation, defined by the above three conditions, and a revolutionary outcome, which is simply "the displacement of one set of power holders by another" (Tilly 1978: 192). The first condition or proximate cause of a revolutionary situation is the advancement of mutually exclusive claims by contenders. Why are these alternative claims advanced by mobilized groups? Tilly offers two possibilities. It is possible that the objectives of a group from the very beginning call for the destruction of the existing polity, a rare event, Tilly suggests. The more likely sequence begins when a polity becomes static in the sense that "challengers are refused access to power" (p. 203). The second condition of a revolutionary situation is the acceptance of these alternative claims by significant portions of the population. Here Tilly relies on precisely the schools of thought he has previously rejected, namely, the social-psychological and structural-functional schools of thought. He suggests that people might accept alternative claims because of the failure of "government to meet specific obligations which members of the subject population regard" as just, such as employment, or because government demands a drastic increase in commitment of resources by the population (pp. 204–205). The third condition of a revolutionary situation is that government fails to suppress the alternative coalition because of a lack of or an inefficient use of coercive resources. A revolutionary situation is only one determinant of a revolutionary outcome. The actual displacement of one set of power holders by another requires coalitions between challenger groups and member groups. These are, as mentioned earlier, ideas also emphasized by Marx and Brinton.

Tilly thus has made three important contributions to conflict theory:

1. an emphasis on mobilization unmatched by other theoreticians

2. a clear distinction between revolutionary situations and revolutionary outcomes
3. a synthesis of elements from structural (Marxian) theories, process theories
(Brinton), and aggregate psychological theories (Gurr)

Intellectually, Tilly is decidedly postbehavioral, if by postbehavioral we mean
a social scientist who is one, firmly grounded in substantive (historical) knowledge
of the subject matter, two, not adverse (and in fact willing) to use empirical tests
of theories, three, questions the global, undifferentiated analysis of conflict phenomena, and four, does not believe in a value-free social science.

Theda Skocpol—The State in the International Arena

Skocpol takes postbehavioralism a step further. Disdaining statistical data, her
analysis of revolutions relies exclusively on a comparative historical analysis of a
small number of cases. She also looks at the international and world historical
contexts of revolutions and thus provides one more essential piece of the puzzle.
We cannot attempt to analyze a phenomenon as complex as revolution by focusing
solely on its domestic context. Four recent events bring this point home: the
revolution in Iran, the overthrow of the Nicaraguan dictatorship, the forced departure
of "Baby Doc" Duvalier from Haiti, and the removal of President Marcos from
the Philippines. Although the latter two events, especially the Haitian case, might
be far from social revolution as Skocpol defines it, the importance of the role of
the United States in both regime changes is nonetheless obvious.

The International Connections: Emergence of a New Paradigm. The idea that
the international system must be considered is not a new one. Studies of imperialism
as early as T. A. Hobson's 1905 work *The Economic Taproot of Imperialism*
discussed the connection between internal and external conflict.[8] Similarly, Johnson's
systems theory approach takes account of international pressures on the division
of labor and the value system in his discussion of the rise of external reference
groups and foreign conquest. Gurr's sources of rising expectations can also originate
in the external environment. What Skocpol does that lends importance to her
treatment of the international connection is to emphasize it and to discuss it within
the transnational political economy, the competing nation-state system, and transnational historical context (Skocpol 1979: 19–24). Skocpol argues the point quite
persuasively:

> If a structural perspective means a focus on relationships, this must include trans-
> national relations as well as relations among differently situated groups within given
> countries. Transnational relations have contributed to the emergence of all social-
> revolutionary crisis and have invariably helped to shape revolutionary struggles and
> outcomes. All modern social revolutions, in fact, must be seen as closely related in
> their causes and accomplishments to the internationally uneven spread of capitalist
> economic development and nation-state formation on a world scale. Unfortunately
> existing theories of revolution have not explicitly taken this perspective. (Skocpol
> 1979: 19)

Figure 2.2 Skocpol's Conceptualization of International Context

International
Context

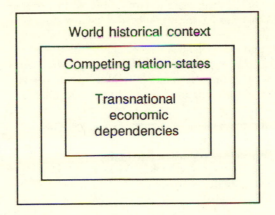

How does this definition relate to her theory? First, structure is what really matters, not individual or group-based discontent or advocacy of a new belief system. Second, there is an element of violent class struggle. What happens in Skocpol's theory is that structural barriers to class-based revolts must be removed or weakened before the revolution can occur. Another critically important point about Skocpol's definition is that it is partly based on outcomes. This aspect is problematic for, if we follow Skocpol, we can never tell when a social revolution is occurring; we must wait for the outcome of the conflict before we can label and explain it. Yet, her emphasis on outcomes (especially state-building outcomes) is also an important contribution.

Skocpol's points are shown graphically in Figure 2.2, and the growing acceptance of such a view in political science can be demonstrated by the following quotation. "Horizontal interdependencies being what they are, it won't do to study China as if there were no Latin America. . . . Vertical linkages being what they are, it won't do to study global energy consumption, international violence, or world hunger and population pressures as if those things did not start in and return to haunt the many households and villages where people work and worship" (Prewitt as quoted in L. Anderson 1982).

Skocpol's Theory of a Social Revolution. A good part of Skocpol's theory is embodied in her definition of a social revolution:

> Social revolutions are rapid, basic transformations of a society's state and class structures, and they are accompanied and in part carried through by class-based revolts from below. Social revolutions are set apart from other sorts of conflicts and transformative processes above all by the combination of two coincidences: the coincidence of societal structural change with class upheaval, and the coincidence of political with social transformation. (Skocpol 1979: 4)

Skocpol argues that for a social revolution to occur, a nation caught in competition with others must have domestic structures that block or resist reforms needed to meet the competition. When these reforms fail to occur, the state apparatus begins to crack. A political crisis has been produced. Now if state coercive controls weaken (a defeat in war can be a cause here), rebellion, specifically peasant rebellion, will occur. Peasants are potentially rebellious at all times, and a political crisis gives them the opportunity to revolt. What is important at this juncture are the specific agrarian structures. Revolution is likely when peasant communities (a) have a high degree of communal solidarity, (b) are quite autonomous as local communities, yet (c) are supervised by a centralized bureaucracy (Skocpol 1979: 116–117). It is the combination of the state's political crisis and the peasant revolt that produces the social revolution.

Skocpol in Perspective: Marx + Barrington Moore + a Theory of the State = Skocpol. My earlier discussion of Karl Marx noted that one of his contributions to conflict theory was his analysis of the division between the countryside and the city. Yet I also noted that such an analytical separation was an indication of the Marxist neglect of the peasantry. When one considers Barrington Moore's *Social Origins of Dictatorship and Democracy* (1966), one notes that the development of regime types is explained by the other half of the title: *Lord and Peasant in the Making of the Modern World.* In other words, agrarian structures are the key in Moore's analysis. Skocpol adds this element to the classical Marxist theory of revolution.

Skocpol also devotes considerable study to the problem of revolutionary outcomes. She argues that social revolutions will result in a state where one, internally the regimes are relatively autonomous, two, externally these regimes are stronger compared to their competitors, three, the revolutionary regimes have incorporated peasants and workers more than the old regimes, and four, the revolutionary regimes are more centralized and bureaucratic than the old regimes. The last three points can be summarized under the general label of state building, which is the focus of Skocpol's analysis (Taylor 1984: 43). In this sense, one might suggest that Marx + Barrington Moore + a theory of the state = Skocpol.

An understanding of the nature of the state and its relationship to civil society is crucial for explaining any sociopolitical outcome. For example, a pluralist liberal view of the state, in which the state is seen essentially as the battleground of different societal groups, tends to understate the importance of the state and consequently focuses on the issue of regime legitimacy rather than on state structures.[9] Skocpol, however, places her emphasis on state structures and sees the primary function of the state as maintaining its own administrative organs within civil society and against military competition abroad. The state is viewed as a "structure with a logic and interest of its own" (Skocpol 1979: 24) and consists of a "set of administrative, policing and military organizations coordinated by an executive authority" (p. 29). Although Skocpol admits that the main function of the state within civil society is to extract surplus from it, she nonetheless argues that the surplus so extracted will be consumed by the state for its own preservation and expansion. In fact, the efforts of the economically dominant classes to block state reforms aimed at extracting this surplus are viewed as an important contributing factor in the development of the revolutionary crisis. The state is therefore viewed as a party to the conflict, not as a battleground for various economic interests.

As pointed out before, Skocpol views the international system of competing states as encompassing both domestic and transnational economic relations. This point is critical because Skocpol argues that the relationship of the state to civil society is shaped by the state's position within the international system. Hence, the nature of the role of the state in domestic instability is partly determined by the structural imperatives of the international system. If, for instance, the state is caught up in military competition, it needs resources to compete. It then must increase the rate of extraction of surplus from the civil society, which puts it in conflict with the economically dominant class, which sees its revenue base taken away by the state. Hence, in contrast to the pluralist liberal perspective, in which the state is either not discussed at all or is analyzed as a battleground for various interests, we come to see the state as an actor in its own right, a party to conflict for its own reasons, and a contributor to the development of revolutionary crisis. Hence, both state structures and the state become critical points of analytical focus.

Summary of Tilly and Skocpol

Tilly and Skocpol recognized the importance of several factors noted by their predecessors: the weakening of the state, both financially and militarily; the development of widespread popular opposition; and the role of organization and opportunity in the triumph of revolutionary forces. But whereas behavioralists aimed chiefly at finding statistical indicators of these factors, Tilly and Skocpol sought to increase our understanding of the detailed historical conditions under which these factors emerged. In particular, Tilly examined the mobilization of contending groups (Tilly 1978), and Skocpol demonstrated the vulnerabilities of states entwined in international competition.

JACK GOLDSTONE: A NEW SYNTHESIS

Jack Goldstone has added to the synthesis provided by Tilly and Skocpol by focusing on intra-elite competition and conflict and by providing a detailed analysis of the impact of urbanization, inflation, and demographic growth on states. Goldstone also focuses on superpower relationships and rivalries with Third World countries in the context of neopatrimonial revolutions.

In his major work, *Revolution and Rebellion in the Early Modern World* (1991), Goldstone points out that Skocpol's discussion of state breakdown does not quite fit the early modern period. Revolutions *did* reflect international pressures on states in some periods, but there were other periods of strong pressure when revolutions did *not* occur. To remedy the problem, Goldstone has offered a new framework, and his work marks a clear shift from the preoccupations of the 1960s and early 1970s. The 1980s witnessed a change in the atmosphere of academia, and some intellectuals began to question the wisdom of radical social change. A number of tragic revolutionary outcomes, such as the tragedy of Cambodia and the enormously costly Iran-Iraq war, seem to have lent empirical support to the intellectual questioning of radical social change. As early as 1980, Terry Nardin pointed out that both the intellectual wisdom and the practice of critical Marxist theory, and the attack on positivist and non-Marxist approaches, were themselves suffering from "epistemological self-righteousness" (Nardin 1980: 469). It was in an intellectual atmosphere in which both the theoretical validity and the practice of Marxist theorizing had become questionable that Goldstone's writings appeared, and he tended to view revolutions, not as a triumph of progressive forces, but as an instance of political failure or state breakdown.

Goldstone was a student of Skocpol when formulating his ideas, and he thus follows her closely in several respects. In particular, Goldstone places the state—as an autonomous organization pursuing its own goals of maintaining and extending its power—at the center of his analysis. Yet he points out several respects in which Skocpol's analysis of social revolutions in France, Russia, and China fails to generalize to other revolutions and revolutionary crises.[10] First, in Europe from 1500 to 1850, international military pressures and revolutions were not closely correlated. Goldstone observes that in this period revolutionary crises occurred in two distinct clusters, from 1580 to 1660 (the Puritan revolution in England, the Fronde in France, the Netherlands revolt, the Catalan, Neapolitan, and Sicilian revolts, the Bohemian revolt, the Ukrainian Khmelnitsky revolt), and from 1770 to 1850 (the French Revolution, the Pugachev revolt, and the many European revolutions of 1830 and 1848), with an intervening period of domestic political stability. Yet international military pressures did not follow this pattern. The wars of Louis XIV (1672–1715) led to no revolutions, and the revolutions of 1830 and 1848 occurred when international conflict was low. Thus, other factors besides the pressures of international military competition cited by Skocpol must have contributed to revolutionary crises in the latter era.

In addition, Goldstone notes that in early modern Europe, as well as in the late twentieth century, revolutions were propelled by urban revolts (Skocpol's emphasis on peasant-driven social revolutions led her to underestimate the problem of urban unrest). And while Goldstone follows Skocpol in seeing the origins of revolutions as primarily determined by a vulnerable "structure" of political and social institutions, he parts with her with respect to outcomes. Goldstone highlights the role of ideologies in revolutionary struggles and observes that the kind of ideology espoused by revolutionary leaders has a decisive impact on the kind of state reconstruction that is attempted after the failure of the old regime.

Goldstone has examined revolutions in both traditional monarchies and in what he labels modern "neopatrimonial" states. The latter are partially industrialized states dominated by a single leader and his patronage, such as Iran under the shah, Nicaragua under the Somozas, the Philippines under Marcos, Mexico under Díaz, and Cuba under Batista. Goldstone makes a sharp analytic division among the processes of state breakdown, the ensuing struggle for power, and state reconstruction. Each process, he argues, is partly independent, has its own dynamics, and thus requires separate causal analysis.

Regarding the origins of revolutions, Goldstone identifies three critical elements whose combination produces a revolution. The first is a crisis of state resources. In traditional monarchies, this is usually a fiscal crisis brought on by a failure of the tax system to meet mounting needs or by defeat in war. The second element is elite disunity and alienation from the state, which leads elites to respond to the state crisis by fragmenting into factions with each seeking control of the government. The third element is a high level of mass mobilization potential. Goldstone notes a number of factors that contribute to this potential—urban concentration, a large proportion of youth in the population, falling real wages, rising real rents. The third element thus subsumes a number of demographic and economic characteristics of the population. When all three critical elements occur at once, Goldstone predicts that a revolutionary crisis will develop.

However, the exact shape of that crisis—whether it leads to a failed revolution (as in 1848 in Germany and Austria-Hungary), to a political revolution (as in England in 1640), or to a social revolution (as in France in 1789)—depends on the power of the various groups and the structure of the social institutions. Goldstone agrees with Skocpol that peasant-driven social revolution is likely only when peasants live in village communities, freed from landlord control, which provide the basis for organized rural action. If other kinds of rural social structure exist, a revolutionary crisis will still develop but with somewhat different results.

Goldstone's approach to the origins of revolution is thus to examine in turn the state and its resources; elites and their aspirations and divisions; and the trends in living conditions, age composition, and urban concentration of the urban and rural populations. In particular, he seeks to identify processes that could lead simultaneously to a state resource crisis, elite disunity, and rising mass mobilization potential.

Goldstone on Early Modern Revolution and Rebellion

In the early modern period, Goldstone finds such a process in long cycles of population change. He first notes that the population grew rapidly throughout Europe from 1500 to 1650, declined slightly from 1650 to 1730, then grew rapidly again from 1730 to 1850 and that these cycles correspond with the pattern of revolutionary crises. He then sets out to demonstrate how these population swings could simultaneously affect states, elites, and the populace. His answer is that in chiefly agrarian states, populations depended mainly on agriculture, elites mainly on rents, and states mainly on land taxes. A rapidly growing population put pressure on the agrarian economy, leading to rising grain prices. Rising prices generally hurt the states, whose traditional tax systems often responded weakly or tardily to inflation. As revenues were eroded by inflation, states had to seek increased taxes or new sources of taxation, both of which alienated elites. Rising prices benefited those members of an elite who were quick to respond to commercial opportunities but were costly to those who were slow or unable to respond. Thus, elite divisions grew, as rising and falling members of the elite competed fiercely for status, wealth, and official positions. A growing population also increased the number of peasants with insufficient land and increased the labor supply, which drove down real wages. Migration to the cities from the land-scarce rural areas swelled the population of political capitals to unmanageable levels. Moreover, as population growth occurred as a result of a greater survival of the young, the population as a whole contained a larger proportion of teenagers and young adults, who were more readily mobilized for radical action. Given the agrarian structure of traditional monarchies, sustained rapid population growth therefore led to increased class conflict, intra-elite conflict, and state and elite competition for resources. State breakdown occurred, not because of military pressures, but primarily because of a combination of factors that can be summarized as a "demographic-structural explanation" (Goldstone 1991).

To illustrate his argument, Goldstone discusses the English, the French, the Ottoman, and the Ming-Ching preindustrial agrarian societies. The English case is treated at length (Goldstone 1986b), and Goldstone rejects the neo-Marxist explanation of the revolution of 1640 developed by authors such as Moore and Immanual Wallerstein. He argues that the growth of capitalist practices in the economy was not the lead cause of factors such as increased intra-elite competition, state fiscal crisis, and the growth of cities. In the case of the English gentry, Goldstone suggests that virtually all the English elite were involved in commercial agriculture before the revolution. As for the growth in the size of cities, using a regression analysis of the growth of London, he is able to demonstrate that 80 percent of London's growth in the century before the revolution was owing to increased migration resulting from an overall population increase. Furthermore, Goldstone argues that the rise in prices in seventeenth-century England was the result of population pressures, not an increased volume of bullion imports, as neo-Marxist authors have suggested. The combined results of population pressure, inflation, and the fiscal crisis of the state drastically affected social mobility in England in the seventeenth century, and for the elite, the result was intense competition for jobs. That in turn produced a fractionalized elite that could not take a unified position when the Crown faced severe financial difficulties. Goldstone then suggests that the frustration caused by social competition and the Crown's measures to raise taxes increased the appeal of radical Puritanism to segments of the elite. He adds that the existence of a mobilizable population—in London and the manufacturing centers of the countryside, which had been hit hard by unemployment and falling real wages—provided the final ingredient for the revolution.

Goldstone compares the case of England with those of the seventeenth-century French and Spanish states. The French case exhibits similar trends: population growth, rising prices, increased rural migration, and declining real wages culminating in the revolutionary crisis of the Fronde. The different outcomes of the French and English state crises are explained by the existence of divergent "national constellations of political and cultural divisions" (Goldstone 1991). In France, the great nobles retained private armies and could be played off against the urban *parlementaires*. In addition, no ideology developed to unite the opposition and to supplant the legitimacy of the Crown. In England, by contrast, the great nobles had no force sufficient to overcome Parliament's New Model Army, and English Puritanism provided an alternative justification for governance, substituting the community of saints for the divine monarchy. In Spain, there was no revolutionary crisis in Castile—revolts took place in the periphery, in Catalonia, Naples, and Sicily. Goldstone shows that in Castile, population growth was slow and ceased after 1600, there was no great turnover in the nobility, real wages did not decline between 1600 and 1650, and the mass mobilization potential was low. Furthermore, state financial demands on the Castilian nobility were nowhere near the state's demands in England or France. Instead, the Spanish monarchy sought to raise revenues from the Netherlands and from Catalonia, Naples, and Sicily. In those regions, population was growing, real wages were falling, and elites were forced to compete for status and position with grandees from Castile, conditions that combined to produce revolts in those regions. The overall framework thus seems to hold true for early modern European state crises.

But does it hold true for non-European agrarian states as well? Taking the Ming and Ottoman crises of the seventeenth century, Goldstone is able to demonstrate the existence of similar situations. In the first half of the seventeenth century, the Ottoman and Chinese states each experienced a tremendous growth in population. However, agricultural output could not keep pace with the growing population, and a price revolution followed. The important point about the price revolution is that it did not reflect primarily the movement of bullion into either China or the Ottoman Empire but was tied to the imbalance between agricultural output and population growth (Goldstone 1988). The tax system in both countries also failed, which in turn led to a weakened ability of each state to enforce its will. As in England, increased population pressure created extensive intra-elite competition for status and jobs. The dissatisfied elites, armed with radical ideology, then provided the leadership for the local uprisings that occurred throughout China and the eastern Ottoman Empire. Calm returned to both empires only when the ecological balance was restored and the states were able to put in place administrative organs and mechanisms that generated sufficient revenues. The framework therefore seems to hold true for non-European states as well.

Goldstone's discussion of state crises in the early modern period is therefore a powerful challenge to the existing neo-Marxist theories. If indeed it was internal ecological shifts that set the stage for revolts in the early modern period, then one has to question the overall validity of neo-Marxist theories. Besides his ecological argument, Goldstone's use of dynamic models and his discussion of the role ideology played also sharply depart from neo-Marxist analyses of the Skocpolian and Mooreian variety. The use of time-series models in particular, which Goldstone uses to test portions of his argument, seems to present an advance in historical sociology, which generally does not rely on any quantitative testing.

Goldstone on Modern Revolution

In an important article, "Revolutions and Superpowers" (1986a), Goldstone examines the origins of revolutions in modern neopatrimonial states. He points out that political crises in such states—e.g., the falls of Batista in Cuba, Somoza in Nicaragua, and the shah in Iran—were not spurred by external military pressures. The international system did impinge strongly, however, for these leaders' problems were in large part the result of their being caught between nationalist domestic elites and pressures from their superpower ally, the United States. Again, Goldstone studies the origins of the revolutionary crises in terms of the failure of state resources—owing to problems of overspending, inflation, excessive debt—plus elite divisions and a rising mass mobilization potential.

Population growth was only one factor leading to these problems. More important was the problem posed by the need to maintain the support of both the superpower, which provided military and financial assistance, and the domestic elites, who sought greater political participation and independence. When domestic elites sought change and superpower support depended on limiting repression and international cooperation, the states faced a dilemma. When this dilemma was compounded by poor economic performance that reduced popular living standards, the regime was faced with the need to orchestrate repression against dissatisfied peasants and/or workers. If, at this juncture, elites withdrew their allegiance and instead supported mass mobilization against the regime, the government quickly collapsed.

Summary of Goldstone

Goldstone's analysis is in many respects a synthesis of earlier approaches. Like Marx, he notes that revolutions reflect broader historical forces—changes in population and prices or superpower competition—that impinge on states and elites, not mere local problems or errors of governance by foolish leaders. The main difference, of course, is that Goldstone cites ecological and international-political factors, rather than the growth of capitalism, as the force that undermines states. Like Brinton, Goldstone divides revolutions into stages—state breakdown, ensuing struggle for power, and state reconstruction—and insists that each deserves analysis and explanation. Like Gurr and Johnson, he emphasizes how external forces may affect the perceptions of states, elites, and the populace that they are faring less well than they should. He notes that radical ideologies gain appeal in times of poor state performance and that although such ideologies may not precipitate the fall of a regime, they greatly influence the state reconstruction that follows. The major difference is that Goldstone is far more concrete. He analyzes the reasons for falls in real wages, for increasing elite competition, and for the failure of state resources by examining how particular external forces—population change and superpower competition—impinge on key groups. Goldstone also differs from Johnson in eschewing "general models" of revolution. Instead, he argues that different state structures—traditional versus neopatrimonial—must be analyzed in somewhat different terms and that similar forces leading to revolutionary crises may nonetheless produce very different outcomes when structural conditions differ. In his insistence that groups, and in particular the state and its administrators, must be the primary unit of analysis and in his careful historical examination of key cases, he closely follows Tilly and Skocpol.

Goldstone's main contribution is that, without at all undermining the advances of Skocpol—an emphasis on states, social structures, and international competition—he has enlarged on her analysis to incorporate demographic forces, urban as well as rural revolt, and shifts in ideology. At the same time, though enlarging the scope of analysis, he has broken down the complex phenomenon of revolutionary origins into a number of manageable components—state fiscal crisis, elite divisions, mass mobilization potential—each of which he carefully examines in a wide variety of contexts. Goldstone's method, which combines comparative-historical analysis of cases with quantitative testing of particular arguments, suggests a future merger of behavioral and qualitative-historical approaches. This combination would be a considerable advance over either purely historical or purely quantitative analyses, which are too often isolated.

CONCLUSION: CHALLENGES THAT REMAIN

The analysis of revolutions has shown considerable development, yet events since 1970 force us to think about this problem anew. Like unexpected celestial phenomena that send astronomers in search for new explanations, the revolutions of the last twenty years pose new challenges to political scientists' understanding of social conflicts. Most of the theoretical thinking on revolutions—from Marx to Brinton to Skocpol to Goldstone—has resulted from the study of revolutions in traditional monarchies or empires. The work of Gurr and Johnson, and Goldstone in his essay on neopatrimonial revolutions, was prompted by the post–World War II wave of Third World revolutions, yet the images of the French, the Russian, and the Chinese revolutions still dominate their writings.

But the revolutions of the last twenty years have been quite different. They have occurred in societies in which urban populations were far larger, and peasant actions much less important, than in traditional revolutions. They have also occurred in states that were subject to enormous influence from allied superpowers. In the case of the Polish Solidarity movement, we saw something hitherto unprecedented—an attempt to expand popular participation in policy formation in a state socialist system without a direct attack on socialism itself. Indeed, what Solidarity called for was real socialism.[11] The fall of regimes that were closely allied with the United States—in Vietnam, Iran, Nicaragua, the Philippines—and the persistence of the Afghan rebellion against the direct and massive intervention of the Soviet Union raise questions about the extent of superpower influence and the consequences of superpower policies. The massive suffering in Ethiopia and Cambodia following the fall of their traditional regimes raises, in stark form, the question of the costs of revolutions and whether those costs are avoidable or inevitable.

The literature that I have reviewed has some of the answers. It is a cumulative literature. We have managed to move from general concepts of inequality, class struggle, and models of conflict to a specific breakdown of factors that would cause social dislocation and unrest. The work of Jack Goldstone, following on the work of Theda Skocpol, points the direction that conflict research should take, but we need to further operationalize the variables that we have identified as important. To give some examples, we need to be aware of the difference in the structures of the states. We need to look carefully at the composition of populations. We need to pay attention to the ideologies of both the state and the revolutionaries.[12] Finally, it is crucial to take note of the conjuncture of events as Skocpol and Goldstone have so aptly pointed out. States suffer in varying degrees from fiscal crises; every state is subject to international pressure. Inflation, unemployment, and popular unrest are often problems. Elites are always competing for power. It is only when these factors intensify at the same time and political institutions are not flexible enough to meet such multiple pressures that a revolutionary crisis occurs.

NOTES

1. The best review of the literature on revolutions is Goldstone's "Theories of Revolution: The Third Generation," Goldstone (1980). Other useful reviews are by A. S. Cohen (1975) and Stan Taylor (1984).

2. For Marx, I relied on the excellent anthology by Tucker (1978) and Marx's *The Civil War in France* (1972) and *Capital* (1967).

3. On the eighteenth century prelude to Karl Marx's world, the Rise of Modern Europe series as a whole is excellent, especially Gay (1971). The latter work shows how the Enlightenment affected revolutionaries. Soboul (1975) and Rudé (1979) are among the most important works dealing with the French Revolution. The work of Stern (1979) offers a fascinating account of the importance of money in Bismarck's endeavors and the role of banking in the rise of the German Empire. Weber (1976), which covers the modernization of France in the late nineteenth and early twentieth centuries, and Holborn (1951), which deals with the decline of European power in the nineteenth century, are also useful and informative works.

4. Although aware of the fact that the first edition of Brinton came out in 1939, I would argue that, in general, the thrust of the argument remains true. The Russian civil war, the Spanish civil war, the civil war in China, the final stages of the Mexican revolution, etc., all occurred after World War I and prior to or during the writing of the first edition. The argument is obviously much stronger for the third edition on which I focus.

5. That is, he looks at how social change affects societal structures and how that in turn affects the functional differentiation of tasks and roles within society.

6. For a review of some of the works that have tested the psychological concepts employed by Gurr and others, see Muller (1980).

7. Page 104 is an extremely important page in *Why Men Rebel* (1970). There Gurr quotes Trotsky to the effect that "existence of privation is not enough to cause an insurrection . . . if it were, the masses would be always in revolt," which is essentially one of the major criticisms of Skocpol (1979: 34): "what society, for example, lacks widespread relative deprivation of one sort or another." Page 104 of *Why Men Rebel* also provides evidence that Gurr is quite aware of the fact that external assessment of RD is not the same as the subjective feelings of deprivation.

8. R. J. Rummel's "Dimensionality of the Nations" project also paid some attention to the nexus issue. This massive literature, quite poor in methodological sophistication, is reviewed by Michael Stohl (1980).

9. This characterization would be true for both Johnson and Gurr.

10. Goldstone's major work is *Revolution and Rebellion in the Early Modern World* (1991). Shorter versions of his arguments have appeared in a series of essays (1986b, 1988): "State Breakdown in the English Revolution: A New Synthesis" and "East and West in the Seventeenth Century: Political Crises in Stuart England, Ottoman Turkey, and Ming China."

11. See Valerie Bunces's (1989) discussion of the Polish case.

12. My own summary of the revolution in Iran (Moshiri 1985) follows some of these specifications.

3

AN ANALYTICAL FRAMEWORK

JACK A. GOLDSTONE

Revolution—the forcible overthrow of a government followed by the reconsolidation of authority by new groups, ruling through new political (and sometimes social) institutions—is a complex process. Although the fall of a government may be sudden, the causal trends leading up to that fall, the ensuing struggle for power among contenders, and the reconstruction of a stable state often span decades.

Many factors implicated in revolutions in the late twentieth century—such as dependent development and superpower competition—are quite different from those faced by the major preindustrial European states. Yet I wish to suggest that if one focuses on causal *processes* and on how revolutions develop over time rather than on individual causes or specific events, the basic patterns of state breakdown, the nature of revolutionary contention, and the challenges of state rebuilding remain largely the same. I therefore believe it is possible to distill from earlier theoretical work, although with some modification, principles for understanding contemporary revolutions.

This chapter presents a process model of revolutions. The model has both forecasting and policy implications; although in some respects, the policy implications are that certain processes, once begun, are unlikely to be altered or deflected. For analytical purposes, I divide the process of revolution into temporal stages, even though in reality these stages overlap and interpenetrate. I first discuss the origins of state breakdown, then examine features of the ensuing struggle for power, and finally consider the factors that affect state reconstruction.

THE ORIGINS OF STATE BREAKDOWN

In my work on early modern revolutions (Goldstone 1986b, 1988, 1991), I identify three conditions whose *conjunction* led to state breakdown: fiscal distress, elite alienation and conflict, and a high potential for mobilization of the populace. Although the particular forces that create these conditions may be quite different in contemporary societies than in earlier ones, I believe these conditions remain central to the development of revolutionary crises.

Conditions of State Breakdown

The first condition is a decline of state resources relative to the state's expenses and commitments, and relative to the resources of potential domestic and international adversaries. Historically, when the revenues of a state become, over time, insufficient to pay the standing army and bureaucracy, award pensions and favors to supporters, and meet the costs of building roads, ensuring the supply of grain to cities, maintaining order, enforcing justice, and overseeing local administration, the authority of the state wanes. The state is then forced to seek new sources of income. Early modern and contemporary Third World states have turned to borrowing, new taxes of dubious legality, and simple corruption—demanding payment for offices, honors, and the right to do business. When expenses still outrun revenues, as debts mount and funding for the military grows strained, the loyalty of the commercial community and of the army grows tenuous. As corruption increases, elites' loyalty to the state becomes more something to be purchased than something offered as a matter of course. The bureaucracy and military become less efficient instruments of the state and more centers of personal advance and peculation. As money becomes both more essential and harder to find, the state grows more dependent on maintaining the goodwill of its creditors, and its freedom of action diminishes. Both the ability to project military force abroad and the ability to control domestic opponents decline. Eventually, a final straw— a war, a collapse of state credit, or superpower pressure—leads the government to yield initiative to the country's elites. It was this dynamic that led to the calling of the English Parliament in 1640 and the French Estates General in 1789, the opening acts of the English and French revolutions.

Yet such a resource crisis is not invariably fatal to states. Elites—individuals who are exceptionally influential owing to their wealth, religious or professional positions, local authority, or celebrity—may, if they are loyal, rally around the government and continue to support it. In France in 1715, the leaders of the regency government developed a plan for recovery from the bankruptcy of Louis XIV. In Prussia, after its defeat by Napoleon at Jena, elites did not abandon the monarchy. Through the support of a conservative military nobility, and the efforts (though only partially successful) of loyal reform ministers to alter and strengthen the army, bureaucracy, and educational and status systems, the monarchy in Prussia emerged stronger in 1815 than before. A crisis of state resources is fatal only when it is accompanied by severe elite alienation. Elite alienation from the government creates resistance to the need for new state revenues and institutional reforms, and thus blocks recovery.

Furthermore, revolutionary struggles arise only when elites are severely divided— a united elite, opposed to a government that is weak in resources, can simply stage a coup d'etat and then alter government policies (Burton 1984; Burton and Higley 1987). Indeed, the near-total withdrawal of elite support, especially when accompanied by popular demonstrations, has sometimes persuaded rulers that they have been abandoned, leading them to flee: e.g., James II in England in 1688,

Charles X in France in 1830, and Louis Philippe in France in 1848. In these cases, substantial elite unity prevented widespread struggles and civil war; there was no wholesale renovation of institutions or destruction of elites. Only when, in addition to widespread alienation from the state, elites are sharply divided over the future direction of institutional change is a revolutionary struggle likely to arise. Thus, a second key condition in the genesis of state breakdown is a certain set of attitudes among the elites—unsupportive of the government yet deeply divided over the degree to which existing institutions need to be merely shored up, moderately altered, or radically overhauled.

One key to this set of attitudes lies in patterns of social mobility. When social mobility is low and the composition and size of elites are stable, there is generally little conflict. However, when social mobility rises, as new groups acquire skills, gain middle-class and professional positions, while social and political institutions still *deny* them higher status and full political participation, conflicts generally arise. These conflicts may pit new aspiring elites against older, dominant elites; they may pit different new elites against each other; and—most important—they may pit a variety of elites against the state, if all groups come to blame the state for the increased insecurity and conflict over elite positions. Thus, it is often precisely when new or oppressed groups seem to be improving their position— as when non-nobles increased their wealth and bureaucratic positions in Old Regime France; when technical professionals increased their importance in modernizing Iran; or when blacks increasingly became skilled workers and township merchants and businessmen in South Africa—that revolutionary pressures increase.

Of course elite disunity is a double-edged sword. Elites who are fragmented into numerous competing and disarrayed groups are unlikely to pose a threat to a regime, much less overthrow it and succeed in reconstructing a stable state. When elites have varying degrees of loyalty to the state and multiple conflicts with each other, the state can play off elite factions against each other and keep the elites divided and weak. A primary policy of absolute monarchies was to promote new men and manipulate court factions to this end. In addition, early modern elites were frequently divided by regional loyalties, by rural versus urban orientation, by religion, by trends in social mobility that advantaged some and disadvantaged others, and in multi-ethnic states such as Austria-Hungary, by race and ethnicity. Indeed, it was such divisions that long sustained absolute rule. It is thus a particular trend in elite divisions that increases the risk of revolution. When, despite their divisions, *many* elite groups are sufficiently alienated from the state that broad anti-state coalitions emerge, *then*—if the state is weaker than its adversaries—revolution becomes increasingly likely. Furthermore, when divided elites begin to polarize into sharply opposed anti-state and conservative coalitions, a revolutionary contest becomes almost inevitable. These two phases in elite dynamics—a broad anti-state coalition of elites followed by polarization into sharply opposed factions—are evident in both early modern and twentieth-century revolutions.

In some twentieth-century situations, such as Turkey in 1921, Peru in 1968, and Egypt in 1952, radical elites who are already in control of powerful state institutions, such as military-based reformers, might triumph over the government and conservative elites in a coup or a brief intra-elite struggle and stage a "revolution from above" (Trimberger 1978). But elites seeking radical change who are not already in influential positions in the state administration rarely can overcome the state and conservative elements in the armed forces without mobilizing support among the populace. Thus, a third necessary condition for revolution is urban or rural popular groups that can be readily mobilized against the state and against counterrevolutionaries. This generally means peasants or urban workers who have grievances against the economic or political regime and who have the autonomy and organization—whether through village communities or urban neighborhoods—to act (Skocpol 1979). A high mobilization potential is generally produced by the combination of adverse trends, such as shrinking access to land or falling real wages, *and* local community structures that give popular groups some freedom of action versus local authorities as well as a basis for organization in support of community goals. Popular support for change, and a willingness to act through demonstrations, riots, and enlistment in revolutionary militias, often makes the difference in the dismantling of existing regimes.

Each of these conditions—state resource failures, elite alienation and divisions, and popular mass mobilization potential—may create political problems and disturbances by themselves. Peasant revolts, urban uprisings, elite rebellions and succession struggles, and state bankruptcies litter early modern history. Yet only when all these conditions *come together* do they have sufficient force to shatter existing institutions and create a revolution.

I have therefore suggested that efforts to forecast political instability leading to revolution should not use an additive framework, simply listing causes that lead to state difficulties, because the key factor is not any one individual source of problems but the *conjunction* of difficulties in several sectors of the society. Thus, I have suggested a model that behaves *interactively*. The risk of revolution should not be seen to rise greatly only if state debt increases, or only if elite alienation and polarization are rising, or only if access to land or real wages in autonomous popular communities falter, but if all three of these elements are rising together, then the risk of revolution increases very rapidly indeed.

I believe this model forms a useful guide to the origins of revolutions in both modern and contemporary states. However, the forces that lead to a decline in state resources, elite alienation, and popular grievances may be quite different in the late twentieth century than in preceding eras, since the composition and aspirations of states, elites, and populations have undergone considerable change.

Forces for Revolutionary Conjuncture

What forces, then, may cause these elements to arise? The answers are as varied as the kinds of resources and tax systems used by states, the status and economic systems that support elites, and the means by which the populace earns its living. Generally, it is some combination of new dynamic forces—that is, some forces that have changed markedly over time—with existing institutional structures that respond poorly to such changes that undermines a manageable status quo.

Two forces that may have either positive or negative impact are price inflation and population growth. Mild inflation may boost government revenues and raise commodity prices for basic producers. If the real economy expands as well, providing jobs and avoiding a drastic fall in popular living standards, inflationary periods may be politically stable. Yet rapid inflation, or inflation in the context of institutions that adjust poorly, may lead to problems. Government obligations and debt may expand too rapidly, and real income may fall for many segments of the elite and the populace. Such conditions are destabilizing. Similarly, population growth may have benefits or drawbacks. If the economy is expanding, population growth can produce a new generation of workers whose successful socialization stabilizes the polity. Yet if the economy is stagnant, population pressures can lead to falling living standards and to downward mobility for members of the elite, whose numbers may increase faster than the growth of positions commensurate with their aspirations and status. In this case, population growth may breed a new generation of discontented radical opponents of the state. In short, there is no simple answer to the question of whether rising population, or rising commodity prices, or *any* single factor is destabilizing or not. The analyst seeking to assess the likelihood of revolution must be skilled in judging the impact of varied forces on a given society, and be aware of their impact on state resources, on elite composition and aspirations, and on the prospects for the population as a whole. The question is not whether a particular economic or demographic trend is present and in what degree. Instead, the question is one of the *interaction* of such trends with the existing structure of a particular society, and whether this interaction is creating, in conjunction, the conditions whose combination leads to state breakdown.

A third, similarly Janus-faced, factor to consider is the impact of the international political and economic environment. Support from international allies may strengthen states, but pressures from foreign allies may also lead states to take actions that alienate domestic elites. International economic trends may strengthen or weaken state finances, either supporting debt or imposing stringent conditions for credit. International firms may invest and increase employment, or drain resources and block the development of an indigenous skilled and managerial class. Again, the political analyst needs to be aware of what impact this factor is having at a particular time on particular groups in the society under consideration before pronouncing a verdict on its stabilizing or destabilizing effects.

Nationalist and ethnic identification can also be a double-edged sword for regime stability. A regime may gain strength, in the form of elite or ethnic sentiment, from such identification, but any number of state policies—obtaining massive aid or loans from other nations, allying with other nations for military or economic gains, favoring particular ethnic groups, or attacking the culture of such groups—can lead to a loss of a regime's nationalist or ethnic credentials. In such cases, regime support can rapidly erode and give way to sharp opposition.

To continue with the list of factors that can lead to revolutionary pressures in modern societies would create a laundry list of factors that, by themselves, may be innocuous or occur in many nonrevolutionary situations. For example, traditional elites may become alienated if their prerogatives are threatened by newly emerging professional groups. Excessive corruption or concentration of power may alienate elites who feel entitled to participate in economic and political decision making. Regional or ethnic rivalries, and orientation toward international markets or toward domestic development, may provide the basis for a polarization of elites. Shifts in commodity prices, export patterns, and land control may greatly affect the real income of large portions of the population, creating widespread grievances. The same factors can also affect state revenues. It is useful to keep such factors in mind, but the critical issue is whether, in a given society, such factors are occurring in isolation, or in a conjunctural pattern that creates multiple threats to the government. Only in the latter case is a revolution likely to occur.

This reasoning suggests that effective strategies to avoid revolution in the face of mounting pressures may be selective. For example, even when popular economic or political grievances are high, a state that has a strong resource base, or has the support of a unified elite, such as South Africa prior to 1990, may be able to weather storms of popular protest. Or a state that has diminishing resources may wish to concentrate them on providing positions for the elite in order to maintain their support. Thus blunting the rise of one essential condition may help a state escape revolution. But an awareness of trends in all three conditions— state obligations and resources, elite alienation, and mass mobilization potential— is necessary. Leaders who have believed themselves secure because they were surrounded by a small circle of supporters and ignored broader elite alienation, or who have believed themselves financially sound because their current income was high and ignored the broader macroeconomic consequences of their fiscal policies (such as Marcos in the Philippines and the shah in Iran), have paid for their oversight.

I thus would argue that approaches to the origins of revolution that pose the simple question, What are the *causes?* and seek a list of items that have destabilizing consequences in most states are misguided and not terribly helpful. As noted above, such factors as population growth, price inflation, and superpower influence may have widely different effects in different societies. Thus, at the level of discrete causal factors, generalizations about consequences for political stability may not be possible. A more productive approach is to examine a particular society and ask, Are there any forces in this particular society that are straining the state's resources, alienating and dividing the elites, or increasing the potential for the mobilization of the populace against the existing regime? It is such a study of *processes* and *conjunctures* that I believe is necessary to forecast revolutionary crises.

Ideological Change and the Process of Revolution

New ideological movements are sometimes also heralded as a cause of revolutions. Yet such an identification again is the result of a search for discrete causes rather than paying close attention to interactions and long-term trends. New ideologies do not suddenly appear—the Enlightenment, liberalism, communism, and fundamentalist Islam were evident for generations before becoming identified with revolutionary activity. Instead, existing ideologies become revolutionary when they are seized on and used by groups that are dissatisfied with their circumstances or with regime performance.

The conditions that give rise to state breakdown—state fiscal distress, usually accompanied by increasing demands on taxpayers, corruption, and military failures;

problems among the elite and aspirants to elite status in achieving positions commensurate with what they feel they deserve; and problems of land scarcity, unemployment, falling wages, and associated unrest among the populace—also give rise to a widespread perception that something has "gone wrong" in society. This perception is expressed as complaints about specific conditions and state actions and through more general diagnoses and prescriptions for society's ills. When the state is perceived as strongly influenced by "foreign" ideas, such ideas are often the target of complaint.

Initially, reactions to such problems are conservative—complaints that traditional rights are being violated or general attacks on "injustice." Yet such conservative complaints can, as Calhoun (1983) has shown, spur revolutionary action, for peasants and artisanal communities may be prompted to seek to rectify injustice themselves by food riots, land seizures, or attacks on landlords. Such "conservative radicalism" was an important element in the French and Russian revolutions.

But some elites also voice their sense that society has gone astray by offering various plans for the renewal of the state. They diagnose current state and social institutions as not merely corrupt and in need of rectification but as being fatally flawed and in need of replacement by a new order. As the state's authority weakens, diverse elements in society each press their own cause without consciously attempting to unite with other groups. Elites seek reforms or resist state authority, artisans stage food riots, and peasants stage land invasions or withhold rents or tithes— all without any further thought than taking advantage of propitious times to rectify personally felt injustices.

Yet all of these actions precipitate further discussions of injustice and social ills. Elite groups seeking change begin to identify themselves with a more "truly just" order and moral reform. As Arjomand (1986), following Walzer (1965), has remarked, "The fact that [revolutionary] social movements are reactions to social dislocation and normative disorder explains the salience of their search for cultural authenticity and their moral rigorism" (Arjomand 1986: 402). Seventeenth-century English Puritans, eighteenth-century Jacobins, and twentieth-century Bolsheviks and Iranian mullahs all responded to perceived social problems by seeking to project greater identification with national aspirations and greater moral rigor than the reigning state.

Once the state's fiscal and political woes reduce its authority further, the situation changes. Instead of merely pressing demands for reform, or resisting state authority, elites (and sometimes the populace, when local control depends on the central government) find themselves with new opportunities and new rivals. The new opportunities appear because of the state's loss of initiative and inability to enforce its views, allowing elites new scope for action. The new rivals appear in the form of competing elite segments and various regional and popular demands seeking to shape the social and political order to replace the current regime.

Taking advantage of the new opportunities requires building coalitions and mobilizing support among the social and political fragments set free by the collapse of the state. It is at this point that revolutions characteristically have a flood of pamphlet literature and popular demagoguery. Instead of particularistic complaints, sweeping social programs come to dominate discourse. New symbols are developed to represent various viewpoints and factions competing for popular allegiance. New enemies are defined, vilified, and condemned in order to sharpen differences among and strengthen support for parties competing for power. The revolutionary struggle has begun.

The rapid spread of radical ideologies is thus an evident symptom of the decline of state authority. It indicates that genuine concrete problems have undermined the belief that the state is capable of maintaining order and balancing the needs of varied groups in the society. Generally, therefore, attempts to combat opposition ideologies merely through counterpropaganda, attacks on opposition leaders, and the like do not succeed, for the appeal of the radical ideologies is rooted in concrete social problems, not merely the rhetoric of a particular leader. Unless the state is able to take actions (or benefit from happy circumstances) that reverse the trends underlying the shift in elite and/or popular perceptions, ideologies opposing the current regime continue to spread.

THE UNFOLDING OF REVOLUTIONARY CRISES AND THE STRUGGLE FOR POWER

Once the state's authority has lapsed, the specific problems that undermined the state's power become less important than the contest among contending groups for the allegiance of the populace. The ideological element of this contest then takes on greater importance, for radical ideologies, even if they, of themselves, "cannot account for the collapse of the societal structure of domination to any significant degree," may yet "shape the political order installed by the revolution to a significant extent" (Arjomand 1986: 384).

Complex societies typically comprise many diverse elements: religious, military, landlord, professional, and commercial elites; urban shopkeepers, artisans, and laborers; and rural peasants ranging from the well-to-do to the desperate. Within each of these "class" designations, segments may be sharply divided by local origin, family background, relation to the state, degree of wealth or status, education, and religious beliefs. Thus, any contender seeking to establish authority in the wake of state breakdown needs to build a "dominant coalition"—that is, a group with sufficient solidarity and resources to defeat all possible combinations of opponents.

It should be clear that the formation of such a coalition is by no means a foregone conclusion. Historically, when such a coalition has not formed—the prime examples in early modern history are the Fronde in seventeenth-century France and Germany in 1848—the old regime has recovered its authority by playing off various social elements against each other. In modern cases, the failure to build such a broad antiregime coalition can lead to a "stalled" revolution as in Afghanistan. To form such a coalition, it is critical to take the various particular complaints, and the various elite and popular ideologies, and forge them into an ideology that has broad appeal.

In the first months following the fall of a government, diverse groups are usually united by the hope that their individual complaints will be rectified and their individual goals realized. This stage is what Brinton (1965) has called the "honeymoon" period of exuberance and superficial unity, which follows the realization that the old state has lost its force and draws on the belief that positive change is on the way. Yet the honeymoon cannot last, for the problems that initiated state breakdown—international pressures, fiscal crisis, elite competition, popular deprivation—do not automatically disappear and still require some solution. As popular groups almost invariably have only local concerns and goals, the task of building a dominant coalition to address these issues falls to members of the elites. Behind the various ideologies that have played a role in revolutions—Puritanism, Jacobinism, constitutionalism, communism (in its Bolshevik, Maoist, Sandinist, and other national variants), Islamic fundamentalism—we can discern three broad themes that have been utilized in the task of mobilization of revolutionary coalitions: rectification, redistribution, and nationalism. Revolutionary struggles are, for the most part, the story of how elite segments seek to appropriate and dominate one or more of these themes while defeating similar attempts by their opponents.

Of course, such struggles are not waged merely in the abstract realm of ideas. It is not merely the content but also the organization that carries an ideology that is responsible for its success or failure. To dominate a revolution, an ideology needs a well-organized carrier able to interpret that ideology for a mass audience. The ideologies of transformation that have dominated Western revolutions—Puritanism, Jacobinism, bolshevism—were only strongly held by a small minority. These individuals played a dominant role in large part by being better organized than their opponents and competitors.

For example, in the decades before the English revolution of 1640, there arose a close-knit network of leading families with Puritan sympathies. They knew each other, they socialized and intermarried, and they corresponded about the political and religious problems of the day (Hunt 1983). When conflict with the king broke out in 1640–1642, and people sought to build new alliances amid the breakdown of the monarchy's traditional patronage network, it was the Puritan leaders who were already equipped with a network for communication and action. Throughout England, while most people sought chiefly to defend their local interests, only the Puritans were able to offer a national program to oppose the king, a program based on defense of "authentic" English law and religion. It should be no surprise that the Puritans, just as many modern revolutionaries, then turned to symbols of foreign threat: the need to throw off the "Norman yoke" of subjugation, the need to defend the "ancient constitution," the need to fight off "papists." This is a typical ideological progression, in which elites seek to mobilize popular support by identifying themselves as custodians of a more "authentic" and truly "national" tradition than their opponents. Only thus can "a movement originally concerned with issues of doctrine . . . be broadened out to become a cultural orientation arousing the emotions of large numbers of people" (Fulbrook 1983: 10). Similarly, in France the Jacobins sought to identify themselves as being the custodians of French "national virtue," as the true voice of the French "nation." They were able to do so, albeit briefly, in large measure because their national network of clubs in major towns allowed them to dominate the news from the capital and offer a coherent program during a time of chaos.

Why, as Brinton noted, do revolutions characteristically show a drift to greater radicalism in the course of the revolutionary struggle? The answer lies in the ensuing ideological conflicts for popular allegiance. Groups that are better organized than their rivals have an advantage in taking a leading role in governance immediately after a revolution. Such groups are usually not the most radical, for the latter have often been suppressed by the former government or have yet to gain a reputation. Instead, articulate professionals who are mostly moderate—the Puritans in the 1630s and the Jacobins in 1789 were moderate, not radical; their radicalization developed later (J. T. Cliffe 1984; Kennedy 1982)—and who have been advocating rectification and some redistribution of opportunities and assets, are best placed to initially assume authority.

Nonetheless, their success in dominating the polity, given the lack of accepted institutions and of adequate military force, rests on their ability to win the allegiance of key groups, which means appealing to desires for rectification of injustice, redistribution, and/or national authenticity. Rectification of formal grievances—reducing ostentation in government, purging corrupt old retainers and unpopular laws, creating a new constitution, and accepting greater popular participation in politics—can usually be quickly accomplished, to the credit of the new authorities. Yet rectification of material grievances usually requires more than mere formal and procedural changes. Generally, it means that a measure of redistribution of assets held by formerly privileged groups is required. This need in turn either forces those groups seeking popular support toward greater radicalism or gives an advantage to groups who espouse more radical measures. Struggles over the pay of the New Model Army in England and over the disposition of church lands in the French Revolution led to the radicalization of the Long Parliament and the National Assembly. On the other hand, the failure of the Provisional Government in Russia to adopt more redistributive measures to favor workers and peasants created an opportunity for the more radical Bolsheviks.

As the struggles by contending groups to achieve political primacy usually take the form of a growing identification and pursuit of "enemies," a period of terror is generally a part of the revolutionary process. This seems to be not merely a regrettable error or an avoidable "excess" but an essential part of the manner in which groups competing for authority in postrevolutionary situations operate. After all, radical redistributive measures, whether undertaken or resisted by the new government, are divisive, and counterrevolutionaries are still around. The collapse of state authority also generally lets social divisions—regional, ethnic, class, factional—that had been submerged initially by the power of the former state, and later by the united struggle against the state, emerge as overt conflicts. These antagonisms then generally become entangled with the revolutionary struggle. Repeated contests between revolutionaries and their opponents thus lead the former to push the revolution to the point where there can be no turning back, and to purge slackers from their midst. The new leadership "ordinarily [has to] establish 'structures of repression' as the instrument of retaining power in the face of renewed challenges" (Gurr 1986a: 150).

It should also be clear why military dictatorship or militarism toward neighbors is often the outcome of revolution. The weakened institutions left in the wake of the fall of the old government are often insufficient to resolve the strife among competing factions that follows. Radical appeals often further divide the polity.

Thus, a nationalist policy, involving strong leadership and action against external "enemies," is often the key to restoring national unity and order.

In such cases, even authoritarian leadership is often initially welcomed. It can be seen as a "plebiscitary" dictatorship, and it appropriates the symbols that the revolution developed to embody national pride. It is thus generally not seen as a revival of the old regime; instead, it embodies the fervent nationalism that is the common denominator to which most revolutions are eventually reduced.

Indeed, much the same struggle—to win allegiance and mobilize on the basis of loyalty to the "nation" rather than the old regime—takes place in the armed forces of a nation during a revolution as takes place in the country at large. As Adelman (1985) has shown, recruitment and promotion in revolutionary armies take on a new principle, emphasizing talent, but also rectification of abuses, redistribution of authority, and national service. The armies of revolutionary states thus embody the state's ideology; their eventual dominance is not merely a triumph of strength but a victory of the revolution, albeit in authoritarian form.

In short, many of the characteristics of revolutions reflect the conditions of revolutionary struggle per se. It is for this reason that revolutions often follow a similar course, despite having diverse origins and espousing ideologies of diverse content.

STATE RECONSTRUCTION
AND REVOLUTIONARY OUTCOMES

Once a new ruling group begins to consolidate its authority, usually through the forging of revolutionary armies, internal repression, and assertive nationalism, the task of reconstructing stable political institutions looms large. The manner in which postrevolutionary elites approach this task is usually conditioned by three factors: the class and economic structures of the prerevolutionary society, the international context of the revolution, and the experiences of the new elites under the old regime and in the revolutionary struggle.

The class and economic structures of the prerevolutionary society set certain constraints on postrevolutionary state building. For example, when there is a substantial commercial and industrial middle class and major economic assets are privately held, building a successful coalition for taking state power generally requires maintaining private property. Thus, the American, English, and French revolutions were unlikely to move in the direction of socialist state reconstruction. (The failure of the French Jacobins to stay in power was largely owing to their failure to build a supporting coalition bridging the urban poor and the commercial middle classes.) On the other hand, when commercial classes are small and weak and major industrial assets are already held by the state, revolutionary leaders can simply seize these assets and, relying on the support of peasants and/or workers and dismissing the middle classes, establish state socialist economies, as occurred in Russia in 1917 and in China in 1949 (Skocpol 1979).

The international context includes both the pressures of distant great powers and the opportunities and threats posed by nearby neighbors. The drift toward an assertive nationalism plays a major role in both respects. To the extent that a country has been dependent on aid or support from a foreign power, the new regime generally seeks to break those ties. Thus, England and France, after their revolutions, broke old alignments and forged new alliances. Other countries, such as Russia, have sought to maintain a nonaligned status. In the contemporary world, however, smaller countries, with a greater need for foreign assistance, may explicitly switch their allegiance to another foreign power, if such a move seems a way of manifesting their new control of foreign policy. For this reason, revolutions in superpower client states often create geopolitical shifts that have implications for strategic rivalry. Moreover, the combination of sudden shifts in external alliances and assertive nationalism often leads to international wars. Even when overt aggression is not immediately chosen, new regimes still lay stress on arming for defense against external threats. Thus, new revolutionary regimes are usually more formidable and more threatening to their neighbors and to international peace than were the prerevolutionary regimes.

This situation is not always the case. Nationalistic and revolutionary fervor may be directed inward, against internal enemies, as the Russians did against kulaks in the 1920s and 1930s and the Chinese did against "capitalist roaders" in the 1960s. To a large degree, the difference depends on how the new revolutionary elites see the world. When the fear of obstruction of the revolution from within is greater, terror may remain primarily internal. Gurr (1986b) has suggested that the deeper the divisions in the domestic society—particularly regional and ethnic divisions—and the greater the resistance faced by the new revolutionary elites in their struggles with internal competitors, the more likely is a high and lasting degree of internal terror.

Regarding internal reconstruction, the choice of a capitalist or a socialist economy, and of a religious or a secular orientation, often reflects deeply held beliefs on the part of new elites. Skocpol (1979) has stressed that revolutionary leaders are generally drawn from groups that were "marginal elites" under the old regime. Marginal elites are groups that have had an upper-class education and have access to national debates over political and social issues; however, they are also restricted— by their personal circumstances or treatment by the government that is unrelated to their merit—from any prospect of active participation at the highest levels of government or society. These groups are, in some ways, discriminated against, excluded, or punished by regimes, and generally resent their treatment. Thus, when they come to power they have a missionary zeal to correct the aspects of the system that wronged them. For example, religious leaders—whether Puritans or Islamic mullahs—who have been marginalized under an old regime are likely to seek to make the role of religion primary. Revolutionaries from the relatively poor intelligentsia, if snubbed by the wealthy and influential, are naturally drawn to an abolition of private property. Revolutionaries who suffer and sacrifice to achieve the overthrow of foreign domination, or overturn a capitalist regime in the name of restoring land to the peasants and freedom to labor, are willing to take extreme measures and demand great popular sacrifices in order to stamp out foreign influence or attain their social goals.

The nature of the revolutionary struggle also influences the shape of postrevolutionary states. Skocpol (1979) has pointed out that when faced with the difficulties of mobilizing economic resources and achieving political ends, revolutionary leaders are liable to turn to the same methods they utilized in initially gaining power—the forcible mobilization of populations in an ideologically extreme and heightened battle to combat particular enemies. It is thus hard for postrevolutionary regimes to tolerate a "loyal opposition." As Gurr has noted, "The first generation of leaders who have seized power by violence are particularly likely to be habituated to its political uses, and to perceive a threat of violent displacement in the actions, even the existence, of potential challengers" (Gurr 1986b: 54). Postrevolutionary states generally become one-party states, and when a significant threat from internal challengers is perceived, they often become police states. This outcome is not merely the product of a particular ideology, such as communism—the biblically inspired English revolution became a military state under Oliver Cromwell, as did Enlightenment France under the Jacobin dictatorship and modern Shi'ite Iran under the mullahs. Rather, the pattern of the revolutionary struggle—and the resulting fear of internal competitors and violent displacement—affect the style of state reconstruction. Only when revolutions are fought primarily against external opponents—e.g., anticolonial revolutions in which there are few strong loyalists or collaborators, as in the United States and Algeria—are postrevolutionary regimes able to reconstruct their states without great fear of attack from internal adversaries, and hence exhibit less of a "garrison" mentality.

Thus, it may be naive to assume that a moderate intervention—in the form of aid or threat of withholding some support—will cause a postrevolutionary elite to take a particular direction in state reconstruction. Certain directions and prejudices, having been forged by past discrimination, humiliation, or punishment or in the heat of revolutionary struggles, are liable to be set firm. Actions taken in the belief that there are "moderate elements" in the postrevolutionary Iranian government, or that Sandinista leaders might change the direction of their policies under moderate military pressure, are therefore likely misguided and unproductive from the outset. Such actions ignore the nature of revolution as a process, in which the impact of past experience and struggles is not easily altered.

SUMMARY: AN ANALYTICAL FRAMEWORK FOR UNDERSTANDING MODERN REVOLUTIONS

The preceding framework offers a partial guide for understanding the development of revolutions. The key originating factor is a *conjuncture of several conditions*: declining state resources relative to expenses and the resources of adversaries, increasing elite alienation and disunity, and growing popular grievances and autonomy. These conditions, however, may be produced by a variety of forces, depending on how they interact with the institutions and structures in particular societies. Forecasting revolutions thus requires that an analyst pay attention to the particular details of the society under study and ask whether current trends are likely to produce those conditions that threaten the state. This framework also suggests that since these conditions work *interactively* to undermine a state, interventions to forestall revolution may be successful if they can effectively counter one of the critical conditions, even though the others may still be present. Thus, this causal model has both forecasting and policy implications.

Once a government has lost the initiative—as evidenced by the wide spread of ideologies advocating radical changes and the emergence of anti-state coalitions of elites whose resources and popular support surpass those of the state—a number of different factors come into play. The chief of these are the organization and ideology of groups competing with the state for authority. Groups that are highly organized at the outset of a revolutionary crisis, and can more effectively deploy their resources to take advantage of opportunities, have a better chance of defeating other contending groups. In addition, groups that develop an attractive, synthetic ideology are likely to gain resources and supporters. In particular, radical and nationalist ideologies are liable to be more successful in this regard than moderate, merely formal rectification programs. One can thus predict that in a state on the edge of collapse, those groups that are the best organized will have an initial advantage. In addition, the group that is able to gain ideological primacy by capturing the aspirations and allegiance of the largest portion of the population is likely to dominate the revolutionary struggle. When moderates are able to capture the ideological high ground as true nationalists, responding to the needs of the population, they may survive. However, when the radicals are able to capture this high ground, they are likely to emerge as the dominant force in the successor regime. This observation suggests a strategy for moderate groups seeking to survive in the postrevolutionary melee. Thus, this model of revolutionary struggle, too, has both forecasting and policy implications.

This framework also, regrettably, suggests that a period of terror and the emergence of coercive and aggressive regimes are likely outcomes of revolutions. The deeper the divisions in the society, and the greater degree of internal struggle and resistance accompanying the emergence and consolidation of revolutionary leadership, the more severe internal terror and coercion are likely to be. The greater the reliance on aggressive nationalism to cement the postrevolutionary regime, the more likely is the "pursuit of enemies" to spill over into arming against external threats or undertaking military engagements.[1]

I have noted that certain features of the prerevolutionary society—the class structure and the concentration and ownership of industrial assets—can constrain the directions of postrevolutionary change. In addition, it is important to examine the experiences of the new postrevolutionary elites under the old regime. Elites that were, in some respect, marginal—owing to discrimination, neglect, or lack of some qualification—are likely to rebuild society in a manner that forcefully overcomes the source of their former marginality. Thus, groups that were discriminated against for their religion may seek to rebuild a state that is guided by, or favors, that religion. Groups that were marginalized because of lack of property or traditional status are likely to abolish such status divisions or property holding. Groups that felt oppressed by the influence of a foreign power are likely to be extremely hostile to that power. This observation suggests that the direction of state reconstruction can be partially forecast from an examination of the dominant postrevolutionary elites—their former positions and grievances. It also suggests that if new elites have emerged from a marginal position and won power through a heated struggle, later policy intervention aimed at changing the direction of state reconstruction is liable to be fruitless, given the deeply held formative experiences of former marginalization and discrimination and the hardening of these beliefs in conflicts against the old regime and other opponents. Thus, this last portion of the model again has both forecasting and policy implications.

Although I have presented this model in general terms, I have stressed that its concrete application to particular cases requires a skilled analyst, one who is capable of examining how varied forces and trends have developed in particular societies. Its value therefore depends on the extent to which it can usefully guide, rather than inhibit, the skill of the area specialist in understanding specific instances of revolution. The following chapters thus test the usefulness of this framework, as area specialists assess the causes, the struggles for dominance, and the developing outcomes of recent revolutions and potentially revolutionary situations.

NOTES

1. The best hope for a democratic outcome in the Eastern European revolutions of 1989 is thus in those countries with few internal divisions and little or no resistance to the new regimes, namely, Hungary and East Germany. Hopes for democratic outcomes are weakest in Romania and the Soviet Union, where such factors are strong. Poland and Czechoslovakia are intermediate cases.

4

VIETNAM: REVOLUTION OF POSTCOLONIAL CONSOLIDATION

H. JOHN LeVAN

U.S. involvement in Vietnam ended on April 30, 1975, with the Vietnamese claim of "complete victory of the General Offensive and Uprising of Spring 1975 that completely defeated the aggressive war and the neocolonialist rule of U.S. imperialism and completely liberated the South." This introductory line to the book *Dai thang mua xuan* [Our great spring victory], by General Van Tien Dung (1977), commander in chief of North Vietnamese forces during the Ho Chi Minh campaign, nicely sums up the principal purposes of this revolution of postcolonial consolidation, the southern phase of the long conflict between Vietnam and colonial powers that began in August 1945.

The August 1945 revolution comprised a number of uprisings throughout Vietnam that took place at the end of World War II, following the Japanese surrender to the Allies. The Japanese had occupied Vietnam since September 1940, along with Cambodia and Laos, together known as Indochina, a French colony since the second half of the nineteenth century (Buttinger 1958). The immediate political result of this revolution was the establishment of the new Democratic Republic of Vietnam (DRV) under the Vietminh, a coalition of Communists and nationalists led by Ho Chi Minh (Lacouture 1968). The new government replaced the imperial institutions that had been preserved and utilized by both the French and the Japanese and headed by Emperor Bao Dai, the last monarch of the Vietnamese dynastic era (Karnow 1984).

The new government did not have time to reconstruct the fractured state before the French returned to Vietnam in force with the intention of reimposing French rule over the former colony. The First Indochina War began in 1946 and did not come to an end until the Vietnamese victory at Dien Bien Phu in 1954 (Fall 1963, 1966), an event that also marked the conclusion of French colonialism in Southeast Asia. With the departure of the French from the scene following

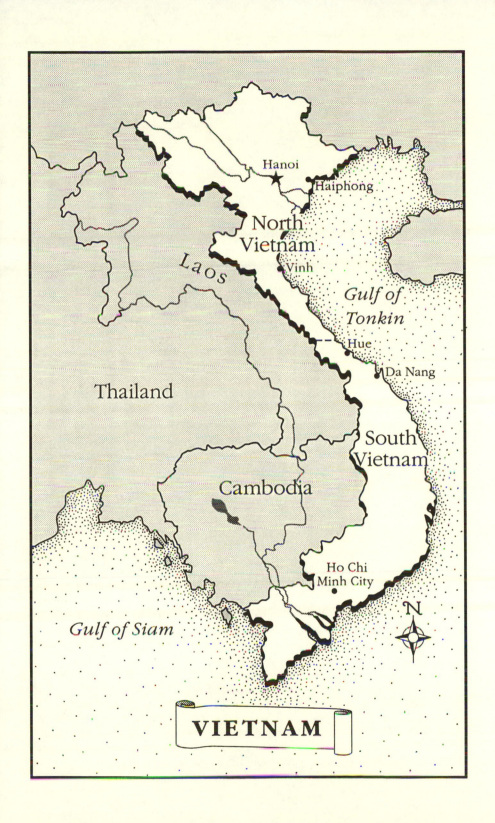

VIETNAM

the Geneva Conference of 1954 (Podhoretz 1980; Karnow 1984) and the partition of the country into two parts at the seventeenth parallel—in the North, the Democratic Republic of Vietnam (DRV) with its capital in Hanoi and in the South, the newly created Republic of Vietnam (RVN) with its capital in Saigon— Vietnam for the first time was placed in the context of superpower competition.

This chapter deals with events between 1957, the year that North Vietnam (DRV) ordered its southern cadres to make plans for a new struggle against the U.S.-backed regime of Ngo Dinh Diem (Karnow 1984: 237), and 1975, when Saigon, the capital of South Vietnam, fell and the country was again reunified as the Socialist Republic of Vietnam (SRV). This period has often been referred to by the Vietnamese Communist leaders as "the national-democratic revolution in the South" (Woddis 1970: 145), but for the southern regime and its U.S. patron, it was "Communist aggression against the Vietnamese people" from the North (Fall 1963: 444). Setting labels aside, I will consider this southern phase of the revolution, like its predecessor, as a peasant-based revolutionary movement.

Overall, the southern phase of the Vietnamese revolution was essentially a renewed struggle for national liberation and reunification led by North Vietnam under the aegis of the Workers' (Communist) party. This fact was constantly exploited by both French and U.S. policymakers in their efforts to induce the South Vietnamese to fight against potential Communist domination of the South, but the French and U.S. tutelage, unfortunately, hurt the South Vietnamese leaders more than it helped them, since to the average Vietnamese, "chinh nghia," or political legitimacy, has traditionally been on the side of those who struggle against invading foreigners for national salvation. As such, no southern government sponsored by either Paris or Washington could count on the wide support of the population against the Vietnamese-led revolutionary forces.

As the war in the South gradually became "Americanized," Hanoi cleverly "Vietnamized" the resistance efforts by frequently emphasizing the indigenous historical culture of the Vietnamese people, especially the heroic insurgencies against the Chinese in the distant past and the more recent efforts against France's attempt to reestablish its colonial rule. This strategy, when coupled with effective Communist organizational tactics, paid off handsomely in the revolutionary struggle for popular support, since it successfully aroused the historical patriotism of the Vietnamese people, who were still searching for a national identity and in whose mind the experience of exploitation and brutality by the French colonialists was still fresh. The southern insurrection was considered by the North as part of the long Vietnamese traditional opposition to foreign occupations: as such, northern leaders stressed the glorious achievements of Vietnamese heroes (*anh hung*) as well as condemning those who chose to collaborate with the enemies as *Viet gian* (Vietnamese traitors). Noticeably, this elaboration on the theme of historical and cultural continuity, which is often disregarded by students of the Vietnamese revolution, is still being echoed by the postrevolutionary government to maintain popular support.

Although the motivation for the expulsion of foreigners was strong, the victory of the Vietminh was still long in coming. Therefore, to understand the timing and development of the southern phase of the revolution, we must examine more closely the resources and the support of the South Vietnam regime.

PREREVOLUTIONARY STATE AND SOCIETY

Goldstone has identified several conditions that act in concert to induce the fracture of an incumbent state structure: state fiscal weakness, elite alienation and revolt, and heightened popular mobilization potential.[1] In the Vietnamese case, circumstances in the collapse of effective state power are different between the August revolution and the southern phase revolution. By 1945, the French colonial regime had been drastically weakened by the Japanese invasion of Indochina and the eventual takeover of the colony's administrative apparatus. State resources had been drained to the bone to support the war machinery rather than ordinary civil needs, and the whole situation was complicated by a massive famine resulting from natural calamities. In effect, the country, especially the northern part, was overwhelmed by economic disaster. This resource crisis was caused in part by the excessive requisition policies of the Japanese and the Vichy French and by their demand that the traditional rice crop be replaced by nonfood planting such as jute, oil seeds, and opium (Hammer 1954: 145). Constant bombing by the Allies had also interrupted the transportation of surplus rice from one part of the country to another that was in dire need.

No such economic situation existed in South Vietnam during the Second Indochina War. Massive U.S. economic aid had created an appearance of prosperity in the southern cities, which acted as a magnet for people from the rural areas who fled the countryside to avoid the danger and insecurity created by armed clashes between the competing forces. It was reported that as early as 1963, South Vietnam had received some $500 million in aid from the United States for the year (Karnow 1984: 681). In this sense, the South Vietnamese state had the resources to sustain both the army and the bureaucracy as well as other essential state needs.

Thus, the initial state crisis in the South was primarily not fiscal distress, but elite disunity. Between the murder of the South Vietnamese president Ngo Dinh Diem in a U.S.-backed coup d'etat in November 1963 and 1967 when Nguyen Van Thieu was able to consolidate his power to become president, the country experienced an atmosphere of factional political instablity induced by a constant struggle within the officer corps of the armed forces, which at that time constituted the ruling elite. In effect, the Saigon leadership was busier manipulating politics and competing for power through factional fighting than it was concerned with the ongoing revolution in the countryside. This situation created a tremendous morale problem in the army, and one of the immediate negative results was a drastic increase in "the South Vietnamese desertion rate, which had reached a total of 93,000 . . . passing over to the enemy . . . in 1965, maintain[ing] a roughly equal rate in 1966" (Fall 1972: 150–151).

The situation also led to what Goldstone refers to as "elite alienation," and by 1960, several influential Vietnamese had joined the revolutionary side. In 1969, the *Who's Who* of the Provisional Revolutionary Government (PRG) of the Republic of Vietnam included several prominent non-Communist South Vietnamese, from a well-known architect who served as its president to several French-educated professors, physicians, lawyers, and artists holding other ministerial portfolios (Giai-Phong Editions 1969). Those who did not leave for the jungle to join the resistance stayed in the city or went overseas, maintaining an indifferent "wait-and-see" (*trum chan*) attitude but completely withdrawing their active support from the government.

Amid this elite factionalism, which at times became polarized, southern politics was anything but unified in the face of the revolutionary threat directed from the North. With tacit endorsement from Washington, the regime—essentially the junta—toughened its repression against non-Communist opposition (Karnow 1984: 444). Although the endorsement was desirable to have from the point of view of the southern elites, it was also a liability for the South Vietnamese leaders, since it undermined their claim to nationalist legitimacy among the southern population, and the question of legitimacy is very important in Vietnamese politics, especially among the peasants in the countryside, who make up the overwhelming majority of the population (Pike 1969: 65–79). In this respect, the revolutionary leaders and their North Vietnamese counterparts enjoyed an enormous advantage, since they could claim a legitimate "righteous cause" (*chinh nghia*) as opposed to the motives of the southern rulers,

> who would sell out their country, sell themselves for dollars, sell their souls to foreigners. In the past there had been those like Tran Ich Tac and Le Chieu Thong,[2] and modern times had seen the likes of Ngo Dinh Diem, Nguyen Van Thieu, Nguyen Cao Ky. Their fate was all the more shameful and vile—some had changed masters as many as three times, and in the end had been killed by those very masters. There were those who killed each other off in their "plot against the prince" and their competition for dollars. (Van Tien Dung 1977: 258)

Regime after regime in South Vietnam, despite the backing of the military might of the United States, thus failed to win the hearts and minds of the Vietnamese population. Some Americans often suggested during the Vietnam war that it was Washington's reluctance to prosecute the war in a more fierce manner—for example, to "bomb Vietnam back to the Stone Age"—that was leading to the U.S. "defeat" in Vietnam. This notion was perhaps correct if the United States was solely interested in occupying Vietnam. The Vietnamese, however, as in the past during their resistance against the Chinese and then the French, just applied their tactic of *tieu tho khang chien*, or burning the land to the ground for struggling against the enemies, and retreated to the jungles to wage long-term guerrilla warfare to wear down the foreign forces. The main mistake committed by Washington policymakers was that they failed to pay attention to the feelings of the Vietnamese masses concerning foreign troops in their own country. This ignorance was perhaps understandable, as a U.S. military occupation had been welcome elsewhere in Asia, particularly in Japan and Korea.

In 1954, when Ngo Dinh Diem returned to South Vietnam to assume power with U.S. political and financial support, he was popular because he was anti-French and determined to root out the corrupt vestiges of the French-backed Bao Dai regime. Yet Diem's nationalism led to his downfall when he refused to simply follow U.S. policy. As is well known, Diem's fall in 1963 was a direct result of his adamant resistance to U.S. policies of political and social reform; thus Washington strategists had no other choice but, in the words of U.S. ambassador to Saigon

Elbridge Durbrow, to "be forced, in the not too distant future, to undertake the difficult task of identifying and supporting alternate leadership" (Karnow 1984: 235).

The task of identifying alternative leadership for South Vietnam following the murder of Ngo Dinh Diem was indeed difficult, if not impossible, for the United States, since as one coup d'etat followed another, those who represented themselves as the only viable ruling elite, the high-ranking officers of the Saigon armed forces, the "brothers-in-arms" according to one of the key actors, were too busy "tearing each other apart for the sake of power" (Nguyen Cao Ky 1976: 156). This behavior did not seem to rest well with the Vietnamese popular mentality, which has traditionally respected the virtues of *trung* and *nghia* ("loyalty" and "righteouness").

However self-centered the dictatorial regime of Ngo Dinh Diem might have been, the generals of South Vietnam were essentially his subordinates, their high positions having been bestowed by him, and their act of toppling and murdering him constituted "plotting against the prince." In Vietnam as in China, usurpation has been historically condemned even if the usurpers were successful in assuming the reign of the country. In addition to being handicapped by this moral judgment in the eyes of their fellow citizens, the majority of the feuding generals never emerged as true national leaders because of either exceptional talent or a reputation that deserved popular respect. In a society in which scholarly achievements of leaders commanded high esteem and admiration, many of the high-ranking officers, except for a few who had received advanced French military training, had not finished the *lycée* (junior college equivalent) or in some cases even a high school education. The corps of junior officers, on the other hand, were essentially drafted from a pool of college students or those pursuing graduate study at universities in Saigon or Hue.

The Saigon generals who recognized their reliance on the United States also perceived that they were forfeiting their credibility to the insurgents by claiming to represent the national cause, since the Communist-backed rebels saw "the war entirely as one of defense of their country against the invading Americans, who, in turn, [were] seen as successors to the French" (Karnow 1984: 460) while the government was being maintained by foreign troops occupying the homeland. In this sense, U.S. support was both an asset and a liability for the South Vietnam regime. Recognizing this dilemma, Nguyen Cao Ky, one of the southern prime ministers in the post-Diem era, later wrote: "We held an ace, and also held a deuce. For while I was preaching the need for freedom, I was not always free myself. . . . How could we have that when every Vietnamese in Saigon referred to the American ambassador as the 'Governor General'?" (Nguyen Cao Ky 1976: 137). One of the U.S. "governors general," Maxwell Taylor, complained General Ky, "had treated top Vietnamese generals like stupid boys" and was "talking to us as errant schoolboys who had been caught stealing apples from an orchard" (Nguyen Cao Ky 1976: 55).

Washington was perhaps aware of this resentment on the part of the Saigon leadership, but it was not ready to allow its "puppets to pull their own strings," since the U.S. strategic stake in South Vietnam was much higher than maintaining the appearance that this former French colony was free from U.S. domination. Former Secretary of State Dean Acheson, in a speech at Amherst College in December 1965, emphasized what Bernard Fall calls the "intellectual underpinning of American new ethics" of neo-Machiavellianism concerning Vietnam when he said that "our . . . actions must be decided by whether they contribute to or detract from achievement of [the end sought by our foreign policy]. They need no other justification or moral or ethical embellishment" (Fall 1972: 236).

RURAL MOBILIZATION POTENTIAL

The situation portrayed above was only one among a host of state difficulties. A still greater challenge to the government of South Vietnam was to find an effective way to deny the revolutionary guerrillas the support of the populace in the countryside, where a high mass mobilization potential among the peasants was also evident. From the Vietnamese revolutionary perspective, this subject deserves consideration in some detail, since it rests in the historical tradition as well as the culture of the vast majority of the country's population, the peasantry. In a review article entitled "What Makes Peasants Revolutionary?" Theda Skocpol has suggested that "cultural factors can help us understand why Asian Communists have been more willing to attempt peasant mobilization than have, say, Latin American Communists or Communists in Moslem countries" (Skocpol 1982: 365). Of the major contemporary U.S. scholarship that Skocpol dealt with—Wolf (1969), Migdal (1974), Paige (1975), and Scott (1977)—evidently none has even alluded to the role of traditional political culture in agrarian revolutions, of which Vietnam often served as a case study.

There existed in Vietnam a traditional cultural tension between the ruling elite and the peasantry. The elite often regarded the culture of the ordinarily uneducated peasants, the village "little tradition" with its absence of complex intellectual and philosophical emphasis, as vastly inferior to the refined finesse and noblesse of the high-society "great tradition."[3] This sociocultural antagonism at times was transformed into political conflicts between the peasants and the elites, the latter often considering rural social behavior as undesirable and potentially troublesome.

The rural cohesiveness of ordinary villagers and the tradition of village resistance to a ruling elite's hegemony were historically evident in the countryside. Conditions leading the peasant to bear arms in insurrection could be a domestic upheaval (such as flood, drought, and other natural calamities) or external pressure (such as a foreign invasion or occupation). Traditionally, even in these situations, the peasants by themselves would not be able to engage in a rebellion of any significant magnitude. Yet when a leader—carrying the banner of *chinh nghia*, "righteous cause"—emerged from the intelligentsia or a landowning class to head an insurgent movement, the peasants' insurrectionary capacities could take on regional or national importance.

It is essential to note the change in the tension between the peasants and the elites after the imposition of French colonial rule. The colonial regime used the Vietnamese imperial court and its mandarinate to carry out its colonial policy, and in so doing discredited the Vietnamese officials and elites even further in the eyes of the peasantry. The preexisting conflict between the "great tradition" and the "little tradition" was inevitably widened, since now the peasants, who still held to some old traditional values, had to deal with a change in social mentality and purposes of the ruling elites. One of the most vivid examples was the drastic 1956 decision of the South Vietnam regime under Ngo Dinh Diem to change the age-old custom of villages electing their own officials by directly appointing village chiefs throughout the country. The Vietnamese proverb *Phep vua thua le lang* ("The emperor codes yield to the village customs") illustrates that this decision was indeed a fundamental error.

When it comes to the question of a revolutionary catalyst for Vietnamese peasant collective actions, Jeffery Paige overemphasizes the peasants' class consciousness, which he argues can precipitate them to emerge "from within" and rise to overthrow landlords and the state. As I have noted previously, the Vietnamese peasants are traditionally conservative and unable to take effective armed action without proper leadership. There have been in Vietnamese history numerous, sporadic, short-lived local revolts of insignificant nature as the result of national calamities or social oppressions, but these incidents were merely temporary reactive or remedial measures taken by desperate villagers without any lasting effects. For a movement to aim at widespread revolutionary consequences or impact, it has needed a revolutionary leader or an organizer from another social stratum—often the intellectuals or landowners—not one from the rank and file of the "cultivator class." In other words, the peasants' revolutionary "political affiliations" are not "internally generated" as Paige suggests (1975: 62). In the case of the recent Vietnamese Communist revolution, the political factor, as Skocpol correctly asserts, was

created and led by urban-educated and middle-class people . . . *come* to agrarian lower classes in search of their support for national political objectives that go well beyond the immediate goals of the vast majority of the peasants, whether small holders or sharecroppers. In Vietnam, the Communists had anti-colonial, nationalist objectives as well as the "revolutionary socialist" goals exclusively stressed by Paige. (Skocpol 1982: 358)

In order to achieve its goals, the Vietnamese Communist party actually played the role that had been played by previous Vietnamese revolutionary leaders who had wanted to tap the most important revolutionary resource of the country, the peasantry. As Communist historian Nguyen Khac Vien succinctly reveals in his essay on "Confucianism and Marxism in Vietnam," the Communist cadres during the revolution assumed the role of the former Confucian scholars in the rural areas as leaders of collective life and, on the cultural and ideological levels, "educated and advised" the peasants daily as they remained in the countryside among the people. To mobilize the villagers to the revolutionary cause, the cadres followed "the tradition of the old-time revolutionary scholars by sequestering themselves in the villages teaching and organizing the peasants over a period of many long years, until the time of land reform and the establishment of agriculture cooperatives. By doing so they raised peasant struggle to a much higher level, opening it up to entirely new perspectives" (Nguyen Khac Vien 1974: 46).

With the presence of these clandestine cadres in the villages, who were known as *can-bo nam vung* ("clandestine cadres who stayed behind in government zone"), the revolution was, in Joel Migdal's words, "created by the impetus from outside the peasant class," which eventually turned the Vietnamese peasants into "active and passive members of a host of revolutionary organizations and groups" (Migdal 1974: 232, 226). Indeed, without this institutionalized peasant support, the modern revolutions, like past ones, would not have been able to arrive at their successful conclusions.

I want to emphasize again the necessity of leadership in Vietnamese peasant movements, since even in the past, peasants never initiated a successful armed struggle without someone to lead them. Culturally, the peasants perceived any spontaneous eruption as *loan* ("chaos"); the group involved was said to act in the manner of *ran khong dau* ("a serpent without a head") and therefore could not be legitimate. The peasantry, even in despair, waited for a leader, an authority, with legitimacy. Except for the resistance supported by the North, no such leadership existed in South Vietnam, as Nguyen Cao Ky readily admitted:

> We never produced a leader to unite the country with its many religious and political factions. The North had one in Ho Chi Minh; rightly or wrongly, the Communists believed in him and fought and died for him. He had a charisma that won many supporters even in the West and not all of them were Communists. Neither [Ngo Dinh] Diem, nor [Nguyen Van] Thieu—both backed by the Americans—won the hearts of even the South Vietnamese. (Nguyen Cao Ky 1976: 137)

The Vietnamese experience has proved that given motivating leadership and effective organization, an insurgency can mobilize, not only the peasants, but also support from all walks of life—during the 1945 August revolution and later during the southern revolutionary phase. There is no question that the movements were essentially peasant based, but the overall revolutionary coalition extended to all kinds of social strata, from intellectuals to illiterates and from city dwellers to village inhabitants. The key factor of this successful mobilization, as Migdal accurately points out, is the "degree to which revolutionary leadership appears, with an organizational framework," capable of appealing to the whole population (Migdal 1974: 231). For the Vietnamese people, after some eighty years of French colonial exploitation and countless abortive resistance efforts during the first four decades of this century, the historical slogan of *Khoi-nghia* ("Uprising for a righteous cause") under a new banner revived and renewed their ethnic pride, which had been suppressed by the white race. Indeed this "exogenous" factor, promoted by the determined and capable leadership of the Communist-led group, complemented by the supporting cadres living among the people—both in the cities and in the villages—was the most important component of the revolution's success.

The customary country-city antagonism was often reinforced by the economic deprivation suffered by the villagers during the war, which was readily exploited by the insurgent force to gain a tactical advantage in winning over the rural population. It is often assumed that in any revolutionary struggle, the economic foundation of the incumbent regime is often one of the primary targets attacked by the rebels. In the case of South Vietnam, it was instead the inherent foundation and direction of the government's economic policy—which was mostly politically motivated—that provided opportunities for the revolutionary side to gain an advantage in their undermining efforts.

ECONOMIC CONDITIONS

I mentioned previously that state fiscal distress was not a direct cause of South Vietnam's downfall, as U.S. aid generously supported the regime. Dependence on this aid, however, *was* a severe liability. In order to understand the progressive deterioration of the political situation of the Saigon regime during the southern phase of the Vietnamese revolution, a brief review of the economic situation is necessary.

Bernard Fall correctly pointed out that "without American aid to Vietnam's military and economic machinery, the country would not survive for ten minutes" (Fall 1963: 289–290), and yet because of this economic assistance, according to Milton Taylor, an economic adviser to the government of South Vietnam, in an article published in the Fall 1961 issue of *Pacific Affairs*, the country had become "a permanent mendicant." Despite these assessments, the official lines of both the U.S. State Department and the government of President Ngo Dinh Diem regarding the southern regime's prospects were quite optimistic. Obviously there were divergent if not opposite, views of the South Vietnamese economic situation, and verification of the correct view is an arduous, if not an impossible, task because of a lack of credible statistics.

The partition of Vietnam at the seventeenth parallel in 1954 created a score of economic and political problems for the South. First, the shaky southern economy had to absorb almost 1 million refugees from the North during a time of political instability, as Ngo Dinh Diem, the new leader backed by the United States, was still facing strong opposition from French-supported politicians as well as from militant religious sects. Second, the economic vacuum created by the departure of the French expeditionary corps, which in 1954 had spent "more than $500 million in Vietnam apart from U.S. aid," also contributed to the uneasiness of the southern economic situation (Fall 1963: 291).

The road and communication networks of South Vietnam, perhaps the finest in Southeast Asia at the time, had suffered heavy damage during the long war with France and needed to be repaired or reconstructed to ease food distribution and other transportation needs. Unless the cities could be linked with the countryside, in the words of Vu Quoc Thuc, a noted Vietnamese economist, in the *Times of Vietnam*, April 1, 1962, "the economic crisis [that] ha[d] its origin in the state of insecurity in the rural areas" would not be resolved despite all the foreign aid that South Vietnam could obtain.

South Vietnam, especially the Mekong delta region, once considered the granary of Indochina and a major rice exporter on the world market, now could not produce enough to feed its own people, and large-scale food imports had to be initiated to meet domestic needs (Dao van Tap 1980: 124). The average rice production for 1954–1955, compared to the yield of 1938, was about 50 percent, according to South Vietnamese official sources, which justifiably blamed the shortfall on the war conditions. Despite optimistic reports from the U.S. State Department asserting that during the above-mentioned period, South Vietnamese "food production rose an average of 7 percent a year and pre-war levels were achieved and passed," the country still had a hard time meeting the food demand of its increasing population, which had grown "more than 50 percent since 1938" (Fall 1963: 294).

Another South Vietnamese export product was rubber from plantations still operated by French owners, who somehow survived both insurgent demands for taxes and heavy fines imposed by the government for alleged "collusion with the enemy" when ransoms were paid to the guerrillas for kidnapped personnel. In spite of these obstacles, the South, according to Bernard Fall, was able to export some 70,000 metric tons annually, which at the 1960 price level brought in an average export income of $80 million (Fall 1963: 295). That figure, however, when compared to the average yearly trade deficit of almost $180 million between 1955 and 1962, was still far from enough to solve the dire economic situation.

Under the circumstances, the export prospects for two of South Vietnam's most important products, rice and rubber, seemed bleak. As an immediate consequence, the deficits in the balance of trade increased drastically, beginning in 1955 when France no longer contributed to the support of the economy. As of that year, the burden of helping Saigon make up its trade imbalance fell on the shoulders of the United States, and South Vietnam's economic survival thus became heavily attached to U.S. aid, in addition to its progressive military dependency.

The Saigon government did make some attempts in the field of industrialization, which up to 1955 was still in its infancy, concentrating mainly on light industries such as soft-drink bottling, cigarette and match production, and rice milling. A "secret" five-year economic plan, announced by the Ngo Dinh Diem government in 1957 to create new industries for South Vietnam, was financed chiefly by U.S. aid and had the declared purpose of producing basic goods for domestic use and thus helping reduce the trade deficit. From the very beginning, even this modest endeavor was a futile effort, as the Vietnamese goods had to compete on the domestic market with superior imported products, mostly from the United States and Japan. Vietnamese retail merchants, while striving to survive the Chinese residents' monopoly of South Vietnamese rice and other food commodity outlets, had to struggle to compete for the lucrative import trade. They often became resigned to exploitation and the "protection" costs that had to be paid to family members of corrupt high officials, while helping turn the South into a consumer society dependent on both U.S. dollars and that country's armed forces.

There was little effort by the government to attract participation from the private sector, and whenever there was legislation on foreign investment, according to the account of independent economist Nguyen Huu Hanh in a somewhat blunt article in the *Journal d'Extreme-Orient*, June 23, 1962, it was "ambiguous because it s[ought] to attract and at the same time limit such investments" (Fall 1963: 301). In addition, there seemed to be a practice of government competition for ownership of industries that were likely to be attractive to foreign and domestic capital. In order to cope with the population increase of 3 percent per year, South

Vietnam would have needed at least 150 times the level of private investment available in the early 1960s to create some half-million jobs annually in its urban areas, but the official regime was too inept to recognize what should have been done to win the economic battle.

The economic picture in the countryside was even more depressing than the situation in the cities. Since 1957, the Saigon government had not been very successful in its agrarian reform effort to win the peasants and tenant farmers to its side, partly because the program was extremely timid, even on paper, and partly because whenever it was promoted, official corruption and rebel disruption often turned it into a symbolic act rather than reality. In the typical province of Long An, it was estimated that "less than 3 percent of . . . tenant families profited from the program in time for it to benefit the government" (Race 1973: 60). Even for this small group of farmers, there was no guarantee that "the benefits which had been conceded to them during the war would [not] be called in question by the landlords" when the central government became weak and the corrupted local authority—which often sided with the rich landowners—became more prevalent (Gettleman 1965: 223–224). The most important concerns of the South Vietnamese peasants were food and security, and while both the government and the insurgents squeezed surplus crops from them, neither side was able to offer complete security both day and night for the villagers. For this reason, the bulk of the rural population chose to flee to the cities to seek security and employment, which created further havoc in the already difficult urban economic situation.

There was an appearance of economic prosperity in the South as long as there were sources of foreign exchange and demands for services from the foreign sector, mainly American. Naturally, supplies of both consumer goods and war materials were readily available from the United States, France, Japan, and other countries in Asia that benefited from the Vietnam war, such as Korea, Taiwan, and Thailand, so the import-export ratio was almost ten to one between 1955 and 1973. Attached to this commercial network was a system of thirty-one privately owned banks with over 150 branches around the country to provide loans for "development of import investments" to facilitate the distribution of foreign goods (Dao Van Tap 1980: 266).

This economic situation turned the cities into magnetic poles attracting large numbers of villagers from the countryside, where the military tactics of "search and destroy" and "free-fire zones" carried out by the allied forces of South Vietnam and the United States often produced serious agricultural labor shortages as well as vast areas of uncultivated land. Urban regions that were already crowded to the limit had to absorb unskilled workers who could neither claim any share in the artificial prosperity nor be integrated into the new social-cultural ambiance of the metropolis. This predicament of the rural people, when reinforced by the age-old resentment against the ruling elite and the insensitivity of the city dwellers, created a time bomb for the insurgents to exploit. In sum, the economy as a whole depended on "intravenous feeding" with imports. The effects, despite the appearance of prosperity, were the abandonment of the countryside and a corrupt, parasitic, and overcrowded urban sector.

THE HISTORICAL EMPHASIS OF
REVOLUTIONARY DOCTRINE

The Vietnamese, with their claimed *bon ngan nam van-hien* ("four thousand years of civilized culture"), have traditionally displayed their spirit of independence by resisting foreign invaders, mainly the Chinese, and bringing down corrupted or illegitimate rulers. The Marxist leaders of the August revolution, led by Ho Chi Minh, dwelling on this tradition to rally the support of the Vietnamese people while using Communist tactics, not only spearheaded a radical revolution but also successfully conducted a thirty-year national resistance struggle against both France and the United States. Although the success of the August revolution may be owing "in great part to the correct leadership of the Indochinese Communist Party" (Truong Chinh 1963: 28), the leaders' ability to mobilize the support of the masses could be attributed to the fact that Ho Chi Minh understood the Vietnamese peasants and knew how "to link the villagers to a new sense of Vietnam as a nation by making their traditions relevant to participation in the modern politics of revolution" (McAlister and Mus 1970: 24).

Since over 80 percent of the Vietnamese population, the majority of them "peasants,"[4] lived in the countryside, any revolutionary movement that expected popular support had to align its political concepts with the traditional values of the Vietnamese peasants. The French had failed to realize this fact, but Ho Chi Minh and the Communist leadership of the August revolution, and eventually of the southern revolutionary phase, understood Vietnam's society well and adapted its traditional characteristics to their revolutionary advantage (McAlister and Mus 1970: 112–113). Thus, in order to understand fully the impact and the nature of these movements one should really consider their indigenous traditional perspectives. In this section we will see, first, that a traditional spirit did exist in the Vietnamese revolutions and, second, that it was one of the driving forces that eventually resulted in the final success of the revolutions. In this sense, I suggest that Vietnamese revolutionary traditions of the historical past could be found in various aspects of the contemporary revolutions and that this heritage was frequently emphasized by Hanoi to increase its legitimacy and to discredit the Saigon regime. For North Vietnam and the revolutionary side, the fact was simple: History was on their side.

Before 1945, the term *cach-mang* ("revolution") was seldom used by Vietnamese revolutionaries as it was used by the French Sûreté agents who hunted them down. *Cach-mang* essentially is made up of two separate words: *cach* means "change," and *mang* means "fate." Literally, the term *cach-mang* reflects some cosmological connotation that may have been associated with the Confucian concept of "mandate of heaven," but this concept was certainly not shared by the Vietnamese Communist writers who advocated that "revolution" is "a movement that destroys the old and changes to the new, destroys the bad and changes to the good." [5] This definition is quoted directly from *Van-kien dang* [Party documents], which also divides "revolution" into two different types: ideological revolution and people's revolution.

Ideological revolution, according to this official work, is exemplified by Galileo's scientific revolution (1633), Stevens's mechanical revolution (1800), Darwin's evolutionary revolution (1859), and Karl Marx's economic revolution. People's revolution is classified into three different categories: capitalistic, nationalistic, and class. The French Revolution in 1789, the American Revolution in 1776, and the Japanese Meiji restoration in 1868 were all "capitalistic revolutions." "Nationalistic revolutions" include the Italian revolt against Austria in 1859 and the Chinese overthrowing of the Manchu Dynasty in 1911. The only movement considered as a "class revolution" is the Russian Revolution of 1917 (VBSBTHTU 1978: 11–12).

Thus, from a Vietnamese viewpoint, "revolution" could be analyzed from the Confucian perspective or the Communist writers' Marxist-Leninist approach, and the August 1945 revolution and its southern phase appear to satisfy both requirements. On the one hand, they seem to fall closely within the historical concept of the pre-Communist perception of revolution, and on the other, they encompass a combination of nationalistic and class revolutions. The August revolution, as such, indeed "ended eighty years of colonial domination, abolished the monarch and restored Vietnam's national independence" (Nguyen Khac Vien 1974: 103). It induced "the people to rise up and seize power" and aroused the people to be "united as one" to foster "the irresistible growth of the revolutionary movement of the entire nation" (Truong Chinh 1963: 14–15) and, finally, to establish a legitimate government and a new political order known as the Democratic Republic of Vietnam.

Although the essence of "legitimacy" was adroitly sought by the leaders of the August revolution, using a number of political manipulations (McAlister 1971: 174–178), it is questionable whether the concept of "mandate of heaven," symbolized by the existence of the royal throne occupied by Emperor Bao Dai in Hue, was ever discussed. Ironically, nature also lent a hand, in a rather drastic manner, to the revolution as described by Truong Chinh:

> The insurrection of March 9, 1945 broke out when the famine was causing frightful ravages among the population. Hundreds of thousands of people starved beside granaries full of rice kept by the Japanese and French. At that moment, a task of the greatest importance for the communist and Viet Minh cadres was to lead the armed masses to seize Japanese rice stores and French concessions full of stocks of agricultural produce. This had the result of inspiring organized and unorganized masses to take an active part in the movement against the Japanese, so that the more actively they struggled, the more they became conscious of their own strength and saw more clearly the real face of the enemy.
>
> It was precisely thanks to these attacks on granaries and colonialist plantations that the national salvation movement could be developed intensely, the people rapidly armed, the self-defense brigade quickly founded. (Truong Chinh 1963: 26)

The modern Vietnamese concept of a revolution involves two basic and important ingredients: independence and freedom. These two factors have served throughout Vietnamese history, up to the present day, as motives for revolutionary action. The ancient revolutionary slogan was effectively repeated by contemporary leaders such as Ho Chi Minh and his followers to rally the people to their revolutionary cause. An example can be found in Ho's "Appeal for General Insurrection," which called upon the Vietnamese people to rise up and regain their independence and freedom (Fall 1967: 141–142). The oft-quoted, Vietnamized Chinese proverb *Quoc-gia huu su, that-phu huu trach* ("When the nation is in trouble, even a social outcast should recognize his responsibility") stresses the solidarity of citizens from all social strata, from both "great" and "little" traditions, for the good of the country. In the same vein, and to be consistent with Marxist ideology while accommodating this nationalistic concept, Communist writers attempt to bridge the gap between nationalistic and class revolutions by relating the themes of independence and freedom to colonial and imperialistic exploitation of peasants and workers. Thus:

> In summary, this oppressing authority forces the other people to serve as slaves, such as the case between France and Vietnam, until the enslaved people could not endure any more. They awoke and united themselves, realizing that it would be better to die in freedom than to live in slavery. They concentrated their will and amassed their forces to get rid of their oppressors; and this is nationalistic revolution. . . .
>
> Our country had this experience as other countries had the same experience, the workers and the peasants could no longer tolerate [the situation] and united themselves to drive out the imperialists such as in the Soviet Union; this is class revolution. (VBSBTHTU 1978: 14–15)

That kind of sentiment is indeed interesting since it is questionable logically but acceptable historically. In the old days, traditional Vietnamese society was divided into four different social groups: *si, nong, cong, thuong* (namely, literati, farmers, artisans, merchants),[6] and the divisions were based on the professions—according to social esteem—rather than on social stratification in terms of privileges or wealth (Le Thanh Khoi 1955: 355–357). From this viewpoint, it is not difficult to visualize a conceptual transition from a nationalist revolution to a class revolution led by peasants and workers, since this "class" of people was more exploited than the others (VBSBTHTU 1978: 16–17). The other classes were also exploited by the French and Chinese "capitalists," but since they did not suffer as much as the working class, their interest in the class revolution was not that vital and accordingly, they could associate with but could not lead the revolutionary movement.

Accounts in the history of Vietnam of ceaseless struggles against foreign invaders and domestic oppressors, and consequently of the preservation of national identity and continuity during these times of crisis, seem to link the past with the present, and indeed, although circumstances may have changed, the same revolutionary spirit and goals are still well preserved. The recent conflicts with France and the United States somehow reflect the ancient wars with China, as noted by a contemporary German writer: "Behind the great Chinese armies, the fleet of junks, stand the French colonial troops, the American invasion host and Seventh Fleet. When the historians trace back the history of Vietnam they clarify the present situation for us. When they speak of historical victories they imply their present confidence in victory" (Weiss 1970: 31). That passage echoes a well-known proverb, *On co nhu tri tan* ("Reviewing the old is like knowing the new"), that older generations of Vietnamese teach the younger ones. Similarly, some historical Vietnamese revolutions may offer case illustrations for the analysis of traditional aspects of modern resistance movements. One example of the latter was the Tet offensive of 1968 (Karnow 1984: 523–566), in which the Communist forces launched a fierce attack against U.S. and South Vietnamese targets throughout the country. One cannot resist comparing this campaign with the one against the Chinese invasion by the legendary hero Nguyen Hue during the Tet celebration of 1789. In fact, one U.S. scholar has named that historical event the "First Tet Offensive, defeat of Chinese invasion" (Whitmore 1980: 13).

COMMUNISM AND THE SOUTHERN REVOLUTIONARY STRUGGLE

Understanding of Communism

As often expressed officially, one of the main concerns of U.S. policymakers was the political snowball effect in the Southeast Asia region should South Vietnam fall into the hands of Communist North Vietnam. The so-called domino theory, frequently repeated by successive U.S. administrations, squarely placed the Vietnamese conflict in the context of great-power confrontations while downgrading indigenous political competition. This unfortunate interpretation created a chain of faux pas in U.S. decisions regarding intervention in Vietnam following the French departure.

The Communist-led victory in South Vietnam in 1975 was indeed impressive, but whether this Vietnamese achievement could be considered as a Communist revolutionary model for insurgency elsewhere, as the domino theorists feared, is still a question for further consideration. The doctrinal intention of communism (*chu-nghia cong-san* in Vietnamese) was—and still is—not well understood among the population. In the old days, under French colonialism, Communists were depicted by French administrators and their Vietnamese mandarinic collaborators as political and social outcasts who were to be hunted down and condemned to the guillotine. Reference to *cong-san* was thus reserved to officialdom for internal security purposes, or speculated upon among the population, especially in the countryside, with both fearful and perhaps folksy admiration. In 1945, during the August revolution, even the Communist-led Vietminh did not openly advocate Communist doctrine, mainly because of the need for alliance with other nationalist forces but partly because of the level of political consciousness of the popular masses.

In fact, Pham Van Dong, prime minister of the DRV during the war years and eventually of the SRV from July 1976 until his retirement, in a collective volume published in Moscow, emphasized that in 1945, although "Communism was the glorious future of mankind . . . , in Vietnam at that time only the insane would have advocated the immediate application of Communism, which was contradictory to the contemporary economic and social conditions of Viet Nam, [and] also contrary to the wishes of the whole Vietnamese population" (Pham Van Dong 1990: 123).

For the Vietnamese villager and ordinary city dweller, "communism" had different connotations. The peasant would perceive communism in terms of the village communal spirit, which had been long practiced by Vietnamese rural society. For example, the enduring institution of "communal land" (*cong dien*) in Vietnamese villages, according to a noted Vietnamese historian, was "probably a survival from an early form of Communism" (Hoang Van Chi 1964: 202).[7] On the other hand, for the city merchant who was more conditioned by the market mentality, Communism perhaps reflected the sharing of surplus with the economically disadvantaged and thus contradicted his profit motives. The level of consciousness regarding the doctrinal implication of Communism could be well illustrated by the remark of the mother of a *can-bo nam vung*, a Communist cadre, who lived clandestinely in the city and who returned to visit his family following the 1975 victory. "Thanks to heaven that the *cach-mang* ['the revolutionaries'] are victors, since if it were the *Viet-cong* [Vietnamese Communists], we would have all been killed." This anecdote illustrates the limited understanding of the general population about both current political concepts and realities.

I do not mean to imply that communism had no significant impact on the revolutionary process or the outcome of the postcolonial southern phase. Although the doctrine of communism had not penetrated deeply into popular consciousness, both Communist personnel and Communist organizations played a key role in the day-to-day revolutionary operations. Yet, even at this operational—rather than doctrinal—level, the seminal source of Vietnamese communism was perhaps neither original Marxist thought, nor classical commmunist ideas, but Lenin's suggestion of a two-stage revolutionary process. Lenin's strategy involved an initial Communist-nationalist alliance in a "bourgeois democratic revolution" followed by a second stage of "socialist revolution."[8]

During the southern revolutionary phase, accordingly, North Vietnam had already completed the first stage and was on the road to socialism, whereas South Vietnam was still going through the first stage of a "national democratic revolution" with all the characteristics of a "national liberation movement." In fact, Ho Chi Minh, in an article written for the *World Marxist Review* (November 2, 1960), summed up the revolutionary guidelines of the Vietnamese Communist party since its inception:

> Educated in the spirit of Marxism-Leninism, the Communist Party pursued a correct revolutionary policy. As early as 1930 it enunciated the tasks of the bourgeois-democratic revolution: *the struggle against the imperialists and feudal lords*, the winning of national independence and the transfer of land to the peasants. This programme was fully in keeping with the aspirations of the peasants, who comprised the majority of the people. (Original emphasis; Woddis 1970: 144)

In the minds of the North Vietnamese leaders, therefore, Vietnam had a two-front revolution, one in the North and the other in the South. As such, "two tasks confront[ed] the Vietnamese revolution: first the construction of socialism in North Vietnam, and second, the completion of the national-democratic revolution in the South" (Woddis 1970: 149).

Southern Phase of the Revolution

The southern phase was thus similar to the August revolution of 1945, in which the Communists realized the necessity of seeking alliance with non-Communist groups opposing the French government. As a result, the same revolutionary strategy of Communist-nationalist coalitions was again employed, first under the facade of the Mat-Tran Dan-Toc Giai-Phong Mien Nam (South Vietnam National Liberation Front, NLF)—an echo of the Vietminh front in 1945—and then the Chinh-phu Cach-mang Lam-thoi Mien Nam (Provisional Revolutionary Government of the Republic of South Vietnam PRG), elected by "the South Vietnamese People's Representatives held in the liberated zone in June 6–8, 1969" (Giai-Phong Editions 1969: 5). Essentially, all policy decisions were made by the Communist leadership in the North and carried out by the southern revolutionary apparatus controlled by key Communist cadres, but the presence of a bonafide southern Communist structure seemed desirable and necessary for both propaganda and practical purposes.

Following the Geneva Accords of 1954, the Communist leadership sought adherence to the terms of the settlement that North and South Vietnam would be unified by general elections within two years. This expectation evaporated with the fierce anti-Communist campaign known as Chien-Dich To Cong (Communist denunciation campaign) of the South Vietnam government under Ngo Dinh Diem, which paralyzed the revolutionary infrastructure left behind when Communist forces withdrew to the North. Ignoring Hanoi's demand for consultations between the two zones, Diem in the summer of 1955 publicly refused to deal with the North.

Despite this adverse action on the part of the southern regime, the Communists were not in a position to advocate revolutionary armed struggle, since the DRV had to be concerned with a host of postwar problems resulting from the First Indochina War against the French, if its socialist goal for the North was to be realized. In addition, the southern Communist apparatus was not strong enough to withstand the newly organized repressive machinery of the Diem regime, which was now strengthened by U.S. economic and military aid. Furthermore, had Ho Chi Minh decided to resume revolutionary violence in the South, it is doubtful whether he could have obtained the necessary assistance from the Kremlin as its leader at the time, Nikita Khrushchev, was charting his own course of peaceful coexistence with the capitalist West and would understandably have had reservations about such a venture.

Thus, the southern phase of the Vietnamese revolution did not take shape overnight. After almost a decade of war with France, the Vietnamese Communist party faced the strenuous task of rebuilding the northern part of the country before there could be any hope of advancing it toward socialism. Consequently, the official Party line was to support the implementation of the Geneva Accords and to wait for peaceful reunification elections. Hanoi did not begin to embark on an active path in South Vietnam until 1956, when it could no longer tolerate the destruction of its southern infrastructure by the Diem government and permitted its followers to take limited measures for self-defense purposes in order to preserve its ability to fight should events dictate. Still, despite appeals from some southern leaders for a renewal of armed insurgency, the Communist party maintained its course of "limited challenge and response," and it was not until May 1959, according to the U.S. State Department's 1968 *Working Paper*, Appendix Item No. 72, that the first groups of party members who had moved North in 1954 were allowed to infiltrate back into South Vietnam to assume leading positions in the preparations for the new struggle.

The level of violent conflict in the South began to intensify during 1959 with several armed raids on South Vietnamese military outposts and mass demonstrations against the Saigon regime, but large-scale uprisings did not occur until the beginning of 1960. In September of that year, during the Third National Congress of the Vietnamese Workers' (Communist) party, the new secretary-general Le Duan, a southerner, commented that the struggle would be "arduous" and combine "many forms," but he made no reference to any direct support on the part of the Democratic Republic of Vietnam (DRV) for the insurgency. Regardless, at this stage the party's southern strategy had been cast, and North Vietnam had decided to expand its national objectives of both building socialism in the North and supporting armed revolution in the South.

During this period, there was a significant development in the socialist camp, which proved to be quite favorable to the policy of the DRV in South Vietnam. As the widening conflict between China and Russia became evident, Moscow became more vocal in its support for Third World revolutions during the Conference of Communist and Workers' Parties held in November 1960. The party leadership decided that it was time to intensify both armed and political struggle and ordered the expansion of activities of revolutionary forces "so that armed violence could play a role equal in size and importance to that of political struggle." Interestingly, Hanoi, in shifting to a more militant policy, also predicted that "the United States might decide to send troops to stem the rising tide of revolution in South Vietnam" (Duiker 1981: 195).

North Vietnam's dilemma as to its southern policy during the reign of Ngo Dinh Diem was quite extensive. From the theoretical perspective, the Communist leadership had always maintained the theme of national unification since, as Ho firmly pointed out, "Vietnam is one, the Vietnamese people are one. As sons and daughters of the same fatherland, our people in the North are bound to extend wholehearted support to the patriotic struggle waged by the people of the South against U.S. aggression."[9] Despite this determination, the question remained whether national unification could be achieved without armed struggle.

Perhaps sensing the urgency of the situation, and in the face of mounting repressive pressure from the Diem government, which meant that procrastination in the South would be detrimental to the southern revolutionary cause, Hanoi was forced to make a decision about its southern strategy. At first, the northern leadership approved organizational improvement of its southern revolutionary organization, while cautioning it against direct confrontation with the government forces (Thayer 1975: 36). It was not until early 1959 that the Vietnamese Communists decided to resume guerrilla warfare against the South, reportedly following visits to Moscow by party leaders in 1956 and 1957, perhaps in an effort to convince Russia that only armed conflict could resolve the current stagnant revolutionary situation in South Vietnam (Turley 1980: 58). There were reports of infiltration by North Vietnamese regular army units of battalion and regiment strength in mid-1961, but as late as May 1964, Ho Chi Minh (1967: 55) still denounced "the U. S. government and its agents" for "slanderous allegations about 'intervention' or 'aggression' by the North in South Vietnam."[10]

The main question that seems to have troubled the Vietnamese Communist leaders involved the degree of armed involvement. They had to decide whether military resources would be used as the revolutionary backbone or just strategically employed as necessary complementary support for political antagonism. Another issue was whether the DRV was ready to bear the burden of a major military venture in the South while pursuing socialist goals in the North.

Events in the late 1950s and early 1960s finally forced the northern leadership into committing the DRV to full-scale armed insurgency in the South, since the entire party organization there was in danger of being wiped out as the Chien-Dich To Cong under Ngo Dinh Diem ferociously intensified. In early 1959, the Fifteenth Plenum of the Central Committee adopted a new policy toward the southern revolution, and this policy was later reaffirmed at the Third Party Congress in September 1960 along with approval for the formation of the National Liberation Front (NLF). The first major armed confrontation took place in late February 1960 when the revolutionary forces, with the assistance of units from religious sects, successfully attacked a regimental headquarters of the South Vietnamese Army located near the Cambodian border in Tay Ninh Province (Ta Xuan Linh 1974: 22–24).

Ironically, the harsh repressive measures of the Diem regime contributed significantly to the revolutionary impetus. During the To Cong campaign, scores of non-Communists were also arrested, persecuted, and some even executed.[11] The hunt for underground Communist cadres and their collaborators took place in the cities as well as in the rural areas, but it was in the countryside that the large-scale persecution and torture of innocent peasants stirred up extensive popular indignation and distrust of the Saigon regime. In addition, the gradually increasing reliance of the southern government on U.S. aid also undercut Diem's credibility as an independent nationalist leader, who back in 1956 had adamantly refused to permit French military bases in Vietnam lest the Vietnamese "concept of full independence" be compromised. Apparently realities and new developments had changed his view on this principle (Fall 1963: 319).

The political vulnerability of the southern government thus presented an opportunity to the revolutionary forces. The view from Hanoi was that as long as U.S. armed forces were not involved, there was reasonable expectation that by a momentous concentrated uprising (Dong Khoi), participated in by peasants in various localities in the Mekong delta such as those of the famed Ben Tre Province, the Saigon government would be caught completely off guard and brought down. In fact, in September 1960, a decision was made by the policymakers of the southern revolution to launch a general uprising throughout the provinces in chosen areas. Nevertheless, as in the case of the August 1945 revolution, external intervention doused any hope for a political victory. With the drastic increase in U.S. aid to the South by the Kennedy administration in 1961, Hanoi was forced to shift its strategic focus to armed violence, with political struggle now becoming a supplementary means to weaken and topple the regime of Ngo Dinh Diem. Even after the murder of Diem in 1963 by his own generals, the new junta, with continued U.S. blessing and affirmation of support for fighting the Communist aggression, just presented Hanoi with the same problem in a different form. In the face of this situation, Hanoi was prepared for a new military escalation in which the armed forces now played the key role in the revolution, but the political force of the masses was also to be intensified to set the stage for the final combined military offensive and political uprising.

On the U.S. side, by late 1962 the United States had spent some $2 billion in helping South Vietnam contain Communist North Vietnam, yet "substantially the same difficulties remain if, indeed, they have not been compounded" (Karnow 1984: 268). Although John F. Kennedy publicly rebutted Senator Mike Mansfield's gloomy report of the situation in Vietnam following a survey trip at the president's request, Kennedy, in private, actually found himself in agreement with the Senate majority leader's assessment. A policy of military escalation was thus in the making if there was to be any hope of saving South Vietnam from communism. The United States, which had played the role of "Pontius Pilate, who washed his hands to keep his conscience clear," regarding the Geneva Agreements in 1954, now had to decide whether it should be directly involved in rebuilding "a truncate land into a viable non-Communist Vietnamese state" by convincing itself in 1962 "that its military commitment in behalf of the Saigon regime was in response to North Vietnamese 'renewal of the aggression in violation of the aforesaid agreements' " (Fall 1972: 145–146).

Despite their successes against the Saigon regime in 1961–1963, the Communists had to cope with new massive U.S. intervention symbolized by the arrival of the first U.S. combat troops in Vietnam on March 8, 1961. From the onset, the North Vietnamese leadership realized that although a total victory against the overwhelmingly superior U.S. forces was not feasible, a continuing high-level combination of military and political struggle by the revolutionary side could perhaps wear down U.S. determination and ultimately compel that country—in the face of mounting antiwar sentiment—into a diplomatic compromise.

The presence of U.S. troops on Vietnamese soil helped the Communists score a significant propaganda victory concerning charges of U.S. "neocolonialism." Although Washington made every effort to formally uphold the integrity, and therefore the legitimacy, of the Saigon regime, reality dictated otherwise. On the one hand, with the prestige of the United States and his own reputation at stake, Lyndon Johnson decided to "Americanize," or to take over, the prosecution of the Vietnam war, which then became a U.S. war. On the other hand, many Vietnamese officials, from top to bottom, keenly aware that their future and even survival depended on the U.S. presence, quickly revived their colonial mentality of the French time, catered to the new U.S. direction, and thus forfeited their claim of Vietnamese nationalist legitimacy. I do not mean to imply that there were no dedicated nationalists among the rank and file of the ruling elites, but their alternatives were either joining their colleagues on the insurgent side or being indifferent to the whole situation and just hoping for the best. For the Communist-led revolution, the main target was no longer the "Saigon puppets" but the "U.S. imperialist aggressors," and the ongoing conflict became "Vietnam's resistance to American aggression for national salvation" (Ho Chi Minh 1967: 87).

Between 1965 and the now famous Tet offensive of 1968, Hanoi lacked the firepower of the U.S. forces, but it did create problems, military and morale, for the U.S. side. On the political front, the influx of refugees to major urban centers, such as the capital of Saigon and the strategic coastal city of Da Nang in central Vietnam, also presented the South Vietnam regime with a time bomb for potential trouble that could destabilize the already weakened government.

The Tet offensive did not achieve the military goals or create the civilian uprisings that North Vietnam had hoped for. It did nevertheless provide the southern revolution with a significant psychological success because of its immense impact on U.S. public opinion, although a Communist general who was a key figure in the Tet campaign later declared to Stanley Karnow that "as for making an impact on the United States, it had not been our intention—but it turned out to be a fortunate result" (Karnow 1984: 545). Obviously the reference was to the ongoing U.S. presidential election campaign. The military cost of the Tet offensive to the revolutionary side turned out to be enormous, and perhaps the Hanoi strategists were forced to scale down the offensive so that it just managed to preserve its revolutionary momentum and propaganda effectiveness, at least until the Easter offensive of 1972 some four years later. Again, the key purposes of that offensive were obviously both the military objective of territorial gain, to be used as leverage at the ongoing Paris peace talks, and the political impact on the 1972 U.S. presidential election.

The Paris agreements, which called for the complete withdrawal of U.S. troops, satisfied one of the main objectives of the southern phase of the Vietnamese revolution. The other revolutionary goal—the unification and territorial integrity of Vietnam—could now be dealt with either through military confrontation with the Saigon forces, which were now "Vietnamized," i.e., without U.S. combat support, or by political and nonviolent means as specified by the Paris accords. Either way, a complete Communist takeover seemed imminent. Communist leaders nevertheless were pragmatic in their perception of a political settlement with all of its inherent problems. Perhaps for this reason, and being confident that they now had "military and political conditions so perfect or a strategic advantage so great . . . [to] complete the national democratic revolution in the South," the Political Bureau of the Vietnamese Workers' (Communist) party decided in January, 1975 to "mobilize the greatest efforts . . . to step up the military and political struggle, in coordination with diplomatic struggle to change the balance of forces on the southern field of battle quickly . . . so that conditions will be ripe to carry out a general offensive and uprising, . . . and liberate the South" (Van Tien Dung 1977: 24–25).

Role of Communist Doctrine

Hanoi's assessments were surpassed by the unexpectedly speedy military successes at the beginning of the 1975 spring offensive in north central Vietnam (Hue, Da Nang) as well as in the highlands (Tay Nguyen). The Communist leaders now were confident that total victory was within their reach and decided on March 31, 1975, that "the time is ripe for carrying [out] the general offensive and general uprising to the enemy's lair . . . at the earliest possible time—best of all in April [1975]" (Van Tien Dung 1977: 132–133). Saigon, the capital of the Republic of Vietnam, fell to the revolutionary forces on April 30, 1975.

Perhaps the main question to be asked now is, How important a role did Communist doctrine play in the Vietnamese revolution of postcolonial consolidation? In discussing the characteristics of Vietnamese revolutionary doctrine, William Duiker suggests three major sources for Communist strategy in the Vietnamese revolution, namely, Leninist, Maoist, and indigenous Vietnamese practices. In Duiker's view, "There is little in the Vietnamese revolutionary arsenal that cannot be traced, in one form or another, to Bolshevik or Chinese experiences," but an "extreme doctrinal flexibility" was also exhibited by the Vietnamese Communist strategists in their "creative applications" of core elements of Leninist or Maoist doctrine to a local Vietnamese setting. Duiker nevertheless disputes the claim by the noted Communist military commander, General Vo Nguyen Giap, that "Vietnamese revolutionary strategy is a linear descendent of the people's wars fought against Chinese invaders in the past." Although conceding, that "the similarities are obvious," Duiker argues that "the contention that the Communists deliberately imitated traditional military strategy is not very persuasive" (in Turley 1980: 66).

Indeed, one of the distinctive hallmarks of the Vietnamese Communist party—or to be more precise, of its founder and leader, Ho Chi Minh—was the remarkable ability to adapt foreign ideology and practice to Vietnamese conditions. However, even though Ho and the Vietnamese Communists faithfully adhered to the principles of Marxism-Leninism—and perhaps even Maoism—during their revolutionary struggle, in their role as native stewards of a national revolution, they had to find a way to connect new revolutionary ideology and practice with old history and culture. Unlike Mao in China, Ho and his followers seemed to realize that the revolutionary process in Vietnam had to be gradually emphasized rather than radically exerted. Thus, any application of Marxism-Leninism to the task of social and cultural transformation must be consistent with the Vietnamese spirit of continuity rather than disruption; in other words, the Communist present must be linked to the Vietnamese past in a continuous connection.

The issue here is, not whether Vietnamese revolutionary doctrines originated from Leninism and/or Maoism, but how those doctrines were applied in the indigenous setting of Vietnam. In this vein, it is quite understandable that the Vietnamese, perhaps out of patriotic zeal, identified their revolutionary strategy, especially the military component, more with the glory of their historical past than with either Leninist or Maoist doctrine. As Georges Boudarel suggests, "the attempt to find solutions to similar problems led to similar conclusions," especially when the strategy was derived "from a common store of socio-political institutions" (in Turley 1980: 150). Should this be the case, we may even further borrow Boudarel's words in concluding that in both revolutionary line and practice, for Vietnam "Marxism merely provide[d] a new language to express old but still dynamic cultural orientations and propensities" (Turley 1980: 166).

REVOLUTIONARY OUTCOMES

With the final triumphal march into Saigon (now Ho Chi Minh City) by North Vietnamese regular units and revolutionary forces technically under the jurisdiction of the Provisional Revolutionary Government (PRG) of the Republic of South Vietnam, the Communist leaders in Hanoi immediately faced the enormous tasks of postrevolutionary planning and state reconstruction. The first order of business was how to wrestle with

the welters of jobs ahead. Were the electricity and water in Saigon still working? Saigon's army of nearly one million had disbanded on the spot. How should we deal with them? What would we do to help the hungry; and find ways for the millions of unemployed to make a living? Should we ask the center [Hanoi] to send in supplies right away to keep the factory in Saigon alive? How would we quickly build up a revolutionary administration at the grassroots level? What policies should we take toward the bourgeoisie? And how could we carry the South into Socialism along with the whole country? The conclusion of this struggle was the opening of another, no less complex and filled with hardship. (Van Tien Dung 1977: 247–248)

Political Consolidation

Since the whole administrative apparatus of the Saigon regime disintegrated as soon as the revolutionary flag was raised on the roof of the Presidential Palace, the vacuum had to be filled to restore civil order. Hanoi's leadership had not anticipated the lightning success of the last offensive drive and apparently had not prepared a takeover plan. When the Communist Political Bureau directed the southern military command in the final days of the war to "attack on Saigon according to plan" and to "dissolve the enemy administration at all levels" (Van Tien Dung 1977: 24), it did not realize that it would need more than elite fighting troops to administer the newly won people and land. The first critical problem to be faced was the shortage of cadres with administrative experience, as the Communist structures in the South had been drastically weakened by the U.S. sponsored Phoenix program as well as by the heavy losses suffered during the Tet offensive of 1968. Scores of thousands of southern Communist cadres had been either liquidated or sacrificed.

The first formal power structure to be established was a Military Management Committee headed by a well-known senior commander, General Tran Van Tra, who had served in 1973 as chairman of the military delegation of the PRG to the Joint Military Committee. It is interesting to note that Tra was a southerner, and his appointment as the head of the transitional postrevolutionary military administration in the South could perhaps have served the dual purpose of restoring civilian order while easing any popular tension in South Vietnam concerning political domination by the North. Yet in June, power was transferred to a civilian government controlled by the Political Bureau in Hanoi.

The northern leaders were fully aware of the challenges and responsibilities they faced in the South and understood well that they had to be flexible in order to dispel any impression of regional conflict, as the southern population had been traditionally sensitive to this issue. Overall, there was undoubtedly general popular relief that the long war had ended, but according to foreign accounts, most South Vietnamese were resigned to the fact that new changes lay ahead and just hoped for a better future. After all, southerners in 1975, as their northern counterparts in 1945 and 1954, were neither ideologically nor politically prepared for an advance to socialism in any near future. During the war, the party leaders had recognized this serious problem, and the revolutionary emphases—as reflected in the NLF program—had been on struggling against the "U.S. imperialists and their Saigon puppets" for national independence and social reforms instead of Communist or Marxist ideologies. In victory, the leaders discovered that the promotion of their socialist goals in the capitalist South, for eventual reunification with the North, required enormous efforts, as the national objectives were no longer armed revolutionary but political and social transformation. The challenge now was how to integrate South Vietnam into northern socialism while preventing southern capitalism from invading the North.

In general, the new regime faced little or insignificant resistance to its new order. Officials of the former government and officers from the Saigon armed forces were instructed to report to the new authorities to be classified in categories and then released or sent to re-education camps for political indoctrination. According to Duiker, "the total number of southerners requiring re-education was well over a million persons" (Duiker 1985: 9). To consolidate its power further, the new government took measures to reduce Western influence in the people's cultural life by banning certain types of music, limiting the availability of Western books, and changing textbooks and curricula in the national school system. Nationally, no political parties other than the Communist party were permitted to continue; existing political organizations that were sympathetic to the revolution were integrated into government-controlled mass organizations.

The Communist leadership was well aware that the population of the South was not ready for socialism and that any strong attempt to immediately impose it would result in political disaster. The southern people's support for the revolutionary cause had been widespread, but as pointed out earlier it was more motivated by a popular desire for reforms than by Communist ideology. With power securely in the hands of the party, the new regime saw no advantage in pushing too early for ideological implementation. Instead, a certain degree of political laissez-faire was allowed within the official "mass line" policies under the overall direction of the united front, the Mat-Tran To-Quoc (Fatherland front).

The task of consolidating revolutionary authority over the whole southern part of the country needed to be carried out as quickly but as smoothly as possible in order to avoid potential chaos. As there was a shortage of trained party cadres, the new regime relied heavily on people's revolution committees. In some locations, this revolutionary power structure had already been in place during the struggle, but in most areas, these political units had to be created at every level, composed mainly of party members and representatives of the local community sympathetic to the revolution. In places where party cadres were not readily available, units of the People's Army were assigned to assume this political responsibility. The first order of business was house visits by cadres or army units to register the local families, but the main purpose was to identify potential sources of opposition and members of the former regime for possible reeducation. Each household was assigned a *ho-khau*, or family registration card, and grouped with other households into *to*, or "family solidarity units," which were directly responsible to the local people's committee. From this local structure a formal administration emerged to prepare for local elections in July 1975 (Duiker 1985: 8–9).

Except for alleged harsh treatment of some officials of the former Saigon government and members of the South Vietnamese armed forces in reeducation camps, the new regime appeared to go out of its way to convey to the world its moderate image by avoiding radical measures such as mass terror and executions. The "Communist bloodbath" that had been widely predicted before the fall of Saigon did not take place, and it was reported that the revolutionary authorities ordered their cadres to refrain from gestures that might cause hostility in the local population, and even severely reprimanded those who zealously acted in a radical manner toward prostitutes and long-haired, Westernized young people. In any case, the party must have had enough confidence in the restored order that it replaced the Military Management Committee with the Provisional Revolutionary Government in June 1975.

At first it was decided that for the foreseeable future, South Vietnam would maintain its separate political status from the North, as previously declared by the National Liberation Front (NLF), but the Communist leadership reversed this early policy at the twenty-fourth plenary session of the Central Committee held in late summer at the mountain resort of Dalat and issued a resolution to move rapidly toward reunification of the country in order to "create a new strength and new advantages for developing the economy and culture and consolidating national defense" (Duiker 1985: 15). Elections for the National Assembly were held in early 1976 for the whole country, and in July the new Socialist Republic of Vietnam (SRV), with its capital in Hanoi, was proclaimed to the world. Vietnam, for the first time since the beginning of French colonialization over a century earlier, was united as a single nation from the Gate of Nam Quan on the Chinese border to the southern tip of the Camau peninsula.

The change of heart by the party leaders concerning the swift reunification of the country, contrary to their earlier announced plan, has puzzled many Vietnam specialists. Following the fall of Saigon, it had appeared that South Vietnam would be allowed to complete its "national democratic revolution"—a necessary transitional period—before uniting with the North. In fact, two individual membership applications had been presented to the United Nations as if the two zones were formally separate. Apparently this move was intended to assure the world community that Hanoi was in no hurry to impose socialism in the South, in the hope that this moderate policy would win tangible international support for the reconstruction of war-torn Vietnam. Although the official reason for accelerating the pace of national reunification as stated by Truong Chinh, one of the most senior party leaders at the twenty-fourth plenary session of the Central Committee, was for better implementation of central planning under a single administration, the true motive for this drastic decision can only be speculated upon.

Looking back to 1945, one may recall that a similar scenario took place then when Ho Chi Minh declared Vietnamese independence in an effort to present the French, the Allies, and the world with a fait accompli that Vietnam was an indivisible single nation from north to south. The rapid process of Vietnam's reunification in 1976 was perhaps designed for the same international effect, lest there be any foreign expectation of a long-term division of the country under two separate economic and political systems. Furthermore, there was evidence that the "corrupted" vestige of South Vietnamese capitalism and life-style had begun to influence the "advanced" socialist North, and unless there was a central administration under the firm control of the party, not only might progress toward socialism in the South have been delayed, but even more damaging, socialist gains in the North could possibly have regressed. It must have been apparent to the party leadership that the longer South Vietnam was politically and economically separated from North Vietnam, the harder it would be to eventually unite the country.

Economic Consolidation

In the economic arena, the revolutionary victory brought with it an immense challenge. The most difficult task for the new government was to reverse the deteriorating economic situation of the South. The southern economy had long been conditioned by U.S. military and economic aid, which had been drastically reduced during the last few years of the war. The situation was further complicated by other war factors, which had created food shortages, unemployment, and most significantly, yet more refugees who poured from the countryside into the cities to seek better livelihood and security. Encouraging the refugees to return to their native villages thus became a postrevolutionary economic priority. As a remedy to the long-term unemployment problem, a program was instituted by the government to relocate people to new economic zones (NEZs) in underpopulated areas, which were to become agricultural and light industrial centers. This farsighted economic plan unfortunately did not turn out as the regime had hoped, and urban dwellers and other refugees formerly from the countryside who had "volunteered" to move to the NEZs began to flock back secretly to the cities where life, although not filled with abundance, was at least not as difficult.

In order to revitalize the southern economy, the Communist leaders faced the enormous task of reviving the urban productive capacity without alienating, but still maintaining control over, the private sector. Several problems had to be resolved before the new government could claim to be in the economic driver's seat. Although there were no harsh measures against the commercial middle class—the national bourgeoisie—some former entrepreneurs were severely punished for their "crimes against the people." This action was allegedly orchestrated to "quieten" the overseas Chinese in South Vietnam, who reportedly "controlled half of all retail trade in the South and were dominant in the export-import sector" and who may have wished to resume the economic power they once enjoyed under the Saigon regime (Duiker 1985: 13).

As a measure to stabilize the monetary system and to exert more control over the business sector, a new currency was circulated in exchange for the old South Vietnamese paper money at a fixed rate determined by the government. A maximum permissible amount of exchange was established, with provisions for depositing extra sums in the Central Bank.[12]

One of the main tasks during this initial postrevolutionary period was to prepare for advancing the South toward socialism, but for the moment the new regime felt it was necessary to be flexible as far as the presence of both a "private capitalist sector" and individual ownership in the postwar economy was concerned. This policy was later affirmed during the Fourth Party Congress in 1976, perhaps because the party was confident that, one, since socialism was so strong in the North, the country could temporarily tolerate some capitalist elements in the South and, two, there was "no chance that capitalism [could] rear its head again in the present conditions of Vietnam" and "individual and family production [would] not necessarily lead to capitalism" (Nguyen Khac Vien 1980: 33).

A five-year plan launched in 1976 was supposed to guide the South on the road toward socialism as commerce and industry were gradually to be placed under the direct control of the state and farm collectivization was scheduled for the early 1980s. In order to halt further degeneration when the economic situation failed to respond to this plan, the party made a swift and decisive move in March 1978 to accelerate the socialization process in South Vietnam by officially banning all private trade and eliminating any nonproductive activities not collectively owned or jointly operated by the state. This policy effectively placed the southern urban economy under strict government control, but its spin-off social effect was also most dramatic as it resulted in the exodus of the "boat people," mostly ethnic Chinese, from both North and South Vietnam. The international impact of this event for the Socialist Republic of Vietnam was both overwhelming and understandably adverse.

International Relations

As to the international situation, the unified Socialist Republic of Vietnam (SRV) was now able to chart a new course in foreign relations. During the revolution, the single main issue had been the "struggle against U.S. imperialist aggression . . . for the independence and reunification of our country, for the security of the socialist camp, for the revolutionary cause and defense of peace of the world peoples" (Ho Chi Minh 1967: 127). From this ideological perspective, the Vietnamese Communists had perceived all support and assistance rendered from "fraternal socialist countries and progressive peoples of the world" during the war as part of their international obligation and had considered the Vietnamese revolution as an integral part of the world revolutions. As such, their victory was also "a worthy contribution to the common victory and the constant growth of the revolutionary forces in the world." This emphasis by Le Duan, general-secretary of the Vietnamese Communist party during a speech before the National Assembly in June 1976, could be seen as a justification for the SRV to adopt an independent course in foreign policy during the postwar period. In this sense, Vietnam's role in global affairs should not be perceived by the "fraternal socialist countries"— mainly Russia and China—as reciprocation in kind for their support and assistance during the Vietnamese revolutionary struggle, because in fighting and winning, the Vietnamese party had already contributed its fair share to the Communist cause and had "fulfilled" its international duty in the common struggle of the world's peoples toward socialist goals. As Ho Chi Minh had said earlier, "the Vietnamese people . . . [in] determin[ing] to fulfill their sacred task of liberating their fatherland, staying the hands of the U.S. imperialist aggressors, [had] firmly defend[ed] the outpost of the socialist camp in South-East Asia and [had] actively contribut[ed] to the movement for national independence and the safeguard of world peace" (Ho Chi Minh 1967: 88).

Having set the tone for its actions on the international scene, Hanoi proceeded with the construction of its own foreign policy to suit its new national needs. This independent spirit, at times resulting in inflexibility, has caused some considerable setbacks for the new regime in the world arena.

One of the most notable and troublesome events in Vietnam's postwar relationships with other countries was its uneasy encounter with its giant neighbor to the north, China. It is still not clear whether Hanoi's attitude toward its former ally and benefactor was merely a reaction to Chinese pressure for Vietnamese allegiance in the Sino-Soviet dispute or whether it was a calculated move to break the tie with a neighboring power that, despite being a Communist state, was a historical threat to Vietnam's independence. This Vietnamese "drift toward an assertive nationalism" is not uncommon for a country, like Vietnam, that has been dependent on foreign aid and support for revolutionary success.[13] Whatever the cause, the Sino-Vietnamese conflict erupted with the occupation of Cambodia (Kampuchea) by Vietnamese troops and the overthrow of the Chinese-sponsored regime of the Cambodian leader, Pol Pot, in 1978 (see Chapter 10). As a direct result, tension between Hanoi and Beijing intensified, and China invaded Vietnam in February 1979 to "teach a lesson" to the "Asian Cuba," "Moscow's junior partner," and the "minor hegemonist" in Hanoi. The Chinese withdrew a month later, declaring that they had achieved their "limited objective," but in Vietnam the bitterness against this fraternal socialist enemy was not soon forgotten.

In addition to its troublesome relations with China, Vietnam has also faced considerable international repercussions as a result of its Cambodian policy. Vietnam's occupation of Cambodia was condemned at the United Nations, and Hanoi has also suffered damaging economic sanctions from the world community. A number of Western aid projects were canceled, and more important, ongoing negotiations for resuming diplomatic ties with the United States were called off, eliminating any hope for potential U.S. help. Amid this mounting difficulty, Vietnam had no other choice but to become more dependent on the Soviet Union.

The Vietnamese realized that they could not rely on China for any postrevolutionary assistance in the reconstruction of their war-torn country, so seeking aid, and to further safeguard their hard-won independence, the Vietnamese entered into a Treaty of Friendship and Cooperation with the Soviet Union. This treaty, signed in November 1978 (before the Chinese invasion), guaranteed, among other provisions, assistance "in case either party is attacked or threatened with attack" for the purpose of "eliminating that threat . . . [by] appropriate and effective measures to safeguard [the] peace and the security of the two countries" (Duiker 1985: 120). This Hanoi-Moscow alliance, although not specifically directed at Beijing, had a warning effect and perhaps was the key factor in the Chinese decision not to enlarge and prolong the border war with Vietnam. It is also interesting to note that before the attack on Vietnam, the vice-premier of China, Deng Xiaoping, paid a well-publicized visit to the United States to put the final touches on the new Sino-American relationship forged only a few weeks earlier. Apparently, Beijing simultaneously decided to invade Vietnam and to resume diplomatic relations with the United States.

Vietnam obviously chose Russia over China out of national interest rather than ideological conviction. After all, Hanoi had seen, during international negotiations participated in by Moscow and Beijing, that Vietnamese interests were at times compromised by both of its two socialist neighbors to accommodate their own foreign policy objectives or their national purposes in dealing with the West (Truong Chinh 1963: 14). It should also be noted that in 1978 Hanoi, before signing the friendship treaty with Moscow, made serious overtures to Washington in an attempt to seek normalization of relations and apparently some principles were agreed to by both sides. Nevertheless, with the breakthrough in the Sino-American rapprochement waiting in the wings, the United States procrastinated, and the Vietnamese impatiently, and perhaps reluctantly, finalized their pact with the USSR.[14]

Before that sequence of events, Hanoi had high hopes of resuming diplomatic relations with the United States and receiving U.S. aid for postwar reconstruction. The U.S. trade embargo caused considerable economic difficulty for the country as it denied Vietnam spare parts for industrial tools and other supplies that the southern sector once enjoyed. In addition, none of the other Western nations were willing to substantially help Vietnam with its needs as long as the U.S. policy of isolating the SRV was in effect. In 1977 Washington, under the new Carter administration, showed signs of a willingness to establish a new rapport with Hanoi, but the Vietnamese leaders—still inspired by the Nixon promise of massive postwar assistance—clung to their demand for a simultaneous approach to both economic aid and diplomatic normalization. At that time, Hanoi felt that it had shown the United States enough goodwill by diverting some of its limited resources to locate American MIAs; in return, it expected U.S. reciprocation, at least in kind. After all, it insisted, since the brutal effect of the war was still fresh, it would be impossible for Vietnam to be friends with the United States without remedial gestures from Washington. This persistent Vietnamese view and the U.S. refusal to make early economic commitment apparently set both sides further apart. In the words of then–Vice Foreign Minister Phan Hien, who had carried out extensive negotiations with Assistant Secretary of State Richard Holbrook, "the United States again missed the boat and another opportunity [in Southeast Asia] completely."[15] Regardless, for the time being, the Washington-Beijing rapprochement took priority, and the issue of resuming diplomatic relations with Hanoi gradually receded into the background.

Closer to home, Vietnam's "special relationship" with the two other Indochinese states of Laos and Cambodia was apparently achieved with the signing of the 1979 Treaty of Friendship and Cooperation between Hanoi and the new Democratic Republic of Kampuchea, following the installation of the Vietnamese-sponsored government in Phnom Penh. Nevertheless, rapport with the five non-Communist members of the Association of Southeast Asian Nations (ASEAN) became uneasy when that group sponsored a UN resolution to demand the Vietnamese withdrawal from Cambodia and, echoing China, accused Vietnam of harboring an expansionist program in the region. Hanoi, in return, charged that ASEAN was but a facade for a military alliance sponsored by the "American imperialists" to impose their "neo-colonialist policy of opposing the patriotic and progressive movements in the region" (Duiker 1985: 105). Despite these outbursts of public distrust, both Vietnam and the ASEAN states have continued their dialogue, reflecting their mutual desire for better relations.

Update

During a month-long visit to both Ho Chi Minh City and Hanoi in September 1990, I observed an atmosphere of artificial economic prosperity on the cities' streets. Domestic foodstuffs and imported goods were abundantly displayed for people who could afford to buy, but underneath, the whole economic situation was still extremely fragile because of the lack of a viable infrastructure as well as of skilled management personnel. Black marketeers and illegal traders, through both the Cambodian and Chinese "opened" borders, coupled with low- and middle-level bureaucratic bribery, corruption, and ineptitude, also undermined any serious effort for postwar economic recovery. Although internal civil restrictions were still quite evident, the official mood of domestic relaxation was also observable. Scores of overseas Vietnamese, including refugees and boat people, some of whom had been high-ranking military officers in the former regime who had fled the country after the fall of Saigon in 1975, have returned for family visits or business ventures.

CONCLUSION

The southern phase of the Vietnamese revolution, like its immediate predecessor, the August 1945 revolution, was a complex event in the revolutionary history of the world. Since both revolutionary phases were led by a Communist party, their radical nature was often emphasized while their nationalistic importance was mostly ignored. This negligence, unfortunately, has frequently led to misconceptions about both revolutionary causes and outcomes.

There was only one original Marxist theory, but its application throughout the years in different parts of the world, with a variety of cultures and political histories, by different Communist groups has resulted in a dilution of Marx's theoretical intention into regional or even national distinctions. Even in Eastern Europe, where most postwar regimes were installed by the Red Army, the initial imposition of uniformity had to be, on occasion, reaffirmed by the use of Soviet troops when local deviations from the intended political and economic directions became too radical for the Russians.

In the case of Vietnam, there is ample evidence that the revolutionary organization and method were mostly those of a typical Communist revolution but the revolutionary goals, as pronounced by the party leadership, were laden with national history and purposes. In effect, one can clearly observe the intertwining of Vietnamese nationalism and Communist ideology. To the fighting revolutionary cadres, the North Vietnamese and the Viet-Cong, party discipline was rigorously implemented and followed, but what made them "formidable foes" of the U.S. and South Vietnamese side was their total conviction that the war was entirely "one of defense of their country against the invading Americans, who in turn, [were] seen merely as successors to the French" (Karnow 1984: 460). In this spirit, as one RAND Corporation expert who interrogated revolutionary prisoners concluded, "neither our military action nor our political or psychological warfare efforts seem[ed] to have made an appreciable dent in the overall motivation or morale" of the enemy (Karnow 1984: 460). This motivation and morale had been originally forged over half a century earlier by Ho Chi Minh, the Vietnamese revolutionary leader, "out of patriotism, not yet Communism" (Woddis 1970: 157).

From this perspective, and in reference to the oft-pronounced "national democratic revolution" as a description for the southern phase and its "national salvation" emphasis, it is not too difficult to place the Vietnamese struggle in the nationalistic context. As such, it is even easier to understand Hanoi's independent behavior during the conflict, relative to both Russia and China, from whom North Vietnam received most, if not all, of its aid to carry out its revolutionary operations in the South. As long as fraternal socialist assistance was rendered without attaching high prices that were harmful to Vietnamese national interests, the aid was welcome; any implications that disrupted the revolutionary goals of national independence, democracy, and socialism (explicitly in that order), or even "advice on how to wage the revolutionary war in the South" were "stubbornly rejected" (Duiker 1985: 94). Vietnamese nationalism during the revolutionary struggle took priority over ideology and socialist solidarity.

I do not deny that the Vietnamese southern revolution had a heavy Communist component. The movement, after all, was directed from Hanoi by veteran Marxist leaders, many of whom had engaged in Communist activities and struggle since 1930, but while subscribing to the tenets of Marxist thought, they did not display much concern about the compatibility between this new ideology and the historical past of their nation, of which they considered the present revolution a continuing part. They were socialists, but first and foremost they were Vietnamese. Therefore, they could afford, even under the hardest conditions and in the most difficult situations, to be optimistic about the future of their country. This spirit sustained their endurance in the face of enormous human sacrifices, for they were convinced that in their struggle, they were "living in the most glorious period of history"; they were "fighting and making sacrifices not only for their own freedom and independence, but also for the freedom and independence of other peoples, for world peace" (Ho Chi Minh 1967: 70). In this same vein, they viewed their continuing struggle, not so much in the light of contemporary class antagonism, but as the essence of revolutionary voluntarism, which embraced a perception of a special human sharing of a common past. Perhaps for this reason, the Vietnamese southern revolution, like its 1945 predecessor, contained less repressive violence during and after the revolutionary period; instead of radically eliminating old traditions and beliefs, these elements were integrated into the building of new social and political institutions. In the struggle for national salvation, the Vietnamese had often been romantically sentimental about the relevance of their people's myths, and it was on this ethnic sensitivity that they built their confidence in an optimistic future (Pham Huy Thong 1975: 67).

The southern phase of the Communist-led revolution in Vietnam, as its predecessor in August 1945, owed its success no less to the chronic weakness and ineptitude of the non-Communist nationalist movements. First, it is essential that one compare the political ability and dedication of the revolutionaries with those of the nationalist elites since colonial times. Before the emergence of Ho Chi Minh and his Communist party, the ineffectiveness of Vietnamese nationalism in challenging French domination was already a matter of historical record. The first "nationalist" regime of "independent" Vietnam was installed by the Japanese near the end of World War II. This regime eventually relegated its nationalist legitimacy to the Vietminh in 1945, with the abdication of Emperor Bao Dai and the transfer of the symbolic imperial sword and royal seal to the government of the new republic. The postwar governments in South Vietnam, up to April 1975, did not come to power as a result of nationalistic struggles against either the Communist government in the North or the returning colonialists but were actually ordained and sustained by foreign powers, first France and then the United States. Second, the initial failure of the non-Communist nationalist movements to attract the allegiance of the Vietnamese urban middle class—from which a whole generation of patriotic scholar-elites emerged—denied them not only a heritage of traditional leadership but also the cultural resource that was most significant in the Vietnamese revolution. Many alienated members of the urban scholar-elites under French colonialism, peculiarly attracted to Marxism as the alternative to the outdated Confucian doctrine, chose to follow Ho Chi Minh rather than his nationalist rivals in the struggle for national independence, and they provided the Communist party with credible early leadership, which proved to be a highly significant asset throughout the revolutionary struggle.

In any revolution, the role of leadership is vital. After the assassination of Ngo Dinh Diem, the leadership crisis in South Vietnam contributed substantially to the eventual downfall of the Saigon regime when the protective shield of the U.S. forces was removed. The Communist success owed no less to the leading role of Ho Chi Minh during the whole of the southern struggle. Ho, the man whom Khrushchev called a "holy apostle" of the revolution, in life as in death, was the sole symbol of the modern Vietnamese revolution. In casting him as a dedicated Communist and a notorious agent of Beijing and Moscow, the West unfortunately overlooked his indigenous impact and his towering moral and political influence in both North and South Vietnam. In looking for nonexistent alternatives for the leadership of South Vietnam to suit its own interests, the United States failed to recognize that successful national leaders derive their support from within, not without, and consequently neglected to compare the viability and quality of its political clients with their counterparts in the North. On this basis, perhaps Washington could have predicted the outcome of the Vietnamese revolution and dealt more carefully with the southern situation.

In summary, the Vietnamese model of revolution, especially the postcolonial consolidation phase, was somewhat different from other agrarian-based movements in the contemporary world, for the revolution had been organized from the beginning, even before the rise to power of the opposing regime in the South, with the remnant of cadres left behind by the North when the country was partitioned into two separate zones. Nevertheless, it exhibited all the temporal phases of state breakdown described by Goldstone for a revolutionary process, perhaps with the exception of authentic fiscal distress—that stage was not truly manifest until near the successful conclusion of the revolution. This chapter also emphasizes a political-cultural dimension that is not often stressed in theories of revolution. This cultural element, which obviously is peculiar to every individual society, nonetheless contributed significantly not only to revolutionary actions but also to revolutionary outcomes. In the case of Vietnam, had this cultural amplitude been seriously considered and understood by the United States, the southern insurgency might not have been totally avoided, but its magnitude, duration, and outcomes perhaps could have been quite different.

CHRONOLOGY

1945–1946: Cach-mang Thang Tam [the August revolution]. Bao Dai, last Vietnamese emperor abdicates. Birth of the Communist Democratic Republic of Vietnam (DRV). French troops return to Vietnam, opposed by the Vietminh. The First Indochina War (1946–1954) begins.

1949–1950: Beijing falls to the Chinese Communists who establish the People's Republic of China (PRC). Bao Dai returns to Saigon as head of the State of Vietnam. PRC and Soviet Union recognize the DRV; the United States recognizes the State of Vietnam under Bao Dai. France requests U.S. military and economic aid for the Indochina War.

1953–1954: PRC accelerates economic and military assistance to Vietnam. Vietminh forces launch full-scale attacks against French forces at Dien Bien Phu.

May 1954: Fall of Dien Bien Phu. Discussions on Indochina begin in Geneva.

July 1954: Ngo Dinh Diem becomes premier of South Vietnam under Bao Dai. Geneva Accords divide Vietnam into North and South at the seventeenth parallel pending reunification elections. Almost 1 million refugees flee from the North to the South. French forces leave Hanoi. United States gives aid directly to Vietnam.

October 1955: Ngo Dinh Diem deposes Bao Dai, proclaims the Republic of South Vietnam, and becomes president. Reunification elections fail to take place between North and South Vietnam. United States begins training South Vietnamese army.

1957–1961: Insurgent activities begin in South Vietnam. North Vietnam infiltrates cadres and weapons into the South. Formation of the National Liberation Front (NLF) of South Vietnam, dubbed by the Saigon regime as the Vietcong. President Kennedy approves counterinsurgency plan for South Vietnam.

March 8, 1961: First U.S. combat troops arrive in Vietnam.

1962: U.S. forces escalate to 11,300. Second Indochina War (1962–1975) begins.

1963: Diem and his brother Nhu are murdered in a coup led by his generals. A military junta is established, which marks the start of a series of coups, countercoups, and military regimes in the years to come.

1964: USS *Maddox* and USS *Turner Joy* report attacks by North Vietnamese gunboats. Congress approves the joint Gulf of Tonkin resolution.

1965: U.S. troops increase to 46,500. Nguyen Cao Ky becomes premier, and Nguyen Van Thieu acts as head of state of South Vietnam.

1966–1967: U.S. bombs North Vietnam. Massive antiwar demonstrations take place in New York and San Francisco. Lyndon Johnson announces ceiling on troop strength of

525,000. Thieu and Ky are inaugurated as president and vice-president of South Vietnam.

January 1968: Insurgent forces launch major attacks on South Vietnamese cities during the Tet Offensive.

May 1968: Washington accepts Hanoi's offer to meet in Paris for preliminary talks.

February 1969: Communist forces launch a general offensive in the South.

March 1969: U.S. troop level peaks at 541,000.

June 1969: Nixon announces troop withdrawal.

September 1969: President Ho Chi Minh of DRV dies.

1970–1971: Kissinger begins secret talks in Paris with Hanoi envoy; no progress is made.

October 1971: Thieu is reelected president of South Vietnam.

December 1971: U.S. intensifies bombing of North Vietnam. U.S. troop level reduced to 160,000.

February 1972: Nixon visits China.

May 1972: Communist forces capture Quang Tri, the northernmost province of South Vietnam; United States mines Hai Phong harbor and intensifies bombing of the North.

December 1972: Paris talks break down. Nixon orders bombing of Hanoi and Hai Phong.

1973–1974: Peace talks resume, and cease-fire agreements are formally signed in Paris. Last U.S. troops leave Vietnam. Nixon resigns to avoid Watergate impeachment and is replaced by Ford. Thieu struggles to defend South Vietnam from Communist forces.

April 1975: Cambodia falls to the Khmer Rouge. Last Americans are evacuated from Saigon, including the U.S. ambassador to South Vietnam. Saigon falls, and North Vietnam proclaims victory and the success of the "Ho Chi Minh campaign."

July 1976: Vietnam formally proclaims the unified Socialist Republic of Vietnam (SRV) with its capital at Hanoi.

NOTES

1. See also Skocpol (1979: chap. 3).

2. Tran Ich Tac was a prince of the Vietnamese Tran dynasty (1225–1400) who served the interests of Kublai Khan's invading Mongolian armies in 1287. Le Chieu Thong was the last emperor of the Le dynasty (1428–1788). After losing his throne to Emperor Quang Trung of the Tay-son (Eastern Mountain) dynasty in 1788, Le invited Mongol forces into Vietnam in an unsuccessful effort to regain his royal domain. See Tran Trong Kim (1954).

3. For a distinction between the "little tradition" and "great tradition," or "Confucianism of the mandarins" and "Confucianism of the people," see Nguyen Khac Vien (1974: 34–41).

4. The term "peasants" here is translated from *nong dan*, which covers a wide variety of farmers or villagers who live in the countryside.

5. See VBSBTHTU (Vu Bien Soan Ban Tuyen Huan Trung Uong) (1978: 11). In some Communist writings the letter *c* was at times replaced by *k*.

6. For the Chinese concept of this "traditional rank order of *shih, nung, kung, shang,*" see Ho and Tsou (1968: 183).

7. Although the institution of *cong dien* ("communal land"), existed in previous times it was not well known until the reign of Emperor Le Thai To (1428–1433) under the form of *quan dien* ("equal field"). See Hoang Van Chi (1964: 202); Ngo Vinh Long (1973: 5); Tran Trong Kim (1954: 237).

8. For the Leninist roots of Vietnamese revolutionary theory, see William J. Duiker (1980: 45–51).

9. This remark was made by Ho Chi Minh during an interview with British journalist Felix Greene on November 18, 1965. See Ho Chi Minh (1967: 105–106).

10. For a description of the morale of the well-disciplined North Vietnamese troops infiltrating into the South who were apparently well motivated and "extremely well briefed" for their mission, see Bernard B. Fall (1963: 350–356); also see Nguyen Cao Ky (1976: 136).

11. See *The Pentagon Papers* (1971: 311).

12. For a detailed analysis of the socialist economy in Vietnam, see Nguyen Tien Hung (1977).

13. When I visited Vietnam in 1977, I was told by some high-ranking officials that during the revolutionary struggle in the South, China had offered Hanoi complete aid and support should the Vietnamese refuse further assistance from the Soviet Union. The Chinese conditional overture was refused. For a Vietnamese view, see Socialist Republic of Vietnam, Ministry of Foreign Affairs (1979).

14. For an analytical discussion of this U.S.-Vietnamese contact, see Robert G. Sutter (1981: 186–188).

15. Personal interview with Phan Hien in Hanoi, September 1977.

5

NICARAGUA: A NEW MODEL FOR POPULAR REVOLUTION IN LATIN AMERICA

DÉVORA GRYNSPAN

Central America entered a period of severe economic and political crisis in the late 1970s, a crisis that first came to the attention of the U.S. public in the form of the 1979 Nicaraguan revolution and later, the civil war in El Salvador. Under the Somozas (1933–1979), Nicaragua was the most dependable ally of the United States in Latin America. When Somoza was overthrown in 1979 by a leftist and anti-imperialist revolution, led by the Frente Sandinista de Liberación Nacional (FSLN), it was the first time since the 1959 Cuban revolution that a revolutionary movement had succeeded in overthrowing a U.S.-sponsored government in Latin America and installing a government committed to social transformation and national independence. It was to be expected, therefore, that the U.S. government and public would become engaged in a debate over the proper response to the new Nicaraguan government. Much of this debate centered around the contra-aid issue, i.e., U.S. funding of anti-Sandinista and counterrevolutionary (thus the label *contra*) military forces led by Nicaraguan business leaders and former Somoza allies.

Although the FSLN successfully fought the contras for a decade, it approached the February 1990 elections worn down by continued economic and political pressures. To the surprise of many observers, the FSLN lost the election to a probusiness coalition, led by Violeta Chamorro. However, the FSLN remains a powerful force and a partner in the new multiparty government. The 1990 elections thus brought about a new stage and a new political experiment in Latin America that is likely to generate further debate: a multiparty political system in which the left (i.e., the FSLN) is the most organized and coherent political party in a region where the state, the military, and the United States have traditionally been geared toward the left's exclusion and repression. In terms of U.S. policy, the debate first centered around the question of whether U.S. foreign policy toward

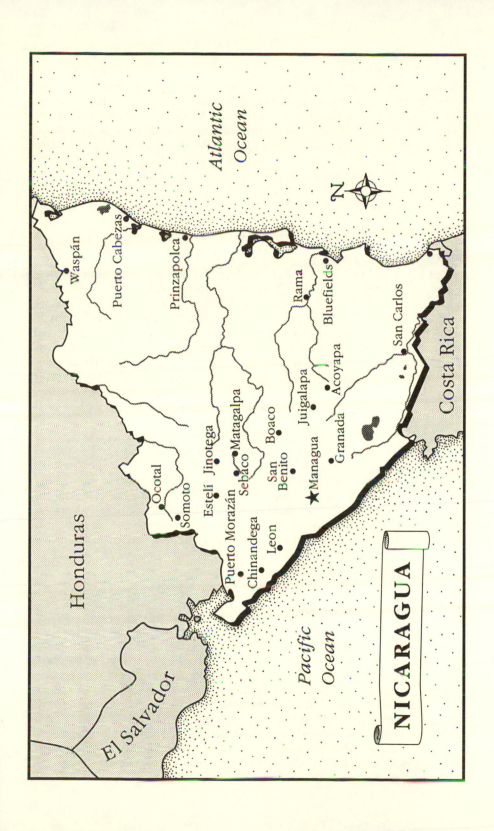

Nicaragua (low-intensity warfare and economic embargo) had indeed been successful. In the future, the debate is more likely to center on U.S. policy responses to the new political configuration in Nicaragua. Whether Nicaragua will present a viable model for El Salvador and Guatemala remains to be seen, as the military in those countries remains under the control of the traditional social and military elites.

This chapter examines the origins of the 1979 Sandinista revolution, the revolutionary process, and the outcome of revolution in Nicaragua, as well as the implications of the 1990 elections for the development of democracy in Nicaragua.[1]

PREREVOLUTIONARY STATE AND SOCIETY

The legacy of Spanish colonialism in Nicaragua was similar in many respects to that in neighboring countries: an oligarchic society based on monopolization of land, forced Indian labor, and the violent economic and political exclusion of the majority of the population. Landowners (i.e., latifundistas) derived not only wealth but also great political power from their control of labor and land. Economic activity after independence in 1821 was based on cattle ranching and the production of cacao and indigo for export and was dominated by landed and merchant elites in the cities of Granada and León. Conflict between these competing elites (in the form of Liberal-Conservative struggles) characterized political life well into the twentieth century, with the Chamorro and Sacasa families playing a central political role.

The consolidation of the export economy came with the introduction of coffee and bananas during the late nineteenth and early twentieth centuries. The Liberal administration of José Santos Zelaya (1893–1909) implemented a series of policies designed to promote coffee production, attract foreign investment in infrastructure, and facilitate labor recruitment. Liberal reforms, both in Nicaragua and throughout the region, resulted in the dispossession of small producers, the proletarianization of the labor force, and the rise to power of the coffee bourgeoisie. These reforms also reinforced Nicaragua's dependence on foreign capital, foreign markets, and imports.

The Nicaraguan State:
Crisis and Foreign Intervention

Throughout Central America, the consolidation of coffee production and its integration into the world economy generated important political changes at the turn of the century. Specifically, the emergence of coffee production as the most dynamic economic sector brought about a relative decline in Liberal-Conservative conflict, greater stability, and the consolidation of state power. The oligarchic state, however, was not a national or a homogeneous state, i.e., it did not represent the consolidation of a legitimate political alliance, of a homogeneous class, or of a national consensus. Nevertheless, the oligarchic state did manage to establish its political and cultural dominance over the majority of the population, relying on the military to put down periodic political and economic challenges.

The emergence of the Nicaraguan state, however, followed a somewhat different path, one that had profound consequences for Nicaraguan development. The consolidation of state power in Nicaragua was achieved, not through a gradual resolution of intra-oligarchic struggles, but through foreign intervention (Torres-Rivas 1984). The United States' early interest in Nicaragua was dictated by a variety of factors, especially a strong English presence and the attractiveness of Nicaragua as the possible site of an interoceanic canal. By the early twentieth century, the United States had been able to displace England militarily and financially by forcing that country's withdrawal from the Atlantic Coast and by forcing the Nicaraguan government to refinance its debt through U.S. banks.

The initial purpose of U.S. military intervention was the overthrow of José Santos Zelaya. Zelaya's anticlerical and procoffee policies had resulted in a major uprising by Conservative landowners, led by Emiliano Chamorro, and his nationalist policies were seen as an obstacle to U.S. investment and efforts to build a canal. The landing of U.S. Marines in support of the Conservatives forced Zelaya to resign in 1909 and inaugurated a period of recurrent U.S. diplomatic and military intervention. This intervention, however, did not guarantee stability or peace. U.S.-dictated governments often faced armed rebellion on the part of both Liberals and Conservatives, in turn leading to new landings of U.S. Marines, so the U.S. military occupation of Nicaragua was almost constant between 1912 and 1933. (See LaFeber 1984; Woodward 1985).

U.S. intervention in Nicaragua had long-term economic and political consequences. U.S. business interests achieved virtual control of Nicaragua's customs and banks, stripping the government of resources and undermining its ability to implement its preferred economic policies, and in the process, weakening—and preventing—the development of autonomous political institutions. Competing oligarchic factions continued to rely on U.S. intervention to settle internal conflict, thus preventing the resolution of intra-oligarchic conflicts and prolonging instability. Moreover, U.S. intervention undermined the legitimacy of the state and promoted anti-U.S. sentiment among the popular classes. The Nicaraguan state, in short, was born in crisis.

Somoza and the National Guard

U.S. concern over the continuing instability and need for intervention resulted in the adoption of an alternative policy toward Nicaragua as well as other Caribbean countries: a combination of internal militarization and supervised elections. In 1926, U.S. Marines intervened to put down a Liberal rebellion and reinstall former President Adolfo Díaz to power; in 1927, the marines again intervened to maintain him in power and in the process, occupied all important Nicaraguan towns. In exchange for his promise to hold supervised elections in 1928, the United States demanded that Díaz finish his term and that the government create a military force to guarantee stability. César Augusto Sandino, one of the Liberal generals fighting President Díaz, refused to accept the pact and continued his fight against U.S. occupation and the newly created National Guard.

Unable to defeat Sandino and restore order in Nicaragua, and faced with increasing opposition at home, the U.S. government proceeded to pull out the marines after the 1932 elections. Newly elected President Juan Bautista Sacasa appointed his nephew, and the U.S. choice, Anastasio Somoza García as commander of the National Guard. Following the withdrawal of U.S. troops in 1933, Sandino agreed to negotiate and was murdered, along with several hundred supporters, by the National Guard in 1934 on his way to a meeting with President Sacasa.

By 1936, Somoza had turned the National Guard into his own political tool and had forced President Sacasa to resign. This time, the United States did not heed the government's pleas for intervention. Through his control of the presidency and the National Guard, Somoza proceeded to impose order and stability and to inaugurate almost forty-five years of Somoza family rule over Nicaragua. National Guard loyalty to the Somozas was guaranteed through corruption, high wages, and other benefits, as well as high levels of U.S. military aid and training. In return, the Somozas became strong and reliable allies in the United States' war against communism and revolution in Central America and the Caribbean, actively supporting U.S.-sponsored invasions of Guatemala and Cuba. With U.S. help, Somoza was able to maintain control of the National Guard, undermine the Liberal party, co-opt the Conservative party, and repress labor unions and the left.

This U.S.-sponsored solution prevented both the resolution of intra-oligarchic conflict and the consolidation of state power in the hands of a cohesive elite. Instead, Somoza established a highly personal dictatorship and proceeded to build a narrow political and economic base that was rather independent of the traditional oligarchic sectors. Somoza's ability to co-opt the traditional parties undermined their legitimacy in the eyes of the population and delayed the emergence of viable, popularly based political institutions. The United States' unwavering support for Somoza, even in the face of increasing repression and corruption, heightened nationalist and anti-U.S. sentiment among the popular sectors and further delegitimized the government.

The Somoza Dynasty: Modernization and Crisis

By the time of his assassination in 1956, Anastasio Somoza had built an economic empire with holdings in industry, banking, and commerce by taking advantage of government institutions and resources, by taking over failing businesses during times of economic crisis, especially in the 1930s, and by outright graft and corruption. His two sons, Luis and Anastasio Somoza Debayle, continued this tradition of repression and corruption through their control of the National Guard and the presidency.

Anastasio ("Tachito") Somoza Debayle, a West Point graduate, controlled the National Guard from 1956 until 1979, using it even more effectively than his father had to repress opposition and maintain himself in power. In the period immediately following his father's assassination, for example, Tachito oversaw a period of intense repression of thousands of Somoza opponents, including the editor of *La Prensa*, Pedro Joaquín Chamorro, who was tortured and then went into exile in Costa Rica. Tachito's older brother, Luis Somoza, was president from 1956 to 1963, and upon his death in 1967, Tachito took over the presidency as well as the National Guard.

The 1950s and 1960s were years of significant economic growth and social change in Central America. In Nicaragua, expanding international markets promoted a degree of agricultural mechanization and export diversification and resulted in increases in the production of sugar, cotton, and meat in the 1950s. At the same time, there was significant investment in infrastructure (e.g., electricity, transportation, and road building), partly financed by outside assistance. Increased agricultural production and the expansion of the infrastructure in turn led to an expansion of financial and commercial activity in Managua, later reinforced by the creation of the Central American Common Market and the adoption of industrialization policies. Real gross domestic product (GDP) growth rates during this period were often impressive: 8.3 percent in 1950–1955, 2.3 percent[2] in 1955–1960, 10.2 percent in 1960–1965, and 4.2 percent in 1965–1970 (Rosenthal 1982: 21). Social indicators also improved during this period, reflecting the expansion of education and the middle class; for example, the literacy rate increased from 38.4 percent in 1950 to 53.1 percent in 1975.

Somoza and the traditional elites were able to use their information and resources to obtain land that would be affected by the development of roads, significantly increasing their land-holdings and leading to the dispossession of large numbers of peasants and small landowners through both legal and forced purchases. At the same time, industrialization and road construction undermined artisan production as urban products reached small towns and villages. The migration to the city by displaced artisans and agricultural producers contributed to the fast rate of urbanization experienced in Nicaragua during this period, the urban population increasing from 19 percent in 1950 to 47 percent in 1970 to 54 percent in 1980 (Rosenthal 1982: 21; Weeks 1985: 42), while the labor force in the service sector expanded from 26 percent in the mid-1960s to 32 percent in 1973 (Booth 1985: 83).

In the 1960s, Nicaragua benefited from an inflow of funds through the Alliance for Progress as well as from the establishment of the Central American Common Market (CACM). The CACM and favorable industrial policies made industrial investment profitable and safe, and the two traditional elites, corresponding to the Liberal and Conservative oligarchic factions, expanded their activities into the financial, manufacturing, and foreign trade sectors and into the processing of agricultural products for export.[3] Somoza and his allies, who were able to benefit more from state agencies, favors, and foreign assistance, constituted the third major economic force in the country. Although entrepreneurs and professionals not associated with these groups also benefited from the rapid economic growth and industrialization, the three major groups controlled about 60 percent of the country's income by the late 1960s (Zamora 1982: 99). Other Central American countries, especially Guatemala and El Salvador, however, were better able to attract foreign investment in manufacturing and to take advantage of the benefits of integration, so Nicaragua soon developed a balance-of-trade deficit not only with its traditional partner, the United States, but also with its regional neighbors.

During this period of economic growth and social change, the Somozas managed to maintain their control of state institutions and co-opt the traditional elites. The Liberal party became Somoza's party, and thus disappeared as a viable opposition.

Excluded from power, sectors of the Conservative party entered into political agreements with Somoza, which led to defections and further internal divisions that weakened the party. The Somoza dictatorship, in short, aided by post–World War II prosperity, prevented the emergence of effective political institutions and contributed to the weakening and loss of legitimacy of the traditional parties. Somoza also achieved social peace through the expansion of social benefits for the working class and the expansion of employment opportunities in industry during the 1960s. At the same time, with increasing U.S. military aid, the Somozas succeeded in repressing leftist opposition, such as the Sandinista guerrilla movement of the early 1960s.

The Crisis of the State

The decline of the CACM and of the international economy in the 1970s highlighted the increasing inequality and deteriorating conditions of the lower-income sectors and brought into the open the conflict between Somoza and the traditional elites. The favorable international conditions and high growth rates that had allowed the concentration of income in the hands of the Somoza, Liberal, and Conservative elite factions, through their participation in highly profitable enterprises, began to disappear in the late 1960s. The process of import-substitution industrialization promoted by the CACM had exhausted opportunities for highly profitable investment, and profit rates declined as Nicaraguan (and Central American) elites were unable to invest in more technologically and organizationally sophisticated industrial sectors. Central America in general was not able to advance the process of industrialization beyond the simple technology of assembly-plant production that is characteristic of import-substitution industrialization.

Although wealthier Nicaraguans had benefited from investment in manufacturing and services, as well as from modernization in the rural sector, conditions for the majority of Nicaraguans had continued to deteriorate. From 1960 to 1975, the population grew at a high average rate of about 3.4 percent, from a total of 1,410,289 to 2,162,262 (Booth 1985: 82). Yet the economic growth of the CACM years—centered on import-substitution industrialization and export agriculture—reduced opportunities for peasant agriculture and provided too small an increase in urban jobs to keep pace with the high rates of population growth and urbanization. The contribution of agriculture and other raw material production to the GDP during this period dropped from 37.4 percent in 1950 to 29.6 percent in 1960, while the contribution of manufacturing and service activities increased from 12.1 percent to 15.8 percent and from 50.5 percent to 54.6 percent, respectively (Rosenthal 1982: 23). However, the small size and capital-intensive nature of the industrial sector generated little employment, which meant higher unemployment levels in the urban areas. Industrial employment increased by only 1.6 percent after 1960, reaching a peak of 11.6 percent in 1965 and decreasing to 9.7 percent after the 1972 earthquake (Booth 1985: 82). In the 1970s, according to UN estimates, 41 percent of the urban population and 80 percent of the rural population were catalogued as poor, with 42.4 percent and 55.4 percent, respectively, living in extreme poverty (cited in Rosenthal 1982: 36). Still, a process of social diversification had taken place with urbanization, along with the expansion of education and the middle class.

Although the traditional oligarchic elites had diversified their economic interests, they continued to be excluded from real political power. Elite opposition to Somoza, although sporadic and often co-opted, had existed since the 1940s. Conservative and Liberal elements remained anti-Somocista throughout this period, but their attempts to depose Somoza did not attract significant elite or popular support. The Conservative party, for example, entered into yet another electoral alliance with Somoza as late as 1971.

The three major economic groups had coexisted by dividing economic opportunities among themselves so that each group tended to invest in particular economic activities. This "understanding" ended in the 1970s with the deterioration in economic conditions, which fueled competition among the two major economic elites as well as between them and the Somoza group. Economic conditions and political conflict were further aggravated by the 1972 earthquake, which destroyed Managua and provided the opportunity for corruption and misappropriation of international aid funds by Somoza and his allies. Most significant was Somoza's use of foreign financial assistance to establish the Banco de Centroamérica, thus breaking the financial monopoly of the two traditional elites and increasingly displacing them through his control of the state. These economic incursions by the Somoza group into activities previously dominated by the two traditional elites, as well as Somoza's attempt to benefit from troubled business sectors after the earthquake, led to intensified elite opposition and defection, which continued until 1979.

The 1970s, therefore, witnessed a rapid deterioration of the state, as all the accumulated contradictions generated by the development model, the political exclusion of the traditional elites, and the lack of institutionalization exploded in increasing unrest at all levels of Nicaraguan society. The crisis of the state was reflected in Somoza's increasing inability to co-opt traditional sectors, repress the popular sector, and maintain order. Although the exhaustion of the economy goes a long way in explaining the defection of the elite and the resulting state crisis, other internal and external factors were also critical for the success of the 1979 revolution. Economic growth and industrialization had had significant impacts on the popular sectors as well, and the process of urbanization had made the income gaps among the various sectors of Nicaraguan society, especially between the lower and upper classes, more obvious. Although there had been a significant increase in the number of blue- and white-collar associations, they remained weak until the 1970s, when they joined the efforts of other popular sectors, especially the FSLN and the clergy. Somoza's inability to control the increasingly combative and effective popular revolutionary forces led by the FSLN represented a threat to elite rule, thus contributing to—and ultimately undermining—the search for alternatives on the part of the elites and the United States.

The FSLN, which had been organized by Carlos Fonseca Amador in the early 1960s, had suffered a series of defeats at the hands of Somoza's National Guard. In the 1970s, however, the FSLN was able to take advantage of the deepening economic and political crisis, especially in the aftermath of the 1972 earthquake.

The FSLN staged a series of daring and successful military actions, both in the rural areas and in Managua, which quickly attracted the support of various popular sectors and movements, including intellectuals, students, teachers, and workers.[4] The spreading social unrest brought about by these combative sectors was met by increasing repression, which contributed to a general sense of crisis and instability. This repression further isolated Somoza and his supporters, both at home and in the international community.

Finally, it is difficult to understand the profound political changes, especially among the lower-income sectors, intellectuals, and small producers, without taking into account the role of the Nicaraguan church during the 1960s and 1970s. Influenced by continent-wide changes within the Catholic church, especially the introduction of the doctrine of Liberation Theology,[5] elements within the Nicaraguan church organized a network of Christian base communities (*comunidades eclesiásticas de base*) that encouraged political demands for human rights, democratization, and social justice. This movement within the church became known as the popular or revolutionary church, in contrast to the more conservative church hierarchy. To a much greater extent than in neighboring countries, the popular church in Nicaragua actively supported the revolutionary struggle and became identified with it. The presence of religious figures in the post-1979 Sandinista government, therefore, was not surprising or contradictory. Unlike the case of the Cuban revolution, the church was an integral part of the Nicaraguan revolution and contributed significantly to the nature and policies of the Sandinista government after 1979.

In addition to the important role played by the clergy in politicizing the popular sectors, the support of the opposition by important sectors of the church contributed significantly to the delegitimization of the Somoza regime. Calls for social justice and land redistribution were just as important as calls for political democracy. To a lesser extent, Protestant groups in Nicaragua also supported the FSLN and the struggle against Somoza. The popular church thus was rightly perceived as a subversive force as it contributed to the radicalization of the popular movement and the legitimacy of the Sandinista revolution.

The Anti-Somocista Alliance, 1974–1979

Although opposition to Somoza had been increasing since the late 1960s, the 1972 earthquake was the main catalyst for popular mobilization and upper-class defection. The earthquake not only aggravated economic conditions but brought into sharp focus the corrupt nature of the Somoza dictatorship and increased the alienation of both the popular sectors and the traditional economic elites.

After the 1972 earthquake, a number of political organizations formed at all levels of society. During the 1970s, an increasing number of entrepreneurs joined in demanding Somoza's ouster and democratization by uniting with some of the upper-class individuals who had obtained a reputation as anti-Somoza politicians. Some joined Pedro Joaquín Chamorro, editor of *La Prensa* and a respected anti-Somocista who established the Unión Democrática de Liberación (UDEL) in 1974. UDEL represented a variety of progressive political sectors, including the socialist parties and labor, and was perceived as the most viable political alternative to Somoza. Still, it failed to gain support from the conservative financial sectors and thus failed in some of its efforts, such as the staging of an entrepreneurial strike in 1977 (Zamora 1982: 102). UDEL was joined by members of the Partido Liberal Independiente (PLI), which had split from the Liberal party in 1944 and had remained in opposition to the Somozas. This party included middle-class elements and small-business interests. A number of other groups also joined UDEL, such as the Partido Socialista Nicaragüense (PSN) and the Partido Social Cristiano Nicaragüense (PSCN), which had organized university students and the working class and had remained in opposition to Somoza throughout the 1960s and into the 1970s.

In 1977, a group of more radical entrepreneurs, clergy, and intellectuals with close ties to the FSLN formed the Group of Twelve (Los Doce). This group, which included important capitalists (e.g., banker Arturo Cruz) and intellectuals (e.g., Ernesto Cardenal and Sergio Ramírez) was to be the basis of the future revolutionary government. Although its members fled the country in 1977, the Group of Twelve continued to provide support from outside until it returned in 1978.

The prospects for a nonrevolutionary alternative to Somoza collapsed with the assassination of Chamorro in January 1978, allegedly on Somoza's order. After this murder, UDEL's call for a "national dialogue" became a demand for Somoza's resignation, and upper-class opposition to Somoza, along with pro-FSLN sentiment and social unrest, increased dramatically. In March 1978, leaders of the banking sector who had continued to work with Somoza and who distrusted the pluralist UDEL alliance organized their own political party, the Movimiento Democrático Nicaragüense (MDN), led by businessman Alfonso Robelo. By May 1978, aware that neither group on its own would be a viable political force, the two groups (UDEL and MDN) joined in the Frente Amplio de Oposición (FAO) and then, lacking the military means and the popular base controlled by the FSLN, entered into an alliance with the pro-FSLN Group of Twelve. The alliance fell apart within months, however, over the refusal of the Group of Twelve and the PSCN to negotiate with Somoza.

As stated by Edelberto Torres-Rivas, the originality of the Nicaraguan revolution was that, for the first time in Latin America, it joined rural guerrilla warfare, urban insurrection, general strikes, political work among peasants and workers, and the support of important sectors of the bourgeoisie, intellectuals, and the church. The FSLN was surrounded by a combination of political mass organizations that provided significant force to its military activities (Torres-Rivas 1982: 58). The crisis of the Nicaraguan state and the 1979 revolution were facilitated by the very broad nature of the anti-Somoza movement. The exclusion of the traditional sectors and the highly personalized and corrupt nature of the dictatorship increasingly alienated upper-class sectors, which in the neighboring countries continue to this day to support the state. This exclusive and narrow power base contributed to the forging of political alliances among social sectors with widely different concerns and policy preferences. With the triumph of the revolution, however, these differences inevitably surfaced (as discussed later).

The political coalition that emerged in the 1970s was more an anti-Somoza alliance than a revolutionary coalition. Social discontent, more than anywhere else in the region, had a clear target in the person of Somoza, who undertook the violent defense of the state without political alliances or the support of the traditional elites. Moreover, the state's violent response to increasing opposition in the 1970s created the conditions for a Sandinista victory rather than for a solution that would allow access to power by the traditional elites. Rising social unrest among all sectors after the earthquake was met with massive repression by Somoza, who imposed a three-year state of siege in 1974. Repression further radicalized and mobilized the population by giving the various sectors a common political experience.

The United States

Just as the United States had played an important role in establishing and maintaining the Somoza dynasty, so it played a role in its overthrow (and in subsequent events). In the aftermath of the 1972 earthquake, Somoza continued to receive growing levels of economic and military aid from the United States, despite increasing elite and popular dissatisfaction. The intensity of the social unrest and state repression after 1976, however, coincided with the Carter administration's focus on human rights as the main element of U.S. Latin American policy. After 1977, the U.S. government refused to support Somoza and slowly joined Somoza's opposition and regional leaders in demanding his resignation. The withdrawal of U.S. support both weakened Somoza's regime and encouraged his opponents.

However, while rejecting Somoza, the United States also rejected any solution that might involve a FSLN-led victory and instead sought a middle-of-the-road, or centrist, alternative based on the entrepreneurial sectors grouped around UDEL. But there was no real center to be found as the Nicaraguan elites did not represent a cohesive alternative but a weak and divided upper class without strong institutions or a popular base of support. Chamorro's assassination had left the upper class without legitimate leadership. Even when confronted by the threat to the system represented by the popular challenge, the Nicaraguan upper classes were unable, during this period, to effectively organize cohesive political parties. As in the past, intra-elite conflicts and competition were expressed, not through popularly based political parties, but by narrow economic-based organizations, such as coffee growers associations, chambers of commerce and industry, and banking associations (Torres-Rivas 1982: 51).

By the end of the 1970s, it was obvious that no solution could exclude the FSLN and the pro-FSLN mass organizations. The U.S. proposal that Somoza resign and that the National Guard stay behind to maintain order was not acceptable to the FSLN and the pro-FSLN elements of FAO. Just as important, the U.S. proposal was not acceptable to Somoza, who decided to continue his violent struggle. Without Somoza's cooperation and with the increasingly strong bargaining power of the FSLN, the United States (and the upper classes) failed in its last-minute attempt to take control of the revolutionary movement.

Although the United States failed in its attempt to impose its own preferred solution (as it had so often done in the past), there is no question that President Carter's refusal to condone Somoza's corruption and human rights violations played an important role in delegitimizing the Somoza regime, strengthening its opposition at home and abroad, and encouraging defections on the part of elites. Left without U.S. military or diplomatic support and unable to control social unrest, Somoza's repressive apparatus was perceived by his opponents to be vulnerable and ineffective.

The Final Offensive, 1978–1979

In October 1977, under pressure from the United States and boasting that government forces had defeated the FSLN, Somoza lifted martial law, only to be confronted by a new explosion of strikes, student unrest, and media attacks. The FSLN followed with attacks on several towns, including Masaya, only thirty miles from Managua. The Group of Twelve, in exile in Costa Rica and supported by the Costa Rican government, called for support for the FSLN and for an FSLN presence in any new government. Somoza escalated the repression by staging an all-out war against villages and the countryside. After Chamorro's assassination and the wave of popular protest that followed, the FSLN again attacked several important towns and National Guard outposts. The popular insurrection took increasing force with whole towns participating in the uprising; for example, the Indian community of Monimbó suffered hundreds of casualties at the hands of the National Guard, only to stage a second uprising weeks later. By mid-1978, the FSLN-led alliance, the Movimiento Pueblo Unido (MPU), had clearly taken control of the anti-Somoza movement, and when the Group of Twelve returned from exile in July of that year, they were greeted by tens of thousands. Popular demonstrations also followed another daring attack on August 22, when the FSLN took over 1,000 hostages at the National Palace in Managua and secured the release of key FSLN leaders, demonstrating not only its military capabilities but also the impotence of the National Guard.

A major FSLN offensive in September 1978 against a number of towns elicited the most violent response from Somoza yet. The National Guard surrounded several cities and, after bombing them, proceeded to carry out on-the-spot executions, especially of young men. The military escalation and political polarization reflected in these events led to a U.S. effort to mediate the crisis through the Organization of American States (OAS), and the FAO selected a three-man commission, constituted by Alfonso Robelo (MDN), Rafael Córdova (UDEL), and Sergio Ramírez (Group of Twelve). The Group of Twelve soon withdrew from the negotiations—and from the FAO—over the U.S. plan, which included a provisional government with members of Somoza's party and the maintenance of the National Guard. Soon other groups, such as the PSN, also left the FAO. More important, Somoza himself was a major obstacle to U.S. mediation efforts by his continuing refusal of U.S. "requests" that he leave the country. His intransigence and the violent repression that followed the September offensive convinced most Nicaraguans of the need for armed insurrection, and thus FSLN leadership, as the only way to depose the dictatorship.

From October 1978 to July 1979, the FSLN received significant external support and trained large numbers of combatants, and Somoza also rearmed the National Guard with external military support. The pattern of FSLN victories and violent National Guard reprisals was repeated in various cities. In April 1979,

Somoza responded to the FSLN capture of Estelí with massive military force, destroying the city and killing more than 1,000 civilians. The FAO supported the FSLN's May 1979 final offensive with a general strike, and by June the FSLN controlled most of the north and was challenging the National Guard in the south. The National Guard continued massive attacks in the north and in FSLN-controlled neighborhoods in Managua, but by mid-July the FSLN controlled most of the country.

Somoza finally fled the country on July 17, 1979, leaving behind a caretaker government that lasted only two days. In the final days of the war, Somoza's government simply collapsed as members of both the National Guard and Somoza's Liberal party fled in fear of popular retribution. However, the revolutionary victory of July 19, 1979, came at great cost to Nicaraguan society. The new revolutionary government inherited a physically ruined country and economic infrastructure, an empty treasury, hundreds of thousands of homeless citizens, and a population decimated by 30,000 deaths.

THE TRANSFER OF POWER

Although dominated by the FSLN, the composition of the Government of National Reconstruction, which took power in July 1979, reflected the broad nature of the anti-Somoza alliance. The five-person executive junta included two private-sector representatives (Alfonso Robelo and Violeta Chamorro—widow of *La Prensa* publisher Pedro Joaquín Chamorro) in addition to Daniel Ortega, as the official FSLN representative, and two other FSLN members (Moisés Hassan and Sergio Ramírez). The legislature (Council of State) inaugurated in May 1980 allocated seats to traditional political parties and organizations as well as to new mass organizations. This arrangement, however, was soon undermined by contradictions inherent in the revolutionary alliance that had overthrown Somoza.

In addition to fissures in the political alliance, the Nicaraguan revolutionaries were confronted with a variety of internal and external constraints that increasingly undermined the power as well as the policies of the new government. The revolutionary government found it increasingly difficult to carry out policies consistent with its ideological preference and of benefit to the lower-income sectors to which it was committed. This section examines the nature of the state and class relations in revolutionary Nicaragua, as well as the major problems and achievements of the Sandinista revolution.

The FSLN-Bourgeois Alliance

The alliance that emerged during the last months of the struggle against Somoza was made possible by a number of factors. Faced with Somoza's intransigence, the bourgeoisie had come to realize that only military force, and thus an alliance with the FSLN, would wrest control from Somoza. At the same time, the FSLN realized the need for upper-class support in designing an urban strategy to complement its military campaign, to undermine the economic base of the dictatorship, and to secure outside support for the revolution. Just as important was the FSLN's awareness of the enormously difficult task of reconstruction that would follow any revolutionary triumph. The new government would have to confront, not only the physical destruction caused by the earthquake and the war, but also long-term structural problems of poverty and dependence. The professional and entrepreneurial skills of the middle class and bourgeoisie would be badly needed in rebuilding the Nicaraguan economy. These considerations shaped the ideology, policies, and organization of the revolutionary government.

Within the FSLN itself there were conflicts over strategy and policy. After several military defeats at the hands of Somoza's National Guard in the 1960s, the FSLN had adopted a long-term revolutionary strategy called prolonged popular war (*guerra popular prolongada*, GPP), i.e., a war of attrition based on a rural popular army. In the 1970s, two other tendencies emerged that complemented (and sometimes clashed with) the GPP strategy. One faction of the FSLN formed the Proletarian Tendency, which emphasized the need to work among the expanding urban working class and to complement rural guerrilla warfare with an urban strategy. The FSLN leadership, mostly supporters of GPP, first disagreed with and then expelled the Proletarians, who continued to fight the dictatorship independently but still under the FSLN banner. FSLN members who tried unsuccessfully to mediate between the two tendencies eventually emerged as a third tendency, the Terceristas, who realized the extent of anti-Somoza sentiment among all sectors of the population and argued for immediate insurrection. For that purpose they concentrated on building a military organization and a broad political alliance.

The three tendencies worked independently until 1978, when they all supported the formation of the MPU out of some twenty pro-FSLN mass organizations that had emerged in the 1970s. As the insurrection developed, the three tendencies within the FSLN coalesced and came to agree with the Terceristas on the need for a multiclass coalition during and after the overthrow of Somoza. Although the Terceristas prevailed, differences among the three tendencies continued over the role of the bourgeoisie, the pace of revolutionary change, and other issues. Daniel Ortega, who emerged as the leader of the FSLN and president of Nicaragua, represented the Terceristas.

The alliance between the FSLN and the bourgeoisie began to unravel almost immediately, as became evident in May 1980 when the Council of State was inaugurated. The program of the Government of National Reconstruction called for the establishment of a legislative body, the Council of State, with thirty-three seats. About half of the seats were to be allocated to traditional parties and organizations, including five seats to the Consejo Superior de la Empresa Privada (COSEP). Under pressure from mass organizations, the FSLN and the executive junta decided in April 1980 to add fourteen seats to be allocated to revolutionary mass organizations. In protest, Alfonso Robelo (MDN) resigned from the junta, and three political parties refused to take their seats in the Council of State.[6] COSEP accepted its five seats after much debate and only conditionally, and the second representative of the bourgeoisie on the junta, Violeta Chamorro, resigned in mid-April.

The clash over the Council of State was symbolic of the contradictions inherent in an alliance between the bourgeoisie and the FSLN. It was clear from the beginning that the FSLN's National Directorate[7] dictated the broad outlines of national policy through its control of the military and key ministries, its majority control of the junta, and now its control of the Council of State. The governing junta and the cabinet, which had appeared to give significant representation to conservative sectors, came under firm Sandinista control within a year. The private sector was allowed to participate and maintain control of the means of production only as long as it complied with FSLN-defined guidelines. Denied real power over national policy, and convinced that the ultimate goal of the FSLN was a transition to socialism and thus an eventual nationalization of private enterprise, the bourgeoisie became increasingly unwilling to work within an FSLN-dominated government that regulated their economic activity through control of marketing, banking, exports, and pricing. By the end of 1980, an opposition coalition had emerged, centered around COSEP and the bourgeois parties and supported by the church hierarchy, the editors of *La Prensa*, and soon the new Reagan administration in the United States.

The conflict between the FSLN and the bourgeoisie was inevitable, as it resulted from the inherent contradiction between revolutionary change and socialist goals, on the one hand, and the interests of a capitalist class, on the other, especially the Nicaraguan capitalist class, which had been accustomed to operating in an environment of complete market freedom and low taxation[8]. It became obvious to the bourgeoisie that its power and interests would be increasingly eroded and could be protected only through control of the state. Some people opted for active opposition through COSEP and traditional parties, and some joined counterrevolutionary forces (contras) operating in neighboring countries.

REVOLUTIONARY OUTCOMES

Sandinista policies underwent important changes during the ten years of FSLN rule. From the beginning, however, ideological preferences gave way to practical economic and political considerations, the urgency of the economic crisis, and external pressures. As in other revolutions, ambitious revolutionary policies were implemented immediately by the new government, with significant popular and external support. As these policies were undermined by domestic and external constraints, support for the revolution declined, and revolutionary transformation took a back seat to economic and political survival.

The Revolutionary Period, 1979–1983

Social and Political Transformation. Immediately after taking power, the FSLN moved to expand and institutionalize its political power. The National Guard was disbanded, and the Sandinista guerrilla forces were transformed into the Sandinista Popular Army (Ejército Popular Sandinista), the name reflecting the reality of Sandinista party (rather than government) control over the military. Through its control of the army, the FSLN sought to protect the revolution from an alliance between the bourgeoisie and the military, such as the one that had overthrown President Salvador Allende in Chile in 1973.

In addition, the FSLN attempted to mobilize support for the revolution through political mobilization and social policy, including education. The FSLN was committed to addressing the low literacy level of the Nicaraguan masses, an effort that was seen as essential to the process of economic development, to the political empowerment of the masses, and to revolutionary democracy. Following the Cuban example, and influenced by Paulo Freire's *Pedagogy of the Oppressed*,[9] the Sandinista government carried out a highly visible literacy crusade in 1980 in which more than 100,000 people, organized into brigades, taught almost 1 million Nicaraguans to read and write. The crusade was also expected to expose and sensitize young urban people to the problems of rural poverty and development. The literacy crusade, however, was seen by the bourgeoisie and the church as an attempt to ideologically indoctrinate both the illiterate masses and the young educators.

The FSLN also encouraged the creation and strengthening of a variety of mass organizations before and after Somoza's overthrow. Mass organizations were represented in the Council of State and played a number of significant roles in the revolutionary process (e.g., coordination and implementation of government policies, mobilization of urban and rural sectors, provision of services, defense of the revolution). Among the most important of these organizations were the Asociación de Mujeres Nicaragüenses Luisa Amanda Espinoza (AMNLAE, which continues to play an important role in mobilizing and providing services for women), Asociación de Trabajadores del Campo (ATC, which represents the interests of small producers and workers and has pushed for land redistribution), and Sandinista Youth–Nineteenth of July (which played a key role in the literacy crusade). Equally threatening to the bourgeoisie was the expansion of mass organizations such as the Sandinista popular militias established at the community level and the Sandinista defense committees (*comités de defensa Sandinista*), modeled after Cuba's committees for the defense of the revolution, which provided political support for the revolution at the community level and worked on the problems of health, education, housing, etc.

Although pro-FSLN, the mass organizations were not subservient to it; they often disagreed over specific policies and pushed for faster, more radical change. What is clear, however, is that the mass organizations were the key to policy implementation, mobilization, and political support for the FSLN. The FSLN gained their support through the implementation of wage and social welfare legislation and by incorporating them into the political system. In the first year of the revolution the government increased workers' salaries, lowered rents, and provided food subsidies. Still, a number of trade unions not associated with the FSLN actively opposed government policies, and even pro-FSLN labor sectors refused to go along with plans that demanded greater sacrifices from labor.

Economic Policy. At the same time that it consolidated and institutionalized its power, the FSLN set about to implement major economic reforms and to take control of the national economy. The stated FSLN goal of establishing a mixed economy was facilitated by its ability to expropriate Somoza holdings without much opposition. Not only Somoza's land-holdings but also more than a hundred commercial and industrial enterprises belonging to the Somoza group were taken over by the state. Subsequent policies, however, such as the nationalization of the banking system and the commercialization of exports, encountered significant opposition because they undermined and constrained the activities of the remaining private sector. Although the Nicaraguan state did not control a greater share of the economy than a number of other Latin American or European states, it differed from them in that its control was used to weaken, not promote, the capitalist class.

Like all Central American countries, Nicaragua's economy relies on agricultural exports as the main source of foreign exchange, and control of land has been the basis of wealth and political power. The FSLN came to power clearly committed to controlling and restructuring the agricultural sector as a source of foreign exchange, income redistribution, employment, and domestic food consumption—not necessarily compatible goals. The National Institute for Agrarian Reform (INRA) was given control of nationalized land, amounting to about 25 percent of the country's cultivated lands. The production of the leading exports, however, remained mostly in the hands of large and small private producers. Large private producers, for example, controlled 67 percent of the cotton production (*NACLA* 1980: 15).

Government policy clearly favored large-scale modern agricultural enterprises in the form of state farms and production cooperatives, and INRA encouraged the formation of such cooperatives among peasants and medium producers, both in the form of production (common ownership of land) and/or service cooperatives (for the purchase and distribution of agricultural inputs). The state also assumed control over the marketing of exports, rents, the purchase and sale of basic grains, and agricultural imports. Although a major goal of the agrarian reform was to increase the living standards of small producers, peasants, and rural laborers, the needs of large producers (both state and private) who generated badly needed foreign exchange often took precedence, absorbing the state's financial and technical resources and forcing it to make economic and political compromises. The FSLN protected private producers from confiscation and discouraged land takeovers by peasants. In the case of cotton, the largest generator of foreign exchange, the FSLN had to provide incentives and benefits to an elite it deeply distrusted. The government's policy was based on a recognition that the highly educated cotton elite could easily emigrate or find alternative economic occupations (Colburn 1986: 51).

The government's policy toward the cotton growers reflected the difficulty of providing incentives for private production, on the one hand, and regulating profits and prices, on the other, all within the context of deep political distrust and antagonism toward large capitalist enterprises. Cotton growers, like all large producers, feared expropriation and resented the production difficulties generated by the government's control of essential agricultural inputs and equipment. They also received decreasing returns as a result of the government's monetary policies and low international prices. Although they continued to produce and make use of government incentives, they increased their political efforts against the FSLN.

From the outset, the FSLN was concerned about possible economic sabotage on the part of the private sector, in the form of both decapitalization of productive facilities and capital outflows.[10] The nationalized banks extended credit to private producers as an incentive, especially to cotton producers, but the government worried that the credit would not be utilized for productive purposes. As private producers inevitably resorted to decapitalization and other tactics to increase their profit and avoid financial risk, the conflict between producers and the government worsened. Poor performance and decapitalization by the private sector were followed by tougher legislation and rhetoric, which in turn generated greater hostility and rhetorical excesses by COSEP. In several instances, the government moved to expropriate idle lands, which it claimed landowners were abandoning to undermine the government's economic program. At the same time, the ATC led a series of land takeovers that were not sanctioned by the government but eventually legalized under popular pressure. Although landowners were offered compensation for these lands, the government's response clearly indicated the decreasing political power of the private sector and further increased the political antagonism between the two.

FSLN policies affected not only the large producers but also medium and small producers producing for export or for internal consumption, especially in the coffee sector where production is characterized by a greater reliance on labor and higher fixed costs. Although the government was committed to benefiting small producers, small coffee growers were particularly hurt by higher wages, government prices, and currency overvaluation as well as by low international prices. According to Colburn (1986: 75), most of the income loss among coffee growers was the result of government policy.

The FSLN attempted to benefit the rural poor by increasing access to land and credit and by promoting the formation of cooperatives. Land rents were lowered, and landlords were required to rent unused land to landless peasants. Land and credit were also made available to those small producers and peasants who joined cooperatives. However, although credit to peasants increased dramatically after the revolution, such measures did not have a dramatic impact on productivity and rural income. As in other agrarian reforms, credit was not accompanied by technical assistance or other government services, partly because of the multiple demands on government resources and know-how and partly because of the priority given to export production. At the same time, the desire to benefit the rural poor often conflicted with the political need to subsidize food consumption in the urban centers, and the low prices paid by the government to meet that need were insufficient to protect peasants' purchasing power in times of inflation. As a result, rural incomes remained low or decreased, even as the government poured resources into the rural sector.

Counterrevolution and War Economy, 1984–1990

Despite serious problems, such as floods in 1982, which caused an estimated $349 million in damage, the Nicaraguan economy experienced significant growth during the first years of the revolution: 10 percent in 1980, 8.5 percent in 1981, 5 percent in 1983.[11] Starting in 1984, however, the Nicaraguan economy entered a prolonged period of contraction. The economic problems encountered by other Latin American countries (e.g., declining terms of trade, a growing foreign debt) hit with equal force in Nicaragua. To those problems must be added others that are typical of revolutionary regimes intent on social transformation and income redistribution, such as the disruption of production caused by nationalization and conflict between the private sector and the government and problems stemming from the government's management of the economy.[12] The Nicaraguan government, however, faced two additional and much greater obstacles to economic growth: the U.S.-sponsored embargo and the contra war.

Armed opposition to the new government, by remnants of Somoza's National Guard, started immediately after the revolutionary victory, and by 1982, U.S. financing and training had turned this poorly organized and isolated opposition into a significant threat. The military pressure on the government was further augmented by opposition from the Miskito Indians and from Edén Pastora, a former Sandinista commander who defected to open a second front along the Costa Rican border. The counterrevolution became a major economic drain on the government, which by 1984 had to devote 25 percent of the budget to defense.

The war presented the government with a number of additional problems as thousands of families were displaced by the fighting and had to be resettled and peasant cooperatives increasingly became targets of contra attacks, further eroding the willingness of the rural population to join such cooperatives. The recruitment of peasants into the military and contra forces also reduced the labor supply, resulting in lower agricultural production. By 1984, the combined effects of weather conditions, contra attacks, and government low food prices had resulted in food shortages, especially of corn, as small producers reduced production or withheld a part for personal consumption. At the same time, Nicaragua's export earnings needed to pay for food imports fell as a result of these and other factors, such as lower international prices. Large private producers also cut back investment, for both economic and political reasons, and state farms proved to be less efficient than private farms (Gilbert 1988: 97).

Agrarian policy after 1983 was intended to redress some of the economic problems and political dissatisfaction created by the government's emphasis on cooperatives and subsidized urban food consumption. The pace of land distribution increased significantly, with more land being granted to individuals instead of cooperatives, and the law also made provisions for the granting of land to women. Both private and state farms taken over by protesting peasants were distributed after 1984, reducing the number of large agricultural producers. But even as the number of medium and small private producers in the agricultural sector expanded, tensions increased further between the government and the bourgeois opposition. The growing threat represented by the contra war and U.S. economic sanctions made the Sandinistas more sensitive to attacks by COSEP leaders, who increasingly and more openly supported the United States and the contras. COSEP leaders, therefore, became the targets of political attacks and confiscation, especially after the 1984 elections.

The November 1984 elections were announced by the government in the face of a rising military threat and international calls for political pluralism and against censorship, particularly of *La Prensa*. Just as the FSLN was confident of victory, the bourgeois opposition, organized in the Democratic Coordinating Committee (Coordinadora Democrática),[13] had no expectation of even a decent showing. COSEP's argument that participation in the campaign would lend legitimacy to the elections prevailed; the Democratic Coordinating Committee instead adopted the strategy of discrediting the Nicaraguan elections at home and, especially, abroad. The elections, then, represented the final break in the FSLN-bourgeois alliance, as the bourgeoisie became "the political wing of the contra movement" (Gilbert 1988: 123).

Other than the FSLN, six parties participated in the elections, including three on the right. The FSLN, with Daniel Ortega as president and Sergio Ramírez as vice-president, won 67 percent of the vote and sixty-one out of ninety-six seats in the National Assembly. Because of the system of proportional representation, all participating opposition parties gained seats in the assembly.[14]

The Split in the Church

The bourgeoisie was not alone in its opposition to the revolution. The church hierarchy had become increasingly vocal in its attacks and also became aligned with the new, more conservative Pope John Paul II in opposition to the popular church and Liberation Theology. Although the church had supported the revolution against Somoza, the hierarchy was deeply suspicious of Sandinista intentions and of Marxism in general. By 1980, the split within the church, pitting the conservative hierarchy against the popular or revolutionary church, was obvious and the subject of heated political debate. The church and the bourgeois opposition resorted to religious symbolism, and so did *La Prensa*, in their attacks on the Sandinistas and in their efforts to mobilize public opinion against the revolution. Political confrontations between the two church factions, and Archbishop Obando's vocal opposition to the FSLN, were utilized effectively to gain international support, especially after Pope John Paul II's chaotic visit to Nicaragua in 1983, which was a public relations defeat for the FSLN.[15] In 1985, Archbishop Obando was elevated to cardinal and became one of the main voices of the opposition.

Still, the popular church maintained a strong presence in the revolutionary government, grass-roots organizations, labor unions, think tanks, and universities.[16] The most visible advocate of the popular church has been Father Miguel D'Escoto, Nicaragua's foreign minister under the Sandinistas. Although the Catholic church has remained strong in Nicaragua, it was the fundamentalist sects that grew the fastest in the 1980s, partly as a result of a dramatic increase in funding from U.S. missions after the revolution. The Protestant community also grew to about 20 percent of the Nicaraguan population, from forty-six to eighty-five denominations between 1977 and 1986 (Lernoux 1989: 390).

The majority of Protestant denominations are represented in the politically moderate Comité Evangélico para la Ayuda y el Desarrollo (CEPAD), which had supported the revolution and proved more flexible than the Catholic hierarchy in its dealings with the FSLN. As with the Catholic church, a number of Protestant ministers, influenced by Liberation Theology, supported the FSLN revolution and became involved in a number of progressive organizations.[17] The majority of fundamentalists, however, remained neutral or actively opposed to the revolution and were associated with the more conservative Conferencia Nacional de Pastores Evangélicos Nicas (CNPEN), which militated actively against the revolution and received significant support from U.S. conservative organizations.

International Actors

From the beginning of the revolution, the FSLN received important economic and diplomatic support from a number of foreign governments. The Soviet Union became the major military and economic supplier, especially after the escalation of the war and the decline in Western assistance, and Cuba provided education and medical personnel as well as technical assistance in a number of economic areas. Additional economic and technical assistance was received from Mexico (the largest aid donor until 1984), Italy, Spain, Canada, and the Scandinavian countries. Aid from the West, in fact, equaled the aid from the Eastern bloc.

Although unsuccessful in the effort to block a Sandinista victory, the United States remained the most important external actor in Nicaragua and the region. Although tense and difficult, U.S.-Nicaraguan relations were relatively friendly until the end of the Carter administration. With the election of Ronald Reagan, however, a shift in attitude occurred on both sides. Within Nicaragua, the U.S. commitment to the overthrow of the FSLN resulted in a hardening in the political position of the bourgeois opposition as well as in the government.

The U.S. Central Intelligence Agency had been funding the contras and organizing a larger paramilitary force since 1981. By 1984, the contras' Nicaraguan Democratic Force (Fuerza Democrática Nicaragüense, FDN) had grown into a well-organized and well-equipped military force led mainly by former National Guardsmen. The FDN's civilian leadership, recruited and paid by the United States, had little control over military planning or behavior on the field. Although the FDN never came close to a military victory and its leadership was never able to attain political legitimacy—both because of its ties to Somoza and its human rights abuses—the contra war was successful in undermining the revolution in several ways. First, the military draft generated enormous political opposition and a decline in support for the FSLN. Second, the war resulted in physical and economic destruction, which further undermined the Nicaraguan economy and increased dissatisfaction in all sectors. Finally, as resources were channeled into the military effort and away from social policies, many of the achievements of the first few years suffered reverses, and the expectations of the population for revolutionary transformation and benefits were frustrated.

In addition to supporting the contra war, the Reagan administration imposed a trade embargo against Nicaragua and used the influence of the United States to block development aid and credits from international institutions and other governments. According to Fitzgerald (1987: 197–200), the cost of U.S. policies was $301.3 million in production losses between 1980 and 1984 alone, before the escalation of the contra war. During the same period, he argues, U.S. military and financial aggression resulted in a balance-of-payments loss of $521 million. The Nicaraguan government put the total cost of military and economic aggression by the United States at $3.7 billion during this period (Gilbert 1988: 168). By any standard, the cost of U.S. economic and military aggression against any country in the region would be enormous, especially one, like Nicaragua, that had just experienced a destructive civil war and was in the midst of revolution. Central American countries are not only dependent on U.S. markets for their exports, they are also dependent on U.S. loans and aid as well as U.S. technology, parts, and consumer goods. Therefore, the impact of an embargo on consumer consumption, industrial production, and transportation would be drastic anywhere in Latin America, and especially so in the smaller and more dependent export-oriented Central American countries.

International actors were also the key to ending the contra war and the potentially dangerous conflicts between Nicaragua and its neighbors. U.S. policies designed to isolate Nicaragua and to use the neighboring countries for military and political purposes were countered by various regional efforts to lower tensions and resolve the various regional conflicts. The January 1983 initiative of the Contadora Group[18] was first rejected but then supported by the Sandinistas in an attempt to undermine international support for U.S. aggression. The Contadora proposals, however, required the cooperation of Guatemala, Honduras, El Salvador, and Costa Rica, and the United States was able to influence those countries and thus block the ratification of any regional peace treaty that would maintain the FSLN in power.

Central American peace efforts were revived in 1987 by the newly elected president of Costa Rica, Oscar Arias Sánchez. This time, conditions were more propitious for the implementation of a regional peace process: deteriorating economic conditions in all Central American countries after years of civil war and regional conflict; the Iran-contra scandal in the United States, which weakened the Reagan administration's efforts; the rise of democratically elected leaders elsewhere in Latin America; and deteriorating economic and political conditions in Nicaragua. Unlike the Contadora efforts, the new Central American peace process (in the form of the Esquipulas Accords signed in Guatemala) emphasized both domestic reform and regional security, in calling for democratization, an end to civil war in all Central American countries, and an end to all outside support for insurgent forces. It soon became obvious, however, that Nicaragua was the real subject of the process and of world attention. Although the Esquipulas Accords called for all countries to implement reforms and negotiations and to protect human rights, neither international nor regional actors seriously pressured the governments of Guatemala and El Salvador to live up to the accords in the same way, especially not after the 1990 Nicaraguan elections.

The Sandinistas supported the Arias plan, agreeing to negotiations with the contras in 1988 and the scheduling of elections in early 1990. Their main goal was to bring an end to the contra war and the U.S. embargo, which had so drained Nicaragua's energy and resources. At the same time, international support for the Nicaraguan revolution had been eroding, and momentum had shifted to the Central American peace process. Finally, there was a belief on the part of the FSLN that it would win the elections, even if by a smaller margin than in 1984, because of its extensive network of mass organizations and its control of state institutions. Still, the FSLN surprised both its supporters and its opponents by showing enormous flexibility and by going beyond the requirements of the Central American accords in organizing and preparing for the elections. The FSLN also allowed a number of international observer teams, especially from the OAS and the UN, to become involved in the preparations and negotiations that led to the elections.

THE 1990 ELECTIONS AND THEIR AFTERMATH

In contrast to 1984, the bourgeoisie decided to participate in the February 1990 elections. Declining U.S. and regional support for the contra war and internal political conditions provided incentives for the opposition to participate. Furthermore, the Bush administration, unable to revive Reagan's contra strategy, shifted its support to the domestic bourgeois opposition, with millions of dollars from the CIA and private conservative groups going to bourgeois parties and organizations. Liberal electoral reform laws, enacted by the FSLN in compliance with the Central American accords, at first led to political atomization, with over twenty parties registering with the National Council of Political Parties. Internal divisions within the opposition often resulted in two or three small parties claiming the same name and the right to bring in funding from external sources. The electoral reform law, in fact, allowed external funding of political parties, but 50 percent of such support was taken by the government for the purpose of financing the extensive personnel and training needs of the electoral process.

In mid-1989, fourteen opposition parties coalesced into the Unión Nacional Opositora (UNO), which selected Violeta Barrios de Chamorro as its presidential candidate and Virgilio Godoy (of the Partido Liberal Independiente) as its vice-presidential candidate.[19] Chamorro and Godoy represented opposing factions within UNO, but despite tensions and disputes between the two during the campaign, UNO won the presidential elections with 55 percent of the vote. The FSLN received 41 percent of the vote, defeating UNO in only two of the electoral regions. The UNO coalition controls the assembly with fifty-one seats, the FSLN has thirty-nine seats, and only two seats went to smaller parties (LASA 1990: 35).

The victory by UNO was a surprise to both supporters and opponents of the Nicaraguan revolution, not only because of the FSLN lead in many polls, but also because of the superior organizational and material resources of the FSLN. On the other hand, the deterioration of the Nicaraguan economy and the inability of the FSLN to end the war had increased dissatisfaction even in sectors previously supportive of the revolution. What seemed evident to all Nicaraguans was that a victory by UNO would not only bring an end to the contra war and the U.S. economic embargo but might also bring in fresh U.S. aid to reconstruct the Nicaraguan economy. To the extent that the U.S.-sponsored war and embargo contributed in a significant way to the erosion of support for the revolution, and to the extent that people perceived a vote for the FSLN as a vote for continued U.S. aggression, it can be said that the United States again had a decisive role in determining the course of Nicaraguan politics.

But the elections and their outcome, even if influenced by U.S. foreign policy, were a radical departure from Nicaragua's—and most of the region's—political history. For the first time, and under a revolutionary regime, Nicaragua experienced free democratic elections and a multiparty system. Unlike elections in most Central American countries, the February 1990 elections were conducted in an environment free of the state terrorism and human rights violations that continue to mark the political process in neighboring El Salvador and Guatemala. Just as important,

President Daniel Ortega and the FSLN honored the results of the elections and allowed for the transfer of power to the opposition.

The Sandinista revolution brought a number of fundamental changes that provide some basis for optimism about the meaning of the elections and the prospects for democracy in Nicaragua. A major structural change concerns the level of political institutionalization in a society with only two weak elite parties and no representation for the lower-income sectors. The Sandinista revolution incorporated the majority of the population into the political process and institutionalized popular participation through the FSLN and through mass organizations. The 41 percent vote received by the FSLN in the elections makes it the largest and best organized single political party in the National Assembly, one that represents the interests of the lower income sectors. There are also all kinds of research centers, labor unions, cooperatives, and a number of political parties on the right that emerged under Sandinista rule. Although most of those parties remain small, divided, and not fully institutionalized, it is to be expected that a few will gain strength through coalitions and through the continued working of the electoral process.

But even these achievements could be reversed by a future Nicaraguan government. The repression of mobilized lower-income or revolutionary sectors at the hands of the government has been common in the past, both in Nicaragua and throughout the region. The FSLN has tried to prevent such repression by maintaining control over the military, which has traditionally been used by the elite to exclude the majority of the population and to repress political opposition. Sandinista control of the military is designed to prevent just such a repressive alliance between the military and the upper class, as well as to prevent the use of terror against the FSLN and pro-FSLN organizations.

An interesting test of that idea took place a few months after the inauguration of President Chamorro. In July 1990, strikes against government policies resulted in violence that left four dead and dozens injured. After the army refused to use force against the strikers, the government settled the strike in consultation with the FSLN. Opponents of President Chamorro's "reconciliation" policy toward the FSLN, including her vice-president, pointed to her lack of control over the military as a reason for their preference for a tougher approach. Had military force been used to settle the strike, however, the number of deaths would have been greater. Throughout the region, the military is used mostly for internal repression rather than external defense. By maintaining control over the military, the FSLN might force the Nicaraguan government to resolve conflict by tools other than military force. By fundamentally changing the nature and role of the military, the Sandinista revolution may prove to have removed one of the major obstacles to democracy in Nicaragua.

On the other hand, FSLN control of the military may be used to give the FSLN veto power over government policies, create instability, or return the FSLN to power. To counter this threat, UNO has made important concessions to the contras and their supporters. In addition to the presence of thousands of still-armed contras in various parts of the country, Chamorro has allowed resettled contras to form autonomous rural security forces, which could in principle be used for political purposes and for creating an alternative paramilitary force to the FSLN-controlled military. The issue of military control, in short, will continue to be the focus of conflict and a source of tension in Nicaragua, with UNO's supporters and the United States trying to gain control of the military and the FSLN threatening to use its significant political resources to prevent control of the military by groups it does not trust.

Although the Sandinista revolution initiated important social and economic reforms, it was not able to solve the problems of widespread poverty and external dependence. The destruction of the Nicaraguan economy brought about by FSLN policies, the war, the embargo, and conflict with the private sector resulted instead in lower production levels, massive inflation, unemployment, and an overall deterioration of living standards. Continuing deprivation and austerity are not conducive to democratic politics and are likely to aggravate economic conflicts over very limited resources, especially land. Furthermore, the expectations of significant new U.S. aid and investment have not yet materialized, making the task of reconstruction much more difficult for UNO.

Another problem is the level of political polarization of Nicaraguan society. The right wing of UNO continues to demand the return of land to landowners, control of the military, and the formation of paramilitary forces. At the same time, more radical elements within the FSLN, including a number of mass organizations, will continue to demand structural change and more militant activism. Although both the FSLN and Chamorro have shown remarkable flexibility, polarization and inflexibility are still present in important sectors.

The FSLN remains the most disciplined and coherent political party while the UNO coalition is internally divided and state institutions are weak. The intrabourgeois divisions that characterized the Somoza period and prevented a unified bourgeois alternative are reflected today in the inability of UNO to adopt a coherent program. There is constant conflict between the right wing of UNO, which is more ideologically intransigent, and the moderate faction of UNO led by President Chamorro and her advisers. The right wing faction, in particular, is unwilling to rely on compromise, national consensus, and political institutions, pushing instead for its own narrow and exclusive interests in a more confrontational style. The balance of power between these two factions within UNO will be an important determinant of FSLN behavior and internal dynamics. Finally, U.S. policy will continue to be important in shaping Nicaraguan politics, especially as the 1996 elections approach with their potential for an FSLN return to power.

CHRONOLOGY

1909–1911: U.S. military force lands in Nicaragua. Liberal president Zelaya resigns. After negotiations with President Díaz, U.S. bankers come to own Nicaragua's National Bank, 51 percent of the railroads, and the customs collection.

1912–1933: U.S. Marines land to keep Díaz in power. U.S. forces used to install and maintain a succession of governments in power.

1927–1933: César Augusto Sandino fights against U.S. Marines and U.S.-sponsored presidents.

January 1933: U.S. troops leave Nicaragua, installing Anastasio Somoza as commander of the National Guard.

1934: National Guard kills Sandino and hundreds of his supporters.

1936: Anastasio Somoza takes over the presidency.

1956: Somoza is assassinated. His oldest son, Luis, takes over the presidency, and the youngest son, Anastasio (Tachito) takes over the National Guard.

1961–1962: Founding of the Frente Sandinista de Liberación Nacional (FSLN).

1967: Luis Somoza dies and Tachito takes over the presidency as well as the National Guard.

December 1972: Earthquake destroys Managua. Somoza misappropriates foreign aid funds.

1974: Founding of Unión Democrática de Liberación (UDEL). FSLN takes hostages at dinner party and obtains $1 million as well as safe passage and the freeing of political prisoners.

1977: Formation of Group of Twelve (Los Doce).

January 10, 1978: Pedro Joaquín Chamorro, editor of *La Prensa*, is assassinated on Somoza's order.

August 1978: FSLN, led by Edén Pastora, seizes National Palace and extracts several demands in exchange for hostages.

September 1978: Repression by National Guard intensifies. Spontaneous anti-Somoza uprisings. Government in exile formed in Costa Rica.

May 1979: FSLN final offensive. National Guard bombs urban areas.

July 17, 1979: Somoza leaves Nicaragua for Miami; assassinated in Paraguay in 1980.

July 19, 1979: FSLN marches into Managua.

January 20, 1981: Ronald Reagan inaugurated as president; suspends aid to Nicaragua.

August 11, 1981: Nicaraguan Democratic Force (contras) formed in Guatemala.

November 1981: Reagan approves $19.95 million for contras.

1982: U.S. blocks credits to Nicaragua from international organizations.

1983: Contadora nations start peace negotiations.

1984: U.S. mines Nicaraguan ports.

November 4, 1984: Daniel Ortega elected president of Nicaragua. Opposition boycotts elections.

May 1985: U.S. economic embargo against Nicaragua.

December 15, 1986: U.S. diversion of funds to contras revealed.

August 7, 1987: Central American presidents approve peace plan of Costa Rican president Oscar Arias.

March 23, 1988: Sandinista and contra leaders sign tentative cease-fire.

February 25, 1990: Violeta Chamorro elected president of Nicaragua as candidate of UNO coalition.

NOTES

1. The widespread interest generated by the 1979 Sandinista revolution is reflected in the volume and breadth of academic research and writings. Refer to Gilbert (1988) for a sample of works, only a few of which are cited in this chapter.

2. The slowdown in real GDP in 1955–1960 was caused by a sharp drop in world market prices for cotton and coffee after 1955, leading to important losses for producers.

3. In the 1950s, entrepreneurs associated with the Conservative elite established the Banco de América, and Liberal interests founded the Banco de Nicaragua. These two major economic groups dominated the financial field, and through it much of industry and commerce, until the 1970s.

4. In December 1974, for example, the FSLN kidnapped a number of high officials and Somoza relatives attending a Christmas party. When FSLN demands were met for $1 million and the freeing of prisoners (including Daniel Ortega), there was an enormous outpouring of popular support for the FSLN, in open defiance of Somoza.

5. Liberation Theology and the progressive church in Latin America emerged out of the broad institutional changes stimulated by the Second Vatican Council (1962–1965), designed to give greater responsibility to the laity and a greater role to the church in the defense of human rights and the promotion of social justice. The concept of Liberation Theology was first developed by the Peruvian theologian Gustavo Gutiérrez. See Gustavo Gutiérrez, *Theology of Liberation: History, Politics, and Salvation* (New York: Orbis, 1973).

6. Robelo's Movimiento Democrático Nicaragüense (MDN), the right-wing Partido Conservador Democrático (PCD), and the Partido Social Cristiano (PSC). See *NACLA* (1980: 16–17) for a detailed composition of the Council of State.

7. The National Directorate of the FSLN consisted of nine members, three representatives from each tendency: the Terceristas were represented by Humberto Ortega, Daniel Ortega, and Victor Tirado López; the GPP was represented by Tomás Borge, Henry Ruiz, and Bayardo Arce; and Luis Carrión, Jaime Wheelock, and Carlos Núñez represented the Proletarian tendency. The leading "pragmatists" in the National Directorate were Daniel Ortega and Jaime Wheelock; the "ideologues" were Borge, Ruiz, and Arce.

8. Except for the corruption and favoritism of the Somoza group, Nicaragua had one of the most unregulated economies in Latin America. The role of the state was minimal, and tax revenues as a percentage of GDP were the lowest in the region. In a visit to COSEP headquarters in 1989, I was surprised by the emotional defense of a free market economy and the absolute attack against government regulation of any kind offered by one of the leaders of COSEP. He also argued that under Somoza, everybody, from the poorest to the wealthiest, had worked together and benefited from the system. The gulf between this position and the reality of 1989 Nicaragua, as well as between this position and Sandinista goals, symbolizes the impossibility of maintaining the FSLN-bourgeois alliance, at least the segment of the bourgeoisie represented by COSEP.

9. Paulo Freire, *Pedagogy of the Oppressed* (New York: Herder and Herder, 1970).

10. Decapitalization refers to a set of practices designed to decrease production and investment, such as leaving land idle; neglecting trees, crops, and pastures; and selling off machinery and livestock. Capital outflow can result when loans obtained by producers from the government are converted into dollars and deposited in foreign bank accounts. Other practices, such as overpricing of invoices for the purchase of official dollars, also result in capital outflow.

11. Although growth rates in Nicaragua were higher than in the rest of the region, where GDP actually contracted by 3.1 percent in 1983 (Gibson 1987: 33), real GDP and export levels remained slightly below 1977 levels. There was barely any investment in commerce and industry, and production levels continued to fall, especially after 1983.

12. See Colburn's (1986) discussion of Third World revolutionary regimes.

13. The presidential candidate chosen by the United States was Arturo Cruz, a member of the Group of Twelve and former head of the Central Bank. Cruz withdrew, arguing that conditions did not exist for fair elections.

14. For a detailed account of the 1984 elections, see the LASA report, *The Electoral Process in Nicaragua: Domestic and International Influences*, Report of the Latin American Studies Association delegation to observe the Nicaraguan general elections of November 4, 1984 (Austin, Texas: LASA, 1984).

15. Although the Sandinistas expected the pope to oppose external aggression against Nicaragua and to praise the role of the popular church, the pope instead supported the position of the hierarchy and called for the resignation of priests from the government.

When the pope proceeded to address these topics at an open-air mass attended by more than half a million people (with the help of free government transportation), the crowd started demanding he address the contra war and support the popular church. His refusal to do so led to a shouting match between the pro-FSLN crowds and the pope, watched on television by millions in Latin America and other countries.

16. In a visit to Nicaragua in 1989, I was somewhat surprised, not only by the number of priests—or former priests—still in all kinds of leadership positions, but also by the deeply religious feelings expressed by supporters of the revolution. In a meeting with a well-to-do producer active in the National Union of Farmers and Cattlemen, for example, he and his wife described how they had become supporters of the revolution through participation in Christian study groups in the 1970s and how they resented the church hierarchy for its efforts to undermine the popular church. "Christians," according to a Jesuit in the Ministry of Education, "make much better revolutionaries than Marxists do."

17. For example the Evangelical Commission for Responsible Social Development (CEPRES) and the Servicio de Paz y Justicia (SERPAJ). For a more thorough discussion of both the Catholic and Protestant churches in Nicaragua, see Lernoux (1989); Laura Nuzzi O'Shaughnessy and Luis H. Serra, *The Church and Revolution in Nicaragua* (Athens Ohio: Ohio University, Center for International Studies, 1986); and Michael Dodson and Laura Nuzzi O'Shaughnessy, "Religion and Politics," in *Nicaragua: The First Five Years*, ed. by Thomas W. Walker (New York: Praeger, 1985).

18. The Contadora Group, composed of Mexico, Venezuela, Colombia, and Panama, met for the first time on Panama's Contadora island, thus the name Contadora. The purpose of the group was to draft a comprehensive peace settlement for the region. In 1985, the Contadora nations were joined by four other countries known as the support group—Peru, Argentina, Brazil, and Uruguay.

19. The UNO coalition included a broad range of ideological positions, from the Communist party of Nicaragua on the left to the Constitutionalist Liberal party (PLC) on the right. Most of the parties were small and new, united only by their opposition to the FSLN. Chamorro represented the more moderate faction of about six parties committed to reconciliation and unity. Godoy led the other eight parties, which were more strongly opposed to any concessions to the FSLN and much more inflammatory in their statements.

6

IRAN: ISLAMIC REVOLUTION AGAINST WESTERNIZATION

FARROKH MOSHIRI

Iran is perhaps the most important country in the Middle East.[1] It contains 10 percent of the proven oil reserves of the world and the second-largest deposit of natural gas. Its population is among the largest of the Middle Eastern countries, and it has a most important geopolitical position. Iran's natural resources and location have made it a point of contention between the superpowers, and for most of this century, concern about the Soviet Union led Iran to ally with the Western powers, in particular the United States. However, the Iranian revolution and its anti-Western outcome took Iran out of the orbit of the Western powers and seems to have pushed the country toward a nonaligned position.

A revolution in Iran would have been an important event solely for geopolitical reasons, but it is also significant as an unusual case that demands we refine our current theories of revolution (Bunce 1988). Additionally, since Iran fits within the general category of neopatrimonial states, a theory of revolutions derived from the Iranian case would be helpful in understanding the dynamics of revolutionary change in other neopatrimonial Third World countries. Finally, because of the importance of Islam in the Iranian revolution, it might augur "populist" revolts to come in the Middle East (Cottam 1986).

The Iranian revolution is best explained by an approach in which competition for resources among domestic groups is embedded in more general trends of super-power competition and changing patterns of global economic interaction. In partic-ular, specific changes in the nature of the state, the position of the elites, and the conditions of popular groups combined to create the revolution. The state sought to completely restructure the Iranian economy while maintaining the authoritarian structure of Iranian politics. It thus lost elite support, for the traditional economic elites gradually lost their economic position and were attacked by the state while the new oil and international-business elites felt politically excluded. In addition, political dependence on the United States and the aggressive economic policies of the state alienated nationalist elites and resulted in debt dependence and high inflation. Elite

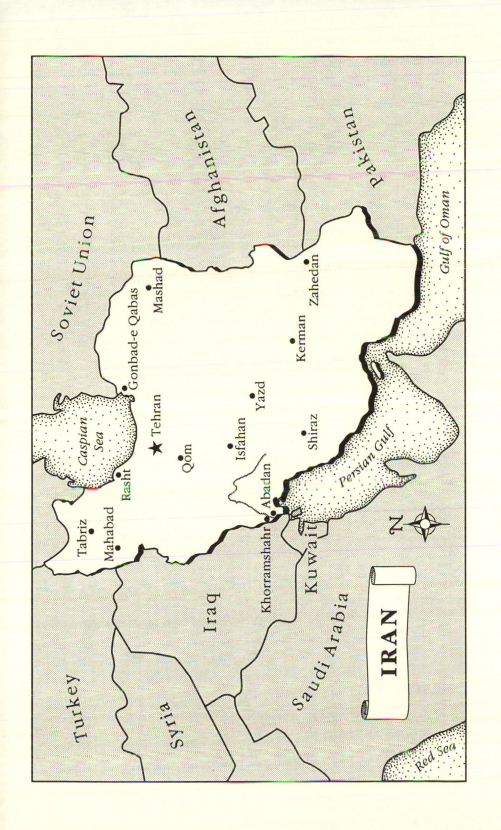

opposition was intensified and abetted by a mild economic crisis in the late 1970s. When high inflation undermined middle-class living standards and hurt portions of the working class and urban poor, the latter were increasingly mobilized to oppose the shah in open demonstrations. The state breakdown that then occurred is easily explained by the vacillating policies of the shah and the contradictory signals from the United States. When alienated elites sought to mobilize the populace against the shah, the state responded with erratic violence while bureaucratic and personal rivalries in the United States gave the shah different policy signals. The state apparatus and the armed forces, which were accustomed to operating under direct orders from the shah and whose institutional autonomy had been inhibited by decades of autocratic rule, could not respond effectively to unrest when they received mixed and indecisive signals from the shah. As opposition grew, the shah shrank from a direct confrontation between his armed forces and his people and fled Iran, leaving the way clear for the revolutionary opposition to seize power.

One can also explain the theocratic outcome of the Iranian revolution within an essentially resource-mobilization approach. The Iranian revolution, from an ideological standpoint, was the product of liberal, socialist, and religious movements (containing factions; Bazargan 1986). The liberal secular movement was led by the National Front, which had gained power in the 1951–1953 period under the leadership of Mohammad Mossadegh. The religious liberals under the leadership of Mehdi Bazargan worked under the banner of the freedom movement. The socialist parties in Iran were never truly significant, but they still represented a portion of the intellectual and working class communities. The religious movement contained both more extreme elements, such as Ruholla Khomeini and his radical interpretation of Islam, and more moderate ayatollahs, such as Shariatmadari. A resource-mobilization approach explains why the religious faction won. It had greater resources in four areas: ideology, manpower, organization, and leadership. The ideology was Shi'ite Islam, which appealed strongly to lower- and lower-middle-class migrants. The masses, and lower-level leaders, were absorbed into religious organizations such as Haya'ts and Mosques and received financial support from bazaar merchants. This grouping provided the religious opposition with more troops than the secular forces could possibly hope for. Finally, Khomeini proved to be a skillful, yet at times uncompromising, leader who gave constant direction to the religious opposition, which enjoyed the organizing efforts of a vast network of mosques, religious schools, and shrines. The liberals and socialists had neither such organization nor ideological appeal to the masses, as much of their organization had been destroyed by the years of police repression.

By 1978, then, a state without a solid class base of support, lacking any political legitimacy, and relying essentially on the army and foreign support was faced with an organized, ideologically motivated, and determined opposition.

PREREVOLUTIONARY STATE AND SOCIETY

The Character of the Political Regime: An Autonomous and Dependent State

The Iranian political regime is best explained as a neopatrimonial state (Goldstone 1986a). In 1921, Reza Khan, the commander of the Iranian Cossack Brigade, seized power, and in 1925, he became king (shah) and established the Pahlavi dynasty. World War II caught Iran unprepared, and despite its declared neutrality, Iran was invaded by the Allied powers. Reza Shah had to leave the country, and his son Mohammad Reza Shah became the king of Iran. Because of the position of Iran at the end of the war and constant interference by foreign occupying powers in its internal affairs, Mohammad Reza Shah began from a very shaky position, yet he gradually managed to concentrate power in his own hands. The historical process that led to this concentration of power began with a coup against the liberal-nationalist Prime Minster Mossadegh in 1953, supported by the British and the CIA. At the time, Mossadegh was involved in a bitter dispute with the Anglo-Iranian Oil Company over the nationalization of the Iranian oil industry. My own detailed analysis of recently released confidential State Department documents shows that the United States (in its support of the shah) was primarily motivated by military security considerations (Confidential U.S. State Department Central Files—Iran: Internal Affairs and Foreign Affairs, 1945–1954). Furthermore, analysis of the documents and other scholarly sources reveals that there was genuine internal opposition to Mossadegh, ranging from the Communists to feudal and reactionary elements. If one follows the minute-by-minute reporting from the United States Embassy during the 1953 coup, it is clear that the course of events was so uncertain that the initial CIA attempt had failed by August 17, 1953. Yet, a constellation of internal opposition forces had swung the balance in the shah's favor by August 19. The point for our purposes, however, is that Iranian nationalists viewed the United States as the subjugator of Iran. As Mossadegh put it in his memoirs, "It is obvious that the United States was not the defender of Iranian freedom and independence and wanted to use the pretext of the prevention of the spread of communism to gain from oil interests" (Mossadegh 1986). After the coup, the shah's government could never adequately claim nationalistic credentials, and thus an important component of a hegemonic ideology was lost to the Iranian government (Confidential U.S. State Department Central Files—Iran: Internal Affairs and Foreign Affairs 1945–1954; Mossadegh 1986; Zabih 1982; Roosevelt 1979; Cottam 1979.)

From 1953 to 1967, the shah had to rely extensively on the United States for military and political support. The special relationship with the United States allowed the shah to purchase any nonnuclear weapons system from the United States that he desired, but his critics charged that the wealth of the nation was wasted on useless weapons systems. By 1967, the United States had poured some $765 million into Iran in economic aid (of which some $464 million were outright grants), apart from establishing training facilities and missions for the Iranian military (Wormser 1981). In approximately the same time period (from 1950 to 1970, to be exact), Iran signed $790 million worth of military sales agreements with the United States (Ramazani 1982). In return, the shah provided exemptions from Iranian laws to U.S military personnel, which caused outrage among Iranian nationalists and brought Khomeini to the center stage of political activity (Bill 1988); permitted U.S listening posts (to spy on the Soviet Union); and provided support for U.S. foreign policy. From 1962 to 1977, Iran provided support for conservative forces in North Yemen, the United Arab Emirates, Oman, North Vietnam, Iraq, Syria, Pakistan, Zaire, and Somalia (Halliday 1979), and Iran's role in the Persian Gulf became especially important after British naval forces withdrew from east of the Suez in 1971. The Nixon doctrine, which wanted to rely on regional powers to pursue U.S. interests, further increased the importance of Iran to the United States. Although it is true that after 1971 the shah achieved some independence vis-à-vis the United States and even began supporting his own candidates in U.S. presidential campaigns (Bill 1988), his image was still one of a U.S. lackey. His attempt to create a nationalist ideology that emphasized Iran's imperial greatness could never succeed in the face of his relationship with the United States.

Although U.S. support cost the shah an ideological base of support, it nonetheless enabled him to move against his opposition. Once the shah had managed to partially suppress the liberal-nationalist movement in 1953, he turned on the landed upper class, and the land reforms of the 1960s were largely designed to destroy the power base of this class. U.S. advisers played a key role in planning the entire political offensive against the landlords, and the U.S.-supported prime minster Ali Amini took charge of the government. The land reforms, however, failed to achieve their other political purpose, which was to create a class of peasant property holders that would support the government. Robert Looney claims that the land reforms produced 800,000 landless laborers and over 1 million poverty-stricken peasants and that by 1976, 1 percent of "peasant property holders" owned one-third of the total "agricultural capital" (Looney 1982: 55). Eric Hooglund (1982) reports that among the beneficiaries of the land reforms by 1971, there were 1,938,728 heads of households who on average had received fewer than 7 hectares (17.5 acres, the land limit considered necessary by Iranian economists to maintain a family of five), while some 180,000 persons owned land-holdings of between 20 and 100 hectares (90–450 acres). The success of the land reforms differed from region to region. For instance, they were more successful in Boyer Ahmad (Loeffler 1986), but in Khuzestan and Turkamanshah, they were outright failures (Afshar 1985). The government also failed to provide credit for the majority of the peasants. The upshot was that while the government did succeed in destroying the power base of the large landowners, it failed to produce an extensive class of peasant property owners that would support it.

With the removal of the landlords and the suppression of the nationalist liberals as a power group, the regime then turned on the religious establishment in what is described as a "frontal attack" (Bill 1988). The regime's strategy here was a combination of co-optation and coercion. Although a religious corps was created that was loyal to the government, land-holdings of the Shi'ite establishment known as *waqf* were increasingly taken over by the government. More and more religious leaders were jailed, exiled, and tortured—including a number of Khomeini's supporters (Bill 1988; Arjomand 1984; Akhavi 1980; Keddie 1981; Fischer 1980; Abrahamian 1982; Moshiri 1985). My calculation from Ervand Abrahamian's analysis of Iranian guerrillas who were murdered between 1963 and 1978 is that over 76 percent of the total had a religious identification of "Islamic," "Islamic Marxist," or "Mujahidin" (Abrahamian 1980). Hence, the liberal nationalists, then the reactionary landlords, and finally, various religious organizations had come under attack by the government. In 1975, the formation of the state-sponsored

Table 6.1   Autonomy of the State in Iran, 1963-1977 (as measured by oil revenues as percentage of government revenues)

1963-1967	48.1
1968-1972	55.2
1973-1977	77.7

Source: From M. H. Pesaran, "Economic Development and Revolutionary Upheaval in Iran," in Haleh Afshar, ed., *Iran: A Revolution in Turmoil* (Albany, N.Y.: State University of New York Press, 1985), p. 24.

Rastakhiz party and the abolition of the nominal two-party system completed the process of state suppression of organized opposition. By 1978, the regime had managed to alienate all power groups in Iranian society but, simultaneously, had failed to produce any social base of support.

At the same time, the state's economic base had shifted from relying on internal taxes to oil income, which permitted the shah to be bolder with his policies of destroying the marginal elites and increasing police repression of the opposition. Indeed, oil revenues as a percentage of government revenues quickly rose from slightly under half to more than three-quarters (see Table 6.1). Meanwhile, the United States continued to support the shah until as late as November 1978 (Bill 1988; Brzezinski 1983; Carter 1982; Cottam 1979; Pahlavi 1980; Ramazani 1982; Rubin 1980; Sick 1985; Huyser 1986).

In sum, the series of events ranging from the 1953 suppression of the nationalist movement to the adoption of modernizing reforms, supported by the United States, produced a Janus-faced political situation. Domestically, the autonomy of the state (the shah) had increased considerably. At the same time, international dependence— oil revenues and U.S. support—had grown. As the state had lost its ideological appeal and had destroyed its traditional class base while failing to generate a new class base of support, the shah had to rely more and more on coercion and support from abroad. Thus isolated, the shah faced a difficult situation. His modernization process had produced a professional middle class that demanded political freedom and participatory democracy, and the religious elite and the secular liberal elite were outraged over the shah's increasing monopoly of power—as early as 1971, Marvin Zonis (1971) argued that Iranian elites were suffering from extreme paranoia and insecurity as a result of the authoritarian system of government. The popular groups, in particular the peasants who had migrated to the cities, were failing to adjust to a rapidly Westernizing culture, and many of them could not find adequate housing or health care.

Basic Social and Demographic Features: Westernization in Iran

One of the programs of the Iranian regime was to transform Iranian society along secular lines. As I mentioned earlier, the secularization program had the dual goals of increasing government control and of destroying the power base of

Table 6.2   Demographic and Social Data on Iran, 1960-1979 (selected years)

	Adult Literacy Rate	Urban Population (in 000)	Total Population	Students Abroad (in 000)[a]	% Women in Labor Force
1960	16.0	7,280	26,085,326		
1961				8,291	
1965					12.0
1966		10,350		10,390	
1970	36.9	12,348	27,150,000	13,575	12.8
1975		13,558[b]	33,390,000	33,021	13.6
1976				40,422	
1978			36,463,000		14.1
1979	50.0				

[a] U.S. statistics.
[b] 1973-1974 estimate.

Sources: World Bank, *World Tables* (New York, various years); UNESCO, *Statistical Yearbook for Asia and the Pacific* (Bangkok: United Nations, various years); *Iran Almanac* (Tehran: Echo of Iran, various years).

the religious establishment. In Table 6.2, I present some social and demographic data on Iran that indicate the speed of the process of Westernization in Iran, and the data indicate that Iran was becoming more urban, more literate, and more open to women's participation in the work force.

The figures on urbanization are particularly relevant. Farhad Kazemi (1980) shows that 35 percent of the increase in the population of cities in Iran between 1966 and 1976 was owing to rural-to-urban migration. Based on his work, I would argue that another 10–20 percent of the increase in urban population was the result of incorporation of rural areas into expanding city boundaries. Regarding the number of students studying abroad, I believe they were a strong source for the spreading of Western influence in Iran. In fact, many of the leaders of Marxists and other left-wing groups had been educated in Western Europe, and many others who did not later assume leadership positions also brought a new and Western outlook back to Iran.

Economic Change: A "Rentier" (Oil-Based) State and a Dependent and Dualistic Development

Table 6.3 shows that Iran's economic development plan resulted in uneven sectoral growth, as Iranian agriculture was neglected at the expense of industry and even services. The shah's economic policies also resulted in a heavy debt burden, which gave political ammunition to the opposition. Furthermore, as already

Table 6.3   Uneven Sectoral Development in Iran, 1963-1977 (mean annual growth rates)

	Third Plan (1963-1967)	Fourth Plan (1968-1972)	Fifth Plan (1973-1977)	Average (1963-1977)
Agriculture	4.6	3.9	4.60	4.4
Domestic Oil	13.6	15.2	-0.07	9.6
Industry & Mines	13.7	13.0	15.50	14.1
Services	8.0	14.2	15.30	12.5

Source: From M. H. Pesaran, "Economic Development and Revolutionary Upheaval in Iran," in Haleh Afshar, ed., *Iran: A Revolution in Turmoil* (Albany, N.Y.: State University of New York Press, 1985), p. 25.

noted, the government became increasingly dependent on oil income (see Table 6.1).

Political dependence again is a key underlying variable. The shah's choice of economic policies was largely influenced by the U.S. development theories of the 1950s and 1960s and by U.S.-trained advisers, such as Jamshid Amuzegar, who at one point was the Iranian oil minister and then became the Iranian Prime Minister in 1978 (Bill 1988; Amuzegar and Fekrat 1971). The purpose of the development plan was not only to incorporate Iran into the international economy but also to increase the political stability of the regime. However, as pointed out above, the political consequences of the development model were disastrous. The economic reforms destroyed the former class base of the regime but did not create a new one. Moreover, they resulted in massive rural-to-urban migration, and in the cities the traditionally minded immigrants felt far stronger support and influence from restive religious leaders (the *ulema*) than from the shah's government.

The data on the uneven sectoral development of the Iranian economy nicely explain the massive rural-to-urban migration. Not only had land reform failed to provide adequate credit and other support facilities to keep the peasants on the land, but also industrial growth offered many better opportunities. Income inequality between the rural and urban sectors increased considerably, and by 1978, the average peasant family made one-fourth the income of the average urban family (Afshar 1985: 68).

An examination of the data on debt, debt service, and the commodity concentration index supports my contention that Iran's economy was not only developing unevenly but becoming more integrated with, dependent on, and therefore more vulnerable to changes in the international financial system. A first look at the data on terms of trade and reserves indicates that the Iranian international financial situation improved substantially, total reserves increasing from $183 million in 1961 to $9,327 million in 1979. Yet Iran's debt burden also increased, from $871 million in 1965 to $7,126.3 million in 1978, and Iran's debt service increased from $76.5 million in 1965 to $1,151.10 million in 1978 (International Monetary Fund 1985, World Bank [various years]).

The political significance of the economic data is that left-wing and nationalist groups could point out that the country was not developing the way it should. The economic plan had failed to give Iran a diversified economy, and therefore a sense of independence from foreign control, so Iran's debt burden and heavy reliance on the export of one item became weapons in the hands of the opposition. An example of an alternative course of development advocated by the left was presented in the writings of Abolhassan Bani Sadar, an Iranian intellectual who became the first president of the revolutionary government. Bani Sadar advocated the exact opposite of the Shah's development plan, as he thought that Iran should cut its dependence on the West and develop its agriculture (Abrahamian 1982: 464). Liberal nationalists did not propose any specific economic plan other than advocating greater national control of resources; most of their concern was with constitutional rights and a nonaligned foreign policy. In fact, the economic development plan of Khomeini's Islamic Republic, and its constitution, emphasized the determination to reduce foreign control and to develop along self-reliant ways.

THE REVOLUTIONARY CRISIS

By 1978, the state's financial resources, with the exception of a minor recess in oil prices, had not decreased, but because of its dependent relationship with the United States, the state had lost a rather intangible, but extremely significant, resource: legitimacy. The Iranian state could no longer claim nationalistic credentials, and was viewed as a surrogate of the United States by many Iranians. Had the state's economic policies succeeded, it could have legitimized its existence by delivering economic rewards. However, the economic data show that the performance of the state fell far short of expectations. Double-digit inflation (a reliable estimate is 18 percent for 1978 [Abrahamian 1982]) and the unemployment rate (10 percent in 1977) created what some economists call stagflation. The effect on the salaried middle classes, mostly professionals, was considerable: Living standards could have declined by as much as one-third from 1973 to 1978 for many of these people. The government also increasingly failed to provide basic services such as electricity and cheap housing for the majority of the young urban population in the capital city. Electricity shortages in Tehran in the summer of 1977 became chronic, and real estate speculators had driven the price of housing so high that most young couples could not afford a decent apartment. At the same time, squatter houses in southern Tehran were developing, and since most of these squatters were frequently attacked by the mayor's office, discontent among them was building up. Bottlenecks in Iranian ports, soaring prices, and the unorganized and unplanned development of cities all indicated an overheated economy.

I must say here that the economic crisis in Iran in 1973–1978 was not owing to a simple lack of revenues on the part of government; it was the result of a distorting economic policy that had overstretched the state's oil wealth. The state was spending beyond its means and therefore falling into more debt and inflating prices while failing to provide basic necessities to the bulk of the population.

These problems were particularly concentrated in the migrant neighborhoods and shantytowns that sprang up to ring Tehran and the other major cities.

Principle Sources of Elite and Popular Grievances

The three principle demands of the elite were economic nationalism, political participation, and an end to the corruption of the royal family. Economic nationalism had been a battle cry of the opposition in Iran since the 1950s. Not only had the liberal Prime Minister Mossadegh pushed for economic nationalism and a nonaligned foreign policy, but the far right, pan-Iran secular nationalist party and Khomeini's radical Shi'ite faction had also emphasized that the shah was selling out the economic interests of Iran to the United States and the West. Khomeini had consistently opposed the shah's government for its oppression and its foreign dependence and had proposed his own brand of government, which would rest on the Koran, get rid of a useless bureaucracy, and be free of foreign domination (see "Islamic Government" in Khomeini [1985], as translated by H. Algar). Indeed, the constitution of the Islamic Republic of Iran makes economic nationalism a law of the country (Algar 1980).

The shah's establishment of a one-party system and the "blank check" given to SAVAK—the shah's repressive secret police, which attacked any opposition— had destroyed any avenues for peaceful change. As an early study of the Iranian elite has shown (Zonis 1971), even the establishment elite were becoming extremely insecure owing to the nature of their position within the structure of power. Furthermore, the shah's expenditures on military hardware and lavish celebrations had caused even his closest advisers to criticize him. By the late 1970s, the corruption within the royal family had reached unbelievable proportions, with the shah's sister Ashraf being involved in international drug trafficking (Bill 1988).

The principal sources of popular grievances have already been noted. The migrant peasants who became mobilized by the religious establishment generally suffered from bad conditions in the shantytowns. The people who had remained in the countryside bitterly complained about a lack of adequate credit, the continuation of landlord abuse, and the growth of multinational and government-owned corporations. For the professional middle classes, the usual democratic freedoms such as freedom of expression and assembly had increasingly become curtailed, and they were also hurt by the stagflation of the mid-late 1970s. Housing prices in particular had gone up considerably, to the extent that most middle-class couples could no longer afford a house. Meanwhile, Tehran was suffering from chronic electricity shortages.

The traditional middle classes, the bazaaris (a Persian term used for the traditional Persian merchants), who had played a key role in earlier anti-state revolts, were particularly badly hurt by the economic policies of the shah, which favored export-import firms. After 1975, the bazaaris became the target of the shah's anti-inflationary campaign, and Abrahamian (1982: 491) reports that up to 8,000 shopkeepers were thrown in jail, 23,000 were exiled, and 250,000 were fined. Although construction workers had benefited from the development policies, the 1977–1978 stagflation decreased their wages. Hence, long-term political grievances were joined by short-term economic grievances.

To these general social grievances must be added the special minority grievances. Of all the minorities in Iran, the Kurds were among the most anti-state, their grievances centering on their inability to preserve their own culture and language, their lack of economic development, and the generally high-handed policies of the central government. Iranian Kurdistan was a particularly underdeveloped region of the country. Illiteracy was as high as 85 percent in rural areas (1975 estimate), and there was only one medical doctor available per 20,000 people (Chaliand, ed. 1980). A major ethnic rebellion in Kurdistan accompanied the national revolution, but the goals of the Kurds soon came into conflict with the goals of the postrevolutionary central government, which wanted to impose conformity. The Arab, Turkoman, and Baluchi minorities inhabiting the southwestern, northeastern, and southeastern parts of the country had similar, yet not as severe, complaints, and these minorities also joined the anti-shah movement as the revolution gathered momentum.

It is important to note that major rural disturbances occurred only when a non-Persian peasant population was organized by an ideological party. In most of the countryside, the peasants remained apolitical until the very end of the revolutionary year. As in the Russian Revolution, rural peasants became politicized only where there was much commuting to the cities or where pro-Khomeini organizers moved to the villages (Hooglund 1982; Afshar 1985). In my own judgment, most of the peasantry remained inactive owing to a tradition of passivity (the only significant national peasant revolt in Iran's history was the communistic Mazdaki movement in A.D. 528), the lack of communication between Iranian villages, and the existence of gendarmerie (rural police) forces.

Revolutionary Mobilization and the Struggle for Power

Relative Significance of Ideological Forces: Shi'ism, Liberal Nationalism, and Leftist Ideology. Fundamentalist Shi'ite ideology and secular liberal nationalism were the most important ideological forces, but Shi'ite Islam provided more troops for the opposition. Less important ideological forces were ethnic nationalism and leftist ideologies (whose anti-imperialist component had obvious nationalistic appeal). The nationalist element of these ideologies assumed significance as the economic development model failed and more attention was focused on the dependent nature of the Iranian regime. There were a number of economic, cultural, migration, and personality patterns that explain why the Shi'ite ideology appealed to more people. First, the migrant peasants, who provided anywhere from 35 percent to over 60 percent of the increase in the urban population, generally relied on the religious establishment for financial and community support. A survey of dwelling units of poor neighborhoods in Tehran showed just how important the religious establishment was for the migrant poor. Health services and more mosques were the two most frequently cited demands of the urban poor (Kazemi 1980: 78), and the fact that there were over 6,000 mosques in Iran as early as 1974 indicates that there were plenty of centers where the poor could be mobilized (*Iran Almanac* 1974: 401, 409).

Second, the bazaaris, who had also been badly hurt by the economic policies of the shah, were closely associated with Shi'ite culture. Furthermore, they had the ability to organize people. The power of the bazaaris lay in their ability to appoint "neighborhood procession leaders," estimated to number 5,000 in Tehran alone. Furthermore, during the revolutionary year, the bazaaris provided financial support for families of the striking workers and the injured or killed revolutionaries. Third, Khomeini provided a key ingredient through his uncompromising leadership and his network of supporters. James Bill summarizes Khomeini's role as follows:

> From the holy Shi'i city of Najaf in Iraq and then from a small home near Paris, Khomeini directed the burgeoning opposition movement. He did so through an extensive personal network, the nodes of which were a large number of key religious and Bazaari followers. It is reliably estimated that over the years Khomeini helped educate hundreds of mujtahids and that during his last years at Qom over twelve hundred students had taken courses from him. The Khomeini network had been in place ever since his exile fourteen years earlier, and over the years it had absorbed and then distributed millions upon millions of dollars among the Ayatollah's followers and the impoverished masses who were his constituents. The Khomeini net was also used as a flexible communications grid to constantly transmit his ideas and teachings. When the revolutionary sparks ignited, this network was firmly in place and served as an extremely effective organizational medium for the movement. (Bill 1988: 238)

Statistics on the number of theology students in the madrasahs (theology schools) in Iran in 1973 indicate that there were some 3,100 theology students in Iran who studied in 111 madrasahs and that all of them were potential organizers (Akhavi 1980: 205). The general trend in the number of madrasahs, however, was one of decline, indicating on the surface the success of the shah's Westernization policies. In the Persian countryside, Khomeini's appeal was transmitted through the urban commuters (Hooglund 1982), and Hooglund's account, based on the province of Fars in southwestern Iran, indicates that in late December 1978, a majority of the peasants joined the opposition. Hooglund suggests that it was the declining power of the central government that caused the peasants to choose to side with the pro-Khomeini faction. Pro-Khomeini factions also gained control in villages near Tehran.

Although Islamic revolutionaries could rely on the mosques and bazaars to mobilize the masses, the left could rely only on the universities and the ethnic regions, which had little power to affect the broader national picture. A breakdown of the guerrillas who were executed by the authorities shows that the majority of the members of these organizations were college students. Accounts of the non-Persian countryside, such as the southwestern province of Khuzestan and the northeastern province of Mazandaran, indicate that left-wing parties launched peasant revolutions in such areas late in 1978 and early 1979 (Afshar 1985). It is important to note that the regions in which leftists won control were non-Persian and therefore not as responsive to Shi'ite cultural appeal.

In contrast to the leftist opposition, the liberal opposition appealed mainly to ethnic Persians. The leadership of the secular liberal opposition was composed mainly of Persian professionals from urban middle-class backgrounds (Abrahamian 1982: 254); the appeal of the religious liberal opposition was mainly to bazaar merchants, particularly in Tehran. Because of the extent of its social base, the liberal opposition presented a more realistic and serious threat to the shah's government than did the left. Yet, since most members of the liberal opposition advocated peaceful and nonviolent means of opposing the government, they were generally treated less harshly by the government than the leftists.

A Chronological Account. The revolution gathered momentum when the Carter administration applied pressure to loosen up the Iranian political system; beginning in 1977, "as Bazargan put it, Carter's election made it possible for Iran to breathe again" (Abrahamian 1982: 500). At first, the liberal and socialist opposition used nonconfrontationalist measures to oppose the government, and an open letter by lawyers in May 1978 set the stage for the moderate opposition's activities. That letter was followed by open letters by poets, leading opposition figures, and the writer's association (Abrahamian 1982: 502). An open letter by the leaders of the National Front in June 1977 summarized the popular grievances. The authors— Karim Sanjabi, Shapour Bakhtiar, and Dariush Forouhar—began by attacking the absolute power of the shah, and then they shifted to a criticism of the housing situation and police brutality. The letter finally ended with a demand for restoration of individual rights, freedom of the press, and freedom of association (Graham 1979: 255–256).

Abrahamian takes mid-November 1977 as the point at which the opposition shifted its tactics from open letters and protest notes to street demonstrations. When the clerical opposition took to the streets in response to an insulting newspaper article against Khomeini on January 7, 1978, the government responded with deadly force to the demonstration in the holy city of Qom and thus began a cycle of violence that ended in the overthrow of the government. In response to government use of force in Qom, and following the Shi'ite custom of commemorating the dead after a forty-day period, the major cities of the country became the scene of major demonstrations. As the government responded with force in Tabriz on February 18, 1978, another occasion for mourning the dead was created. For these forty-day-cycle demonstrations, the bazaar would close, the mosques would organize people, and the liberal opposition would use its networks to spread the news of upcoming demonstrations. Mashhad on July, 22, 1978, witnessed the first major working-class revolt (Abrahamian 1982: 512); the liberal and religious oppositions were now joined by the urban wage earners.

In responding to the national crisis, the government shifted between granting more liberties and coming down hard on the opposition. It finally decided to impose martial law on September 7, 1978, but the most heavily armed Middle Eastern army was unable to restore order. The martial law government failed to achieve its key goals, which were keeping the bazaars open, maintaining key supplies such as gas and heating oil, and banning political meetings in the mosques (*New York Times*, December 13, 1978).

A number of factors were responsible for the failure of the army. The command structure of the Iranian Army, which suppressed local decision making, and the make-up of the army were among the most important. Most army soldiers had been drafted from the countryside and had maintained their peasant culture. They were therefore responsive to the appeal of Khomeini's populist Shi'ism. Furthermore, demonstrators threw flowers on the army soldiers and addressed them as "brothers," so that after a while, the army's rank and file resisted opening fire on the demonstrators and the desertion rate reached as high as 5,000 a day. Sunday, December 10, 1978, was the turning point in the confrontation of the army and the demonstrators. Over a million people marched in Tehran on that day, and the government, which had forbade the demonstration, decided to pull its troops back, in part to avoid a possible refusal by the soldiers to open fire (*New York Times*, December 13, 1978). By this time, the shah had decided that he could not militarily rule the country (Bill 1988: 236), and he left on January 16, 1979, entrusting his government to the newly appointed Shahpour Bakhtiar, who had previously been a leading member of the liberal opposition. Between January 16 and Khomeini's return on February 1, the country was beset by further rioting and fighting. In particular, an attack on university compounds in Tehran by soldiers and the assassination of some officers of the imperial guard by the rank and file were among some of the dramatic events.

Foreign Influence

At this point it is important to discuss the U.S. role in the development of the revolutionary crisis. The Carter administration began pushing for granting more political freedoms in Iran in early 1977, and the U.S. Congress had also become concerned about mounting arms sales to Iran and the large number of U.S. advisers and personnel in Iran. There is also evidence that some people in the State Department might have been thinking along the lines of easing the shah out and replacing him with a more durable and legitimate government. However, once the revolutionary crisis started, the National Security Council and the State Department adopted different positions, which only contributed to the confusion of the reigning monarch.

The National Security Council favored a hard-line approach whereas the State Department favored a softer line. Carter himself was leaning toward the National Security Council line, but his ambassador in Tehran was following a policy of his own. Ambassador William Sullivan wanted to ensure a peaceful transition of power from the shah to a moderate but stable government and he had therefore begun contacting Khomeini supporters and the secular opposition. A number of Iran scholars such as Richard Cottam (Cottam 1979), also urged contact with the Khomeini faction in the hopes of obtaining a peaceful transition of power. While Sullivan was working to ensure a bloodless transition of power to the opposition, President Carter dispatched General Robert Huyser to Iran to coordinate the activities of Iranian generals to prevent a revolutionary takeover. Huyser's biggest problem turned out to be the inability of the Iranian generals to act on their own without direct orders from the shah (Huyser 1986). That problem, as I have stated, was indicative of the problems of a state structure in which, as a result of the tendency to have power concentrated in the hands of the shah, individual initiative and action were generally discouraged. Furthermore, it is now clear that a number of Iranian generals, including General Abbas Qarabaghi, who was the chief of staff, and Hussein Fardust, the shah's boyhood friend who later became the head of the revolutionary secret service SAVAMA, had joined the opposition before the final overthrow of government on February, 11, 1979. The principal problem, however, was that personal and bureaucratic rivalries in the United States and Iran led to increasing paralysis of the government in Iran at a time when Bakhtiar's besieged transition government needed firm support and direction.

THE REVOLUTIONARY OUTCOME

Factional Infighting

Any discussion of the outcome of the revolution must address the factional power struggle within the new ruling elite, which consists primarily of religious figures and technocrats. As of this writing, the eight-year-old war between Iran and Iraq has come to an end, and one reason for Khomeini's acceptance of a cease-fire on July 20, 1988, was the factional infighting that has beset the Islamic Republic ever since its establishment.

The infighting began in 1979 with conflict between the liberal/Islamic moderates, headed by then Prime Minister Bazargan, and the more extreme wings of the revolutionary Islamic party, headed by Bani Sadar and Muhammed Hussein Beheshti. After the resignation of the Bazargan government on November 5, 1979, the factional infighting continued between the fundamentalist wing of the Islamic Republican party and the left wing headed by Bani Sadar. Bani Sadar was finally ousted after a bloody confrontation between the left and the fundamentalist forces in January 1981. The most important leftist organization supporting Bani Sadar was the Mujahedin e Khalq, and that group's attack on the government followed a strategy that was based on (1) "destabilization, elimination of key figures, and the exposure of the regime's vulnerabilities"; (2) "direct confrontation, demonstrations, and strikes to mobilize the people"; and (3) "a mass uprising to bring down the Government" (Bakhash 1984: 219). In my own judgment, the fact that the revolutionary government responded decisively and did not hesitate to execute even children who were accused of having Mujahedin sympathies was only one cause of the Mujahedin's failure. More important, the Mujahedin failed because, by and large, it appealed to the same socioeconomic groups as nationalistic Shi'ism and for most of those people, some components of the Mujahedin's ideology and practices—such as (sexually) mixed safe houses, indiscriminate bombings and assassinations, and alliance with an enemy power (Iraq)—were unacceptable. The wave of assassinations and street battles conducted by Mujahedin members in 1981–1982 failed to bring the government down, and in retaliation, some 7,000 people were executed or tortured to death (Bakhash 1984: 223).

Once the leftist opposition was effectively destroyed (by 1983), the factional dispute within the Islamic Republican party (IRP) centered over the issues of the organization of the economy (in particular land distribution), foreign policy, and the enforcement of Islamic law (Abrahamian 1986). The faction with a more radical position on economic issues and foreign policy was headed by Ayatollah Khomeini, the president of the republic. The faction that was more conservative on social issues and foreign policy was headed by the speaker of the house, Hashemi Rafsanjani. In 1986, both factions agreed that the IRP was no longer an effective organization and decided to dismantle it. In June 1988, the *Iran*

Times reported that with the appointment of Rafsanjani as the commander in chief of the armed forces, it appeared that the power struggle had ended in favor of Rafsanjani (*Iran Times*, Friday, June 17, 1988). However, the signing of the cease-fire accord with Iraq three days later reflected the fact that the factional infighting had destroyed the ability of the Islamic Republic to pursue both the war and the rejuvenation of the economy. On July 20, 1988, Ayatollah Khomeini personally accepted the cease-fire in the "interest of the system." This admission reflected just how bad the situation had become.

The Resources of the Revolutionary Elite

The theocratic outcome of the Iranian revolution is easily explained by the resources at the disposal of the religious elite, namely, the mosques and religious students; The estimated number of mosques was 75,000 in 1982; the estimated number of religious students in 1980 was 1,500 for Qom alone (*Arabia—The Islamic Word Review* 1982). To those religious resources one should add the local committees and the bazaar networks; the network of personnel within the shah's secret service and army who joined the revolutionary government; the revolutionary guards, which had been formed as a counterbalancing organization to the U.S.-trained army; and Sazeman e Basij (Mobilization Organization), Foundations for War Refugees, and the various agencies involved with the reconstruction of the country and land reform such as Jahad e Sazandeghi, Crusade for Reconstruction, and the Dayereh-ye Amr be Ma'ruf va Nahi az Monker (Center for Combating Sin), which functioned as a morals squad. The government also relied on some 2,000 secret agents in the armed forces to gather information on the opposition (Bakhash 1984: 226, 243).

The government controlled the newspapers and television and radio stations after the "cultural revolution" in 1982, which pushed for ideological conformity. The universities were taken over by Islamic students after a series of bloody confrontations in 1979 and were not reopened until 1982. Major newspapers were confiscated, and the offices of the Freedom Movement, which was Mehdi Bazargan's party, were closed. The extent of the push for ideological conformity is evident from the government's attempts to encourage students to spy on their own parents. Islamic education has successfully transformed the new generation of Iranians who were born in the early 1970s and have had no adult exposure to the imperial system. The change in the educational system has been so successful that now "kids teach parents revolutionary values" (Spenser 1988).

Postrevolutionary Economy

The general picture of the revolutionary economy's performance, in my judgment, is a negative one. Two factors, the war with Iraq and continuing internal political arguments, in particular the debate between advocates of the free market and advocates of state control, largely account for the poor performance of the Iranian economy. Some statistics on the war and the worsening condition of the Iranian economy are instructive. Iran's gross national product (GNP) in 1986 was about $82 billion and per capita GNP roughly $1,690. These figures, in constant dollars, represent a substantial decline from prerevolutionary levels—the GNP in the mid-late 1970s approached $85 billion, and per capita income was around $2,500 (Spenser 1988). The cost of the war has been estimated to range anywhere from $250 million to $300 million a month, and each offensive is estimated to have cost the Iranian government close to $500 million (Chubin and Tripp 1988: 128). Despite these negative effects, the war and the imposition of an arms embargo sparked a native Iranian arms industry to supply the government with most of its basic small arms weapons.

A point of interest might be the pattern of Iranian trade. I have looked at the postrevolutionary trade patterns of Iran for the period 1979–1983, when the United States lost its position as Iran's leading trade partner, and the Federal Republic of Germany and Japan came to assume the number one and number two trading roles. West Germany and Japan were also able to maintain a correspondingly good political relationship with Iran. The United Kingdom, Italy, and the Soviet Union also filled much of the gap left by the decline in the trade with the United States.

The Iran-Iraq War

The Iran-Iraq war, which began with Iraq's invasion of Iran in September 1982, has been the most devastating war between two countries in the Third World so far. Iran and Iraq suffered casualties approaching 1 million, and Iranian cities became filled with injured and handicapped people. Moreover, the damage to the Iranian economy was severe. Each side blamed the other for the start of the war, but the goals of each party are quite clear. Iraq's Saddam Hussein saw an opportunity to gain regional hegemony by attacking a weakened, divided, and embattled Iran; Iran sought to spread its revolutionary message and to use the war as a means of reshaping its internal polity (Chubin and Tripp 1988).

Within Iran itself, the consequences of the war are obvious. Initially, the war helped the Iranian government suppress its opposition and rally the people around the flag. Victory in war became the single most important goal of the Iranian government, and various forces were created and mobilized to pursue war aims. New industries were created, and much of the economy's resources went to support the war effort. The war furthermore allowed the government to blame many of Iran's social and economic ills on the aggression by Saddam Hussein and his international supporters. The psychological impact upon the generation of Iranians who lived through war in one form or the other cannot be measured, but it is certain that the constant fighting, the missile attacks suffered by the cities, the displacement of a huge portion of the Iranian population, and the mentality of the war economy as a whole will have a serious impact on the Iranian population for many years to come. Information on Iran reported in *Middle East Reports* (January-February 1989) claims that reconstruction efforts have been severely hampered by the conflict between advocates of free market policies and advocates of greater state intervention.

CONCLUSION

John W. Limbert comments on the tragedy of Iran as follows: "A noble, creative, and humane spirit is no protection against political and social evils. Good people may get bad government" (Limbert 1987: 144). Over a million Iranians, or about 3 percent of the 1978 Iranian population, are dead or disabled because of the revolutionary struggle and the Iran-Iraq war. Over another million, or about another 3 percent of the population, has been displaced and perhaps will never recover from the ills of exile. The country's economic development has fallen back by some twenty years. Per capita income and all other indicators of improvement in conditions of living have declined. Iran's leaders, however, seem to have just now begun to understand the limits of their ideological zeal and to acknowledge the realities of global power. There is no denying that the shah's system was, by Western standards, a brutal system, but suffering and injustice have only intensified in today's Iran. The outcome of the Iranian revolution makes one careful about advocating rapid progressive change.

On the positive side, for the first time in a century, an independent and autonomous Iran has emerged. The regime that exists in Iran today can legitimately claim the support of the masses, and the Iranian government has been able to mobilize the masses and the population to an extent that the shah of Iran could never hope for. Furthermore, despite a complete lack of respect for human rights and the fact that the theocratic nature of the Iranian government must be accepted by all, there is a lively and diversified debate within the theocratic state. According to Ashraf (1989), there are three main currents of thought in today's Iran: the traditionalist element, which has a precapitalist quality to it; the liberal trend, which represents big capital; and the radicals, who have gained more power. The Iranian parliament has therefore become the scene of lively debate among these different factions.

For students of conflict and peace researchers, the lessons of the Iranian revolution are compelling. First, progress along the capitalist lines of development must take account of existing cultural and traditional norms. The shah's frontal attack on bazaar merchants and religious leaders produced fierce opposition rather than reform. Second, economic mismanagement that gives rise to corruption and inflation can alienate even former state supporters. Third, authoritarian systems that produce a growing number of professionals, students, and technical workers yet exclude them from political power create potential radical leaders for the opposition. Fourth, extensive dependence on foreign support can undermine state legitimacy. Finally, a regime that concentrates power in a single leader, with no social class base or bureaucratic loyalties, can crumble with remarkable speed when it encounters even a modest economic/political crisis.

POSTSCRIPT

August 1990 witnessed the occupation of Kuwait (a major financial backer of Iraq during the Iran-Iraq war) by hundreds of thousands of Iraqi troops. The Iraqi invasion followed the ruthless pattern of Iraqi behavior in the war against Iran. The international community, which silently watched Iraq's atrocities during the eight-year war (the Iranian name for the Iran-Iraq war), has only now begun to realize the mistake of financing the Iraqi war machine. Although Iraq was expelled from Kuwait, continued Iraqi militarism, and Iranian zeal to protect Iraq's Shi'ite population and confine its Kurdish problem, may lead to renewed Iran-

Iraq struggles. No matter what the final outcome may be, the situation in the Persian Gulf area in the wake of the Iranian revolution promises further conflict.

CHRONOLOGY

Early 1975: Amnesty International report labels Iran as "one of the world's worst violators of human rights."

Summer 1976: War on profiteers waged against bazaar merchants.

May 1977: Open letter by Iranian lawyers.

November 15, 1977: Demonstrations in Washington against the shah.

December 31, 1977: Carter calls Iran an island of stability.

January 7, 1978: Article attacking Khomeini is published in *Ittili'at.* As a result of Qom protest in response to the article, hundreds are killed.

February 17–21, 1978: Riots in Tabriz on fortieth day of Qom massacre.

February 19, 1978: Khomeini attacks Carter's human rights policy.

March 29, 1978: Fortieth day of Tabriz nationwide protest.

May 10, 1978: Nationwide protest.

September 1978: Major workers' strikes in Ahwaz, Fars, and Tehran.

September 7, 1978: Martial law is imposed.

September 8, 1978: Black Friday. Government uses helicopter gunships and especially trained commandos to kill an estimated 4,000 people. A major turning point in the revolutionary year.

September 9–11, 1978: Oil workers in Tehran, Shiraz, Tabriz, and Abadan go on strike.

November 15, 1978: Kurdish revolt begins

December 23, 1978: General strikes.

late December 1978: Negotiations begin with National Front.

December 30, 1978: Bakhtiar is appointed prime minister.

January 13, 1979: Estimated 2 million people march to demand Khomeini's return.

January 16, 1979: Shah leaves the country.

February 1, 1979: Khomeini returns.

February 9, 1979: Imperial guard is forced to retreat; street fighting continues until February 11.

February 1979: Mehdi Bazargan is appointed prime minister.

June 22, 1981: Bani Sadar loses his presidency.

September 22, 1982: Iraqi invasion of Iran.

May–March 1982: Iranian counteroffensives.

1984: U.S. restores relations with Iraq.

1985: U.S. initiative toward Iran begins.

1986: Iran captures Faw peninsula in southern Iraq.

1987: Iranian Army pushes to within ten miles of Basrah, Iraq's second-largest city.

July 20, 1988: Cease-fire accord is accepted by Khomeini.

August 2, 1990: Iraq invades Kuwait.

November 1990: Iraq accepts all Iranian terms for peace treaty; exchange of prisoners begins.

NOTES

1. The latest information on scholarly research on Iran can be obtained from the Center for Iranian Research and Analysis (CIRA), which is located at Rutgers University, New Brunswick, N.J. 08903. At this writing the latest book on Iranian-U.S. relations is by Bill (1988). Two useful accounts of the Iranian military are the memoirs of Robert Huyser

(1986) and those of the commander in chief of the Iranian armed forces at the time of the revolution, General Abbas Qarabaghi (1984). Graham (1979) and Mottahedeh (1985) provide excellent cultural backgrounds useful for political analysis. Abrahamian (1982) and Arjomand (1984) offer the most complete accounts of the Iranian revolution and society. Akhavi (1980) and Fischer (1980) provide excellent accounts of the religious establishment in Iran. Unfortunately, few works have yet appeared on postrevolutionary Iran. A valuable collected edition is by Nikkie R. Keddie and Eric Hooglund, eds. (1986), and Bakhash (1984) provides a more detailed analysis of the outcome of the Iranian revolution. The most recent collected edition on Iran is by Hooshang Amirahmadi and Manoucher Parvin, eds. (1988).

7

POLAND: NONVIOLENT REVOLUTION IN A SOCIALIST STATE

JAROSLAW PIEKALKIEWICZ

In August 1980, after a summer of strikes and unrest, the Communist government of Poland signed its Magna Charta with Solidarity, the first independent trade union in a Communist country, and granted it the right to exist. But in December 1981, sixteen months after the concordat was signed, the military staged a coup and reimposed absolutist rule. They were to have only moderate success and only for a few years. The general theoretical importance of these events lies in the questions, What were the causes of this particular workers' "revolution" in what purported to be a workers' state? Was the upheaval and its outcome unique to Poland or within the "normal" pattern of the theory of revolution?

Of course, the term "revolution" is used here only in a romantic sense, although the recognition of the independent union contradicted one of the major tenets of a Marxist-Leninist-Stalinist (totalitarian) state, that of the hegemony of the Communist party. The system became pluralistic, changing not only in degree but also in kind. Without any doubt, it was a "state breakdown" with a new system emerging. The process was arrested by a military coup, which, while not returning the polity to its previous state, prevented, and then only for a short time, further pluralization.

PRECRISIS STATE AND SOCIETY

One cannot understand the events of the 1980s without some knowledge of how Poles perceive their history. The story begins in tenth century A.D. with the acceptance of Christianity from Rome and not from Byzantium, thereby making Poland an intrinsic part of the Western world. By federating with Lithuania in the fifteenth century, Poland became a multinational and a multiconfessional state, so that toleration of divergent views became a political necessity and fostered a climate of pluralism. Poland also assumed the role of "defender of the faith," the

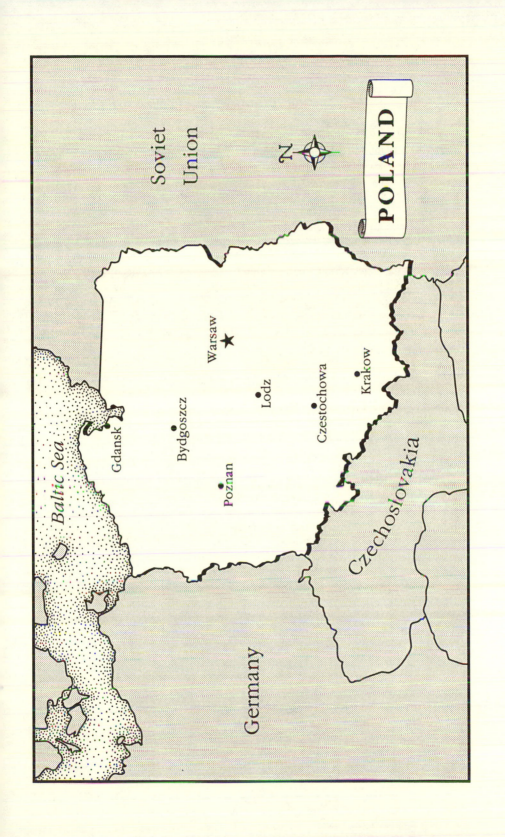

bulwark of the West, protecting it against succeeding invasions from the east: Mongol, Tatar, Russian, and finally Communist. But nearly constant warfare led to more and more privileges being demanded of, and granted to, the fighting men—the gentry—by the Polish kings. By the sixteenth century, the Polish-Lithuanian commonwealth—at that time the largest country in Europe—began electing its monarchs and became the second state in Europe after Iceland to have parliamentary rule.

But in the latter part of the eighteenth century, the Polish republic, with its highly decentralized system, fell prey to its absolutist neighbors who feared that the Polish freedoms would undermine their own strict rule over the populations of their respective empires. Poland was attacked and divided, in three separate partitions, among Russia, Prussia, and Austria. During the next 150 years of subjugation, the Poles fought many times for their freedom, becoming, like the Irish, the scourge of the status quo and participants in all the revolutionary movements of the day. During those years, the Poles developed and honed to a fine degree the art of conspiracy. Since Russia was the initiator of the partitions and since it occupied the largest part of Poland, in the national consciousness the struggle against that country became pivotal and was sung about in Polish arts and letters, so that each new generation was brought up in that spirit.

Only in 1918, after the defeat of Germany and Austria at the end of World War I and with Russia weakened and torn by revolution, did Poland again become an independent nation. But in 1920 it was once more mortally threatened from the east by a Soviet offensive as the Russians undertook to march Marxism-Leninism to the Atlantic. For the last time, Poles were victorious at the gates of Warsaw. "The bulwark of the West" still held, but not for long. In 1939 Poland, armed with little more than British and French guarantees of its borders, was invaded by Germany from the west and, in accordance with the Nazi-Soviet secret pact, sixteen days later by the Red Army from the east. The Poles, attacked on two sides and alone, held out for a month but then saw their country once more fall to partition. In both spheres of occupation, the Poles built an extensive underground state with a secret army (the Home Army, AK), after the Yugoslavs the second largest in Europe. The AK was loyal to the continuing prewar Polish government—the government in exile in London and a militarily participating ally of the Western Alliance. In 1944, when the Soviet Army fought its way into Poland, the Home Army attacked the German forces as the front progressed west. But as soon as the fighting passed certain areas, the NKVD (Soviet political police) would forcibly disband the AK units, arresting the officers and executing many. The largest AK operation was the Warsaw uprising, which broke out in that city on August 1, 1944, with the Soviets broadcasting calls to fight against the Germans and with the Red Army only some twenty miles away. Suddenly the Soviet offensive stopped, leaving the Germans a free hand to finish the Poles. Stalin's plans were working. British and U.S. requests for landing rights in Soviet-occupied territory, in order to supply the Warsaw forces, were denied. After sixty-three days of struggle with the Germans, in which 250,000 inhabitants were killed out of a population of about 1 million, the city capitulated (Zamoyski 1988: 368). On Hitler's order, every building still standing was blown up. Warsaw—

the Polish capital and the emotional symbol of the country—was totally destroyed, once again owing to a combination of German and Russian actions. By 1945, Poland's fate was sealed, as was that of the rest of east-central Europe, by the presence of the Soviet Army and military administration on its territory as well as by the Tehran (1943) and Yalta (1945) agreements between Churchill, Roosevelt, and Stalin, which consigned this region to the Soviet sphere of interest. Polish lands occupied by the Soviets in 1939, in agreement with Nazi Germany, were ceded to Russia, and Poland was rolled west like a mobile home to occupy some of the prewar German lands from which the German population was expelled.

This historical past would have made the establishment in Poland of any type of government coming from Russia extremely difficult. What legitimacy could such a government have? To this problem was added the nature and circumstances of the Polish Communist party itself. Orthodox Marxist and internationalist, not formed until 1894 when the non-Marxist Polish socialist movement was already well entrenched, the Communist party had little appeal for Polish workers and remained composed of intellectuals and minorities. One of its greatest ideological defeats had come in 1920 when the Polish workers fought with great determination against the "liberating" Red Army. Later, in 1938, on Stalin's orders, its most able leaders were executed in the Soviet Union for previously protesting the treatment of Trotsky, and the entire Polish Communist party itself was disbanded. When war broke out in 1939, then, the Polish Communists were leaderless and in disarray. But what was left of them, in blind obedience to their Soviet masters, embraced the Nazi-Soviet pact, which permitted the invasion of their country. After the German attack on the Soviet Union in 1941, the party was hastily reconstructed with most of its leaders parachuted into occupied Poland from the Soviet Union. By then, however, the AK had been fighting the Germans for two years and had the support of the vast majority of the population. By the end of 1945, the party had managed to garner only 65,000 members (Zamoyski 1988: 370) from a population of about 24 million (*Rocznik statystyczny*[1] 1980: 29).

When the war ended, the party by itself was in no position to capture power in Poland as it was too small in size, too alien ideologically, and viewed as a foreign (Soviet) tool, especially for having advocated the ceding of one-third of prewar Polish territory to the Soviet Union. It emerged victorious only through massive Soviet support in what amounted to a civil war, in both political and military spheres, which left many deep scars and put the Communists, despite their contrived victory, in a ruling position of questionable legitimacy—questioned at many times throughout the following forty years by a majority or at least a large number of the Polish people. I do not mean to imply that the Communists lacked support at all. Through skillful tactics and propaganda, mixing promises of social justice, rapid economic development, and economic prosperity with appeals to Polish nationalism, and through mass mobilization, especially of the lower classes and of women and youth, they succeeded in building a large enough and often even fanatical base to maintain their rule with only a residual Soviet backing. By 1948, they were consolidated enough to attempt, on Stalin's orders, to dramatically change Polish political culture. Their policy, employing mass political terror and mass mobilization and indoctrination, survived the death of Stalin in 1953 but ended in nearly complete disaster in the state breakdown in 1956, sparked by an armed uprising of workers and others in the city of Poznan.

The Communist system was saved by the "October revolution" of 1956, in which those of the leaders who were most identified with Stalinism were retired, Russian "advisers" were sent home, and power was transferred to more-moderate Communists, led by Wladyslaw Gomulka, former first secretary of the party immediately after the war, who had been imprisoned in 1948 under the accusation of "national deviation." Gomulka and his lieutenants were "victims" of Stalinism and, as such, could get substantial popular support in the country, which expected the new administration to introduce a large measure of democracy. In fact, Gomulka proved much more conservative, returning to orthodox Communist political and economic solutions as soon as he felt strong enough to do so. The only permanent gain of the October upheaval was the spontaneous decollectivization of agriculture, which the government did not dare or did not want to reverse, leaving this sector of the national economy, and about one-third of the population, outside of socialism. Ruling with a mixture of Communist conservative populism and Polish nationalism, and with a personal honesty—which did not necessarily extend to his subordinates, who became increasingly corrupt—Gomulka survived for fourteen years.

However, by the late 1960s, the system, both politically and economically, was grinding to a halt. The student and intelligentsia revolt of 1968 was temporarily stifled because it was not joined by the general population, but the regime collapsed finally, in December 1970 as the result of a violent workers' uprising in the Polish port cities, which broke out spontaneously because of increases in food prices. The government responded to the uprising with brutal suppression, and many workers were killed, which shocked the country. Gomulka suffered a stroke and resigned.

The new first secretary of the Communist party, Edward Gierek, was different than the previous leaders. As a prewar member of the French Communist party and a wartime member of the Belgian Communist resistance, most Poles regarded Gierek as a "realist" with a "Western" background. Gierek's new political orientation was to deemphasize ideology and to emphasize pragmatism and consumerism. The vehicle for this policy was to be Western loans, which with eventual prosperity the country would have no difficulty in repaying. Even if locked into the socialist camp, Poles were to be Western and wealthy. Important also was the propaganda of optimism and success, which after years of stagnation under Gomulka, but also in comparison to his bland style, felt like a fresh wind of oncoming spring. Relaxed ideological commitment was also to produce an artistic and scientific revival. The new policy, which was generally accepted by a population that had been waiting for a prophet to lead them to the promised land of Western prosperity, brought initial rapprochement between the Communist government and the Polish people and gave Gierek's rule some legitimacy.

CAUSES OF STATE CRISIS

The People

During World War II, the Polish nation was at the gates of hell. In 1938, prior to the war, the population of Poland was 34.8 million; by the end of the war in 1945 it was 23.9 million. The total number of Poles killed during the war and Communist takeover will never be known, but rough estimates put the figure at 6 million, mostly killed by the Germans but also with some substantial Russian contribution. Out of this number, about 3 million were Jewish Poles. The additional population reduction can be accounted for by the Poles who stayed outside the postwar borders of Communist Poland, both those who lived in territory ceded to the Soviet Union and those who remained in the West after the war.

The population decline naturally had a substantial impact on the social composition and on the economic and political development of the country. Socially and culturally, Poland became a highly homogeneous country of people almost exclusively from the Roman Catholic tradition, resembling that of Italy, France, and to a lesser degree, Ireland. The country had lost the linguistic and cultural diversity that had come from large Jewish, Ukrainian, Belorussian, and German minorities and that, over the centuries, had added so much to Poland's dynamism and its overall national development.

The decimation of the population as a result of the war, in combination with rapid industrial growth and the universalization of education and quick urbanization after 1945, leveled Polish society. Like other Communist countries, Poland became an employee community in which, outside of agriculture, most people worked in some way for the state. Class attributes developed, but not on the basis of private wealth. Instead, three factors—education, political position, and employment—came to decide an individual's place on the social ladder. Of the three, political position was the most decisive, and the people at the apex of the Communist party became the "new class" (Djilas 1957) and derived most of the fruits of production. They constituted the power elite. Below them came the intelligentsia—individuals with a university education who occupied "managerial" posts (not in the strict sense, but who managed varied aspects of society) and who could be further subdivided into old and new, and into humanistic and technical groups. The next group could be called the "clerical" class—those who staffed the vast state bureaucracy. These people generally had a high school education or less. The theoretical masters of the socialist state were the workers, in the name of whom the "dictatorship of the proletariat" was exercised, and this group could be divided into two subclasses: skilled and unskilled workers. At the bottom, in the national mind, because of their past serfdom, government propaganda, and the fact that most of the power elite were of this class but wanted to hide the fact, came the peasants, who, after the limited revolution of 1956, had won the right to own their farms. One of the essential attributes of class division is class antagonism, and this attribute certainly existed in Poland, most prominently between the workers and the power elite.

The postwar years also brought a vast shift from rural to urban centers. Although the industrialization and urbanization of Poland had begun in the nineteenth century, these processes accelerated considerably after the war, spurred by the Stalinist model of economic development. In 1938, 60 percent of the population of Poland made its living in agriculture; by 1979, only 22.5 percent remained in the agricultural sector. This tremendous change was accompanied by a dramatic growth of cities, which in 1938 housed only 30 percent of the population and in 1979 57.5 percent.

Between 1946 and 1978, the urban population increased from 7.7 million to 20.2 million (*RS* 1980: 29), but since the net rural-to-urban migration between 1951 and 1979 was only 3.9 million, most of the urban growth was fueled by a spectacular increase in the birthrate. Poles, aware of the population losses, and as if nature was reasserting itself, devoted themselves to having children and maintained a very high birthrate for years. In the first postwar decade, 1946–1956, the average birthrate was 20.4 per 1,000, and in the twenty years following the war, 1946–1966, the average was 16.9 per 1,000 (*RS* 1968: 36–37). As a result Poland's population increased between 1946 and 1979 from 23.9 million to 35.7 million, or 49 percent. This rapid growth meant that by 1980, over one-third of all Poles had been born after the war and that Poland had become a country of young people (in 1978, 63.7 percent were below the age of thirty-nine [*RS* 1980: 35]), and the majority of them lived in urban centers.

Poles, again like many other East Europeans for whom human calamities have come often, dote on children, especially male children. The devastation of war made them a priceless treasure, since males were more likely to have been killed and in 1946 there were 114 females for every 100 Polish males. Many grandmothers saw in their grandsons the image of a lost husband or lost sons. During the many years after the war when shortages persisted, parents would deny themselves the necessities of life so that their children could enjoy luxuries. The children were given the best of everything and promised a future of bounty.

The population losses during the war and the postwar rapid growth affected the economy in two major ways. At least until the 1970s, Poland experienced a labor shortage. Outside of agriculture only 40.8 percent of the population was in the labor force in 1960, the rest being mostly too young to work (*RS* 1980: 41). Combined with rapid economic development and the low productivity of labor characteristic of Communist countries, this labor shortage produced constant pressure on wages and a certain arrogance among the workers, who knew they could not be dismissed from work as they were the essential force for the economic development of Poland—the most important class for the well-being of the Polish economy. After 1970, when the postwar generation was reaching maturity, on average nearly 140,000 young people a year entered the job market, relieving the labor shortage but adding to the consumption pool (*RS* 1980: 52). A rapidly growing population, climbing wages, and the traditional ills of a Communist economy—faulty distribution, shoddy quality of goods, and lack of services and replacement parts—produced constant pressure on the market, especially with regard to consumer goods. The demographic changes also created a society of vigorous youth—radical and impatient; physically fit for the rigors of demonstrations, hardships, and violence; and sure of their own invincibility. They were less likely than their parents and grandparents to be satisfied simply by the government's promises of a better future. They wanted it now and were willing to fight for it.

The Economy

The spectacular postwar growth of the Polish economy cannot be denied. Between 1950 and 1978, national income increased nearly seven times, and industrial output increased sixteen times (*RS* 1980: xxxiii, xxxvii). What was before World War II a predominantly agricultural country that was slowly industrializing became, despite losing 38 percent of its assets during the war (Zamoyski 1988: 371), in a short twenty years a bustling, smoke belching, polluting, industrial giant. But what economists are apt to forget, and political scientists must be so aware of, is that growth of national income is not automatically translated into consumption for all.

After 1948, the Polish economy was structured on the Stalinist model and had three components. First, the so-called socialist sector—by far the largest of the three—was state owned and administered and encompassed most of the mining, manufacturing, transportation and communication sectors. Second, the cooperative component was composed of small workshops, crafts, services, agricultural circles (voluntary associations of private farmers), and some agricultural cooperatives. Third, the private sector included most of agriculture as well as some individuals in small craft and service enterprises.

The Stalinist model of economic development became the curse of the Polish people as well as of the Communist government. It was based on Stalin's theory of "socialism in one country," by which he subjected the Soviet Union to an inhuman pace of forced industrialization. According to this theory, capital was extracted from agriculture by keeping the prices paid to farmers for food low and from labor by paying only "subsistence wages." The resulting state surplus was to be invested and reinvested in industry. The exports of foodstuffs and of raw materials, even to the detriment of the population, were to pay for the importation of advanced Western technology. Collectivization—the confiscation of small private farms and combining them into huge agricultural enterprises run by the state—was to ensure the steady supply of cheap food and was also used as an instrument to drive the rural labor force into industrial employment. In order to achieve consistency, the whole economy was to be planned by the central authority, which would determine, in actual physical terms (since naturally the currency had no objective value), total production, distribution, and consumption. Nothing could or should be produced outside of the plan, which would set social as well as individual needs.

Theoretically, the Stalinist model sacrifices the well-being of one to three generations to the assumption that future generations will have flourishing and productive lives. For this reason, indoctrination and mass mobilization are imperative, but equally important is political terror against people who are or who are perceived to be breaking ranks. In terms of economic strategy, the industrialization is to proceed by the construction, first, of its traditional base—heavy industry and within it, the iron and steel industry. The creator of the theory, Stalin (meaning "man of steel") was most appropriately named. Originally, the total investment level was to be kept at approximately 40 percent of the national income, with 25 percent going to the construction of heavy industry. From the base of heavy industry, the expansion was to "trickle down" to light industry and eventually to the consumer goods industry and to agriculture to provide for a life of unlimited bounty—"to each according to his needs."

Apart from its success or failure in the Soviet Union, the blind application of the Stalinist model in Poland was a total and irreversible disaster. Poland lacks iron ore, so it had to import this bulky necessity from the Soviet Union—a distance of some 800 miles. Much of the steel went, eventually unprofitably, to armaments, shipbuilding, and the construction industry. The shipbuilding industry, concentrated around the cities of Gdansk and Szczecin, was started, according to one theory, to free Soviet yards to concentrate all their efforts on the construction of naval vessels for the expansion of the Soviet Navy. Polish-built ships, including those for delivery to the Soviet Union, were equipped with the newest Western technology, which Poland had to purchase for hard currency—as a result the Soviets had easy access to the latest Western state-of-the-art technology at no cost to themselves. New ships delivered to the Soviet Union were paid for in Soviet currency which, in turn, Poland had to use to pay for Soviet iron ore to make steel to make ships for the Soviet Union. Originally, the shipbuilding industry prospered, earning badly needed hard currency, because its lower labor costs meant it could successfully compete with British and U.S. shipyards. However, the appearance on the international scene of Japanese and eventually smaller Taiwanese and Korean competitors—with their disciplined, low-paid labor and extremely efficient management—made the international shipbuilding trade volatile. At the same time, the Polish working class began to demand a larger share in the declining pie, and the Soviets finished their major naval construction, which freed their own yards for civilian use. Polish shipbuilding then declined drastically, falling 41 percent by 1979 from its peak production in 1975 (RS 1980: 144).

Regarding the construction industry, nobody would deny that Poland desperately needed more transportation infrastructure, buildings of all kinds, and above all, housing for its people. But the heavy use of steel in this sector was, in large part, necessitated by design plans that grossly overemphasized safety and durability rather than cost-effectiveness. Steel was used when better and cheaper substitutes produced by the chemical industry could have been employed, and steel, like all the other raw materials for which there was really no effective accounting, was wasted in incalculable quantities.

The original and continuous focus on the heavy iron and steel industry consistently drew investments away from other aspects of economic development. Poland is rich in natural resources, which could, with intelligent use, produce a rich harvest for the country. Soft coal and other nonferrous minerals are prime examples. They can provide an excellent base for the chemical industry but when, finally, in the late 1960s that industry began to be built, part of it consisted of petrochemicals and had to be based on imported oil from the Soviet Union and from the Arab countries and Iran since Poland has practically no petroleum of its own. The ideological obsession with heavy industry resulted in destructive underinvestment in other branches of the economy: agriculture, forestry, consumer goods, housing, transportation, communication, services. The latter three had the addition of the Marxist bias against them as being nonproductive, because they do not produce "physical" articles. For the whole period 1950–1979, average investment in industry was 39.6 percent of the total investment, investment in building construction was only 4.1 percent, in agriculture and forestry 16.3 percent, transportation and communication 9.6 percent, trade 2.7 percent, communal economy 21.0 percent, and other investment 6.7 percent (calculated from *RS*

1980: 120). In the face of constant and substantial population growth, under-investment in transportation and communication gradually produced a tremendous overload on those two branches of the economy, leading to increased bottlenecks, which stifled economic performance.

Even a cursory glance at the transportation map of Poland reveals that the country is still sadly lacking in modern highways and that its railroad system, still the main means of moving goods and people, has expanded very little from 1939—or even from 1900, when Poland was divided among three countries and its railroad lines followed their international borders. Housing for people became a national disaster. Young married couples had to wait ten, fifteen, or even twenty years to be allocated an apartment, unless their parents or they themselves could pull strings or pay a lifetime's wages for a cooperative one. Agriculture, mostly in private hands since 1956, became a stepchild of the Communist system. People in it lived a life outside the industrial, socialist society, cultivating land by horse and riding by buggy, and they were "raided" by the government through compulsory deliveries of foodstuffs to the state. Outputs lagged far behind those of West Germany, or even the collectivized agriculture of East Germany, both situated on the same north European plain as Poland with comparable soil and climate (Piekalkiewicz 1979: 100). The postwar food shortages were never really eliminated, and for generations, Poles have lived in a constant search for food and for consumer goods. Obtaining the normal necessities of life, which is customary in a modern, industrialized European society, was either a privilege allocated by the government or a lucky find.

One more ideological folly of Marxist economics, and especially of the Stalinist variation, is the emphasis on new projects rather than on conservation and modernization of already existing units by replacing worn-out parts and machinery. The heroic revolutionary march forward does not permit restoration of the past, even if that is much cheaper and more economical. By the end of 1960, many of the enterprises constructed immediately after the war began to crumble, and some of the older machinery had seen "better" pre–World War II, or in some cases, pre–World War I, days. A major overhaul became essential when the old units started to break down and create serious bottlenecks in production. Also, the machinery and whole systems that had become undermined by age increased the level of industrial and other accidents, endangering life and limb. The life of the average Pole was becoming drabber and drabber and was often fraught with danger from industrial accidents and the unchecked pollution marring the skylines of cities, both large and small. Toward the end of Gomulka's period, some of the investment was diverted to renovation, and to increased expansion of housing and the consumer goods industry, but too little. The government's answer was to raise prices to bring supply and demand into equilibrium. Although perhaps economically sound, that decision, as we have seen, was disastrous politically. It brought bloodshed to Poland and led to the fall of Gomulka's regime. Gierek's solutions to the economic problems were radical. He decided that Poles could continue to expand their cake while eating it at the same time. Not slowing investment in heavy industry (e.g., building yet another giant steel mill in his home town of Katowice), he decided to revive Polish industry and to provide consumer goods by borrowing from the West. Western banks, awash in funds from the oil-producing countries, were only too eager to oblige. As a result, net Polish indebtedness to the West by 1975 was about $7.4 billion and by 1980 about $21 billion, or $538 for every Polish man, woman, and child (Lepak 1988: 90, 100).

The idea was, of course, to repay the loans with industrial exports to the West. That sounded feasible on paper. In practice, many investments were wasted by the purchase of the wrong systems (e.g., noncompatible computers or robotics); by mismanagement leading to the destruction of Western equipment; by investment in the wrong projects from the point of view of export; and finally, by considerable graft, which diverted foreign loans to private use. With few exceptions, even those goods for which there could have been a ready market in the West were of shoddy quality, deliveries were uncertain (among other reasons, because of Poland's transportation system), and packing was often careless, which resulted in excessive damage. Western buyers soon became dissatisfied and turned to Asian suppliers (Singapore, Hong Kong, Taiwan, South Korea, and of course, Japan). In Poland imports kept soaring while exports lagged (*RS* 1980: xliv, 305). By the mid-1970s, Polish plans were complicated by a general recession in the West, owing to rising oil prices, which dried up demand for foreign products. The only sure exports for which demand continued were foodstuffs and coal, the latter even increasing in value because of its substitution for oil. Pressed by foreign creditors, the Polish leaders tried desperately to increase the export of those commodities. Coal was to be obtained by any means, even if it meant forcing miners to do an inhuman amount of overtime, including work for long stretches of time without a break, which undermined their health and increased the number of accidents from exhaustion (Hamilton 1983: 255–258). The miners' increased pay could not be spent because of the shortages, even despite special allocations for the mining regions, and that fact added to the general frustration. Coal production increased substantially, from 140 million tons in 1970 to 201 million in 1979, or by 44 percent, and exports continued to climb (*RS* 1980: xxxvii, 317).

The exporting of coal assumed more and more priority over Poland's internal needs which created serious shortages of coal and other products in different parts of the country. The failure to satisfy internal demand for energy led, in the late 1970s, to prolonged brownouts and stoppages of industry. For a time, the shipbuilding industry found itself in the same predicament as coal mining, with tremendous pressure on management and labor to increase output and to shorten the time in which each ship was constructed. Production doubled between 1970 and 1975, from 518,000 to 1,023,000 deadweight tons, but declined again to 602,000 tons in 1979 for the reasons discussed earlier (*RS* 1980: xxxvii). An increased export of foodstuffs was achieved by reducing the amount of goods available on the open market, and what was sold in Poland was of extremely poor quality. The finer and more expensive commodities were shipped abroad. To make matters worse, net agricultural production declined by 2.7 percent between 1970 and 1975 and a further 1.8 percent by 1979, while over the same period the population grew by 2.8 million, or 8 percent (*RS* 1980: 215, 29). The elements did not favor the Communist government, and it had to cope with several years of very bad weather that resulted in wretched harvests. Nevertheless, the export of food rose by 38.7

percent between 1970 and 1975 and an additional 41.3 percent between 1975 and 1979 (*RS* 1980: 307). These measures were nothing more than desperate attempts to save a sinking ship, and by 1980 the economy had virtually collapsed, with the GNP per capita (measured in constant 1981 dollars) declining between 1978 and 1980 from $5,752 to $5,388 (*Research Project on National Income in East Central Europe* 1982: 22).

The Elites

Gierek and his cohorts still belonged to the tightly knit group of "old comrades"—ideological and physical survivors of Polish prisons, Stalinist purges of those who escaped to the Soviet Union, Soviet and Nazi concentration camps—a small group of fighters for what must have seemed at times an unobtainable but still a splendid idea. They had an understanding of one another, and despite their internal differences, they were likely to close ranks when challenged from the outside. In the 1970s, younger men penetrated this group of leaders, individuals who had joined the Communist movement only after the war and who carried out their "battles" for power in the security of a Communist-dominated Poland. One would expect their allegiance to be more to themselves and to the established order than to the "pure" and abstract ideas of their predecessors. For many of these new leaders, party membership meant only access to power and privilege—a managerial "country club."

Like the leadership, the membership of the Communist party also underwent substantial changes. It increased rapidly—reaching 1.1 million by 1960, 2.3 million by 1970, and nearly 3 million by 1978 (*RS* 1980: 25)—but even more striking were the changes in the class composition of the party. In 1945, the party was 61 percent worker, 28 percent peasant, and only 11 percent white collar. By 1960, the white-collar group had grown to 43 percent at the expense of workers, whose share in the ranks had dropped to only 40 percent, and peasants, whose membership had declined to 12 percent. The shifts in class composition are reaffirmed by statistics on education: Members with a completed or partially completed university education increased from a negligible number in 1945 to 15 percent of the party by 1978. In terms of age, the party membership generally became older. Between 1970 and 1978, the share of eighteen-to-twenty-four-year-olds decreased from 11 to 9 percent, and the top age bracket increased from 18 to 23 percent (*RS* 1980: 25). Thus, in 1978 the party was less worker in character and growing older, with its core firmly in the hands of the people who represented the new "managerial" class. Its original roots in the lower, working classes were growing more and more tenuous. From its revolutionary origins, it had become the party of rulers.

Several other factors led to a loss of prestige and effectiveness of the party in the 1970s. First, the loosening of restrictions on travel to the West, the signing of university exchanges with the United States and Western Europe, and increased Western tourism in Poland meant that Poles learned of the great and growing gap between their standard of living and that of people under "capitalism." Second, many Poles, but seldom those in sensitive party or government positions, could travel to the capitalist "paradise" and earn in a few months what they would have to toil for years to obtain in "socialist" Poland. To put it bluntly, now one did not need to be in the party to buy a refrigerator or even a car. Party membership was becoming less and less a privilege and more and more a burden. With popular hostility to the party growing and eventually with the declining economic conditions, its members, and especially those on the factory floor, were on the defensive. Naturally, recruitment of new members became more difficult, and many of those who remained in the ranks yearned for the return to the "good old times" when party members composed a highly privileged elite. That factor again contributed to a certain psychological isolation of the party.

Third, in a series of reforms begun in 1972 and completed by 1976, the composition and nature of local administration was dramatically altered. To provide greater central control, the size of the provinces was reduced, since they were deemed to be too powerful and too independent, and their number was increased from twenty-two to forty-nine. Also, executive power was taken away from the local government councils and given to professional administrators directly nominated by the prime minister or on his authority. The reforms were meant to streamline the administration and to increase its efficiency by the professionalization of its leaders. However, the elimination of the communes, the lowest local government bodies, and the clear separation of the legislative from the executive function in local administration resulted in the destruction of whatever little impact local participation had on central policies. Later, it would be very difficult to assess the nature and the magnitude of local dissatisfaction. The changes in the boundaries of local governments had to be followed by a corresponding restructuring of the party organization and of all specialized bureaucracies, such as the courts, the procuracy, the state control boards (state audit), state censorship, the army territorial headquarters, and various police and state security forces. Some of this restructuring followed the new division; in other cases, overbranching units were formed. The previous role of local government and the local party as the general coordinators of all government functions was lost because of this new hopscotch pattern of overlapping authorities.

The fourth and final factor in the diminishing of party prestige and effectiveness was the human aspect. Party and government officials were demoted or promoted and, in most cases, shifted to new localities, resulting in a vast migration of the ruling elite as well as of lowly bureaucrats. New and more office and living space had to be found—all under conditions of an already severe housing shortage and at the expense of local populations who had been waiting years for new housing and resented the "new families" jumping over them on the waiting lists. Many officials who were transferred from larger to smaller cities, with inferior schools and fewer consumer goods and other facilities, refused to move their families and commuted to work. Thus, they never identified with the territories given into their care. The reforms also disrupted previous networks of personal contacts, which no doubt sheltered local administrators against the pressure of the center but which also permitted them to quickly identify local troubles and to solve them by their own semiofficial local means. In retrospect, the reforms that were intended to bring more efficient controls to a country constantly boiling with dissent may have, in fact, contributed to the eventual inability of the central government to contain the crisis when it did come. They disrupted the well-established patterns of formal and informal rule, made the party and state bureaucrats angry by shifting them around, and created general and unbelievable chaos in the localities as well as in Warsaw.

Why then, in 1980, was Gierek not able or willing to call on the last resort of any government facing extreme crisis—the military? Although the army's allegiance to the established Polish state could not be doubted, unquestioned support of the Communist party, and even more of any particular party leader, could not be automatically assumed. In 1970, the Polish Army high command and especially its chief, Minister of Defense General Wojciech Jaruzelski, complained bitterly about the use of some army units against the rioting workers. Also, as in the case of party membership, the relatively elevated status of professional army men and women declined in relationship to the public as a whole. A career in the military became less and less appealing, especially since it was rare for professional military officers to travel to the West. They could never hope to travel as tourists, not to mention the chance to work and earn hard currency.

Uncertain as to whether the military would defend the government against the population, Gierek, on assuming power in 1970, created special mobile, militarized police units (ZOMO). Recruited from the general pool of military draftees but given very generous pay, these police units attracted the dregs of society. Begun with 30,000 men in the early 1970s, these units comprised 80,000 members by 1976 and 95,000 a year later, nearly one-third the size of the armed forces (Lee 1987: 166). The ZOMO competed with the regular military for men, money, and equipment and encroached on the military's monopoly of control of the means of armed combat. Undisciplined, rowdy, in dirty uniforms, and often drunk, its members were heartily disliked. In contrast, the military continued to maintain high professional standards and to see itself in its traditional role as the defender of the Polish nation.

The Counterelites: The Church, the Intelligentsia, and Skilled Industrial Workers

The most obvious and the most formidable counterelite in Poland was the Roman Catholic church. Apart from its own important role in the politics of the country, the church provided a base and substructure on which many other counterelites could flourish. From 1795 to 1918, while Poland did not exist as an independent state, the Church was the main vehicle for the preservation of Polish national culture and gave hope for the eventual resurrection of the Polish state. Traditionally, the church provided leadership and education for the peasants and later the workers. Most of the clergy was recruited from those lower classes, and like their people, Catholic priests were often persecuted and shared prison cells with other Poles. During World War II, the church stood with the Polish nation in its opposition to the German and the Soviet occupations and terror. The war only made the roots of Polish Catholicism stronger, which enabled it to endure the persecution during the worst years of Polish Stalinism. The church as an institution continued to function, and the terror against it created martyrs and strengthened the resolve of the faithful. After the limited revolution of 1956, the church became gradually, and more and more with every political upheaval, the only legitimate political force in Poland, accepted as such by all sides in the political conflict. Under the masterful leadership of a superb politician, Cardinal Wyszynski, the church became an arbiter between the government and the opposition, and by the 1970s, neither could manage without its cooperation.

The church in Poland is a large organization of close to 7,000 parishes with 14,000 churches staffed by a dedicated and disciplined army of about 20,000 priests (*RS* 1980: 27). It is led by three cardinals, two archbishops, and sixty-five bishops. It extends its influence even to the Polish armed forces, where it maintains a corps of army chaplains led by a bishop with the rank of colonel (Krajowa Agencja Informacyjna 1984: 10). It manages its own education system, capped by the Catholic University of Lublin, the Warsaw Theological Institute, and a number of seminaries. The last produce more priests than the Polish church can use, and some are sent to other countries, including the United States. The church teaches its message in 21,000 centers for religious instruction, which are supported by the government with public funds. In addition to its own press consisting of one weekly and one monthly for the general public and a number of religious publications, the church in Communist Poland had the only uncensored means of communication between the hierarchy and the faithful in the form of pastoral letters read every week in all churches. It had close ties to the lay Catholic association—Chrzescijanskie Stowarzyszenie Spoleczne—which in 1980 had its own small representation in the parliament (about four members). Of course, the final strength of the church comes from the support of the population, of whom 70–75 percent claim to be practicing Catholics, and from its place in Poland's political culture.

The church also has its own specific goals, of which propagation of the faith is the most pivotal. Although in the long run it may desire the complete destruction of communism in Poland, at times it has been as frightened by the prospect of a violent revolution and the ensuing social disorder as the government. Through the 1970s, the state and the church continued to confer with each other on a weekly basis, assuming to some degree coresponsibility for the destiny of the Polish nation.

In addition to the clergy, the ideals of Polish nationalism have been expressed by the secular intelligentsia, and scholars, philosophers, artists, and writers have identified strongly with the Enlightenment and the Western tradition. With the restoration of Polish independence in 1918, it was the intelligentsia who played the dominant role in politics, either in support of the government or in opposition to it. It was also this group that led the struggle against the German and the Soviet occupations. After the war, its influence was greatly diminished as much by physical losses as by the social revolution, which advanced people without education but with the proper "class" origin. Some people from among the intelligentsia, especially younger people, were attracted by the promise of social and economic justice and threw their lot in with the new regime. With the vastly expanded need for university education required by the rapidly industrializing society, the intelligentsia grew in size and complexity.

The intelligentsia is divided into two distinct groups. One, the technical intelligentsia, occupies managerial positions, stays apolitical, and serves whatever master rules in Warsaw. The second group, associated more with the life of research, university teaching, the arts, and the media, has continued to play the traditional and expected role of political commentator, critic, and carrier of the traditional Polish values. As Communist rule in Poland progressed, both groups exhibited increasing alienation from it. The technical intelligentsia became frustrated with the uneducated rulers' inability to comprehend even the simplest scientific and technical notions, especially the growing complexity of the economic system, which was showing up in gross inefficiency and waste. Within the ranks of the second group, even those who originally supported the Communists became disenchanted with the broken promises of their idealistic youth and could not accept the venality and banality of the system. These people were the most likely to find common ground with the workers. The growing radicalization of the intelligentsia and its rejection of the system became especially important in view of this group's specific role in the political culture.

Although the 1980 crisis eventually engulfed all of Polish society, central to that crisis, above all to its beginning, were the industrial workers, who became the party's most formidable opponents. Among them, leadership was often provided by the working class "aristocracy"—the skilled workers. Numbering fewer than 600,000 in 1964, the elite skilled work force increased to over 2.4 million in 1977—a fourfold increase in thirteen years (*RS* 1980: 60). Technically educated and often quite sophisticated with respect to their specific trades, these workers understood the growing complexity of technology better than the Communist leaders and the directors of their enterprises, the latter often chosen for political reliability rather than education. The workers became increasingly cognizant of their importance to the functioning of the economy and realized that economic success could not be achieved without their active and willing cooperation. Their skills, often highly specialized and requiring long-term training, provided them with protection from repression because if they were killed or imprisoned, their employer—the government—would have trouble replacing them. Their position was similar to that of the increasingly technically sophisticated workers in Western Europe and the United States in the nineteenth century, when the suppression of workers in these areas became economically counterproductive. Their importance to the economy was reflected in their wages, which grew faster than those of other workers or even the intelligentsia. They became well paid, which attracted able individuals to their ranks, but like the rest of the population, they had few things to purchase because of the lack of consumer goods. They accumulated large savings, which, ironically, would sustain them during the strikes. Many of them were graduates of vocational high schools, which in Poland, provided good general knowledge in addition to technical education. They knew Polish history and literature and identified with their country's nationalist tradition.

All workers, but especially the worker "aristocracy," deeply resented being treated as only a means of production. They were especially angered by the almost total lack of concern for their well-being on the job, which was exhibited by shortages of protective equipment and apparel and warm clothing, canteens, and warm food and, toward the end of the 1970s, by the greatly declining attention to job safety, which resulted in a growing number of accidents (Hamilton 1983). The pay for the disabled was a pittance, and if nothing else, accidents were dreaded for economic reasons. Unlike in more-established, older industrial societies, Polish workers, including the skilled ones, were of recent, and mostly peasant, origin. That accounted for their nationalism and deep Catholicism, which were reinforced by their own "worker" churches and parishes staffed by priests who, like themselves, were mostly of peasant stock. Many workers still maintained contacts with their families in the farming communities, and during strikes their cousins supplied them with food. All of these factors made the skilled-worker counterelite ready to assume leadership of the working class.

There were additional reasons why Gdansk, and especially its Lenin Shipyard, became a symbol of the worker movement. Authorities should have been warned in 1970 when the uprising in the coastal cities started there. In general, the characteristics of the workers in the shipyards were similar to those of the miners in Silesia. Both places had a high percentage of skilled personnel, but Silesia in southwestern Poland was favored by Gierek (who was Silesian and a former miner himself) and was much better supplied than the rest of Poland. The situation on the coast, and especially in Gdansk, was quite different. Despite initial promises and despite the fact that the blood of the shipbuilders in 1970 had brought Gierek to power, the leaders of that strike were persecuted and eventually removed from the yard (e.g., Lech Walesa was fired from his job as an electrician). Gdansk, as a port city, saw foreign tourists and sailors, who brought news of far-off places, often exaggerated their wealth and well-being, and seemed to have an endless supply of cash, for which the hardworking shipbuilders had to labor long hours. The supply of goods of any kind fluctuated greatly in the coastal communities, with an abundance in summer for the tourists and considerable shortages in winter when the region had to "pay" for its "oversupply" in the previous season, though the brutality of the area's winter climate necessitated a greater supply of calories than in the rest of Poland. The last was especially true for the people who worked in the open areas of the port or in the shipyards, both whipped by sharp north winds with a chill factor far below zero. Freezing ears unprotected by unobtainable mufflers went deaf from the noise of drills in the ship hulls. One believed the workers when they described this life as a hell on earth. In the shipyards, the workers also resented building ships for the Soviets. All of these factors made Gdansk and the Lenin Shipyard a likely spot for the birth of Solidarity and the center of the antigovernment worker opposition.

BREAKDOWN AND STRUGGLE

It is difficult to fix the time when the breakdown of the Polish system began. Was it as early as 1948, or did it begin in 1956? 1970? 1976? or in 1980? One could say that it started with the civil war and that the history that followed was a series of crises. But the Communists won the civil war, and in each successive crisis they managed to rescue their rule, even at times achieving a certain degree of support and stability (e.g., at the beginning of Gomulka's and Gierek's administrations). For reasons that will become evident later, it is convenient to start this analysis of the final disintegration of the Polish Communist system with the upheaval of 1976. On the surface, the workers' riots in Radom and Ursus were very similar to the 1970 events in the coastal cities. Initially, the government lost control since it did not expect such immediate and violent responses to the increase in food prices and had made no preparations to counteract such a reaction, a confirmation of the previous argument that the center was not in touch with the provinces. In both Radom and Ursus, workers won the streets, and in Radom, like their brothers in Gdansk in 1970, they looted and burned the party headquarters. A number of demonstrators and policemen were injured, and one man was killed, perhaps an undercover policeman, in what was most likely an accident. The police, spoiling for revenge and reinforced by ZOMO, went on a riot of their own, killing at least four people, arresting thousands of workers, and beating them severely (Andrews 1985: 18; Ascherson 1982: 113–114).

Although these events were similar to the ones in 1970, there were two important differences. First, workers in Ursus drove tractors onto and dismantled some of the rails of the line connecting the Soviet Army in East Germany with its supply base in the USSR. Rail traffic was disrupted for several hours, which showed the helplessness of the Polish government in such a situation and illustrated, pointedly, the vulnerability of the Soviets to events in Poland. The second difference was that when the government decided to make an example of the arrested workers by putting them on trial as a means to intimidate others, the policy backfired. Fourteen well-known intellectuals formed a committee for the defense of those arrested (Komitet Obrony Robotnikow, KOR), which collected funds for their legal costs and for support of their families, sent observers to the trials, and demanded amnesty and a parliamentary inquiry into police brutality—evidence of which came to light during the testimony of the accused and witnesses. KOR acted in a totally legal manner, publishing the names and addresses of its members, and in a way challenged the government to suppress it. Why didn't the government do so? The KOR actions were not illegal, and attacking the committee would have added an immediate political character to the trial, which the government wanted to conduct as a criminal case. It claimed that the prosecution of the workers was not because of their demands, which might have been justified and accepted had they been expressed through their trade union, but because of their disruption of the public order, which endangered lives and led to the destruction of property. It argued that no government could tolerate such behavior. KOR, while initially small in number, had from the very beginning great support from the Polish intelligentsia and from some in the liberal wing of the party. There was a general feeling that the workers had been brutally and unfairly treated by the police, so the organization grew, adding to its membership internationally known Polish scientists and artists. The government also knew that further terror would have been met by demonstrations and violence, and it could not afford that because of its increasingly difficult international financial position. In its own mind, its ability to obtain more hard currency loans was closely related to its human rights record, especially in view of the emphasis placed on the latter by President Carter when he visited Warsaw in 1977 (Lepak 1988: 101).

The significance of KOR is that it was the first independent organization to defend the rights of people who had been unlawfully arrested, yet it acted within the law. Thereafter, it had to be tolerated by the party leadership even if it was in opposition to some party policies. KOR was an example for other groups that sprang up all over Poland—some acting legally, others semilegally, and some began to issue underground publications. Soon the state, and especially its political police, lost the capacity to monitor and suppress all this activity. It resorted to harassment of KOR and other activists by raiding their apartments, arresting and detaining them, and justifying its actions by labeling those arrested "hooligans." But all this response showed was the growing impotence of the state and a growing split in its elites. Most important, KOR was an expression, for the first time in the history of Communist Poland, of the unity of interests between the workers and the intelligentsia.

The election in 1978 of a Pole to head the Roman Catholic church was at least a technical knockout to what was already a tottering edifice. Politically, for the Polish government the choice of Cardinal Karol Wojtyla was the worst possible one. The new pope, of working-class origin and once a worker himself, a participant in the anti-German resistance during the war, and a former professor of philosophy in the Catholic University of Lublin, was known in Poland for his stubborn, and eventually victorious, fight to establish a church in the new Communist-built city of Nowa Huta. Now the Poles had all the Vatican "divisions" on their side in their struggle against communism. The triumphant visit of the pope to his homeland in 1979 brought millions to his open-air masses and showed the people they had power in numbers and unity.

As the secular intelligentsia and the national church grew stronger, the economic resources of the state grew weaker. The government could no longer "buy" the population with promises of economic prosperity as it had done in the early 1970s. The net hard currency debt had grown to such a magnitude ($21 billion by 1980) that further economic expansion by borrowing from the West was impossible; by the late 1970s, Poland was desperately searching for additional loans just to service its previous indebtedness. To make matters worse, in 1975 the Soviet Union had increased its oil prices by 131 percent and prices for other raw materials by about 52 percent. Since Poland imported most of its oil and raw materials (especially iron ore) from the Soviet Union, it had been forced to begin exporting more of its products to that country instead of sending them to the West in repayment of loans. All factors combined to reduce the general standard of living and the government's ability to "reward" its supporters and "pacify" its opponents. It had to find additional budgetary savings by cutting expenses in social services, education, and the military (Lee 1987: 152–160). The growth in personal consumption and social services from 1970–1975, financed largely by Western loans, came to an abrupt halt. And it was not only that the Poles lived worse in 1979 and 1980 than they had in 1975, but fired by the constant propaganda promising them a spectacularly better life, they now felt cheated when the rhetoric failed to match reality.

At the beginning of summer 1980, the government, falling deeper and deeper into economic disaster, hiked the price of food. In the rash of strikes that followed throughout the country, both sides resorted to different tactics than in previous conflicts. The strikers, rather than demonstrating in the streets where they could be easily dispersed by the security forces, stayed in their factories, daring the government to attack them. They reasoned that it would be much more difficult and bloodier to dislodge them and that the government might be loath to destroy expensive machinery and buildings in the process. In Ursus in 1976, the workers had damaged imported equipment paid for with hard currency; in 1980, the government, with the party disintegrating and the military possibly about to refuse to be used against the people, did not feel strong enough to escalate the conflict. Instead, it chose perhaps the only route open to it—negotiation with individual factories and agreeing to wage increases. That tactic might have worked if 1980 had been 1976, but in 1980 strike committees throughout the country were in constant touch with one another to plan a strategy that would present a united front. The strikes continued, and the final blow was the strike in the huge Lenin Shipyard in Gdansk.

Perhaps to forestall possible workers' unrest, in August the management of the shipyard dismissed a "known troublemaker," Anna Walentynowicz, a forty-year-old crane operator—one of the leaders of the 1970 strike and since 1978 a member of the illegal Free Trade Union of the Baltic Coast. Almost at once the shift sat down on the job and was soon joined by a majority of the workers. Lech Walesa, also a leader of the 1970 events and a member of the same free trade union, who was originally dismissed from his shipyard employment and in August thrown out of his current job, climbed over the shipyard wall to give his active support. He was recognized immediately as one of those charismatic natural folk leaders and was at once elected to lead the strike. He and other strike leaders realized that the government tactics of piecemeal settlements were designed to temporize until the government regained its strength, later to take revenge on the workers and their leaders. The strike leaders therefore refused to accept wage settlements and continued striking in support of other workers.

Regional and national networks developed—the interfactory coordination committees, often based on the illegal free trade unions—and their symbolic center was in the Lenin Shipyard. The Gdansk strike committee was joined by five "advisers" from the intelligentsia who were spokespersons of a much larger group of "progressive" intelligentsia, and they assisted the strikers with their knowledge of Polish law and party affairs. Cardinal Wyszynski, primate of Poland, speaking for the Polish Catholic church, advised both sides to negotiate in good faith but also warned the government against employing violence. The government, fearing all-out revolution, decided to negotiate and sent delegations to Gdansk and another port city, Szczecin. It easily agreed to most economic demands but fought a bitter rearguard battle against the legalization of the independent trade union, Solidarity. Both sides recognized that such a step would be an abandonment by the Communist party of its position as sole ruler and, hence, a systemic change in the Polish political system. Eventual agreements signed on August 30, 1980, in Szczecin, a day later in Gdansk, and on September 3 in Jastrzebia, Silesia, did exactly that and marked the capitulation of the government. Solidarity's consent to recognize the "leading" role of the party, to abide by the principles of the Polish constitution, and to respect Poland's international alliances—meaning Polish ties to the Soviet Union—and its promise not to become a political party were all more of symbolic than of real value. Solidarity's victory was seen as complete at the time.

What followed was a tug of war between the two sides. From its inception in August 1980, Solidarity grew into a national movement, involving eventually not only workers but the whole society. By November, its membership was already about 8.5 million (Ascherson 1982: 201), rising eventually to 9 million (Andrews 1985: 202) out of a working population of 16.5 million and in comparison to a party membership of 3 million (*RS* 1980: 23). Solidarity had branches in all walks of Polish life. There was hardly a workplace or an office, including in the state bureaucracy, without at least some Solidarity membership. It developed a structure of organization based on the regional coordination committees topped by the National Coordination Committee of the Independent Self-Governing Trade Unions. It created its own leadership, in a number of cases dynamic and charismatic individuals elected by their peers who contrasted dramatically with the dour leaders of the bureaucratized party. Led by Walesa, who was acquiring international stature, these union leaders presented an image of a vigorous young force able to lead the Polish nation to a new and better future. They emitted an aura of self-confidence, excitement, and optimism, and the fever was caught by most Poles. The leaders were conscious of their power and knew that there was no way of returning to the previous political system, which is what made them careless and unprepared for what was to come.

While the party and Solidarity were battling with one another—the former declining and the latter growing in power—a third force was becoming dominant—the armed forces, which began to push to the center of the political scene largely unnoticed. The military's growth of power was epitomized by the increase of political functions by its leader, General Wojciech Jaruzelski. Minister of national defense since 1968, Jaruzelski became the Prime Minister in February 1981, and in October of that year he became first secretary of the Communist party. For the first time in the history of any Communist state a professional military man combined in his hands the leadership of the army, the party, and the state, and destruction of Solidarity was essential to his scheme to dominate the country. As prime minister, he filled vacancies at all levels of government with trusted military men, the most important of whom was General Czeslaw Kiszczak, who became minister of internal affairs and thus in control of the police and security forces. With Jaruzelski as the first secretary, the military also took over the leadership positions of the party. In what now appears to have been preparation for martial law, in the spring of 1981 Jaruzelski sent around the country teams of active-duty and retired military officers to assess the economic situation and to fight against "speculation." In September, combined army and police patrols appeared in all public places "to deter" crime, and in November, teams of military officers fanned out to hundreds of villages to identify "all negative developments" (Andrews 1985: 232–233). Finally, on December 13, 1981, the military took over, suspending all activities of the party, the state, and all social organizations, including Solidarity.

Initially, military control was plainly visible as twenty-one generals formed the Council of Ministers, and all important central and local government positions were filled by colonels and majors. In November 1985, however, the military tide receded, leaving only a few generals in crucial positions, and the day-to-day running of the government was turned over to civilian "technocrats." Solidarity was delegalized and replaced by a government-sponsored, new, "independent" trade union. It appeared that Jaruzelski had succeeded in obtaining absolute power, but he had done so only formally. Solidarity went underground and was often aided and abetted by the church. Martial law had struck an unprepared Solidarity and nation swiftly and had netted large numbers of opposition leaders. Enough, however, had avoided arrest and were able to direct activities from their hiding places. Solidarity remained mainly intact in the large enterprises, supported by a loyal working class, and the intelligentsia continued to provide advice, training, and communication. About 600 regularly appearing underground newspapers and magazines were being published, officially censored books were available, and banned films and plays were circulated on video cassette. Conspiracy was once again active in the land, and the volume of these activities was such that the secret police and the penal system could cope with only the tip of the iceberg. After the initial enforcement of martial law, terror was kept to a minimum, with Jaruzelski perhaps fearing armed resistance to his rule.

OUTCOME OF THE REVOLUTIONARY STRUGGLE

With no improvement in the economy, the growing Western debt—$39 billion by 1989—threatened to bring economic collapse, which would lead to mass civil disobedience. Jaruzelski had no option but to work with Solidarity, and in that decision he was aided by the call for reform made by the new Soviet leader, Mikhail Gorbachev. "Roundtable" talks in the spring of 1989 involved all political forces in Poland and led to legalization of Solidarity in April and to the elections in June. In these elections, Solidarity supporters won all but one of the seats in the freely elected Senate and all of the contested seats in the lower house, the Sejm. The roundtable agreement had reserved the majority of the seats in the Sejm for the Communist party and two "minor" parties, which were only fronts for the Communists. However, when President Jaruzelski selected his minister of the interior, General Kiszczak, to form a new government, the two Communist allies deserted and joined Solidarity supporters, giving them a majority in both houses of Parliament. Jaruzelski had no option but to choose a Solidarity candidate, Tadeusz Mazowiecki, as the new prime minister. Thus, with the formation of a coalition government dominated by Solidarity supporters, the transfer of power to the opposition was completed. It was only a question of time when, in preparation for future free elections, the Polish United Workers' party (the Communist party) dissolved itself (by February 1990) and reformed into two separate social-democratic parties. The triumph of Solidarity stunned even itself. The "revolution" has entered its final stage, but its ultimate victory could be in jeopardy if Poland cannot halt its continuous economic decline. If not, there will be fresh strikes and the threat of violent confrontation between the rulers and the disaffected. If that should occur, one should not discard the possibility of yet another military coup.

ANALYTICAL CONCLUSIONS

The final question is, then, What were the causes of the Polish revolution of 1980–1989? Some, which one may call the subjective ones, were specific to

Poland. Others, which could be called objective, fall more in the category of general conditions leading to the collapse of any regime. The post-war Polish Communist government had to face a constant problem of legitimacy. Its ideology and its whole political culture were identified with Russia, a traditional enemy of Poland and a country the Poles considered inferior and despised. The government's inception was rooted in a civil war, which the Communists would have lost without substantial Soviet aid, and in the terror of the Stalinist period—both leaving deep scars on the Polish national psyche. The top leadership was of only mediocre quality, as Stalin had the most able among the Polish Communists killed and the ones left were individuals educated in the hard knocks of life rather than through formal schooling. They accepted Marxism-Leninism as a dogma and had trouble adjusting to changing circumstances, many produced by their own policies of industrialization. On the opposite side was the Catholic church, with its special position within the Polish nation, and the Communists could neither destroy it nor use it for their own purposes. The church provided a wide base for secular dissent, and was firmly anchored in the peasant origins of the contemporary Polish society.

Despite formidable obstacles, the Communists came close to being broadly accepted a few times. Many Poles were attracted to the Communist message of equality; to the policies of industrialization and general economic development, so overdue in the country; and to the argument of necessity of alliance with the Soviet Union in defense of Polish western territories obtained from Germany after World War II. But in the end, the Communists always failed.

At their own peril, they ignored the new objective conditions created by the demographic, social, and economic changes that took place during the thirty-three years of Communist rule (1948–1981). After World War II, the Polish population grew spectacularly, creating a country of young people who did not remember war deprivation and who demanded economic prosperity combined with freedom to decide about their own lives. Most of them went to live in the cities, leaving older people to tend the farms. Expansion of educational opportunities led to a flowering of the intelligentsia, the traditional leaders of the nation, now more and more of peasant or worker origin. Society became less divided by class and, because the country had lost its minority groups during and after the war, very homogeneous—Polish and Catholic and generally united in a hatred of communism.

Economically, the system deteriorated from bad to worse. Continuous investment in nonprofitable heavy industry starved other sectors and resulted in an agricultural system unable to feed the population, a transportation system inadequate to move the raw materials needed and the goods produced, a communications system that failed to facilitate identification of solutions to the growing complexity of demand and supply, and services too meager and too inefficient to distribute the products or to repair those already in use. Failure to invest in the cities despite the fast-growing urban population denied many of the city dwellers decent housing and other amenities that one would expect in a highly industrialized country. The urbanites must have been in an almost constant state of rage, subjected as they were to shortages of almost everything—food, electricity, gas, water, busses, street-cars—while being given government propaganda proclaiming success.

State fiscal problems of the kind that exist in the free market economies cannot plague the centrally planned communist systems. Planning is done in physical terms, and prices are strictly controlled. The Polish state budget always showed a surplus (*RS* 1980: xlviii), hiding the huge subsidies to unprofitable enterprises and to support consumer food prices (but not private farmers). The crisis was indicated by the expanding discrepancy between growing consumer demand, owing to increasing population and steadily advancing monetary income, and the sluggish supply for the internal market, which with the relatively constant prices resulted in rapidly growing personal savings and de facto psychological devaluation of money. (Personal saving calculated per capita and in 1960 zlotys was 1960, 544; 1970, 3,083; 1979, 7,894 [*RS* 1980: xlviii]). This monetary "prosperity" of individuals who could not enjoy its fruits in terms of consumption was bound to produce an acute sense of frustration. The government was unable to remedy the situation because the growing foreign debt owed to the West and to a number of Communist countries, including the Soviet Union, meant it had to withdraw goods from internal consumption to export them abroad. It finally became impossible to pay even the interest on Poland's debts without drastic reductions in the standard of living.

Another problem for the Communist regime was the changing character and fragmentation of the ruling elite. What was in the 1960s and even early 1970s a top elite of "old revolutionary comrades" of lower-class origin who were, in their own simplistic way, devoted to the cause became toward the end of the period a group of white-collar professional politicians who cared more about their own careers than about "building communism." In times of trouble, this new elite split easily, some even joining the opposition. The military elite, its leaders being men who had survived exile during the Stalinist years, was always more professional and nationalistic than communistic. At the crucial moment the military took over instead of defending the tottering edifice, deemphasized ideology, and thus made the transition to the opposition smoother.

The counterelites—the Catholic church, the intelligentsia, and the skilled workers—united in opposition to communism and grew in sophistication, directing the struggle of the huge majority of the Polish nation by combining trade union strike methods with the Martin Luther King strategy of civil disobedience. The revolution would have succeeded in 1980 if it had not been for the threat of Soviet invasion, which gave the Polish military an excuse for its takeover in 1981 to "save the nation." Eight years later, in 1989, Gorbachev made the difference.

The processes identified by Goldstone as leading to a revolutionary situation—fiscal strains on the state, elite alienation and divisions, and mounting popular grievances owing to economic frustrations among a young and growing population—were thus all clearly present in Poland from the late 1970s. These conditions led to ever-greater deterioration of the legitimacy of the Communist regime and repeated clashes with opposition groups. Yet a violent revolution was avoided. As Soviet support faded, the Communist government accepted more and more of the opposition's demands, eventually ceding power.

The Polish "model" of peaceful revolution from communism provided the inspiration to other people living under Communist domination, especially in central Europe and parts of the Soviet Union. The Poles proved that Communist totalitarianism could be overthrown without a shot being fired—"by the power of the powerless" (a phrase coined by the present president of Czechoslovakia, a playwright, Vaclav Havel). Poland is thus the pathfinder, and the success or failure of its post-Communist government will also set an example.

CHRONOLOGY

1795: The last of three partitions of Poland among Russia, Prussia, and Austria. Poland ceases to exist as an independent state.

1918: Poland regains its independence.

1920: Polish-Soviet war.

September 1, 1939: Poland is attacked by Germany and sixteen days later by its ally the Soviet Union. In a month, it is defeated and occupied by the two powers.

June 1941: Germany attacks the Soviet Union, which joins the Allies.

August 1–October 3, 1944: Polish Home Army (AK) fights the Germans for two months for control of Warsaw while the Soviets stand by and watch. Poles are defeated, and the city is totally destroyed.

1945: Poland is "liberated" by Soviet troops. Imposition of the pro-Soviet Communist government begins, followed by armed opposition (civil war), which is finally defeated with Soviet help by about 1950.

1948–1956: Construction of the Stalinist system in Poland.

1956: Workers' and general uprising in Poznan. Polish October, a limited revolution, brings a "liberal" Wladyslaw Gomulka to power.

1968: Students and faculty protest in all universities. Protests suppressed. Many people arrested, dismissed from studies and work.

December 1970: Workers' uprising in the coastal cities of Gdansk and Szczecin. Brutally suppressed (as many as 500–600 workers killed by the security forces). Gomulka replaced by Edward Gierek, who attempts to revitalize the economy by borrowing from the West.

1976: Workers' antigovernment riots in Radom and Ursus are suppressed. Workers accused of violent crimes and put on trial. Small group of intelligentsia forms KOR (Komitet Obrony Robotnikow, Committee for the Defense of the Workers).

1980: After a summer of strikes in many Polish cities, the government capitulates in August and signs, in Lenin Shipyard in Gdansk, an agreement legalizing an independent trade union, Solidarity.

December 1981: The military, led by General Wojciech Jaruzelski, who is also prime minister and first secretary of the Polish United Workers' (Communist) party, declares a state of war (Polish constitution did not have the provision for martial law). Takes over power in a military coup, suspends Solidarity, detains many of its supporters, but also replaces the Communist party.

November 1985: Jaruzelski ends the state of war and nominates a government of civilian party and nonparty technocrats.

1989: Renewed series of strikes and general unrest. Jaruzelski calls in February for roundtable talks, to include all political forces in Poland. Agreement is reached in March to legalize Solidarity and hold semifree elections in June.

June 1989: The opposition, united under the banner of Solidarity, wins all its allotted seats but one. Jaruzelski nominates a military general to head the government, but the minor parties desert the Communist coalition and join Solidarity. Tadeusz Mazowiecki, chosen by Solidarity, becomes prime minister, thus formally ending Communist rule in Poland. The revolution is completed.

NOTES

1. Statistical Yearbook of Poland. Hereafter *RS*.

8

AFGHANISTAN: STATE BREAKDOWN

ANWAR-UL-HAQ AHADY

In April 1978, a military coup overthrew the regime of President Mohammad Daud in Afghanistan and brought the People's Democratic Party of Afghanistan (PDPA) to power. The PDPA is a Marxist-Leninist party, established in 1965, that advocated a revolutionary socioeconomic and political transformation of Afghanistan. Consistent with its long held views, upon the assumption of power, this party quickly introduced programs aimed at the regulation of marriage and wedding expenses, eradication of illiteracy, cancellation of rural debts, and more equal distribution of agricultural land in Afghanistan. The radical nature of these programs, the haste with which they were prepared, and the incompetence of the PDPA cadres, in combination, led to a countrywide rebellion against the PDPA government later the same year. The PDPA's resort to coercion intensified the cycle of violence in Afghanistan, resulting in a likely collapse of the PDPA regime, which led to the Soviet invasion in December 1979.

The Soviet invasion transformed the conflict into a major international crisis. In addition to the general international sympathy for the Afghans, the governments of Pakistan, the United States, Egypt, Saudi Arabia, Iran, and China actively supported the Afghan resistance against the Soviet occupation. The escalation of the conflict forced the Soviets to send into Afghanistan an army of over 120,000 soldiers, at a cost of billions of dollars. Similarly, the U.S. opposition to the Soviet move resulted in the allocation of billions of dollars in military and economic aid to the Pakistan government and the Afghan resistance (the Mujahideen). Over 1 million Afghans have lost their lives in the war, and another 5 million have sought refuge in Pakistan, Iran, and the West. Although the Soviets, under the Geneva Accords signed on April 14, 1988, agreed to a complete withdrawal of their forces from Afghanistan by February 15, 1989, the upheavals of the previous ten years created such a revolutionary situation that even with the withdrawal of the Soviet forces, the conflict is unlikely to cease.

Although the Afghan conflict has attracted the attention of numerous scholars, journalists, and politicians, little effort has been made to analyze the struggle in

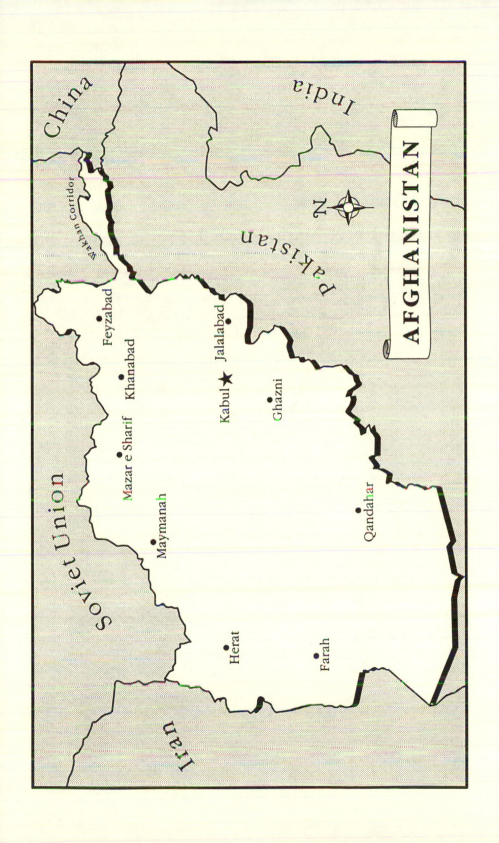

terms of concepts and theories of social revolution. The object of this chapter is to remedy this deficiency. More specifically, this chapter deals with the following questions: What were the salient characteristics of state and society relations before 1978? What were the causes of the crisis of state that led to the PDPA attempted revolution? Why did the PDPA attempted revolution fail? What issues, groups, and ideologies were involved in the revolutionary mobilization in Afghanistan? Why has the anti-PDPA rebellion taken on an Islamist character? What are the consequences of the state breakdown in Afghanistan?

PREREVOLUTIONARY STATE AND SOCIETY

In 1978, Afghanistan was a multi-ethnic nation of over 17 million people, with the Pushtuns accounting for over 50 percent of the population. With the exception of a few Hindu, Sikh, and Jewish families, the entire nation was Muslim. Although ethnic heterogeneity was a major source of conflict, Islam provided a unifying common denominator. However, the Sunni-Shi'ite identification in Islam was divisive. Over 80 percent of the Afghans were Sunni and less than 20 percent were Shi'ite.

With a GNP per capita of $160 in 1978, Afghanistan was a severely under-developed country. Although the capitalist mode of production was beginning to gain momentum, most villages were engaged in subsistence farming. Large land-holdings existed in a few provinces, but more than 60 percent of all farmland was owner operated (L. Dupree 1979: 147). Agriculture absorbed about 70 percent of the employed labor force and contributed about 60 percent of the GDP. Animal husbandry was an important traditional sector of the economy. Although industrial output accounted for 20 percent of the GDP and absorbed about 17 percent of the employed labor force, large-scale industries employing 1,000 workers or more were non-existent. Fresh and dried fruits, cotton, lamb skins, and rugs constituted the traditional major items of export. In the late 1960s, natural gas emerged as the major export item (all to the Soviet Union) and it accounted for $16 million in revenues in 1969 and $39 million in 1977, 10 percent of the government's total receipts. The public sector, which dominated services and industry, accounted for 23 percent of the GDP in 1977 (UNESCO 1984: 47, 56).

Social indicators portray a dismal picture of life in Afghanistan in 1977. Only 10 percent of the population was literate, and less than 30 percent of the school age children attended any school. Life expectancy remained at 40 years, and only one doctor and one hospital bed were available for every 17,246 and 4,020 Afghans, respectively. Despite this unimpressive array of socioeconomic statistics, the Afghan people had experienced tremendous socioeconomic changes since the 1950s, and these changes had dramatically altered the relationship between state and society.

From the founding of the Afghan state in 1747 by Ahmad Shah until the 1950s, Pushtun tribes were the major participants in national politics in Afghanistan. Ahmad Shah's empire was basically a confederation of Pushtun tribes, and he depended on the tribal chiefs, particularly the Duranis, for his army and assigned them rent-free land in return. Ahmad's personal charisma combined with the opportunity for further conquest, particularly in the rich land of India, which usually resulted in a huge bounty for his army, perpetuated this arrangement between the state and the Pushtun tribes. Tribal *jirgas* ("assemblies"), not the state courts, resolved individual and communal conflicts in accordance with the Pushtun code of ethics, and the state intervened very little in the social life of the Pushtun tribes. Ahmad's successors (his son and grandsons) maintained similar relations between the state and the Pushtun tribes until the end of their rule in the 1830s (Kakar 1979: 93–94; Shahrani 1986: 31).

Despite the change of dynasty in 1839, relations between the state and the Pushtun tribes did not alter. Both Dost Mohammed and Shir Ali depended on the tribes for their army and allowed considerable autonomy to the tribal leaders in return (Tapper 1983: 30–34). Only in the 1880s was the state able to reduce its dependence on the Pushtun tribes when the monarch, Abdul Rahman (1880–1901), created a nontribal standing army with the help of British subsidies, which enabled him to centralize his authority. Consequently, the state was able to reduce the power of the tribal chiefs and *jirgas*, and it created state courts to enforce the Sharia (the Islamic law) and collect taxes (Kakar 1978: 195). Despite his success in reducing the power of the tribal chiefs vis-à-vis the state, Abdul Rahman could not alter the dominance of the Pushtun tribes in Afghan politics, and he faced numerous rebellions, which forced him to enter into alliance with some tribes in order to defeat others (Kakar 1979: 168).

This type of relationship continued until the 1920s when King Ammanullah decided to create modern, centralized state institutions and to abolish the privileges of the tribal chiefs, especially the Mohammadzai aristocracy. His sociopolitical modernization program alienated the tribes as well as the religious establishment and led to the 1929 rebellion that resulted in his ouster (Poullada 1973: 160–166). That rebellion once again established the primacy of the Pushtun tribes in Afghan politics. To appease the tribes and the religious establishment, Nadir Shah and his brothers reversed the sociopolitical reforms of the 1920s and built their dynasty (1929–1978) on the support of the Pushtun tribes and the religious establishment. They also established close links with local notables throughout the country. Upon his assumption of power in 1929, Nadir Shah and his brothers closed the schools for women; introduced a strong Loya Jirga (Grand Assembly) composed of tribal chiefs, the *ulema* (religious leaders), and local notables with the power to veto any legislation on taxes; reintroduced the traditional recruitment of the tribal levy for defense forces; allowed the religious establishment to control the country's legal system; declared Hanafi Islamic jurisprudence as the official legal system of the country; and in 1933 declared Pushtu the official language of the country (Halliday 1978: 16). To maintain political stability, Nadir Shah and his brothers at first refrained from interfering in the social life of the tribes and introduced only limited and gradual modernization (Gregorian 1969: 293–296).

A combination of domestic and international political changes altered this situation in the 1950s. Internally, after 1953, the new prime minister, Mohammad Daud, was committed to rapid socioeconomic modernization. Internationally, after Stalin's death in the same year, the new leadership in the Soviet Union adopted a policy of peaceful competition with the United States in the Third World. Consequently, the Afghan government concluded an agreement with the Soviets in 1955 that provided for a $100-million loan to finance Afghan development projects, and it bought $25 million worth of military equipment from Czechoslovakia and the Soviet Union (Lenczowski 1980: 245). Since then, foreign aid has become a major source of government revenues. Even before the PDPA coup, the Soviet Union, Eastern Europe, and China, for the period 1954–1978, provided a total of $1,263 million, $39 million, and $76 million, respectively, in foreign aid to Afghanistan. Similarly, between 1946 and 1977, the United States gave a total of $515 million in aid (Central Intelligence Agency 1986: 112, 118).

With foreign military assistance, the Daud government was able to build a modern army 100,000 strong; with foreign financial aid, the government modernized and expanded national education and built the infrastructure for a modern economy. Consequently, school enrollment rose from 113,000 students in 1954 to 381,000 students in 1965, and major cities were connected by all-weather highways. Other industrial and commercial projects were initiated by the government, and these substantially increased the share of industry in the GNP. Government revenues increased from 188 million afghanis in 1952 to 1,194 million afghanis in 1956 and 1,500 million afghanis in 1958 (*Statesman's Year-Book* 1953: 762, 1958: 796, 1960: 794). Government-owned industries, mining and natural gas, and foreign aid combined to provide 45 percent of government revenues in 1968 (H. H. Smith et al. 1973: xxvii) and about 50 percent in 1975 (UNESCO 1984: 46).

These changes transformed relations between the state and rural society, particularly the tribes. The state was no longer dependent on the tribes to defend itself against internal and external challenges, and the ability of the tribes to challenge the state declined progressively. Moreover, the state was not engaged in extracting resources or imposing nonvoluntary change on the rural population. The state provided social and economic services to urban as well as rural areas, including schools, hospitals, roads, transportation, and agricultural extension programs, and the state also became the largest employer in the country. The rural population experienced tangible benefits from socio-economic modernization and sought even greater services from the government. Local notables (khans) could not possibly compete with the central government in economic or military affairs, and indeed, these notables, including tribal leaders, competed with each other in benefiting from the services offered by the central government and the economic reach of the state.

Thus, by the 1960s, the power base of the state had shifted away from the Pushtun tribes. Indeed, traditional rural elites and the rural population in general became almost irrelevant to politics in the 1960s and the 1970s. The state's financial and military strength did not depend on the extraction of resources from the rural population; conversely, the dependence of the rural areas on the state was also minimal. An unwritten understanding ruled this minimal relation between the state and the society. The state would provide certain services to the rural areas; the state would refrain from imposing socioeconomic change on the rural population; the attraction of socioeconomic modernization would determine the willingness of the rural population to adopt change; the state bureaucracy of law enforcement would continue to gradually penetrate all rural areas; and the state would refrain from imposing programs that were against Islam and Afghan social customs.

In contrast to the declining relevance of the rural population and tribes, the cities became particularly important in Afghan politics in the 1960s and the 1970s, largely because of the success of the government's modernization efforts. The expansion of education in the 1950s and the 1960s created a relatively large professional class, and the professional middle class was dependent on the state for its livelihood. About 90 percent of the professional middle-class jobs were positions with state economic, military, educational, and administrative institutions. Also, a disproportionate number of the middle class was concentrated in the capital, Kabul. Thus, Kabul dominated Afghan politics, and the state became the focus of professional middle-class political activities. The economic stagnation of the 1960s encouraged political activism by the professional middle class, which demanded greater participation in decision making.

Concomitant with the rise of the professional middle class, Afghanistan had become a largely bureaucratic polity. The stable source of political support (tribal and rural) on which the Durani kings had relied for over 200 years (1740s–1950s) was replaced by the autonomy of the state and the absence of a social basis for political power. The structural vulnerability of the regime enhanced the chances of successful military intervention in politics, and while before the 1950s, a successful military coup would have been impossible, in the 1960s and the 1970s, the military coup became the most effective means of political change.

THE ONSET OF STATE CRISIS

Although society experienced significant change during the 1950s and early 1960s, no serious incidents of political instability involving a challenge from alternative elites emerged until the mid-1960s. What triggered the beginning of the state crisis was conflict within the royal family, as a consequence of which Prime Minister Daud had to resign and King Zahir Shah became a ruling monarch in 1963. To strengthen the legitimacy of his regime, Zahir Shah embarked on a rather incoherent policy of liberalizing the polity, including introducing a relatively liberal constitution in 1964 whose precepts he could not totally adhere to later. The limited liberalization of the constitutional decade (1963–1973) brought to the surface new political groups, and they articulated controversial issues that had been either suppressed or nonexistent in the past. These issues included participation, modernization, economic development, Afghan nationalism, and legitimacy.

Controversial Issues

Participation. Until the 1950s, political participation in Afghanistan was largely confined to the tribal leaders, rural notables, and the leaders of the religious establishment, the *ulema*. Only King Ammanullah in the 1920s experimented with a more liberal model of polity, allowing participation for all citizens, which in effect meant greater participation by modern intellectuals, people in the urban centers, and the bureaucrats. However, Ammanullah's experiment with expanded participation abruptly ended when a conservative rebellion overthrew his regime in 1929. In subsequent years, during the rule of Nadir Shah and his brothers, democratic participation was abandoned in favor of the old formula of participation by tribal leaders, rural notables, and the religious leaders (Gregorian 1969: 305).

The limited but successful economic modernization programs of the 1930s and the 1940s, however, produced a sizable middle class, mostly concentrated in Kabul, which demanded greater participation in politics, and after World War II, the regime wanted to attract U.S. interest in Afghanistan's development. Thus, the regime briefly allowed a limited liberalization of the polity, which resulted in the election of 50 liberal deputies (out of 120) to the parliament, and these deputies demanded speedy socioeconomic modernization, democracy, and expanded participation for the people. In 1952, the government dissolved the parliament and arrested a number of the prodemocracy deputies.

For the next ten years, Daud's regime concentrated on socioeconomic modernization and drastically reduced both traditional and democratic participation in politics. The success of Daud's modernization program, in a dialectical way, enlarged the size of the professional middle class, which was mostly interested in democratic participation. The continued success of the socioeconomic modernization programs would have required the cooperation, loyalty, and the further strengthening of this new class, but, although itself a creation of the state, the middle class entertained new ideas of legitimacy in which democratic participation loomed large. Reportedly, Prime Minister Daud correctly analyzed the situation in 1962 and advised the king to replace the old system with a parliamentary democracy, which would dramatically reduce the decision-making role of the royal family and allow genuine participation by the people in the political process (Hyman 1984: 53).

The constitutional decade (1963–1973) that followed saw a significant degree of liberalization and expanded participation. Although ultimate authority rested with the king, the parliament became a far more powerful institution than it had ever been. However, the logical conclusion of expanded participation and democratization would have required a transfer of power to the people and their representatives, but the king was not willing to follow to a logical conclusion his own initiative to liberalize the polity. Thus, the regime's inability to reconcile the contradictions of its own policy of expanded participation reduced its legitimacy even more and added to its vulnerability.

Modernization. Modernization has become a very explosive political issue in most Muslim societies, and there are two different conceptions of it. According to one, Westernization is an integral part of modernization; the other conception confines modernization to the increased relevance of science and technology to economic, military, and educational institutions. Although the first conception is bound to conflict with some Islamic values, the second concept may not satisfy many modernists (Pipes 1983: 105–113).

Afghan leaders have oscillated between these different conceptions of modernization. Between the 1880s and the 1920s, the government was primarily concerned with modernizing the army, bureaucracy, and other state institutions. During the 1920s, Ammanullah adopted a more comprehensive view of modernization, which also included Westernization, but the collapse of his regime in 1929 led to a conception of modernization that excluded Westernization and emphasized a gradual economic and educational modernization. During the 1950s, Daud once again adopted an expanded conception of modernization that included Westernization, and this policy remained in effect during the 1960s and the 1970s.

The promotion of this policy also stimulated a strong Islamist movement that opposed Westernization because the Islamists considered Westernization as de-Islamization. The promotion and defense of Islam had been an essential element of the traditional Afghan theory of legitimacy. Thus, the Islamists' protest against Westernization added to the weakening of the legitimacy, and consequently, the instability, of the regime in the 1960s and the 1970s. In spite of the regime's adherence to the Sharia in legal issues, the alienation of middle-class Islamists and the traditional religious leaders (the *ulema*) from the regime increased in the 1960s and the 1970s.

Economic Development. The state's limited private-capitalist economic development program of the 1930s and 1940s and the expanded industrial state-capitalist development programs of the 1950s were quite successful. A major contributor to the success of the economic modernization programs in the 1950s and the early 1960s was the availability of foreign aid, which was a direct consequence of the cold war competition between the West and the Soviet bloc. However, foreign aid declined in the late 1960s and early 1970s, resulting in economic stagnation. In contrast, educational institutions continued to graduate an increasingly large number of students from high schools and universities, most of whom could not obtain a productive job in the private or public sector. As in other developing countries, this discrepancy between social mobilization and economic opportunities was detrimental to political stability (Deutsch 1961; Huntington 1968: 32–59).

Afghan Nationalism. Although Afghanistan originated as a Pushtun state and Pushtuns have always enjoyed political, military, and cultural dominance in the country, Persian has been the de facto official language of the government. Despite government efforts to base Afghan nationalism on Pushtu and the Pushtun culture, in reality the expansion of education since the 1950s has helped the popularization of Persian.

The relatively liberal constitution of 1964 declared both Pushtu and Persian as official languages and Pushtu as the national language. However, the status of Pushtu in the 1960s and the 1970s alienated both Pushtuns and non-Pushtuns from the government. The non-Pushtun minorities resented the dominance of the Pushtuns in the polity, and they rejected the Pushtu- and Pushtun-culture-based conception of Afghan nationalism in favor of a more state-based conception of nationalism. The Pushtuns, on the other hand, resented the fact that in spite of official support for Pushtu, in reality Persian remained the dominant official language. Many Pushtun nationalists desired a "Pushtu as the only official language" policy, and even the most moderate Pushtuns wanted at least equality of Persian and Pushtu and demanded that parliament pass a law requiring government employees to be proficient in both languages. Non-Pushtuns objected to this demand because while most educated Pushtuns spoke Persian, few non-Pushtuns spoke Pushtu. The issue led to heated exchanges between Pushtun and non-Pushtun members of the parliament in 1971, but the government did not resolve the issue; it simply ignored it. Thus, by the 1970s, non-Pushtuns considered the regime as fundamentally pro-Pushtun and resented their perceived inferior position in the polity. The Pushtuns, on the other hand, found the continuing popularization of Persian a threat to the Pushtu language and Pushtun identity. The language issue constituted one of the most explosive issues of Afghan politics and contributed significantly to political instability in the 1970s.

Legitimacy. The above developments weakened the legitimacy of the regime in the 1960s and the 1970s. Indeed, the changes were so fundamental that the Afghan theory of legitimacy itself suffered a crisis. For over 200 years, in procedural terms, legitimization of a regime in Afghanistan required approval by the Pushtun tribal chiefs and the *ulema*. The Afghan theory of legitimacy also had a number of substantive elements. First, it required that the regime either help the expansion of Islam or at least defend it at home. Second, the theory demanded the enforcement of the Islamic law, the Sharia, although occasionally tribal customs and codes of ethics were observed at the expense of the Sharia. Third, a legitimate government was required to defend the independence of the country, which was closely linked to the defense of Islam—thus, wars of national independence were also religious wars. Fourth, the theory stipulated minimal government and restraint from unnecessary intervention in social life. Fifth, it expected leaders to be pious, generous, and courageous (Ridout 1975).

Since the 1950s, this view of legitimacy itself has suffered a crisis. Although the regime continued to declare its respect for Islam, which was enshrined in the constitutions both of 1964 and 1977, some elements of the government's programs of Westernization were at times in conflict with Islamic culture. The Musahiban dynasty (1929–1978) considered its advocacy of Afghan nationalism to be an essential element of its theory of legitimacy, but its Pushtun-based conception of Afghan nationalism was not shared by the minorities. During the constitutional decade (1963–1973), democracy became the regime's claim to legitimacy, but the king's reluctance to devolve political power and to legalize political parties, combined with corruption and the lack of concern with national issues in parliament, reduced the credibility of democracy as a basis of legitimacy (Kakar 1978: 200–201). Similarly, while the regime's legitimacy benefited from good economic performance in the 1950s and early 1960s, the economic stagnation of the late 1960s and the early 1970s undermined whatever procedural legitimacy the regime may have enjoyed.

The Emergence of Organized Political Groups

During the constitutional decade, the king allowed the de facto formation of political groups without signing into law the bill legalizing the formation of political parties. This development intensified the crisis even more. Many small political groups emerged, but most of them disappeared quickly. Some, however, proved to be more durable, and these groups can be divided into three categories: the Communists, the Islamists, and the nationalists.

The PDPA, the main Communist party, was formed in 1965. In line with its Marxist heritage, the PDPA preached class struggle and considered itself the representative of the workers and the peasants. It subscribed to the noncapitalist model of economic development and advocated close cooperation with the Soviet Union in both economic and political matters. It desired a more rapid development of the economy and blamed the incompetence of the government and the existing semifeudal and semicapitalist mode of production for underdevelopment. It supported a more equal distribution of income and considered land redistribution as essential to this purpose. The party refused to take a stand on the issue of languages. While in opposition, the PDPA took advantage of the liberal political climate during the constitutional decade but did not subscribe to liberal democracy as a permanent feature of the society it envisioned for the Afghans (Arnold 1983: 137–148).

Islamism largely arose as a reaction to the decline of Islamic culture and the rise of communism, and the government was blamed for both phenomena. The Islamists did not offer any coherent prescription for economic development; indeed, economic development and the distribution of income and wealth were not major political issues for them. The Islamists, however, took a clear stand regarding nationalism, participation, and the legitimacy of the government. They rejected the Pushtun-based conception of Afghan nationalism and believed that only Islam could provide a basis for national unity. Indeed, they emphasized the internationalist character of Islam and rejected the legitimacy of territorial disputes between Muslim states. Consequently, they rejected the Afghan government's territorial claim over the Northwest Frontier Province of Pakistan (Pushtunistan), which is mostly populated by Afghans and was detached from Afghanistan by the British in 1893. The Islamists wanted close relations with Muslim Pakistan instead of secular India, and they considered it the religious duty of every Muslim to be politically active and to engage in jihad (holy war) for the defense or expansion of Islam. They believed that the government's commitment to the Sharia determined its legitimacy (Roy 1985: 82).

The Islamists did not have a well-organized political party. The movement started as a student movement and came to include off-campus *ulema*. The Islamists gained organizational discipline after persecution in 1973–1976. They split into three groups in the 1970s and gained prominence only after the Soviet invasion of Afghanistan.

The Afghan Social Democratic Party (ASDP), formed in 1966, was the main nationalist political group, and it advocated a truly representative parliamentary democracy. It supported the extension of participation to all Afghans and considered the expressed support of the people the essential element of political legitimacy. Although the ASDP supported the relatively liberal constitution of 1964, it opposed the king's reluctance to sign into law the bill that allowed the legalization of political parties. The party also objected to the king's unwillingness to devolve power and allow parliamentarism. The ASDP favored a conception of Afghan nationalism in which Pushtu and the Pushtuns loomed large, because although it did not subscribe to granting privileges to any ethnic group, the party believed that Pushtu was essential to the Afghan national identity. Thus, the ASDP was a strong supporter of the right to self-determination for the 10 million Pushtuns living in Pakistan. In this regard, the ASDP totally disagreed with the Islamists. It considered economic development to be the major problem facing Afghan society and supported a mixed-economy model of development. Although the party preached national harmony, it also called for a more equal distribution of income. The ASDP rejected any cultural Westernization of Afghanistan and demanded the strengthening of the Afghan national culture, but at the same time, it supported the modernization of sociopolitical and economic institutions. Regarding these issues, the nationalists considered the government's policy in the 1960s and the 1970s as either inadequate or simply wrong (Afghan Social Democratic Party 1987).

Each group had a few representatives in parliament in the late 1960s and the early 1970s, but parliament was not the focus of their activities. All were busy recruiting supporters among students, teachers, bureaucrats, intellectuals, and army officers. Their open political activities and conflicting views on the major political issues, combined with the indecisiveness of King Zahir Shah, added to the crisis of the state in the early 1970s.

Daud's Coup

With the help of personal friends, nationalists, and leftist officers, the former prime minister Mohammad Daud, a cousin of the king, conducted a successful coup in July 1973, overthrew King Zahir Shah's regime, and declared Afghanistan a republic. Among the organized political groups, the Parcham faction of the PDPA had a strong presence during the first two years of Daud's administration. Perhaps at the insistence of the PDPA, Daud, upon assuming power, quickly launched an anti-Islamist campaign whereby a few Islamists were executed, some were arrested, and many sought refuge in Pakistan. Despite his campaign against the Islamists, Daud's commitment to Islam was not questioned by most Afghans.

After stabilizing his own position, Daud decided to curtail the leftists in his administration, for both internal and international reasons. Internally, Daud was a Pushtun (Afghan) nationalist who believed in modernizing Afghanistan without damaging its Islamic character or its nonalignment. He did not want a close association with the PDPA, which might have damaged his Islamic and nationalist credentials. Furthermore, Daud was a determined autocrat and thought it was time to put an end to the growth of the PDPA's power.

Internationally, Daud wanted close relations with Iran, the Arab countries, and the West, which required some distance from the Soviets and the left. This change in foreign policy was largely determined by the economic development needs of Afghanistan. Because of the initial close relations between Daud and the left, the Soviets increased their economic aid to the Afghan government and provided $450 million in economic development loans in 1975 alone. However, as a consequence of the quadrupling of the price of oil in 1973–1974, Iran and the Arab oil countries became major donors of financial aid to Muslim countries. The shah of Iran promised to invest $2 billion in Afghan development projects over a period of ten years, and the Arab oil countries, such as Kuwait, Saudi Arabia, Iraq, and Libya, also promised financial aid to the Daud regime, although a much smaller amount than Iran. The conservative Arab countries, and certainly the shah of Iran, wanted Daud to reduce his dependence on the Soviets and to abandon Afghan territorial claims against Pakistan. The United States also encouraged close links between Afghanistan and Iran. Although the USSR promised to commit a total of over $600 million to Daud's seven-year development plan, Daud favored close relations with Iran and the Arab oil countries. The PDPA opposed Daud's policy, which led to its elimination from the government by 1975 (Harrison 1980–1981).

Daud was more benign in his relations with the nationalists. He adopted (actually shared) some elements of their socioeconomic program and co-opted some senior members of the ASDP by giving them relatively important posts in his government. However, significant differences regarding democratic rights and the basis of state legitimacy prevented Daud from incorporating the nationalists into his base of power. Daud did not provide a clear-cut answer to some of the major issues of Afghan politics in the 1970s—he was most successful with regard to economic development issues—but he suppressed participation, rejected liberal democracy, banned all organized political activities, and had no coherent theory of legitimacy or clear conception of Afghan nationalism.

To recapitulate, by the late 1970s, the development of state autonomy since the 1950s had separated the state from the rural population and the tribes. The structure of power had changed fundamentally, and cities, especially Kabul, and the professional middle class had acquired a disproportionate degree of influence in national politics. The relative success of socioeconomic modernization in the 1950s and the 1960s had created new political issues, regarding which the politically mobilized strata of the population had conflicting positions. A very few supported the regime, which was unable to offer a coherent theory of political legitimacy or an acceptable conception of Afghan nationalism. The regime could not reconcile its Westernization program with Islamism, and it could not allow or decisively deny genuine political participation. Although the polity was riven by internal conflicts over the nature of government and political structure, the regime lacked any solid social base of power, except for the armed forces and the bureaucracy. Those two institutions had become significantly bureaucratic, with widespread apathy and little loyalty to Daud himself. Thus, when the PDPA mobilized its supporters within the armed forces for a coup, the autonomous, bureaucratized regime of President Daud quickly collapsed.

FROM COUP TO STATE BREAKDOWN

Although Daud came to power with PDPA support in 1973, his relations with the PDPA deteriorated during 1974–1975. The Daud regime, though unable to resolve all the major issues of Afghan politics, was a much more decisive and dynamic regime than Zahir Shah's regime had been. The PDPA was well acquainted with Daud's thoughts, determination, and ruthlessness in eliminating political opponents, and it saw Daud's ban on political activities, his authoritarianism, his efforts to reduce Afghanistan's dependence on the Soviets and his allowing of greater Iranian influence, and his apparent success in diversifying and augmenting the foreign aid sources of the country as a threat to the PDPA's survival. Thus, the two factions of the PDPA—the Khalq and the Parcham—temporarily buried their differences and decided to challenge Daud's regime in a unified manner. They knew very well that the only action possible that could lead to a quick and decisive transfer of power was through the armed forces, and the PDPA had a large number of supporters within the military.

The immediate cause of the coup was the mysterious assassination of a prominent PDPA leader, Mir Akbar Khyber, in mid-April 1978. The PDPA mobilized its members and sympathizers to stage a very large demonstration of 10,000–15,000 people in Kabul for Khyber's funeral, during which the PDPA leadership blamed the Daud regime for his murder. In retaliation, Daud ordered the arrest of the PDPA leadership. However, a prominent PDPA leader in charge of recruitment in the armed forces, Hafizullah Amin, was able to instruct his supporters in the army and the air force to overthrow the Daud's regime. Against all odds, the PDPA supporters were able to defeat the Republican Palace Guard units, kill President Daud and his family members, and transfer power to the PDPA (Bradshaw 1985: 74–77).

Although the success of the PDPA coup was not inevitable, the structural weakness of the Daud regime can explain why it crumbled so quickly and without any major resistance. The state had achieved a significant degree of autonomy. The overwhelming majority of the people, rural as well as tribal, had become almost irrelevant to national politics, and during the first few months of the change, they considered the April coup as an interelite conflict in Kabul without any significance for rural life. Even among the urbanites, Daud's regime had failed to establish a solid social base for itself. The armed forces constituted the regime's base of power, but most army units were either too distant from Kabul or apathetic to the regime. In such a polity, a well-disciplined party of 5,000 members and about 200 supporters in the armed forces could bring about the transfer of power and affect the course of the history of the country and the region. The situation changed when the PDPA attempted to transform this military coup into a social revolution that would end the separation of state and society and reintroduce the rural population, especially the Pushtun tribes, into national politics.

The PDPA Attempted Revolution

The April 1978 transfer of power was not just a military coup but an attempted social revolution aimed at the destruction of the old social structure and the creation of a new order. Decrees No. 6, 7, and 8 of the PDPA government, announced in the summer and fall of 1978, have been described as the "crux of the revolution." Decree No. 6 dealt with rural debt. It stated that land-mortgaged loans were considered amortized at 20 percent of the principal per year, and it canceled all interest. Thus, peasants who had mortgaged their land in return for a loan contracted in 1974 or before could repossess their land without any payment to creditors. Peasants who had mortgaged their land after 1974 were required to repay the principal on a sliding scale over a period determined by the length of the loan (Male 1982: 110).

The PDPA believed that Decree No. 6 would help bring about the destruction of "feudal" and "prefeudal" social relations in Afghanistan and free the peasants from the devastating impact of increasing debt, which was one of the major factors responsible for their poverty. The PDPA also believed the benefits the decree conferred on the peasants would strengthen the position of the PDPA among them (Gupta 1986: 50–54). The actual impact of Decree No. 6 on the Afghan peasantry is quite controversial. Beverly Male (1982: 110) has maintained that the decree had "far-reaching effects," and a PDPA minister, Saleh Mohammad Zeary, has asserted that the decree benefited 89 percent of the rural families. Vladimir Glukhoded, a Soviet economist, has estimated that the decree led to the cancellation of 30 billion afghanis ($1 billion in 1978) of rural debt, but Sadhan Mukherjee, a member of the Communist party of India and a friend of the PDPA, has estimated that the overall peasant debt in Afghanistan in 1978 was 722 million afghanis (about $24 million). Neither scholar provides the basis of his estimate (Shahrani 1984: 13). Fred Halliday (1979: 493) has maintained that the impact of Decree No. 6 was quite minimal because the decree did not cover peasant debt contracted with bazaar merchants and moneylenders, and such transactions, according to Halliday, constituted the lion's share of rural debt. Furthermore, the decree destroyed the old rural credit system without providing an alternative. Thus, it seems that Decree No. 6 actually contributed to the economic hardship of the peasants, and consequently, it did not generate political support among the peasantry for the PDPA.

Decree No. 7 regulated marriage and wedding expenses. It stipulated that marriages should not be contracted without the consent of the couple and specified minimum ages of sixteen for girls and eighteen for boys. It also restricted wedding expenses and reduced the bride price (*mahr*) from an average of 40,000 afghanis to 300 afghanis ($10.00). It also prohibited the custom that the groom should give gifts to the bride and her family on the occasion of major religious festivities (N. Dupree 1984: 323). This decree was supposed to complement Decree No. 6. The PDPA believed that rural debt was contracted largely to pay for peasants' wedding expenses, so the cancellation of rural debt and a ceiling on wedding expenses, the PDPA believed, should improve the economic conditions of the peasants. The second measure was also aimed at changing centuries-old social customs that, according to the PDPA, had institutionalized the subservience of women in Afghan families. Although previous Afghan governments had also attempted to regulate marriage, the PDPA distinguished itself from the previous regimes by vigorously attempting to enforce Decree No. 7. This decree was considered by most of the rural population as an unnecessary government intervention in family life, and when the government supplemented the marriage regulations with a campaign for forced literacy of women, whereby male PDPA members taught Marxism to illiterate rural Afghan women, many rural communities rebelled against the PDPA's rule. Thus, once again, the PDPA attempt at reform backfired.

Decree No. 8 launched the most important program of the PDPA revolution— land redistribution. Since its foundation, the PDPA had supported a radical land reform program, which, the party believed, was essential for the destruction of the old social order and for the promotion of social justice. The PDPA thought that land redistribution would destroy the economic basis of the old dominant class, strengthen the PDPA's position among the peasants, and thus, contribute to the stability and viability of the PDPA regime (Mukherjee 1984: 178).

In spite of the country's large size, arable land is not abundant in Afghanistan. Although 7.8 million hectares (35 million acres, or 12 percent of the country) were cultivable in 1978, only about half were actually cultivated because, generally, Afghanistan's soil is low in productivity and land tilled once has to lie fallow a year or two before the next cropping. Water availability is another major problem, and before 1978, less than half of the cultivable land was irrigated (Mukherjee 1984: 176). Thus, even the most equal distribution of land would not have enabled Afghan peasants to own a sizable tract of land.

The distribution of land is a controversial issue among the scholars of Afghanistan. Louis Dupree (1973: 147) believes that land distribution in Afghanistan was quite equal even before the PDPA revolution. He has estimated that 60 percent of all farmland was owner operated and that only thirty individuals owned over 1,000 *jiribs* of arable land. (5 *jiribs* equal 1 hectare or 4.5 acres). Mohammad Hassan Kakar (1979: 115–118) similarly believes that the combination of a number of factors—including the scarcity of land and the high density of population in most Afghan provinces; the impact of Islamic law, which requires division of inheritance among all family members of the deceased; and the practice of Afghan monarchs, such as Abdul Rahman (1880–1901), of confiscating the land of prominent people in order to prevent a potential threat to the royal family—had resulted in a relatively equal distribution of land. In contrast, the PDPA believed that the distribution of land was highly concentrated in Afghanistan and claimed that 4 percent of the people owned about 50 percent of the arable land and 82 percent of the farmers owned only 35 percent of the land. Glukhoded and Mukherjee, using Afghan government statistics and other sources, have compiled relatively systematic and probably more reliable data on land distribution in Afghanistan in 1978. Their estimates show that while 42 percent of Afghan families owned 1– 6 hectares (4.5–27 acres) of land, more than 75 percent of the families owned some land. Mukherjee's and Glukhoded's data, respectively, indicate that 9 percent and 4 percent of the families owned over 40 percent of the private arable land. However, the average land-holding of even land-rich families was estimated at 15– 18 hectares (67–80 acres), which is quite small compared to land concentrations in Iran, Pakistan, and India (Shahrani 1984: 18–19).

The PDPA announced its land reform program in December 1978 and completed that program's implementation between January and July 1979. It established a maximum land ownership of thirty *jiribs* of first-grade land or the equivalent. The program also stipulated the confiscation, without compensation, of surplus land and its redistribution, without pay, in five-*jirib* parcels among landless and land-hungry peasant families, which the government estimated to total around 630,000, excluding the 2–2.5 million nomads. The PDPA expected 6 million *jiribs* (1.2 million hectares or 5.4 million acres) of surplus land, but the PDPA government was able to confiscate only 840,000 hectares (3.8 million acres) of all-grades land, the equivalent of 330,000 hectares (1.5 million acres) of first-grade land. Consequently, the government was able to distribute a total of only 765,000 hectares (3.4 million acres) of all-grades land, the equivalent of 287,000 hectares (1.3 million acres) of first-grade land, among 296,000 landless and land-hungry peasant families (Shahrani 1984: 18; Hyman 1984: 91). The discrepancy between the PDPA expectation of surplus land and the actual distribution of land to the needy peasants indicates the inaccuracy of the PDPA belief about the inequality of land distribution in Afghanistan. The land redistribution program left many peasants still landless and land hungry, and even the beneficiaries of the reform did not receive adequate land to support a family of five people. Political considerations had loomed large in the initiation of the land reform program, the PDPA leadership believing that land redistribution would strengthen the party's support among the peasants, which would add to the viability of the regime. However, the incompetent implementation of the program instead strengthened rural opposition to the PDPA.

At the symbolic level, the PDPA attempted to reduce the influence of Islam and national traditions and to emphasize Communist symbols. Thus, Decree No. 3 replaced the traditional black, red, and green Afghan flag with a totally red one, and PDPA teachers repeatedly denigrated Islamic symbols in the classrooms. To complete the destruction of the old dominant class, the PDPA government engaged in extensive purges within the state bureaucracy and the armed forces. Consequently, out of sixty-two generals, sixty were either retired or imprisoned. Similarly, most top-level bureaucrats were fired, and others were warned to either join the party or to expect dismissal. These measures caused upheavals that neither the PDPA nor its Soviet allies were able to suppress in subsequent years.

Although the PDPA socioeconomic reforms were prepared in haste, the leadership had a thorough debate about revolutionary strategy. On the one hand, the Parcham faction led by Babrak Karmal argued for a less radical, step-by-step approach, fearing that radical and simultaneous reforms would galvanize a conservative reaction and thus endanger the revolution. The Khalq faction led by Amin, on the other hand, argued for a comprehensive, radical, and immediate revolution, so as to polarize the situation between the revolutionaries and the conservatives. Amin argued that radical reforms would strengthen the PDPA position among the peasants and would ensure the success of the PDPA revolution. Furthermore, he believed that quick action by the PDPA would deny conservatives the time to organize a counterrevolution (Gupta 1986: 45; Edwards 1987: 25–29). The Khalq faction prevailed; Karmal and his Parchamite associates were expelled from the party. Amin consolidated his position within the party by summer 1978 and launched a comprehensive social revolution in the fall. Both the radical substance of his reforms and the incompetent implementation of the programs were important factors in the anti-PDPA rebellion that began in late fall 1978.

Theories of Revolution and the
PDPA Attempted Revolution

Chapter 3 identifies three major clusters of variables as the causes of social revolutions, including a financial crisis of the state, widespread popular discontent, and the alienation of a large number of elites from the regime. Although the alienated elites may sharply disagree among themselves, they are united in their opposition to the regime. The conjunction of these three sets of variables, according to Chapter 3, is likely to result in a revolution.

Although the Afghan economy stagnated in the late 1960s, the state never suffered a financial crisis that would threaten its viability. As Table 8.1 indicates, both state revenues and state expenditures continued to grow in the late 1960s and early 1970s. With the exception of development expenditures, which experienced moderate decline in 1970 and substantial decrease in 1971, every other category of expenditures experienced moderate increase or at least stayed about the same until 1973 (the year of the overthrow of the monarchy). Although state revenues from direct taxes and foreign aid declined substantially in the late 1960s and early 1970s, revenues from natural gas compensated for a large proportion of the decline. Consequently, deficit finance, on the average, remained at the relatively low level of less than 10 percent of the government expenditures.

As Table 8.2 indicates, state financial activism improved substantially during Daud's second administration (1973–1978). Total government expenditures increased from 9.4 billion afghanis in 1972 to over 30.6 billion afghanis in 1977, an increase of over 320 percent. Every major category of government expenditures increased every year by a large percentage. Development expenditures, in particular, experienced phenomenal growth, increasing from 3.4 billion afghanis in 1972 to 20.2 billion afghanis in 1977, a growth of about 600 percent. Although government revenues also increased from 5.7 billion afghanis in 1972 to 16.6 billion afghanis in 1977, an increase of about 290 percent, the difference did not match the increase in expenditures. However, an increase in foreign aid ($425 million from the Soviet Union in 1975) reduced the gap between government revenues and expenditures significantly. Similarly, the state's balance-of-payment situation improved substantially after 1973. The total value of exports increased from $100 million in 1970 to $327 million in 1977, but imports increased even more, rising from $153 million to $523 million. However, the flow of remittances from Afghans working in the Persian Gulf actually created balance-of-payment surpluses after 1973. The appreciation of the afghani in the mid-1970s was reflective of the improved balance-of-payment situation (Ford 1986: 173). Thus, the state did not face any unusual financial problem that would threaten its viability.

Economic conditions are not the only variables affecting the level of popular discontent, but their significance is emphasized in theories of revolution. Declining economic conditions accompanied by high levels of population growth and urbanization are likely to increase popular discontent (see Chapter 3). Although the scarcity of data on Afghanistan does not allow a systematic quantitative assessment of the influence of these variables on the outbreak of the country's revolutionary violence, a quasi-quantitative and qualitative assessment is possible.

Thanks to public health measures, Afghanistan experienced an average population growth rate of 2 percent in the 1960s and the 1970s. Urbanization also increased significantly, resulting in 15 percent of the population living in the cities (International Monetary Fund 1985: 46–47). However, Afghanistan, a large country, still has large tracts of land for reclamation and is mineral rich. As discussed earlier, although the economy stagnated in the late 1960s and inflation was particularly high in 1971 (15 percent), the economy improved substantially after 1973. The improvement was owing to increased public expenditures and private investment as well as consumption. Large public expenditures were financed by

Table 8.1 Government Revenues and Expenditures, Afghanistan, 1968-1972 (in millions of afghanis)

	1968	1969	1970	1971	1972
Revenue					
Direct taxes	556	372	411	469	528
Indirect taxes	2,495	2,083	2,549	2,818	2,806
Government enterprises	613	1,008	996	950	975
Natural gas	73	429	483	720	630
Other revenue	474	573	646	761	760
Total	4,211	4,465	5,085	5,718	5,699
Expenditures					
Current expenditures					
Defense	1,350	1,450	1,550	1,550	1,650
Other expenditures	1,597	1,818	1,864	1,962	2,230
Servicing foreign debt	666	601	867	1,070	1,295
Subsidies		385	451	560	870
Development expenditures					
Local currency	1,707	1,820	1,920	1,743	2,130
Foreign currency	2,808	2,274	2,003	1,249	1,250
Total	8,128	8,348	8,655	8,134	9,425
Government Deficit	-3,917	-3,883	-3,570	-2,416	-3,726
Financing the Deficit					
Foreign commodity assistance	517	1,018	479	627	1,115
Foreign grants and loans	2,808	2,274	2,003	1,249	1,250
Borrowing from the Central Bank	593	592	1,089	540	1,361

Source: H. H. Smith et al., Area Handbook for Afghanistan, 4th ed. (Washington, D.C.: U.S. Government Printing Office, 1973).

Table 8.2 Government Revenues and Expenditures, Afghanistan, 1974-1977 (in millions of afghanis)

	1974	1975	1976	1977
Revenue				
Tax on income & wealth	1,257	1,687	2,144	2,429
Transaction & consumption taxes	720	1,380	1,089	1,226
Import duties	2,315	3,830	4,222	4,661
Export duties	180	300	320	413
Other taxes	113	110	101	389
Service & sale of government property	1,351	2,654	2,847	3,083
Income from government enterprises	1,342	1,350	1,556	1,672
Natural gas	984	841	1,405	2,760
Total	8,262	12,152	13,684	16,633
Expenditures				
Current expenditures				
Defense	1,600	1,912	2,500	2,731
Economic services	452	529	534	667
Social services	1,417	2,403	2,557	5,245
Other current expenditures	1,993	3,811	4,209	1,759
Development expenditures	4,984	9,321	14,027	20,232
Total	10,446	17,976	23,827	30,634
Government Deficit	-2,184	-5,824	-10,143	-14,001

Source: UNESCO, *Statistical Yearbook for Asia and the Pacific* (Bangkok: United Nations, 1984).

increases in foreign aid, foreign loans, and natural gas revenues, and private consumption was largely helped by remittances from Afghans working in the Persian Gulf. The improvement in economic activities was reflected in the very low level (3 percent) of unemployment in 1975—the attraction of high wages in Iran and the Persian Gulf actually resulted in a labor shortage in the countryside. Similarly, consumer prices actually declined in 1972–1973 and increased on the average by only 5 percent between 1973 and 1977 (International Monetary Fund 1985: 46–47).

Although Afghan society in the 1970s was characterized by ethnic, class, and religious inequalities, these inequalities, to some degree, are found in most societies and were certainly not new in Afghanistan. The absence of this form of popular discontent was emphasized in 1975 when the Islamists, with the help of Pakistan, attempted to agitate the people against the Daud regime but completely failed. Elite alienation, however, was strong in the 1970s in Afghanistan. The Islamists and the Communists (after 1975) were openly against the regime, and the nationalists, although closer to the regime, criticized the bureaucratic and authoritarian nature of the Daud regime. The religious leaders and the khans were practically excluded from the regime, and a large proportion of the professional middle class remained apathetic. However, the alienated elites were disunited and probably hated each other more than they hated the regime. The conflict between the Islamists and the Communists, for example, was irreconcilable, and both were closer to the regime than they were to each other.

Thus, there was no financial crisis of the state in Afghanistan in the 1970s nor was there much indication of widespread popular discontent. The elites were alienated from the regime, but they were disunited. It seems that the analytical framework developed in Chapter 3 cannot explain the PDPA's attempted revolution, which is actually not surprising. That framework deals with revolutions that are characterized by mass participation during the outbreak of revolutionary struggle, and the PDPA's attempted revolution did not involve mass participation. It was instead a revolution from above, which differs significantly in terms of preconditions, process, and consequences from revolutions from below.

Revolution from Above

Ellen Kay Trimberger (1978) has constructed an elaborate model of revolution from above that seems quite helpful in analyzing the PDPA revolution. Revolution from above is conducted by high-level military and civilian elites whose main objective is nationalist strengthening and economic development of the country. Trimberger considers the autonomy of the military from the dominant economic class and a high level of cohesion and political consciousness among military officers as necessary preconditions for the outbreak of revolution from above. She also identifies three principles that distinguish the tactics of successful revolutions from above. First, it is essential to consolidate political power before launching the destruction of the old order and the establishment of new institutions. Second, the destruction of the old regime is accomplished gradually, one step at a time. And, third, revolutions from above are relatively nonviolent. Selective repression is used against right- and left-wing dissidents, and political manipulation of the moderates is frequently employed. Revolutions from above avoid mass terror; failure in this regard is likely to alienate the lower classes and facilitate their support for the dominant class, which the revolution wants to destroy.

In the 1970s, the structure of the Afghan political economy was conducive to a revolution from above. Even as early as the 1960s, the military and civil bureaucracy had achieved a significant degree of autonomy, and the old political order, in which the rural notables (khans), tribal chiefs, and religious leaders exercised substantial political influence, had been transformed by the modernization efforts of Prime Minister Daud in the 1950s. The state was successful in diversifying its sources of revenues and in expanding its income. Military officers, although predominantly Pushtuns, were no longer recruited from the old dominant groups of khans and tribal leaders. Indeed, by the 1960s, most military officers were of either lower- or middle-class origin. Nationalism was the dominant ideology within the armed forces, and a large number of military officers exhibited political consciousness and cohesion. Many officers were recruited by the three dominant political activist groups: Communists, nationalists, and Islamists. Both the landed class and the bourgeoisie were relatively weak. Because of the relatively equal distribution of land, Afghanistan never had a very strong landed class, and the modernization of the economy in the 1950s had reduced the strength of that class even further. The bourgeoisie class, which was mainly comprador in nature, itself was a creation of the state and at the mercy of state bureaucrats. The military and civil bureaucrats did not have any strong interest in or loyalty to either one of these classes. Thus, although a military coup had been highly unlikely before the 1950s, dramatic changes in the Afghan political economy in two decades brought the military to the center of Afghan politics and provided the preconditions for a revolution from above. The revolutionary ideology of the PDPA and the valor of its supporters in the armed forces exploited the structural instability of the polity and attempted such a revolution.

However, the PDPA revolution also exhibited strong differences from the ideal model of a revolution from above. In contrast to the model, the PDPA revolution emphasized ideological inflexibility instead of pragmatism, promoted redistribution instead of development, and was led by intellectuals instead of military officers. The most serious difference between the PDPA revolution and the ideal model of a revolution from above, however, was the complete disregard of the PDPA leadership for tactics that Trimburger says are essential for a successful revolution from above. In contrast to the ideal model, the PDPA leadership engaged in the destruction of the old order before consolidating its power, launched socioeconomic and political changes simultaneously instead of one step at a time, and relied heavily on coercion instead of a selective use of force against opponents. It also committed the cardinal error of forcing the lower classes to unite with the old dominant class against the revolutionary regime.

Thus, the PDPA revolution was not a revolution from below, and it had strong commonalities with, and significant differences from, revolutions from above. It was the differences, especially the PDPA's disregard for appropriate tactics, that resulted in the numerous rebellions that culminated in the defeat of the PDPA's revolutionary program.

The Anti-PDPA Rebellion and the
Theories of Revolution

The theoretical framework developed in Chapter 3 is considerably more helpful in analyzing the anti-PDPA rebellion than in analyzing the PDPA attempted revolution. However, its application is not total. Although, as Table 8.3 indicates, government revenues from income and trade taxes declined from 2.4 billion afghanis and 4.6 billion afghanis, respectively, in 1977 to 1.4 billion afghanis and 3.3 billion afghanis in 1979, the state did not suffer any financial crisis. Increased revenues from natural gas and foreign aid from the Soviet Union prevented any serious deterioration in the financial health of the state. Government revenues from natural gas increased from $39 million in 1977 to about $103 million in 1979 and $272 million in 1982. Similarly, foreign aid increased from 2.4 billion afghanis in 1978 to 7.2 billion afghanis in 1981 and 10.4 billion afghanis in 1982. The rebellion against the government increased the defense budget from 2.7 billion afghanis in 1977 to 3.6 billion afghanis in 1979 and 6.4 billion afghanis in 1982. Consequently, the government resorted to deficit finance of 10.2 billion afghanis (about 25 percent of the budget) in 1982. Thus, the rebellion against the PDPA was not the consequence of a state financial crisis; rather, the financial crisis of the state was the result of a continuation of revolutionary violence.

However, elite alienation and popular discontent were instrumental in the anti-PDPA rebellion. The Islamists and the Communists were determined enemies even before the PDPA revolution, and when the PDPA government assumed power, it executed many Islamists, prominent *ulema*, and members of well-known religious families (e.g., the Mujadaddis). Furthermore, it launched a campaign to de-Islamize Afghanistan, and naturally, these developments intensified the old PDPA-Islamist enmity. Although the nationalists had some common objectives with the Communists (e.g., rapid economic development and a more equal distribution of income), the oppressive nature of the PDPA regime combined with its insistence on monopolizing power forced the nationalists to resort to armed struggle against the regime. The same consideration pushed the Maoists into the opposition camp, as well, and intolerance of opposition led the Khalq faction of the PDPA to purge even the Parcham faction of the party. The PDPA had already purged top-level bureaucrats, military officers, and even non-PDPA members of academic institutions. Rural notables, tribal leaders, and religious leaders (mullahs) were considered the most dangerous enemies of the revolution and, thus, were persecuted (Hyman 1984: 96).

Consequently, the PDPA had an extremely narrow basis of power. It had unnecessarily antagonized all segments of the elite—right, left, center, modern, traditional, urban, rural, religious, and ethnic. Despite the considerable differences in their preferred vision of the future Afghan polity, all these segments of alienated elites were united in their opposition to the PDPA regime. Consequently, each group of the alienated elites mobilized some segment of the society against the PDPA.

Widespread popular discontent provided an excellent opportunity for the alienated elites to fight the regime, but scholars of Afghanistan disagree regarding the sources of this popular discontent. Some argue that the PDPA revolution preached class

Table 8.3 Government Revenues and Expenditures, Afghanistan, 1978-1979 and 1981-1982 (in millions of afghanis)

	1978	1979	1981	1982
Revenue				
Tax revenue				
Income and profit taxes	1,419	1,446	1,085	1,282
Trade taxes	4,819	3,257	4,348	5,513
Other	2,614	2,443	3,451	3,992
Nontax revenue				
Public enterprises	1,192	1,406	2,426	1,214
Natural gas	2,697	3,873	13,556	14,792
Other	3,097	3,312	4,985	5,762
Total	15,838	15,737	29,851	32,555
Expenditures				
Current expenditures				
Administration	1,410	1,796	4,320	4,890
Defense	3,000	3,575	5,250	6,370
Education and health	2,807	3,644	4,083	5,050
Social & economic services	1,240	3,225	3,979	5,026
Subsidies and pensions	1,434	1,482	4,020	4,450
Interest payments	684	1,022	1,017	1,835
Development expenditures	8,510	7,150	10,849	11,863
Adjustments		3,097	1,075	9,557
Total	19,085	24,991	34,593	49,041
Government Deficit	-3,247	-9,254	-4,742	-16,486
Financing the Deficit				
Foreign aid	2,362	2,779	7,208	10,441
Foreign debt amortization	-1,809	-2,038	-4,162	-4,196
Domestic finance	2,447	8,513	1,736	10,241

Source: R. F. Nyrop and D. M. Seekins, eds., *Afghanistan: A Country Study* (Washington, D.C.: U.S. Government Printing Office, 1986), pp. 345-346.

conflict and was aimed at the destruction of the old class relations; consequently, the discontent and the upheavals can be understood only in terms of class interest (Male 1982: 116). Others have explained the unrest in terms of conflict between the state and tribes and argue that government attempts to intervene in the social life of tribes have always been unpopular and have led to rebellions. Thus, the PDPA regime's attempt to change social relations caused the rebellion (Halliday 1980: 22). Yet other scholars have emphasized the dominance of Islamic ideology in Afghan social life and the insensitivity or hostility of the PDPA to Islam as the primary motivation for the anti-PDPA rebellion (Shahrani 1984: 25).

A closer examination of rebellions in different parts of the country reveals that certain theories can explain some rebellions better than others. Thus, the regime's insensitivity to Islam was important in the rebellion in Kunar Province (Gupta, 1986: 74). In Paktia Province, the government's intervention in social life, particularly the implementation of Decree No. 7 regulating marriage and wedding expenses and the forced literacy of women, was considerably more important in motivating rebellion against the PDPA government. Forced literacy for women and the insensitivity of the PDPA cadres to centuries-old customs and Islam were also important in the March 1979 uprising in the city of Herat (Hyman 1984: 100–106). The uprising in Hazarajat coincided with the implementation of the land reform program, and the old dominant class (*mirs*), which owned large tracts of land, initiated the rebellion there. Large landowners in other areas also resisted the implementation of the land reform program, and even the peasants were unhappy. Although some peasants benefited from the cancellation of rural debt, they suffered from the destruction of the old rural credit system, which was not replaced by a viable alternative. Similarly, although the land reform program distributed small parcels of land to some landless and land-hungry peasants, it did not provide them with equipment, water, or seed. Consequently, the disruption of rural economic activities, which was also accompanied by rebellions, made the economic conditions of the peasants even worse (Halliday 1980). In the cities, the decline in business confidence, which reduced economic activities; the high rate of inflation; shortages of consumer goods; and, as a consequence of the PDPA purges, job insecurity for government employees, all resulted in widespread popular discontent. The brutality of the PDPA officials contributed even more to popular discontent and outrage, as they frequently resorted to severe beatings of landowners, mullahs, and ordinary peasants (Hyman 1984: 96).

Thus, the PDPA government quickly and completely lost legitimacy with virtually all segments of the population. The regime was considered anti-Islamic, non-Afghan, utterly unjust, and brutally repressive. This situation led to a terrible cycle of violence. The people rebelled against the unpopular government, which led to disproportionately violent government reprisals against the dissidents, which only increased their defiance. By the summer of 1979, the rebellion had spread to fourteen out of the twenty-eight provinces. The government relied heavily on the armed forces, but the support of the army began to disintegrate in 1979.

Although economic and political motivations might have been of great importance in the anti-PDPA rebellion for certain segments of the elites (tribal chiefs, nationalists, and Islamists), for most people, the overwhelming reason for rebellion was their moral disgust with the atrocities committed by the PDPA. This moral outrage provided the objective basis for the emergence of a powerful resistance committed to the destruction of the PDPA regime and the establishment of an Islamic republic in Afghanistan.

The Resistance

To prevent the further deterioration of the political and military situation, and to gain control over the PDPA, the Soviets invaded Afghanistan in late December 1979. The invasion, in turn, spread the rebellion to the entire country and turned the war in Afghanistan into a major international conflict. In 1980, there were twenty-two different nationally and locally organized political groups resisting PDPA rule and the Soviet occupation of Afghanistan. International powers supporting the Afghan resistance sought a unified resistance, one that had established institutions and enjoyed some degree of legitimacy among the people. Pakistan emerged as the main base for the Afghan resistance and unilaterally decided to recognize only six (later seven) resistance groups. This development made it extremely difficult for other Afghan resistance groups to attract any military or financial foreign support, as Pakistan was the main conduit for such foreign aid. Consequently, they could not compete with the seven groups and were thus arbitrarily forced to either merge with one of the seven groups or practically abandon their military struggle for the liberation of Afghanistan.

The seven resistance groups based in Pakistan are divided into two camps: the Islamists and the traditionalists. The Islamist groups include the two Hizb-i Islami (Islamic party) groups led by Gulbudin Hekmatyar and Mohammad Khalis, Burhanudin Rabani's Jamiat-i Islami (Islamic Society), and Abdul Rasul Sayyaf's Itihad-i Mujahideen-i Islam (Union of Islamic Mujahideen). They derive their support from graduates of government-operated *madrasas* (schools for religious studies), secular schools, mullahs, Sufi orders, ethnic minorities, and some detribalized Pushtuns. However, each group has its own niche within this general basis of support (Roy 1985: 110–116). The traditionalist camp is composed of three groups: Mohammad Nabi Mohammadi's Harakat-i Inqilab-i Islami (Islamic Revolutionary Movement), Sayed Ahmad Gailani's Mahaz-i Mill-i Islami (National Islamic Front), and Sabghatullah Mujadaddi's Jabh-i Nijat-i Milli (National Liberation Front). They derive their support from a network of *ulema*, Pushtun tribes, the professional middle class, and bureaucrats of the old regime.

The seven Peshawar-based resistance organizations are all Sunni Muslim. The Shi'ites constitute about 20 percent of Afghanistan's population, with the largest concentration in Hazarajat (central Afghanistan), and they are divided into at least four groups: the Shura (the Council), the Pasdaran (the Guardians), Nasr (Victory), and Harakat-i Islami (the Islamic Movement). These organizations are based in Iran. Although they all receive some weapons and financial help from the Iranian government, Pasdaran and Nasr are favored by the Khomeini regime.

The Shi'ites of Hazarajat played a major role in the war until 1981 when the PDPA and the Soviets decided to withdraw their forces from Hazarajat. Since then, the different Shi'ite groups have been fighting each other for the control of the region. The military and political importance of the Shi'ites is also constrained by the marginal role that Iran has played in the Afghan conflict, the unreliability of the Iranian regime in delivering weapons and financial assistance to the Shi'ite organizations, and the fact that few Shi'ites live near the border area, which increases their dependence on the cooperation of the Sunni organizations.

Thus, the seven Peshawar-based groups constitute the backbone of the resistance. The three traditionalist resistance groups do not even pretend to offer a comprehensive ideology. Mohammadi supports the enforcement of the Sharia but does not advocate an Islamist republic. He opposes the secular orientations of the pre-1978 regimes but finds Islam compatible with monarchy. In short, Mohammadi is "fundamentalist without being Islamist, traditionalist without being secular" (Roy 1985: 114). Mujadaddi, and to a lesser extent Gailani, advocate re-Islamization of cultural life in Afghan cities. Of course, both support the primacy of the Sharia in government and society. Basically, the traditionalists desire a status quo ante (a pre-1978 situation) with minor reforms. They support the return of ex-King Zahir Shah to the leadership position, though not necessarily as a monarch (Roy 1985: 114, 125).

The Islamists share the traditionalists' desire to defend Islam and Afghanistan against communism and Soviet occupation, but they have given the anti-PDPA rebellion an ideological character that emphasizes the abolition of the old monarchy and the creation of a revolutionary Islamic republic. Afghan Islamists consider the enforcement of the Sharia an essential element of their political program—but that is not a radical position in Afghanistan. With the exception of the Communists, all political groups agree with the Islamists on this point.

The emphasis on the Sharia has divided the Islamists regarding the scope of political participation and the role of *ulema* in politics. The *ulema* are the experts of the Sharia, and many Islamic political thinkers, from al-Mawardi in the tenth century to Ruholla Khomeini in the 1980s, argue that because the *ulema* know the Sharia and what is best for an Islamic society, the *ulema* should constitute the ruling class (Khomeini 1981). Yet, in many Muslim societies, the *ulema* have been co-opted by corrupt political leaders and have remained passive observers of creeping secularism and the decline of the Sharia. Consequently, prominent Islamists such as Ali Shariati have been very critical of the view that argues for a special role for the *ulema* in an Islamic regime (Akhavi 1982: 136–137).

Among Afghan Islamists, Hekmatyar opposes theocracy. He is not an *alem* (scholar of Islam), and his supporters are mostly graduates of secular schools. Although Rabani and Sayyaf have not taken a clear position on this issue, Khalis and his associates have frequently (though casually) endorsed the special role of the *ulema* in an Islamic government.

A corollary of the primacy of the Sharia and the leadership of the *ulema* is the negation of meaningful mass participation in politics. The Islamists argue that sovereignty in an Islamic polity belongs to God; the Sharia is the law of God and cannot be changed by the people. Afghan Islamists do not offer a clear and consistent position regarding this issue. They accept the theory of the sovereignty of God but do not specify its meaning in practice. For prominent international Islamists, such as Abdul Ala Maudodi and Khomeini, it means the rule of the *ulema* and the negation of democracy, but Afghan Islamists do not unanimously accept such an interpretation. For instance, contradictory as it may sound, Hekmatyar rejects both democracy and the rule of the *ulema*, but supports general elections with mass participation. In contrast, Khalis restricts political participation to the *ulema*.

Political unity of the Islamic world is another major desideratum of the Islamists (Deckmejian 1985: 22–23, 45). Islamic unity can assume one of two forms: first, solidarity among Muslim states against foreign (non-Muslim) threats or, second, the merger of Muslim countries into one Islamic state. The first conception of unity is not a radical proposal, and the existing Islamic Conference represents the institutionalization of this minimalist conception of Islamic unity. However, in spite of the membership of all Muslim countries in this organization, the Muslim states have rarely adopted a unified stand, even in cases of non-Muslim aggression against a member country. The Soviet invasion of Afghanistan is a good example.

The second conception of Islamic unity is a radical proposal, but it is also highly unrealistic. With the exception of the first forty years of its emergence in the seventh century, the Islamic world has never been politically united. It is inconceivable that Shi'ite Iran would merge with Sunni Turkey and the Arab world. Contemporary Islamists have not addressed themselves to the serious theoretical and practical problems that the conception of unity as a single Islamic state involves.

The principle of the unity of Muslims has a particular significance for the relations of Afghan Islamists with Pakistan. The status of the Pushtuns in Pakistan has always poisoned relations between Afghanistan and Pakistan, and most Afghan political groups support the position of the Afghan government, which advocates the right of self-determination for the Pushtuns living in Pakistan. The Afghan Islamists emphasize Islamic unity between Pakistan and Afghanistan and oppose the Afghan government's position on this issue. Indeed, at one point, Hekmatyar proposed a confederation between Pakistan and Afghanistan. A corollary of the principle of Islamic unity is the rejection of nationalism by the Islamists. Ethnic divisions do not have political significance; only religious differences (Muslims versus non-Muslims) are legitimate (Pipes 1983: 148). Thus, Afghan Islamists reject Pushtun nationalism and minority separatism in Afghanistan.

The Islamists have not been particularly concerned with economic issues. With the exception of usury, Islam is compatible with capitalism. It allows private property, private ownership of the means of production, production for profit, and trading (Rodison 1978: 2–17). But Islam also emphasizes that private property should not be used against the public interest and stipulates certain welfare functions of the state (e.g., public assistance for the needy and sick). Thus, some Islamists have emphasized social justice and redistribution in an Islamic society (Katouzian 1983: 157–159). In contrast, Afghan Islamists have not been insistent supporters of redistribution, which constituted a major thrust of the PDPA revolution. The Islamists, like other resistance groups, have promised to reverse the PDPA's redistributive measures and to return any property confiscated by the PDPA to its original owners. What distinguishes the Islamists is their commitment to cultural authenticity and an Islamic moral order. The Afghan Islamists are united in their rejection of Westernization and any other element of modernization that may contradict Islamic values. In this regard, they have the support of the overwhelming majority of the people.

Thus, although some major elements of the Afghan Islamist program (e.g., the primacy of the Sharia and Islamic unity) do not have radical implications, others would revolutionize sociopolitical life in Afghanistan. For instance, after decades of Westernization, a strict enforcement of the Islamic moral code would radically alter cultural life in the cities. Similarly, the rise of the *ulema*, after decades of decline, would revolutionize the composition of the Afghan elite, and the Islamist objective to destroy tribalism would further strengthen the change in elite composition.

Strengths and Weaknesses of the Resistance

The scope of the resistance is truly extensive. It has used all significant social networks (the *ulema*, Sufi orders, tribes, secular and religious schools) to exploit popular discontent and to mobilize all segments of the population for the overthrow of the PDPA regime. The resistance is particularly strong owing to the legitimacy of its cause. Despite fundamental differences among organizations regarding the structure of a future Afghan polity, they are united in their hatred of the PDPA regime and its Soviet backers. On this point, the resistance has the support of the overwhelming majority of the people. The presence of about 5 million Afghan refugees in Pakistan and Iran immensely strengthens the resistance politically and provides it with an inexhaustible source of recruitment for fighters. The resistance also enjoys certain strategic advantages. The low level of urbanization of the country and the thousands of villages scattered in some of the most inaccessible locations have helped the resistance to withstand the modern army and air force at the disposal of the PDPA and the Soviets. Perhaps equally important is the availability of sanctuaries in Pakistan.

The decision of international powers to oppose the Soviet invasion and to provide military, financial, and political support for the Afghan resistance nicely complemented the other strategic advantages of the resistance. Egypt and China provided very necessary weapons to the resistance in the early years of the war, 1979–1981, and the United States and Saudi Arabia subsequently became the major donors of weapons and financial aid to the resistance. Furthermore, worldwide support for the resistance, especially in the United Nations, the European Community, the Islamic Conference, and the Non-Aligned Conference, increased the isolation of the PDPA regime and the international legitimacy of the resistance (Ahady 1987).

Although the Islamists do not necessarily have the support of the majority of the people, they dominate the resistance. They are (especially Hekmatyar's group) more organized, ideologically committed, militarily superior, and politically more often on the offensive than their traditionalist counterparts. Their dominance is largely the result of their friendly relations with the government of Pakistan, which developed in the 1970s. After the Soviet invasion, Pakistan acquired an unprecedented power to influence Afghan politics. President Mohammad Zia-ul-Haq of Pakistan consistently favored Afghan Islamists (especially Hekmatyar) over other Afghan political groups, and although Prime Minister Benazir Bhutto is an opponent of fundamentalism, she did not have much freedom in formulating her government's policy vis-à-vis the Afghan conflict. The Pakistani military, which favors the Islamists, is still in control of the country's policy toward Afghanistan.

The Islamists have exploited this opportunity and launched an ideological offensive to portray the Afghan conflict as a nonnationalist struggle between revolutionary Islam and communism. However, there is substantial opposition to the Islamists' program, both within the resistance and among the people, and this division frequently prevents a unified political and military position by the resistance, which reduces its effectiveness. The problem was demonstrated by the failure of the resistance's offensive against the PDPA forces in Jalal-Abad after the withdrawal of the Soviet forces. In recent years, interorganizational rivalry and the pursuit of partisan interests, at the expense of the national interest, have also damaged the legitimacy of the resistance groups. The refusal of the political leadership of the resistance to allow the people to elect their representatives to a national council, which was to have elected a provisional government after the withdrawal of the Soviet forces, seriously diminished the legitimacy of the seven Peshawar-based resistance organizations.

INTERIM CONSEQUENCES

The PDPA attempted revolution has failed, but among the opposition, only the Islamists offer a program that has some radical elements. But the Islamists, in spite of their dominance in the struggle against the PDPA and the Soviets, are far from controlling the government, and other forces in the society have also been mobilized, which will complicate an Islamist takeover of power. Thus, neither the PDPA nor the Islamists have been able to institutionalize their values. The conflict has not been resolved yet; thus, no definite outcomes can be identified. However, the interim consequences of the PDPA's attempted revolution are rather the opposite of what the party intended to accomplish.

The PDPA was determined to destroy the old dominant class, which it identified as being composed of local notables, large landowners, big merchants, tribal chiefs (particularly the *Mohammadzai sardars*), and the *ulema*. However, as a consequence of the success of the resistance, the political significance of some of these groups has, if anything, increased. As a class, the *ulema* were a dying species in the 1960s and the 1970s as the forces of modernization were gradually eroding the basis of their sociopolitical influence. The PDPA's attempted revolution politicized the *ulema* and gave them a new purpose and much greater influence in sociopolitical life. The latter is owing to both their role in the war and a fundamental shift in ideology in favor of the role of the Sharia.

The khans and the tribal chiefs have also gained new political importance. As discussed earlier, by the 1960s the autonomy of the state had practically eliminated the independent power of the khans and the tribes in national politics. In competing for support among the various segments of the population, the resistance groups, especially the traditionalists, have found the khans and the tribal chiefs to be efficient intermediaries in expanding their influence. Unlike in the 1950s and the 1960s, foreign aid has not established the autonomy of the resistance organizations from the people and their local leaders because the magnitude of support for a particular resistance group influenced its ability to attract foreign aid, so the resistance organizations sought the support of local and tribal leaders, which enhanced their political influence.

Furthermore, the PDPA reversed its land reform program and passed a bill in 1987 whereby all property confiscated by the government after the 1978 coup was to be returned to the owners if they returned to Afghanistan. The resistance has also committed itself to reversing the land reform program and returning land to its original owners. This policy is bound to strengthen the position of the old dominant class.

The reentry of rural and tribal people into national politics is another major consequence of the PDPA's attempted revolution. As discussed earlier, the autonomy of the state and the modernization of the 1950s and the 1960s drastically reduced the influence of these communities in national politics and allowed the government greater freedom in public policy, but the PDPA revolution reintroduced the relevance of the rural population to national politics. The PDPA intended to mobilize the peasants in support of the revolution; instead, the peasants rebelled against the PDPA government. The reentry of the rural population into national politics is likely to reduce the freedom of any government in the future, and regardless of the final outcome of the conflict, public policy in a post–Soviet occupation and post–civil war Afghanistan will have to reflect the wishes of the rural population at least for a while. This fact is bound to have a very conservative impact on Afghan politics.

The war has thus destroyed most state-building accomplishments of the past 100 years. When the Soviets withdrew in February 1989, the PDPA government controlled less than 20 percent of the national territory, and the bureaucracy of the central government had collapsed in rural areas. The resistance had no unified administrative system to replace the bureaucracy of the central government, so essentially, the country has been divided into hundreds of regions controlled by different political groups, independent commanders, and local elites. The chaos of the past years has facilitated the rise of powerful warlords whose exclusive control over different regions threatens the disintegration of the country.

Even when peace returns to the country, the reestablishment of the authority of the central government over rural areas will be a demanding task. International support, especially from Pakistan, Iran, the United States, the Soviet Union, and Saudi Arabia, for the central government will significantly increase its chances to reestablish the authority of the government throughout the country. It is ironic that while the success of the resistance against the PDPA and the Soviet occupation is likely to deter other regional and international powers from direct intervention in Afghanistan, the war has also enabled Pakistan, Iran, the United States, the Soviet Union, and Saudi Arabia to establish strong relations with important political groups through which they can indirectly intervene in Afghan politics. Indeed, Pakistan's domination of Afghan politics is a real threat. Pakistan has already imposed the seven Peshawar-based groups on the Afghans, and after the Geneva Accords of 1988, President Zia strongly promoted Hekmatyar's leadership within the resistance. Since the Soviet withdrawal in February 1989, despite the drastic decline in the popularity of the seven organizations, Pakistan's continued support for them ensures their dominance within the resistance.

The failure of the PDPA revolution and the success of the resistance have strengthened the primacy of the Sharia in Afghan politics. Even though all Afghan political groups other than the Communists have supported the enforcement of the Sharia, the explicit nature of the recent years of struggle for values dispelled any doubt regarding the dominance of Islam. Even the Communists now accept Islam as the religion of the state.

The revolutionary struggle, however, has not resolved the other major issues of Afghan politics. The conception of Afghan nationalism is still a controversial issue, and the Communists as well as the Islamists and the traditionalists avoid the issue. De facto, they support a status quo, which is unacceptable to many Pushtuns. The weakening of the central government, which is always identified with the Pushtuns, has led to secessionist or autonomist tendencies among minorities. For instance, Hazarajat has had its own organizations since 1982, which encourage Hazara nationalism. A similar tendency is evident among the Nuristanis.

There is no consensus among Afghans regarding political participation or the legitimacy of a government. They all endorse mass participation in politics, but few genuinely believe in the sovereignty of the people. Similarly, while some emphasize procedural legitimacy and others insist on substantive legitimacy, political convenience frequently influences their positions more than any a priori theory.

Most social revolutions resolve major issues of politics that cannot be resolved peacefully. Consequently, despite the destruction, loss of life, and numerous personal and communal tragedies that characterize social revolutions, they are praised for enabling societies to move forward. The revolutionary struggle in Afghanistan has been extremely destructive; but it has not resolved the major issues of Afghan politics. Thus, the Afghan polity will continue to suffer from political instability.

CHRONOLOGY

1965: Formation of the PDPA.

1967: PDPA splits into the Khalq and Parcham factions.

July 1973: Daud, supported by nationalist and leftist (especially Parcham) officers, overthrows King Zahir Shah in a military coup.

1975: Daud purges leftists from his administration.

1977: Khalq and Parcham unite to oppose Daud.

April 17, 1978: An unidentified assassin kills Mir Akbar Khyber, a PDPA Politburo member.

April 27, 1978: PDPA military coup overthrows the Daud regime.

June–August 1978: The Khalq faction purges the Parcham faction.

July 12, 1978: PDPA government issues Decree No. 6, which abolished mortgages on land.

September 1978: First anti-PDPA rebellion in Nuristan, in eastern Afghanistan.

October 17, 1978: PDPA government issues Decree No. 7, which regulated marriages.

November 28, 1978: PDPA government issues Decree No. 8, which launched the land reform program.

December 5, 1978: Afghan-Soviet treaty of friendship signed.

March 1979: The Herat uprising, supported by local garrisons, results in the death of 100 Soviets and 3,000–5,000 civilian Afghans.

Summer 1979: Spread of anti-PDPA rebellion to fourteen provinces.

July 1979: The unpopular land reform is halted.

September 14, 1979: President Noor Mohammad Taraki and the Soviets try to kill Prime Minister Amin but fail. Taraki is ousted.

December 27, 1979: Soviets enter Afghanistan to defend the PDPA.

December 28, 1979: Soviets install Karmal as the new leader of the PDPA and head of state.

January 1980: International condemnation of the Soviet invasion.

January 10–14, 1980: In an emergency meeting, the UN General Assembly calls for the withdrawal of Soviet forces.

January 27–29, 1980: In an emergency meeting, the Organization of the Islamic Conference suspends Afghanistan's membership and calls for the withdrawal of Soviet forces.

May 17–22, 1980: Saudi Arabia donates $25 million to the Afghan resistance.

October 16, 1980: Brezhnev and Karmal call for a political settlement of the Afghan conflict.

September 22, 1981: President Sadat announces that Egypt has supplied arms to the resistance.

June 16–25, 1982: First round of UN-sponsored peace talks between Afghanistan and Pakistan.

Fall 1982: United States decides to dramatically increase both the quantity and the quality of weapons supplied to the resistance.

June 1983: UN peace talks between Afghanistan and Pakistan create great optimism but fail to result in any agreement.

November 19–21, 1985: Gorbachev and Reagan, during their Geneva Summit meeting, discuss the peaceful resolution of the Afghan conflict.

May 4, 1986: Karmal resigns from the leadership of the PDPA; Najibullah replaces him.

January 1, 1987: Najibullah declares a unilateral cease-fire and expresses willingness to share power with the opposition; the resistance rejects both the cease-fire and the power sharing.

April 14, 1988: Pakistan, Afghanistan, the United States, and the USSR sign the Geneva Accords requiring the Soviets to complete the withdrawal of their forces from Afghanistan by February 15, 1989.

August–December 1988: The UN and the USSR intensify efforts to persuade the resistance to form a coalition government with the PDPA, but their efforts fail.

February 15, 1989: The Soviets complete the withdrawal of their forces from Afghanistan, but war between the PDPA and the resistance continues. Factional divisions among resistance groups grow.

9

THE PHILIPPINES: THE MAKING OF A "PEOPLE POWER" REVOLUTION

RICHARD J. KESSLER

In 1986, a combination of popular demonstrations, army defections, and pressure from the United States led President Ferdinand Marcos to flee the Philippines. In succeeding years, Corazon ("Cory") Aquino, who led the opposition, has sought to build a democratic nation. She has had to struggle with a host of obstacles, including attempted military coups, continuing Muslim and Communist rebellions in the countryside, and opposition from the Philippine elite to major social reforms. Although the Philippine revolution began as an inspiring case of popular triumph over tyranny, a variety of conflicts continue, and the story of this revolution is far from over.

PREREVOLUTIONARY STATE AND SOCIETY

The Philippines is an island state still caught in the awkward process of becoming a nation. Over 7,000 islands spread nearly 2,000 kilometers (1,240 miles) north to south between the South China Sea and the Pacific Ocean. With over 57 million people packed into about 300,000 square kilometers (116,000 square miles), a population density that exceeds China's, a mixture of Malay, Chinese, Spanish, Negrito, and Caucasian peoples are divided into forty different tribal groups speaking about eighty languages or dialects.

In prehistoric times Negrito, Proto-Malay, and Malay peoples migrated to the islands. Divided politically along kinship lines, they evinced only a limited sense of nationhood as they engaged in extensive trade with Hindus, Indonesians, Chinese, and Japanese. The spread of Islam, which was well-established by 1500 A.D., brought a heightened sense of political territory, and *datus*, or chieftains, ruled over extended kinship groups. Without Ferdinand Magellan's discovery of the Philippines in 1521 and the subsequent conquest by the Spanish, the islands would

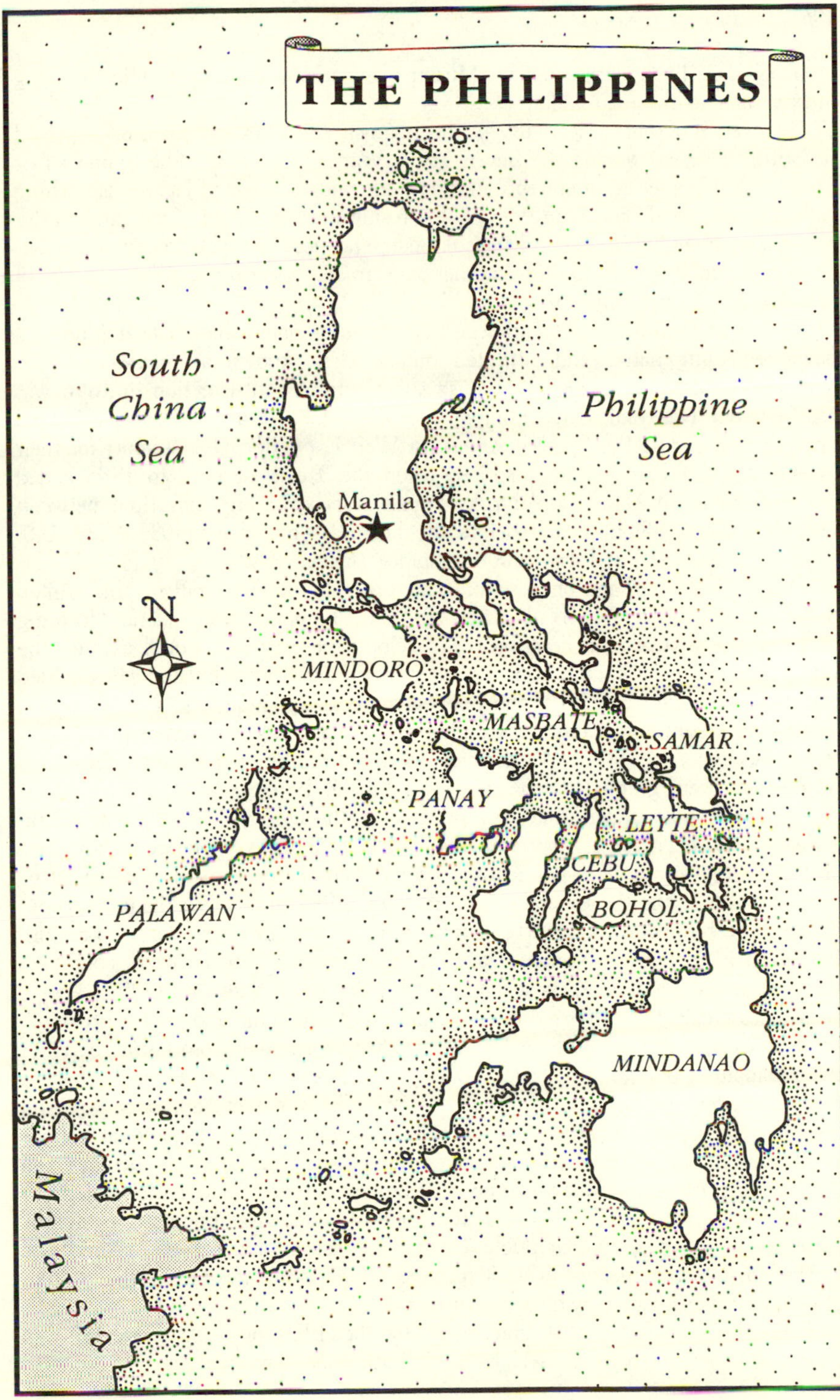

THE PHILIPPINES

South
China
Sea

Philippine
Sea

Manila

N

MINDORO

MASBATE

SAMAR

PANAY

LEYTE

CEBU

BOHOL

PALAWAN

MINDANAO

Malaysia

probably have been dominated by Muslims, eventually evolving politically along lines similar to those in Indonesia.

For over 300 years (1521–1898), the Spanish ruled (except for a brief period of British conquest during the Seven Year's War, 1756–1763). The Spanish first used the Philippines as an entrepôt in their trade with China and Japan, dispatching galleons laden with goods to Mexico for reshipment to Spain. Only after 1785 was trade direct with Spain. Mexico's independence in 1821 forced a further economic reorientation toward international trade, fostering mainly exports of tobacco, abaca, and sugar.

By the end of the nineteenth century, growing native nationalism among a newly emerging native and educated middle class, known as *ilustrados* ("enlightened"), began to challenge Spanish suzerainty. An insurrection in 1896 was crushed, but two years later Philippine rebels joined with U.S. troops to end Spanish rule during the Spanish American War. Expecting U.S. support for their independence, Filipinos were surprised when the Treaty of Paris in 1898 ceded the Philippines to U.S. colonial rule. Again war broke out, this time between U.S. troops and Filipinos, and before the hostilities ended in 1903, 4,234 U.S. troops had died and at least 16,000 Filipinos (Miller 1982).

Despite (and perhaps because of) the brutality of the conflict, the United States indicated its intentions ultimately to grant Philippine independence, forming in 1902 a legislature and describing a development plan that would assure "the Philippines for the Filipinos," but the early introduction of political parties helped institutionalize elite control of the political process. In 1934, the U.S. Congress established a Commonwealth of the Philippines and provided for a ten-year transition to full independence. World War II intervened, but the Philippines, then devastated by the war, were granted independence on July 4, 1946.

The newly independent state was modeled on the U.S. system with a president, a Senate, and a House of Representatives. Instead of states, there were provinces, each with a governor. Two political parties were dominant, the Nacionalista party, formed in 1907, and the Liberal party, created in 1945 from a Nacionalista splinter group. The president could serve a maximum of two four-year terms but until Ferdinand E. Marcos, a Nacionalista, won reelection in 1969, no party controlled the presidential residence, Malacanang Palace, for more than one term.

Marcos's reelection occurred during a period of economic and political turmoil. Student radicals in late 1968 had met secretly to form the Communist party of the Philippines, but this small group was not as threatening as the social malaise that infected a society which, although growing at 5 percent annually, was still less prosperous than any other ASEAN state. A report by the International Labour Organization (ILO) observed "an increasing polarization of rural incomes and . . . a fairly constant urban income distribution pattern" (International Labour Organization 1974: 9). A sense that the political system was impeding economic progress had led to a popular public call for a constitutional convention in 1967, and when it finally met in 1971, it focused on replacing the presidential system of the 1935 constitution with a parliamentary one.

Political dissatisfaction had intensified by the 1969 presidential election, in which Marcos's victory was widely viewed as fraudulent, and in the midterm elections of 1971 the Nacionalistas were badly beaten by the less-well-financed Liberal candidates. The writ of habeas corpus was even briefly suspended after a grenade attack on a Liberal party rally in August. In September 1972, Marcos declared martial law, arresting about 60,000 political opponents—including Senator Benigno Aquino—and announced the birth of a "new society" that would cleanse the Philippines of corrupt elements and remove barriers to economic modernization.

Marcos ruled under martial law until January 1981, during which time he solidified his political and economic control by using executive decrees to reward his cronies and punish his enemies. Although martial law provided the legal veneer for his actions, it was not sufficient to ensure long-term political control, and he engineered periodic national plebiscites to ratify approval of various measures, including in 1973 a new parliamentary-based constitution, in 1977 an interim National Assembly (the first elections for which were held in 1978), and constitutional amendments in April 1981 to provide for a strong, elected president above a prime minister. The slight opening in the political process coupled with a weakening in the economic recovery after a drop of world sugar prices in 1976 and the second international oil crisis in 1978 stimulated more widespread political opposition to Marcos's rule. Indeed, unlike elsewhere in Asia during the 1980s, it was the deteriorating economic situation rather than an improving economic climate that mobilized the middle class to press for a more democratic system (Hawes 1987).

In August 1983, Benigno Aquino was assassinated at the Manila International Airport as he returned from three years of exile in the United States. The wave of protest that followed Aquino's death accelerated political coalition-building among the elite. In National Assembly elections in May 1984, despite cheating by the government, Marcos's New Society Movement party (Kilusang Bagong Lipunan, KBL) was dealt a blow by the relatively unified opposition, which won 61 seats out of 183 despite an early Marcos prediction that his opponents would gain only 20 (Kessler 1984). This political development set the stage for a "snap" presidential election in February 1986, which became a contest among political elites over political control of the future of the Philippines (Simons 1987).

Marcos and his vice-presidential candidate, the former senator Arturo Tolentino, were arrayed against Aquino's widow, Corazon Cojuangco Aquino, a member of an elite landowning family in Tarlac Province, and former senator Salvador ("Doy") Laurel, from Batangas Province, whose father had once been president during the Japanese occupation.

The Elite

Divisions among the ruling elites were rarely for reasons of ideology and often for reason of wealth. As David Wurfel (1988: 38) has observed, nationalism in the Philippines was a form of "unsystemized ideology" used to legitimate the opposition. Thus, it was more often expressed in terms of what it was against rather than what it was for. Political party structures were also weak. Parties were essentially the creation of a small elite and were used only during an election season to mobilize a broader base of support. Marcos, for example, had been a Liberal party member before switching to the Nacionalistas. Traditionally, politics was a means to acquire more wealth and, in practice, was based more on pragmatic alliances than on ideologically based issues.

What Samuel Pepys observed about English government service applied equally to the Philippines: "It was not the salary of any place that did make a man rich, but the opportunities of getting money while he is in place." Disputes among leaders could be attributed to arguments over the distribution of wealth once in power or to some previous business disagreement. Eduardo Cojuangco, Corazon's first cousin, was a strong Marcos supporter, for example, in part because of a falling out with the other part of his clan over business dealings and also because of a dispute with Benigno Aquino over political control of their home province of Tarlac.

One factor contributing to elite cohesiveness was strong kinship ties, a remnant not only of prehistoric custom but also of Spanish influence. Kinship was determined both matrilineally and patrilineally, providing an extensive set of blood relations. Elites were also joined not only by marriage, as in the joining of the Aquinos and the Cojuangcos, but also through the "compadre" system, in which bonds of ritual kinship were sealed through baptism and confirmation as well as marriage. Blood and ceremony served to reinforce a tight system of interlocking alliances between families that both ascended and descended through the social system, in effect tying the elites to less fortunate members of their extended families in the rural areas (see Turner 1978; Lawless 1967; Jocano 1966). Imelda Marcos, for instance, was a poor, distant member of Leyte's distinguished Romualdez clan (Pedrosa 1987).

The system was also more open than it appeared, partly because of American influence. The U.S. colonial rulers brought and actively encouraged universal education in the Philippines, giving it one of the highest literacy rates in Asia. Students who achieved well, especially at the prestigious University of the Philippines, were singled out for co-optation by the elite. Ferdinand Marcos and his predecessor, Diosdado Macapagal, who both came from modest family backgrounds, were "topnotchers" in the Philippine bar exam. Social mobility was thus not entirely determined by initial economic status.

A final factor was the limited pool of elite members. A national elite began to emerge only in the late nineteenth century, and many members of the current ruling elite are the grandchildren or great grandchildren of this original group, tracing their political heritage to the leaders of the 1896 revolution and their economic power to the agricultural and industrial empires created during trade expansion in the nineteenth century or to when the Americans broke up Spanish control of the economy and the Catholic church's landed estates in the twentieth century. Wealth thus has remained concentrated for several generations. For example, in 1956, the top 20 percent of Philippine families controlled 55 percent of the nation's income; in 1971, the figure was 54 percent, and in 1985, 51 percent. Families created broad-based economic empires, spreading their sons and daughters among agricultural and industrial businesses rather than concentrating their holdings in one sector. This system helped protect against economic decline while perpetuating wealth.

Economic and Demographic Trends

The Philippines has traditionally been a primary product exporter and an importer of capital goods. In the 1950s, it began an industrialization policy using import-substitution policies to develop a domestic manufacturing base protected by high tariff barriers and quantitative import controls, which led to the creation of a classic dual economy with a traditional agricultural sector and a more modern industrial base (Hicks and McNicoll 1971). Although this diversification encouraged high rates of growth, import barriers also encouraged inefficiencies and did not encourage manufactured exports as most of the substitution occurred in the light consumer goods sector. Instead of increasing local production of raw materials and intermediate goods, manufacturing inputs were imported with the additional side effect of concentrating manufacturing in the capital region.

Even when these policies brought about severe balance-of-payments crises, little changed. The reasons for failure are multiple, but at least one was social. The elites who controlled the agricultural sector and had diversified into manufacturing as a result of the protected policies of the 1950s were not about to see their economic benefits reduced by foreign competition, so they engineered stratagems to avoid any reduction of their economic power. As a consequence, industrial production further declined, and industrial employment "stagnated" during 1968–1973 (World Bank 1988: 158). This situation changed significantly after 1975, but the underlying economic conditions remained the same.

Between 1975 and 1983, the Philippines' real GNP grew at almost 4 percent, and it increased by 6.4 percent between 1975 and 1979. The reasons were largely external. The 1973–1974 oil crisis stimulated international lending of petrodollars by the commercial banks, and at the same time, the Philippines experienced a boom for some of its principal commodities. The growth in exports, however, was not sufficient to compensate for the growing import demand as the economy expanded, and the total external debt increased fivefold between 1975 and 1982 as foreign borrowing financed the deficit.

The basic structure of Philippine economic growth was also little altered. Growth was in the protected industries, and Marcos's policy of favoring a select few "crony capitalists" forced out many other private entrepreneurs, further exacerbating inefficiencies. Terms of trade began turning against the Philippines in the late 1970s, especially after the second oil crisis in 1978. Political and economic instabilities accelerated private capital flight out of the country, and commercial banks began refusing additional financing. In 1984, per capita real GNP growth was a negative 9.3 percent; in 1985, it was a negative 6.3 percent, and in 1986, it inched up to a negative 0.9 percent.

An International Monetary Fund (IMF) and World Bank–supported stabilization program, begun in late 1983, began to turn the tide in 1985 when external balance was restored. However, servicing the debt required continued restraint of domestic demand through a variety of measures, including reductions in public expenditures, restrictive monetary policies, quantitative import restrictions, increases in import duties, and export taxes. These measures weakened public support for the government and helped coalesce elite political opposition (Blejer and Guerrero 1988).

Adjustment policies worsened the Philippines' long-term economic problem of poverty. Personal income by 1985, when more than 30 million people out of a total population of 56 million were living in poverty, was below the 1971 level. Most of the poor were in rural areas, where 30 percent lived at bare subsistence levels in 1985, and most of the population and labor force lived in the rural areas, although income inequalities were greater in the cities. The causes of increasing poverty and unequal income distribution were unequal asset ownership, rapid population growth, and lack of employment opportunities (World Bank 1988: 12). Current population trends suggest that poverty will remain a problem. About 16 million new workers will be entering the labor market over the rest of the century, and if the present population growth rate continues at about 2.5 percent, then the population will nearly double in the next generation.

International Position

After independence, the Philippines remained closely allied with and dependent on the United States. Filipinos were one of the few colonial peoples to fight for their colonial power during World War II, but after the war, the United States insisted on retaining rights to over 200 military bases and keeping special economic benefits. Even after some of these economic and military privileges were eliminated, the Philippines remained closely allied with the United States, sending troops to fight in both Korea and Vietnam and continuing to host two major U.S. military facilities, Subic Bay Naval Base and Clark Air Base. In exchange, the United States supplied substantial amounts of economic and military assistance, providing more than two-thirds of the bilateral development aid before martial law. Also, the United States remained the most important market for Philippine exports and the source of most foreign capital, accounting for 80 percent of total foreign investment.

U.S. aid increased dramatically in the 1970s. In 1966, U.S. development assistance was about $4 million; six years later in 1972, it was $30.5 million; in 1973, it was $135 million. U.S. military aid made up a substantial portion of the armed forces budget; in essence, it accounted for the Philippines' entire yearly procurement outlays. Military aid in 1966 totaled about $25 million; in 1972, it was only slightly more than $19 million, but the amount increased in 1973 to nearly $40 million. In 1979, the Carter administration renegotiated the base agreement, providing a military and economic aid package that totaled $500 million over a five-year period. This figure was increased to $900 million in the 1983 renegotiations conducted by the Reagan administration. World Bank loans also increased in the 1970s. In 1972, the Philippines owed the World Bank only $142 million; this obligation increased to $576 million in 1978 and totaled almost $2.5 billion in 1985.

After 1972, Marcos used foreign aid and foreign affairs to establish his legitimacy. He became an active proponent of regional cooperation in the Association of Southeast Asian Nations (ASEAN); he pursued the nonaligned movement, sending observers to its meetings; he courted the Islamic countries in the Middle East and Africa; he established diplomatic relations with the Communist bloc countries, especially the Soviet Union and the People's Republic of China; and he periodically threatened the United States with the closing of U.S. military facilities. But while Marcos's often nationalist rhetoric and independent actions were applauded by the elite, they did not add to his credibility and were viewed as cynical attempts to convince the Americans that their financial support should be increased. Ironically, despite dramatic foreign policy initiatives and increased aid, Marcos's legitimacy declined, as did the condition of his country. By 1985, the Philippines was no longer acclaimed, as it had been in the 1950s, as Asia's economic and political showcase for democracy. Its political system was bankrupt, governed capriciously by a dictator in ill health, suffering from kidney disease, and an ambitious wife trying to position herself as his political successor.

THE ONSET OF STATE CRISIS

In the 1980s, President Marcos's rule came full circle, and the Philippines' economic and political disintegration was evident. In the face of massive declines in economic growth, there was renewed talk about returning to pretechnocratic policies of import substitution (Bello, Kinely, and Elinson 1982). The political crisis was aggravated by Senator Aquino's assassination, which encouraged factionalism within the government's ranks, and a spreading Communist insurgency seemed to mark a return to the counterinsurgency atmosphere of the early 1950s.

Opposition to Marcos's rule had been stymied when he declared martial law in 1972, partly because considerable public support emerged for his promise of a "new society." Many people in the middle class, as well as others, had grown disgusted with the political infighting among elites and the violence in the streets, and they had become apprehensive that the Philippines was being left behind economically by the rest of Asia. In 1972, Marcos did the unthinkable by arresting the oligarchy's leaders and weakening their economic power by confiscating their holdings. Private armies also were disbanded and weapons confiscated, leaving the country, especially the capital, with a sense of calm not experienced in many years. The opposition groups that did exist were negligible and isolated. The Communist-led New People's Army, which then consisted of a few score, retreated to the mountains of northern Luzon. The principal military threat came from resurgent Muslim secessionists operating in parts of Mindanao and the Sulu archipelago. By 1976, the Muslim rebels had been tamed, co-opted by Marcos's deft political maneuvers, and the political opposition lived mainly in exile in the United States.

By the late 1970s, however, Marcos's support had begun to weaken significantly. Early expectations that martial law would be a short-term condition followed by the reestablishment of normal political institutions had been disappointed. People began to weary of Marcos's extended rule and began to be wary of the political dynasty he seemed to be establishing through his wife, Imelda, and three children. Also, showcase development programs, including a Westinghouse nuclear power project and large-scale luxury hotel construction in metropolitan Manila for the World Bank and IMF's annual meeting in 1976, struck many as incongruous, given the country's poverty, and also contributed to balance-of-payments problems. Finally, the development of "crony capitalism," in which a few of Marcos's favored businesspeople gained monopoly control of major parts of the country's agricultural and industrial sectors, alienated members of Manila's business elite, who initially had supported martial law in the expectation that a more technocratic approach to development would occur.

In early 1981, a major financial crisis erupted when a Marcos crony, Dewey Dee, fled the country leaving about $100 million in debts. Dee had entangled a number of other cronies in his financial web, and the collapse of his business empire toppled other corporations as well. Although the financial community recovered in the short-term from the Dee fiasco, it was an important turning point as it exposed the financial relationships only previously suspected, making the Manila business elite increasingly outspoken in opposition to Marcos and further accelerating capital flight, which undermined the regime's economic stability. The continued economic difficulties forced a general retrenchment under guidance from the IMF and the World Bank. Stricter economic policies, however, reduced general government outlays. This retrenchment reduced the funds Marcos could use to win support in the rural areas and to spend on the military, which had been an essential part of his power base since he first entered politics after World War II. Marcos's political maneuverability was being limited.

Marcos tried to compensate for this reduction in political space by solidifying his support in Washington, the Philippines' premier economic and military ally. He was aided in this tactic by the election of Ronald Reagan, a conservative eager to demonstrate his support for authoritarian leaders loyal to U.S. interests—unlike the Carter administration, which had withdrawn support from Iran's shah. Reagan had a personal relationship with Marcos dating back to 1969 when Reagan had served as President Nixon's special emissary to Manila. A clear signal of his support was Vice-President Bush's visit to Manila in 1981, during Marcos's inaugural, when Bush saluted Marcos's support for democracy, saying "We love your adherence to democratic principle and to the democratic processes" (Department of State, *Bulletin* 8:2053 [August 1981]). This remark was followed by an invitation for a state visit to Washington in the fall of 1982—only the second such welcome Marcos had received since 1965 (Kessler 1986).

A new military-base compensation package was negotiated in 1983, giving the Philippines $900 million in economic and military assistance over a five-year period. These funds provided financial resources and, more important sent a signal to Marcos's political enemies that they should not expect support from Washington. Even so, external support was insufficient to replenish the depleted treasury at a time when increased demands were being placed upon it. The Communist insurgency became more active in the early 1980s as the deteriorating economic and political situation brought the Communists more recruits and as their 1970s strategy of gradually building a political base among the people bore fruit. Their attacks soon placed the government forces on the defensive, strung out as they were across the archipelago.

In 1981, Marcos officially lifted martial law as a precondition for the pope's visit, and U.S. officials, including congressmen, encouraged Marcos to hold elections to formalize the political system and thus provide a needed sign of political stability for foreign investors. Rather than stabilizing Marcos's control, each action encouraged his opposition. The solution to the debt crisis came only at the great cost of negative growth rates, and economic decline made the people even more disgruntled. The solution to the political crisis only provided more legitimate venues for the opposition to organize and more targets for them to attack as Marcos tried to manipulate the political outcome.

Elite Dynamics

Marcos attempted to centralize political as well as economic control, and in 1978, he created the New Society Movement party (KBL) on a Nacionalista party base to solidify his control as the political system moved toward apparent normality in the post-martial-law period. In December 1972, he had reestablished a system of barangays—neighborhood or village organizations, which had been the principal form of government in the pre-Spanish days—as a means of bypassing normal political structures in order to ratify his actions. The barangay system gave Marcos a grass-roots structure for political mobilization but did not establish legitimacy among the elites or the outside world.

Marcos also expanded the bureaucracy, from 600,000 to 1.2 million (Richter 1987: 58), but a bloated and corrupt bureaucracy was also not the most efficient mechanism through which to enforce centralization. Moreover, Filipinos were not responsive to centralized control. Neither the Spanish nor the Americans had sought or achieved authoritarian control, and even though the central government controlled the purse strings, considerable local autonomy was the norm. In the post-war period, despite a dramatic increase in the size of the government bureaucracy, both central and local governments remained weak primarily for financial reasons. Until 1972, government spending was never more than 10 percent of GNP, and although towns and barrios were allowed to raise some funds locally, they did so on the basis of property tax assessments, which were susceptible to considerable evasion and fraud (Wurfel 1988: 92).

In addition, Filipinos are prone to organization building. For every six Filipinos gathered together there are at least eight parties, goes a standard Filipino joke. In the early years of martial law, Marcos could restrain some of this political activity because of his coercive power and dominance over resources, but as his power weakened, a veritable cornucopia of so-called cause-oriented groups from all sectors sprung up representing the new "parliament of the streets."

In addition, Marcos's control did not extend either to the religious groups, Catholic or Protestant, or to the underground organizations, primarily the Communist party of the Philippines (CPP). The CPP began in the mid-1970s to strengthen its political and propaganda arm, the National Democratic Front (NDF), which used both new and old organizations to mobilize support among a variety of sectors, including labor, students, teachers, and health workers. These groups were directly under the NDF's control, semi-independent, or separate organizations sharing a common agenda with the NDF.

The churches, too, provided support for groups dedicated to social action and, implicitly, political reform. For example, the Association of Major Religious Superiors of the Philippines (AMRSP) created the Task Force Detainees of the Philippines (TFDP) to document human rights abuses. Although church and NDF work affected mainly the lower and middle classes rather than the elites, it helped establish the basis for a broad alternative political agenda once the elites became active, and provided the mass support that was needed later to give credibility to the elite leaders. The mass support was critical because it was precisely what the New Society Movement lacked, as it consisted primarily of bureaucrats, business-people, and politicians trying to curry favor with Marcos, and poor people paid to attend rallies.

Nonetheless, Marcos had reason to be confident about his control in 1985 just before his downfall. Elections in April 1978 for seats in the interim National Assembly gave the KBL 151 out of 165 seats; in local elections in January 1980, the KBL won 95 percent of all positions; and in a presidential election in June 1981, Marcos won 88 percent of the vote against two minor opposition candidates. But the elections also gave elite opponents the opportunity to organize and begin mobilizing their own supporters. Political participation has always been high in the Philippines, and the reawakening of political activity gave people an opportunity to express attitudes long suppressed by Marcos. In 1978 opposition leaders, such as Senators Lorenzo Tanada and Benigno Aquino, formed the People's Power party (Lakas ng Bayan, LABAN), and it won 40 percent of the vote in metropolitan Manila—Corazon Aquino received her first political exposure campaigning for her still-imprisoned husband in that election. In the 1980 elections, which the Liberal party boycotted, several opposition candidates won, including a rump faction of the Nacionalista party controlled by the prominent Laurel family. Stimulated by these victories, opposition leaders signed a Covenant for National Freedom in 1980, and some formed a United Democratic Organization (UNIDO), which became the basis for a surprising opposition victory in the 1984 National Assembly elections. In 1982, UNIDO was renamed the United Nationalist Democratic Organization and now included not only Assemblyman Salvador Laurel but also two exiles, Senators Benigno Aquino and Raul Manglapus. The next year Aquino returned, partly because he believed that continued exile in Boston was threatening to make him irrelevant to the political events occurring in Manila, and his murder encouraged a proliferation of opposition groups, such as the August Twenty-One Movement (ATOM) and the Justice for Aquino–Justice for All (JAJA).

These groups were mostly organizations of middle-class professionals, including students and church officials, whose primary focus was social reform. They formed alliances or, in some instances, shared leaders with the political opposition groups agitating for Marcos's removal, such as the Pilipino Democratic party (PDP) of Mayor Aquileno Pimentel, LABAN, the Social Democratic party (SDP), UNIDO, and the Liberal party (LP). In January 1984, a congress was held to prepare a common agenda for the upcoming assembly election, but unification talks broke apart when some members formed a new opposition umbrella organization called Compact, not to participate in the election, but to boycott the balloting. This group included elements of the LP, PDP-LABAN, and JAJA. The opposition was divided by two principal issues: leadership and strategy. Most of the leaders were pre–martial law politicians, such as former Senators Laurel, Jonito Salonga, Tanada, and Jose Diokno, supplemented by a younger breed of activist busines-speople, including Aquino's younger brother Agapito ("Butz"), who had organized the January congress, and the Benguet Corporation head, Jaime Ongpin (whose brother Roberto served in the Marcos cabinet). These individuals could not easily agree on a common chieftain, but more important were differences over strategy.

Marcos continued to control the playing field despite the titular lifting of martial law. The writ of habeas corpus was still suspended; Marcos could detain anyone in the name of "public safety" or "security of the state"; so-called political offenses were punishable by death or life imprisonment; individuals could be deprived of their citizenship and property if declared political offenders; the president retained concurrent legislative authority with the National Assembly; and Marcos controlled the media and the Commission on Elections (COMELEC), which was responsible for voter lists and balloting. The state's coercive power was thus considerable, and many people in the opposition believed that only an election boycott could undermine Marcos's control.

Marcos's strategy was to divide and conquer the opposition by offering at least the opportunity for political participation in the National Assembly elections, which were recognized as being a precursor to presidential elections later in the decade. He also allowed the appearance of reform by appointing two new members who were not apparently loyalists to COMELEC, and he allowed voter reregistration to purge the list of nonexistent voters. These tactics did succeed in dividing the opposition. Jaime Cardinal Sin, the leader of the Catholic Church, and Corazon Aquino both favored participation although Butz Aquino opposed it. But participation was aided by a powerful external force, the United States—which through congressional hearings, executive branch statements, and emissaries—conveyed the message to Marcos that a credible election process was important if Marcos was to continue to receive support.

Encouraged by the United States but on their own initiative, Filipinos organized the National Movement for Free Elections (NAMFREL) as an independent election oversight group. Led by a Manila business executive, Jose Concepción, and supported by other prominent businesspeople, including Ongpin, all of whom retained close ties to the Catholic church and in some cases were members of Opus Dei (an elite Catholic lay group), NAMFREL organized in a few months a national system of 150,000 poll watchers to supervise balloting and to produce a "quick count" on election day.

NAMFREL was critical to the opposition's strong showings in the 1984 National Assembly elections and the February 1986 "snap" presidential election, and there were both internal and external reasons for this success. Externally, NAMFREL helped energize international public attention. Concepción visited both Europe and the United States to dramatize NAMFREL's work, for example, speaking in Washington to policymakers and journalists at a forum sponsored by the Carnegie Endowment for International Peace. The resulting international press and U.S. congressional attention were extraordinarily effective in focusing world public opinion on Marcos and restricting vote fraud. Internally, NAMFREL provided an institutional setting for hundreds of thousands of previously apolitical Filipinos to participate politically without being overtly anti-Marcos. NAMFREL also provided a venue for many of the cause-oriented groups that were not aligned with a political party to participate in the process.

Thus, although the opposition remained divided and Marcos retained control of the playing field, the large-scale public mobilization that occurred after 1983 supplied a source of mass support for the opposition, as Filipinos at all levels of society were politicized. In addition, the formation of NAMFREL and the intervention of outside observers established more reliable criteria by which to judge Marcos's legitimacy.

Popular Mobilization Potential

An early indicator of Marcos's waning support and control was a January 1984 plebiscite on four constitutional amendments. Although the opposition again failed to unite against them—perhaps giving Marcos unwarranted confidence—voter turnout was much less than COMELEC's predicted 80 percent. Only 38 percent showed up. This low turnout was an early signal of three developments that would be important in the National Assembly and presidential elections. First, the numbers indicated that the government could not deliver the voters. Second, both the church-run Radio Veritas and NAMFREL had accurately predicted the vote, suggesting that they were effective counterpoints to the government's apparatus even though they had had only a short time to organize. Third, government support was weak even among the poor, whose votes Marcos had traditionally been able to buy on the cheap and who were often more responsive to propaganda. Voters from the Bicol region, generally poor and plagued by land tenure issues, rejected two amendments concerning land grants.

Quantitative analysis of recent Philippines elections by Carl Lande and Allan Cigler suggests some of the socioeconomic factors contributing to antigovernment attitudes:

1. Income: Anti-Marcos voting was encouraged by low income levels and high income inequality. Support for Marcos was strongest in areas with the least rural income disparities.
2. Education: Support for Aquino's 1986 candidacy was strongest among voters with an elementary education while uneducated voters and college-educated voters supported Marcos.
3. Basic amenities (e.g., electricity): Aquino's support was strongest in the poorer, more isolated provinces.
4. Land ownership: Aquino's support was strongest among tenant farmers (Lande and Cigler 1988).

These factors and others led Lande and Cigler to conclude that "the strongest support at successive elections for President Aquino and her LABAN alliance came not from the relatively urbanized provinces surrounding Greater Manila, but from those parts of the central Philippines (Bicol and the Visayas) marked by high levels of economic distress, agricultural tenancy, and geographic isolation" (Lande and Cigler 1988: 27–28).

Although the final balloting in 1986 was marked by fraud, making completely accurate tabulations impossible, there is some evidence that the results were much closer than either side was willing to admit. This probability suggests that at the beginning of 1986, Marcos still retained considerable support, even in Manila, and that one of the keys to his fall many have been the marginal increase in urban elite and rural poor opposition to him as a result of the deteriorating economy. Yet, although these two groups were united in opposition, their agendas were separate. The elites wanted a return to a stable political system and a rational economic policy in order to arrest decline. The rural poor were less concerned about political reforms and the cost of imported goods and more concerned about the extent of their economic disenfranchisement, both in terms of tenancy issues and in terms of the prices paid for their produce by government agricultural monopolies controlled by Marcos cronies. In macroeconomic terms, these differences were reflected in the income inequality between the two groups.

In 1985, the poor represented 57 percent of the population, essentially the same as in 1971, with also almost no change in the percentages of poor living in urban and rural areas: 42 percent and 58 percent, respectively (World Bank 1988: 3–4). But the number of poor had increased because of population growth. However, incidences of poverty may have slightly declined between 1971 and 1979 before starting to increase after 1979 when personal income began to decline. Other indicators suggest a similar pattern of improvement in the 1970s and decline in the 1980s.

The poor were typically rural subsistence farmers dependent on rice and corn production. Most lived south of Manila with the greatest concentration in Mindanao. Most were migrants to marginal rainfed and upland areas, where they worked as tenants on farms averaging 1.6 hectares (7 acres). Modern inputs, such as fertilizer and pesticide, were rarely utilized, nor did the farmers use irrigation or credit systems, the average family size was 6.3 people living in homes lacking sanitation facilities or electricity. At least a third of these people had not completed elementary school.

The urban poor resided mainly in metropolitan Manila where their income— earned also by women and children—accounted for half the average urban income. They lived in fetid slums, shack built upon shack, drank polluted water, and washed themselves and their clothes in streams clogged with human excrement. Importantly, the poor spent most of their money on food produced locally, and thus, unlike the elites, they were little affected by the Philippines' balance-of-payment problems.

Thus, although the poor and well-to-do formed an alliance against Marcos, their principal grievances and agendas were radically dissimilar. The poor wanted land reform, improved prices for their produce, basic improvements in living conditions, and personal security from an undisciplined military and a corrupt judicial system. The elites were more interested in wresting political control from Marcos so they could regain their economic power. They opposed anything but the most superficial land reform schemes and preferred low agricultural prices in order to maintain lower living costs. These differences did not weaken the alliance, but they did suggest that once Marcos was exiled, political cooperation between the poor and the rich would cease.

REVOLUTIONARY MOBILIZATION AND THE STRUGGLE FOR POWER

Opposition to Marcos began building momentum after Benigno Aquino's death in 1983, yet it curiously began to slow in 1985. The critical decision point that brought the regime down was determined, not by the opposition, but by Marcos himself when he announced on November 3, 1985, his intention to hold early presidential elections.

Although after Aquino's assassination, opposition voices had begun to be increasingly heard in Manila and in Washington—through street demonstrations and the press, such as the Catholic church's newspaper and radio station, both called Veritas—these only provided an outlet for opposition vitriol. Exposing the regime's corruption was not the same as overthrowing it. Even though the attacks did increase public sentiment against the government, the opposition had little short-term hope for success. Instead, it hoped for success in the then-scheduled May 1987 presidential elections. Characteristic of the opposition's tactics was the preference of the elites to play by Marcos's rules, within the legal and institutional systems he had forged.

Although the poor and more radical members of the middle class joined the Communist-led insurgency, they also had little hope of success. Indeed, an attempt to forge an overt alliance between the left and the right against Marcos in May 1985 failed when the right and some leftist leaders pulled out of the organizing conference, charging that the CPP was trying to infiltrate and control the group through surrogates. A second indicator of the opposition's weakness was a failed effort to impeach Marcos in the National Assembly in the summer of 1985, after a series of U.S. newspaper articles began exposing Marcos's secret investments in the United States.

A third indication that public hostility toward Marcos had yet to reach a boiling point occurred when public outcry was muted after a commission appointed by Marcos to investigate the Aquino assassination concluded in October 1984 that it had resulted from a high-level military conspiracy. By mid-1985, acquittal of the military men, including the military's chief of state, General Fabian Ver, was widely presumed, and they were finally exonerated on December 1.

Perhaps sensing that he still controlled popular opinion and could dominate the political process, Marcos decided to call an early presidential election. He did so for two reasons: First, doing so disrupted the opposition's timetable, and, second, he was under U.S. pressure to stabilize the political system. There were indications in early 1985 of Marcos's intentions when on January 7, 1985, at a KBL caucus, he announced that "as of today, we are a party on a political campaign." Then in February, he returned operational control of the police to the mayors, declaring that this action was not intended for political purposes. After the impeachment effort failed, he suggested that a snap election might be called, which signaled his supporters to prepare and tested the opposition's ability to unite behind a single candidate. The opposition's failure to unite early may have further encouraged Marcos to pursue his strategy.

Marcos had also received a number of U.S. visitors, beginning in January 1985, who pressed for reforms.[1] These visits culminated in Senator Paul Laxalt's (R-Nevada) Manila visit in October as a representative of President Reagan. Laxalt recommended that Marcos hold a snap election, and after returning to Washington he recommended so again during telephone conversations with Marcos. On November 3, Marcos announced this intention in a satellite interview on the David Brinkley television show.

After his announcement, the opposition leaders continued to divide along the previous issue of whether or not to participate. U.S. officials in private contact with them encouraged participation and offered to send election experts and observers to monitor both the process leading up to the election and the balloting. The opposition was also divided over a candidate, despite an effort that had begun early in the year by the formation of a conveners' group, consisting of Corazon Aquino, Jaime Ongpin, and Lorenzo Tanada, to sift through a dozen or so candidates, and choose one.

What the convener-group process had disclosed was the inadequacy of most potential contenders to unite the opposition, but it did highlight Corazon Aquino as the one nonpolitical leader whom most could support. In addition, she gained the powerful backing of Cardinal Sin. Aquino herself, however, was reluctant, and perhaps it was the coincidental acquittal on December 2 of charges against Ver for the murder of her husband that decided her to announce on December 3. But opposition unity was still dependent on the other candidates giving way. Aquino's principal challenger was Laurel, leader of UNIDO and Marcos's major opponent in the National Assembly. UNIDO was the best organized of the opposition groups, and Laurel had invested time and money traipsing about the country, building local alliances as part of a national political structure. In addition, Laurel had substantial political experience whereas Aquino's was limited to the public speaking and political activity begun mainly after her husband's death. What Laurel lacked, however, is what Aquino had—popularity.

Aquino's popularity was derived from her status as a martyr's widow and her lack of political experience. The drama associated with her husband's death and the personal charisma that surrounded the diminutive widow appealed to the common people. Her close association with the Catholic church, typified by her frequent allusion to the power of prayer and periodic sequestering in a convent, attracted a populace attuned to ritual while retaining residual tribal beliefs in magic. There was something mystical about "Cory's crusade." In addition, the church provided her with an institutional mechanism to mobilize supporters, and her lack of prior political experience made Aquino even more appealing to people who had grown disenchanted with the posturing of traditional leaders. Aquino recognized all of this popularity, recounting to me in a private interview in 1985 how she had recently returned from a trip to Negros, distributing relief goods to the poor, where she was greeted gratefully and was told that they would vote for her.

The fragmentation in the opposition continued up to the last moment of the filing deadline. At first, Laurel and Aquino filed separately. Despite the clear majority support for Aquino, Laurel held out, saying he would take the vice-presidential position only if Aquino agreed to run under his party's name. This tactic would assure UNIDO's premier political position in dividing the spoils should they win or would further solidify UNIDO as the dominant opposition party under Laurel's control should they lose. The division was not over ideology— in essence, the only platform was Marcos's removal—but over political supremacy. Aquino and Laurel differed little when it came to issues, both sharing the values and views of the elite.

Only Cardinal Sin's intercession united the opposition. Summoning both principals to the archbishop's palace in Manila just hours before the final deadline, Sin persuaded Laurel to accept the vice-presidential position and Aquino to accept UNIDO. Both sides had engaged in last-minute political brinkmanship, and as each failed to force the other to capitulate, both were forced to agree to each other's demands because both realized that they could not win without the other. Sin's mediation provided a useful means for both sides to save face.

With the opposition united and a date for the election fixed for February 7, 1986, Marcos tried to get out of the situation by asking the Supreme Court to annul the election as unconstitutional. A secretly conducted poll indicating that he would lose the election compelled this tactic. In normal times, Marcos could have been expected to win in the Supreme Court, as he had appointed all thirteen judges and needed only ten votes. But one judge was on leave, and three others refused to oppose the election, deciding that it was the political will of the people. Stymied in this attempt and under domestic pressure because of a building election fever and external pressure from the United States, Marcos acceded to the election.

U.S. pressure was considerable once the election process began. Congressional hearings detailed Philippine election procedures,[2] and other investigative hearings concerned Marcos's hidden wealth and the fabrication of his war record. Several quasi-official groups affiliated with the congressionally funded National Endowment for Democracy were sent to observe the election process, and it was ultimately decided to send a bipartisan group of U.S. observers for election day. Although the membership of this group was picked by the White House to avoid controversial appointments biased against Marcos, the group's leader, Senator Richard Lugar (R-Indiana), played a key role in U.S. public opinion by exposing fraud. All these groups were heavily influenced by NAMFREL's analysis of the election process, which in essence provided the standard by which the fairness and the credibility of the election would be judged. The U.S. embassy in Manila also played a key role in influencing the judgments of observers and participants, meeting frequently with the opposition and providing detailed descriptions of the voting once balloting had occurred.

These actions served to undercut Marcos's control of the process. Although he could still limit the opposition's access to the media and still controlled COMELEC, these levers were no longer critical. An informal network of rumor and information operated throughout the country, using videos, tabloids, and the international news media, to which the elites had daily access through newspaper and television. Filipinos could even receive broadcasts of U.S. news programs from the U.S. military facilities at Clark Air Base and Subic Bay Naval Base. Aquino and Laurel attracted enormous crowds to their rallies, and enthusiasm spread almost by osmosis. COMELEC, too, became less important as NAMFREL had developed into a shadow-COMELEC. Using local citizen-band club radios (an essential method of communication in rural areas), business-donated computers, and a national system of 500,000 volunteers, NAMFREL was able to duplicate COMELEC's work even more quickly as it did not have to wait for the "official" returns.

Marcos's final weapon, the military, was also failing him. In early 1985, a military reform group consisting of junior officers, mainly graduates of the Philippine

Military Academy classes of 1961–1965 and affiliated with the defense minister, Juan Ponce Enrile, began to organize in an attempt to create a shadow military command while plotting a coup against Marcos. This group had become disenchanted with Marcos's rule, angry about the promotion of incompetent officers, and concerned about the growing insurgency. They were fed by Enrile's personal fortune and ambition to replace Marcos with himself. During vote tabulation, the wife of one of these plotters dramatically led a walkout of the computer technicians, charging that Marcos was trying to rig the outcome with false data.

The election on February 7 exposed Marcos's fragile hold on the country, but, although condemned both domestically and internationally, he still held on to power, bolstered in part by Reagan's refusal to withdraw support. On February 10, Reagan said that despite charges of fraud, there was still evidence of a strong two-party system in the islands and he hoped that Marcos and Aquino "could come together to make sure the government works." Instead, political disintegration continued as both sides dug in their heels. Too much was at stake, and too many members of the opposition had been killed to permit compromise.[3]

Possibly (although it is unlikely) Marcos could have survived the crisis despite mounting pressures. If he could outlast his opponents—whose postelection arsenal of weapons was limited to a boycott of companies controlled by his cronies, calls for the formation of a secessionist government, and U.S. congressional pressure to cut aid—Marcos could hope that the tumult would die down. But he had become aware of the military plot against him and while attempting to preempt the plotters by arresting them, he set in motion the very event he was trying to prevent.

On February 22, elements of the military supported by Enrile and the military's vice–chief of staff constabulary general, Fidel Ramos, rebelled. Holed up at the military's headquarters at Camp Aguinaldo and the constabulary's headquarters, Camp Crame, just across the street, this small group called on the rest of the military to join them and appealed to Cardinal Sin to send the people for support. On Radio Veritas, Cardinal Sin called the people out into the streets, and the highway dividing Camp Crame from Camp Aguinaldo became clogged with people of all classes in a festive but periodically tense atmosphere. Matrons and nuns, workers and chief executives all flocked to create a human barricade between the rebels and the Marcos loyalists attempting to move within firing range.

Marcos hesitated to counterattack, partly because he was unsure about the extent of rebel support within the military, partly because it was such an unprecedented action that his first impulse was to negotiate for time, and partly because the Americans insisted that no violent action be taken, fearing that bloodshed would produce further rifts in the military and the political system. As Marcos hesitated, other units joined the rebel cause. Apparently medicated and increasingly isolated in the palace, Marcos equivocated. By the time he finally ordered troops to attack, it was too late; few remained on his side. On February 25, Marcos and his family and aides were airlifted by U.S. helicopters from Malacanang Palace and flown into exile in Hawaii.

In retrospect, clearly no single person or factor was solely responsible for the February 1986 "people power" revolution. It was the result of a combination of factors (internal, external, social, economic, political, psychological) and individuals that eroded the regime's legitimacy and its responsiveness to change and provided the opportunity for an opposition to emerge. It was almost a "bloodless" revolution, although it almost became very bloody when Marcos ordered his tanks and artillery to attack, but it also proved, after Marcos had long gone, to be less a revolution than a restoration of the ancien régime.

REVOLUTIONARY OUTCOMES

During her first four years in office, President Aquino had three major accomplishments: surviving at least six attempted coups, restoring democratic institutions, and improving the economy. The first serious coup attempt, led by Colonel Gregorio Honasan, one of the leaders of the anti-Marcos group, nearly succeeded in toppling her government on August 28, 1987. In December 1989, he tried again and, as before, almost succeeded. After each serious attempt, improvements in military benefits, changes in the command structure, and the arrest of several coup plotters helped quiet the restive military, which was concerned initially about the Aquino government's liberal stance toward the Communist insurgents and later about her government's failure to achieve change.

Following a national referendum in February 1987, which approved a new constitution with a bicameral legislature, congressional elections were held in May 1987 and local elections in January 1988. And with increased amounts of foreign aid, renewed investor confidence, and a spurt in consumer spending, the Philippines' growth rate rebounded dramatically in 1986 and reached almost 8 percent per annum in 1988. Growth, however, began to slow after the December 1989 coup attempt, which seriously damaged investor confidence.

The United States strongly supported Aquino as once it had supported Marcos. She was welcomed in Washington for a state visit in 1986 and addressed a joint session of Congress. In late 1987, a group of congressional leaders proposed a mini–Marshall Plan for the Philippines, known as the Multilateral Aid Initiative (MAI), to demonstrate continued U.S. support for the democratic transition. Bilateral and multilateral aid flowed into Manila from all quarters, so that by the end of 1988, a backlog in aid amounted to about $4.3 billion.[4] In the fall of 1989, Aquino once again visited Washington, and in December, when it looked like her government might fall to a military coup, U.S. planes from Clark Air Base overflew the rebels, discouraging them from further action.

Yet foreign support, new political institutions, and a popular president could not mask continued problems within a polity trying to make a political transition to democracy and an economic transition to industrialization. For while the removal of Marcos had meant an end to dictatorship, it had not meant an end to the deep social divisions between prosperous urban centers and stagnating rural areas or between the rich and the poor. Foreign support also played a role in the continuing fragmentation after Marcos was exiled. Economic and political nationalism enjoyed a resurgence as Filipinos tried to handle the crushing burden of a $30-billion foreign debt accumulated during the Marcos period and as Filipinos tried to define a renewed sense of national identity. New economic planners struggled with programs for development while elites fought for control of the loot

Marcos had left behind in the form of government corporations and bank accounts. Politicians attempted to build mass support by defining themselves as nationalists willing to assert controls over foreign investment and U.S. military facilities—a symbol of repression both by a foreign power and by a fallen dictator long supported by Washington. Nationalism is a common ideology on which to contest political control, and it is one with which Filipinos are well acquainted.

Corazon Aquino came to power, not to revolutionize society, but to restore the political system with which she was familiar. She refused to institutionalize the broad-based support that had characterized the people power revolution; thus, the political party framework that sprang up in response to the elections emulated past elite-controlled structures, and when her government was under attack from the military, she found it hard to call on anyone to support her. Although Aquino did support some candidates, she did not take an active hand in their selection, and ambitious family members, such as her brother Jose Cojuangco, used her popularity to develop their own political machine. Unfamiliar with the levers of government and uneducated about its issues, Aquino found it hard to make the difficult choices necessary in governing, thus allowing many decisions to go unmade as various factions fought over the nation's course.

Midway through her six-year term, although still popular, there were complaints that her government lacked "vision," that corruption, especially in her own immediate family, had crept back in, and that the government had done little to change the basic economic and political structure of the country. In many ways the complaints resembled those heard just prior to the declaration of martial law. Again politicians spoke about abolishing the bicameral legislature and establishing a parliamentary system, and disaffected elements in the military continued to plot Aquino's overthrow.

Much of the dissatisfaction could be traced to the political stasis that had resulted from the Marcos period. The period of one-man rule had hindered but not prevented the continuation of social trends evident prior to martial law, and there were three main ones, as David Wurfel has noted (1988: 21). First, the diversification of a political-economic elite as a result of the rise of commercial and manufacturing sectors brought with it more sources for intra-elite conflict. Second, mass mobilization increased as a result of more education, improved media sources, and higher urbanization. As a consequence, there was, third, a further erosion of the traditional relationships based on a patron-client hierarchy. With the end of Marcos's rule, elite efforts to retake political and economic control were contested by a growing professional class and a politicized and well-organized mass base, heavily influenced by the left if not led by the Communist insurgents.

In the short term, fear of a Communist takeover united the middle and upper classes. Both supported the growth of vigilante movements and the military's efforts to pressure the government to accept more-conservative cabinet members and policies. This alliance undercut support for the left, and it became isolated when several of its key leaders were murdered. But at the same time, a new threat rose from the disaffected ranks of the military, and in their nationalism, many of these people had much in common, ironically, with the Communist insurgents who also sought to cleanse society of its traditional corrupt elements.

An alliance across class lines was incapable of lasting, in part because of the nature of the urban revolt that had forced Marcos from power. It was essentially a Manila-based revolution in which few in the provinces participated, and it did not touch the lives of the majority of Filipinos. Thus it did not in itself bridge the urban-rural chasm. Even in the Manila region, the people agitating against Marcos had had different agendas or visions of the outcome; they were united against something rather than for something. The alliance also could not survive because of the nature of the modernizing process. The middle class wanted to disperse economic and political power, not concentrate it as the elite did.

Although in the short term the fear of a Communist revolution may unite the country, the long-term development of the Philippines depends on the expansion of an entrepreneurial middle class whose interests are profoundly different from those of the traditional elite. If development proceeds, then the elite will be absorbed into an expanded middle class. If development does not proceed, the potential of a military-backed coup may become a reality, this time with the backing of a disaffected middle class.

The most discouraging factor in the Philippines' future remains its poor, whose numbers daily grow larger. By the end of the century, the Philippines may contain close to 100 million people, the vast majority of whom will be poor. There has been little effort by either the Marcos or the Aquino governments to respond to a problem whose dimensions have been long apparent. Population control in this very Catholic country has been essentially nonexistent, and the political and economic conditions that once made the Philippines an attractive home for investors have also deteriorated. Other countries in Asia—South Korea, Taiwan, Singapore, Thailand, and Malaysia—are now more promising. The decline in the quality of the Philippine educational system under Marcos and the new emphasis on speaking local dialects, principally Filipino, rather than English, means that population is no longer the resource it once was. The exploitation of the Philippines' natural resources, the ecological rape of the last decades, has diminished the economic base on which the Philippines must build a strong export economy if it is to compete with other Asian countries. Still essentially a primary-product exporter, without sufficient investment in an industrial base for export, the Philippines has either failed to protect its resource base from destruction or failed to follow the proper economic policies to encourage rational development. These problems, if not altogether reversible as is the case with population growth, can be reduced to more manageable dimensions. To do so, however, will require a level of national and international commitment that has not yet appeared.

CONCLUSION

Clearly, a combination of causes made possible the Philippines' people power revolution. The underlying causes—economic, political, cultural, and international—were in many ways inevitable in their outcome, and Marcos unwittingly reinforced their effects. He was known as a *segurista*, that is, a cautious man who preferred to know the outcome before taking action. He also thought tactically rather than strategically, and the actions he took always had a short-term time horizon. He could not, for example, consider his own mortality and thus would not consider the inevitability of a secession. In failing to consider that event, he helped bring it about.

Seriously ill in the last years of his rule with a kidney disease—systemic lupus erythematosus—which necessitated two secret kidney transplants, other people perceived his demise before he did, and his wife and others, including Enrile, began to jockey to replace him. But Marcos refused to loosen the political controls that would transfer legitimacy to a successor. Indeed, he probably realized that any loosening of controls would probably accelerate the struggle against him both within his official family and in the polity at large. Politically, Marcos was boxed in.

He was also cornered economically. The United States and other donors, including the World Bank, were pressuring him to undertake major economic reforms, such as disbanding government corporations controlling agricultural production. But undoing these economic structures would reduce not only his own financial resources but also those of the cronies on whom he depended for political support.

His coercive power was also hamstrung. He had appointed all the key military commanders to ensure their allegiance but in so doing had weakened the military. Many of the commanders had no combat experience; Ver, for instance, had risen to power after once being Marcos's chauffeur. Junior officers were disgruntled, and a growing Communist insurgency increased their antipathy to their ineffective leaders. The United States, too, played a role both by pressing for military reforms and by insisting that Marcos not use the military against the people. Thus, Marcos could not loosen his controls in one area, such as the economy, while reinforcing it in another, such as against his political opponents. After announcing the end of martial law in 1981, he could not reimpose it without great domestic and international cost in 1986.

Culture also worked against him. Filipinos try to avoid overt conflict, working below the surface to create the appearance if not the reality of consensus. Elite opponents are rarely eliminated. Benigno Aquino was the glaring exception, and perhaps the shock of his death was all the greater because it violated cultural norms so dramatically. More often opponents are co-opted. When his opponents mobilized against him, Marcos's first impulse was to dismiss them as ineffectual or to placate them with minor reforms, buying himself more time to consider outcomes. Yet these tactics only provided his opponents with more political space in which to organize.

In a sense, Marcos was caught in a web of his own making, but he was also caught in a historical continuum. Filipino society had been changing, evolving in ways not easily understood. Population was a key factor in this evolution. The rapid increase in size not only exacerbated rural and urban poverty but also created a pool of youthful recruits for political mobilization, especially in the cities. The Communist party and the Catholic church each provided a rationale and a means for political organization in both rural and urban areas that the government could not duplicate. Once the elites became active as a result of their alienation from a state that could not continue to provide them with economic resources, the masses could be mobilized more overtly. The economic changes fueled dissatisfaction in both the elites and the masses.

Inequality in income distribution and high population growth rates had contributed to an almost continual fall in real wage rates since the 1950s that worsened during the economic decline of the early 1980s. The elites who watched their business empires being absorbed by Marcos cronies and also watched the decline of the Philippines in relation to its major competitors in Asia experienced the psychological equivalent of the wage rate decline. Both the rich and the poor perceived that things were getting worse and that they were being left behind.

The enforced impoverishment of the 1980s needed to resolve the Philippines' balance-of-payments crisis also reduced the state's ability to provide resources. As an example, in the 1986 election, Marcos, in the time honored method, tried to buy votes by paying voters for their support, but even the voters who accepted the funds felt no allegiance to a government that had only made their lives miserable. The government lacked sufficient resources in other instances to pay a voter enough money to justify a switch in allegiance. On another level, the government lacked the resources to undo in a short time the damage already done to the country's economic infrastructure as well as to the state's organizing elements, such as the military and the bureaucracy.

Finally, the state lost its moral force. First Aquino's assassination, then stories about Marcos's and his cronies' hidden wealth stashed abroad in Swiss bank accounts, and finally the accounts of his efforts to forge a war hero's record all helped erode any moral high ground on which Marcos could stand. He tried to impugn his opponent by referring to her as an inexperienced housewife, but this tactic only served to raise Corazon Aquino's stature. The period of her public mourning after her husband's death and her position afterward, seemingly above the political fray, reinforced her moral legitimacy.

All the factors that made it possible to predict the Philippine revolution also make it possible to predict to some degree its outcome. Beyond personality, the issues of population, poverty, elite attitudes toward power, and culture remain. The government can, as Marcos did for many years, postpone a social reckoning by making minor improvements in efficiency—including coercive control—and in economic growth. But without some radical restructuring of political and economic power, bridging the divide that exists between poor and rich, another revolution will occur led by the revolutionary left, the nationalist right, or potentially a combination of both.

CHRONOLOGY

March 1942: Army of Resistance Against Japan (Hukbo ng Bayan Laban sa Hapon, the Hukbalahap) is established.

July 4, 1946: Philippine independence is granted.

1948: The Huks are declared illegal and subversive.

1954: Luis Taruc, the Huk leader, surrenders.

1965: Ferdinand E. Marcos is elected president.

December 1968: Communist party of the Philippines is formed.

January 1969: New People's Army (NPA) is established by Communist party. Marcos wins reelection to a second term.

September 21, 1972: Marcos declares martial law.

April 1978: First elections under martial law are held to elect members of an interim National Assembly.

January 1980: Snap local elections are called by Marcos.

May 1980: Benigno Aquino released from prison and goes to the United States.

January 17, 1981: Marcos formally ends martial law.

June 16, 1981: The first presidential election since 1969 is held. Marcos claims victory with 88 percent of the vote.

May 1982: Elections are held for barangay officials.

August 21, 1983: Benigno Aquino assassinated on his return to Manila.

May 14, 1984: Elections held for National Assembly.

February 7, 1986: Snap presidential election held with Ferdinand Marcos and Corazon Aquino as presidential candidates.

February 22, 1986: Elements of the military launch a revolt.

February 25, 1986: Marcos flees into exile in Hawaii, and Corazon Aquino is inaugurated president.

July 6, 1986: Marcos's former vice-presidential running mate, Arturo Tolentino, takes over the Manila Hotel with military support and declares himself president. He and his supporters surrender after two days.

November 23, 1986: The cabinet is dissolved after the failure of an alleged coup attempt.

January 27, 1987: Military troops attempt a coup.

February 7, 1987: Cease-fire between Communists and the government fails.

April 18, 1987: A military mutiny by former Marcos elements is put down.

May 11, 1987: Congressional elections are held.

July 27, 1987: First session of the new Philippine Congress.

August 28, 1987: Another coup is attempted. Sixty people are killed.

January 18, 1988: Local elections are held.

April 2, 1988: Colonel Honasan, leader of the major coup attempts, escapes a prison ship in Manila Bay.

December 1989: Another military coup is attempted.

NOTES

1. Among whom were Assistant Secretary of Defense Richard Armitage on January 9–12, Assistant Secretary of State Paul Wolfowitz on January 14, another defense official on January 30, and congressional delegations on April 12, with Senator John Kerry, and April 14, with Representative Steve Solarz.

2. See the Center for Democracy, *Report to the Committee on Foreign Relations, United States Senate, on the Presidential Election Process in the Philippines* (Boston: Center for Democracy, December 18, 1985), which was one of several such reports by U.S. election experts.

3. Those killed included the former governor of Antique Province, Evelio Javier, a strong Aquino supporter who was chased, cornered, and gunned down in broad daylight on February 12, 1986. His funeral in Manila was attended by the U.S. ambassador, Steve Bosworth.

4. Aid was slow in actually arriving and being spent. See Nayan Chanda, "A Clogged Pipeline," *Far Eastern Economic Review,* January 5, 1989: 15.

10

CAMBODIA: REVOLUTION, GENOCIDE, INTERVENTION

BARBARA HARFF

In 1975, the Communist Khmer Rouge achieved victory in its revolutionary war against the U.S.-supported government of Lon Nol. Declaring a new state—the Democratic Republic of Kampuchea—the Khmer Rouge sought to totally restructure Cambodian society by eliminating all "modern" elements. The brutality of its efforts, and the Khmer Rouge's own aggression against Vietnam, led to Vietnam's intervention and occupation of Cambodia. The genocidal policies of the Khmer Rouge were unprecedented in Southeast Asia. However, their revolution, and Vietnam's invasion, were rooted in a long Cambodian history of foreign intervention and struggles for independence.

The history of the Cambodian people—the Khmers—goes back to the ancient kingdom of Funan (first–sixth centuries A.D.), which occupied the area that is now Cambodia, southern Laos, Malaya, South Vietnam, and parts of Thailand. It was an Indianized state, but the people were of Indonesian and Chinese stock. The name *Cambodia* derives from the Hindu word *Kambuju*, for Kambu—a figure in Cambodian mythology. The famous Khmer kingdom known as the Angkor Empire, which took shape in the ninth century, was the successor of the Funan kingdom. During its brilliant but relatively short duration, arts and architecture flourished, and Angkor's kings built dikes and canals so that agricultural productivity increased. During this period the magnificent Angkor Wat temple complex was built, and for today's Cambodians, it is a symbol of pride in their ancient culture. From the fifteenth century onward, the Cambodians were attacked by neighboring Siam (present-day Thailand) and Vietnam and eventually yielded large parts of their territory to Siam.

In 1863, the French rescued Cambodia from total annihilation by the Siamese and Vietnamese by declaring it a French protectorate. During World War II, the Vichy French first administered Cambodia and then were replaced by the Japanese,

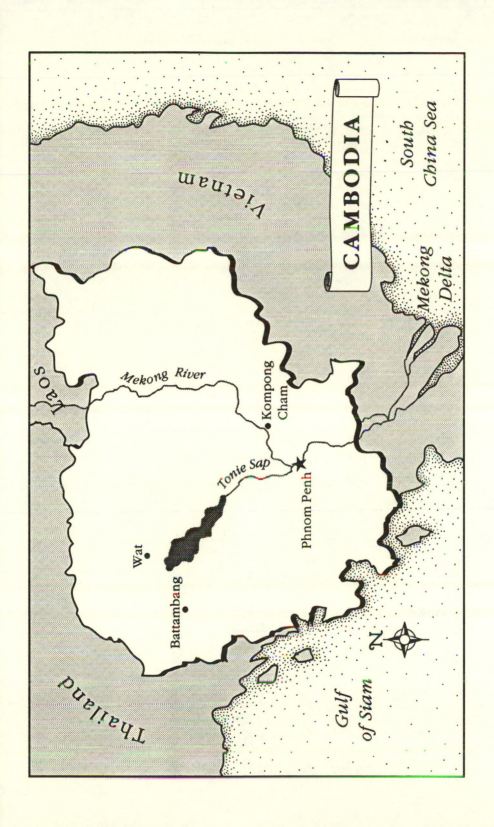

who occupied the area. Prince Norodom Sihanouk declared Cambodia's independence from France after the Japanese withdrawal yet had to yield to the French when they returned at the end of 1945. In early 1946 the status of a protectorate was formally abolished, in 1949 Cambodia became an associate state within the French Union, and in 1953 the country became truly independent. During the interim period Vietnamese forces invaded Cambodia, but following the Geneva Conference of 1954, the French and Vietnamese left and Sihanouk declared the country free of foreign rule.

Norodom Sihanouk, of a branch of the royal family, was chosen king in 1941 by the Buddhist clergy and the French. In 1947, Sihanouk declared an end to the absolute rule of the monarchy and promulgated a constitution that guaranteed popular elections to the newly instituted National Assembly. In 1955 Sihanouk formally renounced the throne in favor of his father and founded Sangkum (Popular Socialist Community), a quasi-socialist party that took 83 percent of the popular vote in 1955, which meant that Sihanouk became prime minister of Cambodia. The Democratic party received 13 percent and the Communists 3.5 percent of the vote. In 1960, after his father's death, he became chief of state but did not assume the title of king. Sihanouk has continued to be referred to as Prince Sihanouk.

The kings of Cambodia played a pivotal role as the brokers of authority patterns. Their rule was personalized to a degree similar to that in preindustrial Europe, and this tradition remained largely intact despite Western penetration in the nineteenth century (McCloud 1986). The king's role also was an integral part of the Hindu religious belief system, as the sovereign was linked to the gods by a complex web of hereditary myths and magic. The degree of supernatural powers ascribed to the king varied with local customs, however, and often the king was seen as the intermediary or transmitter of the Hindu gods. The villagers were protected by the king from pirates and foreigners, and in turn they provided the king with earthly riches in the form of taxes. These taxes often were used to "please the gods" by building elaborate temple complexes and monasteries, thus ensuring the gods' protection and rich harvests. (The occasional poverty and poor harvest could always be blamed on the peasants' bad luck or karma.) The subjects' allotted place in this life could only be altered by "buying" a better existence in the next, giving goods or food to the monks, or by becoming a monk.

CAMBODIA'S ECONOMY AND INTERNATIONAL DEPENDENCIES

During the Angkor Empire, Cambodia's economy was based on a vast hydraulic system of canals and dikes that provided for a relatively high level of productivity for 400 years. After the twelfth century, however, the Angkor Empire entered a long period of decline and disintegration because of floods, lack of irrigation maintenance, and internal dissension (Etcheson 1984: 6). In the nineteenth century, Cambodia was forced to submit to colonial rule under the French, narrowly escaping domination by the Siamese and Vietnamese.

During the 1930s, French colonial authorities began to plant rubber trees, and rubber quickly became the primary commodity of Cambodia and eventually the primary export item. Vietnamese labor was imported because the French saw the Cambodians as lazy. In addition, Chinese and Vietnamese immigrants were employed as lower civil administrators. Later, these immigrant groups became the dominant economic force in Cambodia. The French economic penetration into Indochina (which included Laos, Vietnam, and Cambodia) was achieved through the financing of business enterprises by the French government and through levying taxes on the local population. The French effectively prevented non-French capital from entering Indochina so that in 1938, "they owned 95% of the European capital invested," though there was "a large Chinese investment of 80 million dollars" (Hall 1958: 657). Indochina's exports to France between 1931 and 1938 averaged 57.1 percent of the region's total exports. Thus, the French established a typical colonial economy, which existed predominantly for the benefit of the colonizer. There was no way for local entrepreneurs to compete with French manufactured goods, but on the other hand, the great mass of people could not afford to buy imported goods. Thus, many Cambodians bought local goods, such as cotton and silk, which "continued to be woven on primitive looms . . . pottery and basket making survived as a native craft, but on a reduced scale" (Hall 1958: 658). In general, capital formation was discouraged in favor of exporting profits to France.

However, this led to a marked decline in peasant land holdings. Unable to provide for their growing families, peasants fell into debt and lost their land. From 1930 to 1956, the poorest Cambodians, those who owned less than one hectare of land, nonetheless held a total of 25 percent of the cultivated acreage. But by 1962, this group, amounting to one-third of the population, owned only 3 percent of Cambodia's cultivated acreage (Etcheson 1984: 15). An ever-higher rate of population growth had created for the first time in Cambodian history a landless class of "destitute rural dwellers with very few ties to the land." As Ben Kiernan argues, such a class was much more prone to accept a Communist revolution (in Etcheson 1984: 15). Providing further fuel to increase misery was the practice of royal administrators to squeeze excessive taxes from the peasants. Any poor harvest could push the peasant into the arms of moneylenders, traditionally of Chinese or Vietnamese extraction, and these creditors were free to impose any interest rates they saw fit. Typically, annual interest rates ranged from 100 to 200 percent, and by 1952, one study shows "that 75 percent of the Cambodian farmers were seriously in debt" (Etcheson 1984: 16).

The Khmer village was the center of economic and social life, but its origin is obscure. Some people argue that the villages came about as a result of the powerful court system and perhaps as units to support the kings through taxation. The state was organized as "a collection of revenue-producing regions" allocated to an elite tied to the king by blood or receiving status through royal decree (McCloud 1986: 72). Loyalty of the elite was ensured through binding extended kinship groups to the king, and loyalty of the peasants was ensured by sanctifying the king. Traditionally, the peasants expected little of the court other than protection from foreign invaders so their village life could continue uninterrupted. Only foreign invasions or extreme taxes led to peasant unrest. The French interrupted this functional stability by reducing the king's power, destroying the traditional land-holding system through the introduction of large rubber plantations, and by introducing cash crops, which eventually undermined the existing subsistence agriculture, tying Cambodia, like other colonized countries, into the international political economy.

During World War II, Vichy France was forced to cede nearly one-third of Cambodia's territory to Thailand, territory that contained crucial economic assets. This transfer took place after an emboldened Thai army, encouraged by the Nazi invasion of France and with the support of the Japanese, crossed the border and defeated some French garrisons.

By the end of the colonial period, there was little or no industry in Cambodia other than a few French-controlled rubber processing firms and some plants that processed agricultural and forestry products. In the mid-1950s, independent Cambodia's official policy emphasized industrial development with the help of foreign assistance, which came from the People's Republic of China, Czechoslovakia, the Soviet Union, France, Yugoslavia, and the United States. Some of these ventures failed owing to faulty machinery, miscalculations, lack of competitiveness of the final products, and corruption. Textile plants showed some promise, but machinery plants did miserably. In 1963, the United States canceled all foreign aid at the insistence of Sihanouk, and foreign trade and banking were nationalized.

Rice production was the backbone of the economy and the main source of foreign exchange earnings: 80 percent of the agricultural households in the 1962 census were engaged in rice cultivation, and rice provided 60 percent of export earnings. Production fluctuated markedly because of variations in rainfall and the lack of adequate irrigation systems. It was also hampered by the lack of mechanization: There were only 600 tractors in Cambodia in 1964 (Leifer 1967: 9). In a good year in the 1960s, the country produced over 3 million tons of rice; in a bad year, little more than 2 million tons. Officials estimated that if rice production could be raised to 4 million tons per annum, 1.5 million tons could be exported, thus solving the country's need for development financing (United Nations 1970: 110, 228). A combination of poor harvests and corruption in public life added to what in 1966 Sihanouk publicly called an economic crisis. Although less affected than the city people, the peasants had to endure some hardship, since the government, in an attempt to eliminate the Chinese middlemen, directly purchased rice from the villages. Government-set prices, however, were one third of what could be charged on the black market. Thus, bad harvests in 1966, 1967, and 1969 hurt the peasants, who had less rice to sell yet received a fixed price.

During the mid-1960s, Sihanouk instituted a vigorous development program. The port city of Sihanoukville was modernized, and its capacity was rapidly expanded. Exports increased in most years, and imports were restricted so that the balance-of-payments deficit remained small throughout this period. Although the export of rice, rice products, maize, and rubber remained exclusively in the hands of the government, after 1969 other fields of domestic production and service activity were open to private enterprise. These promising economic trends were undercut by the takeover of the corrupt Lon Nol regime and increased U.S. bombardment. Trying to shift the blame, urban officials exploited the peasants' discontent by making ethnic minorities and foreigners the scapegoats for the increased misery of the peasants. This practice may have added to the fury unleashed by peasant members of the Khmer Rouge against ethnic minorities during the Khmer Rouge's rule.

ORIGINS OF KHMER COMMUNISM

The first known Communist stirrings in Cambodia can be traced to the 1930s, and in the early days, the movement attracted ethnic Chinese and Vietnamese living in Cambodia (Ponchaud 1978: 151). Khmer communism clearly emerged as part of the anticolonialist struggle established by Ho Chi Minh and was probably first enunciated in a student commune in Paris in the late 1940s, which included the later luminaries of the Khmer Rouge—Hou Yuon, Ieng Sary, Son Sen, Khieu Samphan, Saloth Sar (later known as Pol Pot), and Khieu Thirith. The Parisian clique included members of the middle-class and former teachers, one of whom, Khieu Samphan, became a professor of political economy and member of the law faculty in Phnom Penh. Interestingly, some were members of the same family, not atypical for Asian leaders. Thus, Ieng Sary was the brother-in-law of Pol Pot. The close association of these people during the formative years in Paris no doubt laid the groundwork for the later sharing of power among a small number of radical revolutionaries.

From the establishment of the Khmer People's party (KPP) in 1951 and its electoral front, the Krom Pracheachon, in 1954; to what former party officials call the real date of the establishment of the Kampuchean Communist party (KCP) in 1960; to the victory of the Khmer Rouge in 1975, no clear-cut ideological path can be discerned. However, two documents, Hou Yuon's and Khieu Samphan's Paris theses, provide some insights into what later became the strategy for economic policy. The key to economic development was a self-sufficient peasantry, and the objective was a rural-based society, with a rigid adherence to total equality among the masses and a cutting off of all foreign entanglements.

Most important, and often overlooked by Western observers, is the importance ascribed to the destruction of religion by the Khmer Rouge. The systematic effort to close and desecrate temples and to strip Buddhist monks of their traditional role was an attempt by the revolutionaries to replace the old temporal and spiritual symbols of authority. The key to the heart of the peasants was to be the preaching of self-reliance, in contrast to the fatalism preached by the monks. Peasants were urged to become independent—even of the gods; water, the life-giving source of sustenance, no longer belonged in the realm of the gods but to the peasants. Thus, the first task of the Khmer Rouge was to (re)build an extensive network of channels and dikes, most of them made of dirt and built with slave labor. Of similar importance was the role of the king. King (Prince) Sihanouk's popularity with the peasants had not waned substantially, despite an oppressive system of taxation, so the Khmer Rouge was careful at first to cultivate good relations with Sihanouk, who willingly lent his support to the Communists until 1973.

THE REVOLUTIONARY CRISIS

The principal factors leading to the revolutionary victory of the Khmer Rouge in 1975 appear in part to be consistent with the theoretical argument in Chapter

3. These factors, in a nutshell, are the interaction of declining state resources relative to expenses and the resources of adversaries, increasing elite alienation and disunity, and growing popular grievances and autonomy.

The Sihanouk Years

The years following World War II saw the Cambodian leadership under Sihanouk involved in a struggle to throw off foreign domination (French and Vietnamese), and the period between 1954 and 1965 saw the consolidation of the power of Sihanouk's coalition against that of competing nationalist forces. One of the contenders for nationalist leadership was Son Ngoc Thanh, who with Japanese support during their brief occupation of Cambodia, had been minister of foreign affairs and an early nationalist. Forced into the underground after the French returned at the end of 1945, he was influential in forming an alliance among competing factions of nationalist groups fighting renewed French occupation. These groups became known as the Khmer Issarak. Sihanouk was able to gain their tenuous support, and as a result, was able to force the withdrawal of a greatly weakened France, debilitated from the colonial war in Vietnam and harassed by the Khmer fighting coalitions. Under the Geneva Accords of 1954, Sihanouk was obliged to give amnesty to all former opponents. However, Son Ngoc Thanh, who had been exiled to Saigon and then France from 1945 to 1951, and his Khmer Issarak factions, exiled since 1952 because of anti-French and anti-Sihanouk activities, were not allowed any role in Cambodian politics. Thus, Son Ngoc Thanh went into exile once again in 1954, and from exile he formed the Khmer Serei (the Free Khmer), who operated from within Thailand and South Vietnam. Eventually this group was able to gain the support of the United States, Thailand, and South Vietnam, probably because of the escalation of the U.S. involvement in Vietnam and the neutral policies of Sihanouk.

Sihanouk's neutrality was based on necessity: He felt that by establishing good relations with both China and the United States, he could counter any territorial ambitions of South Vietnam or Thailand, but Sihanouk's policies changed when the United States began its strong involvement in Vietnam. He envisaged Cambodia's neutrality as suitable to meet any unforeseen circumstances, so, by associating more closely with China and denouncing the United States, he hoped that Cambodia would be protected by China in case of a North Vietnamese victory. He was, however, unable to prevent the North Vietnamese from using parts of Cambodia as a base against South Vietnam, and this activity eventually led to heavy aerial bombardment by the United States in 1965 (diplomatic relations were then severed), a strengthening of the support base of the nationalist forces fighting Sihanouk, and sweeping reforms in Cambodia.

Most of Sihanouk's reforms were developed to undercut the influence of the competing nationalist elites and, at the same time, to foster good relations with Communists abroad. Thus, the nationalization of the banking system and the nationalization of foreign trade were designed to help curb corruption among the tiny urban elite. However, the sudden decline in foreign exchange earnings led to an economic crisis in the modern sector, and to counteract this development, government officials adopted policies that led to further increases in the taxes levied against the peasants. These tax increases, combined with the expropriation of peasant land—to build a sugar refinery—without adequate compensation in the province of Battambang, led to a spontaneous revolt in 1967. This revolt was suppressed under the leadership of Lon Nol, who was then Sihanouk's acting prime minister, and about 10,000 people (mostly peasants) were killed in a massive effort by government forces. Although Lon Nol was replaced by the more moderate Son Sann, peasant suppression continued well into the 1970s, especially of those thought to support the Communists.

From 1963 onward, Sihanouk had tried to appease the Cambodian Communists by allowing them free movement in Cambodia. But after 1967 and the peasant uprising, his policy changed to one of open oppression, which drove the Communists into the underground. This policy may have increased peasant support for the Khmer Rouge. The Communist party, which had been dominated by the Vietminh in the early 1950s, only slowly evolved into the fighting body it became in the 1970s. Much interfactional fighting had led to the party's near collapse in the late 1950s, but in 1960, twenty-one delegates had met in Phnom Penh and agreed on a common strategy among the factions. In 1963, Saloth Sar (Pol Pot) became secretary-general of the party, and the Paris enclave of the Communist movement thus began its path toward the victory won with the fall of the nationalist government in 1975.

The Lon Nol Regime

It can be argued that Cambodia's civil wars, which eventually led to the victory by the Khmer Rouge in 1975, were a direct result of the Vietnam war. After the massive U.S. troop commitments to South Vietnam in 1965, North Vietnamese fighters often crossed into Cambodia, yet their support for the Khmer Rouge was lukewarm. The People's Republic of China's support for the Cambodian Communists was largely verbal, and simultaneously, it provided Sihanouk with the arms necessary to fight the Khmer Communists.

Sihanouk's careful neutralist policies fell prey to disenchanted officers under the leadership of the former prime minister Lon Nol and royal relatives (Sirik Mataki in particular), who in March 1970, with tacit U.S. support, launched a successful palace coup. Sihanouk, who was then in Moscow to ask for Soviet help against the Vietnamese, suspected CIA involvement, and given U.S. aid to the Lon Nol regime between 1970 and 1975 "totaling more than $2.3 billion" (Etcheson 1984: 93), his suspicions were not without foundation. Whatever the role of the United States was, Sihanouk now made his fateful decision to support the Communists against the U.S.-supported Lon Nol–Khmer Serei coalition. This step encouraged the North Vietnamese and Communist China to give their support to the Khmer Communists. Sihanouk, now in exile in Beijing, called upon the peasants to resist the Lon Nol regime.

It appears that as early as 1968, the United States had knowledge of the coup that was to bring Lon Nol to power in 1970. In August 1969, Sihanouk had given Lon Nol back the prime ministership, but Lon Nol sought the support of the Khmer Serei, which was supported by the United States and by South Vietnam, and Thanh, still in exile and fighting for a pro-Western Cambodia. In addition to the Khmer Serei's direct involvement in the coup, further support came from government officials affected by austerity measures, from urban youth and students, and from those who envisioned a Cambodia free from Communist entanglements. Although Sihanouk, in an effort to stop the North Vietnamese infiltration into Cambodia, had reestablished relations with the United States in 1969, this step was too little and too late for his political foes, who saw it as just another ill-conceived plan.

After the successful palace coup, Lon Nol immediately ordered the Vietcong and North Vietnamese out of the country. Instead, they marched inward, inciting the frontier peasants, with the help of the Khmer Rouge, against Lon Nol. The North Vietnamese invaded two-thirds of Cambodia and played up the peasants' loyalty to Sihanouk, who was still their undisputed leader. The Vitenamese policy was to broadcast openly the peasants' support for Sihanouk, and this program, coupled with Sihanouk's own call from Beijing to fight the Lon Nol regime, made the new regime's position largely untenable. The new government in turn tried to stir the peasants' ancient hatred for the Vietnamese, hoping for peasant support (Ponchaud 1978: 166). The Vietnamese policy was to put Khmer cadres (trained by the Vietminh) into leading positions, and by 1971 much of the land was in Khmer Communist hands. Thus, the government forces were put in the position of fighting their own people, which led to increased demoralization.

The Struggle for Power:
Lon Nol Versus the Khmer Communists

The 1970 coup initiated a period of successive stages of authority breakdown that led eventually to total control by the Khmer Rouge. Etcheson (1984) argues that 1973 was the watershed for a successful revolution in Cambodia. Heavy bombardment by the United States took a great toll on civilian lives and destroyed villages and harvests. As a result of these bombardments and Lon Nol's aggressive and brutal treatment of suspected opponents—including murder and dismemberment of captured villagers—peasants turned against him, and many joined the Communists to fight his regime. Although blaming the Vietnamese for their misery came naturally to the villagers, who had seen their villages destroyed by the Vietminh, especially in areas close to the border with Vietnam, their fury turned against South Vietnam—and against its ally, the United States.

The revolutionary army was regionally dispersed, and seemingly little central control existed prior to 1972 or 1973, other than that exercised by the army's North Vietnamese overlords. However, the Pol Pot group gained firm control of the north and northwest regions, so whatever military faction controlled that area also controlled it politically. Craig Etcheson identifies at least six different factions among the Communists vying for control in the mid-1970s: the Stalinists under Pol Pot; the pro-Vietnamese internationalists; the Issarakists; the Pracheaonists (cadres from the old KPP, Khmer People's party established in the 1950s), regionally concentrated largely in the south, southwest and west; the Maoists, allied with the Chinese Communist party; and the followers of Sihanouk, called Khmer Rumdo, who were not especially anti-Vietnamese (Etcheson 1984: 164). However, by 1975, the Politburo was firmly controlled by the Pol Pot clique. The Lon Nol regime steadily lost rural support and became increasingly isolated in the capital city of Phnom Penh. Although Lon Nol commanded the support of the military, he was never able to gain the full support of the Phnom Penh elite. At the end, the fragmented, disorganized, and corrupt Lon Nol regime faltered in the face of the skilled, highly organized, and strongly motivated united-front fighting machine of the Khmer Rouge.

Democratic Kampuchea

After the Khmer victory, the Pol Pot faction, in true Stalinist fashion, purged most of the dissident cadres from leadership positions (often they disappeared in torture centers), and by 1977, Pol Pot's clique was in full control of the leadership. Records found after the 1978 Vietnamese invasion show that some 20,000 party officers and cadres were executed at the notorious S-21 center, and it can be ascertained that whoever controlled the security apparatus determined the fate of the cadres who fell into disfavor. Even Prince Sihanouk, who returned from exile in September 1975 and became acting head of state, was put under house arrest in April 1976. Given their revolutionary zeal, elite cohesion, and clandestine operations, the Pol Pot clique was able to suppress any internal dissent. The pathological zeal with which the clique went about cleansing the party of those who disagreed with their views contributed eventually to their downfall by making them an embarrassment to the Communist world.

The Khmer Rouge also sponsored frequent incursions into Vietnam, possibly in an attempt to show their invincibility and probably counting on support from Communist China. Some scholars argue that Pol Pot's Vietnam strategy was designed to diffuse public anxiety about the dismal internal situation. Although no explanation seems terribly plausible, in light of the overwhelming superiority of the Vietnamese forces and armament, it seems likely that Pol Pot was persuaded that it was just a matter of time until the Vietnamese would attempt to swallow Kampuchea so an offensive stance while Vietnam was still in the throes of its own revolutionary rebuilding might pay dividends. (A similar situation can be seen in Iraq's attempt to win a quick victory by attacking Iran in 1979, at a moment when the new state was just beginning to consolidate itself.) The response to Pol Pot's ill-advised policy of harassing Vietnam was the full-scale Vietnamese invasion of December 1978.

KHMER ROUGE REVOLUTIONARY GOALS AND POLICIES

There is no single document that elaborates the ideology of the Kampuchean Communist party. What does exist is an amalgam of speeches, actions, a constitution, and public broadcasts delineating a mixture of Communist revolutionary thought, the leader's own conception of a new Khmer society, and select goals that apparently were developed to fit the necessities of the moment. Etcheson (1984: 32) describes the ideology as a mixture of traditional Khmer cultural values, Parisian Jacobinism, and strands of Communist revolutionary thought.

It is exceptionally difficult to identify the conditions inside the country or to decipher the course of policy and action charted by the Communists because of the excessive secrecy shrouding the new regime. The leadership was not even clearly known to the outside world until 1977, when Pol Pot emerged as the undisputed leader. His all-encompassing leadership was comparable to that of Adolf Hitler and Joseph Stalin, and it was he who developed what later became known as Pol Pot's strand of communism. What has emerged, based on the seminal works of Kiernan (1981, 1987), Michael Vickery (1984), Stephen Heder (1979), and Francois Ponchaud (1978) and information attained through hundreds of interviews by David Hawk, Kiernan, and myself, is the realization that the Khmer Rouge acted out the beliefs, experiences, and antipathies of this fragment of the Khmer Rouge leadership.

The case of Kampuchea is complex in that there is no ready-made label that categorizes the type of revolution that was attempted. At times, the Pol Pot clique called it a Communist revolution, and established Communist regimes readily accepted them as comrades. Yet Ieng Sary told ASEAN in 1977 that "we are not communists . . . we are revolutionaries" (Vickery 1984: 288). After the Vietnamese invasion and the fall of Pol Pot, scholars (especially in the West) went about dissecting the Kampuchean experience according to accepted Marxist dogma. Is there value in deciding whether or not the Kampuchean model neatly or roughly fits the various conditions of Marxist thought? Assume we accept Vickery's conclusion that Cambodia's revolution was indeed a peasant revolt led by petty-bourgeois utopians. If this view is correct, the Kampuchean model could serve as a guide to future revolutionaries on how *not* to pursue goals that lead to guaranteed disaster.

The revolutionary elite in Kampuchea, alias the Pol Pot clique, pursued three goals. Goal number one was to eradicate any foreign influence. Goal number two was to forcibly establish a rigidly egalitarian society. Goal number three was to return to an agricultural economy in which modern ways had no place, although the Khmer Rouge paid lip service to the idea that industry should be developed. The most radical policy, implemented immediately after the Khmer Rouge victory, is unique in the annals of modern revolutions: All cities were emptied. Phnom Penh in 1975 was bulging with refugees, it was estimated that close to 40 percent of all Cambodians had fled to the capital to seek refuge from the Communists and from U.S. bombings. Within three days, the Khmer Rouge forced all inhabitants to leave—the old, hospital patients, mothers with newborn children. With little or no prior warning, they were forced to take to the roads with no clear-cut destination. Pushing the urban people into the countryside to fight for their daily bread was part of the Khmer Rouge's strategy of economic leveling. Uncounted numbers of people died in this mass exodus, many of exhaustion, especially the old and sick or wounded, others because they tried to resist their forced deportation. The tiniest infraction of rules (often invented on the spot) led to death by shooting, clubbing, or stabbing. Despite the fact that many of the urban dwellers were peasant refugees, once they arrived at their final destination they were treated as second-class citizens (given lesser food rations) and often were the target of cruel treatment.

The leveling process also proceeded in the countryside. Private ownership was abolished, and all villages were forcibly collectivized. All aspects of life became a communal affair: Meals were eaten in common, there were communal indoctrination centers, and children over the age of twelve were separated from their parents to be educated in pure revolutionary ways. The Buddhist monkhood was destroyed by forcing the monks out of their monasteries and forcing them to till the land (physical labor was prohibited as part of religious duties for the time one served as a monk), and torture and execution of resisting monks were widespread. The organized Buddhist clergy was systematically destroyed, pagodas were closed or destroyed, Buddha's images were defaced. The goal was to defrock all Buddhist monks, and other religions did not fare any better as the constitution strictly forbade the exercise of all reactionary religions, which included Islam and Christianity.

Kampuchea's society consisted of peasants, workers, and soldiers. All other classes, according to official dictum, were to be eradicated. Former urban dwellers became the "new people," second-class citizens in need of reeducation. The former capitalists became superfluous altogether and often were simply killed by the notorious security apparatus. To be considered an intellectual was equally dangerous. Petite bourgeoisie had no place in the new society; thus, former government officials, professionals, and people with a university education fled Kampuchea by the thousands to avoid death at the hands of the Khmer Rouge.

Revolutionary economic policies were equally extreme. The leaders abolished money as a means of exchange and instituted a primitive barter system. Victory was celebrated by setting banks on fire. However, there is some indication that in 1978 the Khmer Rouge considered reinstating some kind of monetary system. All means of production were owned by the state, which is somewhat ironic given that when it destroyed the monetary system, the state lost some of its control over economic dealings in the countryside. There also is clear evidence that those people who were considered "unconditional" (i.e., cadres loyal to Pol Pot) had a privileged position and lived better than their counterparts in the army.

Forced labor was imposed on all Kampucheans regardless of age or state of health. Those previously part of the urban elite now were condemned to the most menial tasks, and others were forced to work in the fields and forests. Twelve- to fourteen-hour days were the norm; inadequate performance was punishable by death. Cadres were installed as supervisors although they often had little experience in agricultural pursuits and even less managerial talent. Not only was production state controlled, distribution of food and consumption ratios for different groups were dictated by the clique and its loyal followers. All "experts" fell victim to the leveling policies, so there were no technicians, doctors, nurses, teachers, or anyone who would willingly admit that he or she had been educated above the most rudimentary level. People now depended on folk medicine and died by the thousands of preventable diseases—e.g., dysentery, diarrhea, fever, beriberi, and tuberculosis. Many others died of starvation and exhaustion. With the advent of renewed hostilities with Vietnam in 1977, some workers knowledgeable about producing military equipment were sought and thus escaped the mayhem inflicted on others.

leveling process included the wholesale massacre of certain groups
:r undesirable or expendable. Part of that policy was dictated by
a....   entiments, so victims included ethnic Chinese (despite the ruling
clique's leaning toward the PRC), ethnic Vietnamese, the Muslim Chams, and
some Burmese and Lao hill-tribe people. Whole families were killed, often even
their servants, evidence that the Khmer Rouge had truly genocidal aims. The
Khmer nation is not of one race. It is a mixture of the Malay, Mongoloid, and,
some argue, Australoid and Negroid family of races. The Chams are considered
a different ethnic group of Malay/Polynesian stock who lived in what was originally
the kingdom of Champa, which was absorbed by Vietnam in the fifteenth century.
Their migration into Cambodia ended sometime during the eighteenth century,
but they have their own language, live in distinct villages or neighborhoods, have
distinct dress styles, and are Muslims. After 1975, they were no longer allowed
to speak their language or wear their distinctive clothes, villages were dispersed,
certain customs were prohibited, and the practice of Islam in any form was banned.
Cham leaders were persecuted and often killed, and those who were killed were
buried so that they would not face Mecca.

Ethnic Chinese, Thais, and others were treated similarly; the least one can
say is that they were forced to assimilate. The Chinese were treated especially
harshly. Many Chinese were merchants, urban people, and better educated, which
made them special targets of the Khmer Rouge, and it is estimated that up to
half of the urban Chinese did not survive the regime. Ethnic Vietnamese, considered
traditional enemies of the Khmer, were forcefully expelled, and those who remained
were often harassed or killed. Even children of mixed marriages were considered
undesirable and often endured the same fate as their Vietnamese parent. Another
part of the Khmer Rouge campaign to rid the country of all foreign influence
was the insistence on total reliance on domestic production. Foreign contacts were
reduced to receiving military aid from China.

Why the extreme use of terror? Given their confused ideology and their years
in the jungle fighting against an array of enemies, the Khmer Rouge fighting
forces and their leaders had little concern for human lives. The policy of taking
youngsters and brutalizing them at a tender age, often by forcing them to kill
their elders, put the Khmer leadership in control of a perfect killing machine.
Once in power, the clique's paranoia and vengeance extended to all people who
harbored an opposing view, whether perceived or real. The regime's extreme vision
of the new Kampuchea inevitably had the result of a reign of terror that far
surpassed the reign of terror under Robespierre.

INTERNATIONAL REPERCUSSIONS

In December 1978, the Vietnamese invaded and occupied Kampuchea; ten
years later, they announced their intention of withdrawing all occupying troops,
and did so, by 1990. Amid the entanglement of international alliances, the
Kampuchean situation is especially complex. There is little doubt that the Pol Pot
clique invited intervention because of its abominable treatment of the people and,
more important to Vietnam, because of its anti-Vietnamese aggression. Kampuchean
guerrillas repeatedly crossed the border into Vietnam, and there exist countless

accounts of their vicious treatment of Vietnamese civilians. They were known to kill pregnant women after they first raped and mutilated them and to decapitate Vietnamese fishermen. Although Communist China openly supported Kampuchea with arms, it also gave aid to Hanoi until the summer of 1978. However, this balancing act became increasingly difficult for the Chinese, in light of Pol Pot's aggressiveness and the treatment meted out against the civilian population. Pol Pot obviously misjudged the willingness of the Chinese to come to his aid when, in April 1977, the fighting between Kampuchea and Vietnam became more serious. In December of the same year, a full-scale war erupted between Vietnam and Kampuchea. At first the Vietnamese seemed to be satisfied with teaching the Pol Pot clique a lesson, so Vietnam withdrew from the border region and asked for a cease-fire and negotiations. The Kampucheans, inspired by what they must have thought was a weakening enemy, escalated their raids into Vietnam. Serious tactical and political errors made by Pol Pot ensured an easy Vietnamese victory in December 1978. One of those errors was the decision to kill and brand as traitors many of the Khmer people living in the border region, a decision that caused the exodus of the remaining border Khmers to Vietnam. It is estimated that some 150,000 crossed into Vietnam to seek refuge from their own government (Etcheson 1984: 193). Surprisingly, the Chinese did not intervene actively on the side of Kampuchea, probably because the Khmer Rouge's excesses against its own people had become a serious international embarrassment.

Some people hailed Vietnam's incursion into Kampuchea as a case of humanitarian intervention—the slaughter stopped. However, others perceived it as a blatant violation of territorial sovereignty. Although human rights violations have not totally abated, there is no comparison between the brutal treatment of Kampucheans at the hands of the Khmer Rouge and the forms of repression endured under the Vietnamese occupation. Ideally, the Vietnamese should have withdrawn after they had driven out the Khmer Rouge regime; instead, they installed a puppet government, led by Heng Samrin and Hun Sen, that seems to enjoy some measure of support from the people.

After the Vietnamese invasion the Khmer Rouge, to the surprise of many astute observers, were able to enter into a rebel coalition fighting the Vietnamese occupation from the outside. What has emerged as a result of the continued occupation of the country are surrealistic alliances. Communist China strongly supports the fighting forces of the Khmer Rouge (estimated at some 40,000 soldiers), and the United States and the ASEAN nations also support the Khmer Rouge (officially they support the rebel coalition, of which the Khmer Rouge provides the strongest fighting force).[1] The other rebel forces consist of Prince Sihanouk, with an estimated 15,000 people under arms, and Son Sann (former prime minister under Sihanouk), with about 4,000 armed rebels. Pressure by China has brought about an uneasy truce among the rebel leaders, at least since 1983 when Pol Pot officially disavowed his former policies, hoping (ironically) for the continued support of the Cambodian people.

In the summer of 1988, China voiced its support for a negotiated settlement in Cambodia after a complete Vietnamese withdrawal, and the Vietnamese signaled their willingness in exchange for much needed economic assistance from the West.

By early 1991, however, intermittent negotiations had produced no binding agreement. By all accounts, the Khmer Rouge leaders will have no place in a future Cambodian government. The question remains whether they will accept nonrepresentation or will continue their guerrilla struggle against a government led by Sihanouk, Hun Sen, or Son Sann. China's willingness to reduce support for the Khmer Rouge can be explained by the thaw in its relations with the USSR (the ultimate supporter of Vietnam), its continued good relations with the United States, and the perception that an economically weakened Vietnam no longer has serious ambitions to extend its hegemony over other parts of Southeast Asia. The losers in the struggle are the Cambodian people, who are pawns in the power struggle between the superpowers and their respective regional partners. It is unlikely that calm will settle over Cambodia once a new government is in place, given the nature of Khmer Rouge leadership and its strong guerrilla forces.

CONCLUSION

What could have been a success story in revolutionary history turned into a disaster for Cambodians and the revolutionary elite. A combination of factors helped to accelerate the downfall of the new revolutionary regime. The immediate factor, of course, was the Khmer Rouge's assault on Vietnam; more fundamental was the single-mindedness with which it attempted to destroy any remnant of the old society to create a classless, self-sufficient agricultural peasant community free of any foreign dependency. By destroying the cities and collectivizing the peasantry, abolishing private ownership, imposing a primitive barter system, depriving the people of education (even in the most rudimentary form), and systematically terrorizing the population, the Pol Pot regime created a situation of total chaos and unleashed a reign of terror similar to that of Stalin. The very young—indoctrinated, alienated from their peers and elders, and with plentiful examples of barbarism exercised by Lon Nol's soldiers—turned savagely against those they perceived to be standing in the way of the revolution. These expendables included ethnic Vietnamese, Chinese, Thais, Chams, Buddhist monks, former cadres, captured foreign soldiers, and especially Cambodians loyal to Lon Nol—almost one-quarter of the country's population. And while Stalin did succeed in creating an industrial power, the Khmer Rouge destroyed the Cambodian economy as well as its people.

Cambodia does not neatly fit Goldstone's model. Of course, it is doubtful that any case will fit precisely the restrictive framework of a theoretical model, so we need to sort out which factors Cambodia had in common with other revolutions and which were unique. The Cambodian revolution occurred in a predominantly rural nation, and broadly speaking, the Cambodian state did not suffer from fiscal distress until it was drawn into the Vietnam conflict. Moreover, the state had few international connections, and under Sihanouk, the peasants were not directly affected by foreign economic penetration. Sihanouk's various policies to pacify the peasants were ill-conceived and came too late, and overall, the government of Cambodia after independence had little ambition to elevate peasants to the level of foreign ethnics living in Cambodia. Attempts to build a modern economy in the 1960s also came too late; thus, economic hardship may have helped precipitate the Lon Nol coup. However, Lon Nol's government received generous support from the United States; it was the corruption, lack of political support, and sporadic brutality of the Lon Nol regime—not fiscal problems—that led to its overthrow. In short, the Lon Nol regime did not lack fiscal resources, but it wasted and abused those resources.

Elite division—particularly between the traditional elite and the new middle class, and foreign-educated youth—played an important role. The traditional political elite in Cambodia, consisting predominantly of members of the former court, including the extended royal family, was closely wedded to the former king (Sihanouk) and totally depended on him. Other elite members were court-appointed provincial officials who perpetuated the colonial system of collecting taxes and meting out penalties to unruly peasants. Foreigners constituted a merchant or middleman elite, a tiny fraction of the population. The future revolutionaries were not part of the preexisting elite; at most they belonged to the tiny marginal elite, part of the lower-middle class, because they were educated, but as such they had no special status among Cambodia's people. They were able to muster the support of enough disgruntled peasants after the incessant bombings by the United States, the ruthless treatment by Lon Nol's soldiers, and the oppressive treatment by Sihanouk's corrupt provincial officials to become a formidable enemy of the incumbent regime. They received only token support from the traditional elite, in the person of Sihanouk, who in the 1960s purged Communists and in 1967 suppressed KCP-led protests. Their support base remained limited until the actual takeover, when, through severe oppression, they were able to eliminate all opposition and thus effectively silence any potential competition.

The Khmer Rouge's confused ideology offered little clue to what was to be expected, and over time it changed character so that now scholars are still unclear whether Pol Pot's vision was a type of Jacobinism or something more mystical. True, the terror that occurred suggests the path of a familiar revolutionary process, but in almost three years it never seemed to abate.

No doubt the Vietnam war had dire consequences for Cambodia. Causing hundreds of thousands of Cambodian casualties, it allowed extreme forces to seek the type of alliances necessary to overcome the wavering policies of Sihanouk. The early support of the North Vietnamese, and the later support of the PRC, allowed a well-armed Khmer Rouge to infiltrate and set up regional governments in areas under heavy bombardment by the United States. The takeover by Lon Nol, a corrupt, U.S.-supported entrepreneur, fueled further support for all those fighting the "foreign devils" and unleashed a peasant fury against urbanites that has few counterparts in modern history.

Cambodia may be the one extreme case that defies comparisons to other modern revolutions.

CHRONOLOGY

9th–14th centuries: Kingdom of Angkor founded by union of Funan (southern Indochina) and Chenla (northeast of Tonle Sap).
12th century: Kingdom of Champa (later Cochin China) conquered by Angkor.
1394: Siamese conquer Angkor—100-year war.

1848: Angkor a tributary state of Vietnam and Siam.

1863: King Norodom accepts French protectorate over the state later called Cambodia.

April 25, 1941: Norodom Sihanouk crowned king.

March 12, 1945: Japanese occupation, Sihanouk proclaims independence from France.

October 1945: Reoccupation of Cambodia by the French.

August 11, 1949: Cambodia achieves limited independence as an associate state within the French Union.

September 11, 1953: Complete independence granted to Cambodia.

February 3, 1955: Sihanouk abdicates to his father and forms Sangkum (Popular Socialist Community), remains head of political institutions.

1956: Sihanouk rejects SEATO membership, and Thailand and South Vietnam impose sanctions; U.S. supports anti-Sihanouk groups.

1960: Sihanouk becomes head of state following his father's death. First Congress of the Kampuchean Communist party; Saloth Sar (Pol Pot) is number three in party hierarchy.

1963: Sihanouk nationalizes banking and foreign trade, severs relations with South Vietnam, rejects U.S. military assistance, and accepts PRC military aid.

January 5, 1965: First U.S. air strikes against Cambodia; Sihanouk breaks diplomatic relations with United States.

April 1967: Peasant revolt in Battambang Province; Premier Lon Nol uses harsh measures.

August 1967: Rebellion ends with mass executions.

January 29 and 30, 1968: Tet offensive in Vietnam begins.

March 1969: Cambodia target of renewed air strikes.

March 1970: Sihanouk is deposed and forms Khmer National United Front.

April 1970: Massive U.S. aid for Lon Nol.

October 1970: Lon Nol proclaims the Khmer Republic.

October 1971: Lon Nol declares state of emergency.

November 1972: Sihanouk rejects cease-fire offer.

February 1973: United States renews bombing of Cambodia.

August 1973: Phnom Penh besieged by national liberation forces.

January 1974: Communists bombard Phnom Penh.

January 1975: United front launches final offensive.

April 1975: Lon Nol leaves for the United States.

September 1975: Sihanouk returns to Cambodia.

January 1976: Democratic Kampuchea declared.

April 1976: Pol Pot becomes prime minister; mass relocation of people begins.

April–May 1977: Vietnamese-Kampuchea border clashes.

December 1977: Full-fledged war against Vietnam; Kampuchea breaks off formal relations with Vietnam.

December 1978: Vietnam invades Kampuchea.

January 1979: Vietnamese-sponsored Heng Samrin regime established in Kampuchea.

July 1989: Leaders of warring Cambodian factions meet in Indonesia in the first of an eighteen-month series of inconclusive peace talks.

NOTES

1. In July 1990, the United States sought to reduce its support for the Khmer Rouge rebels by seeking direct talks with Vietnam regarding free elections in Cambodia.

11

ZIMBABWE: REVOLUTIONARY VIOLENCE RESULTING IN REFORM

JAMES R. SCARRITT

The country now known as Zimbabwe, located in southern Africa, emerged in 1980 out of the former British settler-colonial state of Rhodesia. It will be shown in this chapter that the deliberate isolation of the small white settler ruling elite from the mass of the African population and that elite's utter intransigence against yielding a modicum of either political power or economic privilege created what were in many ways ideal conditions for revolution. Beginning in the late 1950s, Africans mounted a serious challenge to the Rhodesian state based on the model of anticolonial nationalism. After repressing the surface manifestations of this challenge, the settler regime made its Unilateral Declaration of Independence (UDI)[1] from Great Britain in 1965 in order to be able to continue this repression free from the minimal control that Britain had exercised. But seven years later, Africans, whom the settlers thought to be incapable of concerted political to say nothing of military action, began to wage guerrilla warfare in earnest. This action, combined with substantial international pressures, forced the settlers to enter into a series of negotiations that eventually resulted in the creation of Zimbabwe. That the revolutionary crisis was resolved through negotiation is, however, highly significant for the pattern of political and socioeconomic transformation now occurring in that country.

PREREVOLUTIONARY STATE AND SOCIETY

The Origins of Rhodesia

The settler-colonial state of Rhodesia was born in 1890 when a small group of men, originating in South Africa and employed by the British South Africa Company (BSAC), marched across the country and established a fort near the present capital of Harare (formerly Salisbury). This occupation was motivated by

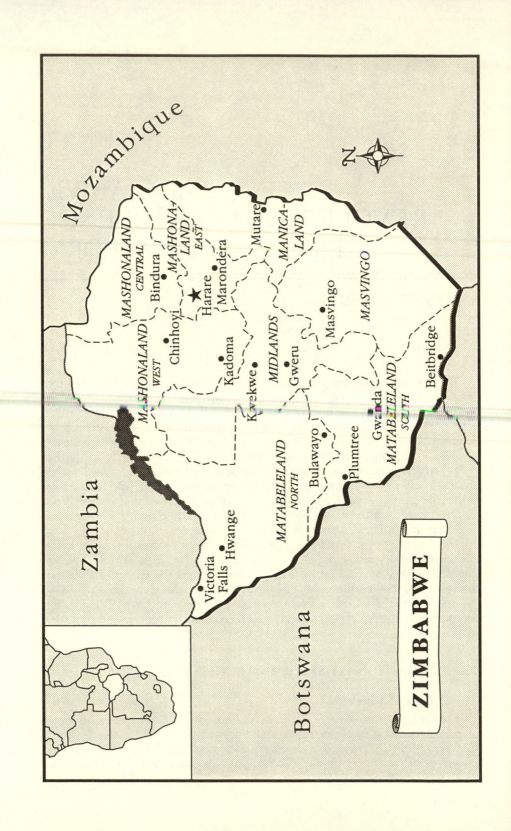

ZIMBABWE

Mozambique

Zambia

Botswana

MASHONALAND CENTRAL

MASHONA-LAND EAST

MANICA-LAND

MASVINGO

MASHONALAND WEST

MIDLANDS

MATABELELAND SOUTH

MATABELELAND NORTH

Bindura

Harare

Marondera

Mutare

Chinhoyi

Kadoma

Masvingo

Kwekwe

Gweru

Beitbridge

Gwanda

Bulawayo

Plumtree

Victoria Falls

Hwange

N

the company's hope of finding great mineral wealth and the British government's desire to extend its influence northward and establish a sphere of influence extending the length of Africa. In 1896–1897, most of the indigenous population rose in rebellion: first the Ndebele in the southwestern part of the country (Matabeleland), who had been the politically dominant group prior to the coming of the Europeans because of their superior military-political organization and who initially thought that they might be able to grant the whites nothing more than mineral rights in their territory, and then the more numerous but politically more decentralized Shona peoples, who had been raided by and forced to pay tribute to the Ndebele in the precolonial period. This rebellion resulted in the death of 10 percent of the European population of the territory and was put down only with the help of British imperial troops, and even then perhaps only because the two indigenous ethnic groups failed to coordinate their efforts and eventually signed separate peace treaties. The 1896–1897 uprising was called the *chimurenga* ("rising") by participants, a term that was to be adopted by the late-twentieth-century rebels who are the focus of this chapter (Ranger 1967).

When the BSAC's expectations for the discovery of vast mineral wealth failed to materialize, the company's desire for an alternative source of profit pushed it to alienate vast tracts of land for sale to European farmers, who either turned the Africans living on these farms into virtual serfs or expelled them to recently created reserves where the available land and water supply were inadequate to support them (Moyana 1984: 38–104; Palmer 1977a, 1977b: 221–245; Yudelman 1964: 57–129). Other sources of profit having failed to materialize, the BSAC was willing, if not anxious, to divest itself of its political responsibilities, if adequately compensated. The white settlers were very pleased to gain greater political control over the territory, and in 1923 they voted in favor of responsible self-government under rarely exercised British sovereignty.

Rhodesian Politics to 1971

Rhodesia remained a self-governing British territory until 1965. The settler government controlled all of the territory's affairs, except that a few types of legislation, the most important of which were laws that subjected Africans to disabilities to which Europeans were not subjected, had to be approved by the British government. Settler control was maintained through the franchise, which, although open in theory to all races, had constantly increasing income and/or property qualifications that excluded all but a handful of Africans until 1961. Having had virtual control of the state for so long, the settlers thought of it as their state, governing the Africans at a distance through their chiefs but not incorporating them into central institutions. The government structure was organized along the lines of a parliamentary system, with a Legislative Assembly, a cabinet headed by a prime minister, and an independent judiciary. Civil servants acquired an unusual degree of political influence through a combination of their importance in implementing government policy, their extensive organization, and their relatively large numbers within the European population (Murray 1970: 20–57). Prior to 1962, there was a substantial concentration of power in the hands of the chief political executive—the prime minister—and this situation also reinforced the influence of civil servants, who were directly or indirectly responsible to him.

Even before UDI, Rhodesian Europeans were highly unified on the general issue of maintaining power in European hands. They assumed without question that they were culturally superior to Africans. Conflicts occurred over the best tactics to use in maintaining power, as well as over policies affecting the distribution of benefits among the Europeans. Colin Leys (1959: 131–177, 202–212) has identified a trend toward greater conservatism on the question of strategy for dealing with the African challenge, and D. J. Murray (1970: ix–xxi, 353–371) and others have pointed out that this trend also involved a rebellion by poorer, less educated whites against the Rhodesian political "establishment" comprised of government party politicians, top civil servants, and representatives of organized business and agriculture.

From 1953 to 1963, Rhodesia, then known as Southern Rhodesia, belonged to the British-inspired Federation of Rhodesia and Nyasaland along with Northern Rhodesia and Nyasaland (now Zambia and Malawi, respectively). The copper wealth and more than 50,000 white settlers of Northern Rhodesia were seen by the leaders of Southern Rhodesia as strengthening their economic and political position while Nyasaland was included only at British insistence. The federal government, generally speaking, took charge of European affairs while the territorial governments retained control of Africans, although the exact division of powers was more complex than this. In retrospect, joining the federation was a major strategic error politically for the Southern Rhodesian settlers, although it contributed substantially to strengthening their economy by redistributing £70 million from Northern to Southern Rhodesia. The other territories of the federation were colonial rather than settler states, and their British rulers became increasingly willing to surrender power to African nationalists, whose agitational activity increased substantially during the years of federation. The alliance formed among nationalists in the three territories to fight the federation strengthened the hand of the Southern Rhodesian Africans.

In 1962, disillusionment over the failure of the federation to protect perceived European interests and determination to preserve white rule in Rhodesia led to the electoral defeat of the United Federal Party (UFP), which had ruled under various names, and with one brief interruption, since 1924. Victory went to the newly formed, more conservative Rhodesia Front (RF) (Hintz 1972). This change of governing party, combined with the consequent installation of Ian Smith as prime minister sixteen months later, was by far the most significant change that occurred within the prerevolutionary regime (Bowman 1973: 91). Party organization became more important and personal leadership less so, and the role of elite interest groups, especially large business, declined with the defeat of the UFP, which they had dominated. The more numerous poorer and less educated Europeans, who felt most directly threatened by African political and economic advancement and who provided the main support for the RF, were now frequently able to get their preferences for more overt segregation, more or less following the South African model, enacted into law.

Although the UFP leaders were also thoroughly racist in their political goals and general view of Africans,[2] they believed that the best way to preserve European rule was to admit a limited number of Africans as junior partners (their interpretation of the official policy of "partnership"), socialize them to accept and defend the notion of a very lengthy political apprenticeship for Africans, and thus obtain both internal legitimacy and formal independence from Britain for a regime that was ostensibly a nonracial meritocracy but would be dominated by whites for the "foreseeable future." As a modest beginning, the UFP had agreed in 1961 to the creation of a second electoral roll with lower educational and income qualifications, which would be dominated by Africans and would elect fifteen out of the sixty-five members of the Legislative Assembly. But in 1969, when it had become obvious that this initial step would produce neither legitimacy nor internationally recognized independence, it was abandoned by the RF, which won all fifty assembly seats representing white constituencies in 1965, 1970, and 1974 (Kirk and Sherwell 1975). The RF established racially exclusive electoral rolls, representation of Africans by chiefs as well as elected politicians, and a constitutional ceiling of parity with whites on the number of African legislators, to be achieved only at the very distant point in time when Africans would pay as much income tax as whites, rather than the less than 1 percent of the total that they then paid.

In the meantime, the RF government, under the strong leadership of Smith and supported enthusiastically by a grass-roots party organization, had unilaterally declared independence (UDI) from Britain in November 1965. This was a psychologically important step for the whites, since they felt that they would easily control the Africans once they had rid themselves of British interference. The complex policy responses required to protect Rhodesia from the international economic sanctions imposed after UDI and from the mounting African political challenge (both of which are described below) greatly reinforced the strength of the bureaucracy within the regime and brought it and the RF closer together.

Rhodesian Economy and Society

As Patrick O'Meara indicates: "Rhodesian society was polarized between a dominant white minority and an African majority that was virtually excluded from effective political participation. For whites, Rhodesia proved to be a country of privilege and ease, while for Africans it was one of subservience and frustration" (O'Meara 1982: 18). This dominance of a racially defined ruling class of approximately a quarter of a million people was by far the most significant characteristic of Rhodesian society, and was manifested in a myriad of ways: income, occupation, land ownership, education, housing, and the right of association as well as political power. Whites, who never accounted for more than 5 percent of the total population (which has grown from less than 1 million in 1890 to more than 8 million today), obtained close to 60 percent of the nation's personal income throughout the 1950s and 1960s and only slightly less during the 1970s. During most of this period, the average monetary income of the whites was more than ten times greater than the income of Africans, and the absolute difference in income was almost constantly increasing.

There were equally stark contrasts in the area of employment. Although all adult Europeans were employed in the money economy, only a small and at times shrinking percentage of adult Africans worked for wages. Thus, the ten to one differential in wages underestimates the actual difference in income. Those Africans who were employed in the money economy were overwhelmingly confined to unskilled and semiskilled jobs, mainly through restrictions, at first legal but later informal, on apprenticeships. A number of Africans owned small businesses in African urban and rural areas, mostly in retail trade or farming, and a very few were able to obtain professional qualifications or capital to start medium-sized businesses. Those Africans who were not employed in the money economy or seeking employment were engaged in peasant agriculture in the Tribal Trust Lands (TTLs, the former reserves) or as squatters, on farms owned by whites.

With over 60 percent of the African population living in the TTLs and having no opportunity to move out of them, the size and condition of those lands, as well as the overall distribution of land, were of major concern to Africans. The alienation of land to the Europeans, started by the BSAC, continued under settler colonialism. The Land Apportionment Act passed in 1930 had assigned essentially half of the country to Europeans and slightly less than half to Africans, with the remainder allocated to national parks or forests. In 1969, this legislation was replaced by the Land Tenure Act, which assigned slightly more land to Africans but made the division between African and European land even more rigid and more closely regulated the behavior of Africans in white areas. In 1969, there were 8.8 acres (3.6 hectares) per capita on African land and 152 acres (62 hectares) per capita on European land (Clarke 1977: Table 49), and subsequent rapid growth of the African population undoubtedly decreased the former. It has been estimated that in 1972, the population of the TTLs exceeded their "safe carrying capacity" by 85 percent, up from 13 percent a decade earlier, and this overpopulation subsequently increased even further (Kay 1976: 53); during the same period, a majority of the European land remained vacant. Furthermore, African land was on the average less fertile and well-watered than European land, as well as provided with less-well-developed infrastructure, and its productivity was further decreased by the effects of guerrilla warfare after 1972. Given the Africans' inability to make a decent living on the land, it is not surprising that 16.5 percent of them had migrated to the cities (versus more than 85 percent of the whites) by 1970 (Kay 1976: 46), and this figure would have been much higher had it not been for legislative restrictions on migration.

Inequalities in education and housing paralleled those in other areas. Per capita spending on European education was ten times greater than spending on African education, and all Europeans had the opportunity to go as far in school as their capabilities would allow while only a small minority of Africans were able to complete primary school and only a handful obtained a university education. Residential areas as well as schools were strictly segregated, and European residential areas were composed of moderately large to very large houses, surrounded by spacious, usually well kept gardens, while African residential areas were almost entirely composed of small houses without gardens or bachelor flats. Overcrowding was very common in the African areas because housing was usually tied to employment and Africans without jobs lived with their more fortunate relatives. Paving, electricity, water, and other services were all far superior in white areas.

The right of association, even in not overtly political organizations, was severely restricted for Africans in Rhodesia, especially with regard to trade unions. The majority of Africans, being employed outside of industry and commerce—most commonly as domestic servants or farm workers—remained under the Masters and Servants Act of 1901 and had no right to organize. The Industrial Conciliation Act of 1934 had initially excluded Africans in industry and commerce from skilled jobs, and thus from collective bargaining machinery, but later amendments did allow them to have an inferior status (legally assigned to skill level rather than race) in white-dominated registered unions or to form unregistered unions; in either case, they were "second class trade unionists" (Austin 1975: 65). African workers were further disadvantaged by the Land Tenure Act provision that allowed them to be in European areas (including all towns) only as long as they were employed and by the limitations placed on strikes and demonstrations by security legislation.

Under these conditions, class formation among Europeans was facilitated while that among Africans was minimized. In spite of the subsidization of European workers, income differentials among Europeans were greater than three to one, and differences in the ownership of assets were undoubtedly much greater than that because of opportunities for the wealthier Europeans to accumulate capital. Duncan Clarke, in the most comprehensive study of inequality among Rhodesian Africans, estimated that approximately 19,000 businesspeople and 9,000 farmers (owning farms in the specially created African Purchase Areas, APAs) had incomes and assets "significantly differentiated from those of workers and peasants" (Clarke 1977: 46). This group formed a minuscule African middle class, even with a few hundred professional people added in, which indicates the failure of the UFP's strategy of creating a black middle class in the face of white "lower-class" opposition.

A more significant cleavage among Africans in settler-colonial Rhodesia—as distinguished from independent Zimbabwe—was ethnicity. Western observers tend to oversimplify the ethnic structure of African societies, seeking to specify a small number of static, mutually exclusive ethnic groups rather than recognizing that Africans think in terms of concentric circles of ethnic identity ranging from the lineage to humanity. In the case of Zimbabwe, this oversimplification has consisted of positing a simplistic dichotomy between the Ndebele and the Shona, who make up 19 percent and 77 percent, respectively, of the country's African population. The former had a single centralized kingdom in the precolonial period while the latter had a number of small chiefdoms. There are, therefore, more pronounced subdivisions among the Shona than among the Ndebele: the Karanga (22 percent of the population), Zezuru (18 percent), Manyika (13 percent), Korekore (12 percent), Rozwi (9 percent), and Ndau (3 percent). The social and political distinctiveness and significance of these linguistic-regional Shona groups have varied over time and from group to group. Another complication in Zimbabwe's ethnic structure involves the Kalanga (5 percent), who were originally Shona speaking but, living along the western border of the country, were conquered and partially assimilated by the Ndebele and are now considered part of the Ndebele, at least for most purposes (M. Sithole 1980: 21–24).

Until the end of World War II, Rhodesia's economy depended almost entirely on exporting primary products—mainly gold, asbestos, and tobacco. Although these products remained important, substantial progress was made after 1945 in developing secondary industry to serve the rapidly growing settler population and, after 1953, the expanded federal market. A second expansion of manufacturing took place in the first nine years after UDI because of efforts made to counter the effects of economic sanctions. The output of manufacturing came to exceed the combined output of agriculture and mining, but this phenomenal growth was achieved only through extensive foreign investment, as is indicated by the fact that 70 percent of the capital stock of the country was still under foreign control in 1980 (Chimombe 1986: 126). The phases of manufacturing expansion were also periods of rapid economic growth, which were followed by periods of economic decline owing to the breakup of the federation in 1963 and the intensification of guerrilla warfare after 1972. The periods of economic growth heightened the regime's confidence but also stimulated the grievances of Africans, who failed to benefit proportionally from the growth. The economic decline after 1974 and the resulting pressure on the Rhodesian regime's resources were major causes of the regime's entering into negotiations for the transfer of power.

International Forces

Official British attitudes about their African colonies underwent rapid change beginning in the 1950s, and decolonization, which had previously been thought likely to occur only in the distant future, became a short run priority for a number of reasons. Rhodesia's whites had been granted self-government in 1923 in very different historical circumstances, but they nevertheless argued that the logical extension of decolonization would be to grant them full independence. Most British leaders did not accept this argument and recognized—with the aid of African pressure—that true decolonization required majority rule. However, there were antidecolonization pressure groups in Britain, and they were especially concerned with colonies in which there were settlers of British extraction. These groups maintained close personal ties to the settlers, especially their political leaders, and were quite influential within the Conservative party. This balance of forces resulted in successive British governments pursuing a compromise settlement of the Rhodesian independence issue.

In 1964, the British government formulated five principles for such a settlement: unimpeded progress to majority rule, guarantees against retrogressive amendment of the constitution, immediate improvement in the political status of Africans, progress toward ending racial discrimination, and acceptability of the settlement terms to the people of Rhodesia as a whole. Later, a sixth principle was added: no oppression of the majority by the minority or vice versa. In a series of negotiations, the British retreated further and further in their interpretation of the six principles until they formulated an interpretation acceptable to the Rhodesian government in 1971. As we shall see below, Africans were able to use the acceptability principle to block this proposed settlement by demonstrating beyond a reasonable doubt that they rejected its terms. After this rejection, and with the subsequent acceleration of guerrilla warfare, the British gradually put greater and greater pressure on the Rhodesian government to make substantial concessions but continued to work for a settlement that would leave as much power in white hands as African political leaders would accept.

There is considerable disagreement among knowledgeable observers about the effects of the economic sanctions on the Rhodesian conflict (R. Good 1973; Minter and Schmidt 1988; Strack 1978), but there is much greater consensus on the fact that the gradual way in which the British implemented the sanctions made them less effective than they otherwise would have been. There was also much criticism of the British by Zimbabwean nationalists, African governments, and their international allies for indicating, prior to UDI, that they would not resort to force to end Rhodesia's rebellion and for not adhering to Labor party leader Harold Wilson's 1964 pledge (given during an election campaign while his party was out of power) of no independence before majority African rule, which sent a uniquely clear signal to the Rhodesian government.

In addition to British vacillation, the major international force that initially postponed successful change was the support given by other settler-colonial states of southern Africa: South Africa and Portuguese Mozambique, which contained the major ports serving landlocked Rhodesia. This support was vital in "sanctions busting," as it enabled Rhodesia to receive necessary imports, especially petroleum products—for which the entire supply had to be imported—and disguised the true source of Rhodesian exports. Furthermore, South Africa provided crucial military equipment and personnel, and Portugal coordinated its counterguerrilla warfare with Rhodesia's until 1974, although not as effectively as the Rhodesians would have liked. The importance of these forms of support from South Africa and Portugal is revealed by the effects of their withdrawal (discussed later).

Zimbabwe's African-ruled neighbors, acting individually and later collectively as the Frontline States, gave indispensable support to the Zimbabwean revolution, although they were much less wealthy and less powerful than Rhodesia's settler-colonial allies (Thompson 1985). Zambia's support was most significant through 1974. That country felt the impact of the anti-UDI economic sanctions more strongly than Rhodesia did, provided a home in exile for the nationalist leaders and a base of operations for guerrillas, and suffered violent retaliation from Rhodesia as a consequence. Tensions developed between Zambian hosts and Zimbabwean guests, especially the largest guerrilla movement, and these led to the replacement of Zambia by Mozambique as the most important guerrilla base and target of Rhodesian retaliation after Mozambican independence in 1975. Both of these Frontline States closed their borders with Rhodesia for several years at great cost to their economies. Because they were paying heavy military and economic costs, these states exerted substantial pressure on the Zimbabwean nationalist revolutionaries to agree to a negotiated settlement in 1980.

THE ONSET OF STATE CRISIS

With one exception, the literature on Rhodesia does not explicitly address the issue of a revolutionary state crisis,[3] but it does contain the data necessary for the utilization of this fruitful concept. The Rhodesian case demonstrates that the existence of a crisis is a matter of degree. The three elements that Jack Goldstone identifies in Chapter 3 as comprising a state crisis—severe economic problems, elite disunity, and popular mobilization—began to appear in conjunction in Rhodesia at the end of the 1950s, became less prevalent after 1964 or 1965, reappeared in 1971, and intensified rather steadily after that date, leading toward state breakdown.

We have already seen that the time period surrounding the breakup of the Federation of Rhodesia and Nyasaland in 1963 was one of psychological uncertainty and economic decline for what was then Southern Rhodesia. Since economic prosperity was the most important reason for whites to come to and remain in Rhodesia, these two factors were closely linked, and an important element in the decline of state resources was the net decline of 25,000 in the European population between 1960 and 1964 (Kay 1976: 45). We have also seen that the whites were disunited at this time, although this disunity was only over tactics since the UFP and the RF agreed on the goal of maintaining white power. The third element of the emerging revolutionary crisis was provided by the organization of a series of African nationalist movements between 1955 and 1962 and the attraction of substantial African popular support to these movements (described in the next section of this chapter). The nationalists' demands would not have been considered revolutionary in most societies, but they came to include majority African rule in the near future, which was a revolutionary demand in the Rhodesian context. Furthermore, the rapid rise of these movements caught the government and its white supporters by surprise and frightened them because of their high degree of isolation from African opinion. The government probably perceived that a potentially revolutionary conjuncture was on the horizon.

In subsequent years, increased electoral support for the RF restored elite unity in fact increased it to a previously unknown level; political repression disorganized the nationalist movements and restricted their leaders to remote rural areas, put them in jail, or drove them into exile; and policies implemented to counter the effects of the sanctions restored a high level of economic growth and produced a net increase in the European population of just over 40,000 between 1965 and 1974. Repression began under the UFP and continued under the RF. The Subversive Activities Act of 1950 authorized the banning of meetings and literature, the Public Order Act of 1955 gave the government the power to detain or restrict people without bringing them to trial or even filing charges against them, and the Unlawful Organizations Act, the Native Affairs Amendment Act, the Preventive Detention Act, the Law and Order Maintenance Act, and the Emergency Powers Act, all enacted in the late 1950s, collectively enabled the government to curb freedom of speech, movement, privacy, assembly, and association and to curb them more severely by declaring a state of emergency. The RF did not need to introduce new legislation, only to amend that passed by previous governments.

Increased white unity, economic growth, and severe repression reduced the degree of state crisis substantially but did not move the society out of a crisis situation entirely. The small size of the white population and its deliberate isolation from Africans made elite unity a less important ingredient of the revolutionary conjuncture in Rhodesia than it is in other potentially revolutionary societies (Bowman 1973: 154–155). Economic growth under sanctions was not achieved without the costs of shifting capital and labor away from crops (especially tobacco), minerals, and light manufactured goods produced primarily for export and coping with perennial shortages of investment capital and foreign exchange. The extent of repression necessary to stifle African protest bothered some white Rhodesians, although the RF and its followers were overconfident about their success in stifling it.

Most important, the state crisis did not cease to exist because African grievances remained intense and limited guerrilla warfare began to occur. Grievances were not concentrated in any subgroups of the African population because all Africans were discriminated against by the inegalitarian structure of Rhodesian society. A survey of black and white university and high school students conducted in 1970 and 1971 found dramatic racial differences regarding regime performance evaluation, political trust, acceptance of regime ideology, sense of obligation to obey laws, and perceptions of regime responsiveness, and 70 percent of the black respondents claimed to have taken part in demonstrations (Maguire 1980: 327–338). Underground political activity of various kinds appears to have remained widespread, although it is impossible to know how widespread it was. A culture of protest had undoubtedly developed among Africans.

The degree of state crisis began to increase again in 1971 owing to African organization to oppose the terms of the settlement negotiated by the British and Rhodesian governments. Under this settlement, Britain would recognize and support Rhodesia's independence, yet the terms fell far short of meeting the "one man, one vote" goal of African nationalism. Africans would obtain at maximum only a ten-vote majority in the Legislative Assembly, and would get that only in the distant future when more Africans than Europeans would meet extremely high educational and property qualifications.

A new organization, described in the following section, rose up to lead the opposition to this settlement, filling the organizational vacuum left by banned nationalist movements and bringing to the fore significant new leaders. Again, the whites were caught by surprise. "The 1971 agreement marked . . . the peak of white fortunes in Rhodesia" (Meredith 1979: 82). Smith had just bragged that Rhodesia's Africans were the happiest in the world, and even some independent observers thought that Africans would accept the benefits of the settlement in the belief that it was impossible to get better terms and that the nationalists would not be able to organize quickly enough to have a significant effect. Yet, when a royal commission under the chairmanship of Lord Pearce visited the country in early 1972 to determine whether the settlement terms were "acceptable to the people of Rhodesia as a whole" in accordance with the fifth British principle, Africans were able to convince the commission beyond a reasonable doubt that the terms were not acceptable to them, and the settlement was not consummated.

In December 1972, a few months after the Pearce Commission issued its negative report, guerrilla warfare began to accelerate substantially, causing the breakdown of administration in the TTLs and psychological uncertainty among white farmers, which led to the abandonment of some farms, as well as raising the defense budget to 40 percent of the total government budget. The GDP began to decline at an accelerating rate, and substantially increased taxation of whites and foreign borrowing became necessary. The net migration of whites again turned negative, and by 1976 the annual decreases in the white population were substantial. Finally, there was also a break, although not a major one, in white unity. In 1977, there was a right-wing revolt within the RF, with the rebels opposing some very modest reforms in segregation proposed by Smith—who had supported legislation increasing segregation as recently as 1972—and favoring a full-scale military offensive, greater repression, and a decisive move toward greater segregation of the races. After being narrowly defeated in the Legislative Assembly, thanks to the votes of a few African members, and then expelled from the RF, the rebels formed the Rhodesian Action party. In elections held shortly thereafter, however, that party's candidates received less than 10 percent of the vote, and it won no seats (Lemon 1978: 527–529; Meredith 1979: 226–229, 294–313).

There is little doubt that Smith and the RF regime now accurately perceived that they were in the midst of a state crisis and that serious reforms would have to be effected in order to prevent what they incorrectly perceived to be a revolutionary Marxist government from taking power. They still believed that they could control the extent of reform and make certain that European privilege was largely maintained. This belief prolonged the crisis, working against the previously conflicting international forces that were now collaborating in the effort to shorten it.

POPULAR MOBILIZATION, STATE BREAKDOWN, AND THE STRUGGLE FOR POWER

Organization and Ideology of Popular Mobilization

African political mobilization increased substantially and its goals and tactics became more radical after the founding of the Salisbury City Youth League in 1955 by George Nyandoro and James Chikerema, its amalgamation into the long-established but nearly moribund African National Congress (ANC), in 1957, and the formation of the National Democratic party (NDP) after the ANC was banned in 1959. Joshua Nkomo, a trade unionist who was generally thought to be a moderate, was president of all of these organizations. They gained substantial support in all areas of the country, which led to increased repression, including the arrest of over 500 ANC leaders in connection with the banning of that organization. The NDP demanded a universal franchise, immediate political parity between the races, and majority rule within a few years. In 1960, major riots occurred in each of the larger towns, and feeling that the momentum of change within the federation as a whole was on their side, the NDP expected that the constitutional conference called by the British in 1961 would go a long way toward the attainment of African goals. But at the conference, the UFP presented proposals very similar to what eventually became the 1961 constitution and would not go beyond them in any significant way; the British government essentially supported them in this position. Nkomo and the other NDP delegates at the conference probably reluctantly agreed to accept these proposals, but massive protests within the party organization caused the leadership to reject the constitution and to hold a referendum among disenfranchised Africans, which overwhelmingly confirmed the rejection. In December, the government banned the NDP.

In the same month, former NDP leaders founded the Zimbabwe African People's Union (ZAPU), with identical aims and tactics. Violence continued through much of 1962, and in September, ZAPU was banned and many of its leaders detained. The Unlawful Organizations Act was then amended to prevent ZAPU from being reconstituted under another name. At this time Nkomo, who was out of the country, wanted to form a government in exile; he thought that the mobilization of international opinion provided the best hope of forcing change in Rhodesia. This plan was the last straw for a number of party leaders—including most of those with a higher education—who had long been dissatisfied with Nkomo's leadership style and his emphasis on international pressures rather than internal mobilization and agitation. In August 1963, these leaders—including Ndabaningi Sithole, Robert Mugabe, and Herbert Chitepo—having been outmaneuvered by Nkomo within ZAPU, formed the Zimbabwe African National Union (ZANU).

The ZANU-ZAPU split had profound and lasting consequences for both the course of the Zimbabwean revolution and the nature of postrevolutionary outcomes. Initially, however, the differences between the two parties in terms of goals and tactics were small, although ZANU's rhetoric was more militant and it was not able to penetrate the Ndebele-Kalanga areas of the country, which remained loyal to Nkomo, as did many Shona speakers, especially in Salisbury. For a year after the founding of ZANU, widespread violence in various parts of the country combined antigovernment protest with interparty conflict. In August 1964, both parties were banned, and many of their leaders—including Nkomo, Sithole, and Mugabe—were detained for a number of years. Other leaders reorganized the parties in exile in Lusaka, the Zambian capital—ZAPU under Chikerema and ZANU under Chitepo (Barber 1967: 20–220; Day 1967, 1969; Meredith 1979: 25–41; Mlambo 1972: 116–216; O'Meara 1975: 98–123).

During this period of intense popular political mobilization, the African trade unions tended to adopt an apolitical stance. They maintained this stance during the subsequent period of guerrilla warfare, and guerrillas were able to penetrate the cities only for occasional sabotage activities. Only a small fraction of the country's 900,000 workers were unionized, the high rate of unemployment meant that strikers could easily be fired and replaced, and the unions were severely restricted by the legislation described earlier. Union members and other workers nevertheless engaged in a number of spontaneous strikes, some of which were obviously politically motivated because they occurred at times of political crisis such as during the Pearce Commission's visit in 1972.

Popular mobilization in Zimbabwe did not occur primarily on the basis of an explicit, well-formulated ideology. During the period of semi-open political organization just described, African nationalism, which had been articulated throughout the continent for more than a decade, was the guiding ideology. This ideology stressed political independence under African majority rule above all else and encouraged the postponement of serious debate about the structure of postindependence society until after this political goal had been attained. European cultural superiority was explicitly rejected, but the nature of the alternative African culture that would become dominant after independence was only vaguely specified (N. Sithole 1959).

During the time that the nationalist movements were in exile, when it had become obvious that settler-colonial Rhodesia was different from the rest of colonial

Africa, and especially after the acceleration of guerrilla warfare beginning in 1972, an uneven ideological radicalization occurred. This change was more evident in political rhetoric and in guerrilla training—especially in ZANU—than in appeals for popular support, whether issued by politicians or by guerrillas. As a result, in the words of one involved observer, "ZANU and the Zimbabwean society are guided by an eclectic ideology that embraces nationalism, pan-Africanism, internationalism, socialism (both in its 'utopian/Fabian' and 'scientific Marxist-Leninist' sense) and . . . capitalism" (M. Sithole 1987a: 96). Marxism-Leninism was officially adopted as ZANU's ideology by the party's Central Committee in 1977 and again by the National Conference in 1984, but nationalism has remained the dominant element in practice (Astrow 1983: 135–144; Mandaza 1986: 29–33; Nyangoni 1978: 118–133; M. Sithole 1987a: 96–99; Stoneman and Cliffe 1989: 37–40). ZANU guerrillas appealed to peasants primarily on the basis of a combination of African nationalism and, with the help of Shona spirit-mediums, traditional respect for the ancestors. The predominance of nationalism exemplifies the generalization presented by Jack Goldstone in Chapter 3 about existing ideologies becoming revolutionary when they are used by dissatisfied groups.

With the option of open popular protest effectively foreclosed after 1964, both ZAPU and ZANU concluded that guerrilla warfare would be necessary to bring down the Smith regime. They continued to believe, however, that British intervention would be the instrument of regime change in Rhodesia, and thus they planned to employ only a limited quantity of violence, because they thought demoralizing the whites and disrupting law and order would be sufficient to force such intervention (Meredith 1979: 67). Small numbers of guerrillas had started going abroad for training in 1963, and the acquisition of weapons had begun in the same year. The numbers of both troops and weapons increased slowly over the next few years. The first isolated guerrilla attack occurred in southeastern Rhodesia in 1964, and the first encounter with the government's security forces—now officially designated as the beginning of the revolution—took place in the north-central part of the country two years later. In 1967 and 1968, both ZAPU's Zimbabwe People's Revolutionary Army (ZIPRA) and ZANU's Zimbabwe National Liberation Army (ZANLA) sent large guerrilla bands—averaging about 100 members—from Zambia across the Zambezi River and the inhospitable and sparsely inhabited terrain that lay between the river and the population centers of Rhodesia. They were easily detected and quickly destroyed, and the collaboration of ZIPRA with the South African ANC brought government troops from that country into Rhodesia for the duration of the conflict. Following these military disasters there was a significant reduction in guerrilla activity for a period of almost four years, and during that time, significant political changes occurred.

Within ZAPU, quarrels over tactics and leadership style took place between leaders from the Ndebele and Shona (Zezuru) areas of the country. The latter—led by Chikerema and Nyandoro—joined with some ZANU dissidents in 1971 to form an insignificant new movement (FROLIZI), which meant that ZAPU—now led externally by J. Z. Moyo—became a party with almost exclusively Ndebele support. Shortly before this occurrence, a group of ZAPU guerrillas calling themselves the March 11 Movement had announced their opposition to both

Chikerema and Moyo and had attempted to take over the party in order to turn it in a more revolutionary direction; they were detained by the Zambian government, however.

The 1971 Settlement and the Pearce Commission

The 1971 constitutional settlement with Britain, whose terms were highly unfavorable to the African population, has already been described. The Smith regime was hopeful that the settlement would end Rhodesia's isolation and the economic sanctions it had endured since UDI. Since 1964, political repression had successfully prevented large-scale political protests, and the African nationalist leadership had been rendered largely ineffective, forced into internal restriction or directing futile guerrilla attacks from exile in Zambia. This substantially reduced level of popular protest convinced Smith and the RF that they, with the help of the 245 chiefs (who were government employees), could persuade a presumably sympathetic Pearce Commission that the "moderate and reasonable" majority of Africans accepted the settlement terms. The twenty-one member Pearce Commission, composed mainly of former British colonial officials, was assigned the task of determining whether the settlement terms were "acceptable to the people of Rhodesia as a whole" by receiving oral and written testimony from all segments of the population in various parts of the country. This occasion prompted a new round of organization by African nationalists to oppose the settlement. The Pearce Commission's visit forced the Smith regime to lift, partially and temporarily, the veil of political repression that had substantially reduced protest for the past seven years. This veil was never to be fully lowered again, for despite the detention and exile of existing leaders, given the opportunity provided by the Pearce Commission, new leaders stepped forward.

The African National Council (also ANC to emphasize continuity with the nationalist past) was founded in December 1971 for the limited purpose of mobilizing African opposition to the settlement. "The national leadership was . . . basically a composite of two elements—former detainees active previously in one or other of the banned political parties, and Africans not previously involved with the nationalist movement" (K. Good 1974: 26). Methodist Bishop Abel Muzorewa was selected as president because he was acceptable to both ZANU and ZAPU as he had used his church role to establish his credentials as an opponent of the regime. The ANC also mobilized a number of relatively elite Africans not previously involved in the nationalist cause and united the African population across class and ethnic lines (Ranger 1985: 258–265).

During their visits to various African rural and urban areas between January and March 1972, members of the Pearce Commission were greeted by a series of strong verbal rejections of the settlement terms by assemblies of Africans, usually numbering in the thousands, and occasionally by rioting when the people perceived that the Rhodesian government was hampering their freedom of expression. It also received a number of written statements expressing opposition. Even many chiefs joined in this negative response. The government attributed the Africans' resounding rejection of the settlement to incomprehension and intimidation, but the commission's report, issued in May, dismissed this argument and found that the settlement terms were clearly not acceptable to Africans. Therefore, the settlement could not be implemented.

Although frequently indecisive and too inexperienced to bargain effectively with Smith, Muzorewa was sufficiently tenacious to hold on to the leadership of the ANC as it evolved into a full-fledged nationalist movement after the departure of the Pearce Commission; in doing so, he constantly faced opposition from more radical leaders more closely associated with the older nationalist movements. These movements viewed Muzorewa and the ANC as their agents, exercising only power that had been delegated by them, but the bishop soon came to reject any such limitation upon him. Leaders who were closely associated with ZANU and ZAPU and their popular followings soon defected from the ANC, which then came to represent more elite African interests (Ranger 1985: 265–275).

Guerrilla Warfare

In December 1972, contrary to the expectations of the Smith regime, guerrilla warfare accelerated substantially. This phase of the guerrilla struggle, which lasted until the end of 1979, differed in several crucial respects from the earlier phase. It was concentrated in the eastern part of the country, with guerrillas and weapons coming across the land border from Mozambique into more favorable, heavily forested terrain, and it was conducted primarily by ZANLA rather than by ZIPRA and involved smaller bands of better-trained and -equipped guerrillas. Most important, it followed the strategy of a people's war, concentrating on winning political support from the Africans who were living in the segregated TTLs and using that support to disrupt the administration of those areas and to attack nearby white farms. At the beginning of the offensive, anti-Portuguese guerrillas of the Mozambique Liberation Front (FRELIMO) had gained a strong foothold in the Mozambican province bordering on northeastern Rhodesia and were able to assist the ZANLA forces; in 1975, FRELIMO became the government of Mozambique, and this assistance increased substantially.

As indicated earlier, the guerrillas appealed to peasants in the TTLs primarily in terms of the peasants' many specific grievances against the neighboring European farmers and the state over the distribution of land and interference with production, backed up by the legitimacy of traditional Shona spirit-mediums. The latter strongly felt that their power and status had been attacked and that the basic values it was their duty to uphold—especially those regarding land—had been undermined by the Europeans. Their importance had, if anything, increased during the period of white rule, in part because they symbolized opposition to that rule and to those chiefs who were viewed as its agents. By conforming to the values and behavioral prescriptions of the mediums, the guerrillas—who were young people in a society that valued age and, in accordance with the ZANLA policy of not assigning fighters to their home areas, were strangers in a society that valued local affiliation—were able to use the mediums to win the peasants' trust and obedience.

ZANLA guerrillas recruited *mujibas* (usually landless and unemployed young men) to act as messengers, spies, policemen, and procurers of supplies, and they recruited *chimbwidos* (young women) to cook and wash for them as well as to help the *mujibas* perform their tasks. Political education and the mobilization of popular support were conducted primarily at *pungwes*, public meetings held at night to avoid detection by the authorities. No area was under full guerrilla control twenty-four hours a day, but many were completely free of government control at night. This situation allowed local people's or party committees to be selected and to undertake a limited range of governmental activities. Of course, relations between peasants and guerrillas or *mujibas* were not always harmonious, and, when it seemed necessary, the latter employed violence to obtain compliance by the former (Ranger 1985: 177–283; Lan 1985; Kriger 1988).

Fighting by ZIPRA guerrillas was confined to the western part of the country and was much more limited, even though they were generally better armed and trained than ZANLA forces. The ZIPRA guerrillas placed more emphasis on sabotage and less on peasant mobilization, and their organization relied mainly on the remaining ZAPU party structure. ZIPRA's relative inactivity allowed ZANLA guerrillas to penetrate parts of Matabeleland (the Ndebele homeland), where they were usually well received until they alienated the local peasants by forcing them to shout "down with Nkomo" (Cliffe, Mpofu, and Munslow 1980: 62–65).

Neither guerrilla army won battles against the regime's armed forces, but that was not their aim. Instead, they sought to avoid open confrontations—in which they suffered kill ratios of up to fourteen to one—and harass the regime's civilian and military institutions, destroying the effectiveness of the former and preventing the latter from stopping this process. After a substantial reduction in activity in 1975 owing to government military successes and some internal problems, ZANLA became increasingly successful in accomplishing both of these goals. By 1979, more than 15,000 guerrillas had infiltrated into the country and had forced the closing down of a majority of cattle dips (which are crucial for the health of cattle) and many local councils, schools, and clinics in TTLs in the eastern half of the country. The government's security forces could go to any part of the country in the daytime and maintained unchallenged control of the towns, but they could not stop the guerrilla infiltration, keep the civilian institutions functioning in the TTLs, or prevent frequent attacks on white farms, which, simply because of their large size, were isolated and were consequently abandoned in large numbers toward the end of the war.

The government's strategy, like that of the guerrillas, was strongly influenced by the racial division of the country. The European areas, including all towns, were declared "vital asset ground" and were to be held at all costs while guerrilla infiltration but not full-time control of the TTLs was considered acceptable. "No go" or "free fire" zones were established along most of Rhodesia's borders, and military-civilian joint operations centers coordinated antiguerrilla operations in each of seven operational zones. Realistic government and military officials realized that gaining legitimacy in the minds of the majority of Africans was neither possible nor necessary to regime survival, although this fact could not be admitted to international audiences. Therefore, the government sought to convince the people that the guerrillas could not win and that they would suffer needlessly by trying to support them. Generous rewards were offered for turning in guerrillas while harsh, collective punishments were meted out for collaborating with them or even not reporting them. Half a million people were forced to move into protected villages surrounded by well-guarded fences in heavily infiltrated areas, and more were moved into essentially unprotected, consolidated villages in lightly infiltrated areas. In the former, standards of living declined substantially because of the government's "scorched earth" policy of destroying crops and selling cattle, and the outbreak of disease was frequent (Gann and Henriksen 1981: 73–76; International Commission of Jurists 1976: 70–77; Weinrich 1977). These devices were much more successful in controlling the peasants than in protecting them from the guerrillas, who managed to infiltrate protected villages regularly at night, with the collaboration of their inhabitants, and even hold *pungwes* in them. Martial law was declared in more and more of the country each year until it applied to over 90 percent in 1979 (Wilkinson 1980: 114).

Although the Rhodesian state had no difficulty in maintaining superiority in sophisticated weaponry, it rather quickly ran short of white manpower to staff both the security forces and the economy. The annual period of military service for white, colored, and Asian males was frequently extended, to the point that those between the ages of eighteen and twenty-four were serving virtually continuously, those between the ages of twenty-four and thirty-eight were serving 190 days a year, and even those between fifty and fifty-nine were serving six weeks (Beckett 1985: 173–174; O'Meara 1982: 45). White manpower was actually reduced each year after 1975 as emigration began to exceed immigration. African volunteers had long been a vital component of the Rhodesian armed forces, and they were now given greater inducements to enlist, so that they made up more than half of the security forces during the height of the fighting. Finally, in 1979, after the limited majority rule of the internal settlement had been implemented, Africans became subject to conscription (although many failed to report), which enabled the state to put 25,000 men in the field at one time. Another indicator of the severe strain that the guerrilla war placed on the state is the sixfold increase in the defense budget between 1973 and 1979, when the cost of the war rose to $1 million a day (Wilkinson 1980: 115), necessitating substantial increases in both the taxation of whites and external borrowing. This expense was especially difficult to tolerate because of the falling GDP and increasing inflation, which resulted from the combination of global recession, international sanctions, and the war. All of these difficulties were greatly compounded by the partial withdrawal of South African military support in 1976.

The Rhodesian state also attempted to remain in power by subjecting the Frontline States that were supporting the guerrillas to military attacks and sabotage and by winning recognition from Western governments. The guerrillas and the parties that supported them were portrayed as Communist terrorists while the government was portrayed as defending the Western way of life. Increasingly draconian censorship of the mass media hid the state's problems and the extent of its repression from not only internal supporters and enemies but also from potential Western allies (Windrich 1979).

After the Pearce Commission report, negotiations over the future of Rhodesia had to include African representatives; negotiations began immediately (with ANC) and occurred with great frequency over the next seven years. The rapidly shifting coalitions among African parties and factions during this period were determined by the terms of the negotiations and the progress of the guerrillas. As indicated above, Ian Smith saw that it was to his advantage to negotiate with those African leaders who would accept minimal concessions in order to isolate the leaders who demanded more and to convince potential Western supporters that he was willing to be reasonable. His conception of minimal concessions evolved over the years, starting from token modifications of the 1971 settlement terms and moving by 1978 to African majority rule based on universal franchise and representation for whites only sufficient to prevent amendment of their constitutionally protected economic privileges. African leaders' terms for an acceptable bargain were a basis of competition among them but became more stringent during the same period, so that no agreement was reached until the internal settlement of 1978.

By 1974, serious splits had developed in ZANU. Sithole had alienated most of the other leaders by renouncing violence in 1969, and the other members of the Central Committee, also in prison in Rhodesia, secretly suspended him as party leader and replaced him with Mugabe. The Central Committee in prison was isolated from the leadership—in exile in Zambia—of the Dare re Chimurenga (War Council, DARE) and the military High Command, and both were somewhat isolated from the guerrilla commanders and forces stationed in Mozambique. All of these groups were also divided along ideological and ethnic lines. Guerrilla leaders from the front who felt inadequately supported by the High Command marched to Lusaka on two occasions and kidnapped several members of that group before they were eventually captured and executed by the high command under the leadership of Josiah Tongogara. Chitepo (a Manyika) was suspected of supporting the rebels, but no firm evidence that he had done so existed; he was certainly a hard-liner on the issue of negotiations. In March 1975, he was assassinated by a bomb placed in his car, and there is still no agreement on whether his ethnic (Karanga) ideological enemies in ZANU or Rhodesian agents were responsible (Astrow 1983: 82–89; Martin and Johnson 1985; Republic of Zambia 1976; M. Sithole 1979: 53–87). The Zambian government thought that the former was the case and detained a large number of guerrillas and their leaders, charging three of them—including Tongogara—with complicity in the assassination. The case was dismissed when evidence was produced indicating that one of the accused had signed a confession after being tortured. Some ZANU leaders raised the possibility that the Zambian government was itself implicated in the rebellion and in Chitepo's murder.

In December 1974, ANC, ZANU, ZAPU, and a briefly resurrected FROLIZI signed the Zimbabwe Declaration of Unity in Lusaka agreeing, under pressure from the Frontline States, to unite under the umbrella of the ANC; the leaders who had been imprisoned in Rhodesia were released because of South African pressure on Smith; and a brief cease-fire occurred. These foreign governments also arranged for a conference the following August in a railway car on the bridge connecting Zambia and Rhodesia, but Smith and the ANC were so far apart that the conference broke up after a few hours without reaching any agreement (Meredith 1979: 145–166, 189–195; Martin and Johnson 1981: 194–195). Competition soon broke out among the various ANC leaders. Nkomo broke from

Muzorewa and began several months of unsuccessful negotiations with Smith. Muzorewa and Sithole attempted to gain control of the ZANLA guerrillas, but the leaders of the latter, including the DARE members imprisoned in Zambia, rejected this attempt and indicated their preference for Mugabe. In January 1976, the rump of the DARE confirmed Mugabe as party leader, with a strong mandate to avoid negotiations and pursue the war vigorously.

By this time, the guerrilla leaders did not trust any politician to pursue the war effectively, so they formed the Zimbabwe People's Army (ZIPA), uniting ZANLA and ZIPRA with strong support from the Frontline States (Martin and Johnson 1981: 215–222). Although the governing committee of ZIPA was carefully balanced between its two component armies, ZANLA guerrillas greatly outnumbered those from ZIPRA in the forces that escalated the war in eastern Rhodesia, and the former became suspicious that the latter were being deliberately held back by their political leaders for later action in the western part of the country if Nkomo's negotiations with Smith did not produce an agreement. Escalation was greatly facilitated by the Mozambique government's closing of its border in March, but ZIPRA forces physically withdrew from ZIPA, so that the latter became merely another name for ZANLA, to which name it soon reverted. In the meantime, its commanders made a brief effort to repudiate Mugabe, Tongogara, and ZANU and form a more radical political organization of their own, but this effort was frustrated by their arrest and detention in Mozambique on the order of the Frontline State presidents (Martin and Johnson 1981: 257–262; Ranger 1980; Saul 1979: 107–122), who had just helped to forge a new ZANU-ZAPU alliance called the Patriotic Front (PF). When ZANU Central Committee elections took place in 1977, a majority of those elected were associated with the military effort, through either the DARE or ZIPA/ZANLA.

The next round of unsuccessful negotiations took place in Geneva and resulted from the intervention of U.S. Secretary of State Henry Kissinger, who was interested in bringing to power a moderate African government in Rhodesia in order to keep the perceived radicals in ZANU from taking over. Kissinger had obtained Smith's acceptance of majority rule in two years in exchange for a dominant white role during the transition period and the ending of sanctions. Although Kissinger and the British were willing to consider amendments to this plan, the Geneva Conference of October–December 1976 broke down because Smith was unwilling to deviate from it and the African nationalists were unwilling to accept it. Yet Smith's acceptance of the principle of majority rule in September 1976 had a profound effect on white consciousness, causing most whites to finally realize that the cause of maintaining white rule indefinitely was lost (Meredith 1979: 251–293).

The formation of the PF offered advantages to both Nkomo—who needed to shore up his waning support and proclaim his militancy—and Mugabe—who was still in the process of establishing control over ZANU and ZIPA and needed to get some of his most important supporters released from jail in Zambia. These leaders took a unified position at Geneva against acceptance of the Kissinger-Smith terms, and after the conference, the Frontline States recognized them as the sole legitimate leaders of the Zimbabwean liberation struggle, thus excluding

Muzorewa's renamed United African National Council (UANC). The PF did not by any means result in complete collaboration between ZANU and ZAPU, however. In 1978, Nkomo once again entered into negotiations with Smith without informing Mugabe that he was doing so, but these negotiations broke down when ZIPRA shot down a Rhodesia Airways plane.

The Internal Settlement and the Muzorewa Regime (1978–1979)

In February 1977, Smith announced that he was working toward an "internal settlement" with African leaders who were not in the PF. To induce these Africans to enter into such negotiations, he enacted some minor reforms affecting racial discrimination (D. G. Baker 1979) and, as described above, obtained an electoral mandate from white voters while silencing his right-wing critics. In response to this tactic, the British and U.S. governments developed, through a process of extensive consultations, comprehensive proposals for a settlement that injected the British government as the supervisor of the transition to majority rule, gave a limited role to UN election supervisors, integrated government security forces and the guerrillas, gave whites special representation in Parliament, and created a billion-dollar Zimbabwe Development Fund. These terms were very similar to those eventually accepted by all parties, but they were rejected by Smith in 1977 because he thought that he could get more favorable terms through reaching an internal settlement the Western powers could be pressured to accept. U.S. and British officials obtained the PF leaders' agreement to most of their proposals, after which Smith accused the Western powers of taking the side of the Marxist guerrillas.

On March 3, 1978, an internal settlement of the Rhodesian conflict was agreed upon by Smith and three African leaders. By far the most significant of the latter was Muzorewa, who retained considerable internal support, but Smith deliberately attempted to limit his power by bringing in competing politicians. Sithole had been allowed to return home the previous year, after he had once again renounced violence, and he regrouped his remaining followers, most of whom came from his home area, into a new party called ZANU (ZANU-Sithole). Chief Jeremiah Chirau, a longtime collaborator with the Rhodesian government, was induced to form his own party of chiefs in order to participate in the settlement. These leaders had been excluded from external support and lacked guerrilla followers, and thus they saw an agreement with Smith as their best hope for obtaining substantial power. The agreement provided for a universal franchise (but limited its effectiveness by also providing for strong protection of private property); a guarantee of white control of the civil service, judiciary, police, and security forces; reservation of 28 out of 100 seats in Parliament for whites, enough to block changes in entrenched clauses of the constitution; membership in the cabinet to all parties in proportion to their parliamentary representation; and a transitional government comprising an executive council composed of the four leaders and operating by consensus, a ministerial council with equal numbers of black and white members, and the existing Parliament, which would rule until elections were held and power was handed over to a black government. The country was to be known as Zimbabwe-Rhodesia. The constitution embodying this agreement was approved by whites in January 1979 by a margin of almost six to one.

During the transitional period, Smith was able to use divisions among the three black executive-council members to block any significant change. Racial discrimination was made illegal in places where it had not been enforced for the past year or more, but otherwise there was very little progress toward its removal for any but the wealthiest Africans, although the Land Tenure Act was eventually repealed. White parents who wished to do so could buy public schools in their neighborhoods and run them, with government support, as virtually all-white "community schools." Undoubtedly the greatest accomplishment of the internal settlement regime was the successful conduct of an election in April 1979. According to official statistics, which undoubtedly underestimated the size of the voting-age population, 64 percent of the eligible voters registered to vote. This turnout in itself was a victory for the regime, for which participation in the election was to be the crucial indicator of legitimacy (Meredith 1979: 357, 365). The election was held in the context of strong pressure from the security forces, local government officials, and employers to vote and pressure from guerrillas and PF officials not to vote. Many Africans voted without being directly pressured to do so in the hope of obtaining peace. Muzorewa won 67 percent of the vote and fifty-one of the seventy-two black seats in Parliament, thus becoming the country's first black prime minister. Ian Smith became minister without portfolio.

But the internal settlement regime failed to attain two of its major goals—getting the guerrillas to lay down their arms and winning recognition from Western governments—and these failures were its undoing. Guerrilla warfare accelerated substantially in 1978 and 1979, as it was the major tactic used by the PF to undermine the internal settlement and obtain better terms under which that coalition could win an election. A substantial majority of the African population, including many people who had voted for Muzorewa, also wanted a better settlement and believed it was possible to attain one. Muzorewa and Sithole, who were completely rejected by the guerrillas, now established their own fighting forces known as auxiliaries. These forces were poorly trained and disciplined, however, and their brutality alienated their leaders even further from the Zimbabwean people. The failure to win the war was primarily responsible for the failure to win Western recognition. Despite strong pressure from ultraconservatives, and because of strong pressure from the Frontline States and oil-rich Nigeria—the latter only recently seriously involved in the Rhodesian question—the British and U.S. governments refused to recognize the internal settlement and continued in their attempts to arrange an all-party conference between the leaders of the internal settlement regime and the PF. Through guerrilla warfare, the PF had achieved what Jack Goldstone calls a "dominant coalition."

The Lancaster House Settlement and the Foundation of the Mugabe Regime

Within two months of the 1979 Rhodesian election, the Commonwealth heads of government met in Lusaka, and the African leaders made it clear to newly elected British Conservative Prime Minister Margaret Thatcher that a solution to the Rhodesian crisis acceptable to the PF was necessary to preserve the Commonwealth and Britain's trade relations with Africa, but also that they would exert pressure on the PF to compromise in order to facilitate the attainment of such a solution. All heads of government present agreed on a set of broad principles for solving the crisis, including placing ultimate responsibility for doing so in British hands. Accordingly, the British government announced in August 1979 that a constitutional conference would convene at Lancaster House in London the following month under the chairmanship of the foreign minister, Lord Carrington, and a draft outline of a new constitution was sent to all parties. Because of the effects of accelerated war inside Rhodesia and throughout southern Africa since the internal settlement, the internal settlement parties, ZAPU, the Frontline States, South Africa, and Britain were all very anxious for the conference to succeed. The UANC, ZAPU, and ZANU were all optimistic about their electoral prospects and thus were willing to fight an election, but ZANU was nevertheless ambivalent about reaching a quick settlement because most of its leaders thought the British would conspire to deny them power and some thought further guerrilla victories might produce better settlement terms in the future. Thus, pressure from the Frontline States, especially Mozambique, was crucial in obtaining ZANU's attendance at the conference and its reluctant agreement to make compromises, although its leaders' fear of a British deal with the other parties in their absence also played a role (Clough 1982: 46–50; Davidow 1984: 44–49).

The Lancaster House Conference was essentially a series of negotiations between Lord Carrington and each of the two Rhodesian delegations—internal settlement and PF. Agreement on a new constitution required both sides to make significant compromises. Muzorewa and the internal settlement government had to surrender power to a British governor and accept the loss of white control over administrative and judicial institutions through an affirmative action program known as the "presidential directive"; the PF had to accept the reserving of twenty seats in Parliament for whites (not enough to block constitutional amendments) for seven years, citizenship for those whites who had immigrated since UDI, and protection of privately owned land and other productive property against expropriation. The last point was resolved only by British and U.S. promises of massive development funds.

Proposals concerning the transitional period and the cease-fire were even more controversial because of the extreme distrust that both sides had for one another and, to a lesser extent, for the British. Carrington's solution was a short transition under the absolute control of a British governor, assisted by limited numbers of British troops and police, but relying heavily on the Rhodesian bureaucracy and security forces, while the guerrillas would be confined to sixteen vulnerable assembly points. The last point made the PF very suspicious, and it presented extensive counterproposals. Before final agreement was reached on these points, Carrington appointed Lord Soames as governor and sent him to Rhodesia, lifting economic sanctions upon his arrival. Under the pressure thus established for the conference to succeed, combined with that of the Frontline States and the Commonwealth, all sides finally agreed in December to a cease-fire commission with little power, a small Commonwealth force to monitor the cease-fire, and a small group of

Commonwealth and other international observers to guarantee that the election to be held less than two months after the cease-fire would be "free and fair" (Clough 1982: 50–55; Davidow 1984: 33–89; Martin and Johnson 1981: 315–320; Verrier 1986: 251–282; Wiseman and Taylor 1981: 4–13).

The cease-fire was effective, although the monitoring force and most international observers acknowledged the existence of intimidation and assigned responsibility for it to both the security forces and the guerrillas who did not report to assembly points. The period leading up to the election was thus one of high tension because the leaders of ZANU—now renamed ZANU-PF because Sithole had been allowed to preempt the name ZANU, and Nkomo, hoping to force a unified ZANU-ZAPU campaign, had been allowed to preempt the name PF—believed, probably correctly, that the British were trying to keep them out of power and knew that the British were dependent for the maintenance of law and order on the Rhodesian security forces, who were certainly intent on keeping them out of power. The governor took several actions against ZANU-PF that hindered the group's campaign activities, especially in comparison to those of the well-financed (largely by South Africa) UANC, but those actions probably increased the group's popular support (Astrow 1983: 156–158; C. Baker 1982; Gregory 1981: 78–89; Verrier 1986: 283–301; Wiseman and Taylor 1981: 20–29, 37–38).

The first of two elections held in February 1980 was for the twenty white seats, all of which were won by the RF. Two weeks later, the election for the eighty African seats was held, and ZANU-PF emerged as the big winner, taking fifty-seven seats on the basis of 63 percent of the vote. The PF (formerly ZAPU) won twenty seats on the basis of 24 percent of the vote, and the UANC won three seats on the basis of 8 percent of the vote. The PF won only one seat in the five predominantly Shona provinces, and ZANU-PF won only one seat in the two predominantly Ndebele provinces; only in the ethnically mixed Midlands Province was there anything close to an even split. Turnout was 2.7 million, up from less than 1.9 million in 1979, casting further doubt on the legitimacy of the earlier election. The results reflected above all the politicization that was carried out by ZANU as part of the guerrilla struggle after 1972 and the widespread presence of ZANLA guerrillas, along with a rejection of Muzorewa as a collaborator (Cliffe, Mpofu, and Munslow 1980; Gregory 1981; Rich 1982). Soames appointed Mugabe as prime minister in a ZANU-PF/PF-ZAPU coalition government as soon as the results were announced.

REVOLUTIONARY OUTCOMES

ZANU-PF's victory was a great shock to many whites, who had expected a UANC (Muzorewa) victory, as it appeared to mark the end of the society they had known. More realistically, two scholars sympathetic to the white cause conclude that "in the history of twentieth-century revolutionary warfare, the indeterminate Rhodesian conflict was *sui generis*" (Gann and Henriksen 1981: 117), and scholars sympathetic to the Africans (Gordon 1984: 129–130; Phimister 1988: 8; "Yates" 1980) agree. As a consequence of guerrilla warfare terminated by an internationally imposed negotiated settlement and the continued operation of extensive international pressures, the new ruling elite had substantial resources at its disposal but faced even more substantial constraints on its efforts to reconstruct society. As Jack Goldstone notes in Chapter 3, the class and economic structure of the prerevolutionary society and the international context of the revolution interact with one another and with the experiences of the new elites under the old regime and in the revolutionary struggle to constrain the directions of postrevolutionary change.

Among the significant resources available to the new African elite were strong support from popular groups owing to the success of the guerrilla struggle, a broad (although not deep) political unity among Africans as represented by the overwhelming electoral victory of the two PF parties in the governing coalition, a strong state structure inherited virtually intact from the previous regime, and an economy that was highly developed by African standards—having been strengthened by measures taken to minimize the effects of sanctions but also having strong potential for further development upon their removal. Among the significant constraints on the new elite were the constitutional limits placed on them in the Lancaster House agreement; the lack of depth of national unity, manifested primarily in the continuation of the long-standing ZANU-ZAPU rivalry but also in factionalism within ZANU-PF; the weakness of party organization (in both parties), particularly with regard to mobilizing popular participation and transmitting the leaders' ideology to the people, especially across class lines; and, above all, continued economic dependence on local white capital, advanced capitalist countries, international lending agencies, and neighboring South Africa—economically and militarily powerful, white-ruled, and thus fundamentally hostile. The fact that efforts to overcome some of these constraints would be likely to exacerbate others should also be considered a major constraint.

There is considerable controversy about where the balance among strengths, constraints, the vigor of the elite's will to reconstruct, and the effectiveness of policies of reconstruction has brought Zimbabwe in the years since its independence. Reconstruction of the state has been extensive, but there have also been major areas of continuity, and the consequences have not led to the thoroughgoing participatory democracy envisioned in ZANU-PF pronouncements. Economic and social reconstruction have been less extensive, although by no means insignificant, and have not created the socialist society also envisioned in those pronouncements. Reconstruction of the southern African environment may be beginning, but the outcome remains extremely uncertain. The actual consequences of reconstruction require a detailed analysis.

The Limits to Postsettlement Change

On the evening of March 4, 1980—the day the election results were announced—Prime Minister Mugabe articulated a policy of national reconciliation under which whites were urged to remain in the country and guaranteed protection of their rights and privileges if they did so. The subsequent implementation of reconciliation policies continued to reassure whites—although not without some setbacks. Mugabe appointed a cabinet that included two whites—one from the RF and one from the Commercial Farmers Union (CFU)—and four ZAPU members, including Nkomo. One reason for the relative success of racial reconciliation has been the emigration of over one-half of the whites—mostly the poorer and less skilled ones who were most economically competitive with Africans—leaving about 100,000 in the country.

ZANU village and (local council) ward committees, established by ZANLA, varied widely in structure and functions but emphasized popular participation and were used by less privileged groups—whether defined in terms of class, traditional status, gender, or age—to challenge more privileged ones with varying degrees of success. These peoples' committees began to become less active around the end of 1981 because they received no official support, and new local party structures, focused on party branches that include several villages, were introduced later from above. Thus, even in areas where there is no opposition, "the party hierarchy stops a little short of being an instrument of central control down to the village level" (Stoneman and Cliffe 1989: 103; see also Lan 1985: 209–215; Ranger 1985: 291–297; Stoneman and Cliffe 1989: 25–26, 100–103). This organizational weakness, combined with the shortage of ideologically committed cadres trained in the techniques of popular mobilization, has placed severe limits on the local ZANU-PF structure as an agent of political and social transformation.

Questions can also be raised about the strength of the national party organization. The party could not operate legally inside the country from shortly after its founding in 1963 until 1980, and party organization did not receive high priority after independence until the selection of delegates for a party congress in 1984 (the first since 1963) initiated a period of greater attention to such organization. At this congress, a new party constitution was adopted, and it declared the supremacy of the party over government, substantially enlarged the Central Committee and created a Politbureau, gave Mugabe increased powers to appoint party officials, appointed five standing committees to oversee various aspects of government policy, and adopted a leadership code that prevented government officials and party leaders down to the branch level from owning businesses, large farms, or rental property and from receiving more than one salary. Very considerable doubt is cast on the effectiveness of these measures in making the central party organization a vehicle of societal transformation by Mugabe's admission in 1988 that neither party control of government nor the leadership code was working effectively and his appointment of two new ministers with reputations as radicals to purely party duties (Stoneman and Cliffe 1989: 79–81).

The serious factionalism within ZANU during the struggle for independence has already been discussed, and this problem has continued in the postindependence period, although at a lower level of intensity. Contemporary factionalism is based on a combination of generational and career differences, ethnicity, personal ambition, and ideology. Most of the major political figures (with the prominent exception of the former secretary-general and alleged radical Edgar Tekere) who had fallen from power in factional disputes have been politically rehabilitated, so that long-lasting, clearly demarcated factions have not emerged. Unlike the earlier period, when Mugabe was a leading partisan in intraparty factionalism, his position has become sufficiently strong—especially since the 1984 party congress—that he is essentially above factional conflicts and able to mediate them in the name of party unity, which he values very highly (Libby 1984; Stoneman and Cliffe 1989: 35–36, 82–86). In spite of its limited intensity, however, factionalism has been a significant factor working against ZANU-PF's transformative capacity.

At least until April 1990, when constitutional guarantees of freedom to organize parties fell away, ZANU-PF had to tolerate opposition parties, and the nature of interparty competition was another factor working against rapid social change. After the 1980 election, the RF renamed itself the Conservative Alliance of Zimbabwe (CAZ) and continued to push for white interests as traditionally defined. Several leaders who favored a more rapid adjustment to postindependence realities split off in the early 1980s to form the loosely knit Independent Zimbabwe Group (IZG), which generally supported the government and worked with Africans who had similar class interests in support of these interests. Collaboration with the CFU, the Chamber of Mines, the Confederation of Zimbabwe Industries (CZI), and the Zimbabwe National Chambers of Commerce (ZNCC)—all dominated by whites—is a crucial part of this strategy; these groups have regained the dominant position in white politics that they lost in 1962 with the rise of the RF (Stoneman and Cliffe 1989: 45–46, 108–110). This influence is unlikely to be significantly diminished by the declaration of a one-party state.

Although several parties continued to exist, by far the most significant opposition to ZANU-PF prior to 1988 came from its sometime coalition partner PF-ZAPU. Fighting between ex-ZANLA and ex-ZIPRA guerrillas within the integrated army began in late 1980 and continued sporadically for more than a year; fighting between supporters of the two parties in the urban townships lasted even longer. In 1982, Nkomo and two of the other four ZAPU ministers were dismissed after a large supply of arms was found on a farm belonging to the party. Nkomo fled to Britain temporarily, saying that he feared for his life. Ex-ZIPRA army deserters, almost certainly supplemented by South African-armed and -trained thugs—collectively designated by the government as "dissidents"—began attacking government officials and white farms in Matabeleland. Nkomo and other ZAPU leaders disowned the dissidents and urged them to surrender, but ZANU claimed that these statements were not entirely genuine. The government's response was to send the newly created, North Korean–trained, Shona-speaking Fifth Brigade to eliminate the dissidents, which they attempted to do, with limited success, by terrorizing the local population and killing an estimated 2,000 people. Prime Minister Mugabe appointed a commission of inquiry in 1984 and began to restrain the Fifth Brigade (Astrow 1983: 167–172; Nkomo 1984: 219–244; Weitzer 1984b: 540–547).

The 1985 elections took place in an atmosphere of some tension because of these developments. ZANU-PF increased its percentage of the vote to 77 percent and its seats in Parliament to sixty-four, emphasizing its accomplishments and the importance of unity and order rather than socialism in its campaign, and winning all seats outside Matabeleland except one in Sithole's home area that went to ZANU-Sithole but losing all seats in the two Matabeleland provinces. Although ZAPU's percentage of the vote declined to 19 percent and its seats to fifteen, ZANU-PF's gains came more at the expense of the other parties, especially UANC. The CAZ won only 55 percent of the white votes but fifteen of the twenty white seats (Kumbula 1986; Lemon 1988; M. Sithole 1986: 86–94; Sylvester 1986: 241–255).

At its 1984 party congress, ZANU-PF passed a resolution to establish a one-party state "in the fullness of time and in accordance with the law and the constitution." Although there are a number of pressures to move in this direction (Shaw 1986; M. Sithole 1987b: 248–249), the most important proximate motive is the perceived need for regime consolidation in light of the winner-take-all conception of interparty politics. Mugabe persuaded Nkomo to reenter unity talks, which had begun in 1983, and applied pressure on him by closing ZAPU offices and detaining opponents of unity. A "unity agreement" was reached in December 1987, providing essentially for the absorption of PF-ZAPU into ZANU-PF. A few months later, Mugabe offered amnesty and resettlement to all dissidents who agreed to surrender; the offer was accepted, putting an end to this serious problem. At the congress of the now-united party held in December 1989, the Politbureau and Central Committee were expanded to include former ZAPU leaders without reducing the number of former ZANU leaders. It is too early to tell how well ZANU-ZAPU unity will work in practice, or what effects it will have for the party's ability to engender social transformation. ZAPU has long been less committed to socialism than ZANU, and thus, whatever influence the former has in the unified party is likely to make it more conservative, but an effective healing of the historic ZANU-ZAPU split would be a significant change in itself. Another indication of the limited potential for radical transformation in Zimbabwe is the formation of a new party—the Zimbabwe Unity Movement (ZUM)—by Tekere in May 1989, which initially attempted to appeal at the same time to student and other radicals and conservative supporters of CAZ, UANC and ZANU-Sithole—renamed ZANU-Ndonga (Meldrum 1989)—but came out strongly in favor of free enterprise in late 1989. Under a one-party system, competitive primary elections may be introduced, as has been done in other African countries with mixed results for popular participation.

In the 1990 elections, which were preceded by a week of violence, voter turnout was down by 300,000 from 1985, with only between 54 percent and 60 percent of those eligible to vote actually doing so. ZANU-PF won 116 of the 119 Parliamentary seats contested, and Mugabe won the presidency by 2,036,976 votes to Tekere's 413,840. But ZUM won close to 30 percent of the votes in urban areas, and the low turnout was widely interpreted as an expression of popular dissatisfaction. Opposition to the declaration of a one-party state on the part of a majority of the members of the ZANU-PF Politbureau and the larger Central Committee has at least delayed implementation of Mugabe's stated intention to ban opposition parties legislatively.

Changes in State Structure

Changes have also taken place in the state itself, and they too are ambiguous in terms of facilitating or constraining societal transformation and participation by popular groups. In December 1987, at the time of the ZANU-ZAPU union, the inherited parliamentary system with a largely symbolic president and a prime minister who was the effective leader of government was replaced by a strong president who is both head of state and government leader. At about the same time, the twenty white seats in Parliament were abolished; their occupants were replaced by twenty ZANU-PF candidates, eleven of whom were whites from the IZG and major interest groups. There is a consensus among observers that Mugabe has been, and will continue to be, relatively cautious in exercising the tremendous power concentrated in the presidency (state and party) but that these powers are subject to abuse by his successors.

State personnel changed fairly rapidly in the first months and years after independence thanks to extensive use of the "presidential directive" to bring large numbers of Africans into positions at all levels of the bureaucracy, although a significant minority of whites remained in their positions for some time (Murapa 1984). The number of state personnel also expanded rapidly, but changes in state structure occurred much more slowly. The size of the cabinet has expanded, and various changes have been made in the allocation of functions among ministries; these have usually been justified as producing a more effective development effort, but some—such as placing development under a senior minister long responsible for finance and still having that responsibility, and reabsorbing the recently created ministries of land reform and manpower planning into more traditional ministries—have in fact protected the status quo. The state has retained its centralization and experienced only a slight decline in its effectiveness.

A crucial change that received high priority at the time of independence was the successful integration of the two guerrilla armies and the security forces into the Zimbabwe National Army (ZNA), with the vital assistance of the British Military Advisory Training Team, after the auxiliaries and the most brutal units of the security forces had been disbanded. A few months after independence, the former Rhodesian commander was removed as commander of the armed forces and expelled from the country, and the ZANLA commander was appointed as head of the ZNA. A number of other whites in the military were dismissed or resigned, and a few were charged with being South African agents. A large number of former guerrillas were also absorbed into the Zimbabwe Republic Police.

Africanization in the judiciary has proceeded more slowly than in the bureaucracy, and the judiciary has "a good reputation for its independence, professionalism, and impartiality" (M. Sithole 1987a: 96). In a few dramatic cases, the higher courts have negated government actions on constitutional grounds (Sklar 1985) in spite of the continuation until July 1990 of the state of emergency established by the Rhodesian regime prior to UDI and extensive use of that regime's infamous Law and Order Maintenance Act (Weitzer 1984a, 1984b). The retention of such legislation and the bureaucratic machinery to enforce it does not bode well, however, for state transformation.

The Lancaster House constitution provided for integrated local government in the towns but separate local governments in the former TTLs, now renamed communal areas, and the former white farming areas. These two systems have now been integrated, and ward and village development committees have been created, but it is too soon to say how effective these new institutions will be. Another significant change has been the replacement of the preindependence authoritarian control of the Ministry of Internal Affairs, its district commissioners, and the chiefs by the more decentralized supervision of the Ministry of Local Government, with reduced powers for provincial and district governors and chiefs although the last have recently regained some functions (Helmsing 1990: 92). In spite of these changes, rural local government does not effectively facilitate local initiatives in social transformation and contains significant elements of a "conservative restoration" (Stoneman and Cliffe 1989: 97–103). This judgment is reinforced by what was said earlier about local party structure.

In the latter part of 1988, rumors of corruption on the part of top government officials were rife, and the press eventually uncovered enough information on the illegal purchase and resale of motor vehicles from a state-owned factory by five ministers and three other officials that these officials were compelled to resign. In the end, Mugabe gained strength from the scandal by disowning those implicated in it, even some longtime political associates, and by appointing a commission of inquiry with a broad mandate to investigate corruption. Part of Mugabe's gain was later lost, however, through failure to prosecute some of the corrupt officials.

Changes in the Economy

New economic opportunities have opened up for several hundred thousand black Zimbabweans since independence, both from the occupancy of positions vacated by departing whites and from the creation of new positions and facilities for capital accumulation that resulted from the expansion of government services and the immediate postindependence economic boom. These opportunities mark a noteworthy change in the social structure and have resulted in significant class formation, but the nature and cohesiveness of the class(es) thus being formed are matters of some controversy, as are the implications of this process for the revolutionary transformation of society. Blacks have entered the previously all-white bourgeoisie, most frequently as professionals or high-salaried employees of government or private firms but also as owners of businesses or farms. A majority of the white petite bourgeoisie has left the country, and their places have been taken by blacks, while many new positions in these categories have been created. Thus, the Rhodesian class structure remains largely intact, although expansion in the size of the most privileged classes and their deracialization have affected their relations with other classes.

Almost all of the political elite—prominent politicians and top-level bureaucrats—came from the petite bourgeoisie, and their current incomes and consequent capital assets—even without corruption—place them in the bourgeoisie. Yet, the cohesiveness of these classes—involving both consciousness and group organization—is relatively low, especially for the recently expanded petite bourgeoisie, and many politicians' and a few bureaucrats' commitment to socialism—ambivalent as it is in some cases—inhibits their pursuit of purely class interests. The combination of Mugabe's genuine commitment and his great power is perhaps an even more important inhibiting factor. If, as most observers believe, class cohesiveness is growing, these inhibitions are weakening (Mandaza 1986: 46–61; D. Moore 1988; Sibanda 1988; Stoneman and Cliffe 1989: 51–63). The Zimbabwean state, under the control of this elite, is "the guarantor of capitalist production; however, it also bears the imprint of the liberation struggle and the class forces it unleashed" (Anonymous 1987: 47, quoted in Sylvester 1990: 475). What does this situation mean in terms of specific policies and their impact on various popular groups or classes?

Michael Bratton (1981; Bratton and Burgess 1987) indicates that the Zimbabwean state has emphasized economic growth and the redistribution of services while moving much more cautiously to redistribute income and even more cautiously with regard to the redistribution of assets. "Growth with equity" has been the theme of the government's economic policies since independence, as has been reflected in the two indicative development plans that have been produced, ineffective as these have been in reaching many of their targets. As we have seen, the economy was relatively developed in African terms at independence, and the government placed a very high priority on maintaining that development. The government has not effectively challenged the capitalist nature of the economy or its high level of dependence on foreign capital and export revenues because it perceived that these givens could not be changed quickly without engendering a temporary economic decline. With the removal of international sanctions, there was a tremendous economic boom in 1980–1981, with the GDP growing 26 percent in two years. Frequent droughts, declining demand and terms of trade for Zimbabwe's exports, minuscule amounts of foreign investment and less foreign aid than initially promised, and a shortage of foreign exchange have combined to produce low to negative levels of growth in all subsequent years except 1985, 1988, and 1989 (Stoneman 1988: 47–48; Knight 1990: 203).

Policies in areas such as expansion of the public sector, control of the private sector, management of the balance of payments, control of trade unions, and agricultural development are directed more toward growth than to equity, and many have a strong element of continuity with the policies of the Rhodesian state. The public sector has expanded rather modestly, mostly through the purchase of South African companies, and the major explanation for this pattern of expansion is the government's desire to increase its control of the economy (Herbst 1989, 1990: 116–122). Zimbabwe has a market economy but one that is controlled by the state in a number of ways, including controls on investment, marketing, prices, and wages. These controls are most stringent in the area of import quotas, although the demand for higher levels of imports to sustain the postindependence economic boom was irresistible and quickly transformed Zimbabwe's favorable balance of payments into a foreign exchange crisis. The combination of meeting rapidly increasing debt obligations without rescheduling, substantial currency devaluation, reduction of overall government expenditures, and reduction of subsidies on basic food and other consumer goods for the poor—an austerity package pursued on internal initiative whatever the state of Zimbabwe's on-again off-again relations with the International Monetary Fund—has clearly been an attempt to stimulate growth at the expense of equity (Nyawata 1988). A recently promulgated investment code that facilitates quick approval of new foreign investment and other economic liberalization measures that have been announced as forthcoming indicate that the emphasis on growth is increasing (Herbst 1990: 133–141; Meldrum 1989).

Social Change

Public services were expanded with great rapidity immediately after independence, and those for the poor were often improved in quality. Education was desegregated, expanded massively at all levels—especially in the rural areas—and made free of charge in the primary grades. In seven years, primary school enrollment almost tripled, and secondary enrollment increased sixfold. This expansion required rapid training of large numbers of teachers and hasty construction of a large number of minimally adequate classrooms, both of which were bound to have a negative effect on the quality of the education presented. The numbers of primary and secondary school graduates now far exceed the number of employment opportunities open to them. Both curriculum reform directed toward making education more relevant to development in Zimbabwean conditions—to say nothing of giving it a socialist content—and a drive for adult literacy have proceeded much more slowly. Management agreements for schools in elite neighborhoods, with relatively high fees, and government subsidies to elite private schools (as well as impoverished village schools) have maintained unequal educational opportunities based on class (Chung 1988; Raftopoulos 1986; Stoneman and Cliffe 1989: 168–172; Zvobgo 1986). Health services were also expanded dramatically, with an emphasis on primary care and preventive medicine, especially in the rural areas, and were made free to those with the lowest incomes. Over 7,000 village health workers have been trained. Dramatic results of this expansion include a 50 percent reduction in the child mortality rate and the highest rate of contraceptive use in Africa. Still, private hospitals continue to provide a higher quality of health care for the elite (Agere 1986; Loewenson and Sanders 1988; Stoneman and Cliffe 1989: 172–175). Educational and health services have both ceased to expand significantly since 1982 because of budgetary constraints.

In the absence of hard data on income distribution, observers disagree on what has happened since independence, but the range of disagreement is narrow— between "a modicum of income redistribution" (Bratton and Burgess 1987: 207) and none (Stoneman and Cliffe 1989: 124), and the initial redistribution has probably been effectively counteracted by more recent developments, at least for workers and poor peasants. There is even more consensus that the redistribution of assets has been slight.

As we have seen, the workers were a peripheral force in the liberation struggle, although prone to spontaneous strikes, and trade unions were extremely weak at that time; also, ZANU-PF had weaker ties to the unions than either ZAPU or UANC. These facts have affected postindependence developments. A wave of spontaneous strikes began in March 1980 and continued well into 1981, which was a predictable reaction to the frustrations of black workers under the Rhodesian labor regime. Initially, the new government was quite unprepared to deal with this behavior; the minister of labor repeated on several occasions phrases from a speech given by one of his Rhodesian predecessors a decade earlier defending the existing repressive antistrike legislation. Soon the government "inserted itself between the capitalist employer and the workers as the guardian of labor discipline" (N. P. Moyo 1988: 209), and it confirmed this role in 1985 by passing the Labor Relations Act and dictating the resolution of strikes in the agricultural processing industry. This insertion involved introducing a legal minimum wage and regulations barring employers from dismissing workers without the approval of the minister of labor, facilitating union organizing, creating workers' committees (which often conflicted with the unions) in all workplaces, establishing the Zimbabwe Congress of Trade Unions (ZCTU), and giving workers and other urban dwellers disguised subsidies through the pricing of goods and services provided by parastatal companies. The government, however, which also froze wages in 1982 and 1987, maintains tight control of both unions and committees, severely limits the right to strike, and preserves many managerial prerogatives. The ZCTU and most unions were internally undemocratic—and thus lacked strong legitimacy—until reforms were enacted in 1987, and they continue to be plagued by corruption at high levels (Sachikonye 1986; Stoneman and Cliffe 1989: 63–68, 104–108; Wood 1988).

The size of the working class—about 1 million people in full-time employment—has not increased since independence, but there has been considerable differentiation within it as black workers have occupied exceptionally well-paid skilled positions. Official estimates classify a slightly larger number of people as unemployed, and this number is increasing rapidly owing to population growth and expansion of educational opportunities. Worker consciousness remains more confined to workplace situations than uniting the whole class (Cheater 1988). Virtually none of the less-well-paid workers—concentrated in agriculture and domestic service—are unionized, so there are fewer than 200,000 union members (Stoneman and Cliffe 1989: 104; Wood 1988: 285), and, if increased union power emerges from recent union reforms, it may well result in further differentiation within the working class rather than increased power for the class as a whole. Because of wage freezes, inflation, and increasing unemployment, the standard of living of the working class has been irregularly declining since 1982. Thus, it must be concluded that Zimbabwe is consolidating capitalist labor relations rather than moving toward a state that is controlled by workers, places their interests above those of other classes, or redistributes income to them.

Land redistribution was the main promise used to motivate peasant participation in guerrilla warfare, although it was closely connected to the provision of better services, and both of these measures were assumed to be means to raise incomes. In recent years, the focus of government policy has shifted from the redistribution of land assets to the provision of services and the realization of higher producer prices. Because of the country's economic problems and the cost of resettlement, only 48,000 households have been resettled (in comparison to the government's initial goal of 165,000)—less than the population increase in the communal areas—and the program has been virtually halted since 1983. Of those resettled, 95 percent have individual smallholdings rather than being in collectivized production units as initially envisioned. Most of the resettlement areas are on relatively poor land, and the performance of the resettled peasant producers—individual or collective—very few of whom had substantial farming skills when they were resettled, has not been encouraging (Bratton 1987: 187–193; Kinsey 1983a, 1983b; S. Moyo 1986; Mumbengegwi 1986: 210–221; Weiner 1988: 79–82). Several political pressures have combined with organizational problems to produce this deemphasis of land reform (Herbst 1990: 37–62).

Although they were the primary white targets of the guerrillas, large-scale commercial farmers have become by far the most politically influential segment of the white population since independence because of their contribution to economic growth and to export earnings and, secondarily, because of the ability of the CFU to work cooperatively with organizations representing small-scale (former APA) commercial farmers and wealthier peasant farmers in the communal areas. Growth in agriculture has been greater than in any other sector, and growth in agricultural exports has been even greater. Commercial farmers have used their influence to obtain high producer prices for most commodities (Bratton 1987: 182–187; Herbst 1988) and to maintain strict adherence to the Lancaster House terms for land reform: resettlement through government purchase of private land on a willing buyer–willing seller basis. The major impact of the former on income distribution has been differentiation within the communal areas as wealthier peasants have been able to increase their production dramatically, especially in the country's staple crop, maize (corn), of which their share of production has increased from 8 percent to almost half. They have been greatly aided in attaining this goal by the immense expansion of extension and marketing services, a policy not opposed by the large-scale commercial farmers, who also receive these services.

Because the peasant National Farmers' Association of Zimbabwe (NFAZ) and, in many cases, local party organization in the communal areas are dominated by the wealthier peasants and because the party itself is weak, landless peasants, including many who are temporarily allowed to be squatters on large-scale commercial farms, are virtually unorganized and remain the least privileged category of Zimbabweans. The group representing producer cooperatives—including those created through resettlement—the Organization of Collective Cooperatives in Zimbabwe (OCCZIM), is weak and has had a history of conflict with the government, but it is a source of potential support for radical change (England 1987; Mumbengegwi 1988; Sylvester 1990: 473; Stoneman and Cliffe 1989: 114–117). Critics of government policy point out that such change will be necessary if rural socialism is to be established and rural class formation is to be impeded. Collective cooperatives need substantially greater funding and technical support to be efficient.

International Effects

The international repercussions of the Zimbabwe revolution have been quite small in the global context but much more extensive in the southern African context, although a fundamental reconstruction of the regional environment has not yet occurred. Because of propaganda produced by the Smith regime, utterances of ZANU and ZIPA leaders, and Soviet aid to ZAPU/ZIPRA combined with a smaller amount of Chinese aid to ZANU/ZANLA, there had been fear in some Western business and government circles that a PF government would take Zimbabwe into the Eastern bloc. In the end, Western governments decided to discount this fear, and it proved to be groundless. As we have seen, economic ties to the capitalist West have been maintained, and Zimbabwe's foreign policy, along with that of most Third World countries, has been nonaligned. In the age of increasing East-West détente, such a foreign policy is not considered a threat to Western interests, and sophisticated Western policymakers consider the outcome of the Rhodesia-Zimbabwe conflict a Western diplomatic success (Davidow 1983), although there have been a few minor, if dramatic, instances of U.S. displeasure at actions of the Zimbabwe government. Relations with the Soviet Union have remained relatively cool because of the latter's support for ZAPU, and the Chinese have been unable to benefit substantially from their support for ZANU because of their own political and economic problems.

Zimbabwean independence strengthened the position of the Frontline States in their confrontation with white-ruled South Africa and its policy of apartheid because it meant that the most developed economy and the largest military force in the region (aside from South Africa itself) were no longer allied with apartheid but were on the side of majority rule. The significance of this change is exemplified by Zimbabwe's dominant position in the Southern African Development Coordinating Conference (SADCC), an international organization dedicated to promoting development and breaking South Africa's economic domination of the region (Thompson 1988); its strong influence in the larger Preferential Trade Area (PTA); and its crucial military assistance to Mozambique in protecting the railway line from Zimbabwe to the port of Beira from antigovernment, South African–supported RENAMO terrorists.

Disengagement from South Africa, participation in international sanctions against it, and support for the overthrow of apartheid are Zimbabwe's official policies, although they have been pursued with great caution because there has been so much to lose from an all-out confrontation. These policies have contributed, at least in a small way, to the recent dramatic developments within South Africa, which will probably lead to the abolition of apartheid there, and have resulted in improved South Africa–Zimbabwe relations. But the internal negotiations among South African political parties over the next few months or, more probably, years will be extremely delicate, and the government of that country may seek to strengthen its negotiating position by destabilizing Zimbabwe (and other Frontline States that support its internal opponents) through various economic pressures and military raids. The Zimbabwe government's commitment to a fundamental reconstruction of the regional environment is genuine, but its power in this arena is even more limited than in domestic socioeconomic reconstruction.

CONCLUSION

Given the ambiguous outcome of the revolution and the many contradictions evident in post-independence developments, it must be concluded that the future of Zimbabwe is uncertain. On the political side, the establishment and organizational form of the one-party system remain the key uncertainties. A number of dedicated activists receiving strong support from Mugabe will be required to make the party more democratic and participatory than the present ZANU-PF structure, and an openness to opposition within the party will be required to accommodate the ambitions of all politicians who have significant numbers of followers, including several prominent ZANU-PF leaders who have come out against the one-party state. It is difficult but by no means impossible to believe that these conditions will materialize, although arrests of some ZUM and ZCTU officials and substantial violence in the period leading up to the March 1990 elections do not bode well in this regard.

On the socioeconomic side, it has been shown that socialism has not been implemented in Zimbabwe, and Marxist-Leninist rhetoric alone, especially if it continues to be accompanied by antisocialist policies, will not be sufficient to implement it. A number of dedicated socialists emerging from within the bourgeoisie and petite bourgeoisie, working within a substantially strengthened party and the state and receiving strong support from Mugabe against technocratic and procapitalist officials, will be required to implement socialism over the opposition of the rapidly consolidating privileged classes (Herbst 1990: 230–242). The substantial improvements that have occurred in race relations, while by no means eliminating white exclusivity, have made it much easier for whites and privileged blacks to work together for common class interests. Again, it is difficult but by no means impossible to believe that the conditions for the implementation of socialism will materialize, although a constitutional amendment has been passed that reduces the protection of private property substantially. A recently announced plan to conscript all males between the ages of eighteen and thirty for a year of political and military training could be addressed to either or both political mobilization or reduction of unemployment.

Finally, on the international side, it has been shown that an increased confrontation with South Africa remains a possibility, and this problem could have profound but difficult-to-predict domestic consequences. Short of radical disruption from this source, it is most likely that future observers will label late twentieth-century Zimbabwe as an unusual case of revolutionary violence resulting in reforms that produced more substantial changes than those occurring in many African countries but that fell well short of producing a genuine socialist revolution.

CHRONOLOGY

1890: Rhodesia occupied and declared a British colony.

1923: Rhodesia granted responsible self-government.

1953: Federation of Rhodesia and Nyasaland formed.

1955: Salisbury City Youth League founded; radicalization of African nationalism.

1957: New African National Congress (ANC) formed, incorporating Youth League.

1959: ANC banned; National Democratic party (NDP) formed.

July 1961: New constitution granted, giving Africans fifteen seats out of sixty-five in legislature.

December 1961: Zimbabwe African Peoples Union (ZAPU) formed after NDP banned.

1962: Rhodesia Front (RF) wins election, replacing United Federal party as governing party.

August 1963: Zimbabwe African National Union (ZANU) formed, splitting ZAPU.

December 1963: Federation dissolved.

April 1964: Smith becomes prime minister.

August 1964: ZAPU and ZANU banned, many leaders detained.

1965: Unilateral Declaration of Independence (UDI); sanctions imposed.

1966: Official beginning of guerrilla warfare.

1969: New constitution enacted, entrenching racial separation.

November 1971: Constitutional settlement negotiated between British and Rhodesian governments.

December 1971: African National Council (ANC) formed to oppose settlement.

May 1972: Pearce Commission report indicates settlement not "acceptable to the people of Rhodesia as a whole."

December 1972: Second phase of guerrilla warfare begins.

1974: ZANU Central Committee elects Mugabe party leader.
March 1975: Chitepo assassination and ZANU factionalism.
June 1975: Mozambique becomes independent, increasing support for ZANU.
January 1976: ZIPA formed but fails to bring unity or radicalization.
September 1976: Smith accepts principle of majority rule.
October 1976: Patriotic Front (PF) alliance between ZANU and ZAPU formed.
October–December 1976: Geneva Conference fails to reach agreement.
1977: Anglo-American proposals formulated, rejected by Smith.
1978: Internal settlement agreement reached.
April 1979: Muzorewa wins election, becomes prime minister.
August 1979: Commonwealth heads of government conference.
September–December 1979: Lancaster House Conference, sanctions lifted.
January 1980: Cease-fire takes place.
February 1980: ZANU-PF wins majority in elections.
March 1980: ZANU-ZAPU coalition formed; Mugabe becomes prime minister.
April 1980: Independence of Zimbabwe.
1982: ZAPU expelled from coalition; dissidents active in Matabeleland.
1985: ZANU-PF increases majority in elections.
1987: ZANU-ZAPU unity agreement signed; Mugabe becomes president; white seats abolished.
1988: Dissidents granted amnesty.
May 1989: Zimbabwe Unity Movement (ZUM) formed.
March 1990: ZANU-PF (now including ZAPU) further increases majority in elections (over 1985).
April 1990: Lancaster House constitutional restrictions fall away, but substantial changes do not occur immediately.

NOTES

1. This event will be referred to as UDI throughout this chapter; *independence* will be used to refer to internationally recognized independence in 1980.

2. In 1961, I asked a UFP official involved in the recruitment of African members what characteristics the party was looking for in potential African recruits. His reply was, "We seek the ones who have come down out of the trees—if only just come down."

3. The exception is Seegers (1984: 97–159), who refers to a "government in crisis" from 1960 to 1962 but does not specify exactly what she means by this term.

12

SOUTH AFRICA: POTENTIAL FOR REVOLUTIONARY CHANGE

C.R.D. HALISI, PATRICK O'MEARA, AND N. BRIAN WINCHESTER

With the electoral victory of the National party (NP) in 1948, South Africa was transformed from a society in which segregation existed more as a matter of custom and practice to one in which the doctrine of apartheid (an Afrikaans word meaning "separateness") became the guiding principle for nearly all social, economic, and political interaction. State intervention became more comprehensive through a system of discriminatory legislation and police enforcement, which coercively restructured society along stricter racial lines. For many years, it has been common wisdom that the gross inequities and injustices between blacks and whites in South Africa would lead to a final confrontation of revolutionary proportions and to the ultimate demise of white minority rule. The prevailing political system has demonstrated remarkable durability despite an ever-increasing spiral of black political violence and white counterviolence, but the question of the continued viability of the system remains, as do the issues of black revolutionary consciousness and the capacity of the majority to end racial oligarchy. The convergence of race and class has shaped South African economic and political history; the response to changing racial and class structures will ultimately determine the outcome of the confrontation.

APARTHEID: THE PRELUDE TO REVOLUTIONARY CONDITIONS

Comprehensiveness of State Intervention

The legal entrenchment of white privilege and racial domination by the National party created a harsh and intrusive security system and extended unequal and

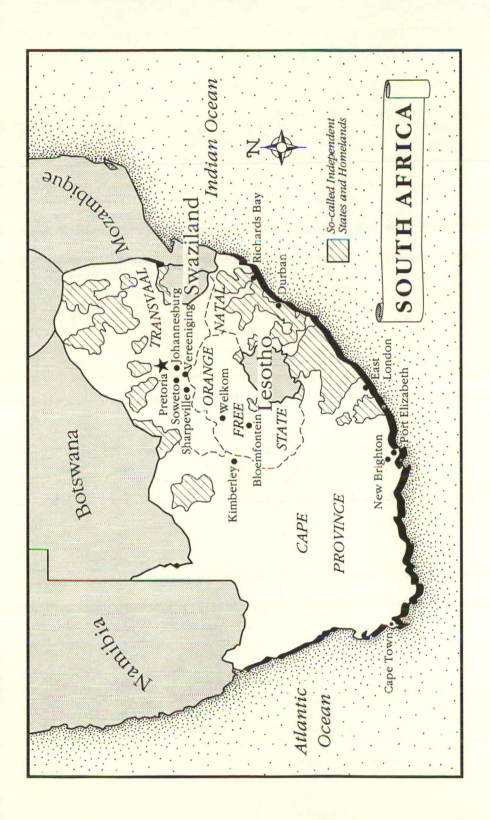

SOUTH AFRICA

So-called Independent
States and Homelands

Indian Ocean

N

Mozambique

TRANSVAAL

Swaziland

Richards Bay

Durban

Pretoria
Soweto
Johannesburg
Sharpeville
Vereeniging

ORANGE

Welkom

FREE

NATAL

Lesotho

STATE

Botswana

Kimberley

Bloemfontein

East
London

Port Elizabeth

New Brighton

CAPE

PROVINCE

Namibia

Cape Town

Atlantic
Ocean

separate education, job reservation, and residential segregation. In the space of a few years, apartheid legislation determined, among other things, whom one could marry, established a racial register of the entire population, prohibited sexual intercourse between races, and restricted ownership of land and property as well as where one could live and conduct business. To preserve white supremacy, such fundamental rights as protection against search without a warrant, detention without trial, and respect for habeas corpus were severely circumscribed, and these were only a few of the laws implemented to structure South Africa along racial lines. In 1954, during a parliamentary debate, H. F. Verwoerd, then minister for native affairs, summed up the National party's basic philosophy when he stated, "There is no place for him [the African] in the European community above the level of certain forms of labor" (Verwoerd in Parliament of South Africa, 1954: June 7).

In a society in which whites represented less than 17 percent of the population, the National party government considered it essential to control the movement of black people for political, economic, and logistical reasons. So-called pass laws, which restricted and controlled black access to white areas, were implemented nationwide in 1952, and two years later, black women as well as black men were required to carry these passes, or identity books, which provided details about their residence and employment status. Blacks who remained in urban areas for more than seventy-two hours without a pass were subject to imprisonment, and millions were arrested for such violations. As was clearly demonstrated by the mass resistance to the pass laws, the black population and a small number of white supporters began to mobilize against racial restrictions by the state. In order to control and intimidate opponents, the government enacted extensive security legislation including the Suppression of Communism Act of 1950 (in which "communism" was so broadly defined as to include the advocacy of any political, social, or economic change brought about by unconventional means), the Riotous Assemblies Act of 1956, the Unlawful Organizations Act of 1960, the so-called sabotage act (General Laws Amendment Act) of 1962, and the Terrorism Act of 1967.

Economic Apartheid

Although the doctrine of political apartheid was predicated on the social and cultural inferiority of blacks, the scope of economic legislation suggests that apartheid was designed to prevent black economic competition with a frightened and vulnerable white working class, as well as to ensure a supply of cheap black labor for farms, mines, and capitalist industry. Africans were barred from skilled mining jobs with the passage of the Mine and Works Act in 1911, and prior to the implementation of apartheid, white workers had already gained economic advantages as a result of the entrenchment of racial privileges, especially in the gold mining industry. This early form of racial proletarianization, according to many historians, shaped future economic discrimination. The slogan of the 1922 Rand rebellion of white mine workers, "workers of the world unite and fight for a white South Africa," was indicative of this "color bar," which divided the working class along racial lines. The Industrial Conciliation Act of 1924 excluded blacks from being designated as employees; they were simply considered "native labor," and therefore white workers could determine their access to training and wages. The so-called civilized labor policy of the 1920s was designed to protect unskilled whites from black competition, and in 1932, the Native Service Contract Act made any breach of contract by African farm and mine workers a criminal offense. In short, whites enacted a battery of legislation to cheapen the cost of black labor while co-opting white workers into its fold by offering them job security and economic protection based on social privilege.

Until 1981, African trade unions could not be officially registered, and African workers could not strike or even hold some skilled occupations, and without legal trade unions and the right of collective bargaining, the wages of Africans have been kept low, and black workers have been excluded from health, training, and unemployment benefits. Nonetheless, if there is one area where blacks have demonstrated growing power, it is in the field of labor. The dependence of the South African economy on both skilled and unskilled black workers has created a potentially powerful political and economic force, and from the 1970s onward, the growing power of the black workers has been demonstrated by a series of legal and illegal boycotts and strikes, orchestrated by a variety of increasingly well-organized black trade unions.

African Homelands: An Illusion of Independence

At the center of apartheid's elaborate system of social, economic, political, and security legislation is the myth of territorial segregation. Laws originally passed in 1913 and 1936 legalized the creation of reserves for Africans and ultimately restricted their ownership of land and property to 13 percent of the country. These laws were updated with the passage of the Bantu Self-Government Act of 1959, and the so-called homelands, or Bantustans, have served a variety of economic and political purposes. By establishing "self-governing" homelands in which Africans could vote and participate in "their own" political process, the government created a legal fiction that it hoped would defuse opposition among black South Africans as well as international criticism. Naively, the crux of government policy was an attempt to make the homelands the central locus for the emerging black middle class by encouraging it to invest its energies in ethnic nationalism rather than in African nationalism. The economic advantage of the policy was that it would absolve white South Africa of welfare obligations to a substantial number of blacks without losing the benefits of an abundant supply of cheap black labor for all sectors of the economy. Thus, ironically, the homeland policy was an important component in South Africa's functioning as an exclusive white welfare state, since Africans were presumed to have an agricultural base in the homelands.

Separate development, as this policy was termed, was vehemently opposed by Africans, who saw the balkanization of the country as a denial of the role they played in its development and as a further erosion of their rights. In conjunction with the battery of apartheid legislation, the enforced "retribalization" of black South Africans has been an attempt to shape the class content and political consciousness of the black community. For example, most homelands enforce labor legislation that is no longer imposed by the South African government.

In the 1970s, South African citizenship was taken away from millions of rural and urban blacks and replaced with the citizenship of a particular "independent" homeland, and four homelands have so far been granted "independence": Transkei in 1976, Bophuthatswana in 1977, Venda in 1979, and Ciskei in 1981. If this policy were to have succeeded, the white South African minority would have become, on paper, the majority in South Africa. A familiar pattern has now emerged: The white South African government provides most of the food requirements of the "independent" homelands and the lion's share of their national budgets, in the form of direct and indirect subsidies, and employs the majority of the migrant workers from the homelands. Clearly, they are neither economically viable nor politically independent, and not surprisingly, none of these so-called independent homelands have received diplomatic recognition from any country other than South Africa itself.

In these regions, a well-subsidized political elite and bureaucracy presides over extremely high levels of poverty and underdevelopment. Homeland governments have become an auxiliary arm of the white state over time, and their bureaucracies, police, and security forces must be seen as a part of the South African government's overall security apparatus. In short, the homeland policy remains crucial to South Africa's counterrevolutionary strategy, so it is therefore not surprising that homeland leaders and officials have become the targets of attacks by the black liberation movement.

Although not forced into homelands, so-called coloreds (people of mixed racial descent who make up about 10 percent of the population) and Asians (predominantly Indians who came to South Africa in the second half of the nineteenth century to work on sugar plantations in Natal Province and now number about 3 percent of the population) have been victimized by the repressive policies of the white regime and have also suffered from forced residential relocation by the government.

Years of Confrontation, Unrest, and Violence

By the start of this century, black opposition in South Africa had begun to take a variety of forms. Dissent increased among religious leaders and among industrial workers whose importance grew because of the decline of whites in the labor force, and economic and political demands increased as black workers were drawn into skilled and supervisory positions. The very system that was created to disperse and control black labor—including workers with urban rights, migrant laborers, commuters, squatters, and those relocated to homelands—also fostered a diversity of popular struggles in urban and rural areas.

The growth of political consciousness has taken place most dramatically among two groups: industrial labor and educated labor. These people have formed a counterelite through organizations such as the African National Congress (ANC), Pan Africanist Congress (PAC), and the Non-European Unity Movement (NEUM), which have mobilized and directed the numerous mass movements against racial domination and have either rejected co-optation or have been alienated from the racially exclusive political system that was, in part, designed to prevent them from joining the ruling elite. Recently, black elites have established good relations with the now-extensive black working class, and this alliance adds a new dimension to the dynamics of revolutionary change. Although it is uncertain how this alliance will affect a postapartheid majority government, even initial reforms have led to increasing demands for further democratization.

In 1912, a black leadership began to galvanize around what was to become the African National Congress. Initially a grouping of traditional and urban elites, the ANC soon had to accept that even more liberal policies, which spawned the small African bourgeoisie, would deliver neither social equality nor full political participation, because the political inclusion of blacks, even on a restricted basis, was vehemently opposed by powerful white farming and mining interests. Black opposition was peaceful for nearly fifty years, consisting of protests and petitions to whites in power, but after decades of white intransigence to black demands for justice and equality, the ANC, under younger and more militant leaders, launched the Defiance Against Unjust Laws Campaign in 1952 in cooperation with the Indian Congress. This campaign was a nonviolent one in which apartheid laws were deliberately broken. After several months of civil disobedience and 8,000 arrests, rioting broke out in a number of cities, which resulted in considerable property damage and forty deaths. Black protests and white repression continued. In 1956, three African women were killed when thousands of women confronted the police because of their inclusion under recently amended pass laws.

In repeatedly foreclosing the possibility of peaceful change, racial repression ensured the inevitability of the eventual resort to ever more radical means by blacks who were in a very real sense offered only two choices: to submit or to resist. Black attitudes toward the tactics of liberation changed dramatically after March 21, 1960, when white police opened fire on a mass demonstration organized by the Pan Africanist Congress. The PAC had broken away from the ANC in 1959 because it wanted to pursue a more exclusively African-based strategy in contrast to the ANC's increasingly multiracial direction. The Sharpeville massacre, in which hundreds of PAC-led protestors were wounded and sixty-seven killed, resulted in demonstrations and thousands of additional arrests all over the country. Given the weight of government repression, civil disobedience and conventional tactics were soon considered ineffective, and in 1961, some members of the ANC and the South African Communist party organized Umkhonto we Sizwe (Spear of the Nation) to conduct an armed struggle against the regime. From its inception, the ANC military wing refused to engage in terrorism and preferred acts of sabotage against symbolic targets, the economic infrastructure, and the police and military, avoiding attacks on white civilians. At the same time, the new PAC formed its military arm, which was more inclined toward direct attacks on whites.

Before police raided the Umkhonto headquarters in the Johannesburg suburb of Rivonia in 1963, the organization was responsible for numerous acts of sabotage. Many of Umkhonto we Sizwe's top leaders were imprisoned, including Nelson Mandela, the single most prominent symbol of resistance among opponents of apartheid. With the government's banning of both the ANC and the PAC in April 1960, South Africa entered more than a decade of enforced calm, but the 1973 wildcat strikes in the coastal city of Durban, involving over 100,000 black workers, brought this period to a decisive end. These strikes marked a new and revitalized phase of black trade unionism. Up until this time, government repression of unions, such as the South African Congress of Trade Unions (SACTU), had contained the political clout of black workers, even though a decade earlier, SACTU had organized over 50,000 black workers and played an important political role in the Congress Alliance, a multiracial grouping of anti-apartheid organizations.

The next major confrontation occurred in the black township of Soweto, near Johannesburg. On June 16, 1976, thousands of African high school students demonstrated against a government ruling requiring that half of all school subjects be taught in Afrikaans, which was seen as the language of oppression and domination. After an undetermined number of school children were killed or wounded during the first several days, rioting and confrontations between youth and police spread throughout the country. Over the next few months, more than 1,000 were killed, and many thousands more were wounded and arrested.

Although the precipitating incident was over instruction in Afrikaans, the intensity and duration of the uprising can be best explained as the result of accumulated grievances over a long period of time. Educational inequities on segregated college campuses had already sparked the growth of the South African Students' Organization (SASO), the harbinger of the black consciousness movement. Influenced by black power and black theology in the United States, writings on African socialism, and Frantz Fanon's perspective on black liberation sociology, black consciousness thought was an attempt by a younger generation of activists to reconstruct the South African black nationalist tradition. Inspired by black consciousness, young blacks from the townships initiated a new period of resistance. This dynamic youth movement found an articulate popularizer in the late Steve Biko, and his death at the hands of security police, while in detention in September 1977, caused yet another round of protests and violence, which was met by further repression and the banning of most black consciousness organizations.

With the Soweto rebellion, black youth had entered the political arena, and they have continued to be a major source of revolutionary fervor. Many black youths left to join liberation movements or were prepared to work underground, and ten years after the June 16 Soweto uprising, the ANC army had grown to over 10,000 combatants stationed at its exile bases, and numerous cells operated inside the country. The exodus of young militants in search of military training under the auspices of either the ANC or the PAC was so great that all could not be accommodated, so the ANC, which recruited the vast majority of these youths, began to establish a more viable underground operation and encouraged many to remain at home to organize mass support.

The growth of militant worker and youth organizations was a clear indication that banning the African nationalist movements had not terminated black resistance. Instead, a younger generation of blacks had been radicalized as a result of government policies. In addition, African, so-called colored, and Indian youths began to reject attempts by whites to divide them through the imposition of separate identities and differential degrees of incorporation into a racially based political economy and a hierarchy of social status. Because of their experiences during the 1970s, many others joined African youths in their move to more militant strategies of protest and confrontation. The developments of the 1970s thus set the stage for the next round of confrontation, which came as a result of government reforms that sought to co-opt more-moderate colored and Indian leaders but left the African majority unrepresented.

Constitutional Change and the Deepening Confrontation of the 1980s

In May 1983, Prime Minister P. W. Botha introduced a constitutional amendment that provided for three racially separate parliamentary chambers for whites, Indians, and coloreds in which each would deal with matters affecting their respective groups. The structure for the new tricameral Parliament gave the appearance of power sharing among these three groups, but white control of the office of the president and the powerful President's Council and the predetermined numerical superiority of the white chamber ensured that real power would remain in white hands. Most important, the tricameral legislature did not include the majority of South Africa's population, those classified as African, who could not stand as candidates or vote.

Prime Minister Botha's office was abolished by the new constitution, and he became South Africa's first executive president on September 14—until then, the presidency had been largely ceremonial. The next day Botha announced a cabinet, which, for the first time in the country's history, included one colored and one Indian member. The Rev. Allan Hendrickse, leader of the Labor party, and Amichand Rajbansi, of the National People's party, were appointed to the cabinet but were given ministries without portfolio. For many observers, their appointments were mere tokens. In a 1986 speech on the occasion of the opening of the third session of Parliament, President Botha saw the new constitution as a new beginning, but for black South Africans, it was nothing more than a cosmetic change: yet another attempt to divide and conquer the black opposition.

In a move to legitimate the proposed constitutional change, the first since the Act of Union had created South Africa in 1910, a referendum for whites, coloreds, and Asians was held in August 1984. Although the new constitution had the general support of the 4.6 million whites, who had voted in favor of the changes in November 1983, it had only minimal support from the 870,000 Indians and 2.1 million coloreds. The United Democratic Front (UDF) led by the prominent black Dutch Reformed church leader, Dr. Allan Boesak, organized a national boycott, which was a clear rejection of the constitution and an indication of the strength of the new UDF coalition of anti-apartheid groups. The legitimacy the government sought was undermined by the 77 percent of the eligible colored voters and 80 percent of eligible Indian voters who boycotted the voting. Africans, who constitute 73 percent of the population, were excluded since no constitutional provision had been made for them.

Reaction to the new constitution was the exact opposite of what the white government had intended: A crisis of unprecedented magnitude and duration was precipitated. Botha had unwisely decided to constitutionally restructure racial domination at a time when the majority of black townships were faced with chronic unemployment, inadequate housing, and staggering rates of crime. At the same time, township administrations were seeking to pass on their growing deficits to residents in the form of higher rents, taxes, and transportation costs. From September

1984 onward, violence erupted in black townships in the Pretoria-Witwatersrand-Vereeniging (PWV) area, the largest metropolitan complex in the country, and hundreds of people were killed or injured. Although angered by the reassertion of white supremacy in the new constitutional order, protestors also expressed a host of local grievances such as rent increases, inferior schools, and the imposition of unpopular, handpicked local authorities in the townships. In October, 7,000 police and defense force (i.e., army) troops conducted house-to-house searches in different townships, and these resulted in the arrest of more than 350 people. The use of the defense force in domestic affairs on an even greater scale than during the Soweto uprising was highly criticized by opposition leaders and even by some progovernment newspapers. As violent confrontations between protestors and security forces spread and as the death toll approached 1,000, the South African government declared a state of emergency in July 1985.

The state of emergency, the first since Sharpeville in 1960, gave the police and army even wider powers of detention without warrant or trial and extensive rights of search and seizure, as well as providing the security forces with full indemnity from all legal claims arising from their actions. The immediate detention of several hundred black political, religious, labor, and educational leaders served only to incite greater violence. Ironically, the declaration of the state of emergency was a clear indication that the police were losing control of the African townships, within which most of the violence was confined. The targets of black rage were frequently those blacks who were believed to collaborate with the apartheid system. Black policemen, by then approximately 40 percent of the force, urban councillors, and suspected informers were often stoned or burned to death, and black police, who once lived peacefully in the townships, had to be placed in barracks. Continued violence, labor unrest, and school boycotts led to the imposition of a second and more draconian state of emergency one year later, which demonstrated the government's determination not to give in to international criticism or to escalating internal dissent. The eventual restoration of law and order through widespread arrests and detention resulted in as many as 24,000 arrested and hundreds killed.

The magnitude of the township rebellions suggests that without a national franchise, the South African government could not easily impose acceptable municipal-level political structures to represent the black urban communities. The resentment of its attempts was reflected in the violent explosions of 1984–1986 within the townships and the attack on black local authorities (BLAs) by radical youth. The government lost all but a modicum of political influence in most black townships; it could intervene in these locations with the help of the police and military but was unable to establish an acceptable institutional framework of local administration. The BLAs, which, like the earlier urban Bantu councils, sought to legitimate segregated black auxiliary structures by promoting a black middle class drawn from conservative elements in black communities such as urban merchants, homeland representatives, and black local-government officials, proved to be a futile political strategy.

Competition for African Leadership

One of the most pernicious of the government's tactics of control has been its covert and overt involvement in the internecine warfare that has erupted in black townships and squatter settlements—the worst examples occurring in Natal and earlier at Crossroads near Cape Town. For decades, the government has sought to thwart the growth of legitimate leaders, favoring only those blacks willing to align themselves with unpopular official policies. This approach unwittingly created a social space for young black radicals, commonly referred to as comrades, to take over political leadership and to extend their control over the political economies of the townships. The government responded by backing black vigilante groups, often organized by progovernment strong men. In South Africa, there are different forms of black opposition. The older generation of African leaders are divided over the proper emphasis that the African nationalists should place on race and class. The African National Congress and the Pan Africanist Congress continue to be divided over such issues, but the younger generation of radicals are divided over a multiracial egalitarian or an African majoritarian solution. In addition, neo-ethnic leaders such as Chief Mangosuthu Gatsha Buthelezi of KwaZulu seek to mobilize ethnic constituencies through such movements as Inkatha in order to consolidate a regional, and in some instances a national, power base. In this sense, Chief Buthelezi transcends being simply a Zulu politician.

After the Soweto uprising and the subsequent death of large numbers of youths at the hands of the police, the turn to armed struggle became more widely viewed as the "highest phase" in the politics of liberation. By the end of the 1970s, the underground was beginning to take on a mass character; the commitment to, and practice of, political violence was widespread among groups of youths and not always controlled from above by the liberation organizations. Many young revolutionaries joined a particular organization because it could provide the training and arms they needed, not because of ideological preference. Furthermore, generational tensions existed within the major black political organizations, causing many people to speculate about the tactics that will be adopted by future leaders.

The ANC continued its multiple strategy for liberation, which included violent confrontation and urban sabotage as well as links with such internal organizations as labor unions and the UDF. The ANC, however, remained estranged from black consciousness groups such as the Azanian People's Organization (AZAPO) and the National Forum Committee (NFC), the black consciousness movement's equivalent of the UDF. At the same time, the Foreign Mission of the ANC pursued diplomatic initiatives and opportunities in the international arena, receiving greater recognition from even conservative administrations in Britain and the United States. The growing popularity of the ANC at home, as well as its acceptability abroad, were directly related to its success in mobilizing international political support.

Limited Political Reforms

The end of the first state of emergency in spring 1986 coincided with modest policy reforms in the midst of repression. A hallmark of the Botha reforms was the attempt to replace overt racial controls with what government planners conceived of as "nonracial," market-oriented control mechanisms. The intent of the government was to repeal a number of apartheid laws, such as restrictions on black freedom of movement, residence, and citizenship, without endangering continued white control. Even before the imposition of the state of emergency in 1985, the prohibitions against racially mixed political parties and interracial marriages had been repealed. Now, restaurants and hotels were permitted, though not required, to serve blacks. The minister of constitutional development and planning was empowered to open central-business districts to businesses of all racial groups, and black South Africans could, for the first time, acquire ownership rights to property in designated black urban areas. This easing of restrictions was accompanied by loans for homeland businesses and by incentives for white businesses to invest in areas bordering the homelands. A limited number of blacks who resided permanently in the townships were granted the right to "reapply" for South African citizenship. Finally, the old system of influx control with its hated pass books was abolished and replaced by a new identity document for both blacks and whites, although, at the same time, the government began to use trespass laws and housing and work permits in order to control the movement of blacks. To this list of reforms must be added the 1981 legalization of black trade unions, strictly as collective bargaining agents with restrictions on participation in "politics." Still, without rights that constrained the security apparatus, the government was the final arbiter of which groups or individuals could operate freely, and few were allowed to exist without constant repression.

These changes were opposed by right-wing whites, who felt that the government was going too far; by white liberals, who felt that the reforms did not go far enough; and by blacks, who did not want apartheid reformed at all but abolished. These mixed signals, and the uncertainty they created, caused increasing numbers of whites to shift their allegiance to right-wing political groups. Although most Afrikaners continued to support the ruling National party, right-wing factions, including the Conservative party (the official opposition in the white Parliament), and the Herstigte Nasionale party (HNP) grew in strength. On the far right, the Afrikaner Resistance Movement (AWB), led by Eugene Terre'Blanche, openly advocated a return to radical white supremacy.

By 1985–1986, it was clear that the government's search for some kind of "corporatist" solution—a reworking of labor legislation, influx control mechanisms, and constitutional arrangements—had failed. Lack of legitimacy forced the government to employ state repression and violence against the indigenous organizations of the black working class, the urban middle classes, and the unemployed in order to impose its version of reform measures.

The state was unable to promote collaboration or to implement institutional arrangements that did not result in widespread protest and a deepening of its crisis of legitimacy. At a time when black South Africans demanded a nonracial social democracy, Botha viewed his administration's reform policy as one component of a counterinsurgency strategy, buttressed by an expanded political role for the military within the State Security Council (SSC). This high-level government body, which gained prominence in the late 1970s, was organized to coordinate the "total strategy," a term used to describe the coordination of all resources of the state against the forces of opposition to white domination. The total strategy was concerned with internal, regional, and international threats. Botha hoped to use the military as an ideological and a political counterweight to the National party in order to place himself in a better position to carry out a limited agenda of nondemocratic reforms from above.

The limitations of the reform program undermined South Africa's diplomatic position with Western nations. In 1986, over the veto of President Ronald Reagan, the U.S. Congress passed the Comprehensive Anti-Apartheid Act, which prohibited new bank loans to South Africa, the sale of nuclear-powered equipment or nuclear technology, the export of computers to government agencies, and the sale of South African Krugerrand gold coins as well as denying landing rights to South African Airways. From 1984 onward, protest and the worsening internal political crisis also adversely affected the continued growth of South African capitalism. South Africa's currency, the rand, fell to its lowest level ever in 1985, and the government reintroduced strict exchange control regulations to avoid a drain on its foreign exchange resources. International bankers refused to lend new money to the government or to renew existing loans, and many international corporations withdrew for either financial or political reasons or both. South Africa's standing as an attractive place for investment by foreigners had been compromised, and the cost of repression at home and of military commitments in the region continued to place considerable fiscal pressure on the economy.

F. W. de Klerk Becomes President and Nelson Mandela Is Released

By 1989, the South African government was able to maintain an uneasy semblance of stability by renewing the existing state of emergency, banning or curtailing a number of black political and labor organizations, and by stifling press freedoms. Despite the stringent controls, there were national strikes, boycotts, protests by church leaders, and acts of sabotage and bombings organized primarily by the ANC. After suffering a mild stroke in January, President P. W. Botha relinquished the leadership of the National party the following month, and he was succeeded by the minister of national education, F. W. de Klerk who had been leader of the National party in the Transvaal Province since 1982. On August 14, Botha resigned as president after ten years in power because of a dispute with his cabinet.

Early in September, the ruling National party won a national election, as it had done in every election since 1948, but it suffered substantial losses to both the right-wing Conservative party and the more liberal Democratic party. De Klerk, citing the combined vote for the National and the Democratic parties, maintained that a majority of the white voters had endorsed a change in direction. On September 14, de Klerk was elected president and sworn in at a church ceremony in Pretoria six days later. Although he was chosen by the electoral college representing all three houses of the tricameral Parliament, in actual fact, the National party, as the majority party of the white Parliament, made the choice. Most white South African politicians saw him as a pragmatist and expected him to expand the limited reforms that had been instituted by Botha.

De Klerk seemed prepared to deal with reforms within a framework of political restructuring whereas Botha had apparently believed that strong law-and-order measures coupled with economic liberalization would be sufficient to deflect black demands for a total reorganization of the state. Soon after taking up office, de Klerk permitted multiracial anti-apartheid demonstrations, and like Botha, he met with important black church leaders, but unlike Botha, these meetings seemed to be preliminary steps toward negotiating fundamental change. He continued to selectively desegregate public facilities and even declared that a limited number of urban neighborhoods could be multiracial. De Klerk also moved to shift control of the national security system away from the security establishment into the hands of politicians. His release of eight of South Africa's most prominent black political prisoners at the end of 1989, including Walter Sisulu, former secretary-general of the ANC, and the subsequent release of Nelson Mandela and the unbanning of the ANC in February 1990 were seen as creating a climate in which "talks about talks" could occur. Although many blacks welcomed these moves, they remained suspicious about de Klerk's commitment to the implementation of an acceptable democratic order. De Klerk's moves were based on a perception that white self-interest coincided with black demands for change and could best be met through negotiation. He had been brought to this point by a number of factors, including South Africa's continuing economic crisis, which was exacerbated by the effects of international sanctions, and the apparent realization that there was no better time to begin talks with legitimate African leaders as a way to stop the violence.

Changes of this magnitude might be assumed to diminish the potential for revolution. However, it should be kept in mind that De Klerk's reforms, like Botha's before him, could be rendered ineffective as they vacillate between more *verligte* (liberal or enlightened) elements, such as the corporate elite, and *verkramptes* (conservative or narrow), who oppose major reform. Initially, significant aspects of the apartheid system remained in place, such as the Group Areas Act and the Population Registration Act, and many members of the military wing of the ANC, Umkhonto we Sizwe, remained in prison while the state of emergency remained in effect. The ANC's bargaining chips included the continuing threat of armed struggle, the power to call for an end to international sanctions, demands for the nationalization of certain industries, and the ability to reinstate South Africa's lost international legitimacy. Mandela's first speeches after his release were a mixture of commitment to the ANC's struggle with a readiness for conciliation. The central tension was between Mandela's call for universal suffrage on a common voters' roll in a united, democratic, and nonracial South Africa and the whites' insistence on entrenched protection for their "group rights" and for some form of continuing control over the police and military.

It is interesting to note that once it became clear, toward the end of 1989, that de Klerk would move to unban the ANC and release Mandela, the ANC's guerrilla campaign of urban sabotage all but came to an end. Some people speculated that this was a calculated move to reassure the white electorate; others saw it as a response to changing international geopolitical conditions since it had by that time become evident to the ANC that Soviet support for a protracted liberation struggle was winding down and that the time had come for it to negotiate for a wedge of political power.

As the ANC began making plans to engage in participatory politics within South Africa, the white right wing was mobilizing a constitutional offensive led by Dr. Andries Treurnicht of the Conservative party who demanded a new election to test the views of the white electorate on the fundamentally changed political environment. The extreme right-wing AWB threatened concrete acts of violence to stem the changes. At the same time, Nelson Mandela made efforts to heal differences between the UDF and the Zulu Inkatha movement and tried to attract to the ANC traditional leaders as well as other groups within the homelands where mass movements and coups d'etat had already begun to challenge those leaders who had gained "independence" from Pretoria.

CONDITIONS FOR REVOLUTION

Demographic and Economic Change

Revolutionary conditions in South Africa are driven by a combination of political, economic, social, and demographic factors. One of the most significant demographic factors is that the white population continues to shrink as a percentage of the total population—from 19 percent to 15 percent between 1960 and 1985 and was expected to be down to 14 percent by 1990 (D. M. Smith 1987: 11). The homelands policy as a partial solution to the white demographic decline has been a failure because the carrying capacity of the land was reached and exceeded in the 1970s and because of domestic and international rejection of the balkanization of South Africa. Efforts to assess demographic trends are complicated by the fact that political boundaries were changed with the establishment of the so-called homelands. Official South African census data excludes homeland statistics (for obvious political reasons), and as a consequence, comparability of census data is skewed. Nonetheless, certain basic trends are apparent.

For the period 1980–1986, for example, excluding the homelands, the annual percentage growth of the white population was 0.95 percent (between 1970 and 1980 it had been 1.8 percent because of increased white immigration at that time). For the African population, the growth rate was 2.39 percent (in the homelands the average growth rate was unusually high, 4.7 percent); for the coloreds, 2.45 percent; and for the Asians, 1.98 percent. It has been projected that by the year 2000 whites will make up only 12.6 percent of the total population and the rest will be composed of Africans, 76.2 percent; coloreds, 8.4 percent; and Asians, 2.8 percent. Moreover, South Africa is predominantly an urban society. In 1985, 89.6 percent of the white population lived in urban areas, and both the coloreds (77.8 percent) and Asians (93.4 percent) were mainly urban dwellers. The percentage of Africans living in cities (approximately 40 percent in 1985) needs to be reassessed. "Soweto, for example, built officially to house 600,000, contained 1.6 million in 1980. There were a staggering 12,500 people per sq. km. compared with only 1,400 in neighboring white Johannesburg" (Brewer 1986: 68, Economic Intelligence Unit 1989: 12). It is projected that between 1985 and 2000, the African urban population will double. Demographic realities have thus forced whites to recognize their diminishing ability to maintain control.

The continuing racial hierarchy within the employment structure also suggests the likely loss of white control in the future. Skilled occupations are filled primarily by white employees despite the fact that they compose less than 20 percent of the total labor force, and conversely, the least skilled occupations are almost exclusively filled by black employees. What job desegregation has occurred in recent years has been largely the result of pressure generated by the shortage of skilled labor. In the late 1970s, it became evident that because of the rapid expansion of the economy, the country was producing less than half the number of skilled workers and technicians needed, and it was estimated in 1980 that even if all the 1.7 million economically active whites had been trained for skilled work, there would still be a shortage of 2 million skilled workers, a direct effect of apartheid labor and education policies (Lipton 1985: 238). Attempts to recruit white skilled immigrants from abroad were unsuccessful, so from an economic point of view, the inequities in the educational system pose a serious threat to future growth.

It has been further estimated that between 1985 and 2000, the whites' share of retail sales will fall from 55 percent to 42 percent while the Africans' share will increase from 31 percent to 40 percent (Bethlehem 1988: 46). Such statistics explain the effectiveness of black boycotts against white businesses. The impact of the demographic and economic changes that have been taking place will be increasingly felt in the 1990s. In particular, as blacks move into more skilled and managerial positions, and as their buying power increases, the pressure for social and political change can be expected to increase dramatically.

Political Structures and Political Power

Although the South African state continues to face a major crisis of political legitimacy, it has attempted to implement a variety of institutional and policy reforms in order to stave off a deepening revolutionary situation. To understand the relationships among revolution, reform, and counterrevolution, it is necessary to consider the basic configuration of political power, which will help to explain why the conditions for revolution persist in South Africa even though most analysts maintain that the black opposition currently lacks the capacity to successfully overthrow the regime.

Elsewhere in this volume, Jack A. Goldstone maintains that revolution is the forcible overthrow of a government followed by reconsolidation of authority by new groups ruling through new political (and sometimes new social) institutions. Moreover, the continuum that includes revolution, reform, and counterrevolution must be seen within the context of the structure of power and is specific to a given society. In South Africa, there are varying degrees of access to political power and privilege structured primarily along racial lines. Whites enjoy laws, legally defined procedures, and social conventions characteristic of Western liberal democracies. Indians and coloreds have been marginally brought into the political system but not on the basis of full equality. Africans continue to be denied access, and political institutional arrangements such as local representative bodies in urban townships and ethnic legislatures in the homelands operate with little popular support and primarily benefit a state-aligned segment of the nascent black bourgeoisie.

Such arrangements reveal a dilemma for the political system with respect to black participation. Although the regime seeks the support of black elites who are prepared to accept white hegemony, it needs black leaders who command support from key segments of the black population. However, antiregime politics is the locus of the revolutionary movement, which is dominated by workers, students, and the most politicized segments of the black middle class. Tom Lodge astutely points out that "if it is a politics without franchise, it is not altogether a politics without power for its constituents live and work their lives in the most strategic positions in the country's economy" (Lodge 1985: 1). To a certain extent, opportunities to engage in extraparliamentary politics are more available to urban blacks, although there was a marked increase of popular unrest in rural areas in the 1980s. Many of the black settlements in the rural areas are on the outermost boundary of the political system, and it is here that South Africa's most powerless, misery-stricken African poor are forced to reside. Either a revolutionary or a genuinely reformist government would have to promulgate social policies to redress the decades of imbalance in these areas.

The pressures on white political parties to realign can best be seen in an evaluation of the 1989 national election, in which none of the country's 28 million blacks were entitled to vote. In the campaign, the National party's "plan of action" proposed bringing blacks into the political system on a limited basis, while the opposition Conservative party called for a strengthening of segregation laws and opposed widening political rights for blacks. Early in April 1989, the newly formed Democratic party said it wished to establish "a true democracy which rejects race as its basis and protects the human dignity and liberty of all of its citizens." The new party brought together the Progressive Federal party, until then under the leadership of Zach J. de Beer; Wynand C. Malan, who had broken away from the National party to form the National Democratic Movement; and Denis J. Worrall, the former South African ambassador to Great Britain who headed the Independent party. There was also moderate black support, including that of Oscar Dhlomo, a high-ranking official in Chief Buthelezi's Inkatha movement. The Democratic party advocated the abolition of all segregation laws and called for universal political rights with entrenched protection for whites and other minority groups. After the election, the National party majority had been reduced from 123 seats to 93 seats, the Conservative party had increased its number from 22 to 39, and the Democratic party seats had increased from 21 to 33. Although the National party won only 47 percent of all the votes cast, the Conservatives 28 percent, and the Democrats 25 percent, de Klerk chose to interpret the election as a white mandate for change.

The racially exclusive control of power placed a major constraint on the ability of the government to negotiate long-term reforms. Large numbers of capitalist elites were disgruntled with many of the government's restrictive policies, but they had failed to decisively influence it to bring about necessary political reforms. In South Africa, the fundamental conflict within the white society—between the interests of capitalism, which seeks to protect accumulation and profit, and the far narrower interests of the white-ruled state, which seeks to protect racial privilege—came to a head in the late 1980s. The white minority regime's search for a way to achieve stability with minimal economic redistribution and with controlled expansion of democratic participation was manifest in de Klerk's release of Nelson Mandela, the unbanning of the ANC, and the beginning of constitutional negotiations.

Revolutionary Consciousness and Mass Mobilization

The important questions regarding the issue of reform versus revolution in the South African context are, Can the link between race and class be abolished? and Can apartheid be dismantled without the total restructuring of the prevailing state and economy? Such questions are at the heart of serious debates within the camps of those people who are committed to reform and to revolution. Blacks trace the source of their personal limitations and frustrations to the structure of political and economic power. Over time, this structure has generated deep-seated discontent and alienation among elites and masses as well as among intellectuals and workers. This discontent, which is the basis of revolutionary consciousness, has led to attempts at mobilization among differing segments of the population.

The Durban strikes of 1973 and the student-led Soweto uprising three years later marked the rapid expansion of black political consciousness after a decade of quiescence. The growth of the black trade union movement and increases in the number of blacks receiving mass public education, albeit inferior education, led to an intensification of the political struggle in factories, townships, and segregated educational institutions. The extension of inferior public education, so-called Bantu education, also turned out to be an important factor in the spread of black political consciousness. Historically, only a small number of Africans were privileged enough to receive an education, often in church-supported schools. However, with mass education, large numbers of students became more acutely aware of their social, economic, and political inferiority. This awareness was further heightened by the unsuccessful attempt by the government to use black public education to foster more politically pliant attitudes among black youths, thereby making them more amenable to the conservative strategies of limited reform.

In South Africa, race and class often fuse to form a distinct liberation consciousness that is most evident among black workers who have experienced a long history of state intervention against their unionization efforts. Black opposition groups have experimented with a range of strategies and tactics, both legal and illegal, violent and nonviolent. The African National Congress, the leading opponent of apartheid rule, established a virtual government in exile. In addition, the military wing of the movement carried on a low-grade guerrilla war against Pretoria, which over time greatly improved in capacity. After the Soweto rebellion of 1976, the ANC underground has become a factor in internal politics, and its popularity and strength have increased, as was dramatized by the number of bombings of economic targets, assassinations of collaborators and informers, and the frequency of political trials involving ANC militants. Still, the perception that capitalism is organically related to apartheid ignites popular resentment and expands political consciousness.

After 1973, there was an expansion of popular resistance to segregation in the areas of labor, housing, education, and urbanization policy. The spread of protest to rural communities and to migrant workers and farm laborers, usually isolated from the urban currents of popular struggle, suggests at least one way in which the migrant labor system may prove to be a Trojan horse. Indeed, the apartheid government's maintenance of the migrant labor system has as much to do with the politics of control as with the economics of exploitation. Black political organizations now face the task of bridging the gap between urban and rural differences.

ANC: From Black Middle-Class Origins to Mass Mobilization

In its early years, the black opposition movement was led exclusively by middle-class, educated urban elites, and one of the perennial challenges to the effectiveness and capacity of the nationalist movement was to mobilize and sustain organization at the grass-roots level. For example, in the 1920s the Industrial and Commercial Worker's Union (ICU), the first important organization of black workers, emerged as a force independent of the middle-class dominated ANC and was drawn into political involvement with Africans who were being displaced from rural areas. The Congress Youth League (CYL) of the 1940s, from which much of the present leadership of both the ANC and the PAC emerged, reflected a generational schism and a usurpation of power by younger members of the ANC against the older and more moderate leadership but was no less plagued by the magnitude of the movement's organizational tasks. In response, Nelson Mandela designed a plan to coordinate black resistance by forming ANC cells in each black neighborhood. The implementation of the so-called M Plan was halted by the suppression of the nationalist movements in 1960, but it regained popularity among some black organizations.

Even more crucial to the effectiveness of black revolutionary action is the participation of workers. In the late 1950s, the African National Congress, through its alliance with the South African Congress of Trade Unions (SACTU), and to a lesser extent the PAC, through its loose alliance with the Free African Trade Unions of South Africa (FOFATUSA), sought to build black political coalitions across class lines. Although the underground relationships between the liberation movements and the student and worker organizations after the 1960s has not been fully defined, it is clear that significant social forces emerged outside of their organizational frameworks. It is likely that if the African nationalists had not been forced into exile, the leadership would have, at a much earlier point, come to grips with the diversity of social forces that were at play and would have taken a path of autonomous development from the 1970s onward. These social forces include not only labor and youth but also women, civic organizations and, more controversially, groups fostering neo-ethnicity such as the Zulu organization, Inkatha. The movements, as a consequence, were obliged to focus on the recruitment of radical youth and to vie for influence among workers and politicized urban dwellers. These groups now provide the primary sources of internal resistance.

After the Soweto uprising, government repression greatly facilitated the recruitment by liberation movements of youths committed to armed struggle, and the banning of all black consciousness movements in 1978 helped to convince some black youth of the futility of open protest and of the necessity to expand underground activity inside the country. Radicalized members of the middle class who did not leave the country worked to organize trade unions and black community organizations. The greater degree of black middle-class radicalization must be seen as a response to the government's attempt to tie black advancement and political rights to its homeland policy. For example, according to government design, the black intelligentsia, which was being educated in segregated universities, was intended to provide the personnel of the homeland bureaucracies, and in urban areas, the government sought to organize the black political leadership into urban Bantu councils as a counterpart to the homeland institutions. Black consciousness activists began to view this strategy as an attempt to form a "Bantustan bourgeoisie." Of course, all members of the middle class were not directly involved in homeland schemes—most of its members were being incorporated in different ways into the expanding economy. Ironically, the *very opening up of political opportunities* for blacks made sections of the black middle class more receptive to radical political alternatives, and government policies, which attempted to control the urban industrial classes by imposing anachronistic ethnic institutions and identities, unwittingly expanded revolutionary consciousness. As a response, a host of new civic organizations, such as the Port Elizabeth Civic Organization (PEBCO), began to coordinate grass-roots or popular struggles, especially those of youth, women, rent payers, squatters, church members, etc. To a certain extent, the constitutional reforms of the 1980s can be seen as a government attempt to stem the tide of middle-class radicalization. In response, new national federations such as the UDF and NFC made successful efforts to coordinate this diversity of local organizations and to begin to narrow differences between Africans, coloreds, and Indians. In most civic associations, student groups were numerically the largest constituency, such as the Congress of South African Students (COSAS) within the UDF.

Black Trade Unions and Political Mobilization

Initially, the trade union leadership was divided over the question of affiliation with the UDF, even though it supported the general thrust of the UDF's anti-apartheid activities and was crucial to its success, and this disagreement was complicated by the two competing organizational strategies that characterized the trade union movement as a whole. So-called community unions, such as the South African Allied Workers Union and the General and Allied Workers Union, advocated affiliation with civic associations while the larger and better organized industrial unions, under the general rubric of the Federation of South African Trade Unions (FOSATU), believed that civic associations were dominated by middle-class elements and that worker control would be compromised by affiliation. Some trade unionists went so far as to accuse the liberation movements of being middle-class organizations and of pursuing a populist strategy designed to subvert worker interests.

Nonetheless, with the establishment of a superfederation, the Congress of South African Trade Unions (COSATU) in 1985, the political divisions among the ideological mainstream of the trade union movement were overcome. However, the National Council of Trade Unions (NACTU), a smaller group of trade unions committed to a black consciousness approach, was not incorporated into COSATU. Altogether a vigilant advocate of the distinct interest of workers, COSATU made it clear that it would not stand aloof from township struggles, since these usually affected the general political conditions under which workers were forced to live.

The federation adopted the ANC's 1955 Freedom Charter, a manifesto for a post-apartheid South Africa, as the basis of its political stance, and in 1986 the leaderships of COSATU and the ANC/SACTU met in Zambia. From Lusaka, COSATU, SACTU, and the ANC issued a joint statement that recognized the autonomy of trade unions but also affirmed the centrality of the working class in the national liberation struggle. Current efforts to define the relationship of the working-class struggle to that of national liberation pervade the ideological debate among black leaders, activists, and intellectuals and are reminiscent of disputes that have embroiled trade unionists and revolutionaries in other parts of the world.

Black Consciousness:
Exclusivity and Political Mobilization

An emphasis on race and class can create competing approaches to mobilization, and the black opposition in South Africa has had to define the complex issues that surround the relationship between reform and revolution as well as the connections among racial domination, capitalism, and socialism. The nonracialism of the ANC, UDF, and COSATU represents the majority tradition, but the black exclusivist tradition, which includes the PAC, AZAPO, the NFC, and the NACTU unions, remains a popular alternative for a smaller number of black South Africans. Advocates of both traditions define their strategies as nonracial, but they differ over interpretation.

Thus, there are two strands of black nationalism, the nonracial or multiracial tradition and the black exclusivist tradition. The latter argues that a liberated South Africa (Azania) has to be uncompromisingly under black rule since the land was forcibly taken from black people; the former calls for the inclusion of all races. The multi-racial ANC and the Communist party of South Africa (CPSA), which developed a close relationship from the 1940s onward, have always been opposed by exclusivist groups such as the Africanists of the PAC and Marxists of the Non-European Unity Movement (NEUM). In contemporary black politics, the NFC has come to host a loose alliance of black exclusivists and black Marxists, and AZAPO, with its origins in black consciousness, and the Cape Action League, with its origins in NEUM Marxism, both function within the NFC framework. The ideological tenets that unite the otherwise eclectic NFC are a rejection of whites in black liberation politics and a rejection of the Freedom Charter.

Inkatha: Moderate Multiracialism

There are also competing multiracial strategies: the social democratic approach of the ANC and the UDF and the more conservative orientation of Chief Mangosuthu Gatsha Buthelezi, whose strategy claims to be nonviolent, moderate, and committed to free enterprise. Buthelezi promises explicitly that his policy will not in any way restructure capitalist production, and hence, it is designed to appeal to the white business community in South Africa. In some fundamental respects, Buthelezi has to be differentiated from other homeland leaders in that he has clearly attempted a unique strategy of multiracial coalition building. Using Inkatha as a source of power, he has pursued an ethnic-based strategy of mobilization within the black community while seeking to bolster his own position in Natal

Province by joining in a multiracial coalition with the more moderate segments of the white community. His main problem is that his political power stems from the narrow ethnic support of Zulus and, further, that he is directly connected to the state as a homeland leader. He has also been severely criticized for his nondemocratic and often violent internal rule of the KwaZulu homeland and for his equally violent confrontations with opposing movements such as the UDF. As a result, he faces tremendous resistance from radical blacks and has limited national support.

Economics and Ideology

The UDF, along with the CPSA and the ANC, perceives of a two-stage theory of revolution in which there will first be a struggle for nonracial democracy and then a struggle for socialism at a future date. The NFC's views on nonracialism sharply contrast with those of the ANC, which are based on the Freedom Charter, which contends that "South Africa belongs to all who live in it, black or white." The ANC's two-stage theory approach to revolution has been challenged by the Azanian Manifesto, which was adopted by the NFC at its 1983 Hammerskraal convention. The manifesto espouses a more radical interpretation of the struggle and directly links racism to capitalism. From this perspective, there cannot be a democratic South Africa without the overthrow of the capitalist economy. Advocates argue that in the South African context, race *is* class and therefore nonracial democracy is socialism; capitalism, by definition, must be eliminated because racism is predicated on capitalist exploitation. AZAPO now argues the radical socialist position, which points out that merely abolishing apartheid will not be a solution since racism is inextricably linked to capitalism, and many black radicals who are not a part of the black consciousness camp also gravitate toward this racial-capitalism argument. These disputes over nonracialism are complicated by different views of capitalism.

The ANC has sought to moderate its socialist position and, in so doing, defines its revolutionary strategy in both multiclass and multiracial terms. With respect to the economic system, there has been a considerable amount of discussion over how the Freedom Charter would be applied in a post-apartheid South Africa. Although the charter calls for the nationalization of some industries, the ANC is prepared to accept certain basic free-enterprise features. This stand is ironic because one interesting fact about South Africa is the degree to which "nationalization" already exists. Even though there is increasing privatization, the government still controls, through parastatals (state-controlled enterprises that would normally be part of the private sector) large sectors of the economy. Since business leaders contemplate the ANC as a possible future government, those leaders who have met with that group in Lusaka and elsewhere have attempted to convince its leadership of the necessity of maintaining the prevailing economic system while dismantling apartheid. More recently, progressive business leaders have begun to meet with the UDF and COSATU inside South Africa. The ANC has never claimed that it would socialize all wealth; what it does claim is that it would fully democratize the political system, more equitably distribute wealth, and ensure protection for minority rights. Thus, the issues of race and class greatly complicate the ideological dimensions of the struggle against white minority rule.

CONCLUSION: SOUTH AFRICA AND THE REVOLUTIONARY PROCESS

Fiscal Pressure

The fiscal crisis in South Africa has been shaped by the requirements of industrial development and the costs of maintaining apartheid. A major source of pressure on the government is overlooked in an assessment of fiscal distress as a political factor in revolutionary change if a distinction is not drawn between the requisites of the capitalist economy and those of the apartheid state, as this difference has placed a severe strain on government-business relations. The benefits that capitalism has derived from cheap black labor should not be underestimated, but South Africa faces increasing black unemployment and is hard pressed to provide the necessary fiscal resources for the demands of black education and housing. It has also had to cope with the influx of more blacks into urban areas—a problem that has grown in intensity since the pass laws were removed in 1986. In addition, there are the high costs of maintaining dual bureaucratic structures, government coercion in what have been described as "ungovernable townships," and military intervention in the region, all of which affect the fiscal stability of South Africa. Government attempts to pass on these costs through increased rents, taxes, and transportation rates have led to the growth of a variety of popular black protests, which indicates that a fiscal problem is not only a cause but often an outcome of revolutionary mobilization. Sanctions, boycotts, strikes, and political violence all directly affect business, which often bears the brunt of the reaction to the government's repressive policies.

The first sign of fiscal distress, according to Goldstone, is the decline of a state's resources in relation to its commitments and expenses, as well as how the state's resources match the resources of potential domestic and international adversaries. Such distress is clearly beginning, if not yet overwhelming, and is a factor pushing the white government toward reform. Like perestroika in the Soviet Union, South Africa's willingness to negotiate settlements in Angola and Namibia has been, in part, prompted by the high cost of maintaining military hegemony in the southern African region. Economic factors also precipitated the fundamental reforms initiated by de Klerk within South Africa.

Elite Cleavages

English-speaking elites have traditionally dominated the South African economy; for example, the mining revolution was heavily funded by British imperial capital. However, after World War II, a significant Afrikaner capitalist class began to emerge and it has been vocal in encouraging reforms (on the whole, the Afrikaner elites are more state-based than their English counterparts). Nonetheless, all business interests were concerned about the flight of capital after Sharpeville in the 1960s and are now deeply concerned about the effects of international sanctions. The vulnerability of South Africa to external pressure, emphasized by advocates of sanctions and disinvestment, affects the ways in which the economy develops and places an additional degree of stress on it. Capitalist elites and government officials, in contrast, remain divided over ways to deal with external pressure.

White elites hold either to a status quo ideology of white supremacy or to a liberal reformist ideology that is often torn between a concern for individual rights and the protection of established property relations that favor white privilege. Significantly, capitalist elites have become increasingly aware that the political system is unable to promote their best interests, in part because large numbers of blacks have targeted the economic sector as an adjunct of racial domination, and these elites are concerned that repressive state policies will compromise the liberalization measures taken within the economic sector. Consequently, some business elites recognize that apartheid jeopardizes the long-term interests of capitalism and support the government's recent reforms as necessary to ameliorate grievances.

In South Africa, the acute tension between white nationalism and capitalism threatens white elite consensus over the "rules of the game" that regulate the system. The problem faced by advocates of reform is that constitutional government, an important arena for change in liberal capitalist regimes, has not been extended to the majority of the population on a nonracial basis. Despite the fact that there has been sufficient consensus among white elites to maintain the white-dominated political system, these same elites have nevertheless been divided by ethnic, cultural, political, and ideological differences. The historic distinctions between English and Afrikaner elites are quite explicit. In the past, Afrikaner elites, as a result of their alienation from an English-dominated political system, sought to unify the Afrikaner people into a tightly knit nationalist movement that mobilized all aspects of Afrikaner society and that tended to mitigate class conflicts that were ever-present beneath the surface. The Afrikaner working class could have become part of a multiracial working-class movement if it had not been for the effectiveness of the Afrikaner elites in mobilizing these workers around nationalist priorities. Implicit in the relationship between the Afrikaner elites and the Afrikaner lower classes has been this ability to organize the *volk* ("people") around an ideology of Afrikaner solidarity rather than class solidarity, which would have necessitated an alliance with English-speaking workers and possibly multiracial cooperation. White workers who clashed with the state in the 1920s had by 1948 been incorporated into what may be referred to as a white welfare state.

To the degree that there has been a liberal movement in South Africa, the English elites have not been successful in mobilizing the more culturally diverse English-speaking lower classes in support of their objectives. Historically, liberal and conservative white elites have been divided over the formation of coalitions with black elites, and indeed, a significant political problem for the state has been its inability to co-opt credible blacks, which would allow it to transcend racially based elite competition in favor of multiracial class formation. This problem was one of the reasons why Nelson Mandela and other ANC leaders were finally released. In the face of the escalation of political confrontation, white elites, especially Afrikaners, have become more divided along class and ethnic lines, and the interests of the capitalists in the business and industrial sectors have often come into conflict with those of the bureaucratic or political elites.

Rising Mobilization Potential

Mobilization against prevailing conditions is propelled by the expansion of mass consciousness, i.e., the increased awareness on the part of an oppressed group that an illegitimate structure of power is the cause of its oppression and that it has the right to contest the illegitimacy through collective action. Although the interplay between spontaneous popular struggles and preestablished objectives is a complex consideration, the success of revolutionary organization is largely measured by the ability to channel mass discontent into effective opposition to a regime. There has been an exponential growth of black revolutionary consciousness in South Africa since the early 1970s as well as an increasing prominence of a seasoned black leadership both inside and outside the country. This black leadership has been animated by a rising class in a racial group whose political aspirations have been blocked by a political system that was unwilling or unable to accommodate their demands. The South African state has been more successful in incorporating some of the workplace demands of black labor, but it has failed to meet the demands of black political elites. Because the prevailing system refused to meet the political demands of most black groups, they were forced to engage in strikes, boycotts, mass movements, and protests. Black mobilization has become pervasive because of participation by youths, disaffected intellectuals, and large numbers of coloreds and Indians, despite their more privileged position within the apartheid system.

Pivotal to this process of black mobilization has been the expansion and diversification of the black working class and the creation of a black leadership based in the trade union movement. The very growth of the South African economy since World War II has necessitated a greater dependency on black industrial workers because of the decline of whites in the labor force, and economic and political demands have increased with the number of black workers drawn into skilled and supervisory positions. The coordination of the popular protest of workers, youth, and other segments of the black population may represent as significant a challenge to black leaders as the confrontation with white power. An emerging black bourgeoisie is divided between those based within the protest structures and those with ties to the state or traditional structures who, the government hopes, might provide the basis for a countermobilization against the more radical black demands. The leadership of the established black opposition, which for years has been largely drawn from the educated and middle classes, has since the 1970s had to respond to mass democratic forces, particularly from black workers and youths. Recently, black elites have established successful relations with the now-extensive black working class, and this alliance adds a new dimension to the dynamics of revolutionary change. Although it is uncertain how this unity will affect a post-apartheid majority government, even minimal reforms have led to popular demands for further democratization.

Can Revolution Be Avoided?

Jack Goldstone maintains that revolution is the product of a combination of state fiscal distress, elite division and alienation, and a heightened potential for mass mobilization. Although we accept this broad view, our concern has been with conditions and consciousness as dimensions of the revolutionary process, and we emphasize the revolutionary process, rather than revolution itself, because of the unfinished nature of the struggle in South Africa. All three of Goldstone's conditions have increased in South Africa in recent years. The black majority considers the government illegitimate because of exclusion from political power on the basis of race. The class structure has been shaped by racial domination and reinforced by the economic deprivation of the black population. Without a redistribution of power, the conditions for revolutionary change will persist, revolutionary consciousness will expand, and the black opposition will seek to improve its capacity to overthrow the regime.

The question remains whether fundamental reforms within the present structure of power will be sufficient to mitigate revolutionary conditions. Despite the facts that a number of whites may now be convinced that some reforms are necessary and that President de Klerk believes that he has a mandate for change, many whites remain fearful and constrained by a political culture based on white supremacy. On the other hand, for most blacks, mere reform within the existing framework is unacceptable. Black demands and political aspirations will not be satisfied by anything less than a fundamental redistribution of political power, which is the basis around which constitutional changes must revolve. The ANC, well aware of the sentiments of its black constituency, has therefore insisted that the remaining pillars of apartheid be removed even before talks begin.

In a volatile political situation, it is difficult to predict any future outcomes. In the Zimbabwean case, political power sharing left whites with substantial economic power, an outcome unforeseen by whites during the independence struggle. South African whites will now carefully watch the outcome of independence in Namibia. In South Africa, a factor complicating change is that racial domination cuts across class conflicts and links the political and economic arenas. Only major reforms will undercut revolutionary conditions, and any government will have to embark on an aggressive policy of social programs and economic reform. Pretoria, the Soviets, Western governments, and the ANC itself all recognize that without such changes revolutionary consciousness and political violence will persist. A particular concern of black leadership is that much of this violence will be internecine, because the present climate of reform has greatly aroused black political and economic expectations and if negotiations fail, there will be even greater cynicism. A realistic assessment of the limitations currently faced by the now-suspended armed struggle against the powerful South African police and military should not diminish our awareness of the determination of black South Africans, and particularly of black youths, to confront the apartheid regime by all means at their disposal and of the continued evolution of innovative modes of black resistance. Although it is rarely stated, generational differences and considerations within the ANC may have been a major incentive for the National party, as well as for many within the ANC itself, to make efforts to transform the system at this point in time. A more radical generation, whose consciousness has been shaped by the events of the 1970s and 1980s, will not simply wait in the wings but will assume leadership if satisfactory progress is not made.

CHRONOLOGY

1910: Establishment of the Union of South Africa.

1911: Mine and Works Act bars Africans from skilled mining jobs.

1912: African National Congress founded.

1913: Native Land Act prohibits Africans from buying land outside of reserves.

1924: Industrial Conciliation Act excludes Africans from being designated as employees.

1932: Native Service Contract Act makes breach of contract by African farm and mine workers a criminal offense.

1948: National party victory over the United party in parliamentary elections.

1949: Prohibition of Mixed Marriages Act and Population Registration Act. ANC Youth League calls for civil disobedience and noncooperation against pass law and apartheid.

1950: Group Areas Act. Police fire on mass labor strike in Transvaal, 18 blacks killed. Communist party declared unlawful.

1952: ANC and Indian Congress deliberately break segregation laws in the Defiance Against Unjust Campaign; 8,000 arrested nationwide, 40 killed.

1955: Freedom Charter adopted.

1956: Thousands of African women protest pass laws, 3 killed by police. Coloreds removed from common voters' roll in Cape Province treason trial of 156 people.

1959: Bantu Self-Government Act prepares the way for homelands (Bantustans).

1960: Sharpeville massacre. PAC and ANC banned.

1961: ANC and South African Communist party organize Umkonto we Sizwe (Spear of the Nation).

1963: Nelson Mandela and Walter Sisulu sentenced to life in prison under the Suppression of Communism Act.

1969: Steve Biko elected first president of South African Students' Organization (SASO).

1973: Black dockworkers strike in Durban and win pay increase.

1976: Soweto uprising, protests spread across country, over 1,000 killed.

1977: Biko killed while in police custody.

1978: Azanian People's Organization (AZAPO) formed.

1981: By this date, "independence" has been granted to the Transkei (1976), Bophuthatswana (1977), Venda (1979), and Ciskei (1981) homelands, but they are not recognized abroad.

1983: Constitutional changes introduced by P. W. Botha.

1984–1986: Violence erupts in different parts of South Africa.

1984: Referendum for constitutional changes.

1985: South African government declares a state of emergency.

1986: End of first state of emergency. Modest reforms, for example, repeal of some apartheid laws. Second state of emergency imposed. U.S. Comprehensive Anti-Apartheid Act.

1989: Botha relinquishes leadership of National party. F. W. de Klerk becomes president of South Africa. Imprisoned ANC leaders released.

1990: Nelson Mandela released. ANC unbanned. Talks about constitutional change begin.

13

THE WEST BANK AND GAZA: THE PLO AND THE *INTIFADA*

JOSHUA TEITELBAUM AND
JOSEPH KOSTINER

The Palestinian uprising that broke out on December 9, 1987, constitutes a new, revolutionary phase in the Palestinian struggle against Israel. The first phase, in the early and mid-1960s, marked the rise of the Palestinian guerrilla movements, led by the al-Fatah guerrilla group and based outside of historical Palestine. In 1968–1969, these organizations took over the PLO, which had hitherto been essentially an Egyptian puppet organization. In the second phase—the *intifada* ("uprising")—the focus of the movement has moved to the Palestinian heartland, the Israeli-occupied West Bank and Gaza Strip. In this phase, the Palestinian masses have been mobilized on a scale unparalleled in the history of the movement and for a longer period of time than ever before. Palestinians have been mobilized for mass acts of collective violence—strikes, stone throwing, firebombing, attacks with axes, and occasional use of firearms—and those who are deemed to be collaborators with Israel have often met their death. Although the PLO was not responsible for the outbreak of the uprising, both the PLO and the Palestinian cause have benefited tremendously, as it has brought them more world sympathy and support than ever before. The uprising is now regarded by both the Palestinians inside Palestine and the outside leadership as the most important aspect of the Palestinian struggle. For the Palestinians, it has to be nurtured, protected, and turned into diplomatic gains that will effect an Israeli withdrawal from the territories.

Our aim in this chapter is to examine the reasons for the emergence of this new phase, namely, the nature of the shift from one pattern of the Palestinian revolution to another, and the interrelation between the two phases. In so doing, we will explain the background to the *intifada*, its structure and its effectiveness, its influence on the PLO, and the extent to which it constitutes a change in Palestinian revolutionary behavior.

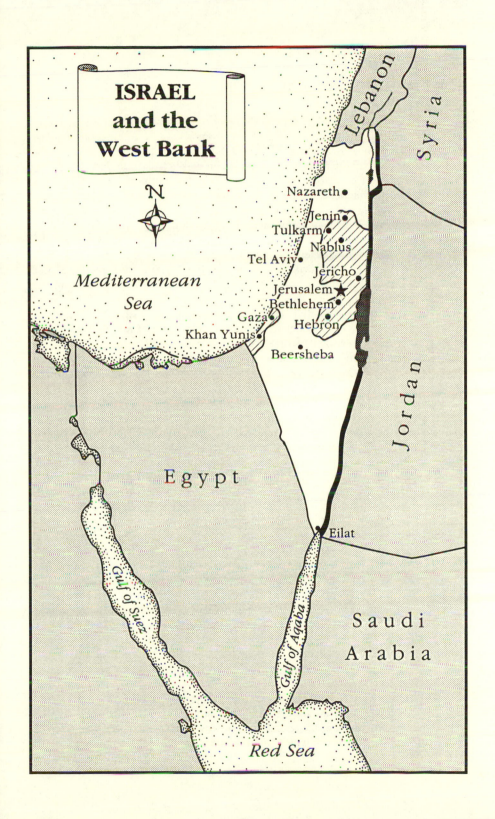

ISRAEL
and the
West Bank

N

Mediterranean
Sea

Lebanon

Syria

Nazareth •

Jenin •

Tulkarm •

Nablus •

Tel Aviv •

Jericho •

Jerusalem ★

Bethlehem •

Gaza •

Hebron •

Khan Yunis •

Beersheba •

Egypt

Jordan

Eilat •

Saudi
Arabia

Gulf of Suez

Gulf of Aqaba

Red Sea

THE REVOLUTIONARY NATURE OF
THE *INTIFADA*

Some underlying theoretical concepts of revolution should be elucidated before we further develop our discussion. Revolution comprises a transformation of social institutions and modes of behavior (Eisenstadt 1978), and therefore it is a process that stretches over long periods and cannot be limited to a short period of political change. During such periods, revolutions develop in fairly recognizable stages (Brinton 1965). Revolutionary guerrilla movements develop in structural and tactical phases, from loosely organized cells using hit-and-run tactics to structures more closely resembling a regular army, and using tactics that are more typical of conventional warfare. This development occurred in China, Vietnam, and the PLO in the early 1980s, when the organization developed the beginnings of a significant conventional infrastructure, such as artillery and a small air force. But these advances were destroyed by Israel when it invaded Lebanon in the summer of 1982, and guerrilla tactics then continued.

But the Palestinian revolution is also a nationalist movement, with much of its constituency under occupation. In a nationalist struggle, a revolution tends to develop over a longer period of time, because the population under occupation undergoes various demographic and social processes that are, by their nature, the products of time. The emergence of the new phase in the Palestinian revolution, as evidenced by the mass uprising, is rooted in changes that evolved in the territories over decades but matured only recently.

Since revolutionary movements evolve over an extended period, each phase is characterized by specific revolutionary tactics and social activity. In various revolutions, there have been periods of mass uprising—witness France in 1789 and Russia in 1917—and in the case of the Palestinian revolution, the present mass uprising constitutes a phase that followed on the heels of an earlier phase, which stressed guerrilla operations. From the mid-1960s to the Israeli invasion of Lebanon in the summer of 1982, Palestinian activity centered on guerrilla actions, accompanied by a degree of international diplomatic activity, and only occasionally included mass involvement in street rioting in the Israeli-administered territories. Following the war in Lebanon in 1982–1983, the activities of the Palestinian revolution shifted focus. Guerrilla activity continued then—as it does today—but it was far less frequent and significant. Diplomacy, particularly attempts at working through Jordan, formed the bulk of Palestinian activity until 1987. With the outbreak of the *intifada* in late 1987, the focus of Palestinian activity shifted significantly to the masses under occupation who engaged in a prolonged uprising; this shift was accompanied by intense diplomatic activity aimed at achieving a dialogue with the United States. Although guerrilla activity has also continued, Yasir Arafat's mainstream al-Fatah has not claimed credit for such activities since November 1988.

The phase represented by the present mass uprising is characterized by the mobilization of practically all sectors of the Palestinian population, rather than of individuals trained in guerrilla operations. Instead of combat skills, the activists of the *intifada* have to know how to regulate the uprising by getting people into the streets, enforcing strikes, and doing away with those people who are considered to be collaborators. Although the phase that concentrated on guerrilla activity involved a small sector of the population operating in a manner that did not necessarily hinge on the cooperation of the masses, the *intifada* phase hinges on the sheer force of numbers, is socially diffuse, and is predicated on demographic, economic, and social changes. These factors are, therefore, of much greater importance in understanding the nature of the *intifada* than of the guerrilla phase. Moreover, a mass uprising constitutes a coalition of different societal groups and also triggers the response of the ruling power. In a mass uprising, the internal hierarchy and structure are less clear than in guerrilla war, and the focus is on the interplay of various groups acting in a fluid situation rather than on organizational factors.

Another point to recall is that the population living in an occupied territory differs from a political-military leadership established outside the homeland. Over the course of a national revolution, opposition leaders are often forced to flee the homeland and establish nationalist organizations in a country of refuge. Those who remain inside are exposed to the occupation, and their concerns emerge primarily from the constant friction with the occupying power. Their perception of how to further the nationalist cause is often different from that of the outside leaders, who most often enjoy freedom of movement and the hospitality of friendly states. The outside leaders are therefore less directly influenced by the trials and tribulations of the occupation, and the relations between those in the interior and those outside are often dialectical. They often cooperate with respect to strategic goals, but, all the same, they frequently differ on tactics. They respect each other but often harbor suspicions of the other. In the cases of the Algerian national movement and that of South Yemen, there were even armed clashes between those inside and outside the occupied areas. Houari Boumedienne used National Liberation Front military units under his command in Tunisia and succeeded in defeating the forces of Ahmed Ben Bella inside Algeria. In South Yemen, the "secondary leadership" inside, with a newly adopted Marxist outlook, succeeded in weakening the power of the old nationalist forces of that country's National Liberation Front. Similarly, the *intifada* represents a dialectical relationship between those inside the territories (in Arabic, *Filastiniyyun al-dakhil*) and those outside (*Filastiniyyun al-kharij*).

The *intifada* thus represents a new phase in the Palestinian revolutionary movement. The interior takes charge, and collective violence predominates over guerrilla activity. Israel, as the occupying power in the territories, has had difficulty in adapting to this new phase of the Palestinian struggle after years of practice in counterinsurgency. Israel's search for a policy to confront the uprising reflects the difficulty of finding a strategy suitable to tackle rioting masses who engage in civil disobedience. This new form of Palestinian struggle, coming as it did on the heels of a stage in which the Palestinians were terrorists and deadly enemies, led to an inchoate Israeli response and added to the complexity of the entire situation.

TWENTY YEARS OF OCCUPATION: SOCIAL AND POLITICAL BACKGROUND OF THE *INTIFADA*

The Social and Economic Dimensions

It is a truism that economic, demographic, and social factors play a significant part in creating the conditions for rebellion, as these factors often contribute to rising expectations and frustration when those expectations are not met (Gurr 1970). Combined with the pressures of military occupation over time, as in the case under discussion, their influence becomes crucial. A brief survey of such developments until the eve of the Palestinian *intifada* in December 1987 is therefore in order.

When Israel captured the West Bank and the Gaza Strip in 1967, it found a population that had been subject to eighteen years of studied inattention to development. Egypt had not physically incorporated the Gaza Strip, with its majority refugee population, and the people had remained under military administration and were supported mainly by the United Nations Relief and Works Agency (UNRWA). Jordan, as part of its policy of trying to undermine a separate Palestinian identity, had preferred to neglect the development of the West Bank, and it had also divided the West Bank into three administrative provinces (Jerusalem, Hebron, and Nablus), each responsible separately to Amman. The status of Jerusalem had been downgraded to that of Hebron and Nablus. The economy of the West Bank, which had been primarily agricultural, received relatively little investment in industry; instead, the Jordanian monarchy developed the East Bank. Even though prior to 1948, the East Bank had no industrial infrastructure, by 1965, about 74 percent of Jordan's gross industrial national product was the result of activity on the East Bank. Moreover, even though about half of Jordan's population lived on the West Bank, in 1966, two-thirds of Jordan's industrial investment occurred east of the river (Sahliyeh 1988: 11–13).

Economic development on the East Bank had created a strong incentive for emigration from the West Bank. From 1948 to 1966, about 400,000 people left the West Bank, but emigration was almost offset by natural population growth. The average annual growth in population under Jordanian rule during the 1952–1967 period was 0.9 percent, but 215,000 people left as a direct result of the 1967 war (Benvenisti et al. 1986: 51–52).[1] When Israel captured the territories, the population of the West Bank was about 586,000, and that of the Gaza Strip was approximately 381,000 (*Statistical Abstract of Israel* 1988: 705).[2]

In the realm of education, under Jordanian rule the West Bank had relatively few people who had completed secondary and higher education. There were no universities in the West Bank or Gaza prior to the Israeli occupation, although what became Bir Zeit University, located near Ramallah, and al-Najah National University in Nablus, did exist previously as teachers' colleges. In 1970, only 1 percent of the population of the West Bank aged fourteen and over had thirteen or more years of schooling; in Gaza, only 0.5 percent (Zakai 1988: 32).

Israel's policy after 1967 was aimed at preventing the development of a strong and independent Palestinian economy, which might compete with the Israeli economy and create the infrastructure for a Palestinian state. Dependency was assured by work in Israel and the integration of road, electricity, and water networks. The territories became a source of cheap labor and an outlet for Israeli goods (Benvenisti et al. 1986: 67–68), and the lack of significant industry in the territories contributed to the ever-growing number of residents who worked in Israel. By 1987, 35 percent of the West Bank work force was employed in Israel, and 46 percent of the Gaza work force was employed there (*Statistical Abstract of Israel* 1988: 728). As a result of employment in Israel and in the oil-producing countries of the Gulf, the standard of living in the territories rose considerably. In the early 1970s, it rose by 8 percent yearly; in the mid- and late 1970s, it hovered at around 3–5 percent; and in the 1980s, the standard of living rose at a rate of 1–2 percent annually, mostly because of a slowdown in the Israeli economy and a decline in the economies of the oil-producing states owing to the oil glut (Zakai 1988: 29).

Another significant development under Israeli rule concerned the demographic changes in the territories, which have been characterized by an increasing number of young people in a growing population. In September 1988, Israel's Central Bureau of Statistics put the population of the West Bank at 885,000, although it may have been closer to 950,000. The official estimate for the Gaza Strip in 1988 was 581,000, but again, the figure may have actually been closer to 625,000 (Yariv et al. 1989: 201, 203). Thus, from 1967 to 1988, the population grew by just over 50 percent, but the most pertinent fact for our study is the increasing demographic weight of the young. Between 1977 and 1986, the number of people in the twenty-to-thirty-four age group doubled in the West Bank and tripled in the Gaza Strip. By the mid-1980s, about half of the population of the West Bank and Gaza was composed of those below fourteen, and one-third was composed of those between the ages of fifteen and thirty-four (Mishal and Aharoni 1989: 11–12).

In the sphere of education, there was a significant change under Israeli rule. In 1987, of those people aged fourteen and over, 11 percent in the West Bank and 15 percent in the Gaza Strip had had more than thirteen years of education (Zakai 1988: 32). This rise was owing to two factors. First, the growing individual prosperity in the territories, particularly in the West Bank, enabled people in a variety of socioeconomic sectors to take advantage of university education. Second, under the Israeli occupation, six degree-granting universities have come into existence: in the West Bank, al-Najah National University, Bir Zeit University, the Islamic College of Hebron, Bethlehem University, and Jerusalem University (comprising the Abu Dis College of Science, the al-Bira Nursing College, and the Religious College in Bayt Hanina); in Gaza, the Islamic University, which is affiliated with al-Azhar University in Cairo.

These demographic factors generated various types of frustrations for the Palestinians in the territories, one of which was economic frustration. The growing number of young people and university graduates have not been able to find employment in Israel or in the territories that meets their educational level—there are about 1,500 university graduates from West Bank institutions and approximately 1,000 graduates returning from overseas each year. For a while, the oil-rich Gulf countries provided a partial safety valve, but with the oil recession that began in 1983, work in those countries became less of a possibility, and in fact, many lost their jobs in the Gulf, and returned to the West Bank, thus raising the local rate of unemployment. According to estimates, only about 15 percent of postsecondary graduates find work in their desired professions (Benvenisti et al. 1986: 213), and according to one source, there were 8,000 unemployed university graduates on the eve of the uprising (Mishal and Aharoni 1989: 13). Whether unemployed or working in Israel as street cleaners, garbage collectors, restaurant hands, or construction workers, educated Palestinians have become frustrated.

A second problem was political, focusing on the frustration engendered by contact with Israeli society. Young Palestinians working in Israel saw not only the prosperity of the Israelis but also the freedom and the civil liberties that the latter enjoy. Yet just a few minutes drive away, they continued to live under military occupation and saw no hope for freedom and independence. Young people—employed in Israel, the West Bank, and Gaza—now form the majority among Palestinians, and they were mostly born just before or during the Israeli occupation. Although their knowledge of what it is to be free grew under occupation, their ability to attain freedom remains limited. What exists is a total absence of a correlation between personal high expectations for political freedom and economic advancement and the ever-present depressing reality—a climate in which the people want political change, and fast.

It is clear that a combination of social, political, economic, and demographic factors formed the background to the uprising. Under Israeli occupation, a new generation arose, and it now constitutes the majority in West Bank and Gaza Palestinian Arab society. These people have been influenced by the benefits offered by Israeli administration as well as by the disadvantages of the occupation, and the result is a rank and file as well as an elite that is better educated and better off economically. The logical result of such developments were aspirations for political and economic independence, yet the occupation remained, effectively preventing Palestinian statehood and thwarting independent economic development. As a result of this socialization process, as well as the openness of Israeli society and the no-holds-barred character of that country's political culture, together perhaps with the example offered by the Iranian revolution, a Palestinian populace developed that is tough, ready to sacrifice, and able to endure hardship. This was the setting for the *intifada*.

The Political Dimension: Political Ideology in the West Bank/Gaza Strip, 1967–1987

One feature of politics in the West Bank and the Gaza Strip[3] that approaches a cardinal rule is that the political elite has followed more or less the political and ideological orientations that have swept the Arab world as a whole since the end of World War I. After the 1948 war, Palestinian nationalism went into a dormant period, and it did not emerge again as a coherent ideology until the 1960s. Many members of the wealthy and prominent families were co-opted and developed an economic and a political interest in their connection to Jordan's

Hashemite monarchy. But the triumph of Nasserism in Egypt and the growth of the Ba'th and Communist parties in Syria in the mid-1950s contributed to a following in the West Bank for these movements. Therefore, during the period of Jordanian rule from 1948 to 1967, some Palestinians were active in political organizations that became current in the Arab world, notably the Arab Nationalists' Movement (*al-Qawmiyyun al-Arab*), the Communist party, the Muslim Brotherhood, and the Ba'th party, all of which were made illegal in the Jordanian-controlled West Bank in 1957.

Most of the political elite saw the Jordanian presence as transitional. The Palestinian identity existed, but the power of the prevailing pan-Arab, Communist, Marxist-Leninist, and pan-Islamic ideologies tended to obscure the Palestinian component of political identity. One researcher has said that this phenomenon was a redefinition of the Palestinian identity through other prevailing identities and ideologies, in what was essentially a "floating identity" (Mishal 1978: 75, 78). Since transnational ideologies overshadowed Palestinian identity, there were few calls by the pro-Jordanian and opposition elite for an independent Palestinian state. This situation, along with the various ideological divisions, accounted also for the lack of an incentive to form a West Bank–wide leadership. Yet it is important to realize that all these organizations were in opposition to the Hashemite regime and constituted, in effect, a kind of disjointed West Bank Palestinian opposition.

Because of its singular role in West Bank politics since 1967, its increasing prominence in the PLO, and its role in widening popular support for the *intifada*, particular attention should be paid to the Jordanian Communist Party (in the West Bank, its name was changed to the Palestine Communist Party only in 1982). Before 1967, it may not have had the most members and supporters, but it was the most active, the most powerful, and had the strongest organizational apparatus. The Communist Party put particular emphasis on recruiting intellectuals, secondary school students, teachers, clerks, and professionals and made inroads, not only in important urban centers like Jerusalem and Nablus, but also in several villages, most notably the village of Salfit near Nablus, which is still a Communist stronghold and a bastion of the *intifada* (Cohen 1982: 57–61).

Moreover, in the early 1950s the Communists had remained committed, albeit with varying degrees of fervor, to the policy long supported by their Soviet patron, namely, the division of Palestine into two states, which implied recognition of Israel and the separation of the West Bank from Jordan. Although this position eventually lost strength after the rise of pan-Arabism and ties with Communists on the East Bank increased, it would come to the fore once again in the early 1970s (Cohen 1982: 70–82; Sahliyeh 1988: 88–92). The West Bank Communists were a crucial factor in influencing the PLO to accept (from that organization's standpoint, a tactical move only) the desirability of a West Bank and Gaza state as well as to take the interests of the West Bank residents more to heart. The political involvement of the masses, political realism, and the assertion of the interests of the West Bank Palestinians vis-à-vis the PLO leadership outside, all particularly characteristic of the Palestine Communist Party, were to become the hallmarks of the *intifada*.

The West Bank/Gaza Strip and the PLO

After less than two years of the Israeli occupation of the West Bank and the Gaza Strip, the PLO underwent a dramatic change. From its inception in 1964 until 1968, the PLO had had relatively little support on the West Bank, and its leader, Ahmad Shuqayri, did the bidding of Egypt's Gamal Abdul Nasser. Although the 1964 version of the PLO's National Covenant ruled out any claim to the West Bank (Article 24), the PLO was hampered in its activities by the Jordanian authorities who correctly saw that such activity could threaten the country's regime. In 1968, the guerrilla organizations, notably Yasir Arafat's al-Fatah, George Habash's Popular Front for the Liberation of Palestine (PFLP), and Na'if Hawatima's Democratic Front for the Liberation of Palestine (DFLP), entered the PLO, and in 1969 Arafat was elected chairman of its executive committee. In theory, the occupation of the territories by Israel was ideal for the launching of a protracted armed struggle. The guerrilla (or *fida'i*) organizations believed that this was the case and attempted to set up a guerrilla network in the territories (O'Neill 1978: 64). Although the organizations succeeded in carrying out numerous guerrilla and terrorist operations during the first couple of years of the occupation, these were accomplished by infiltrators from Jordan and not by local cells. In fact, the combination of successful Israeli counterinsurgency policies and the defeat of the PLO in Jordan in 1970–1971 prevented the emergence of an extensive network of guerrilla cells.[4]

Moreover, it was far from clear before the 1973 war that the West Bank and Gaza represented a constituency for the PLO. Many of the traditional West Bank leaders were pro-Jordanian, others advocated the previously mentioned transnational ideologies, and yet others openly advocated a separate Palestinian entity on the West Bank only, a position that was anathema to the PLO's policy at the time, since it implied coming to terms with the existence of Israel. The PLO was then interested in liberating all of Palestine by military means. In view of the PLO's disappointment in the West Bank and particularly after it lost its base in Jordan in 1970, it did not devote much energy to the West Bank and Gaza, preferring to concentrate on building up its military might in Lebanon (Sahliyeh 1988: 25–34; O'Neill 1978: 115–119; Ma'oz 1984: 86–109; Sela 1978).

A major shift occurred after the 1973 Arab-Israeli war, as the mid-1970s saw a rise in the fortunes of the PLO in the international arena. The blow suffered by Israel in the 1973 war was followed in quick succession by the rise in Arab oil might; the resolutions of the Rabat Arab summit, which recognized the PLO as "the sole, legitimate representative of the Palestinian people" and removed Jordan as a party in negotiating the future of the West Bank; Arafat's appearance before the UN General Assembly (November 1974); and the General Assembly's passing of Resolution 3379, equating Zionism with racism (November 1975). As a result, the pattern we have shown above—West Bank Palestinians following contemporary Arab ideological currents—emerged again, and support for the PLO grew in the territories. The PLO also used threats against people who did not support it and gave material benefits to those who did. Support did not necessarily mean agreement with specific PLO policies, but the PLO was soon to become for many people—if not most West Bank residents—the organizational manifestation of Palestinian nationalism, with Arafat as its personification.

The PLO itself, as early as 1972, had begun to realize the importance of developing a constituency in the West Bank and Gaza. At the tenth session of the Palestine National Council (PNC) in April of that year, the PLO passed resolutions encouraging the organization of the masses in trade unions and cultural and welfare organizations. The next year, the PNC agreed to set up a national front in the territories (Sela 1978: 70). The establishment of the Palestine National Front (PNF) signified three things. First, the PLO was growing more open to the concerns of the people in the territories, particularly programmatically; second, many people on the West Bank began to accept the PLO leadership (whose role was therefore strengthened) while at the same time, they attempted to draw the organization toward more moderate positions that were perceived likely to bring about an Israeli withdrawal; and third, the Communists, who dominated the PNF, had become prominent.

The people who formed the PNF in the territories lobbied the PLO toward positions, such as acceptance of a West Bank/Gaza state, that were more in line with the emerging diplomatic consensus after the 1973 war and with the concerns of West Bank/Gaza residents, who desired realistic policies that had a chance of ending the occupation, positions that were not predicated on the total liberation of Palestine. But these positions were voiced by the Communists, who held the key role in the PNF. Eventually, Arafat's al-Fatah accused the Communists of trying to use the PNF to remove the PLO's representative status for all Palestinians and to create an alternative leadership in the territories (Sahliyeh 1988: 52–62).

Subsequently, at the twelfth session of the PNC in 1974, the PLO adopted its "phased strategy" for the liberation of Palestine, the first phase being the establishment of a "fighting national authority" in any part of Palestine to be liberated. In 1977, the PNC, while remaining committed to this overall strategy, called for the founding of a state in the liberated territory. These were tactical moves, reflecting the PLO's desire to remain relevant to the settlement process in Middle East following the 1973 war. But more important for our purposes, they also reflected a growing response to the concerns of the residents in the West Bank and Gaza, concerns formulated and lobbied for by the Communist-dominated PNF.

The PNF lasted until 1977, by which time, many of its leaders had been deported and it had come into sharp conflict with al-Fatah, which accused it of trying to outmaneuver the PLO in the West Bank. By then, too, the PLO was growing in popularity. In 1976, Israel had permitted municipal elections in the West Bank, which the PLO assented to as it knew that they would result in the election of a slate of pro-PLO candidates. The mayors elected, such as Karim Khalaf, Bassam al-Shak'a, and Muhammad Milhim, represented a new pro-PLO elite, which later coalesced in the National Guidance Committee (NGC)—formed to oppose the Camp David Accords signed in 1978—a kind of successor to the PNF that was not dominated by the Communists. But Israel, generally consistent in its opposition to a pro-PLO West Bank–wide leadership, eventually deported many NGC members and ousted several pro-PLO mayors from their posts. The NGC was outlawed in 1982.

This Israeli policy, and the fact that no elections were held after 1976, contributed to the emergence of a group of more moderate and pragmatic personalities who assumed a kind of self-appointed leadership in the West Bank. Yet they lacked the legitimacy of having been elected, as had the mayors who ran the NGC. People such as Hanna Siniora, editor of the East Jerusalem Arabic daily *al-Fajr*; Sari Nusayba, professor of philosophy at Bir Zeit University; Fa'iz Abu Rahma, a leading attorney from Gaza; and Zafir al-Masri, the mayor of Nablus who was appointed by the Israelis in late 1985—apparently with the assent of both the PLO and Jordan—entered the leadership vacuum. Faysal al-Husayni, the head of the Jerusalem-based Arab Studies Society, should also be included in this group, although he is more closely identified with al-Fatah and his activities have been subject to more restrictions by the Israelis than the other prominent individuals. All of these new leaders were intellectuals from the traditional, notable elite,[5] and it was this group of individuals foreign governments contacted when they wanted to get a sense of the positions of the residents of the territories. These leaders were wholly pro-PLO, in that they identified with the organization, but they were vocal in disagreeing with specific PLO policies or suggesting alternatives. They often suggested a two-state solution: a Palestinian state in the territories alongside Israel. In doing so, they voiced the interests of many people in the West Bank and Gaza whose foremost priority was an end to the occupation and who were willing to co-exist with Israel.

Other factors contributed to the emergence of this pragmatic elite. The PLO defeat at the hands of the Israelis in Lebanon in 1982 and the routing of Arafat's men by the Syrian-backed rebellion within al-Fatah in 1983 in Tripoli turned the West Bank and Gaza into the main PLO constituency and also forced the PLO into more pragmatic positions on the conflict and into attempts at coordination with Jordan. Both of these steps were needed if the PLO was to maintain its political relevancy in any settlement process. These developments advanced the political fortunes of the pragmatists in the territories (Sahliyeh 1988: 165–167).

The PLO related, and continues to relate, to these personalities in an ambiguous fashion. Although Abu Rahma and Siniora were appointed in 1985 to a proposed joint Jordanian-Palestinian delegation for talks with the United States, PLO sources made it clear that they were attached only in an advisory capacity and not as full-fledged members (Susser 1984–1985: 204). These men are useful in that they often convey the position of the PLO and are perceived as working on behalf of that organization. But, as noted by a West Bank Palestinian academic, their "usefulness is directly proportional to their loyalty, obedience to PLO directives and lack of individual initiative" (Abu 'Amr 1988: 24). Al-Masri was assassinated for accepting his post in March 1986 by the PFLP (a deed that was condemned by al-Fatah); Nusayba, who had proposed that the territories be incorporated into Israel as the Palestinians, having been given equal rights, would soon overwhelm the Jewish state, was taken to task by the PLO; and in 1987, thinking along the same lines, Siniora announced his intention of running in the Jerusalem municipal council elections in 1988 and was condemned by the PLO. The PFLP gave him a more graphic warning when they torched his car in front of his house (Teitelbaum 1987). The new leaders have continued to walk a fine line during the uprising, always supportive of the PLO but being called back into line when they go too far astray. Nevertheless, their very prominence and outspokenness put pressure on the PLO to assume a more moderate stance, and when the decision had been made to do so, their presence served to give legitimacy to Arafat's line against that of the PLO hard-liners, particularly the PFLP.

Beginning in the mid-1970s—and the Communists even before that—the various PLO organizations consciously developed support in the territories and made a particular effort to widen their social base. This effort was helped along by Israeli policy, which, while outlawing political parties, tended to ignore the formation of a profusion of student organizations; women's groups; unions; professional associations; welfare, social, and health organizations; literary clubs; etc. Perhaps the most important of these new groups were the various voluntary and popular committees established in all sectors, including the refugee camps. Even though the Israelis were aware that these groups often formed a cover for PLO activities, the thinking was that as long as they did not openly advocate violence or civil disobedience, they performed a useful function in the normalization of life in the territories (Ma'oz 1984: 129). To these groups must be added the growth in the various organizations associated with the Islamic Jihad and the Muslim Brotherhood, which the Israelis allowed to function in order to counterbalance the PLO affiliates.

Each of the four major Palestinian factions developed all-encompassing organizations with influence in the various groupings noted above. Al-Fatah's was the al-Shabiba (Youth), the DFLP developed al-Wahda (Unity), the PFLP established Jabhat al-'Amal (Action Front), and the Palestine Communist party also established such a framework (Frisch 1988). These organizations were evidence of the broadening of the social base of political activity. Activists from them, along with graduates of the Israeli prison system, were to form the Unified National Leadership of the Uprising (UNLU) and to oversee the turning of the Palestinian national movement into a mass movement. This elite, fiercely nationalistic, grass roots in nature, and authentic, competed with and posed an alternative to the staid, old leadership of the PLO outside the territories.

This process—the emergence in the territories of a young, energetic, and politically conscious leadership—stood in stark contradistinction to what was happening in the Arab world in the 1980s, as Arab leaders began to lose interest in the Palestinian issue and were more concerned with the worsening relations with Iran. The Arab summit conference in Amman in November 1987 was illustrative of this trend: The Palestinian issue was ignored, and Arafat was a marginal figure at the gathering. This affront added to the growing frustration of the new, young leadership in the territories.

THE *INTIFADA* AS A MASS MOVEMENT: THE FORMATION OF AGREED STRATEGIES

The first weeks of the *intifada* clearly reflected the sociodemographic conditions of the Palestinian population in the territories: The demonstrations and riots were carried out by young people, mostly under twenty-five years of age. As the uprising developed, it soon became clear that its leadership had organizational skills, probably gained while in high school and while organizing their neighborhoods.

The *intifada* took the form of mob violence, stone throwing and tire burning, accompanied by commercial strikes. Conflagrations sometimes broke out at random, and at other times they were instigated by agitators. In both cases, the demonstrations were ignited by rumors and were also in response to Israeli reprisals. Rank-and-file participants often joined the demonstrations on the spur of the moment, without much forethought. In the first few weeks the center of violence was in the refugee camps of the Gaza Strip, but in March 1988, the refugee camps, villages, and several quarters in the cities of the West Bank became the focal points of mass violence. Evidence of this change can be found in the casualty figures: By the end of March, there were about 80 dead and 700 wounded in the West Bank, while in Gaza there were 31 dead and approximately 300 wounded. By late March, 4,831 incidents of violence had been reported in the West Bank and only 1,370 in the Gaza Strip (Frisch 1988).

Young people were at the forefront of the uprising, so it was no surprise that the four organizations in which they were represented (al-Fatah's al-Shabiba, the PFLP's Jabhat al-'Amal, the DFLP's al-Wahda, and the Communist Party) were catapulted to practical leadership of the *intifada* (*Ha'aretz* [Tel Aviv], November 29, 1988, April 3, 1989). Student activists associated with the Muslim Brotherhood were also involved. These organizations acted in a broad coalition, which manifested no clear dominance by any of them. Two reasons explain this arrangement: In contrast to the situation within the PLO outside the territories, where al-Fatah predominated over the other Palestinian organizations, the leftist fronts inside the territories (as well as the Muslim Brotherhood) had a young, active, and enthusiastic leadership that refused to submit to al-Fatah's overall predominance. Al-Fatah failed to completely dominate the youth of the refugee camps and therefore had to establish a coalition with the other organizations (*Ha'aretz*, April 3, 1989). Moreover, the fear of interorganizational fighting, which would expose the *intifada*'s activists to Israeli countermeasures, further prompted the organizations to act in consensus. Therefore, in the early weeks of the uprising, there was no dominant ideological line or any organizational framework, a general condition that corresponded to the rather disorganized forms of violence that were characteristic of the *intifada* at that time.

Similarly, during the first few weeks, no coherent political platform was proposed. Stone throwing had a symbolic meaning, which was articulated in song and slogans calling for the Israelis to get out of the territories, but the rioters did not propose any specifics for the Israeli withdrawal nor did they have a clear idea of the kind of political settlement they wanted. It was unclear whether the *intifada* was merely echoing the PLO's old call for Israel's destruction or meant to call for coexistence and recognition of the Jewish state. As a result, the uprising's political message was rather vague.

Thus, in its first weeks, the uprising resembled a vehicle with a powerful engine that was not being put to full use; it ran in an unclear direction, toward no identifiable destination. The vehicle needed a driver to guide the vehicle to a safe haven. Politically, the *intifada* was a movement that drew on massive popular participation and had great potential, but it was also beset by ideological disorientation and a power vacuum at its top. Different contenders, well aware of the uprising's potential, sought to fill this vacuum by assuming the leadership. The PLO leadership outside, which the *intifada* had caught by surprise, had initial difficulty in overcoming its lack of direct contact with the Palestinians inside the territories. It attempted to exercise leadership by increasing terrorist attacks in Israel from neighboring states, the most notable of which was the hijacking of a civilian bus near Dimona in southern Israel on March 7, 1988. The PLO leadership also moved on the political level and held highly publicized discussions about the possibility of forming a government in exile.

Both armed operations and political movement had little effect on the course of the riots themselves; at best, they seemed only a display of solidarity with the uprising and at worst, an attempt to compete with the events in the territories in order to show the PLO's dominance of the Palestinian struggle. The activists of the *intifada*, fearful lest their activities be subjugated to outside interests not necessarily relevant to the immediate fate of the territories, refused to harness the uprising to the PLO leadership outside.

Some West Bank personalities—mostly from wealthy, well-known families— who were considered as the Palestinian intelligentsia (most of them were journalists, professionals, and academics) made their own bid for the leadership of the uprising. They enjoyed extensive contacts with the Israeli and Western media and represented mainstream al-Fatah positions. In a press conference in East Jerusalem on January 5, a group including Hanna Siniora and self-professed advocate of nonviolence Mubarak Awad called for civil disobedience, which was to include the refusal to carry identity cards and pay taxes. Moreover, Palestinians were encouraged to exhibit passive resistance to law enforcement authorities. On January 14, a group that included academics from Bir Zeit University, such as Gabi Baramki and Sari Nusayba, called for similar action and also demanded that Israel permit Palestinians to organize themselves politically. Siniora and Gaza attorney Fa'iz Abu Rahma formulated a fourteen-point program along the same lines to present to U.S. Secretary of State George Shultz when he arrived in the region later in the month. But these initiatives met with little response from the rebelling population. Leftist elements objected to the assumption of leadership by prominent notables and their attempt to cooperate with the United States. In addition, many of the rioting youth, including those in al-Fatah's al-Shabiba, feared that these personalities, if given the chance, would overinstitutionalize the *intifada*, thus undermining its violent, spontaneous nature. Finally, it was feared that they would seek a compromise with Israel (*al-Safir* [Beirut], January 15, 1988; Leaflet No. 6 of the UNLU, February 5, 1988).

Given the minimal influence of both the PLO establishment on the outside and the prominent, notable West Bank leadership on the inside during the initial stages of the uprising, the power vacuum was soon filled by representatives of the various above-mentioned PLO-affiliated umbrella organizations that coalesced into the UNLU and began issuing numbered leaflets in mid-January 1988. This development reflected the predominance of the younger generation over their elders and those from established families, and of Palestinians of the interior over those of the exterior. Moreover, violent tactics had won out over mere civil disobedience, and a broad organizational coalition had triumphed over the dominance of al-

Fatah. The UNLU did not impose a clear-cut, comprehensive ideological stand or a structured and hierarchical framework; it was, rather, a leadership that operated only at the top level, devising major strategic lines and boosting the people's morale through emotionally written leaflets. The UNLU had only limited influence over the different committees that ran the uprising locally.

Approximately in late March 1988, however, the UNLU began to institutionalize the *intifada*. By then, the UNLU and other activists saw that although the uprising was developing into a major process in the region, it was also beset by organizational problems that were capable of torpedoing the *intifada's* growing momentum. The leadership, now more self-confident, paused to consider ways to improve the effectiveness of the uprising. These improvements included the establishment of a more formal leadership, a more structured organization, and premeditated activities geared to tangible political results.

At the level of leadership and organizational affiliation, the UNLU embraced the supreme authority of the PLO. The UNLU's fear that the PLO might manipulate the course of the *intifada* and subordinate it to overall PLO interests abated as the uprising gained momentum. At that stage, the movements represented in the UNLU, which in any case considered themselves to be a part of the PLO, finally felt more comfortable and were ready to formalize the links between the UNLU and the PLO. Furthermore, the PLO was the embodiment of Palestinian nationalist aspirations, and Arafat personified the Palestinian struggle (Mandelbaum 1988). The UNLU therefore sought to link the uprising with the PLO and its leader in order to increase the *intifada's* legitimacy and strengthen its political resonance. Also of importance in connecting the UNLU to the PLO was the fear that conflict between the Palestinian interior and the Palestinian exterior might prevent the uprising from continuing. Leaflet No. 6 of the UNLU, dated February 5, 1988, noted for the first time the PLO's role as the embodiment of "the unity of Palestinian representation." At the same time, the PLO and the UNLU found themselves supporting the same position, opposing initiatives by the independent, notable West Bank personalities to meet with Secretary Shultz. The PLO then came out strongly in support of the *intifada* and sent a warning: "The masses of our people have decided to boycott . . . Shultz' visit. Woe unto he who meets with the Zionist Shultz. Our people will have no mercy on anyone who deviates from the will of our giant people" (Voice of the PLO [hereafter, VoP, Baghdad], February 20; Foreign Broadcasting Information Service [hereafter FBIS], February 20, 1988). The UNLU thus received the backing of a true legitimate force, without giving the PLO leadership in Tunis a direct role in regulating the tactics of the uprising.

For the PLO, the uprising had to be kept going at all costs, as it was more successful than years of guerrilla warfare in bringing the Palestinian issue to the center of international concern. But PLO leaders interpreted the *intifada* very broadly, constantly reminding the world that the problem involved more than just the fate of those living in the West Bank and Gaza. Al-Fatah Central Committee member Salah Khalaf (Abu Iyad) expressed it thus: the Shultz plan "helps the Palestinians within [the territories]. . . . There are 1.725m. Palestinians living in the occupied territories and 3.5m. outside. What is the solution for the Palestinians living outside the territories? The Shultz plan gives them no hope. The problem remains" (Agence France Presse, April 15, 1988). Khalid al-Hasan, a member of the al-Fatah Central Committee and an adviser to Arafat, said that the PLO enforced a boycott of the meeting, not because it did not trust the Palestinians living in the territories, but because "our battle is to prevent the separation of the Palestinians living in the territories from the rest" (al-Hasan to *al-Musawwar* [Cairo], April 1, 1988). The PLO was determined that the uprising not end in self-determination only for those in the occupied territories but would lead to self-determination for all Palestinians, wherever they might be, including those living in Israel (VoP [Baghdad], March 7; FBIS, March 8, 1988).

Having effectively stymied local initiatives by the pragmatic West Bank/Gaza elite, it was still important for the PLO to show the unity of the Palestinian people and to portray the *intifada* as the result of its long efforts outside of Palestine. The PLO viewed reports that the uprising was spontaneous as tendentious attempts to rob it of credit due. Arafat often told reporters that the uprising had actually started on October 24, 1986, when there had been demonstrations in the territories in support of the Palestinians under attack by the Shi'ite Amal organization in Lebanon. On one occasion, he stressed that the *intifada* was just another wave among the waves of the uprising since then (Arafat to the *Middle East* [London], March 1988). Arafat was trying to get across the message that the *intifada* was just another event in a long string of events involving Palestinians in other places. When asked if he considered the uprising to be the PLO's greatest achievement, he replied, "It is one of the PLO's greatest achievements" (Arafat on VoP [clandestine], May 10; FBIS, May 10, 1988). Al-Fatah Central Committee member Khalil al-Wazir (Abu Jihad) described the *intifada* as the fruit of a "long struggle . . . inside and outside Palestine" (al-Wazir to *al-Safir*, quoted by Agence France Presse, January 27; FBIS, January 27, 1988). A split between the elite of the Palestinian interior and that of the exterior was thus avoided. As in other revolutions, a broad coalition was formed. Moreover, the partnership with the PLO provided for more sophisticated political action in the future.

Although the *intifada*'s leadership became more formal and broadly based with the establishment of a partnership with the PLO, the UNLU also sought to improve the tactics and organization of the uprising, and it was successful in delivering a blow to Israeli policies. The very outbreak of the *intifada* and the use of nonconventional military means, such as rock throwing and firebombs by civilians against armed soldiers, challenged Israel's attempt to maintain a moral image: Israel's claim to be exercising a "benign occupation" proved immaterial in the face of a mass popular uprising, and Israel was portrayed as brutal in the Western media. Israel's population became divided over the interpretation of the uprising and the amount of force needed to suppress it, with some groups in the Israeli political center and on the left voicing serious doubts about Israel's wisdom and right to act with such force and voices on the right and far right calling for mass expulsions and the use of more force in suppressing the Palestinians. The Israel Defense Forces' (IDF) top brass was apparently beset by doubts about the unusual policing role forced upon the army.

Tactically, Israel was unable to devise a means to properly confront the *intifada*. Trying to stick to a moral viewpoint, Israel did not resort to mass deportations and killings, but the means it chose to use proved insufficient. Army patrols used tear gas, truncheons, gravel-throwing machines, and rubber and plastic bullets against rioters—and live ammunition when the lives of soldiers were in danger. There was a selective deportation of fifty-eight activists in the uprising's first two years, curfews and mass administrative detention, a selective cutting-off of telephone service, and the forced closure of schools, but the Israelis were unable to stop the *intifada*. The masses kept rioting and challenging Israel's authority. They stopped short of steps that might provoke a massive, unbearable Israeli response but continued on a path that assured Palestinian participation and world sympathy. About halfway through the second year of the uprising, activity began to be maintained on a low but constant level, a kind of passive mass mobilization (primarily in the form of commercial strikes) that was conducive to participation over the long term.

A second notable achievement was the emergence of a basic structure within the uprising. The youth movements provided "shock (or strike) troops," which enforced strikes and did away with people who were uncooperative; "national committees" coordinated activities on the national level; and on the local level, "popular committees" coordinated daily economic life, looked after social welfare, and encouraged participation. Women's organizations, students, and trade unions were co-opted in this manner, leading to the mobilization of almost the entire population (*al-Manar* [Cairo], October 1988; *Shu'un Filastiniyya* [Nicosia], December 1988).

Another achievement, was the uprising's remarkable success with the Western media. The rioters were able to shake the traditional image of "terrorists" usually attributed to Palestinian-PLO activists and began to be perceived as legitimate freedom fighters. Moreover, by restricting violence primarily to the use of stones and Molotov cocktails in the face of armed soldiers, the Palestinian activists achieved an image both of bravery and of being the victims, thus giving an entirely new moral dimension to the Palestinian struggle (J. Anderson 1988 is typical of these kinds of reports).

The limitations of the *intifada* also became apparent. Although the uprising proved durable, the *intifada* did not succeed in effecting an Israeli withdrawal or forcing Israel to accept a Palestinian state. What the uprising needed was an effective political platform that had a chance of translating its achievements into tangible results, specifically, a Palestinian state. Another problem was tactical: The mass riots led to too many Palestinian casualties and to mass detention, despite the restraint demonstrated by both sides.[6] The spontaneous mass riots also disturbed the routine of Palestinian daily life. Israel closed down the schools in the West Bank (schools in East Jerusalem and Gaza mostly remained open), so a full school year was lost. Israeli reprisals and directives of the UNLU resulted in damage to the local economy. What was needed was a more rational and predetermined tactical approach that would utilize the advantages of mass violence and full societal mobilization but in a more beneficial and less costly way.

In April 1988, the uprising's leadership decided to embark on what was termed a "civil revolt." It focused on planned small-scale riots, in which youths ambushed IDF personnel and Jewish settlers with rocks, bricks, Molotov cocktails, and occasionally knives. The civil revolt, however, also had long-term, strategic objectives: to curtail the Palestinians' dependence on the Israeli civil administration and economy, to disengage from employment in Israel, and to avoid paying taxes. The Palestinians thus sought to establish an alternative economy and administration that would constitute an infrastructure for a future Palestinian state (*al-Manar*, October 1988).[7] The civil revolt was the epitome of mass mobilization for revolt in a nonguerrilla fashion.

In the next months, the *intifada* developed along two main paths, which drew on the lessons of the earlier months. In the diplomatic arena, the Palestinians sought to gain major international recognition for the establishment of a Palestinian state; inside, the uprising worked to enlarge the civil revolt and prepare the foundation for such a state.

THE PLO AND THE *INTIFADA*: DYNAMICS OF THE RELATIONSHIP BETWEEN THE EXTERIOR AND THE INTERIOR

The PLO was not responsible for the spontaneous outbreak of the uprising, but it was the party to profit from it the most. The *intifada* began at a time when the PLO was at a low point following the Amman Arab summit in November 1987, at which Jordan's King Husayn had publicly snubbed Arafat. Moreover, Arafat was being stymied in his effort to return to Lebanon, as his forces were constantly under attack by the Syrian-sponsored Shi'ite Amal organization. Politically, the *intifada* served to compensate the PLO for the loss of its territorial stronghold in Lebanon following the Israeli invasion in 1982.

The uprising also broke out at a unique time in the history of the PLO. The eighteenth session of the PNC, held in Algiers in April 1987, reunified the PLO after several years with the PFLP and the DFLP outside the organization. Moreover, the 1987 PNC saw the entrance of the Palestine Communist Party into the PLO's fifteen-man executive committee for the first time. This admittance in itself signified a legitimization of the PCP and a serious consideration of West Bank and Gaza interests, since the main constituency of the PCP was in the West Bank (Teitelbaum 1987). Both events were probably crucial in establishing the unity needed to engage in a prolonged uprising.

The *intifada* was responsible for bringing the PLO to declared positions that moved it closer than ever before to an acceptance of a two-state solution to the Israeli-Palestinian conflict. The dynamic at work was similar to that of previous years, and the influence of the Palestinian interior was critical. Palestinians inside the territories wanted an end to the occupation as soon as possible, and it was widely realized, particularly by the pragmatic elite, that this goal entailed recognition of Israel. The PLO, as before, had to respond to these concerns. Furthermore, the organization itself needed to maintain its relevancy to any settlement process, and it was also essential to show those inside the territories that it was advancing the Palestinian cause. The challenge to the PLO leadership, particularly al-Fatah, was, therefore, how to respond to the concerns of the Palestinian interior and maintain the PLO's international relevance as the representative of all the Palestinians, without losing the unity of the organization and without giving up its final claim on all of Palestine and call for self-determination for all Palestinians. It was determined by the PLO leadership that the best way to proceed was to find a way to meet the U.S. conditions for talking to the organization, namely, accept UN Security Council Resolutions 242 and 338, recognize Israel, and renounce terrorism. Finally, breaking the U.S. boycott of the PLO would be a political achievement of momentous proportions.

But statements by PLO leaders made it clear that they were considering a change in tactics, not strategy. Salah Khalaf told the PNC in Algiers: "I am interested in the liberation of Palestine, why not do it step by step? We have to devise a proper method of liberation" (*al-Anba* [Kuwait], December 13, 1988). Khalaf was typical of the al-Fatah mainstream when he told a Palestinian Paris weekly that the resolutions passed by the PLO had to be "sophisticated in rhetoric, but not in content" (Khalaf to *al-Yawm al- Sabi'* [Paris], November 7, 1988).

The resolutions adopted by the PNC in Algiers in April 1988, despite several indications that the PLO was moving toward a recognition of Israel, were so tortuously formulated and so conditional as to render them unacceptable to the United States. Nevertheless, Arafat was able to get unprecedented formulations passed—such as those that mentioned UN Resolutions 242 and 338—without having the PFLP bolt the organization, as it had a few years earlier because of Arafat's political machinations. But al-Fatah's desire to open a dialogue between the United States and the PLO—and thus maintain the organization's political relevancy while showing the interior that it was responsive to its concerns—was so great that Arafat eventually acknowledged Israel's right to exist at a press conference in Geneva in mid-December 1988. The PFLP and part of the DFLP rejected Arafat's statements, correctly maintaining that they were not in line with the Algiers PNC resolutions. But the PLO's executive committee supported Arafat, and just after the press conference, the United States declared that it was opening a dialogue with the PLO.

The other significant move of the PNC was the declaration of the independent state of Palestine on November 15. The PLO had several considerations in mind. First, it needed to pick up the gauntlet thrown down by Jordan's King Husayn when he had announced his country's disengagement from the West Bank at the end of July. Second, if the PLO was to move toward an acceptance of Israel, the sine qua non could be no less than a Palestinian state. Arafat's strategy was to get Israel to an international conference with the Palestinian state as a fait accompli, and then force an Israeli withdrawal.

More than anything, the uprising increased the relative political weight of the Palestinian interior. Not only had the Palestinian movement become a mass movement, but its political center of gravity had shifted. As noted earlier, the uprising focused the conflict on the occupied territories, and the pragmatic elite were seen by many foreign governments as a significant part of the West Bank/ Gaza leadership. These factors led the PLO to be concerned lest these interior leaders act in any way on their own or propose steps that had not been cleared with the organization. In addition to the attempts to meet with Shultz, there were also other occasions during 1988 when these leaders were called back into line by the PLO.

An examination of the leaflets of the UNLU, which exhibit positions that followed the line of the PLO mainstream very closely, nevertheless brings one to the conclusion that this clandestine leadership represents a moderating force on the PLO. The UNLU contains representatives from the more radical factions, and the fact that they are willing to follow the Arafat line strengthens the latter's hand within the organization. So although, as a whole, the UNLU tends to be generally more hard-line than does the pragmatic and intellectual elite, together they constitute an effective lobbying force with respect to the PLO that cannot be ignored. As an authentic leadership in the occupied territories, those groups are reshaping the priorities of the PLO toward a concentration on the specific aspirations of the residents of the West Bank and the Gaza Strip.

The uprising has granted those Palestinians in the territories an unheralded degree of political legitimacy, and the PLO listens to them more than ever before. Although the PLO often tries to move the public discourse from one solely about the future of the West Bank and Gaza, the continued input of the people in the territories will force it to work to ameliorate their plight, which may require the PLO to further moderate its position. The PLO remains the unchallenged leader of the Palestinians in the territories. In general, the dynamic catalyzed by the uprising, by increasing the power of those in the territories, seems to be working toward a solution. But at this stage, it appears that a solution will come about through the PLO, not around it.

THE IMPACT OF CIVIL REVOLT

To what extent has the uprising developed the tangible infrastructure of a political movement preparing for statehood? The *intifada* continues as of this writing, making such an assessment difficult, but enough time has gone by to provide us with some initial answers to this question. The uprising has definitely achieved a structure and developed tactics that serve to feed its nature as a mass uprising and as a movement mobilized for a political goal. This fact is evident in several spheres. First, the uprising's leadership has proved capable of maintaining a level of mass violence, despite Israeli reprisals. This success can be explained by the prestige given to the young demonstrators by local Palestinians, the Arab world, and the Western media for confronting the Israelis. The readiness of the youths for sacrifice and the easy access to rocks, bricks, cinder blocks, and Molotov cocktails have also made continued outbursts of violence possible. The UNLU has successfully used every Palestinian casualty and every possible memorial day to call for more clashes and strikes, in a perpetual, self-feeding process. The hundreds of dead, the thousands detained and arrested, and the expulsions have become a rallying cry for the continuation of the *intifada* rather than a deterrence to the local population.

A second achievement concerns organization. New roles have been formed during the uprising, so there are youths who divert the soldiers (often women), those who ambush them, and those who serve as scouts. The UNLU has succeeded in making each group in society contribute its share to the *intifada*. Students and members of youth movements provide the cadres for the "shock troops" responsible for the clashes with Israeli forces, for writing slogans on walls, and for enforcing strikes. They also punish real and perceived collaborators with the Israeli authorities. Women's organizations and labor and professional associations, all of which have been unofficially affiliated with the various PLO constituent organizations, provide mutual-help services to replace the Israeli administration and compensate people who have been hurt by the uprising. They engage in small-scale industrial work, home farming and education, and medical treatment coordinated by the popular committees at the village and town level. The national committees supervise the violent activities of the shock troops. A PLO journal could therefore boast that all sectors of society participate in the *intifada*: Industrial workers contribute their skills to Palestinian industry and to servicing the local population, villages harbor squads of shock troops and contribute their agricultural produce to the uprising, businesspeople strike when ordered, professionals and students formulate the uprising's ideological message, and the men of religion inflame the emotions of the people (*Shu'un Filastiniyya*, December 1988; Frisch 1988; *al-Qabas* [Kuwait], May 15, 18, 19, 1988).

If the full mobilization of society was aimed at providing the infrastructure for an independent Palestinian economy and administration, disengagement from Israeli administrative and economic institutions was embarked upon in order to provide symbolic independence. Leaflets No. 9 of March 1, 1988, and No. 10 of March 10, 1988, and even more so No. 14 of April 20, 1988, called for the resignation of top civil administration employees, and Leaflet No. 18 of May 28, 1988, called for all employees to resign. The last leaflet also called upon the populace to boycott all Israeli goods and for Gazans to refuse new Israeli identity cards. Leaflet No. 14 called for a full tax boycott. Six hundred or more policemen resigned as did hundreds—but by no means all—of the civil administration employees. One Israeli-appointed mayor, Hafiz Tuqan of Nablus, resigned. The flow of Israeli goods to the territories has also been reduced by 30–40 percent. The UNLU resorts to internal terrorism to enforce its policies; people who refuse to obey are first threatened, then warned, and then either beaten or killed. According to official IDF figures, during the first two years of the uprising, 136 alleged "collaborators" were slain (*Jerusalem Post*, December 8, 1989).

There are, however, several serious obstacles that the uprising needs to overcome before it can establish the infrastructure needed for a state. Mobilization has focused on the actual mechanics of the *intifada* itself—and hinges on its continuity—rather than on serious state building. People have been mobilized by a combination of coercion, terrorism, and an increasing hatred of Israel—in the words of one resigning worker, "we are not willing to be [Israel's] beast of burden and then get killed [by Israeli soldiers]" (*Ha'aretz*, March 20, 1989)—but can this mobilization maintain its momentum beyond the routine of daily clashes and provide a true foundation for a state-based political community? It remains unclear whether the younger generation, which has come to prominence during the *intifada*, will be fully accepted in its new role by other sectors of society. Professionals and intellectuals of notable origins, who usually constitute the backbone of a newly independent political community, have not been fully incorporated into the uprising and may wish for a more central role. Merchants act under duress when they go on strike. It thus still remains to be seen whether these other sectors will mount a challenge to the new order.

Toward the middle of 1989, it became apparent that the uprising had shifted from the active mass mobilization of demonstrators to a more passive type of mobilization consisting of observing strikes. A hard-core group of "professional" activists has emerged, and its members devote most of their time to the *intifada*. It consists of teenagers who wear masks and move about killing collaborators, writing slogans, and seeking confrontations with the army.

Disagreement is also apparent to some extent with respect to the role of guerrilla and terrorist activity alongside the uprising. Although the UNLU and al-Fatah in Tunis have reached an understanding that at this stage the use of firearms in the territories is ruled out, the PFLP and part of the DFLP have called for escalating the armed struggle within and without Palestine (*al-Hadaf* [Damascus], September 18, 1988). Although not taking action to undermine the joint strategy of limited violence within the framework of the *intifada*, both the PFLP and the DFLP, operating from Lebanon, have been very active in attempting to infiltrate Israel's northern border and attack civilian targets.

Intra-UNLU competition has been apparent but has not led as of yet to serious rivalries. Yet competition with another counterelite has increased the level of revolutionary violence. The Palestinian branch of the Muslim Brotherhood movement, which established the Islamic Resistance Movement (known by its Arabic acronym, HAMAS) in 1988, presents a challenge to the unity of the uprising. Although an active participant in the *intifada*, HAMAS—led by a local Gaza divine, Shaykh Ahmad Yasin—is not a part of the UNLU. HAMAS is careful not to directly attack the PLO, but it does not accept that organization as the sole representative of the Palestinians. Yasin has stressed that his movement opposes an organization "that does not operate according to the spirit and laws of Islam. If the PLO grows closer to Islam, so will grow our commitment to the PLO" (*al-Nahar* [Jerusalem], April 30, 1988).

The attempt of the uprising's leadership to establish an administrative and economic infrastructure to replace that dominated by Israel has been successful only in a negative sense, in that many people have boycotted Israeli goods, resigned positions in the civil administration and refused to pay taxes. But the formation of new institutions and alternatives has been less effective. The UNLU has not come up with a comprehensive, "homegrown" system of education or an effective independent system of health services. Vegetable growing at home has also been unsuccessful. The UNLU has not replaced Israel in providing water and electricity and still needs Israel for driving, export, and building licenses. Moreover, by exploiting the requirement for these permits, the Israeli authorities have been able to insist on the payment of back taxes, so sources in the civil administration claim to have collected over 80 percent of the amount collected in the year previous to the *intifada*. The uprising has also hurt the local economy—according to Israeli sources, the Palestinian standard of living has dropped by 40 percent (a contributing factor in this regard was the massive drop in the value of the Jordanian dinar in the spring of 1989)—so in the face of popular demand, the UNLU has consented to permit Palestinians to continue to work in Israel (Frisch 1988; *Shu'un Filastiniyya*, July 1988; *Jerusalem Post*, December 30, 1988). A West Bank Palestinian economist, Hisham Awartani, has nevertheless asserted that owing to the drop in the amount of Israeli goods in the territories and a sense of the need to minimize the consumption of luxury goods, the Palestinians have increased the local manufacture of chocolate, shoes, cigarettes, and clothes and many make an effort to buy only Palestinian products. To a small extent, this activity has substituted for the partial disengagement from the Israeli economy (*Jerusalem Post*, December 30, 1988, April 17, 1989). It therefore seems that the *intifada* can probably continue at a level of basic maintenance, but maintenance alone will not bring about enough of an infrastructure for an independent state.

The Jordanian disengagement from the West Bank acted principally to boost Palestinian independence by minimizing Jordanian authority over local residents. However, the move also added to the economic burden the Palestinians have to bear. With the exception of government-employed clergy and schoolteachers, Jordan cut off the salaries of all other functionaries in various branches of public service. Jordan also forbade the passage of Palestinian goods to Jordan (primarily via the Allenby bridge) or through Jordanian air and sea ports to the rest of the Arab world. Indeed, the lack of independent port facilities is a major obstacle to establishing a self-sufficient Palestinian economy.

Finally, civil revolt has been successful in inhibiting Israeli rule and freedom of movement in the territories. Israelis, particularly civilians, no longer move about freely in the territories. It took until spring 1989 for the Israeli government to define a political strategy to confront the challenge of the *intifada*, by proposing that West Bank and Gaza Palestinians elect negotiators to discuss self-rule in the territories. The plan was stalemated by disagreement about whether it was to include East Jerusalem. Until the plan was proposed, the Israeli government viewed the uprising solely as a problem of crowd control, the leaders of the *intifada* were not seen as being worth talking to, and Israel preferred to use economic and bureaucratic pressures on the populace. In the military sphere, the use of occasional live ammunition and the frequent use of plastic bullets (which began to be used in August 1988) resulted in mounting Palestinian deaths, a development seen in Israeli military circles as counterproductive to calming tensions (*Ha'aretz*, November 10, 1988; *Jerusalem Post*, January 25, 1989). Until late 1990, the government resisted calls by Israelis on the political right for harsher measures to crack down on the uprising.

Israel now shares the practical rule of the territories with the UNLU and the Muslim fundamentalists. Although Israel has military might and an administrative monopoly, the Palestinians enjoy moral and political support, and a small degree of economic independence. The UNLU has used this new balance of power to exercise symbolic independence by declaring villages far from main thoroughfares "liberated areas" and by demonstrating its ability to mobilize the populace. But the UNLU has not succeeded in moving Israel toward relinquishing the territories. The failure here lies, not with the ability of the UNLU to mobilize the Palestinians, but rather with its inability to convince the majority of Israelis that the *intifada* truly represents aspirations for a Palestinian state that would live peacefully alongside the Jewish state and is not just a continuation of the Palestinian goal to weaken and eventually eliminate Israel.

The PLO's success in the territories and its moderation in dealings with the United States and the international community were undermined by the events of the Gulf crisis. The PLO endorsed the Iraqi occupation of Kuwait in August 1990, viewing Saddam Hussein as a champion of the Palestinian cause. Palestinian hopes increased further when Hussein proposed a linkage between withdrawal from Kuwait and an international solution to Palestinian aspirations. As a result of Iraq's crushing military defeat in February 1991, the PLO lost much of its international support in the Arab world and the West. As of this writing, the PLO has virtually no chance of convincing Israel of the sincerity of its desire for peace. Any chances for negotiations that might transform the *intifada* into a real state-building movement now rest with the local leadership in the territories. Ten West Bank and Gaza leaders met with U.S. Secretary of State James Baker when he visited the Middle East in March 1991 to explore long-term solutions for the region.

CONCLUSION

The rise of the *intifada* exhibits several elements of the theory of revolution presented in Chapter 3. Demographic expansion in the occupied territories has brought a new, larger, more youthful generation, and continued Israeli occupation and settlement have sharply limited political freedoms and economic opportunities. Thus, the potential for mass mobilization in the territories has grown. Second, the rise of a new elite in the territories, combined with the PLO's loss of its positions in Jordan and Lebanon, has transferred a substantial amount of initiative to Palestinian leaders within the occupied territories. Together, these two elements created the basis for the *intifada*. However, the third element necessary for a successful revolution—a fiscal or military crisis in the ruling state—has *not* occurred. Although Israel's dependence on U.S. aid and its own political divisions have created some political pressure on Israel to negotiate, to this date the continued strength of the Israeli state has allowed it to retain control of the territories. The *intifada* thus remains an ongoing, though currently stalemated, state crisis.

CHRONOLOGY

June 1967: Israel captures the West Bank and the Gaza Strip.

August 1973: Communist-dominated Palestine National Front established on the West Bank.

October 1973: Arab-Israeli war.

1976: Elections held in the West Bank, with tacit PLO approval, result in a slate of pro-PLO figures.

September 1978: Camp David Accords signed by Israel, United States, and Egypt. Provisions for West Bank and Gaza involve a period of autonomy to be followed by negotiations on the final status of the territories. Rejected by the PLO.

March 1979: Peace treaty signed between Israel and Egypt.

June 1982: Israel invades Lebanon, ousting the PLO from most of the country and putting an end to the ministate it enjoyed there since 1970.

1983–1986: Arafat's al-Fatah mainstream tries to enter the settlement process through coordination with Jordan, a policy that was rejected by the PFLP and the DFLP, which withdrew from the PLO executive committee.

December 1983: Following a Syrian-instigated rebellion in al-Fatah, PLO leader Arafat and his followers are forced out of Lebanon altogether.

April 1987: PLO reunited after Arafat abandons policy of working through Jordan.

November 1987: Arafat snubbed and Palestinian issue ignored at Amman Arab summit.

December 1987: Rioting erupts in Gaza following a collision for which Palestinians blame an Israeli driver. Protests spread to West Bank.

April 1988: PLO military chief Khalil al-Wazir (Abu Jihad) assassinated in Tunis.

July 1988: King Husayn of Jordan announces disengagement from the West Bank to let the PLO take full responsibility for the Palestinian people.

November 1988: PLO declares an independent Palestinian state with Jerusalem as its capital.

December 1988: President Reagan states that the United States is ready to open a dialogue with the PLO.

May 1989: Israeli cabinet approves plan for West Bank and Gaza Palestinians to elect negotiators to discuss self-rule with Israel.

late 1989: Unprecedented number of Soviet Jews begin to arrive in Israel, some of whom settle in the West Bank and Gaza.

August 1990–January 1991: PLO and many Palestinians support Iraq's occupation of Kuwait and proposal to link withdrawal to settlement of the Palestine issue.

October 8, 1990: Seventeen Palestinians are killed by Israeli police on Temple Mount Jerusalem's Haram al-Sharif.

February 1991: Iraq's defeat undermines international support for Palestinians, resulting in an acute leadership crisis in the PLO.

March 13, 1991: U.S. Secretary of State Baker has a first-ever meeting in Jerusalem with ten local leaders from the West Bank.

NOTES

1. Since there has been no census in the territories since 1967, all population figures are based on estimates and statistical models using data provided by Israel's Central Bureau of Statistics. For an explanation of the population data, see *Statistical Abstract of Israel* 1988: 99–100.

2. These figures are based on the Israeli census and are believed by many people to be slightly below the actual figures. The same may hold true for the Central Bureau of Statistics' estimates for the following years.

3. Analyses of political trends and developments in the territories have concentrated much more on the West Bank than on the Gaza Strip, mostly because of the former's larger political elite (most of the Gaza population is composed of refugees living in camps) and greater accessibility to central Israel. Moreover, during the 1967 war, the files maintained by the Jordanian security services on Palestinian political activities fell into Israeli hands and were analyzed by Israeli researchers. The result of this research is to be found in Cohen (1982). Much of our analysis for this period and following is thus necessarily skewed toward the West Bank, which, in any case, is the center of Palestinian nationalism today.

4. A detailed analysis of PLO efforts to form cells and the effect of Israeli counterinsurgency can be found in O'Neill (1978: 64–123). The PLO was more successful in Gaza, where most of the population were poor refugees and not permanent residents. The dense nature of the camps made counterinsurgency more difficult, and consequently, local cells, particularly those of the PFLP, operated well until they were crushed in 1971.

5. Al-Husayni enjoys extra legitimacy, as he is the son of a Palestinian hero, 'Abd al-Qadir al-Husayni, who was killed fighting the Jews at the battle of the Qastel in 1948.

6. According to IDF figures, in the first two years of the uprising (December 9, 1987–December 8, 1989), 535 Palestinians were killed, 8,938 were wounded, 50,000 Palestinian Arabs were arrested, and 58 were deported; 248 houses were demolished, and 118 were sealed. Figures issued by B'tselem, a human rights information center affiliated with the Israeli RATZ party, differ. It said that 616 were killed and cited UNRWA figures of 37,439 wounded (*Jerusalem Post*, December 8, 1989).

7. Initial calls to carry out such a policy were voiced in Leaflet No. 4, January 21, 1988; the slogan "civil revolt" was first mentioned in Leaflet No. 8, February 21, 1988; the strategy of complete disengagement from Israel (including mass resignations from the Israeli-run civil administration) was elaborated upon in Leaflet No. 11, April 2, 1988.

14

COMPARISONS AND POLICY IMPLICATIONS

TED ROBERT GURR AND JACK A. GOLDSTONE

The modern conception of revolution was formed two centuries ago in France, and the political relationship between rulers and ruled has never been the same since. The compelling example established by the French Revolution of 1789 was that a nation's people, by concerted political struggle, could fundamentally transform the political order that governed their lives and, with it, the social and economic structure of society. The revolutionary impulse has far more often been suppressed or diverted into reform than it has succeeded. Of the forty-eight civil and revolutionary wars fought between 1961 and 1965, only nine ended with victory or major concessions for the rebels, compared with thirty-five military defeats and a few protracted struggles that were still going on in 1991, for example, in Eritrea and northern Burma. In 1989, the success of popular revolutionary movements in central Europe was counterbalanced by the brutal suppression of democracy movements in Burma and China. Revolutionary seizures of power often accomplish only limited, sometimes temporary reforms, as happened in Bolivia and Egypt after their 1952 revolutions, in Iraq after the Ba'thist revolution of 1958, and in South Korea after the student-led revolution of 1960. The Philippine revolution of 1986 is going the same way. Nonetheless, the essential idea that rulers are ultimately accountable to their people has persisted and, in uncommon circumstances, has led to political upheavals that profoundly changed for all time the character of the societies in which they occurred.

The contributors to this book have used a common framework to examine ten popularly supported revolutionary movements of the last third of the twentieth century. Seven of these movements thus far have brought down old regimes, and all have had enduring effects on national and regional politics, for better or worse. Our purpose in this concluding chapter is to compare the origins, dynamics, and outcomes of these revolutions. Despite their diversity, we can identify some common or parallel patterns and sequences of events among them, patterns likely to recur in future revolutionary conflicts.

ORIGINS OF REVOLUTIONARY CRISES

The specific conditions that generate revolutionary crises and shape the processes of revolutionary conflict are highly diverse. However, revolutionary movements since the end of the era of the world wars have, in general, differed in three aspects from those that preceded 1945. First, the geopolitical setting has changed. Recent revolutions have occurred in relatively small, often fairly urbanized countries with semimodern colonial or dictatorial governments rather than in large and predominantly rural nations with long-standing traditional governments, such as formed the setting for the "classic" social revolutions of France (1789), Russia (1917), and China (1911–1949). Second, recent revolutionaries have been more often animated by opposition to local colonial, racial, or superpower domination, and specific ethnic or religious claims, than by the quest for universal ideals that motivated most eighteenth- and nineteenth-century European and Latin American revolutions. And third, late-twentieth-century revolutions unquestionably have been more shaped and constrained by international intervention than most of their predecessors.

Nonetheless, these changes seem to reflect more changes in the makeup of the international order than changes in the processes governing the development of revolutionary situations. At the most general level of analysis, we have argued that all revolutions proceed through three phases, beginning with a state crisis, followed by a struggle for power, and efforts by the eventual victors to reconstruct the state. Moreover, no revolutionary crisis occurs until there is a conjunction of three necessary conditions: a crisis in the old state, alienation of a significant segment of the elite, and mass mobilization. In Table 14.1 we summarize the principal sources of these conditions in each of the ten cases, as well as the factors that shaped each revolutionary struggle and its outcomes.

State Crises

Some scholars have argued, after studying the classic revolutions that occurred before 1950, that international competition (Skocpol) and fiscal crisis (Goldstone) are the essential or most important sources of state crisis. We find that serious economic problems beset many of the ten prerevolutionary regimes discussed in this book, including excessive debt (Iran, Poland), economic stagnation and decline (in the Philippines, both African cases, Poland again), and the high costs of fighting internal wars (Nicaragua, Afghanistan, Zimbabwe, Israel). But many other contemporary regimes have confronted similar problems without succumbing to revolutionary pressures.

A full examination of the cases examined in this book reveals a much more diverse set of internal and international conditions that can lead to a crisis which weakens state authorities' grip on power. We think now that a state crisis should not be defined as a specific objective condition but rather as a situation in which significant numbers of elites and popular groups believe that the central authorities

Table 14.1 Summary of Cases

	IRAN	NICARAGUA
SOURCES OF STATE CRISIS	• Excessive debts • Inability to control inflation • Loss of nationalist credentials • U.S. pressure to reduce oppression of regime opponents	• Inability to avoid economic damage from rebellion • Loss of nationalist credentials • U.S. pressure to reduce oppression of regime opponents
SOURCES OF ELITE ALIENATION	• State attacks on *ulema*, landlords, bazaaris • Exclusion of middle classes from power • Corruption • High inflation, uneven development	• State attacks on opposition politicians • Increasing exclusion of middle classes from power • Corruption • Decline of business climate
SOURCES OF MASS MOBILIZATION	• Population growth and urbanization exceeding economic opportunities • Service and support by *ulema* and mosques • Uneven economic growth with lagging traditional sector • Inconsistent persecution by SAVAK • Mobilization by nationalist/Islamic ideology	• Population growth and urbanization exceeding economic opportunities • Service and support by FSLN • Inconsistent persecution by National Guard • Mobilization by nationalist/Sandinista ideology
SHAPE OF REVOLUTIONARY STRUGGLE	• Coalition of traditional and Westernized elites against the shah • Conflict between traditional and Westernized elites	• Coalition of FSLN and church and business leaders against Somoza • Conflict between FSLN and church and business leaders
OUTCOME	• Triumph of traditional elite • Radical Islamization • War with Iraq	• Initial triumph of FSLN • Limited socialization of economy, covert aid to revolt in El Salvador • War against U.S. backed contras • Business elite-backed party wins in 1990

	VIETNAM (Southern Phase)	CAMBODIA
SOURCES OF STATE CRISIS	• Excessive dependence on U.S. • Loss of nationalist credentials • Unfavorable commodity price shifts	• Excessive dependence on U.S. (Lon Nol) • Loss of nationalist credentials • Costs of war incursions from Vietnam war
SOURCES OF ELITE ALIENATION	• Factional conflicts • Corruption • Anti-imperialism	• Factional conflicts • Corruption • Anti-imperialism
SOURCES OF MASS MOBILIZATION	• Population growth and urbanization exceeding economic opportunities • Population service and support by Vietcong • Persecution by U.S./RVN armed forces • Mobilization by nationalist, anti-imperialist, Communist ideology	• Population growth exceeding economic growth • Population mobilization by Khmer Rouge • Costs of Vietnam war incursions • Mobilization by nationalist, Communist-inspired ideology
SHAPE OF REVOLUTIONARY STRUGGLE	• Coalition of rural peasants and middle-class nationalists against U.S.-backed political elites and urban bourgeoisie • Conflict between nationalist/Communist leaders and urban bourgeoisie	• Coalition of Khmer Rouge and Prince Sihanouk against U.S.-backed elites • Conflict between Khmer Rouge and Sihanouk-connected traditional and bourgeois elements
OUTCOME	• Military triumph of North Vietnam-supported nationalist/Communist elites • Continued conflict with southern urban bourgeoisie • War with China, Cambodia	• Genocidal overhaul of Cambodian society • Incursions by Cambodia into Vietnam • Vietnamese armed intervention in Cambodia; continued struggle of Sihanouk, former Lon Nol supporters, and Khmer Rouge to regain power

Table 14.1 (continued)

	PHILIPPINES	AFGHANISTAN
SOURCES OF STATE CRISIS	• Economic decline • Loss of nationalist credentials • U.S. pressure to reduce oppression of regime opponents	• Separation of the state from rural/tribal support • Excessive dependence on Soviet aid • Loss of nationalist credentials (Communists)
SOURCES OF ELITE ALIENATION	• Growing exclusion of middle classes from power • Corruption • Attacks on opponents (especially B. Aquino)	• Attacks on traditional elites • Corruption • Factional conflicts among the Communists
SOURCES OF MASS MOBILIZATION	• Population growth and urbanization exceeding economic opportunities • Urban mobilization by electoral and labor organizations • Rural mobilization by NPA (Communists)	• Rural mobilization by tribal and religious leaders • Persecution and legal disorientation resulting from Communist policies • Mobilization by nationalist, Islamic ideologies.
SHAPE OF REVOLUTIONARY STRUGGLE	• Coalition of military reformers and traditional bourgeois/landed elites against Marcos • Conflict of traditional bourgeois/landed elites with both military reformers and rural Communists	• Coalition of tribal and religious leaders against Soviet-backed Communist regime • Conflicts between tribal/religious factions
OUTCOME	• Triumph of traditional bourgeois/landed elites in people power revolution • No rural reforms; conflicts continue with rural ethnic and Communist movements; repeated coup attempts by military reformers	• Soviet intervention to aid regime, sustained guerrilla war • Soviet withdrawal yields a stalemated war, with severe factional conflicts within tribal/religious opposition

	ZIMBABWE	SOUTH AFRICA
SOURCES OF STATE CRISIS	• Excessive costs of war, inability to end violence, international sanctions • Economic decline • International (chiefly British) pressure to achieve majority rule	• Excessive costs of war, inability to end violence and international sanctions • Economic decline • International pressure to achieve majority rule
SOURCES OF ELITE ALIENATION	• Black elites: exclusion from power persecution • White elites: divisions over policy	• Black elites: exclusion from power, persecution • White elites: international opprobrium, divisions over policy
SOURCES OF MASS MOBILIZATION	• Black population growth exceeding economic opportunities • Black population growth reducing relative weight of the white population • Rural mobilization by nationalist leaders (ZANU, ZAPU)	• Black population growth exceeding economic opportunities • Black population growth reducing the relative weight of the white population • Urban mobilization by ANC, Inkatha, AZAPO, COSATU, etc.
SHAPE OF REVOLUTIONARY STRUGGLE	• Coalition of opposition groups against white-led state • Conflicts between political-ethnic factions (mainly ZAPU versus ZANU)	• Lack of opposition coalition; scattered struggles against white-led regime • Conflicts among opposition movements: ANC, Inkatha, AZAPO, etc.
OUTCOME	• Negotiated settlement under international auspices, bringing majority rule and protection for white rights • Triumph of ZANU-PF over all tribal opponents; incorporation of ZAPU; movement toward a one-party state	• Negotiations seeking to resolve conflicts • Sustained conflicts among Africans and between Africans and white-led regime • Conservative white challenges to de Klerk's reform regime, aimed at undermining negotiations

Table 14.1 (continued)

	POLAND	PALESTINE
SOURCES OF STATE CRISIS	• Excessive Western debts and dependence on the USSR • Loss of nationalist credentials • Economic collapse	• Israel: very mild, chiefly costs of war, dependence on United States • PLO: loss of Lebanese base, creating power vacuum in contiguous areas
SOURCES OF ELITE ALIENATION	• Exclusion of technical elites from power in favor of party • Failure of Poland to keep pace with Western Europe • Corruption	• Israeli: divisions over policy • Palestinian: exclusion from power and economic opportunities; persecution • Palestinian: continued economic stagnation • Palestinian: articulation of nationalist ideology
SOURCES OF MASS MOBILIZATION	• Rapid population growth and urbanization exceeding economic opportunities • Support and services by the church • Urban and rural mobilization by Solidarity	• Population growth far exceeding economic opportunities • Popular support and services through PLO • Mobilization by PLO through nationalist/ ethnic, anti-Zionist ideology
SHAPE OF REVOLUTIONARY STRUGGLE	• Coalition of church, intelligentsia, workers, and peasants against the Soviet-backed Communist regime • Military coup, followed by renewed struggle • Withdrawal of Soviet support, followed by negotiations for limited but free elections	• Coalition of external PLO and internal struggles against Israeli occupation
OUTCOME	• Solidarity victory in elections; Solidarity-led government • Continued conflicts over economic policy between left and center urban, rural, and varied political groups • Search for economic reorganization and political stabilization	• Suppression of overt violence • Continuing low-level mobilization in opposition to Israeli occupation

are acting in ways that are fundamentally ineffective, immoral, or unjust. State crises are, in other words, crises of legitimacy. And standards of legitimacy vary widely across cultures, so we cannot say a priori which actions or failures by authorities will lead to crisis.

A key failing in almost every case is the inability of the state to accomplish major tasks it sets for itself: to promote growth, maintain internal order, defend itself against foreign intrusion. The immediate source of ineffective government usually lies in its administrative structure. Most, but not all, the prerevolutionary states surveyed here were hampered by bureaucratic ineptitude and corruption, most clearly in (South) Vietnam, Cambodia, Nicaragua, Iran, Poland, and the Philippines. Afghanistan is a case in which the revolutionary Marxist regime that seized power in 1978 was even more inept than its monarchist predecessor.

In three contrasting instances—Zimbabwe, South Africa, and Israel—the political will and bureaucratic capacity of the regime were high at the onset of conflict, but internal and external pressures escalated so sharply that they exceeded the capacity of the state to resist without change. The major source of internal pressure in these three countries was the rejection of authorities' legitimacy by subordinate ethnic majorities (in the African cases) or large minorities (in the case of Israel). The critical external pressures have been applied by international supporters of these subordinate peoples.

In many cases, demographic factors affected the state's ability to meet goals or maintain effectiveness. The rapid urbanization of Poland, Iran, Nicaragua, and South Africa created problems of social control over dense working-class neighborhoods. The rapid growth of nonwhite populations in Zimbabwe and South Africa and of the Arab population in the Israeli-occupied territories made sustaining economic systems based on those populations' subordination and exclusion increasingly difficult. Also, rapid population growth in all the countries analyzed has made it more difficult to maintain per capita economic growth or has contributed to sharp regional and sectoral income inequities.

In addition, in every contemporary revolution, international factors have contributed directly or indirectly to state crisis. Economic penetration and exploitation were critical factors in Iran, Nicaragua, and Poland, whose ruling elites were widely perceived to be serving and benefiting from foreign economic interests. The presence of foreign advisers and troops in support of prerevolutionary regimes in (South) Vietnam and Cambodia and in revolutionary Afghanistan undercut their rulers' nationalist credentials. In appearance, and soon enough in fact, these rulers were the local agents of superpower rivalries rather than defenders of their countries' own interests. Foreign economic and political penetration played a critical role in undermining the nationalist credentials of the ruling elites in most of the ten cases.

Foreign economic and military presence are the result of deliberate policies that national leaders can in principle resist; not so the transnational inspiration provided by African decolonization in the 1960s and 1970s, which gave great impetus to African nationalism in Rhodesia and South Africa. It is generally true that dramatic political movements, successful revolutions above all, help convince people in similar situations elsewhere that they are the victims of injustice at the hands of dominant groups. International support for a subject people—Palestinians under Israel occupation, blacks in white-ruled southern Africa—helps translate the sense of injustice into political action.

Elite Alienation

At least some of the political and economic elites supporting an old regime must be sufficiently alienated that they seek revolutionary alternatives. All the sources of state crisis just enumerated have the potential for alienating some of the elite, i.e., people whose skills and positions are such that they are able to influence large numbers of others. Some of the elite are disgusted by corruption and inefficiency, some are responding to economic crisis, many become convinced that their rulers have sold out the country or their class. The crucial added factors are conflicts over culture and ideology and conflicts over the distribution of power.

We consider first the cultural dispositions of the elites supporting the old regime. It is quite clear, for example, that some state authorities have undermined the bases of their legitimacy by undertaking actions and policies that violate fundamental elite cultural precepts. The shah of Iran alienated the religious elite by his policies of secularization. In Afghanistan, the Communist regime alienated religious and tribal elites by its socialist policies. For Cambodians, the state was personified and legitimized by the royal family, in the person of Prince Sihanouk, but he was deposed in 1970 by his premier, Lon Nol—an act that led many Cambodians to support Sihanouk's new nationalist movement or the Khmer Rouge counterelite.

In many contemporary societies, particularly those most affected by global political and economic changes, there are multiple ideological streams of influence on elites. In the face of crisis, growing numbers of the elite, especially younger, university-educated people, are likely to reach for other ideological lenses to interpret their world and find pathways out of crisis. The policies of the discredited old elite often shape, by reaction, the ideology of opposition. Superpower intervention may push radicals into the arms of an opposing ideological camp (the Sandinistas embrace Marxism, Solidarity endorses capitalism) or toward xenophobic rejection of any foreign influence (the Khmer Rouge). Secular materialism in an old regime can stimulate a reaffirmation of religious faith, such as that of Islam in Iran and Afghanistan and of Catholicism in Poland.

Ethnic self-determination is one kind of alternative worldview that has had a natural constituency among the leaders and spokespeople for subordinate majorities in Rhodesia and South Africa, and for the Palestinians in the Israeli-occupied territories. But there are few places left in the world where this kind of self-determination can attract a countrywide following because only a handful of countries are still ruled by ethnic minorities. Ethnic self-determination in the twenty-first century is more likely to fuel civil wars—among the Karen and Kurds, the Tamils and Eritreans, nations fighting to establish their own state—than to motivate revolutionary movements.

However, political nationalism—asserting national integrity and self-determination against foreign occupation or influence—has played a key role in many revolutionary struggles. In Iran, Nicaragua, Vietnam, and Cambodia, political nationalism helped bind diverse elites into coalitions against authorities who were believed to be too subservient to the United States; in Poland and Afghanistan, elite nationalist coalitions similarly formed to oppose regimes that were considered subservient to the Soviet Union. Strong national religious traditions—such as Iranian Shi'ism and Polish Catholicism—may then emerge as the basis for nationalist organizations with political aims.

Although ethnic self-determination and political nationalism have played increasing roles in recent revolutionary movements, universalizing ideologies still retain considerable force. Marxism, though fading in Europe and most of Latin America, remains a potent agent in mobilizing popular groups to revolutionary causes in the Philippines and Peru, and it also retains its appeal among elites in several African nations. Nor should we overlook the persisting influence of Western humanism and political egalitarianism, which led Great Britain to put pressure for change on Rhodesia and which weakened the willingness of ruling elites in Zimbabwe, Poland, South Africa, and Israel to continue to rule by force in the face of popular challenges under the banner of political democracy. The same humanist doctrine, when pressed strongly by the Carter administration on U.S. client states, constrained the repressive actions of the shah of Iran, the Somoza clan in Nicaragua, and Marcos in the Philippines. Arguably, it also helped to ensure their defeat.

Alienated members of the elite do not necessarily act politically on their views. Inertia is a powerful force, especially for people with safe and comfortable positions, and fear of reprisal is an equally strong force, ensuring outward loyalty to an old regime. Widespread, passive alienation within an elite nonetheless weakens an old regime because, in the public sphere, it increases careerism and corruption and thus further reduces efficiency. This situation is precisely what crippled the party and state bureaucracies in Communist Poland and other East European regimes.

The second, more active route of elite alienation is conflict over the distribution of power. To the extent that authorities adopt a policy of narrowly confining political power and participation, and excluding or marginalizing religious, technical, business, and labor leaders, they create active opposition, as such marginal elites often take leadership roles in mobilizing opposition against the authorities. Limited attacks on marginal elites by leaders seeking to cow, but not eliminate, opposition—such as the murders of Pedro Joaquín Chamorro in Nicaragua and Benigno Aquino in the Philippines, or the attacks on bazaar merchants and religious elites in Iran—often backfire, increasing and unifying elite opposition. The increasing narrowness and exclusivity of rule by the shah in Iran, Somoza in Nicaragua, and Marcos in the Philippines helped to antagonize and push into active opposition formerly supportive elements of these nations' elites. Similarly, the efforts of the Khalq faction in Afghanistan, the Thieu regime in Vietnam, the Lon Nol clique in Cambodia, and senior Communist party elites in Poland to systematically exclude all people opposed to the regime's policy from power; the racial exclusiveness of the regimes in Rhodesia and South Africa; and the exclusion of Arabs in the Israeli-occupied territories from full citizenship—all these actions forced educated and influential opponents of regime policies into revolutionary roles.

Elite alienation has its greatest potential effect in the armed forces. Most students of revolution agree that a determined ruling class can rely on force to remain in power, even in the face of revolutionary challenges, so long as it has the unquestioned loyalty of the officer corps and troops. The defection of part of the military to the revolutionary side is usually a fatal blow to an old regime. The two clear-cut examples among our cases are Iran and the Philippines, where key officers decided to disobey orders from threatened autocrats, thus opening the way to revolutionary victory. In three other instances—Cambodia, South Vietnam, and Nicaragua— prolonged combat eroded officers' loyalty and soldiers' willingness to fight, but there was no precipitous shift in support from one side to the other.

Mass Mobilization

In principle, revolutionary change can be attempted "from the top down" by determined leaders committed to using all the instruments of the state to engineer social and economic transformation. Ataturk took such a course in Turkey in the 1920s, making it the most modern and secular state in the Islamic world; Lenin and Stalin imposed revolutionary changes in the Soviet Union by force and at great human cost. In practice, most would-be revolutionaries in the late twentieth century have had to mobilize mass followings as part of their strategy for seizing power and reconstructing state and society. The only exception among our ten cases is Afghanistan, in which urban Marxist revolutionaries took power through a coup and then, in a grotesquely misguided attempt to engineer revolutionary change, inspired mass resistance by a conservative rural population under the banner of Islamic fundamentalism.

A wide and deep sense of grievance among ordinary people is a necessary condition for counterelites who seek to mobilize a mass following. There was no shortage of grievances in the prerevolutionary societies we have studied: widespread dissatisfaction over economic conditions, especially among urban peoples; frustration about the lack of opportunities for real political participation, especially among students and the middle classes; widespread anger about foreign intervention and official corruption; and rural hostility toward the predatory and repressive policies of urban-based regimes.

One of the most striking features of our cases is the frequency with which the old regimes followed policies that intensified grievances and focused popular anger on the state. In virtually every instance, threatened governments used force and violence in ways that increased popular resentment and active support for revolutionary movements. In the Philippines and Nicaragua, the government's assassination of respected spokesmen for the liberal opposition—Senator Benigno Aquino in 1983, editor Pedro Chamorro in 1978—was the catalyst for coalition building and mass mobilization among disaffected urban Filipinos and Nicaraguans. In Cambodia and Vietnam, the government's punitive strikes against villagers suspected of supporting rebels pushed many peasants, out of fear or anger, into the ranks of revolutionary armies. In Iran, a turning point in the revolutionary crisis came in September 1978 when the government used gunships and commandos to kill some 4,000 protestors—an appalling act of repression that far from deterring opposition, intensified it and simultaneously undermined the loyalties of some of the military. The South African and Israeli governments have used the less deadly tactics of restricted movement, imprisonment, and harassment to discourage black and Palestinian activists. The legacy of these tactics is embittered resistance and support for revolution among an entire generation of young people.

The opportunities for revolutionary mobilization vary widely, depending on where grievances are concentrated and which aggrieved groups are most accessible to the potential revolutionary leaders. Three patterns of revolutionary mobilization are discernible among our cases. In the Maoist pattern, seen in Vietnam, Cambodia, and Zimbabwe, a cadre party of revolutionaries followed a long-term strategy of political and organizational buildup, mobilizing a mass base of support before challenging the people in power. In the Leninist pattern, seen in Nicaragua and Iran, a vanguard party built up a disciplined opposition organization, positioned itself to take advantage of a spontaneous upsurge in mass opposition, and briefly allied itself with other regime opponents. Once the revolutionary struggle had begun, the vanguard leaders sought to mobilize their followers to dominate the revolutionary struggle and shape the revolution's outcome. In the third, pluralist, pattern, seen in Poland, the Philippines, and the anti-Communist phase in Afghanistan, a number of distinct counterelites joined in mobilizing their followers against the old regime, but they sought to maintain a coalition or pluralist settlement of the revolutionary struggle rather than having one party embark on purges to eliminate all other elements from the postrevolutionary regime. The South African and Palestinian nationalist movements, at this writing, show elements of both Maoist and Leninist strategies, as nationalist organizations seek to both build revolutionary organizations and take advantage of spontaneous popular mobilization, with different factions vying to dominate each revolutionary movement. It remains to be seen whether, as some supporters hope, these movements will adopt a pluralist pattern of mobilization.

The mass bases of revolutionary power may be either urban or rural or both. All ten of our revolutionary (and counterrevolutionary) movements developed in countries with a disproportionately large number of marginal young people—numerous because of high population growth and marginalized by a relative lack of economic opportunities. In Iran, Poland, and South Africa, mobilization was most effective in the rapidly growing urban areas. In Afghanistan, Cambodia, Vietnam, and Rhodesia, the revolutionaries were recruited mainly in the countryside, and in the remaining three cases—Nicaragua, the Philippines, and the West Bank and Gaza—mobilization cut across the urban-rural division.

The social bases for mobilization vary markedly among our cases. In the classic revolutions envisioned by Marxists, economic class is the only conceivable basis for mobilization, though the possibility of cross-class coalitions is granted. Few of our cases fit this classic ideal. Only the Cambodian and Vietnamese revolutionaries followed Marxist precedents, by using the Chinese Maoist precepts for mobilizing a mass peasant following. Religion and ethnicity, which in Marxist thought are supposed to be only vestigial social forces, have both proved to be potent bases for contemporary revolutionary action. The religious-based mobilization of Poles, Iranians, and Afghans has already been mentioned. The Roman Catholic church also played a supporting role in Cory Aquino's people power revolution; reform-minded Catholic activists, energized by Liberation Theology, were one of the pillars of Sandinista support in the war against the Somozas; and Islam reinforces

Palestinian nationalism in the West Bank and Gaza. Thus, religious commitments and connections played a major role in six of the ten cases.

Ethnically based revolutionary movements developed in the two African cases. Ethnicity is the obvious basis for mobilizing opposition when an old regime has held power on behalf of a dominant ethnic group, as in Rhodesia and South Africa, but ethnic loyalties are not a guarantee of revolutionary solidarity in such societies. Nationalist politics in Rhodesia/Zimbabwe have been often split along the faultline that divides Ndebele from Shona, and in South Africa, some coloreds and Asians have supported the Afrikaner government, some whites have worked for the African nationalist cause, and black nationalists have divided into often-hostile camps, particularly the feuding African National Congress and Zulu-based Inkatha movement.

*   *   *

The specific interactions among state crisis, elite alienation, and mass mobilization affect the timing and character of state breakdown. They also help shape the subsequent process of coalition building and constrain in many ways the outcomes of a revolution.

PROCESSES OF REVOLUTIONARY CONFLICT

The necessary condition for the successful revolutionary overthrow of an incumbent government, even if it is in a state of crisis, is the emergence of a broad coalition among its challengers. Such a coalition typically includes significant elements of the elite and mobilized mass support. Without such a coalition, a seizure of power is unlikely to have revolutionary effects, whatever its leaders claim. They may have to give up revolutionary pretensions as the price of holding on to power or face a counterrevolution in reaction to their policies. The latter was the fate of the Afghan Marxists' attempt to impose a revolution from above.

Democratic Coalitions

Probably the most striking development in contemporary revolutionary practice, as distinct from doctrine, is the emergence in several of our cases of new political coalitions that mobilized a cross-section of mainly urban people on behalf of democracy, economic growth, and social justice. Professional, business, and white-collar groups played a major role in these movements, along with intellectuals, students, and a broad spectrum of blue-collar and service workers. Such alliances brought down the Somoza dynasty in Nicaragua and Ferdinand Marcos in the Philippines and ended Communist party rule in Poland, East Germany, Hungary, and Czechoslovakia.

It may be objected that such coalitions are merely alliances of convenience among people whose main bond is opposition to a repressive old regime. This possibility is belied by the fact that in the examples cited above, supporters tended to agree on general principles of civil and political rights and on the need for social and economic reform. Moreover they have accomplished at least six successful revolutions since 1979—more than Marxists have managed to accomplish in twenty-five years.

Prodemocratic revolutionary coalitions are subject to stress and breakdown like any others. Nondemocratic elements in a coalition may be able to dominate and drive out their coalition partners, as the *ulema* did in revolutionary Iran, and the Polish revolutionary coalition is breaking up because the intellectuals and middle classes support economic restructuring, the costs of which fall disproportionately on blue-collar workers in inefficient, state-protected industries. As a consequence, the remnants of a shrinking Solidarity movement have fragmented into blue-collar, white-collar, and rural segments, and there are increasing calls for more effective, perhaps authoritarian, leadership.

Coalition Breakdown and Stalemated Revolutions

Revolutions seldom have neat endings. Often they get bogged down in factional strife among erstwhile coalition partners, abetted by international intervention. The revolutions in Afghanistan, Cambodia, and Nicaragua are now stalemated because of fragmentation among elites and attempts by foreign powers to manipulate their outcomes. In Afghanistan, a Marxist revolutionary elite headquartered in Kabul, well-supplied by the Soviet Union, opposes a fractious coalition of Islamic revolutionary leaders, some of them in exile, who are amply supported by the United States and the Pakistan military. No coherent program of revolutionary change can be pursued by either party unless and until there is a rapprochement or decisive defeat—neither of which now seems likely.

The first phase of the Cambodian revolution was engineered by the Khmer Rouge leadership, which violently eliminated all potential challengers to its rule until forced out of Phnom Penh by invading Vietnamese forces in December 1978. The Vietnamese withdrew in 1989, in the face of strong U.S., Soviet, and ASEAN pressures, but civil war continues. The reconstituted Khmer Rouge leadership still contends for power, in uneasy coalition with supporters of the old royal regime, with an equally revolutionary but less repressive elite still backed by the Vietnamese. The United States, fearful of Khmer Rouge resurgence, in summer 1990 signaled its willingness to change sides, with highly problematic consequences for the long-suffering people of Cambodia.

The Nicaraguan revolution affords another illustration of the process of revolutionary stalemate: The Sandinista coalition encompassed representatives of virtually all social sectors when it seized power in 1979, but the Marxism of the populist Sandinistas soon drove the middle-class moderates out of the coalition, and some of them went shopping for foreign support to strengthen their hand. The Sandinistas, meanwhile, lacked the instinct for the jugular that would have enabled them, like the Bolsheviks in revolutionary Russia, to terrorize their opponents into submission.

These three cases illustrate vividly that protracted civil war is the price of the failure to build and hold together a coalition that encompasses the revolutionary elite and a broad popular base. Narrowly based coalitions may be sufficient, but only if they are ruthless enough to eliminate or drive into impotent exile all potential rivals and schismatics. All three stalemated revolutions demonstrate the crucial role of international support and intervention in shaping revolutionary strategies and outcomes. Each of the revolutionary parties, once in power, had foreign champions prepared to supply material and military support, and groups that opposed or defected from the revolutionary coalition found competing foreign powers who were ready to support counterrevolutionary challenges. Thus, the protracted postrevolutionary struggles in Afghanistan, Cambodia, and Nicaragua are jointly the result of fractures in the revolutionary coalition and competition among foreign supporters of elite factions. In all three countries, the people on behalf of whom the revolutions were fought have ended up as victims rather than victors. More than 1 million noncombatants have died in Afghanistan, as many as 3 million in Cambodia.

Coalitions in Ongoing Revolutions

The ongoing revolutionary struggles in South Africa, in the Philippines, and by the Palestinians also can be characterized in terms of coalitional politics within the revolutionary leadership. In South Africa, the Afrikaner government has acknowledged the African National Congress as the representative of black South Africans, but what looked at first like a move that strengthened the revolutionary coalition led instead to a sharp increase in factional fighting between ANC supporters and the Zulu-based Inkatha—which in August 1990 proclaimed that it was a national political movement. We speculate that there are other, so far less visible, fracture lines that threaten to divide the leadership of the black nationalists from some of the colored and Asian elites and to divide the nascent black bourgeoisie from more radical and less privileged groups in the urban townships.

The Palestinian nationalists have had a dominant coalition headed by Yasir Arafat since 1969, though significant factions have remained outside the umbrella of the PLO. The *intifada* threatened to disrupt the coalition because it gave rise to a new, militant local leadership in the occupied territories, but the thrust of Teitelbaum and Kostiner's analysis is that the PLO has reached out to accommodate and incorporate this grass-roots leadership in the dominant coalition. It is now the Israeli political leaders—the inheritors of what was once a highly cohesive revolutionary elite—who are increasingly in disarray, divided against themselves over how to respond to an opponent who both fights and campaigns for negotiations.

The greatest disarray is evident among the Filipino revolutionaries. The popular movement that brought Cory Aquino to power represented the reforming impulses of the urban middle and professional classes. Efforts to extend the ruling coalition to incorporate significant elements of the left evidently have failed. The Marxist and populist leadership of the New People's Army is again committed to insurgency, and neither the middle-class reformers nor the revolutionary insurgents have much to offer to the Muslim separatists of the southern Philippines. It is now evident that the Aquino revolution of 1986 was simply one dramatic phase of a revolutionary conflict that can be expected to continue indefinitely.

The Role of Violence in Revolutionary Conflict

The use of violence for political ends is central to most definitions of revolution, but the evidence of our ten cases suggests that this is a misplaced emphasis.

Events of the 1980s demonstrate that in some circumstances, revolutions occur without substantial resort to deadly force and that when violence is an intrinsic part of the revolutionary struggle, it is not necessarily of high magnitude. Revolutionary conflicts are, on average, less deadly than civil wars and politicides—the mass murder by the state of its political opponents; the most deadly of our ten revolutionary conflicts are those that attracted foreign military intervention. Finally, the cases provide no consistent evidence that any one kind of armed struggle, or armed defense of an old regime, is likely to be successful.

The Communist win in Vietnam and the Khmer Rouge triumph in Cambodia illustrate the classic revolutionary model of military victory following a protracted period of revolutionary political mobilization and armed struggle. African nationalists in Rhodesia were on the same course when the Smith regime decided to negotiate a settlement. This kind of armed struggle is still a plausible model in predominantly rural, peasant-based societies.

The 1979 overthrow of the shah of Iran was regarded at the time as signaling a new model of revolutionary action, but historically minded scholars could equally well have evoked parallels with events in Paris that led to the French Revolution of 1789. What happened in Iran was an urban-based revolution in a modernizing society in which the peasantry played no significant role. The revolutionaries relied mainly on street demonstrations rather than armed force, and the Iranian regime's attempt to restore order by using violence against unarmed demonstrators illustrates the principle that repression in revolutionary situations is a double-edged sword. As we noted above, that decision widened and intensified support for the revolutionary coalition and led to crippling defections in the Iranian military.

Although it is true that elites who command an old regime seldom give up without a fight, the struggle is not necessarily a violent one. The Communist regime in Poland gave up power to Solidarity after a protracted political contest in which there was virtually no violence, and Poland provided a scenario for more rapid transitions from Communist to multiparty democracy elsewhere in central Europe. The Aquino people power revolution in the Philippines, incomplete though it has proved to be, is another example in which the revolutionary drama was played out in nonviolent street confrontations. In both these situations, though, some members of the old regime were disposed to make a bitter and bloody fight of it—as the shah did for a while in Iran and Ceausescu in Romania. The Filipino and most central European transfers of power were nonviolent because of policy shifts by the United States and the Soviet Union. It was made clear to Marcos and the old-line Communist rulers of central Europe that they no longer had the political or military support of their foreign patrons. So they chose not to fight.

We might wish that the Philippines and central European examples are the bellwether of future revolutionary struggles, but the bloody suppressions of China's democracy movement in June 1989 and of a similar movement in Burma the same year demonstrate that older methods of responding to revolutionary pressures are still part of threatened elites' repertoires of action. Neither the Chinese nor the Burmese regime was susceptible to foreign pressures or withdrawal of support, and both were willing to use overwhelming, unrestrained violence against unarmed demonstrators.

In two of our cases, Zimbabwe and Nicaragua, international pressures were crucial in bringing about a negotiated resolution of what had been militarized revolutionary conflicts. In the Nicaraguan case, the United States and other Central American countries pressured the Sandinista regime into an electoral process that ended in its unexpected defeat in 1990. In Rhodesia, pressure from Great Britain and the United States, reinforced by international sanctions, led the white-settler regime headed by Ian Smith to accept the transfer to majority rule in 1978–1979. Violence was instrumental to both outcomes. It is unlikely that the Rhodesian regime would have made the crucial concessions it did without the escalating pressures caused by the guerrilla warfare of African nationalists. Similarly, the costs of fighting the U.S.-backed contra guerrilla insurgency were instrumental in the Sandinista's decision to put that government to the electoral test.

*   *   *

These comparative observations indicate how diverse the revolutionary process and its immediate outcomes can be, but four general observations can be made. First, the process of revolutionary struggle is largely one of coalition formation and maintenance or breakdown. Second, the extent and duration of violence in the revolutionary process is a function of the decisions and tactics of both (perhaps one should say, all) parties to the conflict. Revolutions are not intrinsically or inevitably violent.

Third, there is a detectable trend away from militarized revolutionary conflict, as in Vietnam and Cambodia, Nicaragua and Afghanistan, toward confrontational tests of political will between revolutionary political movements and old regimes. The alternative winning strategy for modern revolutionaries is to mobilize enough political force, with credible threats of disruption and violence, so that the old leaders are persuaded that the costs and risks of resistance are greater than the costs of early retirement.

The fourth observation, already made but worth repeating, is that international involvement is critical in shaping the revolutionary process and its outcomes. The waning of the cold war has been accompanied by increased reliance in the international community on peaceful means of managing local conflicts that threaten regional stability. In revolutionary situations, this change is manifested in a shift away from military intervention by the superpowers and regional powers toward reliance on pressures and persuasion to bring about negotiated settlements and nonviolent transfers of power. Vietnam, Afghanistan, and Cambodia are examples of the old pattern. The new pattern is exemplified by the course of events in Zimbabwe in 1978–1979, central Europe in 1989, and Nicaragua in 1990. Moreover, there is ample evidence that public and private international pressures, economic and political, have been instrumental in weakening the commitment of the South African government to apartheid. It is less certain whether international pressures can bring the Israeli government to negotiate with Palestinian nationalists.

CONSEQUENCES OF REVOLUTION

The revolutionaries' seizure of power is the necessary precondition for any kind of directed revolutionary change. Their objectives are not necessarily clearly formulated, but they usually face the immediate imperative of consolidating political power. The ten revolutions surveyed in this book include seven in which revolutionaries seized power but only three that are complete as of late 1990, in the sense that the new leadership has consolidated power by either co-opting or eliminating all potential competitors (Vietnam, Iran, and Zimbabwe). The final step in the postrevolutionary consolidation of power took place in Zimbabwe as this chapter was being written: President Robert Mugabe now claims overwhelming electoral support for establishing a one-party state. Poland could be added to this list, except for the evidence cited earlier that the revolutionary coalition has begun to crack.

Whatever the fate of the revolutionary coalition, the longer-term question is how effective the new leaders are in implementing their revolutionary program. Most of our cases are too recent to permit an assessment of these long-term achievements, but their relative progress can be judged along four general dimensions: reconstruction of the state, socioeconomic structure, international position, and prospects for political democracy.

Reconstruction of the State

All ten of the revolutionary seizures of power occurred in states paralyzed by crisis. The question is whether, how, and to what extent the new leaders can create state institutions that are more resilient than those they overthrew. The clearest cases of enhanced state capacity are in Vietnam and Iran, both of which have dealt more or less successfully with international challenges and the postrevolutionary succession of new leadership. Both also have survived considerable economic hardship. Zimbabwe has faced no great internal or external challenges, and Poland's new government confronts extraordinary economic challenges with a state apparatus that is still undergoing drastic changes. The greatest failures of state making occurred in Afghanistan and Nicaragua, where the potential legitimacy of the new institutions was quickly (in Afghanistan) or slowly (in Nicaragua) undermined by the disastrous policies pursued through those institutions.

Socioeconomic Structure

Revolutions invariably are built on popular grievances over socioeconomic issues harnessed to elite ambitions for societal change. This statement suggests two test questions to be asked about the social and economic consequences of revolutionary seizures of power:

- To what extent do the revolutionary leaders remain committed to their original program of revolutionary change?
- To what extent do revolutionary changes address the causes of the popular grievances, and at what cost?

We must recognize that the contents of revolutionary programs virtually always change along the way, not primarily because leaders "sell out" the revolution, but because shifting domestic and international circumstances require "mid-course adjustments." The Vietnamese, Iranian, and Zimbabwean leaders seemingly have remained loyal to their revolutionary ideals. So have Poland's new leaders, but their term in office has been very brief. There have been remarkably few allegations of corruption about the leaderships of Vietnam and Iran and fewer than the African norm in Zimbabwe—one possible indicator of the continuing authenticity and legitimacy of the revolutionary leaders in these states. Nonetheless, the solution of fundamental social and economic problems has largely eluded leaders in all countries. In Afghanistan, Cambodia, Iran, Nicaragua, and Poland, majorities are clearly worse off materially than before the revolution. In the Philippines, most people are no better off, and the traditional land-holding elite still dominates the rural areas. Only in Zimbabwe have economic grievances been even partly met, and the white commercial farming elite there still exercises a disproportionate economic influence.

The Sandinista leadership in Nicaragua enthusiastically pursued a program of socioeconomic change, but it was hampered by external (military) and internal (social) resistance and eventually was voted from office because of economic ruin. Analogously, the Khmer Rouge leaders followed what was unquestionably the most radical program of social and economic reconstruction of the contemporary era, including the virtual annihilation of the old urban and middle classes, and the results were far short of the autarchic and egalitarian, agrarian utopia to which they aspired. They created instead a nightmare that alienated most of the presumed beneficiaries and even many of their own cadres. In Nicaragua and Cambodia, the failures of policies of revolutionary change helped discredit the revolutionary leadership in each country and contributed to their replacement by new leaders. The same fate probably is in store for the Marxist government in Kabul.

The one positive accomplishment of most of the ten revolutions is intangible: They reasserted national identity and autonomy. The two major exceptions on this count are Afghanistan and Cambodia, whose regimes lack authenticity because of their continued dependence on foreign support. Unfortunately, however, the nutritional value of national pride is low.

International Position

One issue is whether any postrevolutionary regime has substantially improved its international standing. The revolutionary governments of Afghanistan, Cambodia, and Nicaragua declined in international standing because through international intervention, they lost much of their old regimes' limited freedom of political action. Vietnam can claim the greatest gains. Its revolutionary forces stalemated the United States, defeated the Saigon regime, and later bloodied the Chinese army in a 1979 border war. By managing to consolidate its two peoples and establishing regional dominance over Laos and Cambodia, this regime has unquestionably gained in international stature. Grudging U.S. moves toward accepting the regime in 1989 and 1990 can only enhance its international position. But its war involvements, and hostility toward China, have badly hurt the country's prospects for development.

Revolutionary Iran has established its credentials among Muslim fundamentalists throughout the world by asserting the primacy of Islamic principles in social and political life and by distancing itself from Western and Soviet influences. On the down side, the costly war with Iraq and hostility toward Western countries have precluded most technological and developmental assistance. Iran almost certainly stands to gain materially and politically by tacitly siding with the West and conservative Arab states against Iraq in the current Gulf crisis.

Zimbabwe has joined the respectable ranks of independent African states and succeeded in maintaining reasonably satisfactory relations with Great Britain and, much more tentatively, with South Africa. But the international stature of the independent, European-dominated Rhodesia could scarcely have been lower. Poland also has improved its international standing from a position that could scarcely have been worse. Its revolutionary politics have been widely praised throughout Europe and the West and emulated in other central European countries. Its radical and abrupt shift toward a free-market economy is being closely scrutinized by policymakers from Moscow to Prague and Bonn to Washington, D.C. The Poles may be admired now for undertaking a massive economic experiment affecting 39 million people, but the country's international position will eventually depend on how well the experiment succeeds.

Prospects for Political Democracy

The most significant revolutionary gains enumerated thus far are political ones: dictators deposed, more effective state institutions founded, national identity re-affirmed, international stature enhanced. One or more such gains can be claimed in six of the eight countries where revolutionaries have already gained power. The final question is whether and under what circumstances revolution can improve the prospects for Western democratic institutions and the defense of civil and political rights. The revolutions in Zimbabwe, Poland, and the Philippines had prodemocracy outcomes, and the same can be claimed for Nicaragua, too, now that the electoral counterrevolution has occurred. The other completed or stalemated revolutions have had very different outcomes. The successful revolutions in Iran and Vietnam spawned authoritarian and repressive regimes that are the antithesis of democracy.

Three circumstances and conditions of revolution jointly determine the chances for revolutions to have prodemocratic outcomes. One is whether the prerevolutionary society has any democratic experience. Democratic values and institutions are far more likely to take root in societies with some democratic traditions, like Poland and the Philippines, than in societies like Vietnam, Iran, and Afghanistan whose political traditions are almost wholly autocratic.

Second are the ideological commitments of the revolutionaries and their sup-porters, domestic and international. Most of the new leaders in central Europe and the Philippines are serious about democracy and are strongly encouraged in their commitment by the United States and Western Europeans. African and Palestinian nationalists and Nicaraguan revolutionaries have more conditional attitudes about democracy: They are prepared to accept democracy if and when it helps maintain popular support, but they may abandon it when it is expedient to do so. In the South African and Palestinian instances, external support and the policies of the South African and Israeli governments can make or break the prospects for a democratic future. There is no discernible elite support for democracy whatsoever among the revolutionary elites of Iran, Afghanistan, Vietnam, or Cambodia.

The most inimical condition for democracy is a protracted and violent revolutionary conflict. Intense conflict hardens attitudes on all sides and convinces the victors that they must rely on force to suppress potential opponents. It takes a full political generation or more to overcome the battle-hardened revolutionaries' habit of relying on force to maintain power. We know of no clear exceptions to this principle in this century, and certainly there are none among the ten cases surveyed.

In Poland and elsewhere in central Europe, the present prospects for democracy are on the positive side of the ledger, but only if their revolutions are not discredited by economic collapse. The revolution in the Philippines and the electoral counterrevolution in Nicaragua initially seemed to improve the chances for democratic outcomes, but these countries' economic problems are so severe that they are at serious risk of more conflict, and intensified conflict can be expected to lead to authoritarian solutions. Aside from the Philippines, none of the Asian revolutions, from Iran to Vietnam, show any potential for democratic political developments in the foreseeable future, and the prospects for democratic outcomes in the revolutionary conflicts under way in South Africa and Palestine hang in the balance. The longer and more bitter those two conflicts are, the less the chances are for settlements that establish democratic institutions and rights.

POLICY IMPLICATIONS

Revolutions threaten local, regional, and international stability. *Most* recent and ongoing warfare in the Third World—the Iran-Iraq war, the Nicaraguan contra war, the wars in the Horn of Africa involving Ethiopia and Somalia, the Tamil war in Sri Lanka, the Shining Path guerrilla war in Peru, the FSLN guerrilla war in El Salvador, the Cambodian and Afghan wars—is the result of revolutionary struggle. At the very least, unexpected regime changes can undo decades of diplomacy spent building alliances and send streams of refugees across borders. Thus, it is unsurprising that the great powers have repeatedly intervened in recent revolutionary situations to try to avert undesirable outcomes.

Yet some of the greatest policy debacles in modern history have arisen from superpower efforts to intervene in revolutionary conflicts. The Bay of Pigs invasion in response to Castro's revolution in Cuba, U.S. intervention in the Vietnam war, the hostage crisis in Iran, the Soviet invasion of Afghanistan, and the Soviet-backed Polish government's initial attempts to suppress Solidarity are efforts that have become synonymous with futility and failure. Indeed, these interventions proved far more harmful to the administrations that attempted them than to the revolutionary actors they sought to control. We do not mean to say that all interventions produce unintended adverse consequences. Great Britain's efforts in resolving the crisis in Zimbabwe, the United States' actions in demanding elections and assisting Marcos's subsequent departure from the Philippines, and the efforts— led by Costa Rica's President Arias—of the Central American states to resolve the Sandinista-contra war demonstrate that some forms of international action can be effective. These examples suggest that effective policy requires selecting reasonable goals and carefully tailoring policy actions to meet those goals.

The goals of reasonable policy with regard to revolutions are first, avoiding being surprised by totally unexpected revolutionary crises; second, seeking to achieve nonhostile relations with the government that emerges to deal with that crisis; and third, seeking to minimize international spillovers, such as wars and disruptive refugee flows. Unreasonable goals include seeking to reverse or arrest a well-advanced revolutionary process. It is precisely in pursuit of such goals—in Cuba, in Vietnam, in Iran, and in Afghanistan—that superpower interventions, even with massive commitments of force, have come to grief.

However, even in pursuit of reasonable goals, the requirements for outstanding intelligence and subtlety of action are quite high. The following suggestions, based on the preceding case studies and the process model of revolution presented in Chapter 3, may therefore often be difficult to follow. In the event of incomplete information, and given that intervention actions so frequently backfire, it may be wise for policy analysts to recommend a "hands off" approach until the smoke of a revolutionary struggle clears and a well-informed policy can be formulated.

Avoiding Unexpected Crises

Although the falls of the shah in Iran, Somoza in Nicaragua, and Marcos in the Philippines and the crises of the Communist regimes in Afghanistan, Poland, and throughout Eastern Europe came as great surprises, the signs that pointed to these revolutionary crises were, in retrospect, quite clear. Indeed, in our current state of knowledge, it is evident that the superpowers supported and encouraged actions by their client regimes that helped to precipitate their downfall.

We have noted that one essential element of a revolutionary situation is a state crisis, involving widespread belief that the ruling regime is ineffective, immoral, or unjust and has lost the nationalist credentials that legitimize its rule. Such views may be difficult to detect by simply querying individuals as to their beliefs—after all, prior to the outbreak of a revolution, individuals have a vested interest in concealing any antiregime sentiments. Thus, the absence of clearly expressed widespread hostility does *not* imply the absence of a state crisis, though the presence of such expressed hostility almost certainly *does* imply a crisis. Since the absence of expressed hostility is not a good indicator of attitudes, it is necessary to seek more objective evidence of state legitimacy. The following five questions provide a useful means of probing a state's legitimacy and vulnerability to crisis.

1. Does the regime have accomplishments to its credit that create a reserve of good will and faith in its effectiveness? Examples are a recent victory in war, prompt action with regard to a famine or earthquake or other crisis, or recent progress in meeting publicly expressed goals of economic growth and equitable development. An affirmative answer suggests prima facie legitimacy. Conversely, a defeat in war, failure to cope effectively with disaster, or clear failure to meet publicly expressed goals are indicators of a regime whose legitimacy may be wearing thin.

2. Does the regime have control of resources in its own society to support its actions in pursuit of its expressed goals, and does it have sufficient fiscal health

to effectively manage its economy? If not—if the regime is excessively dependent on foreign support or foreign borrowing or is seen as helpless or irresponsible in the face of high inflation or recession—the regime is again likely to suffer reduced legitimacy.

3. Does the loyalty of the bureaucracy and army depend on discipline or corruption? A well-disciplined civil service and military can help a regime cope with grave difficulties. By contrast, a corrupt administration both builds contempt for the regime and leads to immediate ineffectiveness in the event that the flow of funds that underwrites the corruption—whether from foreign support or exploitation of resources—suffers any interruption. Thus, a corrupt regime is doubly vulnerable to state crisis.

4. Are elites outside the central government—business and labor leaders, religious leaders, local politicians—well integrated into the framework of power, or do they feel excluded, indifferent, or hostile to the regime? As no government can govern effectively without the support of local political and economic leaders, disaffection or hostility on the part of such leaders carries the potential for a sudden crippling of the regime, which is compounded if effective opposition leaders emerge.

5. Finally, is there evidence of a popular mobilization led by counterelites? The absence of such mobilization is *not* a guarantee of stability, for the previous four conditions have often been sufficient to topple a regime. However, the presence and growth of such mobilization are indicators of the weakening effectiveness and legitimacy of the current rulers.

Those regimes whose recent fall was so "astonishing"—the shah, Somoza, and Communist regimes in Eastern Europe—all were clearly crippled by several of the above problems. Yet the response of the superpowers was, not to consider such multiple problems as symptoms of deeper, possibly unavoidable, crises, but to believe that the regimes were basically sound and only needed treatment for the symptoms. Thus, lack of domestic support or losses to corruption were countered by the provision of additional foreign aid and loans, and such measures only further undermined the nationalist credentials of regimes with already shaky legitimacy. The United States responded to the hostility of business, labor, and local political elites to the shah and Somoza by pressuring those autocrats to reduce their oppression of such elites; it did not (until those leaders had already clearly lost power) insist on the elites' effective incorporation into structures of authority. U.S. policy thus gave counterelites more freedom to mobilize but ignored a root cause of their grievances, and thus, it hastened the fall of those client regimes.

The most effective response to such a situation came in the Philippines, where U.S. policy leaders—particularly in Congress—recognized the multiple indicators of failing regime legitimacy. They successfully urged the U.S. administration not to seek to shore up the Marcos regime but to insist on new elections, and then facilitate Marcos's departure when his lack of support was fully demonstrated. Mikhail Gorbachev took a similarly far-sighted approach in response to prodemocracy movements in East Germany and Czechoslovakia in 1989: He encouraged Communist leaders in those countries to choose political reform rather than violent response.

In sum, concrete signs of impending state crises are not invisible, although the actual attitudes of people may be concealed. Thus, rather than wait for clear signs of widespread overt opposition, superpowers should realize that regimes that show multiple symptoms of an impending crisis, such as a lack of positive accomplishments, inadequate resources or foreign dependency, corruption, exclusion, and counter-mobilization, are in deep trouble and cannot be shored up indefinitely. If the basic regime attitudes and structures that produced these symptoms cannot be rectified, one should brace for the emergence of a revolutionary struggle in such states.[1]

Achieving Nonhostile Relations During and After Revolutionary Struggles

A state crisis blossoms into a revolutionary struggle when a regime is reduced to reacting to opposition actions it can no longer discourage or control. At this point, latent elite opposition is likely to emerge in full, and mass mobilization—if not already well under way—will accelerate. When facing such a struggle, several outcomes are possible. If the regime retains sufficient military reserves and popular support to restore control, it has three options: massive repression; reform to alleviate the reasons for the state crisis and popular opposition; or creating divisions among the opposition to the regime so that the opposition is paralyzed by infighting and the regime has the opportunity to eliminate opponents one at a time, or to pose as the sole unifying force and peacemaker. The first option is an effective, albeit temporary, solution, for it does nothing to change the structural conditions that led to the crisis. If such conditions continue, further weakening the state and increasing elite and popular opposition, a similar situation will reemerge in relatively short order, perhaps in a decade or two at most.[2] To the extent that foreign powers are involved in supporting such repression, their action is liable to accelerate the return of a crisis, as such support further deprives the regime of nationalist credentials. Moreover, such support almost guarantees that in the next crisis, the foreign supporter will encounter hostility and distrust from the opposition, which makes future friendly relations difficult, if not impossible, to achieve.

The option of reform has been effective—from the reform movement of 1832 in Great Britain to the resolution of the Polish Solidarity, Zimbabwean, and Nicaraguan-contra struggles—but such reform is possible only when a precise balance of power prevails. First, if the old regime is sufficiently weakened that its demise seems imminent, the opposition has no incentive to accept reforms in lieu of a forceful seizure of power. Thus, reforms must be undertaken while the old regime is still strong enough to undertake a long fight in its defense. Second, the opposition must be strong enough to pose a credible threat of continued disruption if the regime does not undertake reform, and have sufficient mobilized support and resources to be able to participate in the offered reforms (electoral or administrative), but not so strong that it believes it can get a better deal by continued exercise of force. In other words, reform is most likely when a still militarily dominant regime is bogged down in a costly struggle with an opposition that, although able to inflict damage, is unlikely to attain victory in the near future. These conditions obtained in Zimbabwe and Sandinista Nicaragua prior to their internationally-brokered settlements, and roughly obtain today in South Africa, the Philippines, Afghanistan, Cambodia, and the Israeli-occupied territories.

However, the examples of Zimbabwe and Nicaragua suggest two other conditions that are vital for reform. First, both the regime and the opposition must relax ideological claims that prevent compromises. Thus, the regime must be willing to make real reforms, which involve power sharing, rather than cosmetic reforms aimed merely at defusing conflict; similarly, the opposition must be willing to respect and maintain key interests of the regime and its supporters, rather than using reforms as a prelude to future radical change. Such "covert agendas" can disable efforts to achieve stable reforms. Pressure on both regimes and oppositions to make such compromises can come from broad international sanctions or from direct pressure by supporters—such as the Soviet Union's pressure on Poland's government to deal with Solidarity or the United States' pressure on the contras to disarm if the Sandinistas held elections. Second, the transition to reform is greatly aided by the mediation and intervention of trusted third parties who can supervise disarmament, elections, and the construction of a new administration. Without such a trusted intermediary, suspicion of covert agendas may undermine any peace process. However, a major obstacle is that powers that are putting pressure on one party to compromise by threatening to reduce bilateral support are generally unable to also act as impartial mediators of reform. One of the reasons that revolutionary struggles have reached ongoing stalemates in Afghanistan, Cambodia, and Palestine is that most potential mediators had already committed themselves to supporting one or another party to the conflict. Nonetheless, one of the most welcome lessons of this volume is that even long-standing revolutionary struggles can be resolved through reform, provided that pressure is put on actors to accept compromise terms (via international sanctions or by bilateral pressure) and trusted third parties can be found to mediate and supervise their implementation. The United Nations and regional organizations may be particularly valuable in the latter role.

The third strategy—taking advantage of divisions among regime opponents—is, like massive repression, at best a short-term expedient and does not prevent the likelihood of future crises (as is evident in South Africa, which has tried for decades to substitute this strategy for massive repression). This strategy is most effective in the long run for a regime facing a narrow opposition (such as a regional or an ethnic separatist movement) while the bulk of the population still considers the regime to be legitimate. When the regime's legitimacy is already widely questioned, encouraging and playing on opposition divisions—although such a strategy has great appeal to weakened regimes and their allies, who may see no other recourse for holding on to power—tends to discredit both the regime and its supporter in the long run. This was the result, for example, of the 1953 U.S.-supported coup against Mossadegh in Iran, which was intended to restore the stability of the shah's regime. A more successful interventionist strategy in the case of a severely weakened regime facing a divided opposition may be to encourage the opposition factions to unite and assist the smooth departure of the discredited regime, in a manner similar to the U.S. policy that led to Marcos's departure from the Philippines.

However, dealing with factions in a revolutionary struggle is a precarious task. Foreign support for a particular faction may backfire and end up discrediting that faction's nationalist credentials. Miscalculating the strength and coherence of different factions may lead to futile policies, such as the Reagan administration's "arms for hostages" deals with Iranian "moderates." Thus, policy actions are best taken with a bias toward caution. When a weakened regime faces an opposition whose coherence, and factional dominance, are shifting and unclear, the best action for an outside party may be to distance itself from the conflict and await an outcome. In such situations, any more interventionist actions are likely to be counterproductive. The United States' initial caution in response to Shi'ite and Kurdish resistance to Saddam Hussein's regime in postwar Iraq (March 1991) seems based on recognition of this principle.

Once a new regime has established itself in power following a revolutionary struggle, further diagnoses must be made—Is the new regime moderate or radical? and Does it have a mass-mobilized base and a willingness to undertake aggressive reforms? It is often the case that the first group to take power in the course of a revolutionary struggle is a moderate leadership with wide ideological appeal but limited mass-mobilized support and a limited willingness to implement radical change to resolve the structural problems that delegitimized the former regime. A classic example is the Kerensky regime of 1917 in Russia; a modern example is the Aquino regime in the Philippines. Such regimes are unstable. Lacking their own mass-mobilized base, they leave space for countermobilization by more radical or conservative groups; moreover, the continuation of economic weakness, corruption, and lack of accomplishments will, in time, undermine their appeal as it undermined the former regime. Thus, if a new regime is of this unstable, moderate type and its continuation is desired, it is essential to press the regime into efforts toward mass mobilization, reform, and attainment of secure accomplishments. Without these actions, mere provision of financial or military support will not create stability; indeed, as in the case of support for any regime of dubious stability and declining legitimacy, such support is likely to backfire and undermine the nationalist credentials of the aided regime and increase opposition hostility to the regime's supporter. This is the pattern unfolding in the Philippines as this chapter is written.

If a new regime is radical and hostile, there is little that interventionist policy can do. Any attempts to undermine or overthrow the regime simply add to the new regime's ability to draw on patriotic sentiment to ensure its support, as was the case in Iran and Nicaragua. A better policy may be to disengage and allow the radical regime to undermine its own legitimacy if it should pursue extreme domestic policies, as happened quickly to the Sandinista regime in Nicaragua and the Pol Pot regime in Cambodia and more slowly to the Communist regimes in Vietnam and Cuba. However, the rise of radical regimes raises great risks, and therefore crucial policy issues, with regard to international war.

Minimizing the Threat of War

There is a vast, largely inconclusive, literature on the relationship between revolution and war, though the studies that are broadest in scope clearly and strongly link new revolutionary regimes to an increased likelihood of war. The limitation of most of this literature rests in its treatment of revolutionary regimes as unitary; considerably richer insight is gained by focusing, as in this volume, on the dynamics of revolutionary coalitions.

The risks of international war in the wake of revolutionary struggles vary according to whether the factional conflicts within the revolutionary coalitions are strong or weak and whether or not a major role is played by radical factions— that is, factions whose goal is a major transformation of political and economic structures. If a united, moderate regime emerges from the revolutionary struggle, with few counterrevolutionary or radical threats to face, the risks of international war are decreased (although a moderate regime may continue to fight to expel an invasion begun under the old regime, as Kerensky fought Germany in World War I, and the Yugoslav partisans fought Germany in World War II.) For example, the resolutions of the Zimbabwean conflict and that in Namibia have reduced the pressures for war in southern Africa, and the electoral settlement of the Nicaraguan contra conflict has reduced war fears in Central America.

However, if a revolutionary coalition has sharp divisions among moderates, conservatives, and radicals, leading to drawn-out power struggles, and especially if the radicals obtain power, the risks of international war rise sharply. War then can arise from a wide variety of causes. One, any faction (including old-regime supporters who see an opening in continued conflict) may call on foreign powers for support in their struggle. Two, any faction may seek to start a foreign war to marshal patriotic support and distract from flaws in its domestic program (radicals seem particularly likely to do this). Three, foreign powers may act aggressively, seeking to take advantage of a nation that seems weakened by internal factional problems. Four, foreign powers may act defensively, fearing the spread of radical ideology and power into their states or because they are overwhelmed by a flood of refugees (again this possibility seems particularly likely if a radical faction takes power). Adding to these multiple risks of war is the paranoia common to radical factions who have achieved power only after a sustained struggle against a determined regime. Such factions are likely to see counterrevolutionary threats everywhere and to feel threatened unless they are successful in subverting neighboring countries to their cause.

In the face of such strong risks for war, can policy actions achieve any reduction of risk? The best solution lies in international cooperation to discourage aggression, both by the revolutionary regime and by opportunistic neighbors. Such discouragement requires relieving the fear of revolutionary regimes that they may be attacked by extending normal diplomatic relations and relieving the fear of neighboring regimes by promising strong international support in the event of aggression by the revolutionary regime. Conversely, opportunistic neighbors should be restrained with the threat of a weapons embargo or other sanctions if they act aggressively toward the revolutionary state. In the event that international cooperation can achieve a pact not to interfere in a revolutionary struggle, situations such as those in Afghanistan and Cambodia, where internal faction struggles have spilled over into international conflicts, might be avoided.

When a strong radical faction establishes control of a revolutionary regime, war becomes highly likely. In this circumstance, the best strategy for minimizing war's impact may be to respond to revolutions with a reduction of armament shipments to the affected region. Had the United States reacted to the weakening of the shah's regime in the 1970s by reducing, rather than increasing, the flow of sophisticated weapons to Iran and carefully limited its arming of Iraq in response to the Iranian revolution, Iraq's aggression, and the eventual consequences of the Iran-Iraq conflict, might have been greatly reduced. In short, the superior strategy for minimizing international conflict seems to be to limit the adverse consequences of revolution rather than to support war in pursuit of the unreasonable goal of reversing or arresting a well-entrenched revolution. In addition, early preparation of international support for coping with refugee flows may help prevent such refugees from becoming sources of war passions or recruits for armies, as has occurred in Afghanistan, Cambodia, and Palestine.

THE FUTURE OF REVOLUTION

In the 1960s, revolutions were viewed through the prism of the cold war; regime changes were seen as the consequence of superpower interventions for their advantage. From the perspective of the 1990s, it is evident how often such interventions have miscarried, creating unwanted wars and hostility rather than policy gains. Moreover, it is evident that revolutions are created and driven by internal regime dynamics, so the end of the cold war will not mean the end of revolutions.

In Africa, Latin America, Eastern Europe, Asia, and the Middle East, there are many regimes of dubious legitimacy and stability, and even in currently sound regimes, failed domestic policies can lead to state crises. Revolutionary situations continue, at this writing, in South Africa, Angola, the Horn of Africa, the Philippines, Sri Lanka, Burma, Peru, El Salvador, Palestine, Iraq, most of Eastern Europe, and many republics of the Soviet Union. Analyzing revolutions therefore is not simply a means of understanding the past—it remains vital to comprehending the present and the future.

NOTES

1. It is interesting to examine the history of the Soviet Union in light of these factors. Stalin's regime, despite its severe tyranny, was by this analysis quite stable, with its achievements in rapid industrialization, victory in World War II, a vast bureaucracy disciplined by fear, and the extension of loyal local party commissars throughout society. In contrast, Brezhnev's regime, which was marked by a lack of economic or military accomplishments, growing corruption, and hostility of the technocratic factory managers and intelligentsia, was beginning to store up the ingredients of a legitimacy crisis. Gorbachev's regime—with few accomplishments outside of international peace treaties; with rapidly shrinking resources; unable to control either the economy or the rampant corruption; drawing the hostility of skilled labor, and to an increasing degree that of technocrats and the intelligentsia, and to an unprecedented degree the hostility of local governments; and experiencing rapid and extensive countermobilization—is unlikely to escape from its current crisis. Given these conditions, current U.S. policy orientation, which deals primarily with Gorbachev and seeks to encourage and rely on his continued influence while downplaying his opposition, may be repeating the same mistakes that were made in dealing with the shah and Somoza.

2. The long-term futility of repression is most evident in the history of France. Following the French Revolution, when foreign powers sought to restore the Bourbon monarchy, it took the entire concert of Europe and the Russian winter to defeat Napoleon. The restored Bourbon monarchy then collapsed in just over a dozen years. Moreover, the continued conflict among royalist, Orleanist (those groups favoring a constitutional monarchy), and republican parties, whose resolution was arrested by the restoration of the monarchy, continued to destabilize French politics and led to further revolutions and coups until the establishment of the Third Republic in 1870. The legacy of the Bourbon Restoration in 1815 was thus fifty-five years of further instability.

REFERENCES AND
SELECTED BIBLIOGRAPHY

Abrahamian, Ervand. 1980. Structural Causes of the Iranian Revolution. *Middle East Research and Information Project (MERIP)* 87:21–26.
———. 1982. *Iran Between Two Revolutions*. Princeton: Princeton University Press.
——— 1986. Discussants Remarks. In N. R. Keddie and E. Hooglund, eds., *The Iranian Revolution & the Islamic Republic*, pp. 84–86. Syracuse, N.Y.: Syracuse University Press.
Abu 'Amr, Z. 1988. Notes on Palestinian Political Leadership: The "Personalities" of the Occupied Territories. *Middle East Report* 18:23–25.
Adelman, Jonathan R. 1985. *Revolution, Armies, and War: A Political History*. Boulder, Colo.: Lynne Rienner.
Afghan Social Democratic party. 1987. Representation, Democracy, and the Afghan Resistance. *Janata* (India) 6:11–14.
Afshar, Haleh, ed. 1985. *Iran: A Revolution in Turmoil*. Albany: State University of New York Press.
Agere, S. T. 1986. Progress and Problems in the Health Care Delivery System. In I. Mandaza, ed., *Zimbabwe: The Political Economy of Transition 1980–1986*, pp. 355–376. Dakar: CODESRIA.
Ahady, A. 1987. Prospects for Peace in Afghanistan. Paper presented at the Sixteenth Annual Conference on South Asia held at the University of Wisconsin, November 8–11.
Akhavi, Sharoough. 1980. *Religion and Politics in Contemporary Iran*. Albany: State University of New York Press.
———. 1982. Shariati's Social Thought. In N. Keddie, ed., *Religion and Politics in Iran*, pp. 125–144. New Haven: Yale University Press.
Algar, Hamid. 1980. *The Constitution of the Islamic Republic of Iran*. Berkeley, Calif.: Mizan Press.
Amirahmadi, Hooshang, and Manoucher Parvin, eds. 1988. *Post-Revolutionary Iran*. Boulder, Colo.: Westview Press.
Amuzegar, J., and M. Ali Fekrat. 1971. *Iran: Economic Development under Dualistic Conditions*. Chicago: University of Chicago Press.
Anderson, J. 1988. They Who Throw Stones. *Harper's Magazine* (July):60–66.

Anderson, Lee. 1982. *Alternative Perspectives on Global Systems*. Evanston, Ill.: North-western University, Department of Political Science.

Andrews, Nicholas G. 1985. *Poland 1980–81: Solidarity Versus the Party*. Washington, D.C.: National Defense University Press.

Anonymous. 1987. The Political Economy of Zimbabwe: Is Zimbabwe in Transition to Socialism? *South African Labor Bulletin* 12:39–47.

Arabia—The Islamic World Review. Various years.

Arjomand, Said Amir. 1984. *The Shadow of God and the Hidden Imam*. Chicago: University of Chicago Press.

———. 1986. Iran's Islamic Revolution in Comparative Perspective. *World Politics* 38:383–414.

Arnold, A. 1983. *Afghanistan's Two-Party Communism*. Stanford, Calif.: Hoover Institute Press.

Ascherson, Neal. 1982. *The Polish August: The Self-Limiting Revolution*. New York: Viking Press.

Ashraf, Ahmad. 1989. There Is a Feeling that the Regime Owes Something to the People. *Middle East Report* 19:13–18.

Astrow, A. 1983. *Zimbabwe: A Revolution That Lost Its Way?* London: Zed.

Austin, R. 1975. *Racism and Apartheid in Southern Africa and Rhodesia*. Paris: UNESCO.

Baker, C. 1982. Conducting the Elections in Zimbabwe 1980. *Public Administration and Development* 2:45–58.

Baker, D. G. 1979. Time Suspended: The Quenet Report and White Racial Dominance in Rhodesia. *Zambezia* 7:243–253.

Bakhash, Shaul. 1984. *The Reign of the Ayatollahs: Iran and the Islamic Revolution*. New York: Basic Books.

Barber, J. 1967. *Rhodesia: The Road to Rebellion*. London: Oxford University Press.

Barron, John, and Anthony Paul. 1977. *Murder of a Gentle Land: The Untold Story of Communist Genocide in Cambodia*. New York: Reader's Digest Press.

Bazargan, Mehdi. 1986. *Enghelab e Iran dar do Harkat* [The two phases of the Iranian revolution]. Tehran.

Beckett, I.F.W. 1985. The Rhodesian Army: Counter-insurgency, 1972–1979. In I.F.W. Beckett and J. Pimlott, eds., *Armed Forces & Modern Counter-Insurgency*, pp. 163–189. New York: St. Martin's Press.

Beckman, G. M. 1962. *The Modernization of China and Japan*. New York: Harper and Row.

Bello, Walden, David Kinely, and Elaine Elinson. 1982. *Development Debacle: The World Bank in the Philippines*. San Francisco: Institute for Food and Development Policy.

Benvenisti, M., et al. 1986. *The West Bank Handbook: A Political Lexicon*. Jerusalem: West Bank Data Project.

Bethlehem, Ronald William. 1988. *Economics in a Revolutionary Society*. Cape Town: Donker Publishing.

Bill, James. 1988. *The Eagle and the Lion: The Tragedy of American-Iranian Relations*. New Haven: Yale University Press.

Blake, David, and Robert Walters. 1983. *The Politics of Global Economic Relations*. Englewood Cliffs, N.J.: Prentice-Hall.

Blejer, Mario I., and Isabel Guerrero. 1988. Stabilization Policies and Income Distribution in the Philippines. *Finance & Development* 25 (December):6–8.

Booth, John. 1985. *The End and the Beginning: The Nicaraguan Revolution*. Boulder, Colo.: Westview Press.

Boudarel, G. 1971. Essai sur la pensee militaire Vietnamienne. In J. Chesneaux, ed., *Tradition et revolution au Vietnam*, pp. 460–495. Paris: Anthropos.

Bowman, L. W. 1973. *Politics in Rhodesia*. Cambridge: Harvard University Press.

Bradshaw, H. 1985. *Afghanistan and the Soviet Union*. Durham: Duke University Press.

Bratton, M. 1981. Development in Zimbabwe: Strategy and Tactics. *Journal of Modern African Studies* 19:447–475.

————. 1987. The Comrades and the Countryside: The Politics of Agricultural Policy in Zimbabwe. *World Politics* 39:174–202.

Bratton, M., and S. Burgess. 1987. Afro-Marxism in a Market Economy: Public Policy in Zimbabwe. In E. J. Keller and D. Rothchild, eds., *Afro-Marxist Regimes*, pp. 199–222. Boulder, Colo.: Lynne Rienner.

Brewer, John D. 1986. *After Soweto*. Oxford: Clarendon Press.

Brzezinski, Zbigniew. 1983. *Power and Principle: Memoirs of the National Security Advisor, 1977–1981*. New York: Farrar, Straus and Giroux.

Brinton, Crane. 1965. *The Anatomy of Revolution*. Rev. ed. New York: Vintage.

Bunce, Valerie. 1989. The Polish Crisis of 1980–81 and Theories of Revolution. In T. Boswell, ed., *Revolution in the World System*, pp. 167–188. New York: Greenwood Press.

Burton, Michael G. 1984. Elites and Collective Protest. *Sociological Quarterly* 25:45–66.

Burton, Michael G., and John Higley. 1987. Invitation to Elite Theory: The Basic Contentions Reconsidered. In G. William Domhoff and Thomas R. Dye, eds., *Power Elites and Organizations*, pp. 133–143. Beverly Hills, Calif.: Sage.

Buttinger, J. 1958. *The Smaller Dragon: A Political History of Vietnam*. New York: Praeger.

Calhoun, Craig. 1983. The Radicalism of Tradition: Community Strength or Venerable Disguise and Borrowed Language? *American Journal of Sociology* 88:886–914.

Carney, Martin. 1984. *The State and Political Theory*. Princeton: Princeton University Press.

Carney, Timothy M. 1983. Kampuchea in 1982: Political and Military Escalation. *Asian Survey* 23:1:73–83.

Carter, Jimmy. 1982. *Keeping Faith: Memoirs of a President*. Toronto and New York: Bantam.

Central Bureau of Statistics. *See Statistical Abstract of Israel*.

Central Intelligence Agency. 1986. *Handbook of Economic Statistics*. Washington, D.C.: U.S. government.

Chaliand, Gerard. 1977. *Revolution in the Third World: Myths and Prospects*. New York: Viking.

Chaliand, Gerard, ed. 1980. *People Without a Country: The Kurds and Kurdistan*. London: Zed.

Chandler, David P. 1975. An Anti-Vietnamese Rebellion in Early Nineteenth-Century Cambodia: Pre-Colonial Imperialism and a Pre-Nationalist Response. *Journal of Southeast Asian Studies* 6:1:16–24.

————. 1983a. *A History of Cambodia*. Boulder, Colo.: Westview Press.

————. 1983b. Strategies for Survival in Kampuchea. *Current History* 82 (April):149–153.

Cheater, A. P. 1988. Contradictions in Modelling "Consciousness": Zimbabwean Proletarians in the Making? *Journal of Southern African Studies* 14:291–303.

Chimombe, T. 1986. Foreign Capital. In I. Mandaza, ed., *Zimbabwe: The Political Economy of Transition 1980–1986*, pp. 123–140. Dakar: CODESRIA.

Chomsky, Noam, and E. S. Herman. 1979. *After the Cataclysm: Postwar Indochina and the Reconstruction of Imperial Ideology*. Boston: South End Press.

Chubin, Shahram, and Charles Tripp, eds. 1988. *Iran and Iraq at War*. Boulder, Colo.: Westview Press.

Chung, F. 1988. Education: Revolution or Reform? In C. Stoneman, ed., *Zimbabwe's Prospects*, pp. 118–132. London: Macmillan.

Clarke, D. G. 1977. The Distribution of Income and Wealth in Rhodesia. *Mambo Occasional Papers*, Socio-Economic Series no. 7. Gwelo, Rhodesia: Mambo Press.

Cliffe, J. T. 1984. *The Puritan Gentry*. London: Routledge and Kegan Paul.

Cliffe, L. 1988. The Prospects for Agricultural Transformation in Zimbabwe. In C. Stoneman, ed., *Zimbabwe's Prospects*, pp. 309–325. London: Macmillan.

Cliffe, L., J. Mpofu, and B. Munslow. 1980. Nationalist Politics in Zimbabwe: The 1980 Elections and Beyond. *Review of African Political Economy* 18:44–67.

Clough, M. 1982. From Rhodesia to Zimbabwe. In M. Clough, ed., *Changing Realities in Southern Africa*, pp. 1–60. Berkeley: University of California Press.

Cohen, A. 1975. *Theories of Revolution: An Introduction*. London: Nelson.

———. 1982. *Political Parties in the West Bank Under the Jordanian Regime*. Ithaca: Cornell University Press.

Colbert, E. 1985. The Great Powers and Cambodia. In *Southeast Asia: Problems and Prospects. A Conference Report*. Washington, D.C.: Center for Strategic and International Studies, Georgetown Univeristy.

Colburn, Forrest. 1986. *Post-Revolutionary Nicaragua: State, Class, and the Dilemmas of Agrarian Policy*. Berkeley: University of California Press.

Cole, Juan R. I., and Nikki R. Keddie, eds. 1986. *Shi'ism and Social Protest*. New Haven and London: Yale University Press.

Confidential U.S. State Department Central Files. 1945–1954. Iran: Internal Affairs and Foreign Affairs. Washington, D.C. Microfilm.

Cottam, Richard. 1979. *Nationalism in Iran*. Pittsburgh: University of Pittsburgh Press.

———. 1986. The Iranian Revolution. In J.R.I. Cole and Nikki R. Keddie, eds., *Shi'ism and Social Protest*, pp. 55–87. New Haven: Yale University Press.

Dao Van Tap. 1980. *35 nam kinh-te Viet-Nam (1945–1980)* [Thirty-five years of the economy of Viet-Nam (1945–1980)]. Hanoi: Nha Xuat-ban Khoa-hoc Xa-hoi.

Davidow, J. 1983. Zimbabwe Is a Success. *Foreign Policy* 49:93–106.

———. 1984. *A Peace in Southern Africa: The Lancaster House Conference on Rhodesia, 1979*. Boulder, Colo.: Westview Press.

Davies, R. 1988. The Transition to Socialism in Zimbabwe: Some Areas for Debate. In C. Stoneman, ed., *Zimbabwe's Prospects*, pp. 18–31. London: Macmillan.

Day, J. 1967. *International Nationalism*. London: Routledge and Kegan Paul.

———. 1969. Southern Rhodesian African Nationalists and the 1961 Constitution. *Journal of Modern African Studies* 1–2:221–247.

———. 1980. The Insignificance of Tribe in the African Politics of Zimbabwe Rhodesia. *Journal of Commonwealth and Comparative Politics* 18:86–109.

Deckmejian, R. H. 1985. *Islam in Revolution*. Syracuse, N.Y.: Syracuse University Press.

Deutsch, K. 1961. Social Mobilization and Political Development. *American Political Science Review* 55: 493–514.

Dix, Robert. 1983. Varieties of Revolution. *Comparative Politics* 15:281–293.

Djilas, Milovan. 1957. *The New Class*. New York: Praeger.

Dollard, J., L. W. Doob, N. E. Miller, O. H. Mowrer, and R. R. Sears. 1939. *Frustration and Aggression*. New Haven: Yale University Press.

Doran, Walter. 1971. *Competition for Empire: 1740–1763*. New York: Norton.

Duiker, W. J. 1980. Vietnamese Revolutionary Doctrine in Comparative Perspective. In W. Turley, ed., *Vietnamese Communism in Comparative Perspective*, pp. 45–73. Boulder, Colo.: Westview Press.

———. 1981. *The Communist Road to Power in Vietnam*. Boulder, Colo.: Westview Press.

————. 1985. *Vietnam Since the Fall of Saigon.* Athens, Ohio: Ohio University Press. Monographs in International Studies—South East Asia Series no. 6.

Dunn, John. 1972. *Modern Revolutions: An Introduction to the Analysis of a Political Phenomenon.* Cambridge: Cambridge University Press.

Dupree, L. 1973. *Afghanistan.* Princeton: Princeton University Press.

————. 1979. *The Democratic Republic of Afghanistan, 1979.* Hanover, N.H.: AUFS.

Dupree, N. 1984. Revolutionary Rhetoric and Afghan Women. In M. N. Shahrani and R. Canfield, eds., *Revolution and Rebellion in Afghanistan,* pp. 306–340. Berkeley, Calif.: Institute of International Studies.

Easton, D. 1957. An Approach to the Analysis of Political Systems. *World Politics* 9:383–400.

————. 1969. The New Revolution in Political Science. *American Political Science Review* 63:1051–1061.

Eckstein, Susan. 1982. The Impact of Revolution on Social Welfare in Latin America. *Theory and Society* 11:43–94.

Economic Intelligence Unit. 1989. *South Africa, 1989–1990.* London: Economic Intelligence Unit.

Edwards, D. B. 1987. Origins of the Anti-Soviet Jihad. In G. M. Farr and J. M. Merriam, eds., *Afghan Resistance: The Politics of Survival,* pp. 21–50. Boulder, Colo.: Westview Press.

Eisenstadt, S. N. 1978. *Revolution and the Transformation of Societies: A Comparative Study.* New York: Free Press.

England, R. 1987. Zimbabwean Co-ops and Class Struggle. *South African Labour Bulletin* 12:122–148.

Etcheson, Craig. 1984. *The Rise and Demise of Democratic Kampuchea.* Boulder, Colo.: Westview Press.

Falk, Richard, and Samuel Kim. 1980. *The War System, An Interdisciplinary Approach.* Boulder, Colo.: Westview Press.

Fall, B. B. 1963. *The Two Viet-Nams.* New York: Praeger.

————. 1966. *Hell in a Very Small Place: The Siege of Dien Bien Phu.* Philadelphia: Lippincott.

————. 1967. *Ho Chi Minh on Revolution.* New York: Praeger.

————. 1972. *Last Reflections on a War.* New York: Schocken Books.

Farhi, Farideh. 1990. *States and Urban-Based Revolutions: Iran and Nicaragua.* Urbana and Chicago: University of Illinois Press.

Fischer, Michael. 1980. *Iran: From Religious Dispute to Revolution.* Cambridge: Harvard University Press.

Fitzgerald, E.V.K. 1987. An Evaluation of the Economic Costs of U.S. Aggression: 1980–1984. In Rose Spalding, ed., *The Political Economy of Revolutionary Nicaragua,* pp. 195–213. New York: Allen and Unwin.

Ford, R. 1986. Growth and Structure of the Economy. In R. F. Nyrop and D. M. Seekins, eds., *Afghanistan: A Country Study,* pp. 139–208. Washington, D.C.: Government Printing Office.

Foreign Broadcasting Information Service (FBIS). *Reports.* Washington, D.C.: U.S. Government.

Frisch, H. 1988. The West Bank and the Gaza Strip. *Middle East Contemporary Survey* (*MECS*) (Tel Aviv: Dayan Center for Middle Eastern and African Studies, Tel Aviv University) 12:277–305.

Fulbrook, Mary. 1983. *Piety and Politics.* Cambridge: Cambridge University Press.

Gann, L. H., and T. H. Henriksen. 1981. *The Struggle for Zimbabwe: Battle in the Bush.* New York: Praeger.

Gay, Peter. 1971. *The Party of Humanity*. New York: Norton.

Gettleman, M., ed. 1965. *Viet Nam*. New York: Fawcett Publications.

Giai-Phong Editions. 1969. *Who's Who of the Republic of South Viet-Nam*. South Vietnam: Giai-Phong Editions.

Gibson, Bill. 1987. A Structural Overview of the Nicaraguan Economy. In Rose Spalding, ed., *The Political Economy of Revolutionary Nicaragua*, pp. 15–41. New York: Allen and Unwin.

Gilbert, Dennis. 1988. *Sandinistas: The Party and the Revolution*. Oxford: Basil Blackwell.

Goldstone, Jack. 1980. Theories of Revolution: The Third Generation. *World Politics* 32:425–453.

———. 1986a. Revolutions and Superpowers. In J. R. Adelman, ed., *Revolutions and Superpowers*, pp. 38–48. New York: Praeger.

———. 1986b. State Breakdown in the English Revolution: A New Synthesis. *American Journal of Sociology* 92:257–322.

———. 1988. East and West in the Seventeenth Century: Political Crises in Stuart England, Ottoman Turkey, and Ming China. *Comparative Studies in Society and History* 30:103–142.

———. 1991. *Revolution and Rebellion in the Early Modern World*. Berkeley and Los Angeles: University of California Press.

Goldstone, Jack, ed. 1986. *Revolutions: Theoretical, Comparative, and Historical Studies*. San Diego: Harcourt Brace Jovanovich.

Good, K. 1974. Settler Colonialism in Rhodesia. *African Affairs* 73:10–36.

Good, R. 1973. *UDI: The International Politics of the Rhodesian Rebellion*. Princeton: Princeton University Press.

Goodwin, Jeff, and Theda Skocpol. 1989. Explaining Revolutions in the Contemporary Third World. *Politics and Society* 17:489–509.

Gordon, D. G. 1984. Development Strategy in Zimbabwe: Assessments and Prospects. In M. G. Schatzberg, ed., *The Political Economy of Zimbabwe*, pp. 119–143. New York: Praeger.

Graham, H. D., and T. R. Gurr, eds. 1979. *Violence in America: Historical and Comparative Perspectives*. Beverly Hills, Calif.: Sage.

Graham, Robert. 1979. *Iran: The Illusion of Power*. New York: St. Martin's Press.

Gregorian, V. 1969. *The Emergence of Modern Afghanistan*. Stanford: Stanford University Press.

Gregory, M. 1981. Zimbabwe 1980: Politicisation Through Armed Struggle and Electoral Mobilisation. *Journal of Commonwealth and Comparative Politics* 19:62–94.

Gugler, Josef. 1982. The Urban Character of Contemporary Revolutions. *Studies in Comparative International Development* 17:60–73.

Gupta, B. 1986. *Afghanistan: Politics, Economics, and Society*. London: Frances Pinter.

Gurr, Ted Robert. 1970. *Why Men Rebel*. Princeton: Princeton University Press.

———. 1973. The Revolution—Social Change Nexus: Some Old Theories and New Hypotheses. *Comparative Politics* 5:359–392.

———. 1986a. Persisting Patterns of Repression and Rebellion: Foundations for a General Theory of Political Coercion. In Margaret Karns, ed., *Persistent Patterns and Emergent Structures in a Waning Century*, pp. 149–168. New York: Praeger.

———. 1986b. The Political Origins of State Violence and Terror: A Theoretical Analysis. In Michael Stohl and George A. Lopez, eds., *Government Violence and Repression: An Agenda for Research*, pp. 45–71. Westport, Conn.: Greenwood Press.

Gurr, Ted Robert, ed. 1980. *Handbook of Political Conflict: Theory and Research*. New York: Free Press.

Hall, D.G.E. 1958. *A History of South-East Asia*. London: Macmillan.

Halliday, F. 1978. Revolution in Afghanistan. *New Left Review* 112:3–44.

———. 1979. A Revolution Consumes Itself. *Nation* 229:492–494.

———. 1980. War and Revolution in Afghanistan. *New Left Review* 119:20–41.

Hamilton, Christopher Ryland. 1983. A Comparative Policy Analysis of Coal Mine Safety Regulation in the United States and Poland. Ph.D. dissertation, University of Kansas.

Hammer, E. J. 1954. *The Struggle for Indochina.* Stanford: Stanford University Press.

Harff, Barbara. 1986. Genocide and State Terrorism. In George Lopez and Michael Stohl, eds., *The Yearbook of State Violence and State Terrorism*, pp. 165–187. Westport, Conn.: Greenwood Press.

———. 1987. The Etiology of Genocide. In Michael N. Dobkowski and Isidor Wallimann, eds., *The Age of Genocide*, pp. 41–59. Westport, Conn.: Greenwood Press.

Harff, Barbara, and Ted Robert Gurr. 1988. Toward Empirical Theory of Genocides and Politicides: Identification and Measurement of Cases Since 1945. *International Studies Quarterly* 32:359–371.

Harrison, S. 1980–1981. Dateline Afghanistan: Exit Through Finland. *Foreign Policy* 41:163–187.

Hawes, Gary. 1987. *The Philippines State and the Marcos Regime: The Politics of Export.* Ithaca: Cornell University Press.

Heder, Stephen R. 1979. Kampuchea's Armed Struggle: The Origins of an Independent Revolution. *Bulletin of Concerned Asian Scholars* 11:2–24.

Helmsing, A.H.J. 1990. Transforming Rural Local Government: Zimbabwe's Postindependence Experience; Environment and Planning. *Government and Policy* 8:87–110.

Herbst, J. 1988. Societal Demands and Government Choices: Agricultural Producer Price Policy in Zimbabwe. *Comparative Politics* 20:265–288.

———. 1989. Political Impediments to Economic Rationality: Explaining Zimbabwe's Failure to Reform Its Public Sector. *Journal of Modern African Studies* 27:67–84.

———. 1990. *State Politics in Zimbabwe.* Berkeley: University of California Press.

Hicks, George L., and Geoffrey McNicoll. 1971. *Trade and Growth in the Philippines, An Open Dual Economy.* Ithaca: Cornell University Press.

Higonnet, Patrice. 1981. *Class, Ideology, and the Rights of Nobles During the French Revolution.* Oxford: Oxford University Press.

Hintz, S.E.C. 1972. The Political Transformation of Rhodesia, 1958–1965. *African Studies Review* 15:173–183.

Ho, Ping-ti, and Tang Tsou, eds. 1968. *China in Crisis: China's Heritage and the Communist Political System.* Chicago: University of Chicago Press.

Hoang Van Chi. 1964. *From Colonialism to Communism.* New York: Praeger.

Ho Chi Minh. 1967. *Against U.S. Aggression for National Salvation.* Hanoi: Foreign Languages Publishing House.

Holborn, Hajo. 1951. *The Political Collapse of Europe.* New York: Alfred Knopf.

Hooglund, Eric. 1982. *Land and Revolution in Iran.* Austin: University of Texas Press.

Hunt, W. 1983. *The Puritan Moment: The Coming of Revolution in an English County.* Cambridge: Harvard University Press.

Huntington, S. 1968. *Political Order in Changing Society.* New Haven: Yale University Press.

Huyser, Robert E. 1986. *Mission to Tehran.* New York: Harper and Row.

Hyman, A. 1984. *Afghanistan Under Soviet Domination.* New York: St. Martin's Press.

International Commission of Jurists. 1976. *Racial Discrimination and Repression in Southern Rhodesia.* London and Geneva: CIIR and ICJ.

International Financial Statistics Yearbook. Various years.

International Labour Organization. 1974. *Sharing in Development: A Program of Employment, Equity, and Growth for the Philippines.* Manila.

International Monetary Fund. 1985. *International Financial Statistics*. Washington, D.C.: United Nations.

Iran Almanac. Various years. Tehran: Echo of Iran.

Israel, Central Bureau of Statistics. *See* Central Bureau of Statistics.

Jocano, F. Landa. 1966. Rethinking "Smooth Interpersonal Relations." *Philippine Sociological Review* 14:282–291.

Johnson, Chalmers. 1966. *Revolutionary Change*. Stanford: Stanford University Press.

Kadhani, X. M. 1986. The Economy: Issues, Problems, and Prospects. In I. Mandaza, ed., *Zimbabwe: The Political Economy of Transition 1980–1986*, pp. 355–376. Dakar: CODESRIA.

Kakar, H. K. 1978. Fall of the Afghan Monarchy in 1973. *International Journal of Middle East Studies* 9:195–214.

———. 1979. *Government and Society in Afghanistan*. Austin: University of Texas Press.

Karnow, S. 1984. *Vietnam: A History*. New York: Penguin Books.

Katouzian, Homa. 1980. *The Political Economy of Modern Iran: Despotism and Pseudo-Modernism, 1926–1979*. New York: New York University Press.

———. 1983. Shi'ism and Islamic Economics: Sadr and Bani Sadr. In N. R. Keddie, ed., *Religion and Politics in Iran: Shi'ism from Quietism to Revolution*, pp. 145–165. New Haven: Yale University Press.

Kay, G. 1976. Population. In G.M.E. Leistner, ed., *Rhodesia: Economic Structure and Change*, pp. 42–56. Pretoria: Africa Institute.

Kazemi, Farhad. 1980. *Poverty and Revolution in Iran: The Migrant Poor, Urban Marginality, and Politics*. New York: New York University Press.

Keddie, Nikki R. 1981. *Roots of Revolution*. New Haven: Yale University Press.

Keddie, Nikki R., and Eric Hooglund, eds. 1986. *The Iranian Revolution & the Islamic Republic*. Syracuse, N.Y.: Syracuse University Press.

Kennedy, M. L. 1982. *The Jacobin Clubs in the French Revolution: The First Years*. Princeton: Princeton University Press.

Kessler, Richard J. 1984. Politics Philippines Style, Circa 1984. *Asian Survey* 24:1209–1228.

———. 1986. Marcos and the Americans. *Foreign Policy*, no. 63 (Summer):40–57.

———. 1989. *Rebellion and Repression in the Philippines*. New Haven: Yale University Press.

Khomeini, R. 1985. *Islam and Revolution: Writings and Declarations, Imam Khomeini*. Translated and annotated by H. Algar. London: Routledge and Kegan Paul.

Kiernan, Ben. 1981. Origins of Khmer Communism. *Southeast Asian Affairs*, pp. 161–180.

———. 1987. *How Pol Pot Came to Power*. Thetford, Eng.: Thetford Press.

Kinsey, B. H. 1983a. Emerging Policy Issues in Zimbabwe's Land Resettlement Programs. *Development Policy Review* 1:163–196.

———. 1983b. Forever Gained: Resettlement and Land Policy in the Context of National Development in Zimbabwe. In J.D.Y. Peel and T. O. Ranger, eds., *Past and Present in Zimbabwe*, pp. 92–113. Manchester: Manchester University Press.

Kirk, D. 1971. Cambodia's Economic Crisis. *Asian Survey* 9:239–243.

Kirk, T. 1974. The Rhodesian Front and the African National Council. *Issue: A Quarterly Journal of Africanist Opinion* 4:14–23.

Kirk, T., and C. Sherwell. 1975. The Rhodesian General Election of 1974. *Journal of Commonwealth and Comparative Politics* 13:1–25.

Kissinger, Henry A. 1957. *A World Restored: Mettternick, Castlereagh, and the Problems of Peace, 1812–1822*. 2d ed. Boston: Houghton Mifflin Company.

Knight, V. C. 1990. Zimbabwe a Decade After Independence. *Current History* 89:201–204, 224–226.

Kohn, Hans. 1965. *Nationalism, Its Meaning and History*. Rev. ed. New York: Van Nostrand Company.

Krajowa Agencja Informacyjna. 1984. *Biuletin Prasowy*, May 21–27. Warsaw: Polish Press Agency.

Krasner, Stephen. 1978. *Defending the National Interest: Raw Material Investments and the United States' Foreign Policy*. Princeton: Princeton University Press.

Kriger, N. 1988. The Zimbabwean War of Liberation: Struggles Within the Struggle. *Journal of Southern African Studies* 24:304–321.

Kumbula, T. 1986. A Mandate for Mugabe. *Africa Report* 31:70–73.

Lacouture, J. 1968. *Ho Chi Minh—A Political Biography*. New York: Random House.

LaFeber, Walter. 1984. *Inevitable Revolutions: The United States in Central America*. New York: Norton.

Lan, D. 1985. *Guerrillas and Spirit Mediums in Zimbabwe*. Berkeley: University of California Press.

Lande, Carl H., and Allan J. Cigler. 1988. *Recent Philippines Elections: A Quantitative Analysis*. Lawrence: University of Kansas Press.

Latin American Studies Association (LASA). 1990. *Electoral Democracy Under International Pressure: The LASA Commission to Observe the 1990 Nicaragua Election*. Pittsburgh: University of Pittsburgh Press.

Lawless, Robert. 1967. The Foundation for Culture-and-Personality Research in the Philippines. *Journal of Asian Studies* 5:101–136.

Lee, Dae-Kyu. 1987. A Causal Analysis of Military Intervention in Polish Politics. Ph.D. dissertation, University of Kansas.

Lefebvre, Georges. 1947. *The Coming of the French Revolution*. Princeton: Princeton University Press.

_____. 1962–1963. *The French Revolution*. 2 vols. Translated by E. M. Evanson. London: Routledge and Kegan Paul; New York: Columbia University Press.

Leifer, Michael. 1967. *Cambodia: The Search for Security*. New York: Praeger.

_____. 1971. Peace and War in Cambodia. *Southeast Asia* 1:59–73.

Lemon, A. 1978. Electoral Machinery and Voting Patterns in Rhodesia, 1962–1977. *African Affairs* 77:511–530.

_____. 1988. The Zimbabwe General Election. *Journal of Commonwealth and Comparative Politics* 26:3–21.

Lenczowski, G. 1980. *The Middle East in World Affairs*. 4th ed. Ithaca: Cornell University Press.

Lepak, Keith John. 1988. *Prelude to Solidarity*. New York: Columbia University Press.

Lernoux, Penny. 1989. *People of God: The Struggle for World Catholicism*. New York: Penguin.

Le Thanh Khoi. 1955. *Le Viet-Nam: Histoire et Civilization*. Paris: Edition de Minuit.

Leys, C. 1959. *European Politics in Southern Rhodesia*. Oxford: Clarendon Press.

Libby, R. 1984. Developmental Strategies and Political Divisions Within the Zimbabwean State. In M. G. Schatzberg, ed., *The Political Economy of Zimbabwe*, pp. 144–163. New York: Praeger.

Limbert, John W. 1987. *Iran: At War with History*. Boulder, Colo.: Westview Press.

Lipton, Merle. 1985. *Capitalism and Apartheid: South Africa, 1910–1984*. Totowa, N.J.: Rowman and Allanheld.

Liu, Michael. 1988. States and Urban Revolutions: Explaining the Revolutionary Outcomes in Iran and Poland. *Theory and Society* 17:179–210.

Lodge, Thomas. 1985. Introduction. In Shelagh Gastrow, ed., *Who's Who in South African Politics*, pp. 1–26. Johannesburg: Raven Press.

Loeffler, R. 1986. Economic Changes in a Rural Area Since 1979. In N. R. Keddie and E. Hooglund, eds., *The Iranian Revolution & the Islamic Republic*, pp. 93–108. Syracuse, N.Y.: Syracuse University Press.

Loewenson, R., and D. Sanders. 1988. The Political Economy of Health and Nutrition. In C. Stoneman, ed., *Zimbabwe's Prospects*, pp. 133–152. London: Macmillan.

Looney, Robert E. 1982. *Economic Origins of the Iranian Revolution*. New York: New York University Press.

McAlister, J. T., Jr. 1971. *Vietnam: The Origin of Revolution*. New York: Knopf.

McAlister, J. T., Jr., and P. Mus. 1970. *The Vietnamese and Their Revolution*. New York: Harper and Row.

McCloud, Donald G. 1986. *System and Process in Southeast Asia*. Boulder, Colo.: Westview Press.

Maguire, K. 1980. Prospects for Reactionary and Revolutionary Change in Zimbabwe. In J. R. Scarritt, ed., *Analyzing Political Change in Africa*, pp. 301–343. Boulder, Colo.: Westview Press.

Male, B. 1982. *Revolutionary Afghanistan*. London: Croom Helm.

Mandaza, I. 1986. The State in the Post–White Settler Colonial Situation. In I. Mandaza, ed., *Zimbabwe: The Political Economy of Transition 1980–1986*, pp. 21–74. Dakar: CODESRIA.

Mandelbaum, M. 1988. *Israel and the Occupied Territories*. Personal report for the Council on Foreign Relations.

Ma'oz, M. 1984. *Palestinian Leadership on the West Bank: The Changing Role of the Arab Mayors Under Jordan and Israel*. London: Frank Cass.

Martin, D., and P. Johnson. 1981. *The Struggle for Zimbabwe: The Chimurenga War*. London: Faber and Faber.

———. 1985. *The Chitepo Assassination*. Harare: Zimbabwe Publishing House.

Marx, Karl. 1967. *Capital*. Edited by Frederick Engels. New York: International Publishers.

———. 1972. *The Civil War in France*. Introduction by Frederick Engels. Moscow: Progress Publishers.

Meldrum, A. 1989. Mugabe's Maneuvers. *Africa Report* 34:38–40.

Meredith, M. 1979. *The Past Is Another Country: Rhodesia 1890–1979*. London: Andre Deutsch.

Migdal, J. S. 1974. *Peasants, Politics, and Revolution: Pressure Toward Political and Social Change in the Third World*. Princeton: Princeton University Press.

Miller, Norman, and Rod Aya, eds. 1971. *National Liberation*. New York: Free Press.

Miller, Stuart Creighton. 1982. *"Benevolent Assimilation": The American Conquest of the Philippines, 1899–1903*. New Haven: Yale University Press.

Minter, W., and E. Schmidt. 1988. When Sanctions Worked: The Case of Rhodesia Reexamined. *African Affairs* 87:207–237.

Mishal, S. 1978. *West Bank/East Bank: The Palestinians in Jordan, 1949–1967*. New Haven: Yale University Press.

Mishal, S., and R. Aharoni. 1989. [Speaking stones: The words behind the Palestinian intifada]. In Hebrew. Tel Aviv: Ha-Kibbutz Ha-Meuhad and Avivim Publisher.

Mlambo, E. 1972. *Rhodesia: The Struggle for a Birthright*. London: C. Hurst.

Moore, Barrington, Jr. 1966. *Social Origins of Dictatorship and Democracy: Lord and Peasant in the Making of the Modern World*. Boston: Beacon Press.

Moore, D. 1988. Review Article: The Zimbabwean "Organic Intellectuals" in Transition. *Journal of Southern African Studies* 15:96–105.

Moshiri, Farrokh. 1985. *State and Social Revolution in Iran: A Theoretical Perspective.* New York: Peter Lang.

Mossadegh, M. 1986. [Memoirs and writings of Dr. Mohammed Mossadegh]. In Farsi. Tehran: Paiez.

Mottahedeh, Roy. 1985. *The Mantle of the Prophet: Religion and Politics in Iran.* New York: Simon and Schuster.

Moyana, H. V. 1984. *The Political Economy of Land in Zimbabwe.* Gweru, Zimbabwe: Mambo Press.

Moyo, N. P. 1988. The State, Planning, and Labor: Towards Transforming the Colonial Labor Process in Zimbabwe. *Journal of Development Studies* 24:203-217.

Moyo, S. 1986. The Land Question. In I. Mandaza, ed., *Zimbabwe: The Political Economy of Transition 1980-1986*, pp. 165-202. Dakar: CODESRIA.

Mukherjee, S. 1984. *Afghanistan: From Tragedy to Triumph.* New Delhi: Sterling Publishers.

Muller, Edward N. 1980. The Psychology of Political Protest and Violence. In T. R. Gurr, ed., *Handbook of Political Conflict*, pp. 69-99. New York: Free Press.

Mumbengegwi, C. 1986. Continuity and Change in Agricultural Policy. In I. Mandaza, ed., *Zimbabwe: The Political Economy of Transition 1980-1986*, pp. 203-222. Dakar: CODESRIA.

_____. 1988. The Political Economy of Agricultural Producer Cooperative Development in Post-Independence Zimbabwe. In H. Hedlund, ed., *Cooperatives Revisited*, pp. 153-172. Uppsala: Scandinavian Institute of African Studies.

Murapa, R. 1984. Race and the Public Service in Zimbabwe: 1890-1983. In M. G. Schatzberg, ed., *The Political Economy of Zimbabwe*, pp. 55-80. New York: Praeger.

Murray, D. J. 1970. *The Governmental System in Southern Rhodesia.* Oxford: Clarendon Press.

NACLA *Report on the Americas.* 1980. *Nicaragua's Revolution.* 14 (May-June).

_____. 1981. *Central America: No Road Back.* 15 (May-June).

Nardin, Terry. 1980. Theory and Practice in Conflict Research. In T. R. Gurr, ed., *Handbook of Political Conflict*, pp. 461-489. New York: Free Press.

Ngo Vinh Long. 1973. *Before the Revolution.* Cambridge: M.I.T. Press.

Nguyen Cao Ky. 1976. *Twenty Years and Twenty Days.* New York: Stein and Day.

Nguyen Khac Vien. 1974. *Tradition and Revolution in Vietnam.* Washington, D.C.: Indochina Resource Center.

_____. 1980. *Vietnam '80.* Hanoi: Vietnam Courier.

Nguyen Kien Giang. 1960. *Les Grandes dates du parti de la classe ouvriere du Viet-Nam.* Hanoi: Foreign Languages Publishing House.

Nguyen Thi Dinh. 1976. *Khong con duong nao khac nua* [No other road to follow]. Translated by Mai Elliott. Ithaca: Southeast Asia Program, Cornell University.

Nguyen Tien Hung. 1977. *Economic Development of Socialist Vietnam 1955-1980.* New York: Praeger.

Nkomo, J. 1984. *Nkomo: The Story of My Life.* London: Methuen.

Nyangoni, W. W. 1978. *African Nationalism in Zimbabwe.* Washington, D.C.: University Press of America.

Nyawata, O. I. 1988. Macroeconomic Management, Adjustment, and Stabilisation. In C. Stoneman, ed., *Zimbabwe's Prospects*, pp. 90-117. London: Macmillan.

Nyrop, R. F., and D. M. Seekins, eds. 1986. *Afghanistan: A Country Study.* Washington, D.C.: Government Printing Office.

O'Meara, P. 1975. *Rhodesia: Racial Conflict or Coexistence?* Ithaca: Cornell University Press.

_____. 1982. Zimbabwe: The Politics of Independence. In G. M. Carter and P. O'Meara, eds., *Southern Africa: The Continuing Crisis*, pp. 18-56. Bloomington: Indiana University Press.

O'Neill, B. 1978. *Armed Struggle in Palestine*. Boulder, Colo.: Westview Press.

Pahlavi, M. R. 1980. *Answer to History*. New York: Stein and Day.

Paige, Jeffery. 1975. *Agrarian Revolution: Social Movements and Export Agriculture in the Underdeveloped World*. New York: Free Press.

Palmer, R. 1977a. The Agricultural History of Rhodesia. In R. Palmer and N. Parsons, eds., *The Roots of Rural Poverty in Central and Southern Africa*, pp. 221–254. Berkeley: University of California Press.

———. 1977b. *Land and Racial Domination in Rhodesia*. Berkeley: University of California Press.

Parliament of South Africa. 1954. *Senate Debates*. Pretoria: Government Printer.

Pedrosa, Carmen Navarro. 1987. *Imelda Marcos*. New York: St. Martin's Press.

The Pentagon Papers. 1971. Senator Gavel Edition. Boston: Beacon Press.

Pesaran, M. H. 1985. Economic Development and Revolutionary Upheaval in Iran. In H. Afshar, ed., *Iran: A Revolution in Turmoil*, pp. 15–50. Albany: State University of New York Press.

Pham Huy Thong. 1975. Ba lan dung nuoc [Three times establishing the nation]. *Hoc Tap* 237:67.

Pham Van Dong. 1990. *Chien si cach mang loi lac: Nhung hoi ky ve Ho Chu Tich* [The outstanding revolutionary fighter: Reminiscences about President Ho]. Moscow: Nha Xuat Ban Tien Bo.

Phimister, I. 1988. The Combined and Contradictory Inheritance of the Struggle Against Colonialism. In C. Stoneman, ed., *Zimbabwe's Prospects*, pp. 8–17. London: Macmillan.

Piekalkiewicz, Jaroslaw. 1979. Kulakization of Polish Agriculture. In Ronald Francisco, Roy Laird, and Betty Laird, eds., *The Political Economy of Collectivized Agriculture*, pp. 86–107. New York: Pergamon Press.

Pike, D. 1969. *War, Peace, and the Viet Cong*. Cambridge: M.I.T. Press.

Pipes, D. 1983. *In the Path of God*. New York: Basic Books.

Podhoretz, N. 1980. *Why We Were in Vietnam*. New York: Simon and Schuster.

Ponchaud, Francois. 1978. *Cambodia Year Zero*. New York: Holt, Rinehart and Winston.

Porter, G. 1975. *A Peace Denied*. Bloomington: University of Indiana Press.

Poullada, L. B. 1973. *Reform and Rebellion in Afghanistan, 1919–1929*. Ithaca: Cornell University Press.

Qarabaghi, 'A. 1984. *Haqayaq dar bareh-ya bohran-e Iran*. Paris: Soleil.

Quinn, K. 1976. Political Change in Wartime: The Khmer Krahom Revolution in Southern Cambodia. *Naval War College Review* 28:3–31.

Race, J. 1973. *War Comes to Long An*. Berkeley: University of California Press.

Raftopoulos, B. 1986. Human Resources Development and the Problem of Labor Utilization. In I. Mandaza, ed., *Zimbabwe: The Political Economy of Transition 1980–1986*, pp. 275–318. Dakar: CODESRIA.

Ramazani, Rouhollah K. 1982. *The Foreign Policy of Iran, 1500–1941*. Charlottesville: University of Virginia Press.

Ranger, T. 1967. *Revolt in Southern Rhodesia 1896–1897: A Study in African Resistance*. London: Heinemann.

———. 1980. The Changing of the Old Guard: Robert Mugabe and the Revival of Zanu. *Journal of Southern African Studies* 7:71–90.

———. 1985. *Peasant Consciousness and Guerrilla War in Zimbabwe*. Berkeley: University of California Press.

Republic of Zambia. 1976. *Report of the Special International Commission on the Assassination of Herbert Wiltshire Chitepo*. Lusaka: Government Printer.

Research Project on National Income in East Central Europe. 1982. OP-70. New York: L. W. International Financial Research, Inc.

Rich, T. 1982. Legacies of the Past? The Results of the 1980 Election in Midlands Province, Zimbabwe. *Africa* 52:42–55.

Richter, Linda K. 1987. Public Bureaucracy in Post-Marcos Philippines. *Southeast Asian Journal of Social Science* 15:57–58.

Ridout, C. 1975. Authority Patterns and the Afghan Coup of 1973. *Middle East Journal* 29:165–178.

Rocznik statystyczny (RS) [Statistical yearbook]. 1968, 1980 editions. Warsaw: Glowny Urzad Statystyczny.

Rodison, M. 1978. *Islam and Capitalism*. Austin: University of Texas Press.

Roosevelt, Kermit. 1979. *Counter Coup: The Struggle for the Control of Iran*. New York: McGraw-Hill.

Rosenthal, Gert. 1982. Principales rasgos de la evolución de las economías centroamericanas desde la posguerra. In Trinidad Martínez-Tarragó and Mauricio Campillo Illanes, eds., *Centroamérica: Crisis y política internacional*, pp. 19–38. Mexico City: Siglo XXI.

Roy, O. 1985. *Islam and Resistance in Afghanistan*. London: Cambridge University Press.

Rubin, Barry. 1980. *Paved with Good Intentions: The American Experience and Iran*. New York: Oxford University Press.

Rudé, George. 1979. *The Crowd in the French Revolution*. New York: Vintage.

Russell, D.E.H. 1974. *Rebellion, Revolution, and Armed Force*. New York: Academic Press.

Sachikonye, L. M. 1986. State, Capital, and Trade Unions. In I. Mandaza, ed., *Zimbabwe: The Political Economy of Transition 1980–1986*, pp. 243–274. Dakar: CODESRIA.

Sahliyeh, E. 1988. *In Search of Leadership: West Bank Politics Since 1967*. Washington, D.C.: Brookings.

Saul, J. S. 1979. *The State and Revolution in Eastern Africa*. New York: Monthly Review Press.

Scott, J. C. 1977. Hegemony and the Peasantry. *Politics and Society* 7:267–296.

Seegers, A. 1984. Revolution in Africa: The Case of Zimbabwe (1965–1980). Ph.D. dissertation, Loyola University of Chicago. Ann Arbor: University Microfilms International.

Sela, A. 1978. The PLO, the West Bank, and the Gaza Strip. *Jerusalem Quarterly* (Summer):66–77.

Shahrani, M. N. 1984. Introduction: Marxist Revolution and Islamic Resistance in Afghanistan. In M. N. Shahrani and R. Canfield, eds., *Revolution and Rebellion in Afghanistan*, pp. 3–57. Berkeley, Calif.: Institute of International Studies.

———. 1986. State Building and Social Fragmentation in Afghanistan: A Historical Perspective. In A. Banuazizi and M. Weiner, eds., *The State, Religion, and Ethnic Politics: Afghanistan, Iran, and Pakistan*, pp. 23–74. Syracuse, N.Y.: Syracuse University Press.

Shaw, W. H. 1986. Towards the One-Party State in Zimbabwe: A Study in African Political Thought. *Journal of Modern African Studies* 24:373–394.

Shawcross, William. 1980. *Sideshow: The American War in Cambodia*. New York: Simon and Schuster.

Shugart, Matthew S. 1989. Patterns of Revolution. *Theory and Society* 18:249–271.

Sibanda, A. 1988. The Political Situation. In C. Stoneman, ed., *Zimbabwe's Prospects*, pp. 257–283. London: Macmillan.

Sick, Gary. 1985. *All Fall Down: America's Tragic Encounter with Iran*. New York: Random House.

Simon, Sheldon W. 1978. Cambodia: Barbarism in a Small State Under Siege. *Current History* 77:197–201.

Simons, Lewis M. 1987. *Worth Dying For*. New York: William Morrow.

Sithole, M. 1979. *Zimbabwe Struggles Within the Struggle.* Salisbury: Rujeko Publishers.
———. 1980. Ethnicity and Factionalism in Zimbabwe Nationalist Politics 1957–79. *Ethnic and Racial Studies* 3:17–39.
———. 1986. The General Elections: 1979–1985. In I. Mandaza, ed., *Zimbabwe: The Political Economy of Transition 1980–1986,* pp. 75–98. Dakar: CODESRIA.
———. 1987a. State Power Consolidation in Zimbabwe: Party and Ideological Development. In E. J. Keller and D. Rothchild, eds., *Afro-Marxist Regimes,* pp. 85–103. Boulder, Colo.: Lynne Rienner.
———. 1987b. Zimbabwe: In Search of a Stable Democracy. In L. Diamond et al., eds., *Democracy in Developing Countries,* Vol. 2, *Africa,* pp. 217–257. Boulder, Colo.: Lynne Rienner.
Sithole, N. 1959. *African Nationalism.* New York: Oxford University Press.
Sklar, R. L. 1985. Reds and Rights: Zimbabwe's Experiment. *Issue: A Journal of Africanist Opinion* 14:29–33.
Skocpol, Theda. 1979. *States and Social Revolutions: A Comparative Historical Analysis of France, Russia, and China.* Cambridge: Cambridge University Press.
———. 1982. What Makes Peasants Revolutionary? *Comparative Politics* 14:351–375.
Smith, David M. 1987. *Update: Apartheid in South Africa.* Cambridge: Cambridge University Press.
Smith, H. H., et al. 1973. *Area Handbook for Afghanistan.* 4th ed. Washington, D.C.: Government Printing Office.
Soboul, Albert. 1975. *The French Revolution, 1787–1799: From the Storming of the Bastille to Napoleon.* Translated by A. Forrest and C. Jones. New York: Vintage.
Socialist Republic of Viet-Nam, Ministry of Foreign Affairs. 1979. *The Truth About Vietnam-China Relations Over the Last Thirty Years.* Hanoi: Ministry of Foreign Affairs.
South Africa, Parliament. *See* Parliament of South Africa.
Southeast Asia Chronicle. 1978. Two Views on the Vietnam-Kampuchea War. (Sept.–Oct.). Special issue.
———. 1981. *Kampuchea Survives . . . But What Now?* 77 (February). Special issue.
Spenser, William, ed. 1988. *Global Studies: The Middle East.* Guilford, Conn.: Dushkin Publishing.
Statesman's Year-Book. 1953, 1958, 1960 editions. London: Macmillan.
Statistical Abstract of Israel. 1988. Jerusalem: Central Bureau of Statistics.
Stern, Fritz. 1979. *Gold and Iron: Bismarck, Bleichroder, and the Building of the German Empire.* New York: Vintage.
Stohl, Michael. 1980. The Nexus of Civil and International Conflict. In T. R. Gurr, ed., *Handbook of Political Conflict,* pp. 297–331. New York: Free Press.
Stoneman, C. 1988. The Economy: Recognising the Reality. In C. Stoneman, ed. *Zimbabwe's Prospects,* pp. 43–62. London: Macmillan.
Stoneman, C., and L. Cliffe. 1989. *Zimbabwe: Politics, Economics, and Society.* London: Pinter Publishers.
Strack, H. R. 1978. *Sanctions: The Case of Rhodesia.* Syracuse, N.Y.: Syracuse University Press.
Sullivan, William. 1981. *Mission to Iran.* New York: Norton.
Summers, L. 1975. Consolidating the Cambodian Revolution. *Current History* 74:218–222.
Susser, A. 1984–1985. The Palestine Liberation Organization. *Middle East Contemporary Survey (MECS)* (Tel-Aviv: Dayan Center for Middle Eastern and African Studies, Tel Aviv University) 9:181–233.

Sutter, R. G. 1981. China's Strategy Toward Vietnam and Its Implications for the United States. In D.W.P. Elliott, ed., *The Third Indochina Conflict*, pp. 163–192. Boulder, Colo.: Westview Press.

Sylvester, C. 1986. Zimbabwe's 1985 Elections: A Search for National Mythology. *Journal of Modern African Studies* 24:229–255.

———. 1990. Simultaneous Revolutions: The Zimbabwean Case. *Journal of Southern African Studies* 16:452–475.

Tapper, R. 1983. Introduction. In R. Tapper, ed., *The Conflict of Tribe and State in Iran and Afghanistan*, pp. 1–82. London: Croom Helm.

Ta Xuan Linh. 1974. Ben-Tre: The Land of Concerted Uprisings. *Vietnam Courier* 27:6.

Taylor, Stan. 1984. *Social Science and Revolutions*. New York: St. Martin's Press.

Teitelbaum, J. 1987. The Palestine Liberation Organization. *Middle East Contemporary Survey (MECS)* (Tel Aviv: Dayan Center for Middle Eastern and African Studies, Tel Aviv University) 11:201–243.

Thayer, C. A. 1975. Southern Vietnamese Revolutionary Organizations and the Vietnam Workers' Party: Continuity and Change 1954–1974. In J. Zasloff and M. Brown, eds., *Communism in Indo-China: New Perspectives*, pp. 27–55. Toronto: D. C. Heath.

Thompson, C. B. 1985. *Challenge to Imperialism: The Frontline States in the Liberation of Zimbabwe*. Boulder, Colo.: Westview Press.

———. 1988. Zimbabwe in Sadcc: A Question of Dominance. In C. Stoneman, ed., *Zimbabwe's Prospects*, pp. 238–256. London: Macmillan.

Tilly, Charles. 1973. Does Modernization Breed Revolution? *Comparative Politics* 3:436.

———. 1978. *From Mobilization to Revolution*. Reading, Mass: Addison-Wesley.

Tonnies, Ferdinand. 1974. *Karl Marx: His Life and Teachings*. Translated by C. P. Loomis and I. Paulus. East Lansing: Michigan State University Press.

Torres-Rivas, Edelberto. 1982. Notas para comprender las crisis política centroamericana. In Trinidad Martínez-Tarragó and Mauricio Campillo Illanes, eds., *Centroamérica: Crisis y política internacional*, pp. 39–69. Mexico City: Siglo XXI.

——— 1984. Quién destapó la caja de Pandora? In Daniel Camacho and Manuel Rojas B., eds., *La Crisis Centroamericana*, pp. 23–51. San Jose, Costa Rica: EDUCA.

Tran Trong Kim. 1954. *Viet-Nam su-luoc* [History of Viet-Nam]. Hanoi: Tan-Viet.

Tran Van Tra. 1982. *Ket thuc cuoc chien-tranh 30 nam* [Conclusion of a thirty-year war]. Ho Chi Minh City: Nha Xuat-Ban Van-Nghe.

Trimberger, Ellen Kay. 1978. *Revolution from Above*. New Brunswick, N.J.: Transaction Books.

Truman, D. B. 1965. Disillusion and Regeneration: The Quest for a Discipline. *American Political Science Review* 59:865–873.

Truong Chinh. 1963. *Primer for Revolt*. New York: Praeger.

———. 1966. *President Ho-Chi-Minh: Beloved Leader of the Vietnamese People*. Hanoi: Foreign Languages Publishing House.

Tucker, Robert C., ed. 1978. *The Marx-Engels Reader*. 2d ed. New York: Norton.

Turley, W. S., ed. 1980. *Vietnamese Communism in Comparative Perspective*. Boulder, Colo.: Westview Press.

Turner, Mark M. 1978. Interpretations of Class and Status in the Philippines: A Critical Evaluation. *Cultures et developpement* 10:265–296.

United Nations. 1970. *Economic Survey of Asia and the Far East 1969*. Bangkok: Economic Commission for Asia and the Far East.

United Nations. Various years. *Statistical Yearbook*. New York: United Nations.

United Nations. Statistical Office. Various years. *Population and Vital Statistics Report*. New York: United Nations.

United Nations Educational, Scientific, and Cultural Organization (UNESCO). 1984. *Statistical Yearbook for Asia and the Pacific*. Bangkok: United Nations.

United States, Central Intelligence Agency. *See* Central Intelligence Agency.

United States Committee for Refugees. 1985. *Cambodians in Thailand: People on the Edge*. Issue paper. Washington, D.C.: U.S.C.R.

United States, State Department. *See* Confidential U.S. State Department Central Files

van der Kroef, Justus M. 1979. Political Ideology in Democratic Kampuchea. *Orbis* 22:1007–1030.

Van Tien Dung. 1977. *Dai thang mua xuan* [Our great spring victory]. Translated by J. Spragues, Jr. Hanoi: Nha Xuat-Ban Quan-Doi Nhan-Dan; New York: Monthly Review Press.

VBSBTHTU (Vu Bien Soan Ban Tuyen Huan Trung Uong). 1978. *Lich-su dang Cong-san Viet-Nam* [History of the Communist party of Viet-Nam]. Hanoi: Nha Xuat-Ban Giao-Khoa Mac Le-Nin.

Verrier, A. 1986. *The Road to Zimbabwe 1890–1980*. London: Jonathan Cape.

Verwoerd, H. F. 1954. *Senate Debates*. June 7, Parliament of South Africa. Cape Town: Government Printer.

Vickery, Michael. 1984. *Cambodia 1975–1982*. Boston: South End Press.

Vietnam, Socialist Republic of. *See* Socialist Republic of Vietnam

Vo Nguyen Giap. 1970. The South Vietnamese People Will Win. In R. Stetler, ed., *The Military Art of People's War: Selected Writings of General Vo Nguyen Giap*, pp. 185–225. New York: Monthly Review Press.

Vu Quoc Thong. 1952. *La Decentralisation administrative de Viet-Nam*. Hanoi: Presses Universitaires.

Walton, John. 1984. *Reluctant Rebels: Comparative Studies of Revolution and Under-development*. New York: Columbia University Press.

Walzer, Michael. 1965. *The Revolution of the Saints*. Cambridge: Harvard University Press.

Weber, Eugene. 1976. *Peasants into Frenchmen*. Stanford: Stanford University Press.

Weeks, John. 1985. *The Economies of Central America*. New York: Holmes and Meier.

Weiner, D. 1988. Land and Agricultural Development. In C. Stoneman, ed., *Zimbabwe's Prospects*, pp. 63–89. London: Macmillan.

Weinrich, A.K.H. 1977. Strategic Resettlement in Rhodesia. *Journal of Southern African Studies* 3:207–229.

Weiss, P. B. 1970. *Notes on the Cultural Life of the Democratic Republic of Vietnam*. New York: Dell Publishing Company.

Weitzer, R. 1984a. Continuities in the Politics of State Security in Zimbabwe. In M. G. Schatzberg, ed., *The Political Economy of Zimbabwe*, pp. 81–118. New York: Praeger.

———. 1984b. In Search of Regime Security: Zimbabwe Since Independence. *Journal of Modern African Studies* 22:529–557.

Welch, Claude. 1980. *Anatomy of Rebellion*. Albany: State University of New York Press.

Whitmore, J. K. 1980. Communism and History in Vietnam. In W. S. Turley, ed., *Vietnamese Communism in Comparative Perspective*, pp. 11–44. Boulder, Colo.: Westview Press.

Wilkinson, A. R. 1980. The Impact of the War. *Journal of Commonwealth and Comparative Politics* 18:110–123.

Windrich, E. 1979. Rhodesian Censorship: The Role of the Media in the Making of a One-Party State. *African Affairs* 78:523–534.

Wiseman, H., and A. M. Taylor. 1981. *From Rhodesia to Zimbabwe: The Politics of Transition*. New York: Pergamon Press.

Woddis, J. 1970. *Ho Chi Minh: Selected Articles and Speeches*. New York: International Publishers.

Wolf, Eric. 1969. *Peasant Wars of the Twentieth Century*. New York: Harper and Row.

Wood, B. 1988. Trade-Union Organization and the Working Class. In C. Stoneman, ed., *Zimbabwe's Prospects*, pp. 284–347. London: Macmillan.

Woodward, Ralph Lee, Jr. 1985. *Central America: A Nation Divided*. New York: Oxford University Press.

World Bank. Various years. *World Debt Tables*. Washington, D.C.: World Bank.

————. 1988. *The Philippines, The Challenge of Poverty*. Report No. 7144-PH, October 17. Washington, D.C.: World Bank.

Wormser, Michael A., ed. 1981. *The Middle East*. 5th ed. Washington, D.C.: Congressional Quarterly.

Wurfel, David. 1988. *Filipino Politics, Development, and Decay*. Quezon City: Ateneo de Manila University Press.

Yariv, A., et al. 1989. *The West Bank and Gaza: Israel's Options for Peace*. Tel Aviv: Jaffee Center for Strategic Studies, Tel Aviv University.

"Yates, P." 1980. The Prospects for Socialist Transition in Zimbabwe. *Review of African Political Economy* 18:68–88.

Yudelman, M. 1964. *Africans on the Land*. Cambridge: Harvard University Press.

Zabih, S. 1982. *Iran Since the Revolution*. Baltimore: Johns Hopkins University Press.

Zakai, D. 1988. *[Economic development in Judea, Samaria, and the Gaza District.]* In Hebrew. Jerusalem: Bank of Israel.

Zambia, Republic of. *See* Republic of Zambia

Zamora, Oscar. 1982. Comentario sobre el trabajo de Edelberto Torres-Rivas. In Trinidad Martínez Tarrago and Mauricio Campillo Illanes, eds., *Centroamérica: Crisis y política internacional*, pp. 93–105. México City: Siglo XXI.

Zamoyski, Adam. 1988. *The Polish Way: A Thousand-Year History of the Poles and Their Culture*. New York: Franklin Watts.

Zonis, Marvin. 1971. *The Political Elite of Iran*. Princeton: Princeton University Press.

Zvobgo, R. 1986. Education and the Challenge of Independence. In I. Mandaza, ed., *Zimbabwe: The Political Economy of Transition 1980–1986*, pp. 319–354. Dakar: CODESRIA.

ABOUT THE BOOK

Departing from the "Great Revolutions" tradition, Jack A. Goldstone, Ted Robert Gurr, and Farrokh Moshiri have drawn together a variety of area experts to examine contemporary revolutionary crises in light of recent social and political developments. The result is a wide-ranging compendium of cases placed in current theoretical perspective.

The book opens with a survey of theories of revolutionary conflict, ranging from Marx and Engels to Skocpol and Tilly. Next, Goldstone lays out an analytical framework for understanding contemporary revolutions that traces a sequence from processes of state breakdown and the ensuing struggle for power to the process of state reconstruction. The framework is then used to examine ten very different revolutionary crises—in Vietnam, Nicaragua, Iran, Poland, Afghanistan, the Philippines, Cambodia, Zimbabwe, South Africa, and the Palestinian uprising in the West Bank and Gaza. Factors implicit in state breakdown and reconstruction such as political and fiscal crisis, elite divisions, and mass mobilization are highlighted in the analyses of the individual crises.

The concluding chapter, coauthored by Gurr and Goldstone, compares the origins, dynamics, and outcomes of the revolutions in the case studies and applies the findings to ongoing and prospective cases. Taken together, the contributors' and editors' work shows that the end of the cold war does not signal the end of revolution and that with proper attention to certain conditions and factors, revolutionary "surprises"—such as those in Eastern Europe—need not catch us off guard in the years ahead.

ABOUT THE EDITORS
AND CONTRIBUTORS

Anwar-ul-Haq Ahady received his Ph.D. in political science from Northwestern University and is currently assistant professor of Middle East politics at Providence College. He has written extensively on the peace process in Afghanistan, with articles appearing in the *Christian Science Monitor*, the *Atlanta Constitution*, and the *Guardian*.

Jack A. Goldstone is professor of sociology and director of the Center for Comparative Research at the University of California, Davis. He is the author of *Revolution and Rebellion in the Early Modern World* (1991) and the editor of *Revolutions: Theoretical, Comparative, and Historical Studies* (1986). Dr. Goldstone's articles on theories of revolution have appeared in *World Politics*, *Theory and Society*, *American Journal of Sociology*, *Comparative Studies in Society and History*, and other scholarly journals.

Dévora Grynspan is director of development for International Programs and Studies at the University of Illinois at Urbana-Champaign. She is also assistant professor of political science and is currently serving as acting director of the Center for Latin American and Caribbean Studies. In addition to her interest in Central American revolutionary movements, she has done research and published on the impact of foreign investment and technology transfer patterns on Costa Rican development.

Ted Robert Gurr is professor of government and politics and Distinguished Scholar of the Center for International Development and Conflict Management at the University of Maryland, College Park. He has written or edited more than a dozen books, including *Why Men Rebel* (1970), *Handbook of Political Conflict* (1980), and *Violence in America* (1969, 1979, 1989 editions), and sixty scholarly articles and chapters. His current project, a global survey of 230 minorities at risk, focuses on the escalation, internationalization, and resolution of minority conflicts since 1945.

C.R.D. Halisi is an assistant professor at Indiana University. He has done extensive research in South Africa and has written several chapters in edited volumes on South Africa. These include: "Popular Struggle: Black South African Opposition in Transformation," *Radical History Review* (1990); "Racial Proletarianization and Political Culture in South Africa," in *South Africa in Southern Africa* (1989), and "Soviet-US Cooperation for Southern African Development and Regional Security," in *Agenda for Action: African-Soviet-US Cooperation* (1990). He is currently completing a book on black political thought in South Africa.

Barbara Harff is associate professor of political science at the United States Naval Academy. She has written a series of theoretical and empirical articles and chapters on

371

the causes and processes of gross human rights violations and a monograph, *Genocide and Human Rights: International and Political Issues* (1984). She is now working on a book-length comparative study, *Victims of the State*.

Richard J. Kessler is a professional staff member with the Senate Committee on Foreign Relations. Prior to joining the Senate staff, he taught Asian politics and U.S. foreign policy at the American University and was a senior associate at the Carnegie Endowment for International Peace. He has written extensively on the Philippines and U.S. foreign policy and is the author of *Rebellion and Repression in the Philippines* (1989).

Joseph Kostiner is lecturer in the Department of Middle Eastern and African History and research fellow, the Moshe Dayan Center for Middle Eastern and African History, both at Tel Aviv University. He has been a visiting scholar at the Center for Middle Eastern Studies, Harvard University. Dr. Kostiner is interested in the modern political and social history of the Middle East, especially with regard to the Arabian Peninsula and Arab revolutionary movements. His recent publications include *South Yemen's Revolutionary Strategy: From Insurgency to Bloc Politics, 1970–1985* (1990) and *The Making of Saudi Arabia: From Chieftaincy to Monarchical State* (forthcoming), and he is coeditor, with Philip S. Khoury, of *Tribe and State Formation in the Middle East* (1991).

H. John LeVan is an established physical and medical scientist who returned to graduate study in political science in 1981 and received his Ph.D. from Northwestern University in 1989. Although continuing his academic career in radiology and medical radiation physics, he is preparing for a transition to teaching and research in the social sciences. Dr. LeVan is currently working on two biographies: *Ho-Chi-Minh: A Cultural Biography,* and *Vo-Nguyen-Giap: From History Professor to Revolutionary General*.

Farrokh Moshiri is the author of *State and Social Revolution in Iran: A Theoretical Perspective* (1985) and has served as a lecturer and research associate at Northwestern University.

Patrick O'Meara is director of the African studies program and professor of political science and public and environmental affairs at Indiana University. He has published extensively on Africa and has served as project director for *Living Africa: A Village Experience*, a film on African life that was a finalist in the New York Film Festival. His books include *Rhodesia: Racial Conflict or Co-existence* (1975), *Southern Africa in Crisis* (1977), with G. M. Carter, *African Independence: First Twenty-Five Years* (1985), with G. M. Carter, and *International Politics in Southern Africa* (1982). He is currently working on a book on violence in contemporary Africa.

Jaroslaw Piekalkiewicz is professor of political science and of Soviet and East European studies at the University of Kansas. He came to the United States to start a university-to-university student and faculty exchange program with Poland and remained the program's director for many years. Dr. Piekalkiewicz is the author or coauthor of *Communist Local Government: A Study of Poland* (1975); *Public Opinion Polling in Czechoslovakia, 1968–69* (1972); *Politics of Ideocracy: The Rise and Fall of Totalitarian Governments* (forthcoming); and a number of chapters and articles on east-central European politics. He is also a coeditor of *Soviet Invasion of Czechoslovakia* (1972) and *Theory of Socialist Public Bureaucracy* (1991).

James R. Scarritt is professor of political science, director of conflict and peace studies, faculty research associate at the Institute of Behavioral Sciences, and professor adjoint at the Center for Studies of Ethnicity and Race in America, all at the University of Colorado, Boulder. He has written extensively on Zambian politics and on the theory and comparative study of African development and human rights. He is editor and coauthor of *Analyzing Political Change in Africa* (1980) and coeditor of *Global Human Rights* (1981). He is currently finishing a book entitled *Rulers, Conflict, and Change in Zambia* and collaborating in Ted Robert Gurr's project on minorities at risk.

Joshua Teitelbaum is research fellow at the Moshe Dayan Center for Middle Eastern and African Studies, Tel Aviv University, and is visiting acting assistant professor of international studies at the Middle East Center of the Henry Jackson School of International Studies, University of Washington. He has written articles on the Palestine Liberation Organization and the Druze in Israel, and he also has a keen interest in the early modern history of the Arabian Peninsula.

N. Brian Winchester is a political scientist and associate director of the African studies program at Indiana University. He is the author of numerous articles in reference works and academic journals and several book chapters on African politics, including a chapter in *The South African Quagmire: In Search for a Path to Peaceful Pluralism* (1987) with P. O'Meara.

INDEX

374